# Adobe ColdFusion Anthology

Clear and Concise Concepts from
the Fusion Authority

Michael and Judith Dinowitz

Apress®

**Adobe ColdFusion Anthology: Clear and Concise Concepts from the Fusion Authority**

ISBN-13 (pbk): 978-1-4302-7215-1

ISBN-13 (electronic): 978-1-4302-7214-4

Printed and bound in the United States of America 9 8 7 6 5 4 3 2 1

President and Publisher: Paul Manning
Authors: Charlie Arehart, Peter Bell, Mike Brunt, Doug Boude, Raymond Camden, Sean Corfield, Pete Freitag, Hal Helms, Mike Henke, Doug Hughes, Kevin Jones, Wally Kolcz, Dave Konopka, Boyan Kostadinov, Brian Kotek, Mark Kruger, Mark Mandel, John Mason, Nathan Mische, Adrian J. Moreno, Jake Munson, Ben Nadel, Jim Pickering, Jim Priest, Joe Rinehart, Jared Rypka-Hauer, Terry Ryan, Chris Scott, and Matt Woodward
Lead Editor: Matthew Moodie
Technical Reviewers: Mark Drew, Brian Kotek, Mark Mandel, and Sean Corfield
Editorial Board: Clay Andres, Steve Anglin, Mark Beckner, Ewan Buckingham, Gary Cornell, Jonathan Gennick, Jonathan Hassell, Michelle Lowman, Matthew Moodie, Duncan Parkes, Jeffrey Pepper, Frank Pohlmann, Douglas Pundick, Ben Renow-Clarke, Dominic Shakeshaft, Matt Wade, Tom Welsh
Coordinating Editor: Debra Kelly
Copy Editor: Marilyn Smith
Production Support: Patrick Cunningham
Indexer: Brenda Miller
Artist: April Milne
Cover Designer: Anna Ishchenko

Distributed to the book trade worldwide by Springer-Verlag New York, Inc., 233 Spring Street, 6th Floor, New York, NY 10013. Phone 1-800-SPRINGER, fax 201-348-4505, e-mail orders-ny@springer-sbm.com, or visit www.springeronline.com.

For information on translations, please e-mail rights@apress.com, or visit www.apress.com.

Apress and friends of ED books may be purchased in bulk for academic, corporate, or promotional use. eBook versions and licenses are also available for most titles. For more information, reference our Special Bulk Sales–eBook Licensing web page at www.apress.com/info/bulksales.

The source code for this book is available to readers at www.apress.com.

# Contents at a Glance

Foreword ........................................................................................................... xxv

About the Authors................................................................................................ xxvi

About the Technical Reviewers ........................................................................ xxxvii

Acknowledgments............................................................................................ xxxviii

Introduction ...................................................................................................... xxxix

PART 1: COLDFUSION FUNDAMENTALS................................................................1

Chapter 1: Working with Application.cfc................................................................3

Chapter 2: Application.cfc Reference ................................................................. 15

Chapter 3: From User-Defined Functions to ColdFusion Components ................... 17

Chapter 4: onMissingTemplate()— Error Handler and So Much More ................. 47

Chapter 5: "Say What?" Handling Unknown Messages
with onMissingMethod() ................................................................................. 61

PART 2: DOCUMENT CREATION IN COLDFUSION................................................. 73

Chapter 6: PDF Support in ColdFusion................................................................. 75

Chapter 7: Image Processing in ColdFusion ........................................................ 89

**PART 3: ESSENTIALS TO SERVER PRODUCTIVITY** ...................................................................101

**Chapter 8: Tuning Your Java Virtual Machine:**
 **Finding Your Ideal JVM Settings Through Metrics Log Analysis** .........................103

**Chapter 9: The Shoemaker and the Asynchronous Process Elves** ......................111

**Chapter 10: Asynchronous Gateways  Step-by-Step** ...........................................117

**Chapter 11: You Might Have a Performance Bottleneck If.** ....................................121

**PART 4: COMMUNICATION AND INTEGRATING WITH OTHER TECHNOLOGIES** ...........143

**Chapter 12: An Introduction to Consuming**
 **and Deploying Web Services  in ColdFusion** .........................................................145

**Chapter 13: Web Services and  Complex Types** ...................................................157

**Chapter 14: Type Validation When Returning an Array of Components** ..............179

**Chapter 15: Sending E-mail the Right Way** ...........................................................181

**Chapter 16: ColdFusion and  Microsoft Exchange** ...............................................189

**Chapter 17: BlazeDS** ...............................................................................................199

**PART 5: OBJECT-ORIENTED PROGRAMMING (OOP)** ..................................................211

**Chapter 18: Object-Oriented Programming: Why Bother?** ...................................213

**Chapter 19: The Object-Oriented Lexicon** ............................................................217

**Chapter 20: Design Patterns: Exposing the Service Layer** ..................................225

**Chapter 21: Beans and DAOs and  Gateways, Oh My!** ........................................231

**Chapter 22: SOA for the Rest of Us** ......................................................................239

**Chapter 23: How Base Classes Can Help You Generate Your Applications** .........249

**PART 6: COLDFUSION FRAMEWORKS** .........................................................................257

**Chapter 24: An Introduction to Frameworks** ........................................................259

▓Chapter 25: Fusebox 5 Fundamentals .......................................................... 265

▓Chapter 26: Mach-II Fundamentals ............................................................ 281

▓Chapter 27: Model-Glue Fundamentals ....................................................... 299

▓Chapter 28: ColdSpring Fundamentals ........................................................ 315

▓Chapter 29: Reactor Fundamentals ............................................................ 321

▓Chapter 30: Developing Applications with Transfer ...................................... 331

▓Chapter 31: FW/1: The Invisible Framework ............................................... 347

PART 7: DESIGNING THE USER INTERFACE ............................................... 359

▓Chapter 32: Separating Layout from Logic .................................................. 361

▓Chapter 33: Creating Dynamic Presentations in ColdFusion .......................... 369

▓Chapter 34: Working with JSON and cfajaxproxy ........................................ 375

▓Chapter 35: Prototyping for Interface Driven Architecture:
Easing the Transition from Prototype to Application ..................................... 385

PART 8: DEVELOPMENT TOOLS ................................................................ 389

▓Chapter 36: Turbo Charging Eclipse .......................................................... 391

▓Chapter 37: An Introduction to ColdFusion Builder ..................................... 407

▓Chapter 38: The ColdFusion Debugger Explained:
Interactive Step Debugging for ColdFusion 8 and 9 ....................................... 421

▓Chapter 39: Getting Started with Subversion ............................................. 433

▓Chapter 40: Subversion in the Workflow .................................................... 445

▓Chapter 41: Advanced Subversion ............................................................. 451

▓Chapter 42: Automating Your Development with Ant .................................... 461

Index ....................................................................................................... 477

# Contents

Foreword ............................................................................................ xxv

About the Authors ............................................................................ xxvi

About the Technical Reviewers ...................................................... xxxvii

Acknowledgments .......................................................................... xxxviii

Introduction .................................................................................... xxxix


PART 1: COLDFUSION FUNDAMENTALS ................................................ 1

▆Chapter 1: Working with Application.cfc ........................................... 3

What Is an Application? .................................................................... 3

Adding Application Variables ............................................................ 5

The onApplicationStart Method ................................................................ 5

The onSessionStart Method ...................................................................... 6

The onRequestStart Method ...................................................................... 7

The onError Method .................................................................................. 8

The onApplicationEnd Method ................................................................ 10

The onSessionEnd Method ...................................................................... 10

The onRequestEnd Method ...................................................................... 11

The onRequest Method ............................................................................ 11

A New Application Structure .......................................................... 13

▆Chapter 2: Application.cfc Reference ............................................. 15

■**Chapter 3: From User-Defined Functions to ColdFusion Components** ..................**17**

  User-Defined Functions ...................................................................................17

    Creating UDFs .............................................................................................18

    Executing UDFs and Passing Parameters.....................................................27

    Error Handling............................................................................................30

    A Full UDF Example ...................................................................................31

  ColdFusion Components ..................................................................................32

    Creating CFCs.............................................................................................33

    The CFC Container: The cfcomponent Tag ...................................................39

    Implementing Security ...............................................................................39

    Defining Properties: Variables and This.......................................................40

    Understanding Encapsulation......................................................................41

    Caching Components...................................................................................41

    Using Inheritance.......................................................................................43

  Parting Words ................................................................................................45

■**Chapter 4: onMissingTemplate()— Error Handler and So Much More** .................**47**

  404 Missing Template Handling: Step-by-Step Basics.....................................47

  Setting Global Handlers ..................................................................................48

  What Is the onMissingTemplate() Method, and When Is It Called?.....................49

  Method Invocation within onMissingTemplate() ................................................51

  When Errors Occur..........................................................................................52

  Reasons for Calling onMissingTemplate() .........................................................53

    Request Errors and Corrected Requests.......................................................53

    Content Redirects.......................................................................................54

    Dynamic Page Generation ..........................................................................55

    Fusebox URL..............................................................................................58

    Model-Glue URL.........................................................................................59

Mach-II URL ....................................................................................................... 59

We're Not Done Yet, but .................................................................................. 59

▓**Chapter 5: "Say What?" Handling Unknown Messages
with onMissingMethod()** ............................................................................ **61**

Get the Message? ............................................................................................ 61

Message Received ........................................................................................... 63

Defining onMissingMethod() .......................................................................... 64

Using onMissingMethod() ............................................................................... 65

    Automatic get/set Methods ........................................................................ 66

    Method Injection ........................................................................................ 68

    Aspect-Oriented Programming .................................................................. 70

Summary ......................................................................................................... 72

Further Reading .............................................................................................. 72

**PART 2: DOCUMENT CREATION IN COLDFUSION** ............................................ **73**

▓**Chapter 6: PDF Support in ColdFusion** ................................................... **75**

PDF Support in ColdFusion MX 7 (and Earlier) ............................................... 75

PDF Support in ColdFusion 8.0.1 and beyond ................................................ 76

The isPDFFile and isPDFObject Functions ...................................................... 77

What Exactly Can We Do with the cfpdf Tag? ................................................. 79

    Getting and Setting Information .................................................................. 80

    Adding a Watermark .................................................................................. 84

    Using DDX ................................................................................................. 86

Where to Go Next ............................................................................................ 88

**▨Chapter 7: Image Processing in ColdFusion**....................................................**89**

The cfimage Tag ..........................................................................................89

Getting Image Dimensions with cfimage..............................................................89

Resizing an Image with cfimage ........................................................................90

Multiple Operations with cfimage.......................................................................91

Creating a CAPTCHA Image with cfimage............................................................91

The New Image Processing Functions ............................................................92

Image Drawing Functions.................................................................................92

Image Manipulation Functions ..........................................................................96

Image Information Functions.............................................................................97

Image I/O Functions......................................................................................100

Summary ...................................................................................................100

**PART 3: ESSENTIALS TO SERVER PRODUCTIVITY**................................................**101**

**▨Chapter 8: Tuning Your Java Virtual Machine:**
**Finding Your Ideal JVM Settings Through Metrics Log Analysis** ........................**103**

How the JVM Fits into ColdFusion ...............................................................103

Enabling Metrics Logging ...........................................................................104

Editing the jrun.xml File.................................................................................105

Splitting Up the JRun Logs ............................................................................106

Examining the Metrics Logging Output .............................................................107

Finding the Proper Start and Maximum Heap Memory Size....................................108

The New Metrics..........................................................................................109

Summary ...................................................................................................110

**Chapter 9: The Shoemaker and the Asynchronous Process Elves.....................111**

by Doug Boude.........................................................................................................111

The Experiment.......................................................................................................112

Before Employing Those Elves.............................................................................115

The Moral of the Story ...........................................................................................115

Further Reading on Asynchronous Gateways .....................................................115

**Chapter 10: Asynchronous Gateways  Step-by-Step .......................................117**

**Chapter 11: You Might Have a Performance Bottleneck If..............................121**

If You Can't Tell a Manager from an Employee,
You Might Have a Performance Bottleneck ........................................................121

If Your Foreign Key Values Are Not Defined in the...........................................123

Database . . ..............................................................................................................123

If You Relate Data Between Tables, but Neglect to  Inform the Database . . ......125

If You Store a Comma-Delimited List of Foreign Keys in a Single Column . . ..126

If You Use SELECT MAX( ID ) to Get the Primary Key of
a Newly Inserted Record . . ...................................................................................129

If Your Only Transactions Are Between You and a Cashier . . ...........................130

If You Think the Difference Between Char and Varchar
Is Typing Three More Letters . . ...........................................................................132

If You Think UTF-8 Is One of Those TV Channels
You Used to Get with Rabbit Ears . . ....................................................................134

If You Use More Than One Query to Read Data  from Multiple Tables . . ..........135

If the Only Index Your Database Knows Is Next  to Your Middle Finger . . ........137

If You Run Calculations on Data Using  Your Application Code . . .....................139

If the Contents of a Table Depend  on the Phase of the Moon . . .......................142

Build It Correctly from the Beginning..................................................................142

**PART 4: COMMUNICATION AND INTEGRATION WITH OTHER TECHNOLOGIES............143**

**Chapter 12: An Introduction to Consuming
and Deploying Web Services  in ColdFusion.......................................................145**

Deploying a Web Service from a CFC ..............................................................146

Using a Remote Proxy Object............................................................................147

Deploying a Web Service from a Standard ColdFusion Page.........................148

Invoking Web Services in ColdFusion .............................................................151

    Using the cfinvoke Tag ...............................................................................151

    Using the CreateObject() Function .............................................................152

    Using the cfhttp Tag ...................................................................................153

    Invoking a CFM-Based Web Service ...........................................................154

Error Handling....................................................................................................155

And Finally... .....................................................................................................156

**Chapter 13: Web Services and  Complex Types..............................................157**

Consuming Web Services ..................................................................................157

Passing Complex Types as Input Parameters.................................................157

    Nested Complex Types ...............................................................................159

    Arrays .........................................................................................................160

    Attributes ....................................................................................................162

Going to the Source ...........................................................................................164

    When Structures Are Not Enough ..............................................................169

    WSDL2Java..................................................................................................171

Working with Complex Return Values...............................................................172

Publishing Web Services ...................................................................................173

Other Resources ................................................................................................177

**Chapter 14: Type Validation When Returning an Array of Components** ............. **179**

Validating a Component ................................................................................... 179

Validating an Array of Components ................................................................. 180

**Chapter 15: Sending E-mail the Right Way** ............................................... **181**

The From Conundrum ...................................................................................... 182

Checking E-mail Origins .................................................................................. 184

Sender Policy Framework (SPF) ................................................................... 184

DomainKeys Identified Mail (DKIM) ............................................................ 185

Real-Time Blacklists (RBLs) ......................................................................... 185

Checking Sender Behavior ............................................................................. 185

Checking the Content ................................................................................... 186

Miscellaneous Commandments ..................................................................... 187

**Chapter 16: ColdFusion and  Microsoft Exchange** ................................... **189**

ColdFusion and Exchange Integration Requirements ..................................... 189

ColdFusion Exchange Tags ............................................................................. 190

Using cfexchangeconnection .......................................................................... 190

Using cfexchangecalendar, cfexchangecontact, and cfexchangetask .............. 191

Using cfexchangemail .................................................................................... 194

Using cfexchangefilter ................................................................................... 195

ColdFusion and Exchange Interaction Best Practices ..................................... 196

Connections ................................................................................................... 196

Service Accounts ........................................................................................... 197

SSL ................................................................................................................ 197

Conclusion ...................................................................................................... 197

**Chapter 17: BlazeDS** .................................................................**199**

  Messaging Patterns ...................................................................199

    BlazeDS vs. LCDS ...................................................................... 200

    What's in a Name? ...................................................................... 200

    Installing BlazeDS with ColdFusion ............................................... 202

  Messaging Framework ...............................................................202

    Running BlazeDS with a ColdFusion Event Gateway ......................... 204

  Concluding Thoughts .................................................................209

**PART 5: OBJECT-ORIENTED PROGRAMMING (OOP)** ...............................**211**

**Chapter 18: Object-Oriented Programming: Why Bother?** ..............**213**

  OOP Fundamentals ...................................................................213

    Inheritance................................................................................. 214

    Polymorphism............................................................................. 214

    Encapsulation............................................................................. 214

  So What?...................................................................................215

  Where Do I Start?......................................................................215

**Chapter 19: The Object-Oriented Lexicon** .................................**217**

**Chapter 20: Design Patterns: Exposing the Service Layer** ...............**225**

  Model-View-Controller (MVC) .....................................................225

    Handling Sessions ...................................................................... 226

    Returning Data............................................................................ 228

    Accessing the Application ............................................................. 229

  Conclusion ...............................................................................229

**Chapter 21: Beans and DAOs and Gateways, Oh My!** ........................................ **231**

A Four-Layer Cake ............................................................. 231

A Review of Recipes ............................................................. 233

What Are Those Ingredients? ............................................................. 236

Eating Well or Poor Diet? ............................................................. 237

Real-World Web Applications ............................................................. 238

**Chapter 22: SOA for the Rest of Us** ............................................................. **239**

SOA Components ............................................................. 239

SOA vs. OOP ............................................................. 239

SOA Code Organization ............................................................. 241

Web Services ............................................................. 241

Data Formats ............................................................. 242

Security ............................................................. 243

Error Handling ............................................................. 245

Discoverability ............................................................. 246

Service Interfaces ............................................................. 247

**Chapter 23: How Base Classes Can Help You Generate Your Applications** ..........**249**

Base Class Basics ............................................................. 249

It's All About the API ............................................................. 251

A Simple Example ............................................................. 252

The Variables Define the API ............................................................. 252

Types of Methods ............................................................. 254

Metaprogramming ............................................................. 254

Summary ............................................................. 255

Resources ............................................................. 255

## PART 6: COLDFUSION FRAMEWORKS .................................................................................. 257

### Chapter 24: An Introduction to Frameworks .............................................................. 259

Can Someone Just Tell Me What They ARE Already? ............................................... 259

Frameworks that Focus on HTML and the User Interface ....................................... 260

Fusebox ................................................................................................................. 260

Model-Glue ........................................................................................................... 261

Mach-II .................................................................................................................. 262

ColdBox ................................................................................................................. 262

Back-End and Service Frameworks .......................................................................... 263

ColdSpring ............................................................................................................ 263

Reactor .................................................................................................................. 263

Transfer ................................................................................................................. 264

Summary ................................................................................................................... 264

### Chapter 25: Fusebox 5 Fundamentals ........................................................................ 265

Fusebox—What and Why .......................................................................................... 265

Fusebox Concepts ................................................................................................ 266

Fusebox Benefits .................................................................................................. 268

What's New in Fusebox 5 and 5.5 ............................................................................ 270

Compatibility ......................................................................................................... 270

Coding Styles ........................................................................................................ 270

Multiple Applications ............................................................................................ 272

Application Initialization ....................................................................................... 273

Custom Lexicons ................................................................................................... 273

XML Grammar ....................................................................................................... 276

Dynamic Do ........................................................................................................... 278

Application.cfc Support ......................................................................................... 278

The event Object ................................................................................................... 278

The myFusebox Object ......................................................................................... 279

Search-Engine-Safe URLs ......................................................................................... 279

Runtime Control ..................................................................................................... 279

Why Upgrade? ............................................................................................................ 280

**■Chapter 26: Mach-II Fundamentals ................................................................. 281**

Introducing the Mach-II Framework ........................................................................... 281

Installing Mach-II ....................................................................................................... 283

The Mach-II Application Skeleton .............................................................................. 286

Mach-II's XML Configuration File ............................................................................. 286

Properties ............................................................................................................ 290

Listeners .............................................................................................................. 291

Event Filters ........................................................................................................ 291

Plugins ................................................................................................................. 292

Event Handlers .................................................................................................... 292

Page Views ......................................................................................................... 292

Hello Mach-II .............................................................................................................. 292

Let's Get Personal ...................................................................................................... 294

Conclusion ................................................................................................................. 297

**■Chapter 27: Model-Glue Fundamentals ........................................................... 299**

A Recipe for Spaghetti ............................................................................................... 300

Fun with Front Controller ........................................................................................... 301

Installing Model-Glue ................................................................................................. 301

Starting a New Model-Glue Application ..................................................................... 302

Creating the Application Manually ...................................................................... 302

Automating Application Creation ......................................................................... 303

Model-Glue XML Files in a Nutshell .......................................................................... 304

ColdSpring XML Configuration File ..................................................................... 304

The Model-Glue XML Configuration File ............................................................. 305

Your First Model-Glue Application ..................................................................309

    Setting Up the Form..................................................................................309

    Adding Functionality.................................................................................310

    Finishing Up.............................................................................................312

Conclusion ...................................................................................................313

**Chapter 28: ColdSpring Fundamentals** ....................................................**315**

The Problem of Dependency in System Design ..........................................315

ColdSpring and Component Management ...................................................316

Some Development Concepts.......................................................................318

    Unit Testing..............................................................................................318

    Test-Driven Development ..........................................................................318

    Too Many Dependencies Can Spoil the Model............................................318

    Back to ColdSpring...................................................................................319

Using ColdSpring to Architect Your Application in Logical Tiers.................319

**Chapter 29: Reactor Fundamentals** .........................................................**321**

The Origin of Reactor....................................................................................321

A Look at Reactor .........................................................................................322

Installing Reactor .........................................................................................323

Some Simple Reactor Examples....................................................................324

How Does Reactor Work? ..............................................................................325

Slightly More Interesting Reactor Examples .................................................326

Using Iterators .............................................................................................328

Learning More About Reactor ......................................................................329

■**Chapter 30: Developing Applications with Transfer** ....................................................**331**

Transfer—An ORM for ColdFusion ..............................................................................332

Installing and Configuring Transfer ............................................................................332

    The Transfer Data Source Configuration File................................................................ 332

    The Transfer Object Configuration File ........................................................................ 333

    Mapping Objects to Tables .......................................................................................... 335

Using Transfer ...........................................................................................................338

    Creating the TransferFactory...................................................................................... 338

    Creating a New Object ................................................................................................ 339

    Saving an Object......................................................................................................... 339

    Retrieving an Object ................................................................................................... 341

    Deleting an Object ...................................................................................................... 342

    Using List Queries...................................................................................................... 343

Other Transfer Functionality ......................................................................................344

Conclusion .................................................................................................................345

■**Chapter 31: FW/1: The Invisible Framework** .........................................................**347**

What Happened to ColdFusion's Simplicity? ...............................................................348

    Initialization with Application.cfc................................................................................ 348

    Convention over Configuration ................................................................................... 348

Getting Started with FW/1 ..........................................................................................349

A Real Application.......................................................................................................351

Beyond the Basics ......................................................................................................355

Summary ...................................................................................................................357

## PART 7: DESIGNING THE USER INTERFACE ........................................................... 359

### Chapter 32: Separating Layout from Logic ........................................................ 361

Why Does Separation Matter? ........................................................................... 361

More Maintainable Business Calculations ..................................................... 361

Less Formatting Duplication ........................................................................ 362

Template Simplification ................................................................................ 362

Better Support for Specialization ................................................................ 362

Three Helpful Techniques ................................................................................ 362

Business Objects ........................................................................................... 362

Custom Data Types ....................................................................................... 363

View CFCs ...................................................................................................... 365

Conclusion ........................................................................................................ 368

### Chapter 33: Creating Dynamic Presentations in ColdFusion ........................... 369

Overview ............................................................................................................ 369

cfpresentation - The Shell ................................................................................ 370

cfpresenter - The People ................................................................................... 371

cfpresentationslide - The Message .................................................................. 371

Putting It All Together ...................................................................................... 373

The Amazing Potential ...................................................................................... 373

### Chapter 34: Working with JSON and cfajaxproxy ............................................ 375

Working with JSON ............................................................................................ 375

Special Considerations with JSON Serialization ............................................ 379

Working with cfajaxproxy ................................................................................. 379

A More Complex Example .................................................................................. 382

Conclusion ........................................................................................................ 384

**■Chapter 35: Prototyping for Interface Driven Architecture:
Easing the Transition from Prototype to Application** .................................................**385**

Introduction..................................................................................................385

The Challenges ...........................................................................................385

Suggestions ................................................................................................386

    CSS ..............................................................................................................386

    Tables ..........................................................................................................386

    Complete Your Prototype ..............................................................................387

    AJAX ............................................................................................................387

Conclusion ..................................................................................................387

**PART 8: DEVELOPMENT TOOLS**.................................................................**389**

**■Chapter 36: Turbo Charging Eclipse** .......................................................**391**

The Right Eclipse Package .........................................................................392

Preparing for Turbo Charging .....................................................................392

    Getting a Fresh Instance of Eclipse ..............................................................393

    Setting Eclipse Preferences..........................................................................393

    Installing Core Tools ....................................................................................395

    Refresh Eclipse Data ...................................................................................396

Initial Benchmark........................................................................................397

    Diagnosing Plug-in Issues ...........................................................................397

    eclipse.ini ....................................................................................................398

Switching Eclipse from the Default JVM......................................................400

Conclusion ..................................................................................................401

References ..................................................................................401

   More Learning ...................................................................401

   SUN JVM Information...........................................................402

   BEA JRockit Information......................................................402

   Products/Downloads............................................................402

Eclipse Runtime Commands and Various JVM Options ...............402

   Eclipse Runtime Commands................................................403

   JVM Options......................................................................403

   Sun JVM OPTIONS ............................................................404

   JRockit JVM Options...........................................................405

**Chapter 37: An Introduction to ColdFusion Builder ...................407**

Why Eclipse?.............................................................................407

Installation ................................................................................408

Learning Eclipse .......................................................................408

   Projects............................................................................408

   Rearranging Your Workspace ..............................................409

   Ask for help .....................................................................409

ColdFusion Server Integration ...................................................409

   Configuring Your Server .....................................................410

   RDS Dataview ...................................................................411

   Services Browser................................................................411

   CF Admin and Server Monitor..............................................411

CFC Wizard................................................................................412

CF Builder Extensions ...............................................................412

   Building an Extension .........................................................413

Debugging Applications .............................................................417

   Configuring Your Application for Debugging .........................417

Conclusion ................................................................................419

▓ **Chapter 38: The ColdFusion Debugger Explained:**
**Interactive Step Debugging for ColdFusion 8 and 9** ............................................**421**

What Is Interactive Step Debugging? ...........................................................421

Getting Started with the CF8 Debugger ......................................................424

First Stop: Setting a Breakpoint ...........................................................425

Observing Program State Information (Variables) ..................................426

Stepping Through Lines of Code .........................................................427

Configuration and Security .....................................................................430

Configuring RDS in both Eclipse and ColdFusion's Administrator Page ..........430

Configuring the Multiserver or J2EE Configuration .............................431

Differences Between the Debugger and FusionDebug ...............................431

Summary ................................................................................................432

▓ **Chapter 39: Getting Started with Subversion** .....................................**433**

Introducing Subversion ..........................................................................433

Setting Up Subversion on a Windows Server ...........................................434

Creating Your First Repository ............................................................436

Importing a Web Site Project into a Repository ..................................438

Setting Up the Client Machine ...........................................................441

Updating, Committing, and Resolving with Subversion ...........................442

Always More to Learn .............................................................................444

▓ **Chapter 40: Subversion in the Workflow** ...........................................**445**

The Advantages of Subversion ...............................................................445

Terminology ...........................................................................................446

Using Subversion ...................................................................................446

Creating Your First Repository ............................................................447

Setting Up Your Project ......................................................................447

Creating Your First Revision ...............................................................448

Branching and Tags.................................................................................................448

Synchronizing Changes Between Branches and the Trunk...............................................449

Taking Advantage of Advanced SVN Features in Your Workflow...................................450

Reverting to a Previous Version.................................................................................450

Working with Locks................................................................................................450

Exporting from SVN................................................................................................450

Conclusion ...........................................................................................................450

▓**Chapter 41: Advanced Subversion**.................................................................**451**

Branching ...........................................................................................................451

Creating a Branch.................................................................................................452

Successful Branching.............................................................................................453

Tagging ...............................................................................................................454

Switching .............................................................................................................455

Merging................................................................................................................455

Blame Game ........................................................................................................458

Properties .............................................................................................................458

Where to Go From Here .........................................................................................460

▓**Chapter 42: Automating Your Development with Ant**.......................................**461**

Ant Installation......................................................................................................462

Eclipse Integration ................................................................................................463

The Ant Buildfile ..................................................................................................464

Buildfile Components.............................................................................................464

A Hello World Buildfile ..........................................................................................466

Ant Properties.......................................................................................................468

Dynamic Data in Ant.............................................................................................469

Copying and Zipping Files.................................................................................470

Interacting with Subversion............................................................................473

Sending E-mail ................................................................................................474

Some Ant Guidelines.......................................................................................475

Conclusion .......................................................................................................475

Index.................................................................................................................477

# Foreword

ColdFusion has evolved and changed since its creation a decade and a half ago, and so have the applications being built using it. Simple, loosely coupled scripts have been replaced with carefully architected applications. Cobbled-together projects have been replaced with sophisticated, design-pattern-based solutions. Lightweight, database front ends have been replaced by tiered ORM abstractions providing greater power and flexibility. ColdFusion has grown up, and both the product and language have matured to provide the capabilities today's developers need.

In some ways, being a ColdFusion developer was a whole lot simpler back then. As long as you knew a little SQL, a little more HTML, and the basics of CFML, well, you could build and deploy applications that worked and solved real problems. But as the needs and requirements of applications have grown, so has the complexity involved in building these applications, and so have the demands on ColdFusion developers. While it is indeed still possible to build quick and simple applications, and there remains a legitimate need for this type of rapid application development, many ColdFusion developers are finding that their repertoire has had to grow to include lots of other supporting and complementary products and technologies.

*Fusion Authority* has been at the forefront of ColdFusion knowledge and ongoing education for many years, encouraging developers to fully appreciate the power and capabilities of their chosen development platform, and introducing them to vital skills and opportunities that they otherwise might have missed. Along the way, *Fusion Authority* has published content and knowledge created by the thought leaders in the ColdFusion world, on topics as diverse as framework use to effective Ajax user interfaces to JVM optimization to the mechanics of `Application.cfc` use to automated deployment and a whole lot more.

As such, I am really pleased to see that the *Fusion Authority* team has taken their hard work to the next level, compiling the best and most important articles from the printed journal, updating them, and publishing them all together in one comprehensive anthology. The ColdFusion community has long been seeking this type of higher-end content and will be well-served by the book you are holding in your hands.

Ben Forta
*Director of Platform Evangelism*
*Adobe Systems Inc.*
Author, *The ColdFusion Web Application Construction Kit*

# About the Authors

**Michael Dinowitz** is a longtime ColdFusion expert (since early 1995) and is well-known for his troubleshooting, experimentation, and ability to take complex topics and break them down into simple elements. He is President of House of Fusion, Publisher of *Fusion Authority*, and a founding member of Team Allaire/Macromedia/Adobe Community Professional.

**Judith Dinowitz** is the Master Editor-in-Chief of the *House of Fusion* magazines and journals, where she enjoys serving up ColdFusion and Flex goodness on a weekly and quarterly basis.

A veteran ColdFusion developer since 1997, **Charlie Arehart** is a longtime contributor to the community and a recognized Adobe Community Professional. He's a certified Advanced ColdFusion developer and instructor for each release since ColdFusion 4. Now an independent contractor living in Alpharetta, GA, Charlie provides high-level troubleshooting/tuning assistance and training/mentoring for ColdFusion teams (carehart.org/consulting). He runs the Online ColdFusion Meetup (coldfusionmeetup.com, an online ColdFusion user group with 2,000+ members), runs the CF411.com site and other resources, and is a contributor to each of the three-volume series *ColdFusion 8 WACK* books by Ben Forta, et al.

▨**Peter Bell** presents internationally and writes extensively on Flex, CFML, Groovy, and JavaScript development. He's best known for his expertise in code generation, domain-specific modeling, and agile/lean/XP best practices. He heads up Railo US (www.getrailo.com), a fast, open-source CFML engine. His popular application generation blog is at pbell.com, and he also blogs at gettinggroovy.wordpress.com.

▨**Mike Brunt** has been coding web applications since 1993 and began using ColdFusion at version 1.54 in 1995-6. He designed and created the first online international industrial equipment mart in 1997 (Power Bank International) at the request of a Cummins Engine Company subsidiary. In 1998 he worked with Kodak and Lucent Technologies to create a pioneering web-based TeleRadiology cross-consult portal where Radiologists and Primary Care Physicians could review patient medical images. Allaire recruited Mike in 1999 to join a ColdFusion-JRun consulting team. This team was dispatched world-wide to help Allaire and then Macromedia clients design and troubleshoot ColdFusion applications. In 2001, Mike co-founded his own company, Webapper Services, LLC. He now works independently, helping ColdFusion users worldwide to create strategies that ensure that Enterprise-level ColdFusion applications can be scaled effectively and efficiently.

Having spent four years disarming bombs for the Air Force, **Doug Boude** is currently a Senior Web Application Architect living in San Antonio, TX. He blogs at http://www.dougboude.com, is co-manager of the San Antonio RIA User Group, and is a frequent speaker for his local ColdFusion User Group. He has been developing with ColdFusion since version 4.0.

▓**Raymond Camden** is a software consultant focusing on ColdFusion and RIA development. A long-time ColdFusion user, Raymond has worked on numerous ColdFusion books including the *ColdFusion Web Application Construction Kit* and has contributed to the *Fusion Authority Quarterly Update* and the *ColdFusion Developer's Journal*. He also presents at conferences and contributes to online webzines. He founded many community web sites, including CFLib.org, ColdFusionPortal.org, ColdFusionCookbook.org, and is the author of open source applications, including the popular BlogCFC (www.blogcfc.com) blogging application.

Raymond can be reached at his blog (www.coldfusionjedi.com) or via email at ray@camdenfamily.com. He is the happily married proud father of three kids and is somewhat of a Star Wars nut.

▓**Sean Corfield** is currently Chief Technology Officer for Railo Technologies US, the consulting group that provides professional services and support for the free open source Railo CFML engine. He has worked in the IT industry for about 25 years, initially in database systems and compilers and then mobile telecoms. Since 1997, Sean has architected large-scale, high-availability web systems for Macromedia (now Adobe), Oracle, Thomas Cook, Toshiba, Toyota and Vodafone, among others. He is a staunch advocate of software standards and best practices, and is a well-known and respected speaker on these subjects. Sean has championed and contributed to a number of ColdFusion frameworks, and is a frequent publisher on his blog, http://corfield.org/.

▓**Pete Freitag** is the owner and principal consultant of Foundeo Inc., a company specializing in ColdFusion consulting and products. Pete has been involved in the ColdFusion community for nearly a decade and has been blogging about ColdFusion since 2002 on his blog at www.petefreitag.com.

▓**Hal Helms** writes, teaches, and consults on software development. His podcasts with Jeff Peters can be downloaded from http://helmsandpeters.com. His popular "Occasional Newsletter" is available at http://halhelms.com. Hal can be reached at hal@halhelms.com.

▓**Mike Henke** has worked with ColdFusion since 1999 for several companies. He is an advocate of Eclipse, Source Control, Mylyn, and anything that makes developing ColdFusion more productive and easier. His main focus currently is learning Git, Ruby on Rails, and ColdFusion on Wheels. An Adobe Community Professional, Mike has spoken at several user groups and enjoys discussing ColdFusion with anyone.

▓**Doug Hughes** is a ColdFusion programmer, small business owner, husband, and proud parent of two wonderful kids. When not trying to find ways to get more sleep, Doug busily spends his spare time programming and writing technical articles. Doug is the creator of the Reactor ORM framework for ColdFusion and the well-known Alagad Image and Captcha Components.

▓**Kevin Jones** is a Senior .NET Consultant in Washington, D.C., and a Microsoft ASP.NET MVP.

▓**Wally Kolcz** has been a web developer for six years and currently serves as the ColdFusion Architect and Flex Developer for University of Michigan Health Systems. He is married to a tolerant wife, has an amazing son, and has three wonder dogs. In his free time, he donates web sites and printed materials to local and national animal rescues and causes.

▓**Dave Konopka** lives and works in the Philadelphia, PA, area. He builds web applications for students and faculty of the Wharton School by day. He also helps administer the school's web environment. You can find him on Twitter @davekonopka and read his web development blog at http://imakewebjunk.com.

■Boyan Kostadinov is a software engineer with 10 years of experience whose career has centered around developing web and Windows applications in a wide variety of languages. He received a bachelor's degree in Computer Science from Alfred University with a minor in Management Information Systems, and has worked with Perl/CGI, ColdFusion, SQL, ASP, PHP, JSP, a little Java, and .NET. Currently, he develops mainly in ColdFusion and .NET with a heavy use of Ajax. In his spare time, he wonders how to spend his little time away from the computer on the computer. You can read more of his thoughts on ColdFusion and programming on his blog at http://blog.tech-cats.com.

■Brian Kotek has been developing web applications for more than 12 years, using ColdFusion, Java, Groovy, Flex, and AIR. He's worked as a consultant or employee on a wide range of projects for private companies and government agencies. Brian is a regular speaker at industry conferences, as well as a blogger and author. He has contributed to a number of community endeavors, including Fusebox, ColdSpring, Swiz, and several RIAForge projects.

■Mark Kruger is the owner and CEO of CF Webtools (http://cfwebtools.com), a ColdFusion development company. Starting as a network engineer, Mark discovered ColdFusion in 1998. He founded the Nebraska ColdFusion User Group (http://necfug.com) in 1999 and started CF Webtools in 2000. CF Webtools has grown to 12 developers and works with high-profile customers such as ACS Inc, Lincoln Financial, and the City of San Francisco and Pasadena, CA. As an avid ColdFusion programmer and advocate, Mark blogs at ColdFusion Muse (coldfusionmuse.com), and he lives in Omaha, NE with his wife, Ann, and three children - Jasmine, Aaron, and Matthew.

■**Mark Mandel** is a full-time consultant and lead developer on several open-source projects, most notably Transfer ORM, ColdSpring, JavaLoader, and ColdDoc. He has been working with ColdFusion for a number of years, including at his very own dot-com back in the late 90s.

Mark can often be found blogging on ColdFusion, Java, and various aspects of software development at www.compoundtheory.com. He is also a regular poster on ColdFusion mailing lists and generally causes havoc in the #coldfusion channel on Dalnet irc network.

When he's not too busy writing open source software and consulting, he spends his extra time training in the martial arts in a wide variety of disciplines and reading way too much fantasy literature.

■**John Mason** works at FusionLink, a ColdFusion and Flex hosting provider based in Atlanta, GA. John has been building web applications with ColdFusion since 1997 and is a Certified Advanced ColdFusion Developer. He currently serves as the president of the Atlanta Flash/Flex User Group. He actively blogs at www.codfusion.com.

■**Nathan Mische** is a Senior Programmer/Analyst for the Wharton Learning Lab, where he develops technology-enhanced learning materials for The Wharton School of the University of Pennsylvania using ColdFusion and Flex. He is also the lead developer of the ColdFire Firebug extension and blogs at www.mischefamily.com/nathan.

■**Adrian J. Moreno** is an Enterprise Web Architect and Business Analyst who specializes in ColdFusion applications. He is the assistant manager for the Dallas / Fort Worth ColdFusion User Group and in his spare time plays Texas Hold'em and studies Pekiti Tirsia Kali. You can find his blog at `www.iknowkungfoo.com`.

■**Jake Munson** has been programming ColdFusion for eight years, and works for Idaho Power doing the same. He is the manager of the budding Boise ColdFusion User's Group. He is also the creator of CFQuickDocs and CFFormProtect.

■**Ben Nadel** is the chief software engineer at Epicenter Consulting, a boutique software company in New York City that specializes in developing high-end, customized business solutions. He is also an Adobe Community Professional as well as an Adobe Certified Professional in Advanced ColdFusion. In his spare time, he co-manages the New York City ColdFusion User Group and blogs extensively about all aspects of obsessively thorough web application development on www.bennadel.com.

A Gulf War Veteran of the United States Navy, **Jim Pickering** is a self-taught ColdFusion programmer with more than a decade in the field, and he runs his own business at PickeringProduction.com. He is a loving husband and a proud father of five daughters. He is the founder of Kansas City's first RIA Community, KCDevCore (www.KCDevCore.org), helping with its leadership and management, and is Co-Founder of KCCoreGroups (www.KCCoreGroups.org), an umbrella organization that assists and organizes all four Adobe User Groups in Kansas City. Visit his blog at www.PickeringProduction.com. You can contact Jim at jim@PickeringProduction.com.

■**Jim Priest** is a husband, a father of two, a developer, and an avid motorcyclist. He currently works for Lockheed Martin as a senior software development analyst.

■**Joe Rinehart** has been designing and developing applications based on Adobe products for more than 10 years. By participating in the Adobe community, blogging and developing open-source development tools like Model-Glue, Joe has built a reputation as a leader in the Adobe development community. Published in magazines such as *Dr. Dobbs' Journal* and *The Fusion Authority Quarterly Update*, he's also a regular speaker at technical conferences such as Adobe MAX. Find out more by reading Joe's blog, Firemoss, at www.firemoss.com.

▨Jared Rypka-Hauer has been a member of ColdFusion's community support network since 2005 when he was invited to join Team Macromedia (later Adobe Community Professionals). He is founder of cf.Objective(), the world's only Enterprise Software Engineering conference for ColdFusion developers, and has authored or contributed to numerous articles in many publications. He is a member of the development teams for Model-Glue, ColdSpring and Fusebox and has taught classes and workshops on framework use and best practices in his efforts to evangelize modern software engineering best practices to the ColdFusion community. He lives in the Minneapolis area with his wife and daughter.

▨Terry Ryan is a Flash Platform Evangelist for Adobe. He specializes in ColdFusion. Previously he was a ColdFusion developer for more than 10 years, working at the Wharton School of Business. He's been blogging about ColdFusion since 2004 at both Aarrgghh and TerrenceRyan.com. He's started and contributed to several open source projects on RIAForge.com. When he's not traveling the world touting the advantages of ColdFusion and the Flash Platform, you can find him in his home office in Philadelphia, PA.

▨Chris Scott is an independent consultant in the Philadelphia area with nine years of coldfusion development experience and a strong interest in the implementation of open source solutions. Chris recently joined the development of the ColdSpring cfc container and began work on ColdSpring AOP, the first Aspect Oriented Programming framework for coldfusion.

■**Matt Woodward** is Principal IT Specialist for the Office of the Sergeant at Arms at the United States Senate in Washington, D.C., and is the Community Manager and a Contributing Developer for the Mach-II framework. He has been working with CFML since 1996 and also develops in Java and Grails. Matt is also a member of the Free Software Foundation, the Association for Computing Machinery, the League for Programming Freedom, and serves on the Open BlueDragon Steering Committee and the CFML Advisory Committee.

# About the Technical Reviewers

■Sean Corfield is currently CEO of Railo Technologies, Inc. He has worked in IT for more than 25 years, starting out writing database systems and compilers then moving into mobile telecoms and finally into web development in 1997. Along the way, he worked on the ISO and ANSI C++ Standards committees for 8 years and is a staunch advocate of software standards and best practice. Sean has championed and contributed to a number of CFML frameworks and was lead developer on Fusebox for 2 years. He released his own framework (FW/1) in 2009.

■Mark Mandel is a full-time consultant and lead developer on several open-source projects, most notably Transfer ORM, ColdSpring, JavaLoader, and ColdDoc. He has been working with ColdFusion for a number of years, including at his very own dot-com back in the late 90s.

Mark can often be found blogging on ColdFusion, Java, and various aspects of software development at www.compoundtheory.com. He is also a regular poster on ColdFusion mailing lists and generally causes havoc in the #coldfusion channel on Dalnet irc network.

When he's not too busy writing open source software and consulting, he spends his extra time training in the martial arts in a wide variety of disciplines and reading way too much fantasy literature.

■Brian Kotek has been developing web applications for over 12 years, using ColdFusion, Java, Groovy, Flex, and AIR. He's worked as a consultant or employee on a wide range of projects for private companies and government agencies. Brian is a regular speaker at industry conferences, as well as a blogger and author. He has contributed to a number of community endeavors, including Fusebox, ColdSpring, Swiz, and several RIAForge projects

# Acknowledgments

Michael and I could not have done this book without the help and support of a multitude of people. *Fusion Authority* is not just a labor of love for Michael and myself, but for the ColdFusion community as a whole, and we would not be able to do any of this without their support.

We'd like to thank our wonderful staff – Dana Tierney, Dee Sadler, Charlie Griefer, Brian Rinaldi, Mark Mandel, Sean Corfield, Adam Tuttle, Tom Chiverton, Jake Munson, and Ryan Hartwich – who work tirelessly to make sure that the articles are error-free and as readable as humanly possible.

We owe a special debt of gratitude to two people. The first is Dana Tierney, our Senior Editor, whose sharp eye and wicked red pen have made many an article leaner and clearer. The second is Sean Corfield for his tireless support of the journal, above and beyond the call of duty. This does not, of course, subtract from the gratitude we have for the rest of our staff.

Thank you to our technical reviewers for finding the places that needed improvement.

We'd like to acknowledge all of our authors, whose insight, enthusiasm, and knowledge are the key to the success of our journals. Thank you: Sean Corfield, Raymond Camden, Peter Bell, Doug Boude, Pete Freitag, Mike Brunt, Ben Nadel, Adrian J. Moreno, Terry Ryan, Nathan Mische, Mark Kruger, John Mason, Brian Kotek, Hal Helms, Dave Konopka, Jared Rypka-Hauer, Matt Woodward, Joe Rinehart, Chris Scott, Doug Hughes, Mark Mandel, Wally Kolcz, Mike Henke, Jacob Munson, Charlie Arehart, Jim Pickering, Boyan Kostadinov, Kevin Jones, and Jim Priest.

Thank you Jeff Peters, Ezra Parker, and Kurt Wiersma for updating articles when the original authors did not have the time themselves.

Finally, we'd like to thank the highly professional staff at Apress, especially Steve Anglin for getting Apress interested in the first place, and Debra Kelly, Caroline Rose, and Matthew Moodie for their editorial efforts.

Judith Dinowitz

# Introduction

Almost as long as there's been ColdFusion, House of Fusion has been there to support the ColdFusion community. This support started with the House of Fusion web site, mailing lists, and forums, then logically led to the Fusion Authority News Alerts, which in turn led to the *Fusion Authority Quarterly Update* (FAQU). FAQU was designed not to give just the latest news but to give in-depth technical articles, professionally edited and designed to give readers of every level an understanding of the topic at hand.

This book takes the best articles from the Fusion Authority issues, updates them with the latest information, and provides them to you with the same quality editorial that Fusion Authority is known for. Our goal, as always, is for you to understand what's going on. If you don't, we've failed. Articles are divided into the following sections: ColdFusion Fundamentals, Document Creation in ColdFusion, Essentials to Server Productivity, Communicating and Integrating with Other Technologies, Object-Oriented Programming, ColdFusion Frameworks, Designing the User Interface, and Development Tools.

### ColdFusion Fundamentals

The five articles in this section touch on topics that are key to understanding and creating effective ColdFusion applications: Application.cfc, User-Defined Functions (UDFs) and ColdFusion Components (CFCs), onMissingTemplate(), and onMissingMethod().

### Document Creation in ColdFusion

The two articles in this section focus on key elements of document creation: PDFs and images. Recent advances in ColdFusion have made PDF and image manipulation easier and more versatile.

### Essentials to Server Productivity

How you handle the elements in this section – the Java Virtual Machine (JVM), asynchronous gateways, and the organization of your database code – can boost or hinder your server productivity.

### Communicating and Integrating with Other Technologies

In this section, we group together articles about technologies external to ColdFusion – web services, email, Microsoft Exchange and BlazeDS – that can add power and flexibility to the ColdFusion application.

### Object-Oriented Programming (OOP)

Learning to create object-oriented applications requires a shift in thought about the architecture of your application as a whole. In these articles, our authors help you make this shift, addressing such issues as "Why bother?", learning the terminology of OO, and then looking at specific, more advanced techniques in object-oriented design.

### ColdFusion Frameworks

Frameworks organize your application, reduce the amount of work that has to be done, and standardize the application, allowing multiple developers to work on the same application with less confusion. These articles cover most of the major frameworks in ColdFusion: what they are, why you'd use them, and how to get started.

### Designing the User Interface

ColdFusion provides many tags, functions, and techniques to help create rich front ends for your applications. Two of the articles -- "JSON and CFAJAXPROXY in ColdFusion" and "Creating Dynamic Presentations in ColdFusion" – are hands-on tutorials on how to use ColdFusion's layout and presentation functionality, while the other two articles take a higher-level look at user interface design and architecture.

### Development Tools

In our last section, we look at the tools that will increase your productivity. We cover IDEs (Eclipse and ColdFusion Builder), the ColdFusion Debugger built into ColdFusion 8 and 9, and source control and automation tools (Subversion and Ant).

This book is another step toward our goal of making ColdFusion programmers more knowledgeable, more successful, and in the end, more salable.

Michael and Judith Dinowitz
*Publisher and Master Editor-in-Chief*
*House of Fusion, Inc.*

# PART 1

# ColdFusion Fundamentals

# CHAPTER 1

■ ■ ■

# Working with Application.cfc

## by Raymond Camden

*Application.cfc, introduced in ColdFusion MX 7, revolutionized ColdFusion programming because it allowed for a more modular, ColdFusion Component (CFC)-based approach to application management. Although some people still use Application.cfm, Application.cfc is the preferred method, and with good reason. Raymond Camden sheds some light on what's possible using Applicationc.cfc.*

ColdFusion MX 7 added a number of really cool features to the ColdFusion developer's toolkit. One of the most powerful of these was support for a CFC-based approach to application management. Prior to ColdFusion MX 7, ColdFusion applications were typically defined by the existence of a `cfapplication` tag, usually contained within an `Application.cfm` file. While this worked well enough, there were a lot of things that we either couldn't do or couldn't do easily with these tools. For example, setting memory variables once and only once usually involved a check for existence, a lock, and another check, or other strange coding techniques.

The `Application.cfc` file changes all of that. It improves our options for designing ColdFusion applications. In this article, I will show you how to leverage ColdFusion's new event-driven methods in your own `Application.cfc`. We will build a new application and slowly "grow" the `Application.cfc` file as we add features. You may want to follow along, and have your ColdFusion server up and running, as well as a good editor (ColdFusion Builder, of course, available from `http://labs.adobe.com/technologies/coldfusionbuilder/`).

## What Is an Application?

ColdFusion defines an application as a collection of files that all contain a `cfapplication` tag with the same name attribute. In the "old days," the easiest way to make sure the `cfapplication` tag was part of each file was to place the tag within an `Application.cfm` file, which ColdFusion automatically prepends to any page called in the same directory and any subdirectories. ColdFusion automatically runs the `Application.cfm` file and creates the *Application* scope, and potentially a *Session* scope and a *Client* scope. The data is unique to and contained within that particular application. The code would look like this:

```
<cfapplication name="myApplication" sessionManagement=true>
```

As long as you didn't have any other `cfapplication` tags, all the files in the folder containing the `Application.cfm` file, and in any subfolder, would be considered one application.

So how did we typically use the `Application.cfm` file? Most of us used it as an "auto-include." In other words, since we knew it was always run, we would use it to do the following:

- Initialize application variables like the database source name (DSN) and the administrator's e-mail.

- Include user-defined functions (UDFs) for other pages to use.

- Control what happens when an error occurs with the `cferror` tag.

- Add security to the application (or to parts of the application).

Let's take a quick look at a simple, old-school `Application.cfm` file (Listing 1-1).

*Listing 1-1. Example1.cfm*

```
<!--- define application --->
<cfapplication name="oldSchool" sessionManagement=true>

<!--- initialize application variables --->
<cfif not isDefined("application.init") or isDefined("url.reinit")>
  <cfset application.dsn = "foo">
  <cfset application.adminemail = "ray@camdenfamily.com">
  <cfset application.init = true>
</cfif>

<!--- load UDFs that my pages may need --->
<cfinclude template="udfs.cfm">

<!--- If something goes wrong, run this file and blame the management --->
<cferror type="exception" template="error.cfm">

<!--- secure the admin folder --->
<cfif findNoCase("/admin", cgi.script_name) and not isDefined("session.loggedIn")>
<cfinclude template="login.cfm">
<cfabort>
</cfif>
```

I won't spend a lot of time on this file because it represents the old way of coding, but it does provide an example of all four uses of `Application.cfm`. (Of course, you can do more with `Application.cfm`, but this resembles what most of us are doing out there in the real world.)

Now let's look at how this code can be rewritten in the new `Application.cfc` format. We'll start simple and expand piece by piece. The first version (Listing 1-2) has a grand total of two lines.

*Listing 1-2. Application.cfc (version 1)*

```
<cfcomponent output="false">
</cfcomponent>
```

Woohoo! We have a file that does absolutely nothing. (But boy, does it run fast!) You will want to save this file in a folder by itself somewhere under your web root. It doesn't really matter what you name the folder.

The next thing you probably will want to do is configure the application. In the past, this would have been done with attributes in the `cfapplication` tag. In our component-based `Application.cfc` file, we simply use the *This* scope. Let's add a few more details to the application (Listing 1-3).

*Listing 1-3. Application.cfc (version 2)*

```
<cfcomponent output="false">
  <cfset this.name = "OurApplication">
  <cfset this.applicationTimeout = createTimeSpan(0,2,0,0)>
  <cfset this.clientManagement = false>
  <cfset this.sessionManagement = true>
</cfcomponent>
```

So what did we do here? We named the application, set a specific application timeout, turned off client management, and turned on session management. In the past, this would have been done as shown in Listing 1-4.

*Listing 1-4. Old-style application management using the cfapplication tag*

```
<cfapplication name="OurApplication" applicationTimeout="#createTimeSpan(0,2,0,0#"
 clientManagement="false" sessionManagement="true">
```

Although the CFC version has more lines, it's a bit easier to read. We should quickly check to make sure everything is working OK, so let's create a simple `index.cfm` (Listing 1-5). This should be saved in the folder where you saved the `Application.cfc` file.

*Listing 1-5. A simple index.cfm*

```
<cfdump var="#application#" label="Application Scope">
```

If you run the index file, you should see a dump of the Application scope. Since we didn't actually put anything in it, you should see just the application name.

# Adding Application Variables

Next let's look at how to add application variables. This section describes eight methods for doing so.

## The onApplicationStart Method

The "old-style" code would do something like the code shown in Listing 1-6.

*Listing 1-6. Old-style method of adding application variables*

```
<cfif not isDefined("application.init")>
  lots of application variables
  <cfset application.init = true>
</cfif>
```

This works, but it is a bit of a hack. It would be nice if there was a way to have code that would run only once, when the application started. Luckily, we can do that by simply adding the onApplicationStart method to the Application.cfc file. Listing 1-7 is the next version of the Application.cfc file.

*Listing 1-7. Application.cfc (version 3)*

```
<cfcomponent output="false">
  <cfset this.name = "OurApplication">
  <cfset this.applicationTimeout = createTimeSpan(0,2,0,0)>
  <cfset this.clientManagement = false>
  <cfset this.sessionManagement = true>
  <cffunction name="onApplicationStart" returnType="boolean" output="false">
    <cfset application.dsn = "foo">
    <cfset application.adminEmail = "ray@camdenfamily.com">
    <cfreturn true>
  </cffunction>
</cfcomponent>
```

The method we added, onApplicationStart, will be called by ColdFusion automatically the first time a user hits the application. Notice there is no isDefined or wasted application variable to check. We just set the application variables for our site, and we're finished with it.

Also notice that the method returned true. If you return false, the application won't start. Why would you ever return false? Well, you might write some code that checks to make sure the data source is working. If not, you could fire off an e-mail to the administrator, and then return false.

## The onSessionStart Method

An Application.cfm file is also commonly used to initialize Session variables, typically using the same type of logic. The code checks for some Session variable used as a marker, sets some variables, and then sets the marker. Once again, we can do this a lot easier by adding the onSessionStart method to the Application.cfc file. Listing 1-8 shows version 4 of our application.

*Listing 1-8. Application.cfc (version 4)*

```
<cfcomponent output="false">
  <cfset this.name = "OurApplication">
  <cfset this.applicationTimeout = createTimeSpan(0,2,0,0)>
  <cfset this.clientManagement = false>
<cfset this.sessionManagement = true>
```

```
<cffunction name="onApplicationStart" returnType="boolean" output="false">

    <cfset application.dsn = "foo">
    <cfset application.adminEmail = "ray@camdenfamily.com">
    <cfreturn true>

</cffunction>

<cffunction name="onSessionStart" returnType="void" output="false">
    <cfset session.started = now()>
    <cfset session.numberofpagesvisited = 0>
</cffunction>

</cfcomponent>
```

The onSessionStart method is much like the onApplicationStart code. We set a few random Session variables, and we're finished. But unlike onApplicationStart, the onSessionStart method doesn't return a value.

## The onRequestStart Method

So far, we've covered how to handle creating variables at startup. Now let's look at how we can load templates that contain information that we want associated with the page.

At the beginning of each request, ColdFusion will look for a method named onRequestStart. We can use this method to load a template containing all of our UDFs. Listing 1-9 is the next version of our Application.cfc file.

*Listing 1-9. Application.cfc (version 5)*

```
<cfcomponent output="false">
  <cfset this.name = "OurApplication">
  <cfset this.applicationTimeout = createTimeSpan(0,2,0,0)>
  <cfset this.clientManagement = false>
  <cfset this.sessionManagement = true>

  <cffunction name="onApplicationStart" returnType="boolean" output="false">

    <cfset application.dsn = "foo">
    <cfset application.adminEmail = "ray@camdenfamily.com">

    <cfreturn true>
  </cffunction>

  <cffunction name="onRequestStart" returnType="boolean" output="false">
    <cfargument name="thePage" type="string" required="true">

    <cfinclude template="udfs.cfm">
```

```
    <cfreturn true>
  </cffunction>

  <cffunction name="onSessionStart" returnType="void" output="false">

    <cfset session.started = now()>
    <cfset session.numberofpagesvisited = 0>

  </cffunction>
</cfcomponent>
```

When the onRequestStart method is called, ColdFusion passes it an argument that contains the script name of the file being requested. You could use this for security and check for an admin folder. If it exists and the user isn't logged on, you could forward the user to a login page. Or you can ignore it, as we did here. You don't need to do anything at all with it.

Like the onApplicationStart method, onRequestStart has a returnType of boolean, and if you return false, the request will abort. All we did in the method here was include a file of UDFs.

You should know that if you set a variable in the onRequestStart method, it will *not* be available in the page. I know that this is confusing. (And it gets even more confusing when you use the onRequest method, which is why I'll cover it at the end.) So why bother including the UDFs file at all? In my case, I used the *Request* scope for my UDFs, as shown in Listing 1-10 (udfs.cfm).

*Listing 1-10. udfs.cfm*

```
<cfscript>
  request.udf = structNew();
  function doNothing() {
      return "";
  }

  request.udf.doNothing = doNothing;
</cfscript>
```

Most folks use UDFs by including them in the Request scope, as I did here. The only difference is that I copied the UDFs to a structure. This has two benefits:

- It means that when onRequestStart loads the file, I'll have access to the UDFs in my pages. I'll just need to use the Request scope.

- If I use any custom tags that need the UDFs, they will be accessible from the Request-scoped structure, especially if I have deeply nested tags.

So remember to use a non-Variables scope if you want to use the onRequestStart method to initialize some variables for your pages.

## The onError Method

So far, we've covered everything from our list except error handling. You could simply use the cferror tag in your Application.cfc file. That is perfectly fine. But if you really want to move into the future, use the onError method. As you can guess, this error handler runs whenever an exception that is not captured within a cftry/cfcatch is thrown by your site's code. Let's look at the latest version of our Application.cfc file, in Listing 1-11.

*Listing 1-11. Application.cfc (version 6)*

```
<cfcomponent output="false">
  <cfset this.name = "OurApplication">
  <cfset this.applicationTimeout = createTimeSpan(0,2,0,0)>
  <cfset this.clientManagement = false>
  <cfset this.sessionManagement = true>

  <cffunction name="onApplicationStart" returnType="boolean" output="false">

    <cfset application.dsn = "foo">
    <cfset application.adminEmail = "ray@camdenfamily.com">

    <cfreturn true>
  </cffunction>

  <cffunction name="onRequestStart" returnType="boolean" output="false">
    <cfargument name="thePage" type="string" required="true">
    <cfinclude template="udfs.cfm">
    <cfreturn true>
  </cffunction>

  <cffunction name="onSessionStart" returnType="void" output="false">

    <cfset session.started = now()>
    <cfset session.numberofpagesvisited = 0>

  </cffunction>

  <cffunction name="onError" returnType="void" output="false">
    <cfargument name="exception" required="true">
    <cfargument name="eventname" type="string" required="true">

    <cfmail to="#application.adminEmail#" from="#application.adminEmail#"
     subject="Error!" type="html">
      <cfdump var="#exception#" label="Exception">
      <cfdump var="#cgi#" label="cgi">
      <cfdump var="#form#" label="form">
    </cfmail>

    <cflocation url="error.cfm" addToken="false">
  </cffunction>

</cfcomponent>
```

When the `onError` method is called, two arguments are passed to it. The first is the exception object. The second is the name of the event that threw an error, if—and only if—it was another event in the `Application.cfc` file. We've done nothing special here, except to e-mail the administrator some details about both the error and the current request.

Note the `cflocation` tag in the `onError` method. Why did we add that? When you use `cferror` and an exception occurs, the layout that had already been displayed is cleared. When the `onError` method is called, any previously generated HTML isn't cleared. Using `cflocation` will let you present a clean error page to the user.

## The onApplicationEnd Method

Still with me? So far, we haven't done anything that couldn't be done in an `Application.cfm` file. Now let's take a look at some things that would *not* have been possible with `Application.cfm`.

The first method we added to the `Application.cfc` file was `onApplicationStart`. There is a corresponding method named `onApplicationEnd`. This method will be run when the application times out. Since the file is getting a bit large now, I'll just paste in the method in Listing 1-12.

*Listing 1-12. onApplicationEnd*

```
<cffunction name="onApplicationEnd" returnType="void" output="false">
  <cfargument name="applicationScope" required="true">

  <cflog file="#this.name#" text="Application timed out.">
</cffunction>
```

Note two important things here:

- An application "dies" when no one hits the site for a certain period of time (the application's timeout). Because no one is actually at the site, you can't use the method to display a message. Who would the message be displayed to? As you can see, all we did in this method was to `cflog` the event.

- Officially, at this point, the Application scope no longer exists. But since ColdFusion passes in the Application scope as the one and only argument to the method, if you wanted to e-mail the address specified in `application.adminEmail`, you would need to use `arguments.applicationScope.adminEmail` instead.

The names for the arguments that you use in these methods are up to you. While ColdFusion has a specific API for what it sends to each method, you can use whatever names you desire.

## The onSessionEnd Method

Besides knowing when an application ends, the `Application.cfc` file gives you access to the end of the session event. As with the previous listing, we'll look at just this new method in Listing 1-13.

*Listing 1-13. onSessionEnd*

```
<cffunction name="onSessionEnd" returnType="void" output="false">
  <cfargument name="sessionScope" type="struct" required="true">
  <cfargument name="appScope" type="struct" required="false">
  <cfset var duration = dateDiff("n", arguments.sessionScope.started, now())>
  <cflog file="#this.name#" text="Session timed out after #duration# minutes.">
</cffunction>
```

As with the onApplicationEnd method, we can't use onSessionEnd to display a message, but we can use it to log information. Also, as with the onApplicationEnd method, we don't actually have access to the Session scope (after all, it did end), nor do we have access to the Application scope. Both scopes are passed to the method, however. Note that since the Application scope is passed as a pointer, if you modify the Application scope via the argument, you will be modifying the "real" Application scope.

In Listing 1-13, we use the fact that we stored the session start time to log the duration of the session. This is an excellent use of onSessionEnd, as you can see how long people are sticking around your site.

## The onRequestEnd Method

Since we are talking about "end" methods, let's look at one more: onRequestEnd. This is the opposite of onRequestStart. Technically, this type of operation was possible in the past using the onRequestEnd.cfm page. As with Application.cfm, if the onRequestEnd.cfm file existed, it would be included automatically at the end of a request. Listing 1-14 is a simple example of the onRequestEnd method.

*Listing 1-14. onRequestEnd*

```
<cffunction name="onRequestEnd" returnType="void" output="true">
  <cfargument name="thePage" type="string" required="true">
  <cfoutput>
    <p align="right">
    Copyright #year(now())#
    </p>
  </cfoutput>
</cffunction>
```

In this example, we're using the onRequestEnd method to display a copyright notice that will run on each and every page request.

Let me be clear. I do *not* like, nor approve of, doing outputs like this in the Application.cfc file. I typically use custom tags to do my layout outputs. However, this was a simple enough example of how to use the method.

## The onRequest Method

The onRequest method is definitely the "problem child" of the Application.cfc family. It can be a bit confusing to use and has some serious side effects that I'll talk about later.

Let's start with a very simple and bare-bones example (Listing 1-15).

*Listing 1-15. A simple example of the onRequest method*

```
<cffunction name="onRequest" returnType="void">
  <cfargument name="thePage" type="string" required="true">
  <cfinclude template="#arguments.thePage#">
</cffunction>
```

As it does in the onRequestStart method, ColdFusion passes the name of the script being executed to the onRequest method. However—and this is very important to note—you *must* actually include the file. If you don't, it won't be processed. The reason for this is that the onRequest method overrides the normal behavior of how files are processed. It gives you precise control over the entire request, and therefore, you must do the work that ColdFusion would normally do—in this case, simply including the template.

To be honest, I haven't seen very many uses for onRequest, and I rarely use this method myself. In the past, I've used it to enable a printable version of a site. I did this by building my page templates to use HTML comment markers. I then used the onRequest method to check for a URL variable. If it existed, I simply used regular expressions to remove the header and footer, which was easy with the markers I had in the layout. Listing 1-16 is a simple example of this use.

*Listing 1-16. onRequest with print functionality*

```
<cffunction name="onRequest" returnType="void">
  <cfargument name="thePage" type="string" required="true">
  <cfset var buffer = "">
  <cfset var thisPage = "">
  <cfif isDefined("url.p")>
      <cfsavecontent variable="buffer">
          <cfinclude template="#arguments.thePage#">
      </cfsavecontent>
      <cfset buffer = reReplace(buffer,".*?<!-- Page Body -->","")>
      <cfset buffer = reReplace(buffer,"<!-- Page Body -->.*","")>
      <cfoutput>#buffer#</cfoutput>
  <cfelse>
      <cfinclude template="#arguments.thePage#">
  </cfif>
</cffunction>
```

The code in Listing 1-16 simply notices a URL variable. When the variable exists, I used a regular expression to remove everything before and after a set of HTML comments.

Another possible use is to strip out the extra whitespace generated by ColdFusion. (One thing ColdFusion likes to do is generate whitespace.)

Using onRequest has two negative side effects, though. The first "gotcha" is the fact that all of the methods and the This scope for the Application.cfc will be copied to the local Variables scope for your script. While this isn't a huge big deal, it may be surprising if you dump the Variables scope.

The other negative side effect affects versions of ColdFusion prior to 9. The mere presence of the onRequest method will immediately break Flash Remoting and web service calls to CFCs in the application. This is because certain data transformations take place as part of a Flash Remoting or web service request, and these are not included in the execution of the onRequest method. This *is* a big deal! There are two ways you can get around it:

- Place your CFCs in a subdirectory and add another `Application.cfc` (one without the `onRequest` method, of course) within the same folder as the CFCs.

- Use the work-around developed by Sean Corfield.

The work-around is a bit weird looking, but it works well and I recommend it. The idea is simple. In the `onRequestStart` method, notice a call for a CFC and hide the `onRequest` method. We do this by taking advantage of how methods are stored inside a CFC. All methods are stored to a structure called `this`. The `this` structure holds all of the information about the CFC and what it contains.

Listing 1-17 is a code sample that can be used in the `onRequestStart` method. It checks to see if the page requested is a CFC or if it uses the Flash Services gateway URL. It then deletes the `onRequest` method from the `this` structure. This is done only for the current request. It doesn't remove the method permanently.

*Listing 1-17. Check for web services or Flash Remoting calls within onRequestStart*

```
<cfif listLast(arguments.thePage,".") is "cfc" or arguments.thePage is↵
 "/flashservices/gateway">
  <cfset structDelete(this,"onRequest")>
</cfif>
```

ColdFusion 9 avoids this problem with the inclusion of the `onCFCRequest` method. This method is run in place of the `onRequest` method when the request is a web service or flash remoting call. If the `onCFCRequest` method is not defined and an `onRequest` method is, the work-around will still be needed.

# A New Application Structure

The `Application.cfc` feature has truly added a good deal of power to our ColdFusion applications. It pulls together all the pieces of an application into a single, streamlined template that provides us with functionality we previously didn't have. We can finally determine how many sessions are active in an application. We can determine when a session ends and when an application times out. We can determine both the start time and end time of any application or session. We have these new powers and the benefit of a much more organized application structure.

While this article has barely scratched the surface of what you can do to take advantage of the new `Application.cfc` features, I highly recommend you begin today to convert your `Application.cfm` files to the new format. If you need a handy reference, you can find a skeleton `Application.cfc` PDF at `http://www.coldfusionjedi.com/downloads/application.cfc.txt`. Personally, I find `Application.cfc` files much easier to parse than older `Application.cfm` files.

# CHAPTER 2

# Application.cfc Reference

**by Michael Dinowitz**

This visual aid and reference to the Application.cfc gives you the order of operation as well as the methods that are available in an Application.cfc template.

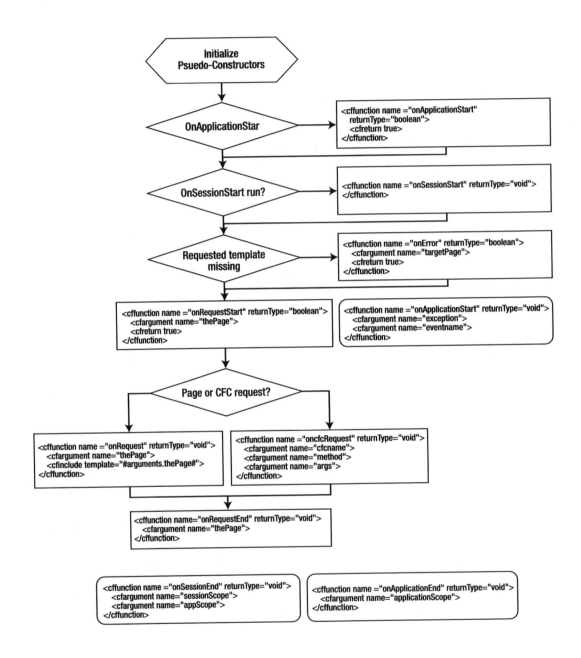

# CHAPTER 3

# From User-Defined Functions to ColdFusion Components

## by Michael Dinowitz

*ColdFusion Components (CFCs) and user-defined functions (UDFs) have become the cornerstones of ColdFusion applications. It is almost impossible to use many of the latest capabilities of ColdFusion without knowing how to use UDFs and CFCs. In this chapter, Michael Dinowitz introduces you, step by step, to these cornerstones.*

In order to use object-oriented programming (OOP) in ColdFusion, you need to understand ColdFusion Components (CFCs). In order to understand CFCs, you need to understand user-defined functions (UDFs). These two concepts are at the root of almost every ColdFusion framework, and they are the starting points for any use of OOP in ColdFusion.

Some people have never used either UDFs or CFCs; others may use them only because they've been told to use components, but they don't truly understand how these technologies work. Even those who know nothing about UDFs or CFCs will gain a full understanding of what they can do from this article. We'll also examine some of the best practices and dogma that have sprung up around these technologies. Only by understanding how things actually work can you know how to use them.

## User-Defined Functions

UDFs were first introduced in ColdFusion 5 as a feature of the CFScript language. This language, designed to be used within the `cfscript` tag, was originally limited in functionality to standard flow control and logic. This, combined with its JavaScript-based syntax, reduced its popularity and usage. With the introduction of ColdFusion functions, originally available *only* in CFScript, the language got a lot more attention. This has evolved to the point where CFScript can be used to create much richer UDFs and even be used to create full components.

When ColdFusion MX 6 was released, UDFs received a major boost with the inclusion of the `cffunction` tag. This allowed people to write UDFs using the full range of ColdFusion tags and functions and provided other advantages as well.

# Creating UDFs

UDFs are composed of two parts: a function definition and a function call. The function definition is composed of a `cffunction` tag block, which will contain all of the operations that the function is expected to perform. This tag also has a unique name that will be used when executing the function.

A function definition is not executed in line with other code in a ColdFusion template, but instead is executed by a function call. In most cases, a UDF function call will look and act exactly like a standard ColdFusion function call and can be used in all the same places and ways. The differences between the two will be discussed later.

## Naming a UDF

Every UDF is defined by a name that will be used to execute it. The UDF cannot have the same name as an existing ColdFusion function. There is currently no way of overriding a standard ColdFusion function with a custom one.

When a template containing a UDF is processed, the UDF code is compiled into memory, and a reference to it is placed in the template's Variables scope. For this reason, all of the standard rules for creating a variable name also apply to the UDF name. The UDF name must have as its first character a letter, underscore (_), or dollar sign ($), which may be followed by any number of additional letters, underscores, dollar signs, and/or numbers. As there is no real cost to having a long name, it is a best practice to make the name as descriptive as possible. It is far easier to understand what a function called `getdate()` does than one that is called `i()`.

Because a UDF is stored in the Variables scope, it will overwrite any variable of the same name that was set before the UDF definition. In addition, any variable of the same name set after the UDF will in turn overwrite the UDF, effectively erasing it. This has been known to happen when someone creates a UDF and then uses it to set a variable of the same name, as in this example:

```
<cfset nextdate=nextdate()>
```

One exception to this behavior is when two UDFs of the same name are defined in the same template. Doing this will always throw a compile-time error, preventing the template from running at all. This will happen no matter how many variables of the same name exist in the template or where they are defined.

When a standard variable is created with a period within the variable name, ColdFusion will assume that what comes before the period is a structure to which that variable will be assigned. If the structure does not exist, ColdFusion will automatically create it. The following assignment:

```
<cfset today.date =now()>
```

is the same as this:

```
<cfset today=StructNew()>
<cfset today.date=now() >
```

This does not apply to UDFs. A period in a UDF name will cause an error.

## Assigning UDFs to Other Scopes

There are times when a UDF will need to be assigned to a different scope. One such time is when you want to make the UDF available to a custom tag. Custom tags do not have access to the Variables scope of a template, but they do have access to the Request scope. Assigning a UDF to the Request scope not only makes it available to the custom tag, but also to any and all code being used by the template, such as CFCs.

To assign a UDF to another scope, simply do a `cfset` with the UDF name as the value being assigned, as shown in Listing 3-1.

*Listing 3-1. Setting a UDF to the Request scope*

```
<cffunction name="nextdate">
    Function code
</cffunction>
<cfset request.nextdate = nextdate>
<cfset tomorrow = request.nextdate()>
```

This will create a variable in the Request scope containing a reference to the `nextdate()` UDF. There is no difference in the behavior of the reference and the original UDF. The only difference is in how they are called. `nextdate()` is called without a prefix; `request.nextdate()` uses the `request` prefix.

## Placing the UDF Definition

A `cffunction` tag can be placed anywhere in the same template as its function call. It does not matter if the tag is placed before or after the call. On the other hand, if a `cffunction` is being included in some way, it must always be included before the function call.

There are four basic ways in which a `cffunction` can be included into a template:

- `Application.cfm`: A `cffunction` in the `Application.cfm` file will be available to any function call in that template or in any template associated with it, such as the template being processed. This is the simplest type of include.

- `cfinclude`: It is a common practice to place a number of `cffunction` tags within a separate template and use the `cfinclude` tag to include that template in the requested page. If this is done, the function call must always be after the `cfinclude` tag.

- `OnRequestEnd.cfm`: If a UDF is placed within an `OnRequestEnd` template, it will be available only to function calls within the `OnRequestEnd` template.

- `Application.cfc`: A UDF placed within a CFC is referred to as a *method* of the CFC, rather than as a function or UDF. This is just a difference in terminology and should not bother you at all. A UDF is the same as a custom function, which is the same as a CFC method.

Because `Application.cfc` is a component and not a template, a few special issues come up when you want to define a UDF within it. The first issue is that while a UDF can be defined in the `Application.cfc` file, it will be accessible only by other methods of the component. It will *not* be automatically accessible by the template that was being requested. In order to make the UDF accessible by the requested template, you will need to use the `onRequest()` method of `Application.cfc` to explicitly include the requested template into the component. This makes the Variables scope of the component available to the requested template, including any UDFs that are stored within it.

If you can't use the `onRequest()` method, another option is available. Directly after the UDF definition, you can assign a reference to the UDF to the Request scope (see Listing 3-1). While this requires you to access the UDF as `request.nextdate()`, it is a small price to pay.

This issue comes up often when people try to replace their `Application.cfm` templates with the `Application.cfc` component. The new placement of the UDFs is probably the major stumbling block to this move. For more information about `Application.cfc` functionality, see Chapter 1, "Working with Application.cfc."

## The cffunction Tag

To create a UDF, you place the code you want executed within a `cffunction` tag. This block tag acts as a container for the code and has a number of attributes that relate directly to the calling of the function. Some of these attributes are useful only when a UDF is used within a CFC. Others are not really useful and are usually ignored. The only required attribute is `name`, which is used when executing the function.

Listing 3-2 creates a basic UDF.

*Listing 3-2. Basic UDF creation*

```
<cffunction name="GetUser">
     Function code
</cffunction>
```

Other than the `name` attribute, the only other attributes of importance are `hint`, `returntype`, and `output`.

The `hint` attribute is used to document the UDF. It should be used in all UDFs as a best practice. While there is also a `description` attribute, most people ignore it in favor of `hint`.

`returntype` is an optional attribute that validates the data being returned from the UDF and throws an error if the validation fails. The value of this attribute can either be the name of a data type that the return data is being tested against or a special validation type. The first special validation type is `variableName`, which checks if the return data is a string formatted as a valid ColdFusion variable name. The second special validation is used when a CFC reference is being returned from a UDF. The value is the name of a component, which should be the same name as the component in the CFC reference being passed.

The `returntype` validates only the data actually returned by the UDF. If no data is returned, no validation is done, and no error is thrown.

The `returntype` attribute has two additional possible values, neither of which will trigger any validation. The first is `any`, which indicates that the UDF may return something, with no restrictions on what that might be. The second is `void`, which not only indicates that the UDF will return no data, but actually prevents the UDF from returning data even if it wants to.

Some feel that `returntype` validation is an unnecessary overhead, and therefore avoid using it. Even when no validation is desired, this attribute should be used. Using a `returntype` of `any` when data is to be returned is more efficient than not having a `returntype` at all. The same efficiency occurs with the `returntype` of `void` for a UDF that will not return any data. This overhead was partially addressed in ColdFusion 8 with the inclusion of an administration-based switch to ignore `returntype` validation when returning a component reference, which is suggested only for production servers. This switch *does not* turn off other types of `returntype` validation output is a very important attribute. Omitting it may lead to problems when a UDF is executed. When no output attribute is defined, any content within the cffunction block will be output as if it were at the location of the function call. See Listing 3-3 for an example of a function with an undefined output attribute.

*Listing 3-3. cffunction with an undefined output attribute*

```
<cffunction name="showme">
    <cfset test="test value">
    this text will be outputted to the screen. #test# will not be evaluated
    <cfoutput>#test# will be evaluated</cfoutput>
</cffunction>
```

When the example in Listing 3-3 is executed, all of the text inside the cffunction tag will be output exactly as it appears inside the tag. The first #test# will be treated as plain text, while the second one will be evaluated just like any other variable in a cfoutput block. In addition, the cfoutput tags will be replaced with whitespace, as is standard for page output.

One thing to pay particular attention to is the whitespace inside the UDF, as well as the whitespace generated by ColdFusion tags. This whitespace will not only be output when the function is executed, but will also be added to any returned data in the form of a leading space. This space can alter the data being returned from the UDF, and, as its origin is not clear, debugging it can be frustrating.

While it sounds like outputting data from a UDF is a bad thing, there are times when you want to do so. Having a UDF output debugging information about itself is a perfect example.

The output effect can be enhanced by adding the output attribute to the tag and setting its value to Boolean true (true/yes/!0), as shown in Listing 3-4. This will have the same effect as just described, with one alteration: All of the content will be treated as if it were inside a cfoutput block.

*Listing 3-4. cffunction with its output attribute set to true*

```
<cffunction name="showme" output="true">
    <cfset test="test value">
    this text will be outputted to the screen. #test# will be evaluated without↵
a cfoutput
</cffunction>
```

If you do not want any output, and especially not the extra space in the return value, all you need to do is set the output attribute to a value of Boolean false (false/no/0). This will prevent any output when the UDF is executed. Even if you had explicitly set content within the UDF for output, it will be suppressed. Listing 3-5 shows an example.

*Listing 3-5. Effect of setting the output attribute to false*

```
<cffunction name="showme" output="false">
    <cfset test="value">
    #test#
</cffunction>
```

Here's a quick summary of the effects of the `output` attribute on the `cffunction` tag:

- *No* `output` *attribute:* Returns  `#test#` (the word #test# as plain text, with a leading space).

- *The* `output` *attribute set to* `true`: Returns  `value` (the value of the test variable, with a leading space).

- *The* `output` *attribute set to* `false`: Returns nothing.

If the `output` attribute is used, it must always have a Boolean value. Any other value, including no value, will cause an error.

There is a disagreement in the community over whether a UDF should output data. On one side, people say that a UDF should be limited to data processing, and that any data that it would output should instead be returned as a variable and output by its caller. On the other side are those people who feel that there is no reason why a UDF should not be used to display content. I belong to the latter group, but have a firm rule when writing a UDF that outputs data. Such a UDF should not have a `cfreturn` tag and should have little to no ColdFusion code within it. This results in pure user interface-generating UDFs and pure data-processing UDFs. This clean and clear distinction helps me avoid problems.

## The cfargument Tag

The `cfargument` tag is a subtag of `cffunction` that handles assignment and validation of data passed into the UDF. When used, it must be the first ColdFusion tag inside the `cffunction` block. You can use as many `cfargument` tags as you want, with the single restriction that each `cfargument` tag must have a unique variable name in its `name` attribute, which is required.

The primary purpose of the `cfargument` tag is to take data and assign it to the Arguments scope of the UDF, while is contained within the local scope of the UDF. In most cases, the data used by a `cfargument` will come from a passed parameter.

When the parameter is passed by position, the first parameter will be assigned to the first `cfargument` tag, the second to the second, and so on. Once a parameter has been assigned, its associated `cfargument` tag sets the parameter's value to the Arguments scope using a variable name equal to the `cfargument`'s `name` attribute.

When parameters are passed by name, ColdFusion will attempt to match the name of a passed parameter with the name of a `cfargument` tag. If a match is found, the parameter is assigned to that `cfargument` tag and is set to the Arguments scope.

A `cfargument` tag without an associated parameter will still create a variable in the Arguments scope. If the optional `default` attribute is set, then its value will be set as the variable's value. If no default exists, an empty variable will be created in the Arguments scope. Any data set to this variable location later in the UDF will keep this reference.

In addition to assigning variables, the `cfargument` tag can perform two different types of validation on the data being passed. These two validation options are not mutually exclusive. Either or both can be used.

The first validation makes use of the optional `required` attribute, which can take a Boolean value. When this attribute is set to `true`, the `cfargument` tag will throw an error if no parameter is assigned to it. The value or size of the data contained within the passed parameter does not matter as long as it exists. Having a default attribute set in the tag will prevent the required check from ever failing, thus defeating its purpose. Each of the following examples is designed to cause an error because a required value was not set. In Listing 3-6, no parameter is passed to the UDF, and the `cfargument` tag requires one.

*Listing 3-6. Error due to a missing single required parameter*

```
<cfset nextdate()>
<cffunction name="nextdate">
  <cfargument name="date" required="yes">
</cffunction>
```

In Listing 3-7, both `cfargument` tags have the `required` attribute defined, but only one parameter is passed in. The parameter will be assigned to the first `cfargument` tag, leaving the second to throw an error.

*Listing 3-7. One of two required parameters is missing*

```
<cfset nextdate('1/11/1971')>
<cffunction name="nextdate">
    <cfargument name="date" required="yes">
    <cfargument name="offset" required="yes">
</cffunction>
```

Listing 3-8 is much the same as Listing 3-7, but the parameter is passed in by name. The name of the parameter will be matched to the name of the second `cfargument` tag. Because the first `cfargument` tag will not be assigned a parameter, an error will be thrown.

*Listing 3-8. One of two required named parameters is missing*

```
<cfset nextdate(date='first value')>
<cffunction name="nextdate">
    <cfargument name="date" required="yes">
    <cfargument name="offset" required="yes">
</cffunction>
```

The second type of validation looks at the data being passed in and checks to see if it fits the criteria set in the `type` attribute. This attribute can have the same values as the `returntype` attribute mentioned earlier. When data is being passed to a UDF from an outside source such as a form or URL, checking the data type is a very good idea and highly recommended. You should never trust data that is not under your direct control. Some people still ignore the `type` attribute in order to save on overhead. Others ignore it and instead do type validation within the UDF itself.

The `cfargument` tag also has a `hint` attribute that allows you to document what the tag expects passed to it. The few seconds it takes to write a parameter description in this attribute could save you a ton of time later when altering or debugging the UDF.

## The Arguments Scope

When a UDF is executed, the Arguments scope will automatically be created to contain any information passed into the UDF. This scope is private to the UDF and will exist until the UDF has finished processing. The scope is actually a subscope of the UDF's local scope.

The easiest way to add variables to the Arguments scope is to use the `cfargument` tag. Any parameter passed to the UDF that is not assigned to a `cfargument` tag will still be added to the Arguments scope, but will not have any of the other advantages that come from the `cfargument` tag. If the unassigned parameter is passed in by name, it is added to the Arguments scope using that name and is treated as a normal variable in every way. Parameters passed in by position treat the Arguments scope as an array, and each parameter is added in positional order. In Listing 3-9, we pass parameters to a UDF without the use of the `cfargument` tag. Figure 3-1 shows how these arguments are added.

*Listing 3-9. Passing parameters to a UDF without the cfargument tag*

```
<cfset today=nextdate('1/11/1971', 35) >
```

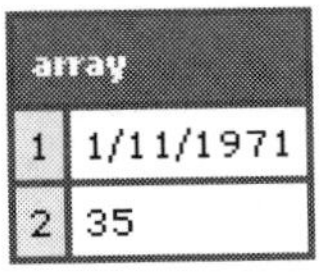

| array | |
|---|---|
| 1 | 1/11/1971 |
| 2 | 35 |

*Figure 3-1. The nextdate UDF after Listing 3-9 has been run*

Arguments stored in this manner can be accessed using standard array syntax:

```
arguments[argumentposition]
```

Using arguments in this way can be painful, which is why `cfargument` tags are so important. If an argument has a name, then it is treated like any other variable, with data being read from it or set to it using the Arguments scope name as a prefix. In Listing 3-10, we use the Arguments scope to set the value of the variable date to 3/29/1972 and then output that variable.

*Listing 3-10. Using the Arguments scope*

```
<cfset arguments.date="3/29/1972">
<cfoutput>#arguments.date#</cfoutput>
```

When an argument is defined using the `cfargument` tag but has no data assigned to it, a variable space will be reserved in these scopes with the name of the `cfargument`, which can later be assigned a value. Listing 3-11 contains an example of a `cffunction` tag that sets variables to the Arguments and local scopes.

*Listing 3-11. Scope of variables*

```
<cffunction name="testfunction" output="true">
    <cfargument name="variable1" default="set to Arguments and local scope">
    <cfargument name="variable2">
    <cfset arguments.variable3="set to the Arguments scope">
    <cfset variable2="load variable 2">
```

```
  #variable1# is the same as #arguments.variable1#<BR>
  #variable2# is the same as #arguments.variable2#<BR>
  #Arguments.variable3# needs the arguments prefix<BR>

  <cfset variable1="new value">
  #arguments.variable1# now has a different value
</cffunction>
```

Listing 3-11 contains two **cfargument** tags. The variable names defined in them will be set to the Arguments scope. If no parameters are passed into this UDF, **variable1** will be assigned the default value that is set in the tag. **variable2**, on the other hand, will have no value and will not be available until a value is assigned to it. Note the use of the **output="true"** attribute of the **cffunction** tag to cause the tag content to be evaluated and output to the screen.

Finally, once inside a UDF, you can set variables to the Arguments scope directly by adding the **Arguments** prefix to the variable name being set. An argument can also be accessed without using the **Arguments** prefix; however, if a local variable of the same name exists, that variable will be used instead. It is a best practice to always access your arguments using the Arguments scope to avoid this potential problem, and also to add self-documentation to your code.

## Local Variables

A UDF's local scope is private to the UDF, allowing variables set to the local scope to exist only as long as the UDF exists. Variables set within a UDF that is not assigned to the local or Arguments scopes are automatically assigned to the Variables scope of the page containing the UDF. This is of utmost importance when dealing with cached components.

Prior to ColdFusion 9, the local scope was virtual and could not be accessed using a prefix. The only way to assign variables to it was by using the **var** keyword. When this keyword was used as part of a variable assignment operation, it made the variable local to the UDF. A variable set in this manner could be accessed anywhere within the UDF, but had no prefix available to it.

An additional limitation was that any assignment using the **var** keyword had to be done at the top of the UDF, after any **cfargument** tags. This separated the creation of a local variable from where it would be used, which, combined with the lack of prefix, could lead to confusion as to what scope a variable belonged to when it was used without a prefix. To combat this, the best practice was to always prefix all variables that were not set using the **var** keyword—in other words, any variable not local to the UDF.

The local scope, added in ColdFusion 9, changed all of that. Any variable can be set using the **local** prefix, which will assign it to the local scope. This acts in the exact same way as a variable set using the **var** keyword. A variable set using the **local** prefix is *exactly* the same as a variable set using the **var** keyword. In addition, when outputting or operating on the variable, the **local** prefix can be used to specify where the variable is from, removing confusion and helping to self-document the code. Finally, variables can be set with the **local** prefix or the **var** keyword anywhere within the UDF. Listing 3-12 demonstrates using **var**.

*Listing 3-12. Using var*

```
<!--- The second cfset will work in CF9 and throw an error in earlier versions. --->
<cfset var test=structnew()>
<cfset var test.variable="local variable">
```

```
<!--- This CFSET will assign the variable name to the user structure in the variables scope
--->
<cfset test.variable="Michael">

<!--- Local variable setting example: --->
<cffunction name="testfunction">
    <cfargument name="variable1" default="set to Arguments ">

    <cfset var variable2="set to local scope">
    <cfset local.variable2="overwrites variable2 in the local scope">

    <cfset variable3="set to Variables scope">
    … function code…
</cffunction>
```

When the function in Listing 3-12 is executed, it will create a variable in the Arguments scope with the name variable1. If no parameters are passed to this UDF, variable will be assigned the value of "set to Arguments scope". Then a local variable named variable2 will be set using the var prefix. This variable will then be overwritten by explicitly using the local prefix. The next line will set a variable named variable3 without using the local prefix or var keyword. This will cause the variable to be assigned to the Variables scope of the page from which the UDF is called, showing that *any* variable created within a UDF and not set to the local or Arguments scope will be set to the global Variables scope.

This may not be what you expect and is the source of many UDF and CFC-based errors. If you are setting a variable that will be used only within the UDF, you must always make sure that it is set to the local scope, whether by using the var keyword or the local prefix. ColdFusion 9 does not remove the need to either var your variables or explicitly use the local prefix.

## The cfreturn Tag

The cfreturn tag is used within a cffunction block to return a variable or value to the UDF call. A UDF can have multiple cfreturn tags, each returning a different value based on some programmatic logic or event. When a cfreturn tag is run, the UDF ceases operation, and its local variables are cleared from memory. If a returntype is defined in the cffunction tag, any data passed through a cfreturn tag will be evaluated against the returntype criteria. If this validation fails, an error will be thrown.

## UDF Variable Protection

There are many times when a variable set in a UDF is accidentally set to the global Variables scope, rather than to the local scope. While people may be scrupulous about variables set using the cfset tag, they tend not to think about the variables created by ColdFusion tags such as cfquery or even cfloop. These variables should also be declared as local to the UDF. Let's look at Listing 3-13, where we use var with a cfquery tag.

*Listing 3-13. Using var with cfquery*

```
<cffunction name="GetAllAuthors" output="false" hint="Query Authors DB and
        Returns all authors">

        <cfset var authors="">
        <cfquery name="Authors" datasource="authordsn">
            Select *
            from Authors
        </cfquery>

    <cfreturn authors>
</cffunction>
```

The first thing to happen within the UDF is that a local variable named authors is created. A query is then run with the same name, overwriting the local variable userquery and making the results of the query local to the UDF. The query in Listing 3-14 bypasses the step of creating a local variable first by directly assigning the query results to the local scope.

*Listing 3-14. Assigning query results to the local scope*

```
<cffunction name="GetAllAuthors" output="false" hint="Query Authors DB and
        Returns all authors">

        <cfquery name="local.Authors" datasource="authordsn">
            Select *
            from Authors
        </cfquery>

    <cfreturn authors>
</cffunction>
```

## Executing UDFs and Passing Parameters

Standard ColdFusion function calls are limited in the way they can pass parameters into a function. All parameters are passed by position, where the physical order of the parameters is important. UDF function calls can pass parameters by position, but they can also pass parameters by name, by data collection, and even by using the cfinvoke tag.

Passing parameters by name is a simple change to the way standard functions pass them. Rather than passing the parameters in a specific order, you assign each parameter a variable name in a *name=value* format. The advantage of this is extra documentation in the UDF function call as well as assigned names for the parameters inside the UDF. For instance, note the two cfset statements in Listing 3-15.

*Listing 3-15. Two examples of passing parameters*

```
<cfset GetAuthor('Michael')>
<cfset GetAuthor(name='Michael')>
```

The first line is a standard pass-by-position setup, where you simply send the parameter into the UDF and trust that the UDF will handle the naming and other details of the parameter. The second line explicitly says that the parameter being passed in has a variable name associated with it and that this is the name it will have inside the UDF.

Another option for passing named parameters to a UDF is to assign all of them to a structure, and then pass the structure to the UDF. The structure is passed by name to the UDF using argumentCollection as the variable name and the structure name as the value. When a UDF receives a parameter named argumentCollection, it will know that this is actually a collection of variable/value pairs and treat them as if they were named parameters passed to the UDF. Listing 3-16 shows how to use argumentCollection to pass named parameters.

*Listing 3-16. Using argumentCollection to pass named parameters*

```
<cfset User=StructNew()>
<cfset User.Name="Michael">
<cfset User.Password="MyPass">
<cfset UserID=GetAuthor(argumentCollection=User)>
```

## The cfinvoke Tag

In addition to the standard manner of calling functions, a UDF can also be called using the cfinvoke tag. This tag, normally used with components, will not only call a UDF, but will also allow you to have more control over the parameters being passed. The only required attribute of the tag is method, which is the name of the function being called. If the UDF returns data, the returnvariable attribute must be set with the name of the variable that will be created to store the return value. If no returnvariable is defined, no variable will be created, even if the called UDF returns data. Listing 3-17 shows a cfinvoke tag calling a UDF but not capturing the return data. Listing 3-18 uses the same UDF as Listing 3-17, but captures the data returned from the UDF.

*Listing 3-17. invoking a UDF with no return variable*

```
<cffunction name="nextdate">
    <cfargument name="date" default="#now()#">
    <cfargument name="offset" default="1">

    <cfreturn DateAdd('d', arguments.offset, arguments.date)>
</cffunction>

<cfinvoke method=" nextdate">
```

*Listing 3-18. Creating a variable using the results from a function*

```
<cfinvoke method="nextdate" returnvariable="tomorrow">
```

The cfinvoke tag is stricter than standard function calls when passing parameters to a UDF. Parameters can be passed only by name or by argumentcollection, never by position.

There are two ways that parameters can be passed by name: within the tag as pseudo-attributes or by using the cfinvokeargument tag.

To pass parameters as pseudo-attributes, each parameter is treated as an attribute of the tag. This is frowned upon as being messy and prone to errors, as well as being an eyesore. Listing 3-19 shows the date and offset parameters being passed into the nextdate UDF.

*Listing 3-19. Placing parameters to pass directly into a cfinvoke tag*

```
<cfinvoke method="nextdate" returnvariable="tomorrow" date="1/11/1971" offset="1">
```

In the example in Listing 3-19, it is very hard to tell that date and offset are parameters of the UDF and not normal attributes of the cfinvoke tag.

In all of the examples so far, the cfinvoke tag has been used without any optional closing tag. When using the second way of passing parameters to a UDF, the closing tag is required. The cfinvokeargument tag is a subtag of cfinvoke and can be used only within a cfinvoke block. Each cfinvokeargument tag has a name attribute, which contains the name of the parameter being passed, and a value attribute, which contains the passed data. Listing 3-20 runs the UDF from Listing 3-17 and passes in a new date and offset.

*Listing 3-20. Creating a variable using the results from a function with multiple parameters*

```
<cfinvoke method="nextdate" returnvariable="dayafterbirthday">
    <cfinvokeargument name="date" value="1/11/1971">
    <cfinvokeargument name="offset" value="1">
</cfinvoke>
```

The explicit nature of the cfinvoke tag makes it easier to debug, as there is little question as to where the UDF function call is located, what is being passed, and what is being returned. On the other hand, this syntax is still not the norm, and is rarely seen outside CFCs.

One minor restriction of the cfinvoke tag is that is can run only UDFs that are local to the page (in other words, in the Variables scope) or within a structure local to the page. In addition, it is not possible to use the bracket notation to run a UDF contained within a structure; you can use only the dot notation. Listing 3-21 shows the various results of trying to run a UDF stored in different locations:

*Listing 3-21. Invoking a UDF stored in different locations*

```
<cffunction name="nextdate">
    <cfargument name="date" default="#now()#">
    <cfargument name="offset" default="1">

    <cfreturn DateAdd('d', arguments.offset, arguments.date)>
</cffunction>

<!---set UDF to an array -
<cfset testarray=arraynew(1)>
<cfset testarray[1]=nextdate>

<!--- set UDF to the request scope -
<cfset request.nextdate=nextdate>
<cfset testlocal= request.nextdate>
```

```
<!--- set UDF to a structure -
<cfset teststruct=structnew()>
<cfset teststruct.nextdate=nextdate>

<!--- fails -
<cfinvoke method="testarray[1]" returnvariable="tomorrow">
<cfinvoke method="teststruct['nextdate']" returnvariable="tomorrow">
<cfinvoke method="request.nextdate" returnvariable="tomorrow">

<!--- succeeds -
<cfinvoke method="teststruct.nextdate" returnvariable="tomorrow">
<cfinvoke method="testlocal.nextdate" returnvariable="tomorrow">
```

## Passing by Reference Versus Passing by Value

When variables are passed to a UDF, it is important to remember the difference between passing by reference and passing by value. When a variable containing a complex data type such as a structure, query, and object reference is passed to a UDF, the variable created within the UDF contains only a reference to the original variable. Any changes to the variable's data within the UDF will automatically be reflected in the data contained in the original variable. They are essentially the same variable.

If there is a need to pass a copy of a complex data type to a UDF, the `duplicate()` function can be used. This will create a clone of the data, and the clone will be passed. Note that the only object types that can be duplicated are components—never Component Object Model (COM), Common Object Request Broker Architecture (CORBA), Java, or .NET objects.

In contrast to passing by reference, passing by value creates a full copy of the data contained within the variable being passed. This occurs only when simple data types (strings, numbers, and so on) or arrays are being passed. Any change to the variable within the UDF will not be reflected in the original variable.

Knowing the differences between passing by reference and value can have a major impact on an application's design. If a request includes a large array of information, and that array is being passed to multiple UDFs, then each time the array is passed, the memory used by the request will increase. This increase might not seem like a lot, but with enough requests, that increase can become significant. If at all possible, pass structures rather than arrays.

## Error Handling

When an error occurs within a UDF, it can usually be handled internally using a standard `cftry/cfcatch` block. The only cases that cannot be handled internally are validation issues with data being passed to and from the UDF. There are three types of validation failures:

- A `cfargument` with the `required` attribute set to `yes` and no data being passed in
- A `cfargument` with the `type` attribute set and data being passed in that is not of the specified type
- A `cffunction` with the `returntype` attribute defined and data being passed by the `cfreturn` tag that is not of the specified type

In all of these cases, the error will not exist inside the UDF, but will instead be passed back to the UDF call. In order to handle the error, the function call itself must be within a `cftry`/`cfcatch` block. Listing 3-22 shows such error-handling code.

*Listing 3-22. Using cftry and cfcatch*

```
<cffunction name="testfunction" output="true" returntype="struct">
      <cfreturn variable1>
</cffunction>
<cftry>
    <cfset testfunction ()>
    <cfcatch>
        <cfreturn "error">
    </cfcatch>
 </cftry>
```

The specific type of error returned is `application`. There is no specific error type.

# A Full UDF Example

Let's assume that our web site has a number of pages that use the same query. If the database changed in some way that affected the query, we would need to find every place where the query is used to update it. One solution would be to put the query into a separate template and include that template everywhere the query is to be used. We will be doing something similar, but instead of including the query into the page, we will place the query in a UDF and return the query data to the UDF call. In the next part of this article, we will expand on the function and make it even more useful.

Let's start with a UDF with a basic query, as shown in Listing 3-23.

*Listing 3-23. Using a query variable*

```
<cffunction name="QueryLists" returntype="any" output="false" hint="Run a query of the
        lists table and return any data.">
    <cfargument name="DSN" hint="The datasource needed for the query call">
    <!--- make the qLists variable local to the UDF. No need for a local structure
        as only one variable is going to be created --->
    <cfset var qLists="">

    <cfquery name="qLists" datasource="#arguments.DSN#">
        Select ListID, Listname
        From Lists
    </cfquery>

    <cfreturn qLists>
</cffunction>
```

When the function in Listing 3-23 is executed, it will query a database for information and return the query data to the function call. We are not checking the value of the data being passed in, as we know it is a string. We are also not checking whether the data being returned is a query. If the **cfquery** is successful, then a variable of the query data type will be returned. The only question is how many rows it will contain (zero or more). If the cfquery fails due to a database issue, we will handle it gracefully somewhere else. A database connection failure, which can affect an entire site, is one of the situations that should be handled on a global level, rather than in individual queries. Listing 3-24 shows the same function with the query being assigned directly to the local scope.

*Listing 3-24. Using a query variable with direct assignment to the local scope*

```
<cffunction name="QueryLists" returntype="any" output="false" hint="Run a query of the
        lists table and return any data.">
    <cfargument name="DSN" hint="The datasource needed for the query call">

    <cfquery name="local.qLists" datasource="#arguments.DSN#">
        Select ListID, Listname
        From Lists
    </cfquery>

    <cfreturn qLists>
</cffunction>
```

The query in Listing 3-24 returns all of the rows from the table queried. The query in Listing 3-25 will return a specific row.

*Listing 3-25. Querying a specific row*

```
<cffunction name="QueryListRow" returntype="any" output="false" hint="Run a query of
        the lists table and return any data.">
        <cfargument name="DSN" hint="The datasource needed for the query call">
        <cfargument name="RowID" hint="The row to return from the lists table.">

        <cfquery name="local.qLists" datasource="#Arguments.DSN#">
            Select ListID, Listname
            From Lists
            Where ListID = <cfqueryparam value="#Arguments.RowID#"
                cfsqltype="CF_SQL_INTEGER">
        </cfquery>

        <cfreturn qLists>
</cffunction>
```

Now that we have a solid grounding in UDFs, we can move on to CFCs. We will also expand on our sample function and turn it into a full CFC that will handle both the retrieval and caching of a query.

# ColdFusion Components

CFCs were introduced in ColdFusion MX 6 . They were first used by many simply as containers for UDFs. This was a waste of the power of CFCs, but it took time for the community to learn how to use them properly. As understanding of CFCs grew, certain limitations became apparent, certain ideals and dogmas were voiced, and many new concepts were introduced to the ColdFusion community (such as

OOP and design patterns). Subsequent releases of ColdFusion have removed many of the early limitations of CFCs and added new features. As of ColdFusion 7 and later, CFCs are seen as a cornerstone of the language.

A CFC is a template with an extension of `.cfc` that usually has a `cfcomponent` tag, one or more functions (referred to as methods), and one or more variables (referred to as *properties*). None of these are actually necessary—it is possible to have a CFC with all, some, or none of these elements.

When you want to use the component, you create an instance of it in memory. This instance can be stored in a variable for future use, stored in a memory scope for long-term caching, or just used to invoke a method.

One of the biggest hurdles when learning to use CFCs is the terminology associated with them. Because CFCs were created to be object-like, many terms from OOP are used. These terms can be confusing to people who do not have a background in OOP. The following are definitions of some key terms associated with CFCs:

- *Child*: The CFC using the `extends` attribute of the `cfcomponent` tag to inherit another CFC (the parent). A child is a more specific version of its parent. A child is also known as a *derived class*.

- *Class*: The CFC file.

- *Constructor*: A method that is invoked automatically when a component is instantiated.

- *Instance*: A unique copy of a CFC held in memory. Multiple instances of a CFC can exist, with each being independent of the other.

- *Instantiation*: The act of creating an instance of the CFC in memory. This instance can be used once or assigned to a variable for multiple usages.

- *Invocation*: The act of running a method.

- *Method*: A UDF inside a CFC.

- *Object*: A CFC instance in memory.

- *Parent*: The CFC that is extended when using inheritance. A parent is a more general version of the child. A parent is also known as a *base class*.

- *Property*: A variable that is part of the CFC. CFCs have two scopes that can contain properties: Variables and This.

- *Pseudo-constructor*: Any ColdFusion code in a CFC that is outside a `cffunction` tag. This code will be run when a CFC is instantiated.

You can read more about OOP terminology in Chapter 19, "The Object-Oriented Lexicon" by Hal Helms.

## Creating CFCs

Any file with a `.cfc` extension is automatically a CFC, no matter what it contains. Let's begin with the simple CFC shown in Listing 3-26.

*Listing 3-26. A simple Authors CFC*

```
<cfcomponent output="false">
    <cfset Variables.DSN="cfbookclub">
    <cffunction name="GetAllAuthors" output="false" hint="Query Authors DB and↵
 Returns all authors">

        <cfquery name="local.Authors" datasource="#Variables.DSN#">
            Select *
            from Authors
        </cfquery>

        <cfreturn Authors>
    </cffunction>
</cfcomponent>
```

Listing 3-26 shows the basic elements of a CFC: a cfcomponent tag block to contain all of the component code and options, a cfset tag to create a global property for the CFC, and a cffunction tag to define a method.

## Instantiation and Constructors

A component's life cycle starts with instantiation. This is where the component is read into memory and an instance of it is created for use.

As part of a component's instantiation, ColdFusion will execute any code that is contained within the cfcomponent tag block but is not part of a cffunction. This code, referred to as the *pseudo-constructor*, can be used to set variables within the component or even to invoke one (or more) of the component's methods. The use of pseudo-constructors is seen as a poor substitute for true constructors, a feature that did not exist in the language prior to ColdFusion 9.

A *constructor* is a method of an object that will be invoked automatically when the object is instantiated. Constructors are usually used to initialize variables within the object instance for later use. In this regard, constructors work much like the pseudo-constructors in ColdFusion. The major difference is that a constructor can accept arguments as part of the component's instantiation, which is not possible with pseudo-constructors.

The need for a constructor method in versions of ColdFusion prior to 9 was addressed by the creation of a community standard. This standard said that all CFCs should contain a method called init(), and that this method should be the first thing called when instantiating the CFC. It also said that the init() method should always return the This variable scope, which contains a component reference. Listing 3-27 shows a basic init() method.

*Listing 3-27. Basic init() method*

```
<cffunction name="Init" returntype="any" output="false">
    <cfreturn This>
</cffunction>
```

To use the `init()` method as a constructor, the component had to be instantiated using the `createobject()` function. When the function was executed, the `init()` method was invoked using standard method chaining (covered shortly). The component reference returned from the `init()` method could then be used as normal.

Constructors were added to ColdFusion 9 along with a new approach to instantiating components: the `new` keyword. When a component is instantiated using this approach, ColdFusion will invoke any constructor method that the component may have. This invocation occurs in addition to and immediately after the execution of any pseudo-constructors. In such a case, any parameters passed to the constructor will not be available to the pseudo-constructor. They run sequentially.

In most cases, the instantiation of a component will result in a component reference being returned. A component reference is a link to a component instance in memory. Usually, a component reference will be stored in a variable, which will be used when invoking one of the component's . methods. As long as the component reference exists, the component instance can be used. This allows us to instantiate a component once and then use it multiple times within a page request. The variable containing the component reference can also be assigned to other scopes. If it is assigned to a long-term scope, such as Session or Application, the component instance will continue to exist as long as the scope does. This allows a single component instance to be used across multiple pages and is the cornerstone of caching in ColdFusion.

There are currently four ways in which a component can be instantiated: the `cfobject` and `cfinvoke` tags, the `createobject()` function, and the `new` keyword.

## The cfobject Tag

The `cfobject` tag will instantiate an object and return a variable that contains a reference to the object instance. The tag's `type` attribute defines what type of object will be instantiated. This attribute is optional; if it is missing, a value of `component` is assumed. Some still use the `type` attribute to avoid any confusion when using the tag.

The tag's required attributes include the `component` to be used and the `name` of the variable to contain the component reference. The tag is limited to instantiation and returning a component reference variable. No methods can be invoked directly. Listing 3-28 gives an example of instantiating and creating a component reference with `cfobject`.

*Listing 3-28. Instantiating and creating a component reference with cfobject*

```
<cfobject type="component" component="Authors" name="AuthorComponent">
```

Once a component reference exists, it can be used as the base from which its methods can be run. This acts in the same way as a standard ColdFusion function call, but uses the component reference as a prefix to the method call. Listing 3-29 shows an example.

*Listing 3-29. Invoking a method using a component reference*

```
<cfset author = Authorcomponent.GetAuthor(5)>
```

## The cfinvoke Tag

When the `component` attribute is added to the `cfinvoke` tag, the tag will instantiate the component defined within the attribute and try to invoke the method defined in the `method` attribute. Other than specifying that the method to be invoked is in a component rather than local, the tag operates as described earlier in the UDF section of this article. When a component is instantiated using this tag, no component reference is returned. In effect, the component is destroyed after use and cannot be used again without instantiating it again. Listing 3-30 shows an example of using the cfinvoke tag.

*Listing 3-30. Instantiating and invoking a method using cfinvoke*

```
<cfinvoke component="Authors" method="GetAuthor" returnvariable="Author">
```

When the component attribute is used, the component defined will always be instantiated. When invoking a method that is within the same component, the attribute should be removed, unless the new instantiation is intended.

If a component reference exists, an additional option becomes available to the cfinvoke tag. The component reference variable can be used at the value of the component attribute. When this is done, there is no component instantiation, as the component we're using already exists. In addition, after the method is run, the component reference is left unaltered and is not destroyed. In Listing 3-31, we invoke the method GetAuthor() using the AuthorComponent variable as the value of the component attribute.

*Listing 3-31. Invoking a method from a component reference*

```
<cfinvoke component="#AuthorComponent#" method="GetAuthor" returnvariable="Author">
```

## The createobject() Function

createobject()is usually seen as the functional equivalent to cfobject, but because it's a function, there are more things that we can do with it. As with cfobject, the function can instantiate an object and then return an object reference that can be stored in a variable. To do this, the function needs to know what type of object will be instantiated and the object's name. Unlike cfobject, the type of object must be explicitly stated; there is no default. In addition, the name of the variable that will contain the object reference is not part of the function itself. This will become very important in a moment.

Listing 3-32 is the functional equivalent of Listing 3-31.

*Listing 3-32. Instantiating and creating a component reference with createobject()*

```
<cfset AuthorComponent = CreateObject('component', 'authors') >
```

The most important thing to notice about Listing 3-32 is that it is a two-step process. First, the createobject() function is run, and then the result of the function—a component reference—is assigned to a variable. Before we assign the component reference to a variable, we can use it to perform some special operations, such as method chaining.

## Method Chaining

Using a concept called *method chaining*, we can invoke methods contained within the component reference returned from the createobject() function. In theory, this is the same as invoking a method from a component reference as seen in Listing 3-29. Instead of using the variable containing the component reference as a prefix to the method, we are using the component reference directly. Listing 3-33 shows basic method chaining.

*Listing 3-33. Invoking the init method from a returned component reference*

```
<cfset AuthorComponent = CreateObject('component', 'authors').Init('cfbookclub')>
```

In Listing 3-33, `createobject()` will instantiate the `authors` component and then pass the component reference over to the next item in the chain, the `init` method. The `init` method will be invoked from the passed reference, and any value that it returns will be assigned to the `AuthorComponent` variable. If the `init` method does not return the component reference, the component instance is, in effect, destroyed. In order to return a component reference, the invoked method must return the component's This scope. Listing 3-34 shows a sample `init` method that returns a component reference.

*Listing 3-34. Sample init method*

```
<cffunction name="Init" returntype="any" output="false">
    <cfargument name="DSN">
    <cfset Variables.DSN=Arguments.DSN>
    <cfreturn this>
</cffunction>

<cfset AuthorComponent = CreateObject('component', 'authors').Init('cfbookclub')>
```

Because the `init` method is returning a component reference, it can be also be used as the base for another method from the same component to be invoked. There is no limit to the number of times this method chaining can be used. Listing 3-35 uses the component reference returned from the `init` method as the base for the `deleteallauthors` method.

*Listing 3-35. Chaining two methods after the function*

```
<cfset CreateObject('component', 'authors').Init('cfbookclub').deleteallauthors()>
```

In Listing 3-35, we simply want to instantiate a component, invoke its `init` method, and then invoke its `deleteallauthors` method. Because we are not assigning the results to a variable, any value returned from the `deleteallauthors` method is lost. This is very much like using the `cfinvoke` tag with a component, except we can use multiple methods; the `cfinvoke` tag is limited to one.

## The new Keyword

As noted earlier, ColdFusion 9 introduced a new way of instantiating components: by using the `new` keyword. This keyword can be used anywhere that a variable can be evaluated, but is usually used as part of an assignment statement. Listing 3-36 shows a simple example of instantiating with the `new` keyword.

*Listing 3-36. Instantiating with the new keyword*

```
<cfset AuthorComponent = new authors() >
```

The new keyword is followed by the name of a component to instantiate, which must always be followed by a set of parentheses. This component name can use dot path notation, but if there is a dash anywhere within the component name/path, the entire name/path must be contained within parentheses (see Listing 3-37).

*Listing 3-37. Instantiating with the new keyword where the component name/path has a dash*

```
<cfset AuthorComponent = new "book.my-authors"() >
```

Upon instantiation, any constructor method defined in the component will be invoked automatically—a feature that is unique to this method of instantiation. Any parameters placed within the parentheses after the component will be passed into the constructor method as arguments.

ColdFusion will determine the component's constructor by first checking for the new `initmethod` attribute in the `cfcomponent` tag. This attribute takes the name of a method that will be used as a constructor; if that method does not exist, an error may be thrown. Listing 3-38 shows some constructor examples.

*Listing 3-38. Constructor examples*

```
<cfcomponent output="False" initmethod="newinit" extends="initparent">
        <cffunction name="newinit">
                        initmethod used as constructor
        </cffunction>

        <cffunction name="init">
                        init used as constructor
        </cffunction>

        <cffunction name="onmissingmethod">
                <cfargument name="missingMethodName" type="string">
                <cfargument name="missingMethodArguments" type="struct">
                        init method missing
        </cffunction>
</cfcomponent>
```

When the component in Listing 3-38 is instantiated using the new keyword, the `newinit()` method will be invoked. This method can either exist within the component itself or be inherited from another component. If the `newinit()` method does not exist, `onmissingmethod()` will be called in its place. If there is no `onmissingmethod()` defined, an error will be thrown. If the `initmethod` attribute has not been set, ColdFusion will look for a method called `init()`. If this method does not exist, then no constructor will be invoked.

By default, the constructor is expected to return a component reference. This is handled automatically, and the `init()` method does not need a `cfreturn` tag. In fact, it is possible to set a return type of `void` for the method without causing any problems. If a `cfreturn` tag is used, the tag's value, rather than a component reference, will be returned.

The reference returned when instantiating a component with the new keyword can be used to chain methods in the same way as the `createobject()` function. Listing 3-39 takes the method chain used in Listing 3-35 and removes the explicit invocation of the `init()` method. Otherwise, it operates in exactly the same manner.

*Listing 3-39. Method chaining with the new keyword*

```
<cfset new authors('cfbookclub').deleteallauthors()>
```

▓ **Note** the syntax used when instantiating components with the new keyword mirrors the syntax used by most other scripting languages. Not only is the syntax analogous, the capabilities are the same as well. Keep this in mind when converting applications to ColdFusion.

## The CFC Container: The cfcomponent Tag

The final tag to be discussed in reference to CFCs is the cfcomponent tag itself. This tag acts as a container for all other ColdFusion code that is part of the CFC. Any ColdFusion code placed outside the tag body will cause an error. On the other hand, plain text can be placed before or after the tag, and it will be ignored when the component is used.

While the cfcomponent tag has no required attributes, a few are important. The output and hint attributes are exactly as described in the UDF section, and it is considered best practice to use both. The initmethod attribute was discussed in the previous section. This leaves the extends attribute, which is used when inheriting from another component and allows the child component to use the methods and properties of the parent. We will cover this attribute later when talking about inheritance.

When a cfcomponent tag is used, the CFC automatically inherits from the base component.cfc, which is stored in the \WEB-INF\cftags directory. Normally, this component is empty—it doesn't even have a cfcomponent tag. It is possible to place code here and have it automatically used by every CFC on the server. This is rarely done, as the code would be in a nonstandard location, and the base component.cfc would be overwritten when a new version of ColdFusion was installed. Those who do place code here tend to limit it to basic methods like init() that should be used by all components.

It is possible to have a CFC that does not use a cfcomponent tag. When you do this, you lose all of the attributes of the tag, including extends and output. This means that no inheritance is possible, and the automatic inheritance of the base component.cfc is eliminated. It also means that there is no output control outside the cffunction tags. Any text that is not contained within a cffunction block will be output, and all pseudo-constructor code will generate whitespace. (ColdFusion 9 does allow for components to be written completely in CFScript, which you may want to look into after learning the basics of CFCs.)

## Implementing Security

In the UDF portion of this article, we skipped over one attribute of the cffunction tag that has no use outside CFCs. This attribute, access, is used to control which templates can invoke a method. This attribute allows for the following levels of access:

- The default value is public, which means that any code on the server can invoke the method.

- The next level of security is called package, which means that the method can be invoked only by code in the same CFC or from a template in the same directory (.cfc or .cfm).

- The most secure level, called private, allows only code within the same CFC to invoke the method.

- A fourth type of access, called remote, is actually more permissive than public. This access allows the method to be invoked through a URL, form, or web service, as well as through Flash Remoting.

It is considered a good practice to limit access to methods using private or package when you do not expect to invoke it directly from a ColdFusion template. This allows you to control when and where a method will be used, which for some methods (such as credit card processing) is a must. Using private and package access greatly helps when you need to upgrade or debug the code. The more restricted the access to the code, the easier it is to hunt down a bug.

Some frameworks require that you define an access attribute, even if it will only be set to the default value of public.

## Defining Properties: Variables and This

Properties are the variables defined by the CFC itself. A CFC automatically creates two variable scopes when it is instantiated: the Variables scope, which is much like a standard template's Variables scope, and the This scope, which is special to the CFC. Both of these scopes will exist for the life of the component, are accessible to all pseudo-constructors and methods in the component, and can store any type of ColdFusion data. Beyond this, the differences between the scopes have to do with public versus private access.

### Variables Scope

The Variables scope is private to the CFC and can be used only from within the CFC. Any variable set inside the CFC that is not declared local to a method or is not set to a specific scope prefix is automatically assigned to the Variables scope. In addition, data in the Variables scope can be accessed without using a prefix, though ColdFusion will check for a local variable in the method before looking in the Variables scope. As with all nonlocal variables in a CFC, it is a good practice to use the Variables prefix, even if it's not needed.

If you want to expose information from the Variables scope to the template that invoked the CFC, you will have to create methods to do so. The standard terms for these methods are *getters* and *setters*. Getters allow information from the Variables scope to be retrieved by the invoking template. Setters allow variables to be set in the Variables scope of the CFC.

### This Scope

The This scope differs from the Variables scope in that it is public to the template that called the CFC. This means that the calling template can read data from and write data to the This scope at will. Because there is no control over who or what can read and write to the scope, there is a dogmatic view that says never to use the This scope. Others are a little more lenient and say that the scope should be used only for unimportant data.

The problem is that the This scope is totally open. There is no control over what code can read data from the scope and what code can write to the scope (even overwriting other data).

If you don't have a reason, don't use the This scope. On the other hand, if you have a perfectly good reason to use it, don't let dogma stand in your way.

# Understanding Encapsulation

The reasoning behind not using the This scope is that it breaks encapsulation. This OOP concept says that a component should:

> *Operate only on data passed into the CFC, and never assume that data will exist in the environment.* A CFC has access to all of the environmental data that a standard ColdFusion template has. While it could use a server, Common Gateway Interface (CGI), or other variable directly, it is a good idea to make use of only data that has been explicitly sent into the CFC. This helps avoid errors that are based on a false assumption that an environment variable will exist. While some variables, such as standard Server scope variables, will always exist, it is better not to assume. The application of this rule is referred to as *loose coupling* or *decoupling*, as the CFC is not directly connected to or dependent on another variable, component, or anything else. The less a CFC is coupled to another, the easier it is to debug (theoretically) and reuse.

> *Allow changes only to properties that you want changed.* This rule says that the This scope should not be used. Because variables in the This scope can be added, manipulated, and deleted directly without control, it breaks encapsulation. Those who hold by this rule suggest placing data only in the Variables scope, and using getters and setters to manipulate the data.

> *Expose only those methods and properties that you want seen.* This rule stresses that if there is a method that should be called only from within the CFC, rather than directly, the method's access should be set to private or package.

For each of these rules, there is an exception. The key is knowing if the exception should be used or not. An example of one such exception would be a component designed to manipulate and process CGI information. The component would be used in a place where CGI information exists.

# Caching Components

Caching a component after it has been instantiated is a simple matter of assigning the variable containing the component reference to a variable in a memory scope. The most commonly used memory scopes are Application for application-specific components and Session for components specific to a particular user. It is also possible to cache a component in the Server scope, and this is actually a good idea when dealing with components that will be needed by all applications on the server, such as logging. There is a strong dogma against caching components in the Server scope that is a holdover from the pre-MX days when there were locking issues with memory scopes. This has not been an issue for years, but the dogma persists.

One reason for caching a component is that as long as it exists, all of its properties will exist. This means that if a component has a query stored in its Variables or This scope, it will continue to exist and not need to be called again. We will use this as the basis for an example (see Listings 3-40 and 3-41) that builds on the UDF example in the previous section.

*Listing 3-40. A CacheQuery CFC (CacheQuery.cfc)*

```
<cfcomponent output="false">
    <cffunction name="Init" returntype="any" output="false" hint="Set the DSN and return
            the object reference.">
        <cfargument name="DSN" hint="(String - Required) The Data Source name to be set
            to the Variables scope">
        <cfset Variables.DSN=Arguments.DSN>
        <cfinvoke method="QueryDB">
        <cfreturn This>
    </cffunction>

    <cffunction name="QueryDB" returntype="void" output="false" access="private"
            hint="Query the Authors table and cache the query">
        <cfquery name="Variables.CacheQuery" datasource="#Variables.DSN#">
            Select *
            from Authors
        </cfquery>
    </cffunction>

    <cffunction name="GetQuery" returntype="any" output="false" hint="Return the query
            to the template">
        <cfif Not StructKeyExists(Variables, 'CacheQuery')>
            <cfinvoke method="QueryDB">
        </cfif>
        <cfreturn Variables.CacheQuery>
    </cffunction>

    <cffunction name="ResetCache" returntype="any" output="false" hint="Resets the
            cached query">
        <cfinvoke method="QueryDB">
    </cffunction>
</cfcomponent>
```

*Listing 3-41. Testing the CacheQuery CFC (test.cfm)*

```
<!--- Example Data Source - cfbookclub↩
 (\CFIDE\gettingstarted\community\db\bookclub.mdb) --->
<cfif Not StructKeyExists(Server, 'Authors')>
    <cfset Server.Authors=new CacheQuery('cfbookclub')>
</cfif>
<cfset Authors=Server.Authors.GetQuery()>
<cfoutput query="Authors">#authorid# #firstname# #lastname#<BR></cfoutput>
```

The second line of test.cfm in Listing 3-41 checks if a variable called authors exists in the Server scope. If not, it instantiates the CFC in Listing 3-40, invokes the init() method, and saves the results of the function into the Server.Authors variable. We can then run the GetQuery() method of the cached CFC and make use of the data. No matter how many times we use the CFC, it will always have the same data in it, without needing to go back to the database. When we want to refresh the cached query, all we need to do is run the ResetCache() method.

While CacheQuery is a useful component, it has a problem, in that it is meant for a single use with a single query. In a moment, we'll make it a lot more useful by allowing it to be used by multiple queries without an increase in complexity. How? By using inheritance.

# Using Inheritance

Inheritance is one of the basic concepts of OOP where you have a more general parent component that has a more specific child component. The child has all of its parent's methods and properties, as well as its own specific methods and properties. In this way, the child *is* the parent, but an enhanced version of it, leading to the use of the term "is a" to describe inheritance relationships.

Inheritance can be one of the hardest OOP concepts to learn because it is usually described in a very abstract manner. Here, I will describe a use of inheritance that is practical, which should help you get a better understanding of it.

It should be noted that when a component is inherited, it effectively becomes part of its child. There are no restrictions on the parent using the Variables scope of the child and vice versa. Additionally, all methods from either the parent or child are considered part of the same CFC when it comes to methods with a private access.

## Overriding and Super

When a child inherits from a parent, all of the methods and properties of the parent become methods and properties of the child. If the child already has a method or property of the same name, it is not inherited. This is referred to as *overriding*, as in the child's methods and properties are overriding those of the parent's.

When a parent's properties are overridden, they can no longer be accessed in any way. They have been totally eliminated from memory.

This is not the case when it comes to the parent's methods. The overridden methods can still be invoked by using the prefix super before the method call, as shown in Listing 3-42.

*Listing 3-42. The super prefix in action*

```
<cfset oldmethodresult=super.getuser(1)>
```

Even if a parent method has not been overridden, using super will allow you access to it. On the other hand, when super is used, the child methods are rendered inaccessible. In addition, super can be used only from within the child component.

## Two Different Views

Inheritance can be viewed from either the top down or the bottom up.

For the top-down view, we will look at our general CacheQuery component and say that we will need to change the QueryDB() method if we want to use this component to cache anything other than authors. By taking the QueryDB() method and placing it in its own CacheAuthors component, and having that component extend (inherit from) the CacheQuery component, we can create as many database-caching components as we want, each having the same general functionality but with different specific querying functionality.

From the bottom-up view, we would take our original CacheQuery component and say that we also want to cache poll information. To do so, we will copy everything from the CacheQuery component into a new component called CachePolls. To make things neat, let's also rename the CacheQuery component CacheAuthors to keep its name in line with its sibling component. We will then change the CachePolls component so that it is caching poll information.

We now have two very similar components that perform very similar functions. If we compare these two operational components, we will find that some or most of the methods and properties are the same. We can then move these duplicate methods and properties into a separate, more general CacheQuery component (Listing 3-43), and set that component as the parent of both CacheAuthors (Listing 3-44) and CachePolls (Listing 3-45).

In the first example, we are removing what is unique from the parent component and placing it into more specific children. In the second example, we are taking what is similar between two components and moving it into a more general parent. In both cases, we have more specific children inheriting from a more general parent.

*Listing 3-43. CacheQuery.cfc (the parent)*

```
<cfcomponent output="false" hint="allows for the caching and use of queries that↵
   will be defined in a child component">
   <cffunction name="Init" returntype="any" output="false" hint="Set the DSN and return
         the object reference.">
      <cfargument name="DSN" hint="(String - Required) The Data Source name to be set
            to the Variables scope">
         <cfset Variables.DSN=Arguments.DSN>
         <cfinvoke method="QueryDB">
         <cfreturn This>
   </cffunction>

   <cffunction name="GetQuery" returntype="any" output="false"
         hint="Return the query to the template">
         <cfif Not StructKeyExists(Variables, 'CacheQuery')>
            <cfinvoke method="QueryDB">
         </cfif>
         <cfreturn Variables.CacheQuery>
   </cffunction>

   <cffunction name="ResetCache" returntype="any" output="false"
         hint="Resets the cached query">
         <cfinvoke method="QueryDB">
   </cffunction>
</cfcomponent>
```

*Listing 3-44. CacheAuthors.cfc (child)*

```
<cfcomponent extends="cachequery" output="false" hint="child component for
    cachequery that handles author data">
    <cffunction name="QueryDB" access="private" output="false" hint="Query the Authors
        table and cache the query">
        <cfquery name="Variables.CacheQuery" datasource="#Variables.DSN#">
            Select *
            from Authors
        </cfquery>
    </cffunction>
</cfcomponent>
```

*Listing 3-45. CachePolls.cfc (child)*

```
<cfcomponent extends="cachequery" output="false" hint="child component for
    cachequery that handles poll data">
    <cffunction name="QueryDB" access="private" output="false" hint="Query the Authors
        table and cache the query" >
        <cfquery name="Variables.CacheQuery" datasource="#Variables.DSN#">
            Select *
            from Polls
        </cfquery>
    </cffunction>
</cfcomponent>
```

## Type Checking Parents and Children

An interesting aspect of the parent/child relationship comes into play when components are being validated.

Let's use the CachePolls component and invoke the init() method (which is inherited from CacheQuery). init() returns a reference to the This scope, which contains a reference to the component itself. If the init() method had a returntype defined, and the returntype was set to CachePolls, then the component would validate as true because the data being returned from init() *is* a reference to CachePolls. On the other hand, if we set the returntype to CacheAuthors, we would expect it to fail, as they are not the same component.

But what would happen if we set the returntype to CacheQuery? We're calling the CachePolls component, which is not the CacheQuery, but does inherit it. Will the validation work?

The answer is yes. This is because by inheriting the CacheQuery component, CachePolls effectively becomes both itself and CacheQuery. On the other hand, if we were calling the CacheQuery component directly and tried to validate it as a CachePolls component, it would fail. A CachePolls is a CacheQuery, but a CacheQuery is not a CachePolls. A child is its parent plus; a parent is its children minus.

# Parting Words

While this article is jam-packed with information, it is not the be-all and end-all of UDF and CFC documentation. It focused on what you need to know to get started using UDFs and CFCs properly. Here are some additional topics to look into:

- Calling CFCs from a URL or form
- Calling CFCs from Flash
- Using CFCs as web services
- Securing CFC methods with role-based security
- Using introspection and metadata
- Building UDFs and CFCs with CFScript
- Creating interfaces
- Using getters and setters
- Using serialization

Also, please remember that while I preach against dogma, I also don't want to become a source of it. Just because I say something does not make it right. Go out and test it out yourself. Only by building UDFs and CFCs will you truly understand them.

# CHAPTER 4

■ ■ ■

# onMissingTemplate()— Error Handler and So Much More

## by Michael Dinowitz

*No matter how good your code is, it will fail. The question is how to minimize the effect of that failure and recover from it. ColdFusion provides many levels of code error handling ranging from cftry/cfcatch blocks all the way up to a site-wide error handler. This is great if the error is code based, but what if the error is due to a missing template? Coldfusion 8 has answered that question by introducing onMissingTemplate(), and in this article Michael Dinowitz examines missing templates and explains how this predefined method works.*

Until ColdFusion 8 we had only one recourse when faced with an error due to a missing template: a global missing template handler. Any missing template error was routed through this single handler, which greatly limited our ability to gracefully handle the error. Numerous hacks have been created to make this more effective over the years, but there was a limit to what could be done. This limit has been removed with the introduction of the onMissingTemplate() handler in ColdFusion 8. Implemented as a predefined method in Application.cfc, onMissingTemplate()allows us to handle missing template errors on a per-application and even per-directory level. Not only does onMissingTemplate() allow for tighter control of missing template errors, it can even be used for redirects and dynamic page generation—a cornerstone of search engine optimization.

Before we examine onMissingTemplate(), however, we should cover how missing templates are handled in ColdFusion without it, how to set up the global error handler, and look at an example of what can be done with the global error handler. We will then examine the implementation of onMissingTemplate() in Application.cfc with specific areas of usage and code. Our final goal is to turn onMissingTemplate() into much more than just an error handler.

## 404 Missing Template Handling: Step-by-Step Basics

When a visitor requests a specific file from a web site, the web server first checks if the file's extension is mapped to an application server. When ColdFusion is installed, it automatically maps the following extensions in the web server: cfm, cfc, cfml, cfr, cfswf, jsp, jws. If the requested file has any of these extensions, the web server hands the request off to ColdFusion, usually not caring if the file actually exists. If it doesn't exist, ColdFusion will do one of three things.

1. If an `Application.cfc` is associated with the location of the missing template and it has an `onMissingTemplate()` method, then ColdFusion will run that method.

2. If that's not the case, ColdFusion will run the global 404 handler, if it exists.

3. If ColdFusion can't find either `onMissingTemplate()` or a global 404 handler, a very ugly general missing template error will be shown.

If the request was for a directory rather than a specific file, then the web server will try to provide a default document. IIS and Apache check for the existence of the default document before trying to process it. If the default document doesn't exist, then the web server will either show the directory (if directory browsing is turned on) or throw a "403 Forbidden" error saying you can't browse the directory. The request is not sent to ColdFusion and cannot be handled by `onMissingTemplate()`. That's why it is a good idea to include a default document in any directory that could be accessed but is not designed to be browsed.

Certain web servers, notably the JRun web server that comes with ColdFusion, do not check for the existence of a default document before sending the request to ColdFusion. If a default document does not exist, the directory's contents are shown as normal. But what if there's no default document and an `onMissingTemplate()` is associated with the directory? The method will always run, preventing the directory from being shown. To combat this, a new variable has been created for use within an `Application.cfc`: `This.welcomeFileList`. This variable can be set with a list of the default documents that are expected (usually `index.cfm`, `index.htm`, and `index.html`) and the request for the directory will (supposedly) bypass the `onMissingTemplate()` if a default document does not exist. I say supposedly as I've never gotten it to work correctly.

# Setting Global Handlers

The new ability to handle missing template errors on a per-application basis does not mean that the global missing template handler can be ignored. As stated above, errors happen. And if an error occurs within the `onMissingTemplate()` method and is not handled in some way, the global handler will be run. This is our last line of defense and, if all else goes wrong, may be the only thing between a cleanly handled missing template error and an ugly Java dump. If you have access to the ColdFusion administrator, you should make sure that both the missing template handler and the site-wide error handler are set. They can be found at the bottom of the Server Settings ➤ Settings page. See Figure 4-1.

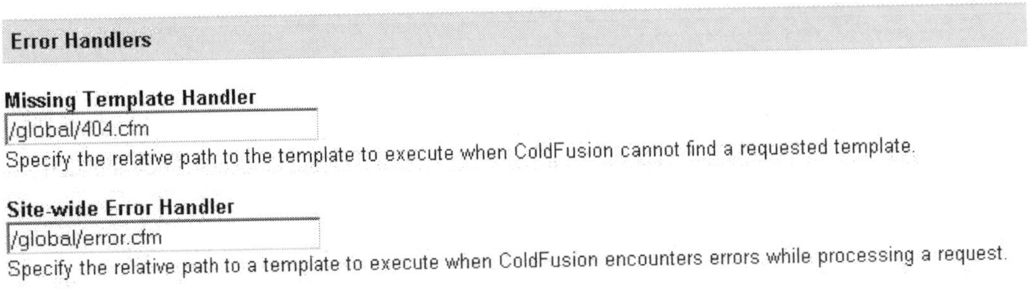

**Error Handlers**

**Missing Template Handler**

/global/404.cfm

Specify the relative path to the template to execute when ColdFusion cannot find a requested template.

**Site-wide Error Handler**

/global/error.cfm

Specify the relative path to a template to execute when ColdFusion encounters errors while processing a request.

*Figure 4-1. ColdFusion Administrator error handler section*

There are cases where you may want both the onMissingTemplate() method and the global missing template handler to run at the same time. For example, you might use the onMissingTemplate() method to cleanly handle a missing template error and the global missing template handler to log or report that the error occurred. Just because a missing template request can be cleanly handled does not always mean that it is fixed. A single bad link, even for a moment, can sit in a search engine's records and be tried again and again indefinitely and you wouldn't know about it.

Using the code in Listing 4-1 to send an e-mail about the bad request not only informs you that there was a bad request, but also forces you to fix it immediately. Logging the request means that someone has to read the log file eventually—which may mean today, next week, or next year. If you get 100 e-mails because of an error, you're going to fix it fast!

*Listing 4-1. Using onMissingTemplate() to Send Error Reports*

```
<cfmail to="erroradmin@mydomain.com" from="erroradmin@mydomain.com"
    subject="#CGI.HTTP_Host# 404 error - #CGI.Script_Name#" type="HTML">
    <cfdump var="#CGI#" label="CGI">
    <cfif NOT StructIsEmpty(URL)>
        <cfdump var="#URL#" label="URL">
    </CFIF>
    <cfif NOT StructIsEmpty(Form)>
        <cfdump var="#Form#" label="Form">
    </cfif>
</cfmail>
```

# What Is the onMissingTemplate() Method, and When Is It Called?

When an Application.cfc is run, all of its pre-request operations are run no matter what. This usually includes the setting of variables to the This scope and running the onApplicationStart() and/or onSessionStart() methods as needed. ColdFusion decides what to do with the requested template only after it has finished with these pre-process operations. If the template exists, then the onRequestStart(), onRequest(), and onRequestEnd() methods are run, with the entire operation ending after the last of these methods are run. If the requested template does not exist, then the onMissingTemplate() method is run in place of the onRequest trio. This is the only difference between a request for an existing or missing template. Figure 4-2 shows the flow of a request that uses Application.cfc.

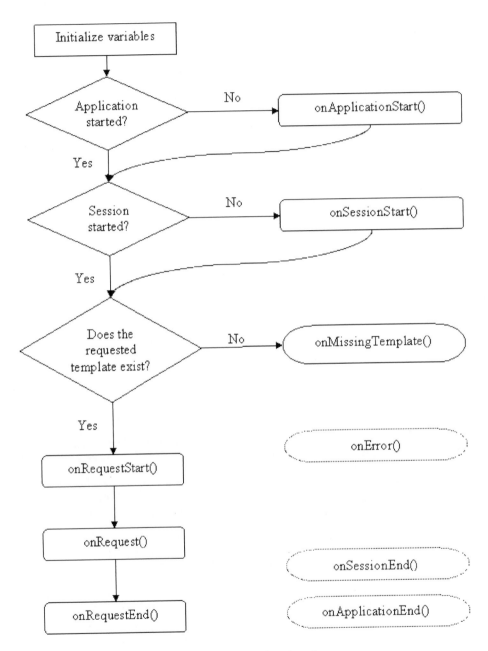

*Figure 4-2. Standard flow of a request using application.cfc*

When the `onMissingTemplate()` method is called, ColdFusion will automatically pass the path information for the requested template, which includes the file name, in as an argument. If the `cfargument` tag is set, then this path information will be assigned to the value of the `cfargument name` attribute (`targetpage`). If the `cfargument` tag is missing, then the path information will be contained in the first elements of the arguments structure (`arguments[1]`).

Listing 4-2 shows the most minimal `onMissingTemplate()`, which uses no attributes other than the method name and contains no code or content. Even the closing `cffunction` tag is collapsed into the starting one. When this method is run, nothing will be returned from it and the page request ends immediately.

*Listing 4-2. Very Minimal onMissingTemplate() Method*

```
<cffunction name="onMissingTemplate" />
```

Listing 4-3 fleshes out the `onMissingTemplate()` method with some attributes and tags, as well as some content to be displayed. Note that the `output` attribute is not set. This is where some people trip up, as they either put the `output` attribute in and set it to `false` out of habit, or use a pre-built method skeleton that has it set by default. The `returntype` and `hint` attributes have been added for self-documentation.

*Listing 4-3. Minimal onMissingTemplate() Method*

```
<cffunction name="onMissingTemplate" returnType="boolean" hint="outputs a general
  missing template message">
  <cfargument type="string" name="targetPage" required="true">
    The template you want is missing
      ---other code here---
    <cfreturn true>
</cffunction>
```

After the method's code is run, one of two things will happen. If no `cfreturn` tag is used or a `cfreturn` tag is used to return a value of `true`, the request is ended—nothing else happens. If the `cfreturn` tag returns a value of `false`, then the global missing template handler will run before the request is ended.

In Listing 4-3, the code to deal with the missing template error is embedded directly into the `onMissingTemplate()` method. If we're only returning a message or doing a single operation, this should not cause a problem. Once we start getting into more complex missing template processing, we're going to have to segment the code. The first thought that comes to mind is to put the code in a separate file and include it in the method using `cfinclude`. This works without a hitch and is even suggested in the documentation. When including code within the `onMissingTemplate()` method, always use the `cfinclude` tag. If the code is included using the `getPageContext().include()` function, an error will occur. For those working in a more OOP (object-oriented programming) or framework mind-set, the missing template processing code can be placed within another component and invoked.

# Method Invocation within onMissingTemplate()

An error message is site content and should be treated as such. The message should have as much of the site's normal layout and formatting as possible. One option is to include all of the layout in the onMissingTemplate() method along with the error message. A better alternative is to make use of the already-existing layout that may be contained within the onRequest methods. When a normal request is processed, ColdFusion passes the requested template's path information to the onRequest() method. When the method is called directly, the method call has to provide that information (see Listing 4-4, line 3).

*Listing 4-4. Direct Call to onRequest() for Error Formatting*

```
<cffunction name="onMissingTemplate" returntype="boolean" hint="calls onrequest to
    output a general missing template message">
    <cfargument name="targetPage" type="string">
    <cfset onrequest('/missingtemplate.cfm')>
    <cfreturn True>
</cffunction>

<cffunction name="onRequest" returnType="void">
    <cfargument name="thePage">
    <cfinclude template="/global/meta.cfm">
    <cfinclude template="/global/header.cfm">
    <cfinclude template="#arguments.thePage#">
    <cfinclude template="/global/footer.cfm">
</cffunction>
```

In Listing 4-4 we are calling the onRequest() method directly from within the onMissingTemplate() and passing /missingtemplate.cfm as the path information.

# When Errors Occur

If the onMissingTemplate() method or any code within it has an error, one of a number of things will happen. If the error is not handled within a cftry/cfcatch block, then the onError() method will be called, followed by the global 404 template. The same thing will happen if the error is passed out of a cftry/cfcatch block using the cfthrow tag. If you want to have the error captured by the onError() method but not call the global 404 error handler, you will have to call the onError() directly. The onError() method expects two variables passed to it: a structure with the error information and a string with a title for the error.

In Listing 4-5, my onMissingTemplate() method uses a general cftry/cfcatch around all of the method's code, with a direct call to the onError() method. The only reason this is done is to make sure that the global 404 template is not called after the onError() executes. If I want the global 404 template to run, I'll use a cfreturn tag with a value of false. Note that if I set a cfabort tag at the end of the onError() method it will prevent the global 404 from being called when an error occurs, but I prefer not to do this.

*Listing 4-5. Using cftry/cfcatch within onMissingTemplate*

```
<cffunction name="onMissingTemplate" returnType="boolean">
    <cfargument type="string" name="targetPage" required="true">
```

```
<cftry>
    <!--- Your code here --->
    <cfcatch>
        <cfset onError(cfcatch, 'onMissingTemplate')>
    </cfcatch>
</cftry>

    <cfreturn true>
</cffunction>
<cffunction name="onError" returnType="void">
    <cfargument name="exception">
    <cfargument name="eventname">
    ---error code---
</cffunction>
```

# Reasons for Calling onMissingTemplate()

The `onMissingTemplate()` method is presented in the ColdFusion documentation as an error handler that is invoked in response to a request for a missing template. The focus is on the fact that the requested template does not exist. In order to make the most use of this method, however, we have to stop thinking about it as an error handler and instead think of it as a request handler. What's the difference? A request handler looks at the request as something to be fulfilled rather than focusing on the existence of the requested template. How the request will be fulfilled is the question. We can break this down into four categories.

- Request errors

- Corrected requests

- Content redirects

- Dynamic page generation

## Request Errors and Corrected Requests

We will define a request error as a request for a template that fails to find that template, and that failure is not expected. The definition does not say that the template does not exist but only that it could not be found. This takes into account the times when the URL to the template is malformed in some way. Here is one such example.

A URL is sent in a post to a mailing list, which archives the post to a web page. The archive program takes long lines, looks for a place where they can be broken up, and then wraps them. If this is done within a URL, it may result in a space, a new line, or something else being placed inside the URL. The URL now contains unexpected characters and when clicked will force a missing template error even though the template exists. This is what the requests might look like—one with a `<br>` tag in the URL and the other with a space.

```
http://www.houseoffusion.com/tutorials/regular<br>-expressions/index.cfm
http://www.houseoffusion.com/groups/flex- jobs/index.cfm
```

The first step in correcting this is to know that it's happening. The reporting code mentioned above is perfect for this. The second step is to think about how we can transform the failed request into a successful one. That should always be our goal—not to capture errors but to handle them and provide the requested content if at all possible.

*Listing 4-6. Handling Known Request Errors*

```
<cffunction name="onMissingTemplate" returntype="boolean" hint="redirect malformed
        requests or handle the error">
    <cfargument name="targetPage" type="string">

    <!--- check for html tag in request --->
    <cfif REFind('<[^>]+>', arguments.targetPage)>
        <cflocation url="#REReplace(arguments.targetPage, '<[^>]+>', '', 'all')#"
                statuscode="301" addtoken="No">
    </cfif>

    <!--- check for space character in request --->
    <cfif REFind('\s', arguments.targetPage)>
        <cflocation url="#REReplace(arguments.targetPage, '\s', '', 'all')#"
                    statuscode="301" addtoken="No">
    </cfif>

    <!--- include template to handle unexpected errors --->
    <cfinclude template="/missingtemplate.cfm">

    <cfreturn True>
</cffunction>
```

The code in Listing 4-6 checks to see if a specific type of malformed URL exists, corrects it, and then forces a 301 redirect. This is done so that any search engine knows that the record for the malformed URL should be replaced with the one for the redirect location and that the change is permanent.

Note that the ColdFusion documentation says that a cflocation should not be used within an onMissingTemplate() method. To date I have not seen cflocation to be a problem but, as with including files mentioned previously, using getPageContext().forward() to do a redirect will cause an error. Please note that this limitation has been since removed in later point releases of ColdFusion 8.

# Content Redirects

A redirect was used in Listing 4-6 to correct an error, but the reasons for redirection go beyond errors. There are times when templates and directories on a web site will be shuffled around. This is great for organization but terrible for external links, especially when it comes to search engines. As we saw in Listing 4-6, a 301 redirect tells a visitor that the link has permanently changed and then sends him to the new content location.

*Listing 4-7. Handling 301 Redirects*

```
<cffunction name="onMissingTemplate" returntype="boolean" hint="redirect pages or
        handle the error">
    <cfargument name="targetPage" type="string">

    <cfswitch expression="#arguments.targetPage#">
        <cfcase value="/regex.cfm">
            <cflocation statuscode="301" url="/tutorials/regular-expressions/index.cfm"
                    addtoken="No">
        </cfcase>
        <cfcase value="/cfscript.cfm">
            <cflocation statuscode="301" url="/tutorials/coldfusion-script/index.cfm"
                    addtoken="No">
        </cfcase>
      <cfcase value="/bit.cfm">
            <cflocation statuscode="301" url="/tutorials/bitmask-functions/index.cfm"
                    addtoken="No">
        </cfcase>
        <cfdefaultcase>

            <!--- include template to redirect known request errors --->
            <cfinclude template="/expectederrors.cfm">

            <!--- include template to handle unexpected errors --->
            <cfinclude template="/missingtemplate.cfm">

        </cfdefaultcase>
    </cfswitch>

    <cfreturn True>
</cffunction>
```

In Listing 4-7 we have renamed three templates and moved them to new directories. When a request comes in for the now-missing templates, the onMissingTemplate() will check to see if the missing template is expected and redirect it.

# Dynamic Page Generation

Dynamic page generation is the ultimate expression of onMissingTemplate() as a request handler and is a standard practice when it comes to search engine optimization. The idea is that a request is made for a template. That template returns content. The visitor sees the template's content and thinks that the template exists as a physical file, but in reality it does not. A virtual page is being dynamically generated based on the request, and the visitor has no way to tell that the page is virtual rather than physical. This allows us to create an almost unlimited number of unique pages on the site, even though none of them actually exist.

---

▨ **Note** A dynamically generated page is one that does not physically exist but if requested, will act as if it does.

---

## Examining Template Requests

Let's use an example blog application to better understand this technique. The application will use a template called entry.cfm to display blog entries, each of which is stored in a database with an ID. When a variable called entryid is passed to the template, it is used to get the information from a database and display it. If the ID does not correspond to an entry, then an error page will be returned saying that the entry does not exist. If we look at how the template is requested and how the entryid is passed, we'll see an evolution of requests that end with a dynamically generated page.

An entry can be called as

```
/entry.cfm?entryid=999
/entry.cfm/999
/999-this-is-the-entry.cfm
/entries/999-this-is-the-entry.cfm
```

When the site was first created, the entryid was passed on the URL in the standard variable=value format, usually referred to as question mark variables. This format makes a clear distinction between the template being requested and the variables being passed to it. The problem is that this is not very search engine friendly. A search engine will recognize that entry.cfm can have different content based on the variable passed in but will give that content a relatively low ranking. This gets worse if the variable name used is ID or contains ID. In addition, if multiple pieces of information are passed on the URL, it can get long and rather ugly.

To get around these problems, programmers looked at a number of ways to mask the variables inside the URL to create "search engine-safe URLs." All of the techniques depended on placing the variables after the requested template in what is referred to as the extended or slash-path information. This was better than the question mark-based variables, both for search engine optimization and cleanliness. The only real work was in decoding the extended path information back into URL variables. It is still an effective method for masking passed variables and results in higher content ranking, but search engines are not 100% fooled. It's not perfect.

The next level up is dynamic page generation. Rather than having a URL that points to the entry.cfm template, a unique URL is generated. Something about the URL will be used in place of the entryid to look up the content from the database. In the previous entry examples, the third and fourth show the entryid encoded into the template name portion of the URL. When the template is requested, the onMissingTemplate() method will strip the entryid from the path information and use it. This allows us to both pass a masked entryid and have a template name that is descriptive of the content that will be displayed—a boon to search engine ranking. The subdirectory is used in the fourth example to show that the requested template is the important thing, not where it is located.

Now that we have a clear understanding of how things are supposed to work, let's look at the code. Listing 4-8 will allow any of the four example URLs to be used and will attempt to display an entry based on the passed entryid. The onMissingTemplate() method will be used to handle dynamically created pages, and the onRequestStart() method will handle any call to entry.cfm, whether the entryid was passed as question mark variables or in the extended path information. Either method is expected to return an entryid that will be used by the onRequest() method, which will try to display the entry.

*Listing 4-8.Entry Based on the Passed entryid*

```
<cfcomponent displayname="Entry handler" output="False">
   <cffunction name="onMissingTemplate" returntype="boolean">
      <cfargument name="targetPage" type="string">

      <cftry>
         <!--- if the entry is called using a dynamic page starting with 999-title --->
         <cfset url.entryid=val(listlast(arguments.targetPage, '/'))>
         <cfset onrequest('entry.cfm')>
         <cfcatch>
            <cfset onError(cfcatch, 'onMissingTemplate')>
         </cfcatch>
      </cftry>

      <cfreturn True>
   </cffunction>

   <cffunction name="onRequestStart" returnType="boolean" output="false">
      <cfargument name="thePage">

      <cfif Not StructKeyExists(url, 'entryid')>
         <!--- Only check these if the entryid is not defined on the URL   --->
            <cfif refindnocase('^/[0-9]+', CGI.PATH_INFO)>
               <!--- if the URL passes the entryid like entryid.cfm/999 --->
               <cfset variables.entryid=val(removechars(CGI.PATH_INFO, 1,1))>
            <cfelse>
               <!--- something went wrong with the URL --->
               <cfthrow>
            </cfif>
      </cfif>

      <cfreturn true>
   </cffunction>

   <cffunction name="onRequest" returnType="void">
      <cfargument name="thePage">
      <CFQUERY name="qEntry" datasource="blogdb">
         SELECT *
         FROM Entries
         WHERE EntryID =<CFQUERYPARAM value="#url.entryid#"
                 cfsqltype="CF_SQL_INTEGER">
      </CFQUERY>
      <cfif qEntry.Recordcount>
         <cfinclude template="/entry.cfm">
      <cfelse>
         <cfinclude template="/missingentry.cfm">
      </cfif>
   </cffunction>
   <cffunction name="onError" returnType="void" output="true">
      <cfargument name="exception">
```

```
        <cfargument name="eventname">
        <cfmail to="errors@site.com" from="errors@site.com"
                subject="Error: #arguments.eventname#" type="HTML">
            <cfdump var="#arguments.exception#"
                    label="Error: #arguments.eventname#">
        </cfmail>
    </cffunction>
</cfcomponent>
```

If the requested template does not exist, then we will assume that this is on purpose and that we're dealing with a dynamically generated template. The `onMissingTemplate()` method will try to turn the path information passed into it into an `entryid`, set to the URL scope. This will be done in a rather unconventional manner. First we will treat the `arguments.targetpage` as if it were a list with a forward slash (/) as a delimiter and get the last item. This will always return the actual file name requested, stripping off any directory information. The `val()` function will then be used to remove any non-number characters, starting from the left. The assumption is that the file name starts with the `entryid`, so this will have the effect of stripping off anything that is not the `entryid`. If the file name starts with anything other than a number, the value returned from the function will be 0. The returned number will be assigned to the `url.entryid` variable and the `onRequest()` method will be called.

If the request was for the existing `entry.cfm`, the `onRequestStart()` method will first check to see if the `entryid` was passed on the URL. If it wasn't, `onRequestStart()` will try to parse the `CGI.path_info` into a value that will be assigned to the `url.entryid` variable. This is done by first checking if the `CGI.path_info` starts with a forward slash followed by one or more numbers. If the `CGI.path_info` is properly formatted, the leading forward slash will be removed and then a `val()` function will be used as explained previously. If the `CGI.path_info` does not have the proper format, then an error will be thrown using the `cfthrow` tag.

If no error is thrown, then the `onRequest()` method will be run. This method will use the `url.entryid` to look up a database record and either display it or show a message that the entry does not exist.

## Attractive URLs for Frameworks

The example `Application.cfc` code in Listing 4-8 can easily be integrated into a framework, and this is where the dynamic page-generation concept really shines. Frameworks tend to suffer from long, cumbersome URLs that are all routed through a single template (usually `index.cfm`). This not only limits the framework's value to search engines but results in URLs that average people just can't read, let alone type in. An attractive and informative URL can be the difference between someone visiting your site or skipping it for someone else's. The following examples show three different frameworks with a short URL followed by two possible alternatives.

## Fusebox URL

```
/index.cfm?fuseaction=public.viewentry&id=1
/public/viewentry.cfm?id=1
/fuseactions/public/viewentry.cfm?id=1
```

## Model-Glue URL

```
/index.cfm?event=viewentry
/viewentry.cfm
/events/viewentry.cfm
```

## Mach-II URL

```
/index.cfm?event=blog:viewentry
/blog/viewentry.cfm
/events/blog/viewentry.cfm
```

# We're Not Done Yet, but ...

As an error handler, onMissingTemplate() fills a gap that has existed for a number of releases. As a request handler, onMissingTemplate() allows us to turn bland requests into informative ones, ugly URLs into pretty ones, and pages with low search engine rankings into pages with high ones. If it did the dishes, too, you might want to marry it. Until it does, I'm hoping it'll be a lure for you to move up to the latest version of ColdFusion and start using Application.cfc.

■ ■ ■

# CHAPTER 5

# "Say What?" Handling Unknown Messages with onMissingMethod()

## by Sean Corfield

*Among the new functions introduced in ColdFusion 8, onMissingMethod() is one of the more unappreciated ones. Most people see and use it as an error handler, if they use it at all. But the function really has so much more to offer. When it came to finding an author for this article, we didn't have to go far. We didn't have to go anywhere, actually. Sean Corfield eagerly volunteered before we could even ask him.*

If you are using ColdFusion Components (CFCs), you probably think in terms of calling methods on objects. A CFC has a collection of methods defined within it using the `cffunction` tag, and those declared with `access="public"` can be called by other code. For the purposes of this article, there is another way to look at methods and method calls—as messages sent to objects—which I think will help you write better object-oriented code.

## Get the Message?

The literature on object-oriented programming (OOP) sometimes refers to the concept of objects passing messages to each other. Instead of describing the objects as interacting by calling methods on each other, some books and articles describe a series of autonomous objects that pass messages around back and forth—messages that request that actions be done (method calls) and messages containing information (return values).

Thinking of object-oriented systems in this manner helps us focus on the interactions within the system rather than on calling a series of functions, which is inherently procedural. Some OOP languages use this message-passing idiom more than others. Smalltalk and Objective-C are classic examples of languages where what we might think of as methods on objects are described, instead, as the behavior triggered when a message is received—and the language syntax reflects this idiom. Listing 5-1 is a small example of Objective-C code.

*Listing 5-1. An Example of Objective-C Code*

```
// WebHistory Notification Messages
- (void)historyDidAddItems:(NSNotification *)aNotification
    {
        // Get the new history items
        NSArray *items = [[aNotification userInfo] objectForKey:WebHistoryItemsKey];
        NSEnumerator *enumerator = [items objectEnumerator];
        id historyItem;

        // For each item, create a menu item with the history item as the represented object
        while (historyItem = [enumerator nextObject])
            [self addNewMenuItemForHistoryItem:historyItem];
    }
```

The bracketed expressions in Listing 5-1 represent messages being sent to objects. The following expression means "Send the message userInfo to the object aNotification":

```
[aNotification userInfo]
```

We would write that in ColdFusion as follows:

```
aNotification.userInfo();
```

When a message contains data, Objective-C uses colons to introduce the data:

```
[self addNewMenuItemForHistoryItem:historyItem];
```

In Listing 5-1 you see the behavior for the message historyDidAddItems, which contains the data aNotification (which has type NSNotification *). Let's look at another message declaration:

```
- (void)addObserver:(id)observer selector:(SEL)aSelector name:↵
 (NSString *)notificationName object:(id)anObject;
```

This message contains four pieces of data, and the message name is essentially broken up into four parts. The full message name is addObserver selector name object, and it would be sent like this:

```
[nc addObserver:obs selector:s name:n object:obj]
```

Looking back at the message declaration, we can see it has four named arguments: observer (of type id), aSelector (of type SEL), notificationName (of type NSString *), and anObject (of type id). An approximate ColdFusion equivalent is shown in Listing 5-2.

*Listing 5-2. Approximate ColdFusion Equivalent of Listing 5-1*

```
<cffunction name="addObserverSelectorNameObject" returntype="void">
    <cfargument name="observer" type="id" >
    <cfargument name="aSelector" type="SEL" >
    <cfargument name="notificationName" type="NSString*" >
    <cfargument name="anObject" type="id" >
...
</cffunction>
```

Note that `NSString*` is not a valid ColdFusion type—we don't have pointers. This is just to show the approximate equivalent message declaration.

We would write the message passing code as follows:

```
nc.addObserverSelectorNameObject(obs,s,n,obj);
```

# Message Received

At this point, I hope you can think of method calls as somewhat equivalent to sending messages and a method definition as the declaration of the behavior when a message is received.

Now we can ask the question: What happens when an object receives a message that it does not understand?

It is not a question that we think to ask when dealing with method calls because the answer is obvious: The method call fails because the method cannot be found. In a statically typed language, the compiler determines whether or not the method exists and will not compile calls to unknown methods. In a dynamically typed language, the runtime determines whether or not the method exists and will not execute calls to unknown methods. We're familiar with this error in ColdFusion.

```
The method bogus was not found in component /Library/WebServer/Documents/missing/alpha.cfc.

Ensure that the method is defined, and that it is spelled correctly.
```

If we think in terms of sending messages to objects and objects responding to those messages, the question makes a lot more sense. It's the object's responsibility to respond to a message; the object knows its own capabilities. In other words, we shift the responsibility from the system into the object, which is really where it belongs in OOP. With that mind-set, we would expect the error message to read more like this.

```
I am the /Library/WebServer/Documents/missing/beta.cfc object and I received

a message bogus which I did not understand!
```

Smalltalk directly supports this by allowing you to define a behavior within an object for `doesNotUnderstand`, which is essentially a handler for messages that the object does not otherwise understand. There is even a French Smalltalk blog at `http://doesnotunderstand.free.fr/`.

Ruby also supports this, but calls it `method_missing`. In both languages, this feature allows you to write smarter objects that can fully take on the responsibility for all messages that their environment might send them. Since you can write smarter, more responsible objects in Smalltalk and Ruby, you might reasonably claim they were "more OOP" than languages that do not let you write objects that take on this responsibility—more OOP than languages such as Java, for example.

Where does ColdFusion sit in this world? ColdFusion MX (6.x and 7) sat squarely in the Java camp, because the system decided whether or not you could call a given method on an object. ColdFusion 8 moves our favorite language into the Smalltalk/Ruby camp by adding a small feature: the ability to define a function called `onMissingMethod` inside any CFC. ColdFusion is now more OOP than Java.

# Defining onMissingMethod()

The `onMissingMethod` handler takes two arguments, which are also shown in Listing 5-3.

- The name of the method that is missing

- The arguments supplied in the call to that method

*Listing 5-3. Minimal onMissingMethod() Declaration*

```
<cffunction name="onMissingMethod">
    <cfargument name="missingMethodName" >
    <cfargument name="missingMethodArguments" >
</cffunction>
```

■ **Note** The two arguments must be named exactly as shown, unlike other handlers in ColdFusion where you are free to use your own names for arguments.

If you call

```
obj.bogus(a=1,b="two");
```

and the method `bogus()` is not defined, then ColdFusion will call

```
obj.onMissingMethod("bogus", { a=1, b="two" } );
```

In the previous example, `onMissingMethod` is automatically passed the information with which it needs to work. This is the name of the method that was being called (`"bogus"`) and all the arguments that were being passed to it (a=1 and b="two"). These are passed as `missingMethodName` and `missingMethodArguments` respectively, as shown in Listing 5-4.

*Listing 5-4. A More Complete Declaration of onMissingMethod()*

```
<cffunction name="onMissingMethod" returntype="any" access="public">
    <cfargument name="missingMethodName" type="string" required="true">
    <cfargument name="missingMethodArguments" type="struct" required="true">
</cffunction>
```

You can specify output="true" or output="false" on the cffunction tag, depending on whether the handler should produce output or not, just like any other function.

The contents of the missingMethodArguments struct will depend on how the original method was called. If named arguments were used, the struct will contain those same named keys

```
obj.bogus(a=1,b="two");
```

which produces (via <cfdump label="missingMethodArguments" var="#missingMethodArguments#">)

---

missingMethodArguments - struct

a 1

b two

---

If positional (unnamed) arguments were used, the struct will contain numeric keys

```
obj.bogus(1,"two");
```

which produces

---

missingMethodArguments - struct

1 1

2 two

---

# Using onMissingMethod()

At this point, you're probably wondering "What on Earth would I use this for?" The preceding narrative talks about handling a message that is not understood—a missing method—and that might make you think that this is all about error handling. If you want to get an exception when an unknown method is called, you already have a perfectly acceptable way to do that: Just don't define onMissingMethod. ColdFusion MX has always behaved like that, and ColdFusion 8 is no different: If you call a method that doesn't exist, an exception is thrown.

No, onMissingMethod—and its equivalent in Smalltalk and Ruby—is about much more than error handling. Let's look at a couple of possibilities to see the new world this opens up to us.

## Automatic get/set Methods

If you're tired of writing all those getFoo() and setFoo() methods but you still want encapsulation, onMissingMethod() is your friend. You can define onMissingMethod() to look for getFoo() and setFoo() calls and implement them in a base class. Listing 5-5 shows an example.

*Listing 5-5. Implementing Get and Set Calls in a Base Class*

```
function onMissingMethod(missingMethodName,missingMethodArguments) {
    var name = "";

    // if the missing method is getXyz(), return the xyz variable if it exists
    if (left(missingMethodName,3) is "get") {
        name = right(missingMethodName,len(missingMethodName)-3);
        if (structKeyExists(variables,name)) {
            return variables[name];
        } else {
            // getXyz() but xyz does not exist - throw an exception
            throw("Expression_",
            "Element #name# is undefined in a Java object of type class
            coldfusion.runtime.TemplateProxy.");
        }

    // if the missing method is setXyz(), set the xyz variable
    } else if (left(missingMethodName,3) is "set") {
        name = right(missingMethodName,len(missingMethodName)-3);

        // if xyz argument was passed by name...
        if (structKeyExists(missingMethodArguments,name)) {
            variables[name] = missingMethodArguments[name];
            // ...else if xyz argument was passed by position
        } else if (structKeyExists(missingMethodArguments,1)) {
            variables[name] = missingMethodArguments[1];

        // no matching argument
        } else {
            throw("Application",
            "The #uCase(name)# parameter to the get#name# function is required but was not
            passed in.");
        }

    // not a getXyz() or setXyz() method call... throw an exception
    } else {
        throw("Application",
        "The method #missingMethodName# was not found in component #expandPath("/"
        & replace(getMetadata(this).name,".","/","all"))#",
        "Ensure that the method is defined, and that it is spelled correctly.");
    }
}
```

Assuming the throw() function is defined elsewhere in the component, this provides generic get and set methods for arbitrary properties in an object. It even replicates the exact exceptions you would see if you actually had the get/set methods instead.

I've used the raw variables scope, but you could just as easily use variables.instance to keep the data packaged within a structure inside your object, as in Listing 5-6.

*Listing 5-6. Getter Logic Using variables.instance*

```
if (structKeyExists(variables.instance,name)) {
    return variables.instance[name];
} else {
    throw("Expression_",
    "Element #name# is undefined in a Java object of type class
    coldfusion.runtime.TemplateProxy.");
}
```

■ **Note** You would need to add some code to ensure variables.instance existed as a struct.

If you want to restrict this to a specific list of valid property names, it would be relatively straightforward. Just include an additional check for some instance variable that lists the gettable or settable fields in your structKeyExists() section, as shown in Listing 5-7.

*Listing 5-7. Getter Logic Restricted to Specific Fields*

```
if (structKeyExists(variables,name) and
    (not structKeyExists(variables,"readableFields") or
    listFindNoCase(variables.readableFields,name) neq 0)) {
        return variables[name];
} else {
    throw("Expression_",
    "Element #name# is undefined in a Java object of type class
    coldfusion.runtime.TemplateProxy.");
}
```

Your component can just set variables.readableFields to a list of variable names that can be read from the object via the implicit get method. You can also do this for the implicit set method with variables.writableFields, as shown in Listing 5-8.

*Listing 5-8. Setter Logic Restricted to Specific Fields*

```
if (structKeyExists(missingMethodArguments,name) and
    (not structKeyExists(variables,"writableFields") or
    listFindNoCase(variables.writableFields,name) neq 0)) {
        variables[name] = missingMethodArguments[name];
```

```
} else if (structKeyExists(missingMethodArguments,1) and
    (not structKeyExists(variables,"writableFields") or
    listFindNoCase(variables.writableFields,name) neq 0)) {
        variables[name] = missingMethodArguments[1];

} else {
    throw("Application",
    "The #uCase(name)# parameter to the get#name# function is required but was not
    passed in.");
}
```

The nice thing about implementing these generic get/set methods is that you can easily override the behavior by defining an explicit method. For example, you could define getAge() to calculate age based on date of birth but still allow getDOB() and setDOB() to be handled generically.

This sort of automation is one of those rare cases where I would even consider modifying WEB-INF/cftags/component.cfc so that this behavior is available in every object.

## Method Injection

Another possibility is that the onMissingMethod() handler could automatically generate explicit get/set methods and add them to the object. Then subsequent calls would call the actual get/set method instead of onMissingMethod(), increasing your application's performance. This object would adapt, changing its behavior over time depending on how it was used, much as the Java HotSpot compiler optimizes parts of the code that are executed frequently.

You may have heard of the term "method injection" in conjunction with Reactor, Transfer, or other frameworks where objects are created and then new methods are added at runtime. As hinted at in the preceding commentary, this technique generally relies on writing CFML code to a file, including that file to get access to a new function, and then adding that to the object.

For example, Listing 5-9 shows some simple code that generates a new method called hello() in the current object.

*Listing 5-9. Generating a New Method Using the File System*

```
<cfset here = expandPath(".")>
<cfset temp = getTempFile(here,"cfm")>
<cffile action="write" file="#temp#"
    output="<cffunction name=""hello""><cfreturn ""Hello  World!""></cffunction>">
<cfinclude template="#right(temp,len(temp)-len(here)-1)#">
<cffile action="delete" file="#temp#">
<cfoutput>#hello()#</cfoutput>
```

Instead of generating the code for a number of methods and including it, you could just generate a single onMissingMethod() handler and inject that. This can actually give you more dynamic control over the behavior of the injected methods.

Listing 5-10 is a simple example of adding a handler to an object.

*Listing 5-10. Direct Injection of onMissingMethod()*

```
function newfunc(missingMethodName,missingMethodArguments) {
    return "New method (" & missingMethodName & ")";
}
obj = createObject("component","someobj");
obj.setFoo(42);
obj.onMissingMethod = newfunc;
writeOutput(obj.wibble() & "<br>");
writeOutput(obj.getFoo() & "<br>");
```

This example assumes that someobj does not have a method called wibble() and does not already have an explicit onMissingMethod() handler; someobj inherits the implicit get/set handler shown above, so that the call to setFoo() uses the base class onMissingMethod(), but then the call to getFoo() uses the injected version. The output of the above is as follows:

```
New method (wibble)

New method (getFoo)
```

In general, you would be more likely to define a new handler to intercept certain messages and delegate to the parent handler for messages that it does not understand, as Listing 5-11 shows.

*Listing 5-11. Delegation to Parent Class Method Handling*

```
function newfunc(missingMethodName,missingMethodArguments) {
    var result = 0;
    if (missingMethodName is "wibble") {
        return "New method (" & missingMethodName & ")";
    } else {
        result = super.onMissingMethod(argumentCollection=arguments);
        if (isDefined("result")) {
            return result;
        }
    }
}
```

Since you don't know whether the parent handler will return a value or not, you have to handle a possible null return value. With this new handler, the output would be

```
New method (wibble)

42
```

The new handler intercepts wibble() and returns a string but passes all other methods up to the parent handler (which is the get/set example in Listing 5-5).

If the object has an explicit onMissingMethod() handler, you need to move it out of the way and that's more complicated. I'll leave that for you to tackle if you're so inclined.

## Aspect-Oriented Programming

You may have heard of this term in conjunction with the ColdSpring framework. The idea is that some functionality in an application, such as logging and security, is common across many otherwise unrelated points in the code. These are often called "cross-cutting concerns" or "aspects." Aspect-Oriented Programming (AOP) provides a way to write these cross-cutting concerns in a single, isolated place (an object) that is then applied automatically wherever it is needed.

ColdSpring works by generating new objects that wrap around your original objects and provide versions of your objects' methods that first invoke the code for the aspect you want (logging or security or whatever) and then invoke your original method.

But onMissingMethod allows you to write AOP-style code without needing to worry about code generation and a lot of the complexity that goes along with it. Consider the component in Listing 5-12.

*Listing 5-12. Proxy.cfc*

```
<!--- proxy.cfc --->
<cfcomponent output="false">
    <cffunction name="init">
        <cfargument name="object">
        <cfset variables.object = arguments.object>
        <cfreturn this>
    </cffunction>

    <cffunction name="onMissingMethod">
        <cfargument name="missingMethodName">
        <cfargument name="missingMethodArguments">
        <cfset var result = variables.object.call(arguments.missingMethodName,
        arguments.missingMethodArguments)>
        <cfif isDefined("result")>
            <cfreturn result>
        </cfif>
    </cffunction>

</cfcomponent>
```

This assumes there is a call() method in the object or its base component. But this simple, two-method component is a complete proxy for the underlying object, allowing you to call methods on this component that are automatically forwarded to the specified object, as shown in Listing 5-13.

*Listing 5-13. Demonstration of proxy.cfc*

```
a = createObject("component","alpha");
p = createObject("component","proxy").init(a);
writeOutput(p.a() & "<br>");
writeOutput(p.echo(data="named data") & "<br>");
writeOutput(p.echo("unnamed data") & "<br >");
```

This code creates an instance of the alpha component that has methods `a()` and `echo()`. Then it creates a proxy for the `alpha` object—as shown above—and calls `a()` and `echo()` on the proxy. The proxy's `onMissingMethod()` handler intercepts those calls and passes them on to the `alpha` object with which it was initialized.

That's not very exciting, but look at the logging component in Listing 5-14.

*Listing 5-14. Logging Proxy Component*

```
<!--- logging.cfc --->
<cfcomponent output="false">

    <cffunction name="init">
        <cfargument name="object">
        <cfset variables.object = arguments.object>
        <cfreturn this>
    </cffunction>

    <cffunction name="onMissingMethod">
        <cfargument name="missingMethodName">
        <cfargument name="missingMethodArguments">
        <cfset var result = 0>
        <cflog text="> #arguments.missingMethodName#()" log="console">
        <cfset result= variables.object.call(arguments.missingMethodName,
        arguments.missingMethodArguments)>
        <cflog text="< #arguments.missingMethodName#()" log="console">
        <cfif isDefined("result")>
            <cfreturn result>
        </cfif>
    </cffunction>

</cfcomponent>
```

If we use this logging proxy instead of the bare-bones proxy, not only will it call the methods but it will trace each call, as shown in Listing 5-15.

*Listing 5-15. Using the Logging Proxy*

```
a = createObject("component","alpha");
p = createObject("component","logging").init(a);
writeOutput(p.a() & "<br>");
writeOutput(p.echo(data="named data") & "<br>");
writeOutput(p.echo("unnamed data") & "<br>");
```

This displays the results in the browser as before, but it also displays the following in the console log:

```
08/24 00:36:31 Information [jrpp-71] - > a()

08/24 00:36:31 Information [jrpp-71] - < a()

08/24 00:36:31 Information [jrpp-71] - > echo()

08/24 00:36:31 Information [jrpp-71] - < echo()

08/24 00:36:31 Information [jrpp-71] - > echo()

08/24 00:36:31 Information [jrpp-71] - < echo()
```

With a little more work, it could also log the arguments and return values.

A similar approach could allow security to be applied transparently to existing components, or simple adapters to be written that map arguments and/or return values for selected methods, or whatever takes your fancy.

# Summary

These are all very powerful techniques that are available in dynamic languages such as Smalltalk, Ruby, and ColdFusion. These techniques are not available in static languages such as Java and C#. (AOP is implemented in Java through a preprocessor that rewrites your code prior to compilation, so you cannot apply aspects at runtime like you can with dynamic languages.)

The addition of the onMissingMethod() handler to ColdFusion is a very important and powerful change that opens up new possibilities, allowing us to write more intelligent objects and take advantage of sophisticated techniques from other dynamic languages.

# Further Reading

Travis Griggs on Smalltalk's doesNotUnderstand handler:
http://www.cincomsmalltalk.com/userblogs/travis/blogView?searchCategory=Smalltalk:%20doesNotUnderstand:

Maurice Codik on emulating dynamic multiple inheritance in Ruby with method_missing: http://www.nach-vorne.de/2007/3/18/multiple-inheritance-without-mixins

# PART 2

# Document Creation in ColdFusion

# PDF Support in ColdFusion

**by Raymond Camden**

### Updated by Michael Dinowitz

*The PDF standard, created by Adobe, is a great way to keep documents consistent across digital and print media. When Adobe acquired Macromedia in 2005, we all hoped that sooner or later we'd have native PDF manipulation in ColdFusion. Version 8.0.1 brought us this ability with the cfpdf and related tags. ColdFusion 9 did not add any new PDF related tags, but it expanded the capabilities of the cfpdf tag family with some new actions, and it added the capability to create PDF packages or portfolios. In this article, updated by Michael Dinowitz, Raymond Camden takes us on a tour of the new PDF features in ColdFusion 8.01 and 9.*

I have to admit it: PDFs bore me. In the grand scheme of things, when you compare PDFs to CFCs, Ajax, event gateways, UDFs, and other cool ColdFusion features, PDF support probably falls somewhere between 0 and 1 on the excitement scale—at least, that's what I used to think. Like most folks, I had only experienced PDFs as a consumer. I appreciated the fact that they looked pretty, but I never really knew about the full complexities of a PDF document. As ColdFusion has matured and expanded its PDF support, I've found a new appreciation for this "boring" file format, and I hope this article will help awaken others to the coolest boring feature of ColdFusion. Let's begin by taking a look at the history of PDF support in ColdFusion.

## PDF Support in ColdFusion MX 7 (and Earlier)

Native PDF support began in ColdFusion MX 7. The **cfdocument** tag is probably the easiest way to create PDF documents. Consider the simple example in Listing 6-1.

*Listing 6-1. cfdocument Example*

```
<cfdocument format="pdf">
    <h2>TPS Form</h2>
    <p>
    Please fill out your TPS form.
    </p>
</cfdocument>
```

We could create PDFs from almost any dynamically generated HTML code, including images. We had header and footer support to allow for things like page numbering and copyright notices, and we could divide PDFs up into sections as well. This all made the creation of PDFs pretty trivial, but that was the extent of PDF support native to the platform.

Outside of the built-in tags, developers could use third-party products to work with PDFs. Companies such as activePDF have had ColdFusion support for years and offer a good option for people who need advanced support or have older versions of ColdFusion.

# PDF Support in ColdFusion 8.0.1 and beyond

Let's take a look first at the PDF features added in ColdFusion 8 and then the new ones in ColdFusion 8.0.1. ColdFusion 8 added numerous new PDF-related features. We will start by looking at updates to cfdocument, and then move to the new tags and functions introduced in ColdFusion 8. At a high level, the following changed in cfdocument (and its siblings, cfdocumentitem and cfdocumentsection) in ColdFusion 8:

- You could add bookmarks to your PDF. This change really mattered to people generating large PDF documents. For example, the *ColdFusion Cookbook* (http://www.coldfusioncookbook.com) has close to 150 entries and features a PDF version you can download and view offline, but the length of the PDF made it hard to find specific content; bookmarks made this significantly easier.

- A localURL attribute was added to cfdocument, potentially speeding up the creation of a PDF that includes images. It tells ColdFusion to load the images from the file system instead of making an HTTP call to retrieve the image data. Since PDF creation can seem a bit slow at times, anything that speeds it up is a good thing.

- You could embed PDF forms into a PDF generated by cfdocument.

- Document sections could have their own page numbering independent of any other section, no matter where they are in the PDF. Prior to ColdFusion 8, the PDF had to have incremental numbering across the entire document.

- You could specify a saveAsName attribute for the cfdocument tag, letting you specify a file name for the PDF when the user downloads it.

This list does not include everything that got updated in cfdocument and its siblings, but it gives a good idea of how the tags changed. Now let's take a quick tour of the new tags and functions introduced in ColdFusion 8.0.1:

- **cfpdf**: The monster tag, which adds so many features that we can only cover a portion of them. This article will focus on this tag.

- **cfpdfparam**: Helps configure the **cfpdf** tag.

- **cfpdfform**: Allows you to manipulate data from PDF forms created with Acrobat or LiveCycle.

- **cpdfformparam**: Helps configure the **cfpdfform** tag.

- **cfpdfsubform**: Works with subforms within PDF forms.

- **isDDX**: Determines if a string is a valid DDX (Document Description XML) item.

- **isPDFFile**: Determines if a file is a PDF.

- **isPDFObject**: Determines if a variable is a PDF object.

We'll start with the last two, **isPDFFile** and **isPDFObject** functions, and then turn our focus to the **cfpdf** tag. We'll see what ColdFusion 9 added when we cover the **cfpdf** tag.

# The isPDFFile and isPDFObject Functions

The **isPDFFile** function checks a file on the file system to determine if it is a valid PDF. This is useful for simple file upload forms where you want to require the user to upload a PDF. Once you have determined that a file is a PDF, you can read it into a ColdFusion variable. PDF has become a proper variable data type in ColdFusion 8, much like images, and you can see if some variable is a PDF object by passing it to **isPDFObject**.

Let's wrap this up into a simple example (see Listing 6-2).

*Listing 6-2. isPDFObject Example*

```
<cfdocument format="pdf" name="mypdf">
    This is a PDF document.
</cfdocument>

<cfif isPDFObject(mypdf)>
    <p>
        The variable mypdf is a PDF object.
    </p>
</cfif>

<cfset mystring = "I am not a PDF">
<cfif not isPDFObject(mystring)>
    <p>
        The variable mystring is not a PDF object.
    </p>
</cfif>
```

```
<cfset fileWrite(expandPath("./mypdf.pdf"), mypdf)>

<cfif isPDFFile(expandPath("./mypdf.pdf"))>
    <cfoutput>
        <p>
            The file #expandPath("./mypdf.pdf")# is a valid PDF.
        </p>
    </cfoutput>
</cfif>
```

This template creates a simple PDF using cfdocument. Note the use of the name attribute; this stores the PDF data into a variable. We first check to see if the variable is a PDF object, and display a message if so. Then we check some other variable — in this case, a simple string variable — and check whether it's a PDF object, this time displaying a message if not. Next we save the data to the file system and use the isPDFFile function to check it.

When you run this, you will see something interesting, similar to the following:

```
The variable mystring is not a PDF object.

The file /Users/ray/Documents/Web Sites/webroot/pdfarticle/mypdf.pdf is a valid PDF.
```

Whoa, what happened? Shouldn't the code have recognized mypdf as a PDF object? Remember that I said ColdFusion considers PDF a variable type now, much like images? In Listing 6-2, the cfdocument tag stored the binary data into a variable. ColdFusion didn't consider this a PDF object, but rather a binary object, so it failed the test. We'll modify the code a bit and use it as an excuse to introduce the cfpdf tag (see Listing 6-3). I mentioned earlier that this tag does quite a bit, but for now we will simply use it to read in a PDF object from a file.

*Listing 6-3. Reading a PDF object from a file with cfpdf*

```
<cfdocument format="pdf" name="mypdf">
    This is a PDF document.
</cfdocument>

<cfset fileWrite(expandPath("./mypdf2.pdf"), mypdf)>
<cfpdf action="read" source="./mypdf2.pdf" name="mypdfob">

<cfif isPDFObject(mypdfob)>
    <p>
        The variable mypdfob is a PDF object.
    </p>
</cfif>
```

In Listing 6-3, we immediately save the binary data to the file system. We then use the cfpdf tag to read the PDF file into a variable named mypdfob. This variable will pass the isPDFObject test because we used the cfpdf tag to create the variable.

# What Exactly Can We Do with the cfpdf Tag?

Now that we've been introduced to the `cfpdf` tag, let's take a closer look at it. Here are all the things you can do with it:

- Add a Watermark: Watermarks help protect documents in a simple way by adding a marker to a file, visible in the background on the page, that can help trace it when it's been released on the Internet. When ColdFusion 8 first came out, you could add only images as watermarks. Version 8.0.1 provided the ability to add an HTML watermark, since most people prefer to use text for their watermarks. You now have options for rotation, opacity, positioning, and other attributes. You can also remove a watermark.

- Delete Pages: This feature lets you remove pages from an existing PDF. You can specify specific individual pages, or a range using a format like 5-* (pages 5 to the end). You could use this to provide a trial version of a PDF to unregistered users; once they pay for the content, you can provide the full length PDF.

- Get Information: This returns a structure of information about the PDF, including useful metadata like author and the number of pages. Of course, you can also update information about a PDF.

- Merge: Merging can be useful if you have a set of template documents, like company title pages or legal PDFs. You can easily merge these templates into dynamic PDFs to create a final product.

- Manipulate PDF Security: You have full control over the security of a PDF document. You can enable or disable permissions for operations such as printing, and you can set passwords.

- Generate Thumbnails: This cool feature allows you to provide a graphical preview of a PDF document by generating a set of thumbnails from it.

- Read and Write: You perform the operations listed previously by reading and then changing PDF data. Once you change a PDF you have the ability to write these changes back out to the file system.

- Process DDX: Basically, if you want to do something that is not listed previously, DDX most likely has a way to do it. I'll show an example of this later.

ColdFusion 9 added the ability to:

- Add or remove headers and footers

- Extract text or images: This will extract the text or images from the PDF.

- Optimize - This will optimize the PDF by removing unneeded elements such as bookmarks and JavaScript.

- Transform - The PDF can be resized, rotated, or repositioned.

- Create PDF packages or portfolios using the merge action. Different types of files, such as images, multiple PDFs, and PowerPoint slides, can be bundled together into a PDF package.

# Getting and Setting Information

Let's take a look at the metadata information returned from a PDF. Listing 6-4 creates a PDF and then uses the getinfo action of the cfpdf tag to return a structure of information.

*Listing 6-4. The getinfo action of the cfpdf tag*

```
<cfdocument format="pdf" name="mypdf">
    <cfloop index="x" from="1" to="90">
        This is a PDF document.
        <cfif x mod 5 is 0>
            <cfdocumentitem type="pagebreak" />
        </cfif>
    </cfloop>
</cfdocument>

<cfset fileWrite(expandPath("./mypdf3.pdf"), mypdf)>
<cfpdf action="getinfo" source="./mypdf3.pdf" name="info">
<cfdump var="#info#">
```

This isn't much different from the previous example. We've added a cfdocumentitem type="pagebreak" tag just to make the PDF a bit bigger than it normally would be. As before, we save the PDF to the file system, and finally we get information about it using cfpdf. Figure 6-1 shows the dump of the variable where we stored the information. Note that the Producer key in the following output, which has the value iText 1.4, reveals what ColdFusion is using behind the scenes to generate PDFs.

| struct | |
|---|---|
| Application | [empty string] |
| Author | [empty string] |
| CenterWindowOnScreen | [empty string] |
| ChangingDocument | Allowed |
| Commenting | Allowed |
| ContentExtraction | Allowed |
| CopyContent | Allowed |
| Created | D:20081229071235-06'00' |
| DocumentAssembly | Allowed |
| Encryption | No Security |
| FilePath | /Library/WebServer/Documents/../mypdf3.pdf |
| FillingForm | Allowed |
| FitToWindow | [empty string] |
| HideMenubar | [empty string] |
| HideToolbar | [empty string] |
| HideWindowUI | [empty string] |
| Keywords | [empty string] |
| Language | [empty string] |
| Modified | D:20081229071235-06'00' |
| PageLayout | SinglePage |
| Printing | Allowed |
| Producer | iText 1.4 (by lowagie.com) |
| Properties | [empty string] |
| Secure | Allowed |
| ShowDocumentsOption | [empty string] |
| ShowWindowsOption | [empty string] |
| Signing | Allowed |
| Subject | [empty string] |
| Title | [empty string] |
| TotalPages | 19 |
| Trapped | [empty string] |
| Version | 1.4 |

*Figure 6-1. cfdump Results from Listing 6-4*

Now let's modify the example and see how easily we can update the information (see Listing 6-5).

*Listing 6-5. Updating our document's information using the setinfo action*

```
<cfdocument format="pdf" name="mypdf">
    <cfloop index="x" from="1" to="90">
        This is a PDF document.
        <cfif x mod 5 is 0>
            <cfdocumentitem type="pagebreak" />
        </cfif>
    </cfloop>
</cfdocument>

<cfset fileWrite(expandPath("./mypdf4.pdf"), mypdf)>
<cfpdf action="getinfo" source="./mypdf4.pdf" name="info">

<cfset info.title = "Modified PDF">
<cfset info.author = "Darth Doohicky">
<cfpdf action="setinfo" info="#info#" source="./mypdf4.pdf"
    destination="./mypdf4_modified.pdf" overwrite="true">

<cfpdf action="getinfo" source="./mypdf4_modified.pdf" name="info2">
<cfdump var="#info2#">
```

This time we modify the structure returned by the getinfo action and use the setinfo action to update the document's information as we create a new PDF file from the previous PDF file. Finally, we read the new PDF's information into the info2 structure and dump info2 to screen (see Figure 6-2).

| struct | |
|---|---|
| Application | [empty string] |
| Author | Darth Doohicky |
| CenterWindowOnScreen | [empty string] |
| ChangingDocument | Allowed |
| Commenting | Allowed |
| ContentExtraction | Allowed |
| CopyContent | Allowed |
| Created | D:20081229071605-06'00' |
| DocumentAssembly | Allowed |
| Encryption | No Security |
| FilePath | /Library/WebServer/Documents/././mypdf4_modified.pdf |
| FillingForm | Allowed |
| FitToWindow | [empty string] |
| HideMenubar | [empty string] |
| HideToolbar | [empty string] |
| HideWindowUI | [empty string] |
| Keywords | [empty string] |
| Language | [empty string] |
| Modified | D:20081229071605-06'00' |
| PageLayout | SinglePage |
| Printing | Allowed |
| Producer | iText 1.4 (by lowagie.com) |
| Properties | [empty string] |
| Secure | Allowed |
| ShowDocumentsOption | [empty string] |
| ShowWindowsOption | [empty string] |
| Signing | Allowed |
| Subject | [empty string] |
| Title | Modified PDF |
| TotalPages | 19 |
| Trapped | [empty string] |
| Version | 1.4 |

*Figure 6-2.* `cfdump` *Results from Listing 6-5*

## Adding a Watermark

As I mentioned before, watermarks are a good way to secure a document. If you are working on the next big movie hit (let's say, *Godfather Part IV*) and want to share a copy of the script with an agent, you can use a watermark to clearly label that the document was given to a certain person. If the PDF ends up on the Internet, you can then identify who leaked it.

The cfpdf tag supports this feature with the addWatermark and removeWatermark actions. When ColdFusion 8 was released, adding a text-based watermark required a small workaround: since you could use only images, you needed to create a dynamic image, paste the text onto it, and use the resulting image for the PDF watermark. The 8.0.1 update made this process much easier by allowing you to use any string of HTML for the watermark input. Listing 6-6 gives a simple example.

*Listing 6-6. Creating a watermark using a string*

```
<cfdocument format="pdf" name="mypdf">
    <cfloop index="x" from="1" to="90">
        This is a PDF document.
    </cfloop>
</cfdocument>

<cfpdf action="addwatermark" source="mypdf" destination="mypdf5.pdf"
    text="Documented generated for Darth Vader's eyes only" foreground="yes"
    overwrite="yes">
```

As with the previous examples, we begin by creating a simple PDF filled with text (though we didn't bother saving it this time). Next, for the cfpdf tag, we can point to a binary PDF variable as the source and use a destination file name. Pretty handy. The watermark is provided in the text and can also include HTML, but we've kept it simple. We didn't change the default opacity but did specify that the watermark should be in the foreground. That's it! This generates a PDF with a nice, very obvious watermark (see Figure 6-3).

*Figure 6-3. Watermark on PDF Generated by Listing 6-6*

# Using DDX

Now let's step it up a notch and take a look at DDX, which is a part of LiveCycle Assembler, another Adobe product. You can think of it as batch (.bat) files — or bash scripts for those of you not raised on Windows — for PDF files. In DDX you can define inputs, operations, and outputs. I do not have the room for a full exploration of its incredibly powerful feature set in this article, but a full reference for DDX may be found online (http://www.adobe.com/go/learn_lc_DDXReference_82). ColdFusion has a few restrictions on what you can do with DDX, and a list of restricted tags may be found on Adobe LiveDocs (http://livedocs.adobe.com/coldfusion/8/htmldocs/Tags_p-q_02.html - 2938002).

Let's look at an example of DDX in action doing something kind of cool. Have you ever wondered how search tools such as Verity can index the contents of PDF files? When Verity encounters a PDF file, it must use some type of API to get the text content of the PDF for indexing. We can use DDX to mimic that API ourselves in ColdFusion (see Listing 6-7).

*Listing 6-7. Using DDX to get the text content of a PDF*

```
<cfdocument format="pdf" name="mypdf">
    <cfloop index="x" from="1" to="90">
        <cfoutput>
            <p>
            This is a PDF document. Dynamic row #x#.
            </p>
        </cfoutput>
    </cfloop>
</cfdocument>
<cfset fileWrite(expandPath("./mypdf6.pdf"), mypdf)>

<!--- Create DDX --->
<cfsavecontent variable="ddx">
    <?xml version="1.0" encoding="UTF-8"?>
    <DDX xmlns="http://ns.adobe.com/DDX/1.0/"
xmlns:xsi="http://www.w3.org/2001/XMLSchema-instance"
xsi:schemaLocation="http://ns.adobe.com/DDX/1.0/ coldfusion_ddx.xsd">
        <DocumentText result="Out1">
            <PDF source="doc1"/>
        </DocumentText>
    </DDX>
</cfsavecontent>

<!--- Set parameters --->
<cfset inputStruct = {doc1="#expandPath('./mypdf6.pdf')#"}>
<cfset outputStruct = {Out1="#expandPath('./mypdf6.xml')#"}>

<!--- Process DDX --->
<cfpdf action="processddx" ddxfile="#ddx#" inputfiles="#inputStruct#"
    outputfiles="#outputStruct#" name="ddxVar">
```

Listing 6-7 builds on the previous examples. We've modified our cfdocument tag to be a bit more dynamic; we actually use the variable x in the output. As I mentioned, DDX is XML-based, and in this case our XML uses a few root tags — xml and DDX — that each DDX action we use must contain.

ColdFusion also has an isDDX() function you can use to confirm that a given string is a valid DDX XML packet. In this script, we use the DocumentText element as a command. It basically says that we want to suck the text out of the specified source PDF(s). The only child tag defines the input.

Don't worry if this doesn't make complete sense. You can consult the DDX documentation to learn about all of the available features, but for now you should focus on two parts: the source (doc1) and the result (Out1). We need to provide information on input and output files to ColdFusion. In the section where we set the parameters, we define that information as structures so that we can use it later on. We used shorthand structure notation for this script.

- The first structure, inputStruct, has a key with the same name as the source defined in the DDX XML: doc1. The actual value is the PDF we created in this process.

- The next structure, outputStruct, has a key with the same name as the result in the DDX XML: Out1, and in this case represents where we want to save the result.

This brings up an important limitation with DDX: You cannot use ColdFusion variables as input and output sources but instead must provide real file names.

The last line uses the processddx action of the cfpdf tag and passes in the values we previously defined. The last attribute of cfpdf, name, stores the result of the output operation. Its value will partially depend on the DDX operation used, but you can check it at runtime to see if everything worked. The end result of this action will be stored as the file specified by outputStruct. The important portion of the contents of mypdf6.xml is shown in Listing 6-8.

*Listing 6-8. Example result from the processddx action in Listing 6-7*

```
<?xml version="1.0" encoding="UTF-8"?>
<DocText xmlns="http://ns.adobe.com/DDX/DocText/1.0/">
    <TextPerPage>
        <Page pageNumber="1">This is a PDF document. Dynamic row 4. ...</Page>
        <Page pageNumber="2">This is a PDF document. Dynamic row 62. ...</Page>
        <Page pageNumber="3">This is a PDF document. Dynamic row 90. ...</Page>
    </TextPerPage>
</DocText>
```

This listing omits a bit of text in order to focus on the result itself. As you can see, it is an XML packet in which each page has its own XML text. We can then write some simple CFML to parse this XML into an array where each array element represents a page of text (see Listing 6-9).

*Listing 6-9. Parsing the XML into an Array*

```
<!--- This is a continuation of Listing 6-8 and not a standalone program --->
<!--- Read in and parse XML --->
<cffile action="read" file="#outputStruct.out1#" variable="myxml">
<cfset myxml = xmlParse(myxml)>
<cfset results = []>
```

```
<!--- Ensure valid stuff --->
<cfif structKeyExists(myxml, "DocText") and
    structKeyExists(myxml.DocText,"TextPerPage") and
    structKeyExists(myxml.DocText.TextPerPage, "Page")>
    <cfloop index="x" from="1"
        to="#arrayLen(myxml.DocText.TextPerPage.Page)#">
        <cfset node = myxml.DocText.TextPerPage.Page[x]>
        <cfset text = node.xmltext>
        <cfset arrayAppend(results, text)>
    </cfloop>
</cfif>
<cfdump var="#results#">
```

To index the text for searching purposes, you could take that final array and turn it into a string: `<cfset text = arrayToList(results, " ")>`. What's really cool about this is that anything that ColdFusion didn't provide to us directly with the `cfpdf` tag, we can potentially accomplish with DDX. This brings up my last point: As I mentioned at the beginning of this article, these PDF-related features actually got me excited about PDFs, something I never thought would happen. While playing around with these features, I found things that I wanted to do that weren't as easy as they could be. For example, consider the DDX read operation we did before to index the content of a PDF. While certainly not hard to do, wouldn't it be nice if we could just do `<cfset text = somepdf.getText()>`? With that in mind, I built a CFC called `pdfutils` (`http://pdfutils.riaforge.org`) to wrap up some of these ideas into an easy-to-use component (which is 100% open source and available for free). This CFC supports the following features:

- `getExtraInfo`: Returns a bit more information than `getInfo` does, including the size of pages.

- `getPage`: Lets you get one PDF page from a document by deleting every page except the one you want.

- `getText`: Wraps the DDX operation used in Listing 6-7.

- `readXMP`/`writeXMP`: Submitted by David Griffiths; allow you to work with XMP data in PDFs.

# Where to Go Next

ColdFusion has really opened the world of PDFs to me and exposed me to how deep their functionality goes. In this article we didn't even touch on forms and form processing, a whole other set of features you can use as well. If you had previously ignored new PDF features — perhaps thinking, like me, that they weren't really worth your time — I highly encourage you to make the time to play around with these tags and see what you can create!

■■■

# CHAPTER 7

# Image Processing in ColdFusion

## by Pete Freitag

*Built-in image resizing functionality has been on the ColdFusion developer's wish list for years, and boy, has Adobe delivered! Not only did they give us the cfimage tag, with built-in image processing functionality, such as image resizing and getting the dimensions of an image, but they added advanced functionality with more than fifty additional image processing functions. In this article, Pete Freitag introduces you to the cfimage tag and several of ColdFusion's image processing functions.*

## The cfimage Tag

The cfimage tag supports nine action attributes, which allow you to

- add borders to an image
- create a CAPTCHA image
- convert an image file from one format to another (e.g., jpg to png)
- get image information such as dimensions
- read an existing image
- resize an image to specified height and width
- rotate an image
- write an image to disk; and finally
- serve up the image to the browser dynamically with the writeToBrowser action

## Getting Image Dimensions with cfimage

Listing 7-1 shows how to display image dimensions with cfimage. The info action populates the structure specified in the structName attribute. The source attribute can either be the absolute path of an image file on the server, a URL of an image, an image object variable, or a Base64 string. (Base64 is an algorithm for encoding binary data, such as a binary image file, as an ascii string.)

*Listing 7-1. Display Image Dimensions*

```
<cfimage action="info" source="#ExpandPath("lobster.jpg")#" structName="imageInfo">
<cfoutput>
   <p>Image Dimensions: #imageInfo.width# x #imageInfo.height#</p>
</cfoutput>
```

The most useful keys in the `imageInfo` structure are width and height because they contain the image dimensions. See Figure 7-1 for a full dump of the `cfimage imageInfo` structure.

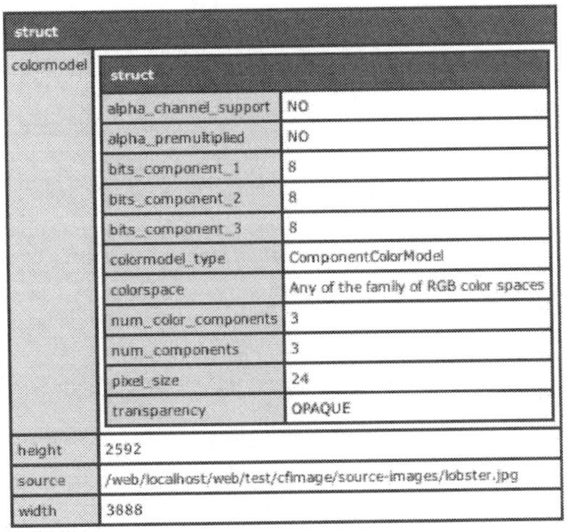

| struct | | |
|---|---|---|
| colormodel | alpha_channel_support | NO |
| | alpha_premultiplied | NO |
| | bits_component_1 | 8 |
| | bits_component_2 | 8 |
| | bits_component_3 | 8 |
| | colormodel_type | ComponentColorModel |
| | colorspace | Any of the family of RGB color spaces |
| | num_color_components | 3 |
| | num_components | 3 |
| | pixel_size | 24 |
| | transparency | OPAQUE |
| height | 2592 | |
| source | /web/localhost/web/test/cfimage/source-images/lobster.jpg | |
| width | 3888 | |

*Figure 7-1. Screenshot of a cfdump of the imageInfo structure*

## Resizing an Image with cfimage

When the `action` attribute is `resize`, we must again populate the `source` attribute. Since we are manipulating the image, we must also specify where the resized image will go. In Listing 7-2, I use the `destination` attribute to set a new path for the resized image. The `width` and `height` attributes take either a pixel value or a percentage value. Finally, the `overwrite` attribute specifies whether we should overwrite the destination file if it already exists.

*Listing 7-2. Resize an Image Using the cfimage Tag*

```
<cfimage action="resize"
   source="#ExpandPath("lobster.jpg")#"
   destination="#ExpandPath("lobster-sm.jpg")#"
   width="150" height="100" overwrite="true">
```

# Multiple Operations with cfimage

If you wanted to perform additional manipulations to the image, you could use the `name` attribute instead of the `destination` attribute to specify a variable name for a `cfimage` object. Listing 7-3 illustrates the use of a `cfimage` object with the `cfimage` tag.

*Listing 7-3. Manipulate an Image Using cfimage*

```
<cfimage action="read" source="#ExpandPath("lobster.jpg")#" name="myImg">
<cfimage action="info" source="#myImg#" structName="imgInfo">
<cfif imgInfo.width GT 50>
    <cfimage action="resize" source="#myImg#"
          width="25%" height="25%" name="myImg">
    <cfimage action="border" color="red" thickness="3"
          source="#myImg#" name="myImg">
    <cfimage action="rotate" angle="15" source="#myImg#" name="myImg">
    <cfimage action="writeToBrowser" source="#myImg#">
    <cfimage action="write" source="#myImg#"
          destination="#ExpandPath("lobster-3.jpg")#"
          overwrite="true" quality="0.8">
</cfif>
```

Let's run through the code in Listing 7-3. On the first line, the read `action` loads an image (`lobster.jpg`) into the variable name specified by the `name` attribute (`myImg`). At this point, we can pass this value into other `cfimage` tags through the `source` attribute by adding pound signs to the variable name.

Listing 7-3 also exemplifies how the `border` and `rotate action` values are used. The `border action` supports two new attributes: `color` and `thickness`. The `color` attribute should be given a hexadecimal color name, or a simple color name such as red, white, or black (see http://livedocs.adobe.com/coldfusion/8/htmldocs/Tags_i_02.html#4004168 for a full list of supported named colors). The `thickness` attribute specifies, as you might imagine, how many pixels thick the border will be. The rotate `action` simply adds an `angle` attribute denoting the number of degrees (0-360) to rotate the image.

This example uses the `writeToBrowser action`, handy for outputting dynamic images you have no intention of saving to the file system. It works by outputting an HTML `Img` tag with a dynamically generated `src` attribute value.

Finally, the `write action` is used to save an image to the server's file system. It uses the `source` and `destination` attributes and adds an additional attribute called `quality`. The value of the `quality` attribute should be a number between 0 and 1, where 1 generates a file of the highest quality. We've used a value of 0.8, which is equivalent to 80% quality. The `quality` attribute is only used when you are writing a JPEG image.

# Creating a CAPTCHA Image with cfimage

Up to this point we have seen seven out of the nine possible values for the `action` attribute. The eighth `action` value is CAPTCHA. The word CAPTCHA is an acronym that means Completely Automated Public Turing test to tell Computers and Humans Apart. CAPTCHA images are often used on web forms to prove that a human, and not an automated process such as a spam-bot, is filling out the form. The user is asked to type in the word or text that is printed in the image. See Figure 7-2 for an example of a CAPTCHA image.

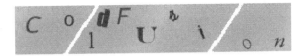

*Figure 7-2. A CAPTCHA image*

Because it is difficult for a computer to read text from an image file, this test does a good job of separating humans from computers. However, the CAPTCHA test can also be hard for humans to complete, and CAPTCHA images do not comply with Section 508 accessibility standards. Regardless of how you feel about CAPTCHAs, creating CAPTCHA images with ColdFusion is quite simple.
The code in Listing 7-4 almost speaks for itself. Simply use the text attribute to specify the text you want to display in the CAPTCHA image. Be sure to specify a width large enough to display the text or an error will be thrown.

*Listing 7-4. Generating a CAPTCHA with cfimage*

```
<cfimage action="captcha" text="ColdFusion" height="50" width="300">
```

Because CAPTCHAs can sometimes be difficult for humans to read, a `difficulty` attribute was added to allow you to control how hard it will be to solve. To change the default setting of "low," make the difficulty equal to "medium" or "high." You may also want to set the `fonts` attribute, which takes a comma-separated list of font names and uses them randomly to display the text. If you don't specify the fonts attribute, any font installed on the server may be used. This may pose a problem if a symbols font, such as Wingdings, is selected randomly, as you will not be able to read the CAPTCHA.

# The New Image Processing Functions

While the `cfimage` tag is great for basic image manipulation, you will need to employ the image processing functions for more advanced operations. With the image functions, you can draw shapes, lines, and text on top of an existing image or onto a blank image canvas. You can also crop, blur, flip, grayscale, rotate, overlay images, and more.

## Image Drawing Functions

Let's start by looking at image drawing functions, which include drawing an image from scratch, using a custom drawing stroke, and drawing text on an image.

### Drawing an Image from Scratch

The first line of Listing 7-5 creates an empty, white canvas, 200 pixels wide by 100 pixels high using the `ImageNew` function. The first argument of `ImageNew` allows you to optionally specify a source image object.

This can be handy if you want to duplicate an existing image, but in most cases you will simply pass an empty string to create an empty image from scratch. The second and third arguments are used to define the width and height of the new image respectively. Next, the color type is specified, and possible values for this argument are rgb, argb, and grayscale. Finally, the fifth argument specifies the canvas color of the new image. The ImageNew function returns a cfimage object that we can now manipulate using cfimage or any of the image manipulation functions.

*Listing 7-5. Drawing a Rectangle*

```
<cfset myImg = ImageNew("", 200, 100, "rgb", "white")>
<cfset ImageSetDrawingColor(myImg, "blue")>
<cfset ImageDrawRect(myImg, 0, 0, 50, 25, true)>
<cfimage action="writeToBrowser" source="#myImg#">
```

On the second line of Listing 7-5, we set the drawing color of our new image to blue using the ImageSetDrawingColor function. This will tell any subsequent drawing functions what color to use.

The third line is where things start to get interesting and we are actually using ColdFusion to draw! There are 11 drawing functions from which to choose, and we are starting with the ImageDrawRect function. This function draws a rectangle on our blank image canvas. As in nearly all image processing functions in ColdFusion, the first argument of the ImageDrawRect function is the cfimage object variable. The second and third arguments tell ColdFusion where to start drawing the X and Y respectively. By passing zeros into the X and Y arguments we are instructing the function to start in the top left corner of the image. The fourth and fifth arguments specify the width and height of the rectangle, while the sixth argument is a Boolean value indicating whether or not the rectangle should be filled or remain an outline. In Figure 7-3 you can see the results of this code.

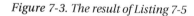

*Figure 7-3. The result of Listing 7-5*

## Using a Custom Drawing Stroke

Now suppose we wanted to draw an unfilled rectangle with a 4-pixel line thickness. We can employ the ImageSetDrawingStroke function to define the pen width, as well as several other options including dashes, line joins, end caps, and miters.

*Listing 7-6. Drawing an Unfilled Rectangle*

```
<cfset myImg = ImageNew("", 200, 100, "rgb", "white")>
<cfset ImageSetDrawingColor(myImg, "blue")>
<cfset stroke = StructNew()>
<cfset stroke.width = "4">
<cfset ImageSetDrawingStroke(myImg, stroke)>
<cfset ImageDrawRect(myImg, 5, 5, 100, 50, false)>
<cfimage action="writeToBrowser" source="#myImg#">
```

To use the `ImageSetDrawingStroke` function, you must first create a structure that contains the parameters you wish to define. In Listing 7-6, we are setting the pen thickness to 4 pixels by setting the width key of our structure. Next, we pass in the structure to the `ImageSetDrawingStroke` function. Finally, we call the `ImageDrawRect` function and set the filled argument to false. The results are seen in Figure 7-4.

*Figure 7-4. The result of Listing 7-6*

## Drawing Text on an Image

The ability to draw text on an image is one of the most useful drawing functions available. The `ImageDrawText` function accepts a string of text in the second argument to print on the image. The third and fourth arguments define the X and Y position where the text begins. In Listing 7-7, a function named `ImageSetAntialiasing` was used on the third line. You can see the results in Figure 7-6.

*Listing 7-7. Drawing Text on an Image*

```
<cfset myImg = ImageNew("", 120, 50, "rgb", "white")>
<cfset ImageSetDrawingColor(myImg, "red")>
<cfset ImageSetAntialiasing(myImg, "On")>
<cfset ImageDrawText(myImg, "ColdFusion!", 20, 20)>
<cfimage action="writeToBrowser" source="#myImg#">
```

You can see the results in Figure 7-6.

ColdFusion!

*Figure 7-6. Result of Listing 7-7*

This function toggles antialiasing, which, in essence, makes rounded corners appear smoother and crisper. It's a good idea to turn on antialiasing whenever you are drawing objects that may be rounded, including text, circles, and arcs.

## Text Drawing Options

The optional fifth argument of the ImageDrawText function allows for a structure containing text drawing options including font, size, style, strikethrough, and underline. Listing 7-8 illustrates the use of the text options structure.

*Listing 7-8. Changing the Text Drawing Font*

```
<cfset myImg = ImageNew("", 150, 50, "rgb", "white")>
<cfset ImageSetDrawingColor(myImg, "green")>
<cfset ImageSetAntialiasing(myImg, "On")>
<cfset textOptions = StructNew()>
<cfset textOptions.font = "Georgia">
<cfset textOptions.size = "16">
<cfset textOptions.style = "bold">
<cfset textOptions.strikethrough = false>
<cfset textOptions.underline = true>
<cfset ImageDrawText(myImg, "ColdFusion!", 20, 20, textOptions)>
<cfimage action="writeToBrowser" source="#myImg#">
```

## Additional Image Drawing Functions

We have only scratched the surface of the available image drawing functions in ColdFusion. Here's a list of the drawing functions in ColdFusion:

- ImageDrawArc ( imgObj, x, y, width, height, sAngle, arcAngle [, filled ] )

- ImageDrawBeveledRect ( imgObj, x, y, width, height, raised [, filled ] )

- ImageDrawCubicCurve ( imgObj, cx1, cy1, cx2, cy2, x1, y1, x2, y2 )

- ImageDrawLine ( imgObj, x1, y1, x2, y2 )

- ImageDrawLines ( imgObj, xArray, yArray [, isPolygon, filled ] )

- ImageDrawOval ( imgObj, x, y, width, height [, filled ] )

- ImageDrawPoint ( imgObj, x, y )

- ImageDrawQuadraticCurve ( imgObj, cx1, cy1, cx2, cy2, x1, y1, x2, y2 )

- ImageDrawRect ( imgObj, x, y, width, height [, filled ] )

- ImageDrawRoundRect ( imgObj, x, y, width, height, arcWidth, arcHeight [, filled ] )

- ImageDrawText ( imgObj, text, x, y [, options] )

- ImageClearRect ( imgObj, x, y, width, height )

- ImageAddBorder ( imgObj, thickness [, color, borderType ] )

In addition to ImageSetDrawingColor, ImageSetDrawingStroke, and ImageSetAntialiasing, there are several other functions that affect the output of the drawing functions. These functions are:

- ImageSetAntialiasing ( imgObj, onOff )

- ImageSetBackgroundColor ( imgObj, color )

- ImageSetDrawingColor ( imgObj, color )

- ImageSetDrawingStroke ( imgObj, strokeOptions )

- ImageSetDrawingTransparency ( imgObj, percent )

- ImageRotateDrawingAxis ( imgObj, angle [, x, y ] )

- ImageShearDrawingAxis ( imgObj, shearX, shearY )

- ImageTranslateDrawingAxis ( imgObj, x, y )

- ImageXORDrawingMode ( imgObj, color )

# Image Manipulation Functions

I've shown you image functions that allow you to draw new images or draw text on images. The next group of image functions alter the entire image object and may be classified as image manipulation functions. Examples include ImageBlur, ImageCrop, and ImageGrayscale.

## ImageScaleToFit

ImageScaleToFit is one of the more useful manipulation functions. This function resizes an image, yet maintains the aspect ratio. It ensures that the resulting image fits inside the dimensions you specify, but it will also keep the same height-to-width ratio of the original. So, if you have an image that is 200 x 100, as in Listing 7-9, the result of ImageScaleToFit(myImg, 100, 75) would be a 100 x 50-pixel image. You can also pass additional options on this function to control interpolation and the blur factor.[1]

*Listing 7-9. Resizing While Maintaining Aspect Ratio*

```
<cfimage action="read" source="lobster.jpg" name="myImg">
<cfset ImageScaleToFit(myImg, 100, 75)>
<cfimage action="writeToBrowser" source="#myImg#">
```

---

[1] Digital Photography Preview online defines interpolation as "an imaging method to increase or decrease the number of pixels in an image." (Source: http://www.dpreview.com/learn/?/key=interpolation)

## Additional Image Manipulation Functions

Here are some additional image manipulation functions:

- `ImageBlur ( imgObj [, blurRadius ] )`
- `ImageCrop ( imgObj, x, y, width, height )`
- `ImageFlip ( imgObj [, transpose ] )`
- `ImageGrayscale ( imgObj )`
- `ImageNegative ( imgObj )`
- `ImageOverlay ( imgObj, imgObj2 )`
- `ImagePaste ( imgObj, imgObj2, x, y )`
- `ImageResize ( imgObj, width, height [, interpolation, blurFactor ] )`
- `ImageRotate ( imgObj, [x, y,] angle [, interpolation] )`
- `ImageScaleToFit ( imgObj, width, height [, interpolation, blurFactor] )`
- `ImageSharpen ( imgObj [, gain ] )`
- `ImageShear ( imgObj, shear [, direction, interpolation ] )`

# Image Information Functions

The next class of image functions allow you to obtain many different types of information from an image object.

The `ImageInfo` function returns the same image information structure as the `cfimage info` action attribute. However, if you only need the image width and height, you can use the `ImageGetWidth` and `ImageGetHeight` functions. Simply pass in your `cfimage` object as the first argument, and the height or width will be returned by the function.

## Displaying the Digital Camera Model and EXIF data

One of the more interesting image information functions is the `ImageGetEXIFMetadata` function illustrated in Listing 7-10. EXIF stands for Exchangeable Image File Format and is a standard for storing information within image files. Most digital cameras write EXIF data when you take a picture, so you can extract information such as the camera make and model, shutter speed, focal length, and exposure time.

*Listing 7-10. Dump EXIF Metadata*

```
<cfimage action="read" source="lobster.jpg" name="img">
<cfset exif = ImageGetEXIFMetaData(img)>
<cfoutput>
   <cfif StructKeyExists(exif, "Model")>
      <p>Camera Model: #exif["Model"]#</p>
   </cfif>
</cfoutput>
<cfdump var="#exif#">
```

The ImageGetEXIFMetadata function returns a structure containing keys set by your camera or image software. If no EXIF data is present, an empty structure is returned. You can also use the ImageGetEXIFTag function; however, if the tag is not present or the image is not a JPEG image, ColdFusion will throw an exception.

Figure 7-6 shows the result of a cfdump tag on the EXIF metadata.

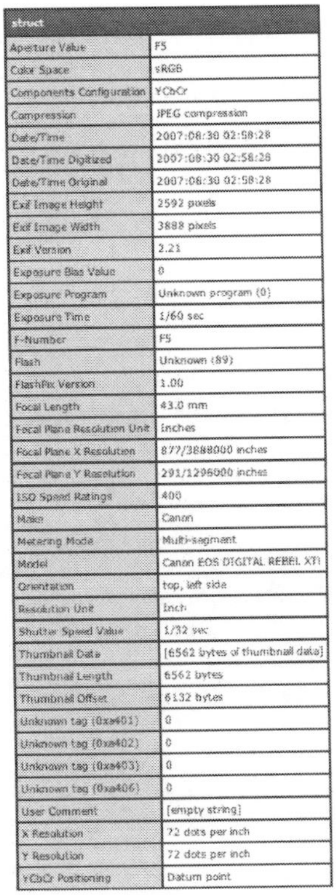

| struct | |
|---|---|
| Aperture Value | F5 |
| Color Space | sRGB |
| Components Configuration | YCbCr |
| Compression | JPEG compression |
| Date/Time | 2007:06:30 02:58:28 |
| Date/Time Digitized | 2007:06:30 02:58:28 |
| Date/Time Original | 2007:06:30 02:58:28 |
| Exif Image Height | 2592 pixels |
| Exif Image Width | 3888 pixels |
| Exif Version | 2.21 |
| Exposure Bias Value | 0 |
| Exposure Program | Unknown program (0) |
| Exposure Time | 1/60 sec |
| F-Number | F5 |
| Flash | Unknown (89) |
| FlashPix Version | 1.00 |
| Focal Length | 43.0 mm |
| Focal Plane Resolution Unit | Inches |
| Focal Plane X Resolution | 877/3888000 inches |
| Focal Plane Y Resolution | 291/1296000 inches |
| ISO Speed Ratings | 400 |
| Make | Canon |
| Metering Mode | Multi-segment |
| Model | Canon EOS DIGITAL REBEL XTi |
| Orientation | top, left side |
| Resolution Unit | Inch |
| Shutter Speed Value | 1/32 sec |
| Thumbnail Data | [6562 bytes of thumbnail data] |
| Thumbnail Length | 6562 bytes |
| Thumbnail Offset | 6132 bytes |
| Unknown tag (0xea01) | 0 |
| Unknown tag (0xea02) | 0 |
| Unknown tag (0xea03) | 0 |
| Unknown tag (0xea06) | 0 |
| User Comment | [empty string] |
| X Resolution | 72 dots per inch |
| Y Resolution | 72 dots per inch |
| YCbCr Positioning | Datum point |

*Figure 7-6. cfdump of EXIF MetaData*

## Image I/O Functions

This final group of image functions includes `ImageRead`, `ImageReadBase64`, `ImageWrite`, and `ImageWriteBase64`. The `ImageReadBase64` and `ImageWriteBase64` functions both work with Base64, which is a good format for transmitting binary objects over web services or a text-based network protocol. E-mail attachments sent over SMTP are often encoded in Base64.

# Summary

This article has only addressed a portion of the image processing functionality ColdFusion has to offer. Adobe has given us a toolkit for both basic and advanced image manipulation. However, Adobe has kept things simple by standardizing the invocation of these new features. The examples above demonstrate how easy image manipulation has become. If you understand the concepts presented here, learning the remaining functionality should be a straightforward task.

# PART 3

# Essentials to Server Productivity

CHAPTER 8

■ ■ ■

# Tuning Your Java Virtual Machine: Finding Your Ideal JVM Settings Through Metrics Log Analysis

**by Mike Brunt**

*The Java Virtual Machine underlying the ColdFusion server is probably one of the least understood things about ColdFusion. Yet this mysterious "black box" is key to keeping ColdFusion operating efficiently. In the ColdFusion world, Mike Brunt is one of the best-known experts on taming this beast, and he presents many insights in this article.*

Tuning the Java Virtual Machine (JVM) can deliver dramatic benefits. For instance, a client recently called with severe stability issues: ColdFusion froze regularly and needed multiple restarts daily. We initially found that both thread and heap memory utilization reached 100% regularly. After we spent five days on-site tuning the JVM, overall heap memory utilization did not go beyond 30% and threads cycled well—a totally different world!

When I help clients with problems like this, I use a two-step process. First, I analyze the client's metrics logs, which measure memory and thread usage over time. Second, I use these logs to help me pinpoint, implement, and test the JVM settings that are ideal for the client's particular server.

In this particular case, the client had not done anything more than accept the default JVM settings. This organization also ran an older version of ColdFusion, which meant it could not run the latest JVM.

Often, simple changes, such as fine-tuning the JVM settings and upgrading to a newer JVM, will do wonders to restore a server's efficiency—even before analyzing and correcting issues in the client's codebase. In this article, I will detail how to go about tuning the JVM to improve performance and stability.

## How the JVM Fits into ColdFusion

ColdFusion moved squarely into the standards-based Java Platform, Enterprise Edition (Java EE) world with version 6.1. The greatest benefit of that move was the ability to run multiple instances of

103

ColdFusion—effectively multiple ColdFusion servers—on the same physical machine. This common practice in the Java EE world was not possible in ColdFusion before version 6.1.

The JVM enables the claim "write once, run anywhere" for Java (and ColdFusion) applications to come very close to reality. In essence, it abstracts the host operating system, such as Windows, Macintosh OS X, or Unix.

In the Java application server world, which includes ColdFusion 6.1, 7, 8, and 9 as standards-based Java EE application servers, three layers sit within the host operating system. As shown in Figure 8-1, ColdFusion sits at the center of it all. And in a ColdFusion Enterprise installation, we might well see multiple Java application server <COLDFUSION> instances in that central position, each totally encapsulated.

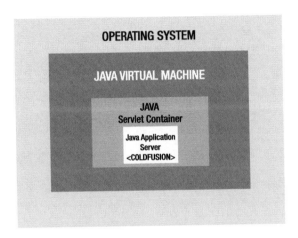

*Figure 8-1. The JVM with ColdFusion*

---

■ **Note** The Sun JVM is the default that comes with ColdFusion 6.1, 7, 8, and 9, with JRun as the default Java servlet container. The principles I will show here for tuning the JVM apply to any of the standards-based Java EE JVMs, although the location and names of the basic configuration files may differ.

---

# Enabling Metrics Logging

The root needs of the JVM revolve around memory use and threads. In my experience, the perfectly tuned JVM recycles threads quickly (in milliseconds) and rarely uses more than 50% of the total heap memory available. To that end, the first thing I do with a client is see how the memory and threads are behaving, by enabling metrics logging within the JVM, which provides me with a running log of the threads and memory state on the client's server. In fact, I have found this so safe and useful, I often recommend setting up metrics logging and leaving it running permanently.

# Editing the jrun.xml File

You enable metrics logging by editing the `jrun.xml` file for the ColdFusion server or instance. If you are on a Standard installation, you'll find this file here:

`{drive-volume}\{coldfusionRoot}\runtime\servers\cfusion\SERVER-INF`

where *drive-volume* is the name of the drive where ColdFusion is installed, and *coldfusionRoot* is the directory on that drive that holds ColdFusion. On a standard Windows installation, this would be `C:\ColdFusion9`.

On an Enterprise installation, `jrun.xml` will be here:

`{drive-volume}\JRun4\servers\{instancename}\SERVER-INF`

Save a copy of the original `jrun.xml` file in case you need to roll back to it. Then open the original file in a text editor and locate the first set of metrics-logging entries, which will look like Listing 8-1.

*Listing 8-1. Default jrun.xml*

```
<!-- To enable metrics: uncomment this service
and in LoggerService set metricsEnabled to true -->

<!--
<service class="jrunx.metrics.MetricsService" name="MetricsService">
    <attribute name="bindToJNDI">true</attribute>
</service>
-->
```

Uncomment the lower block of code so it now looks like Listing 8-2.

*Listing 8-2. Uncommented metrics section in jrun.xml*

```
<!-- To enable metrics: uncomment this service
and in LoggerService set metricsEnabled to true -->

<!-- myemailaddress 10/25/2008 "enabled metrics logging" -->
<service class="jrunx.metrics.MetricsService" name="MetricsService">
    <attribute name="bindToJNDI">true</attribute>
</service>
```

Next, enable the metrics, once again in the `jrun.xml` file. Locate the block of settings shown in Listing 8-3.

*Listing 8-3. metricsEnabled attribute in jrun.xml*

```
<!-- You may also need to uncomment MetricsService
    if you want metrics enabled -->
<attribute name="metricsEnabled">false</attribute>
<attribute name="metricsLogFrequency">60</attribute>
```

```
<attribute name="metricsFormat">Web threads (busy/total):
    {jrpp.busyTh}/{jrpp.totalTh} Sessions: {sessions}
    Total Memory={totalMemory} Free={freeMemory}</attribute>
```

Finally, make the changes shown in Listing 8-4 for the ColdFusion Enterprise edition, or make the changes shown in Listing 8-5 for the Standard edition.

*Listing 8-4. metricsEnabled attribute set to true in jrun.xml (Enterprise edition)*

```
<!-- You may also need to uncomment MetricsService
    if you want metrics enabled -->

<attribute name="metricsEnabled">true</attribute>
<attribute name="metricsLogFrequency">60</attribute>
<attribute name="metricsFormat">Web threads (busy/total/delayed):
    {jrpp.busyTh}/{jrpp.totalTh}/{jrpp.delayTh} Sessions: {sessions}
    Total Memory={totalMemory} Free={freeMemory}</attribute>
```

*Listing 8-5. metricsEnabled attribute set to true in jrun.xml (Standard edition)*

```
<!-- You may also need to uncomment MetricsService if you want metrics enabled -->

<attribute name="metricsEnabled">true</attribute>
<attribute name="metricsLogFrequency">60</attribute>

<attribute name="metricsFormat">Web threads (busy/total/delayed):
    {busyTh}/{totalTh}/{delayTh} Sessions: {sessions}
    Total Memory={totalMemory} Free={freeMemory}</attribute>
```

In Listings 8-4 and 8-5, we are changing the metricsEnabled flag to true and adding a metric to show delayed threads. This important step helps to determine the number of threads an application needs under x amount of load. The difference between the Standard and Enterprise editions is that the Standard edition does not use the jrpp. prefix in the thread variable declaration (compare the last line of both listings).

## Splitting Up the JRun Logs

Now we will improve organization and human-readability of the JRun logs by splitting different information into separate logs. In the jrun.xml file, make the bolded addition to the logging settings shown in Listing 8-6.

*Listing 8-6. Separate groups of information in jrun.xml*

```
<attribute name="filename">
{jrun.rootdir}/logs/{jrun.server.name}-{log.level}-event.log</attribute>
```

Next, restart the server to get the changes to take effect. Then look for the extra logs that are now being created, as shown in Figure 8-2.

| 📄 cfusion-event.log | 6 KB | Text Document | 10/2/2008 6:01 AM |
| 📄 cfusion-out.log | 17 KB | Text Document | 10/3/2008 9:45 AM |
| 📄 go2rialab1-event.log | 38 KB | Text Document | 10/26/2008 7:42 PM |
| 📄 go2rialab1-info-event.log | 3 KB | Text Document | 10/27/2008 4:10 PM |
| 📄 go2rialab1-metrics-event.log | 2 KB | Text Document | 10/27/2008 4:21 PM |
| 📄 go2rialab1-out.log | 131 KB | Text Document | 10/27/2008 4:21 PM |
| 📄 go2rialab1-user-event.log | 4 KB | Text Document | 10/27/2008 4:10 PM |
| 📄 go2rialab2-event.log | 33 KB | Text Document | 10/24/2008 3:09 AM |
| 📄 go2rialab2-out.log | 123 KB | Text Document | 10/27/2008 3:25 PM |

*Figure 8-2. New logs after server restart*

Here, we have three ColdFusion instances, and we can see that both cfusion and go2rialab2 have only two log files, while go2rialab1 has more, created as a result of our enhanced settings.

Now that we've split the logs, it's time to look at the data.

# Examining the Metrics Logging Output

Listing 8-7 shows an example of metrics-logging output from a server under load.

*Listing 8-7. Metrics before making changes*

```
10/29 16:42:32 metrics Web threads (busy/total/delayed): 9/98/57 Sessions: 1 Total
Memory=122848 Free=20640
10/29 16:43:32 metrics Web threads (busy/total/delayed): 9/112/75 Sessions: 1 Total
Memory=122848 Free=19567
10/29 16:44:32 metrics Web threads (busy/total/delayed): 9/142/101 Sessions: 1 Total
Memory=122976 Free=1847510/29 16:45:32 metrics Web threads (busy/total/delayed): 9/156/109
Sessions: 1 Total Memory=123104 Free=21705
10/29 16:46:32 metrics Web threads (busy/total/delayed): 9/157/84 Sessions: 1 Total
Memory=123104 Free=43526
10/29 16:47:32 metrics Web threads (busy/total/delayed): 9/158/104 Sessions: 1 Total
Memory=123348 Free=69981
10/29 16:48:32 metrics Web threads (busy/total/delayed): 9/173/119 Sessions: 1 Total
Memory=144552 Free=57853
10/29 16:49:32 metrics Web threads (busy/total/delayed): 9/195/143 Sessions: 1 Total
Memory=154480 Free=43064
10/29 16:50:32 metrics Web threads (busy/total/delayed): 9/216/162 Sessions: 1 Total
Memory=154544 Free=37209
10/29 16:51:32 metrics Web threads (busy/total/delayed): 9/226/170 Sessions: 1 Total
Memory=154608 Free=74059
10/29 16:52:32 metrics Web threads (busy/total/delayed): 9/226/150 Sessions: 1 Total
Memory=154608 Free=9180
```

The logging collects these metrics at 60-second intervals. From this portion of the log, we can deduce that the default heap total memory size is too small. Let's examine the first metrics line:

```
10/29 16:42:32 metrics Web threads (busy/total/delayed): 9/98/57 Sessions: 1 Total
Memory=122848 Free=20640
```

10/29 16:42:32 represents the date and time the metric was collected. In the Web threads (busy/total/delayed): 9/98/57 portion, the first number shows the amount of free memory (9 MB), which is uncomfortably low. The second number represents the total number of threads. The third number represents delayed or queued threads. (Threads are roughly equivalent to requests.) This number shows that in its current state of long-running requests, the application needs a higher concurrent request number than its current value of 8. At this point, we can start to pinpoint the desired start and maximum heap memory size in the JVM.

## Finding the Proper Start and Maximum Heap Memory Size

Armed with the information from the metrics-logging output, I would change the start and maximum heap memory size. To do this, change the jvm.config file. On a Standard ColdFusion installation, you'll find the file here:

{*drive-volume*}\{*coldfusionRoot*}\runtime\bin\

On an Enterprise installation, look in this directory:

{*drive-volume*}\JRun4\bin\

The default values from a ColdFusion 9 Enterprise installation look like this:

```
# Arguments to VM

java.args=-server -Xmx512m -Dsun.io.useCanonCaches=false -XX:MaxPermSize=192m
    -XX:+UseParNewGC -Dcoldfusion.rootDir={application.home}/
```

At present, we have no start value for the heap, and the maximum size -Xmx512m does not really help us. We will double the value of the maximum heap size and set the start value at the same level, as follows:

```
# Arguments to VM

java.args=-server -Xms1024m -Xmx1024m -Dsun.io.useCanonCaches=false
-XX:MaxPermSize=192m -XX:+UseParNewGC -Dcoldfusion.rootDir={application.home}/
```

Over many years of tuning the JVM up to Sun Java 1.6, I have found it beneficial to set the start (Xms) and maximum (Xmx) to the same number. The school of thought on this is that there is more effort expended by the JVM in gradually taking more memory than if we simply start it at the maximum in the first place.

After making this change, we have much more free memory available at all times during the test. Requests are still queued, but not as many; response times improve; and errors diminish.

From the number of queued requests and the good amount of memory still available, we can see that we should increase the number of threads using ColdFusion Administrator. In this case, let's change the "Maximum number of running JRun threads" setting from 8 to 25, as shown in Figure 8-3.

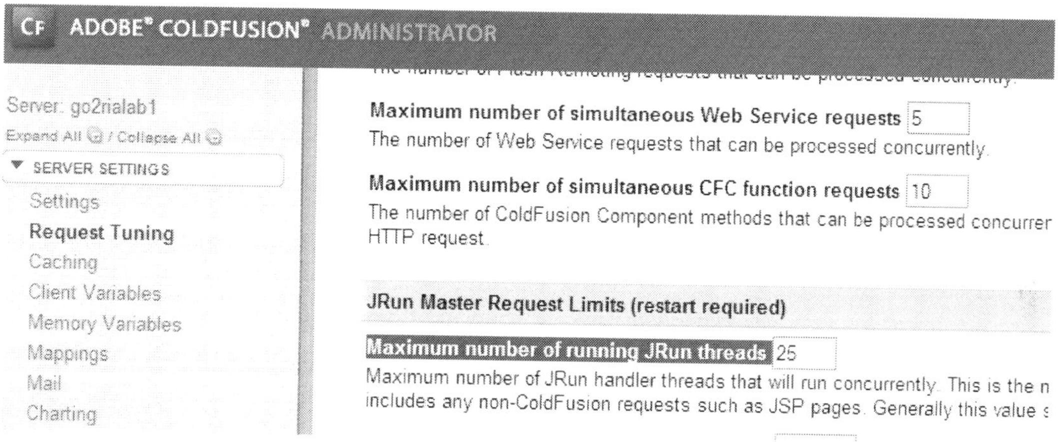

*Figure 8-3. Setting the maximum number of running JRun threads in ColdFusion Administrator*

For this change to take effect, you must restart the server instance.

## The New Metrics

After our changes to the memory and maximum thread settings, the metrics look like Listing 8-8.

*Listing 8-8. Metrics after making changes*

```
10/29 21:27:02 metrics Web threads (busy/total/delayed): 22/86/0 Sessions: 0 Total
Memory=1028928 Free=826205
10/29 21:28:02 metrics Web threads (busy/total/delayed): 17/85/0 Sessions: 0 Total
Memory=1028928 Free=854949
10/29 21:29:02 metrics Web threads (busy/total/delayed): 13/85/0 Sessions: 0 Total
Memory=1028928 Free=824296
10/29 21:30:02 metrics Web threads (busy/total/delayed): 14/85/0 Sessions: 0 Total
Memory=1028928 Free=860022
10/29 21:31:02 metrics Web threads (busy/total/delayed): 21/85/0  Sessions: 0 Total
Memory=1028928 Free=866417
10/29 21:32:02 metrics Web threads (busy/total/delayed): 24/85/0  Sessions: 0 Total
Memory=1028928 Free=875053
10/29 21:33:02 metrics Web threads (busy/total/delayed): 24/85/0 Sessions: 0 Total
Memory=1028928 Free=912602
```

```
10/29 21:34:02 metrics Web threads (busy/total/delayed): 26/85/0 Sessions: 0 Total
Memory=1028928 Free=868403
10/29 21:35:02 metrics Web threads (busy/total/delayed): 26/85/0 Sessions: 0 Total
Memory=1028928 Free=921888
```

The requests still run too long, but not as long as before, since now we do not get any queued threads. At this point, we would move on to check both code and any database query issues.

## Summary

In this article, I have shown what I do to enable enhanced metrics logging and how I use the logging information to find a server's optimal JVM settings. These are actual results from a live production server. I hope to produce more articles in the future covering garbage-collection logging and the use of SeeFusion, both critical components of the work that I do, day in and day out.

■ ■ ■

# CHAPTER 9

# The Shoemaker and the Asynchronous Process Elves

## by Doug Boude

*This article was based on an experiment—a bit of impromptu testing by the author on the viability of using ColdFusion's asynchronous processing, a feature introduced in ColdFusion MX 7. The effectiveness of the experiment and the power he discovered in asynchronous processing inspired and excited Doug and prompted this article.*

It was the last session at the two-day cf.Objective() conference where speakers had been exploring en masse new ways of approaching application development using ColdFusion. I had found the sessions inspiring and enlightening and had no reason to believe that the one called "Asynchronous Logging" would be any different. Indeed, as Michael Dinowitz began to artistically weave what would later serve as a catalyst for his audience's understanding, an analogy began to form in my mind. To further my understanding, I likened "Asynchronous Logging" to an old story that was told to me as a child—"The Shoemaker and the Elves."

Taking the liberty of modernizing and modifying the tale a bit to better apply to the subject at hand, I saw it like this: The shoemaker worked steadily, night and day, working his way down a very long list of customer shoe orders, yet the list grew ever longer. Given enough time and processing power the shoemaker would eventually complete his list of orders, but at what cost in time to the customers waiting patiently for their new shoes to arrive? How long would they wait before finding another site to make their shoes?

Then late one night help arrived. A company of process elves begged the shoemaker to let them help. There they stood, tools in hand, looking up at the obviously worn out shoemaker, ready to start work as soon as he gave the word. The elves didn't wait long, as the shoemaker immediately began doling out shoe orders to be filled. Under his direction, each elf began to pound away toward the completion of his individual piece of work. By the time the shoemaker had delegated all of his shoe orders, the sound of the hammers was deafening. And in a very brief time, every single order had been "automagically" filled. It was nothing short of a miracle for the shoemaker, who vowed never again to settle for serial processing when parallel processing was an option. He ran every other shoemaker in town out of business and, of course, lived happily ever after.

Armed with this inspiration, I arrived back at my office on Monday ready to see just how much faster it is to make shoes with the help of elves. When I shared my epiphany with my coworkers, it spawned some debate over whether or not the work would actually occur in less time or just appear to be completed in less time, because once a process is handed off to an elf, it is completely out of sight, leaving no clue as to how long it actually took. So I came up with an experiment to settle that debate.

# The Experiment

I inserted the contents of a text file into a database table using two different methods: First, I inserted one record at a time, essentially having the shoemaker do all of the work himself. Then I gave the shoemaker the sole job of handing off one record to each elf for insertion. After the insertions were complete, for each method I subtracted the time when the first *insert* occurred (noted by a *datetime* field in the target table) from the time when the last *insert* occurred to see which method required the least amount of time to complete.

My incoming file consisted of 256 records, each with three *varchar* fields. Two additional fields were also inserted: a *datetime* stamp set within the *insert* statement and an integer indicating which method had performed the insertion (synchronous or asynchronous).

Listing 9-1 shows the code I used to read in the data.

*Listing 9-1. Code to Read in Data (asynctest.cfm)*

```
<!--- Read in our data file --->
<cffile ACTION="read" FILE="#expandpath(".")#/testfile.txt"
    VARIABLE="incoming">

<!--- Treating the file like a list, use the following (line feed/carriage return)
    characters as delimiters --->
<cfset mydelim = chr(10) & chr(13)>

<!--- Grab number of lines in file and display for informational purposes --->
<cfset filelen = listlen(incoming, mydelim)>
<cfoutput> lines: #filelen# </cfoutput>

<!--- Put the data file into an array --->
<cfset thisdata = ListToArray(incoming, mydelim)>
```

The template I used, `asynctest.cfm` shown in Listing 9-2, contained both the synchronous processing and the asynchronous process handoff, segregated within a *cfswitch* that I manipulated via a URL expression.

*Listing 9-2. cfswitch Statement (asynctest.cfm)*

```
<!--- Data put into array. Start the test (testtype value of 1
    indicates synchronous processing, 2 indicates asynchronous). --->
    <cfswitch expression="#url.test#">
        <cfcase value="batch">
            <!--- Perform insertions the old-fashioned way --->
            <!--- First purge existing records --->
            <cfquery name="qryDelete" datasource="#dsn#">
                delete from TestTable where testtype = 1
```

```
        </cfquery>
        <!--- Loop over the data array and perform an insert for each item --->
        <cfloop from="1" to="#arraylen(thisdata)#" index="j">
            <cfquery name="qryInsertRec" datasource="#dsn#">
                insert into TestTable (txt_groupid, txt_code,
                txt_description, inserttime, testtype)
                VALUES (
                <cfqueryparam value="#listfirst(thisdata[j])#"
                    CFSQLTYPE="CF_SQL_VARCHAR">,
                <cfqueryparam value="#listgetat(thisdata[j],2)#"
                    CFSQLTYPE="CF_SQL_VARCHAR">,
                <cfqueryparam value="#listlast(thisdata[j])#"
                    CFSQLTYPE="CF_SQL_VARCHAR">,
                <cfqueryparam value="#now()#"
                    CFSQLTYPE="CF_SQL_TIMESTAMP">,
                <cfqueryparam value="1" CFSQLTYPE="CF_SQL_TINYINT">)
            </cfquery>
        </cfloop>
        <!--- Retrieve the max and min times so we can calculate total
            insertion time --->
        <cfquery name="qryGetMaxMin" datasource="#dsn#">
            select max(inserttime) as maxtime, min(inserttime) as mintime
            from TestTable where testtype=1
        </cfquery>
        <cfoutput>total time for linear insertions:
#datediff("s", qryGetMaxMin.mintime, qryGetMaxMin.maxtime)# seconds</cfoutput>
    </cfcase>

    <cfcase value="async"><!--- Perform inserts via gateways --->
        <!--- Purge existing data --->
        <cfquery name="qryDelete" datasource="#dsn#">
            delete from TestTable where testtype = 2
        </cfquery>
        <!--- Loop over data array and call the gateway for each item,
            passing in the data --->
        <!--- Set up the structure we'll be handing over to the gateway --->
        <cfloop from="1" to="#arraylen(thisdata)#" index="j">
            <cfscript>
                stData = structnew();
                stData.dsn = dsn;
                stData.theData=thisdata[j];
                sendGatewayMessage(gateway, stData);
            </cfscript>
            <!--- To give the gateways time to complete their work, call
            this page with a separate request where test=checkAsyncTime
            to see the total insertion time for the gateways --->
        </cfloop>
    </cfcase>

    <cfcase value="checkAsyncTime">
    <!--- Go back and see how long it took to perform all inserts
```

```
        via gateway --->
            <cfquery name="qryGetMaxMin" datasource="#dsn#">
                select max(inserttime) as maxtime, min(inserttime) as mintime
                from TestTable where testtype=2
            </cfquery>
            <cfoutput>
              total time for asynchronous insertions:
              #datediff("s", qryGetMaxMin.mintime, qryGetMaxMin.maxtime)# seconds
            </cfoutput>
        </cfcase>
    </cfswitch>
```

The actual elf itself (asynchronous process code) lived in a CFC, shown in Listing 9-3, that had been associated with a ColdFusion gateway set up within the ColdFusion Administrator. Both methods were given the responsibility for splitting the incoming record into individual field values before performing their insertions, so that work was also part of their total insertion time. The back-end database was Sybase, which was accessed via ODBC instead of a native Sybase ColdFusion driver.

*Listing 9-3. Asynchronous Process Code (aTest.cfc)*

```
<cfcomponent>
    <cffunction access="public" name="onIncomingMessage" output="false">
        <cfargument name="CFEvent" type="struct" required="yes">
        <cftry>
            <cfquery name="qryInsertRec" datasource="#CFEvent.Data.dsn#" dbtype="ODBC">
                insert into TestTable
                (txt_groupid, txt_code, txt_description, inserttime, testtype)
                values (
                    <cfqueryparam value="#listfirst(CFEvent.Data.theData)#"
                        cfsqltype="cf_sql_varchar">,
                    <cfqueryparam value="#listgetat(CFEvent.Data.theData,2)#"
                        cfsqltype="cf_sql_varchar">,
                    <cfqueryparam value="#listlast(CFEvent.Data.theData)#"
                        cfsqltype="cf_sql_varchar">,
                    <cfqueryparam value="#now()#" cfsqltype= "cf_sql_timestamp">,
                    <cfqueryparam value="2" cfsqltype="cf_sql_tinyint">)
            </cfquery>
            <cfcatch>
                <cfmail to="dougboude@gmail.com" from="gateway test"
                    subject="Candygram for Mongo">
                    #cfcatch.error#<br>#cfcatch.message#<br>#cfcatch.detail#
                </cfmail>
            </cfcatch>
        </cftry>
    </cffunction>
</cfcomponent>
```

I ran each method three times and found that the results favored the asynchronous method much more than I had expected. What took on average 20.7 seconds using the standard synchronous methodology took only 1.7 seconds when handing each insert to the gateway. That's 12 times faster!

When run under ColdFusion 8 and ColdFusion 9 beta, the same test performed a little better during standard insertion (13 seconds on average), but yielded the same results as MX 7 when performing the work asynchronously. Needless to say, I'm now a fan of using the elves whenever and wherever I can find a creative place to do so.

To see the experiment in action, download my files from http://www.apress.com and save them to the same directory. Execute the tests at

```
http://yourserver/asynctest.cfm?test=
```

Here `test` can be `"batch"` (linear processing), `"async"` (gateway processing), or `"checkAsyncTime"` (to retrieve the time results for the last asynchronous processing test).

# Before Employing Those Elves

There's always a competing shoemaker in town, so you are probably thinking of at least two places in your application where an elf or two would be just the ticket. But before you start delegating functionality to ColdFusion gateways, take a few moments to consider the prerequisites.

The most important prerequisite for using asynchronous gateways is that your ColdFusion server must be MX 7 Enterprise or ColdFusion 8 (Enterprise or Standard)—MX 7 Standard, as well as previous versions of ColdFusion, does not have built-in support for gateways. And before deciding how much work to delegate to a gateway, consider how beefy your server is. While we can sometimes mistake our servers for the latest Cray prototypes, they do have their limits, and we can all too quickly discover those limits if we aren't careful. For some insight to help balance your zeal, read Sean Corfield's blog post "Asynchronous Development—How Much Parallelism?" listed in the resource section at the end of this article.

---

■ **Note** ColdFusion 8 Standard allows gateways, but limits them to a single thread.

---

# The Moral of the Story

Although every speaker at the cf.Objective() conference had different topics, styles, and approaches, I was able to glean the same message from all of them: be creative in my coding, think outside the box, make the time to experiment with ColdFusion, and let my creativity manifest itself in what I produce. Their examples taught me that I should always strive for elegance and efficiency in my code. It was inspiring, to say the least.

I leave you with a bone to chew on: How would you recreate or simulate asynchronous processing using a version of ColdFusion that does not support that feature? Let that question be fodder for your creativity and experimentation next time you have a few minutes to "play."

# Further Reading on Asynchronous Gateways

- Matthew Woodward, "The Asynchronous CFML Gateway": http://coldfusion. sys-con.com/read/101326.htm

- Adobe LiveDocs on Asynchronous Gateways: http://livedocs.adobe.com/ coldfusion/7/htmldocs/wwhelp/wwhimpl/common/html/wwhelp.htm?context= ColdFusion_Documentation&file=00000622.htm

- Sean Corfield, "Asynchronous Development—How Much Parallelism?": http://corfield.org/entry/Asynchronous_Development__How_Much_Parallelism

- Sean Corfield, "Asynchronous Development—Things to Consider": http://corfield.org/entry/Asynchronous_Development__Things_to_Consider

- Ben Forta, "Understanding Asynchronous Processing": http://www.forta.com/ blog/index.cfm?mode=entry&entry=A61BC2EE-3048-80A9-EF50D0AA3896B282

- Raymond Camden, "Using ColdFusion's Asynchronous Gateway": http://coldfusionjedi.com/index.cfm/2006/9/7/Using-ColdFusions- Asynchronous-Gateway

- Raymond Camden, "Using ColdFusion's Asynchronous Gateway – 2": http://coldfusionjedi.com/index.cfm/2006/9/7/Using-ColdFusions- Asynchronous-Gateway--2

- Raymond Camden, "Using ColdFusion's Asynchronous Gateway – 3": http://www.coldfusionjedi.com/index.cfm/2006/9/14/Using-ColdFusions- Asynchronous-Gateway--3

# CHAPTER 10

■ ■ ■

# Asynchronous Gateways Step-by-Step

## by Michael Dinowitz

*Asynchronous gateways were one of the key additions to ColdFusion MX 7. Originally, gateways were limited to the Enterprise version, but in ColdFusion 8 and 9 this limitation has been removed. (ColdFusion 8 and 9 Professional allow gateways but limit the number of threads in use.) In this short article, a companion piece to Chapter 9, Doug Boude's "The Shoemaker and the Asynchronous Process Elves," Michael Dinowitz takes us, step-by-step, through setting up a gateway.*

Despite its awe-inspiring power, setting up an asynchronous gateway in ColdFusion is actually very simple. All you need is a CFC that will be called by the asynchronous gateway, a place to put that CFC (and where you place it is more important than you may think), and access to the ColdFusion administrator in order to register the CFC.

It is best to put all asynchronous gateways in a directory separate from the rest of your application. There is a really good reason for this, and it has to do with context. A normal ColdFusion page runs in one context with access to the sitewide error handler. A gateway runs in a different context, and if an error is ever thrown from the gateway CFC it will not be caught by the sitewide error handler.

The solution to this is to place an `Application.cfc` in the same directory as the gateway. Using an `onError` method, we can now capture error events and do something about them, such as emailing an administrator. In addition, we can use the `Application.cfc` to create application and server variables for use by the gateway. Application variables set inside an `onApplicationStart()` method will run once. Variables set inside a gateway CFC will run every single time the gateway is run. In other words, there is no caching of the gateway CFC. It's possible to use the gateway CFC as a "stub" to call a cached CFC, but the technique is outside of the scope of this article.

Our asynchronous gateway will look like Listing 10-1.

*Listing 10-1. Sample Asynchronous Gateway CFC*

```
<CFCOMPONENT output="false">
        <CFFUNCTION name="SiteLog" returntype="void" output="false">
                <CFARGUMENT name="CFEvent" required="yes">
                   ... lots of logging code ...
        </CFFUNCTION>
```

```
        <CFFUNCTION name="listbanners" returntype="void" output="false">
        <CFARGUMENT name="CFEvent" required="yes">
                ... lots of logging code ...
        </CFFUNCTION>
</CFCOMPONENT>
```

When we create an asynchronous gateway in the administrator, we will map its unique name to the specific CFC. In Listing 10-1 we have two different methods (SiteLog and listbanners), which means that two different asynchronous gateways can use this same CFC.

The only thing that will be passed into any gateway method is a structure called CFEvent. This structure contains all of the data that the gateway method will use. While this is required, we really do not have to check its data type. If it's not a structure, an error will be thrown before we even get to the method. Not checking the data type saves us memory and processing, and in cases like this, where we have total control over what's going into the CFC, it's warranted.

Now that we have created our asynchronous CFC and the methods it contains, we have to register it in the ColdFusion Administrator. Open up the Event Gateways tab (see Figure 10-1) and select Gateway Instances. All we need here is the name of the gateway, which does not need to be the name of the method being called. We select "CFML - Asynchronous Events via CFML" as the gateway type (there are others) and then put in the full server path to our CFC.

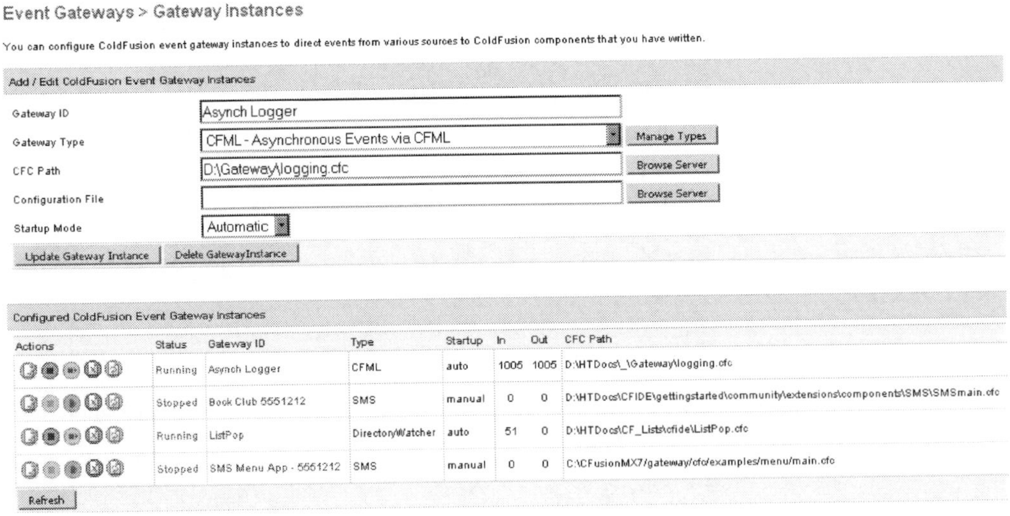

## Event Gateways > Gateway Instances

You can configure ColdFusion event gateway instances to direct events from various sources to ColdFusion components that you have written.

**Add / Edit ColdFusion Event Gateway Instances**

| | |
|---|---|
| Gateway ID | Asynch Logger |
| Gateway Type | CFML - Asynchronous Events via CFML  [Manage Types] |
| CFC Path | D:\Gateway\logging.cfc  [Browse Server] |
| Configuration File | [Browse Server] |
| Startup Mode | Automatic |

[Update Gateway Instance]  [Delete Gateway Instance]

**Configured ColdFusion Event Gateway Instances**

| Actions | Status | Gateway ID | Type | Startup | In | Out | CFC Path |
|---|---|---|---|---|---|---|---|
| ⊙⊛⊙⊙⊙ | Running | Asynch Logger | CFML | auto | 1005 | 1005 | D:\HTDocs\_\Gateway\logging.cfc |
| ⊙⊛⊙⊙⊙ | Stopped | Book Club 5551212 | SMS | manual | 0 | 0 | D:\HTDocs\CFIDE\gettingstarted\community\extensions\components\SMS\SMSmain.cfc |
| ⊙⊛⊙⊙⊙ | Running | ListPop | DirectoryWatcher | auto | 51 | 0 | D:\HTDocs\CF_Lists\cfide\ListPop.cfc |
| ⊙⊛⊙⊙⊙ | Stopped | SMS Menu App - 5551212 | SMS | manual | 0 | 0 | C:\CFusionMX7/gateway/cfc/examples/menu/main.cfc |

[Refresh]

*Figure 10-1. Setting up Your Gateway in the ColdFusion Administrator*

We don't need a configuration file, so we can skip over that. We do need to decide if the gateway should start automatically or be turned on by hand.

Once you have done all this, click submit. You now have an asynchronous gateway.

Having a gateway set up is only half the battle. To use it, you must call it. Listing 10-2 contains some sample code that will call an asynchronous gateway to log user information.

*Listing 10-2. Calling the LogPage Gateway*

```
<CFFUNCTION name="LogPage" returntype="void" output="false">
    <CFSCRIPT>
            var sLogData=StructNew();
            sLogData.Query_String=CGI.Query_String;
            sLogData.Path_Info=cgi.Path_Info;
            sLogData.Script_Name=cgi.Script_Name;
            sLogData.REQUEST_METHOD=CGI.REQUEST_METHOD;
            sLogData.HTTP_REFERER=cgi.HTTP_REFERER;
            sLogData.REMOTE_ADDR=cgi.REMOTE_ADDR;
            sLogData.http_user_agent=cgi.http_user_agent;
            sLogData.method="SiteLog";

            SendGatewayMessage('Asynch Logger', sLogData);
    </CFSCRIPT>
</CFFUNCTION>
```

The function in Listing 10-2 creates a structure containing some visitor information that we want to log. The structure also includes the method that we want to run in the gateway CFC, "SiteLog". Finally, in the last line of the `cfscript` section, we send the structure to the asynchronous gateway using the SendGatewayMessage, and we're done. The gateway gets the data and uses it, the page that calls the gateway doesn't have any of the overhead of logging, and everything is smooth.

The whole purpose of an asynchronous gateway is about performance and savings. Rather than doing 1,000 operations sequentially in a single template, you have an asynchronous gateway do them individually and get them done quicker. Rather than have a complex and resource-intensive logging operation take place as part of a user's session, you throw the information you want to log "somewhere else" to be worked with. The only limit is knowledge and imagination.

# CHAPTER 11

■ ■ ■

# You Might Have a Performance Bottleneck If...

by Adrian J. Moreno

*Many a flame war has started over the argued performance of a web application based solely on the language with which it was programmed. You may hear "X scales better than Y," or "No real programmer uses Z." More often than not, poor performance in a web application can be traced to data management. The application could be performing tasks better suited to the database, or the database could be poorly designed. Taking a cue from Jeff Foxworthy's "You might be a redneck if..." jokes, this article will introduce terms and concepts related to data normalization and application optimization in order to help you pinpoint poor database structures, data-storage processes, and data-retrieval techniques.*

## If You Can't Tell a Manager from an Employee, You Might Have a Performance Bottleneck

Most developers know that the *primary key* (denoted as PK) of a database table is a unique value that identifies each row. For the example in this article, Listing 11-1 creates a table named USERS with columns named USER_ID, FIRST_NAME, and LAST_NAME. The USER_ID column holds the table's primary key, which is an auto-incrementing numeric value, also called an *identity*, that increases as new records are added.

---

■ **Note** The SQL contained in this article pertains to Microsoft SQL Server. Consult your documentation for syntax specific to your database.

---

*Listing 11-1. Creating the USERS table*

```
CREATE TABLE USERS(
    USER_ID int IDENTITY(1,1) NOT NULL,
    FIRST_NAME varchar(50) NOT NULL,
    LAST_NAME varchar(50) NOT NULL,
    CONSTRAINT PK_USERS_USER_ID PRIMARY KEY CLUSTERED ( USER_ID ASC )
)
```

Figure 11-1 shows the USERS table, including a yellow key icon next to the USER_ID column. That key icon is a common way of denoting the primary key of a table.

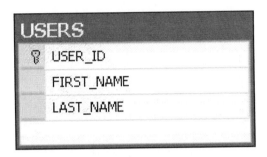

*Figure 11-1. The USERS table created by Listing 11-1*

In this article's example, your application's requirements include restricted sections, such as user management and order processing. In order to allow certain people into restricted sections, the application code could be written to recognize one user from another, as shown in Listing 11-2.

*Listing 11-2. User access in the application code*

```
<cfif (session.first_name eq "John") and (session.last_name) eq "Doe")>
    <!--- run restricted functionality --->
</cfif>
```

This creates a performance bottleneck in the application, because it's possible for there to be more than one "John Doe" in the system. In addition, you would need to manually add a CHECK condition for each new user allowed into a restricted section. If you can tell a manager from an employee, you eliminate this bottleneck.

You need to classify each user as a specific type. A beginning developer might create a list of user types and add a column to the USERS table that stores the first character of each user type, as in Listing 11-3. Figure 11-2 shows the altered USERS table.

*Listing 11-3. Altering the USERS table to add a USER_TYPE column*

```
ALTER TABLE USERS ADD USER_TYPE CHAR(1) NOT NULL;
```

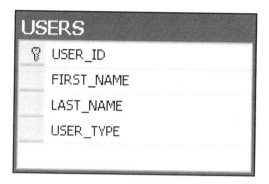

*Figure 11-2. The USERS table, altered by Listing 11-3, with a USER_TYPE column*

For the user types of Admin, Manager, Supervisor, and Employee, by application logic, the elements of USERS.USER_TYPE would now have only the values 'A', 'M', 'S', or 'E'. But this presents the problem that nothing keeps other values for USER_TYPE out of that table. The wrong solution, if your database allows, would be to add a CHECK constraint to the table, restricting the value of USER_TYPE to those four values, as in Listing 11-4. If any value other than 'A', 'M', 'S', or 'E' were attempted, the INSERT or UPDATE would fail.

*Listing 11-4. The wrong way: adding a CHECK constraint to the USERS table*

```
ALTER TABLE USERS ADD CONSTRAINT CK_USER_TYPE CHECK ( USER_TYPE IN ('A','M','S','E') );
```

Unfortunately, adding this constraint creates a new performance bottleneck related to the scalability of your application. You've limited yourself to exactly four types of users. If you wanted to add a Contractor user type, for example, you would need to change the constraint on the USERS table to allow USER_TYPE value 'C.' You would need to repeat this process for each new user type required.

The best solution to this problem lies in creating another table.

# If Your Foreign Key Values Are Not Defined in the Database . . .

The problem with the USER_TYPE column described in the previous section may seem trivial with so few user types, but experienced developers know that an application's scope can grow with little notice, and soon you'll have a dozen or more user types.

Rather than store user types in you're the USERS table, the solution is to create a separate table called USER_TYPES with a primary key named USER_TYPE_ID, as in Listing 11-5. Figure 11-3 shows the new table.

*Listing 11-5. Creating the USER_TYPES table*

```
CREATE TABLE USER_TYPES (
    USER_TYPE_ID int IDENTITY(1,1) NOT NULL,
    USER_TYPE_DESC varchar(20) NOT NULL,
    CONSTRAINT PK_USER_TYPES_USER_TYPE_ID PRIMARY KEY CLUSTERED
        ( USER_TYPE_ID ASC )
)
```

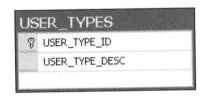

*Figure 11-3. The USER_TYPES table created by Listing 11-5*

Once you have a USER_TYPES table, give the USERS table a column named USER_TYPE_ID (a numeric data type), instead of USER_TYPE (a string data type), as in Listing 11-6. Figure 11-4 shows the modified USERS table.

*Listing 11-6. Altering the USERS table to replace USER_TYPE with USER_TYPE_ID*

```
-- Delete the Check Constraint on the USER_TYPE column
ALTER TABLE USERS DROP CONSTRAINT CK_USER_TYPE;

-- Add a new column USER_TYPE_ID
ALTER TABLE USERS ADD USER_TYPE_ID int;

-- Delete the column USER_TYPE as it is no longer used
ALTER TABLE USERS DROP COLUMN USER_TYPE
```

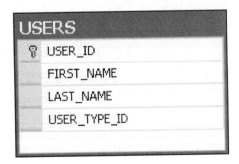

*Figure 11-4. The right way: the USERS table with a USER_TYPE_ID column (Listing 11-6)*

While the column USER_TYPE_ID is the primary key of the USER_TYPES table, it is now also a foreign key in the USERS table. A *foreign key* (denoted FK) is basically any column in a table that relates back to a primary key in another table.

Tables like USER_TYPES are often called *lookup* or *control* tables, since they're used to look up certain values for use in other tables. Storing data in this manner describes a *one-to-many relationship*. Each record in USER_TYPES is linked to many records in USERS, but each record in USERS is linked to only one record in USER_TYPES.

Now you can update the application code to check for the user's type ID in order to allow access to restricted areas, as shown in Listing 11-7.

*Listing 11-7. User type access in the application code*

```
<cfif session.user_type_id eq 1>
    <!--- run restricted functionality --->
</cfif>
```

While adding the foreign key USERS.USER_TYPE_ID solves the performance bottleneck related to the CHECK constraint, another issue now exists. This new problem is related to the integrity of the data that the USER_TYPE_ID column can contain.

# If You Relate Data Between Tables, but Neglect to Inform the Database . . .

The intended function of table structure described so far is that for every record in USERS, the value of USERS.USER_TYPE_ID must exist as a value of USER_TYPES.USER_TYPE_ID. The problem is that nothing currently prevents the USERS table from containing USER_TYPE_ID values that are not defined in the USER_TYPES table. To fix this, add a FOREIGN KEY constraint to the USERS table, as shown in Listing 11-8.

*Listing 11-8. Adding a FOREIGN KEY constraint to the USERS table*

```
ALTER TABLE USERS WITH CHECK
    ADD CONSTRAINT FK_USERS_USER_TYPES FOREIGN KEY( USER_TYPE_ID )
    REFERENCES USER_TYPES ( USER_TYPE_ID );
ALTER TABLE USERS CHECK CONSTRAINT FK_USERS_USER_TYPES;
```

This constraint limits inserted values for the foreign key USER_TYPE_ID to the primary key values defined in the USER_TYPES table. The FOREIGN KEY constraint is represented by a chain with a key icon, as shown in Figure 11-5.

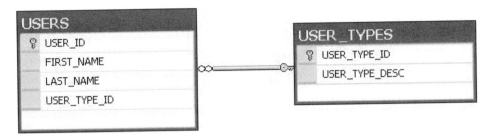

*Figure 11-5. Adding a FOREIGN KEY constraint*

Now the USERS.USER_TYPE_ID column can contain only values that exist in USER_TYPES.USER_TYPE_ID. In addition, you cannot delete a row from USER_TYPES when its USER_TYPE_ID is used by one or more rows in USERS, thus enforcing *referential integrity*. Along with ensuring data integrity, using foreign keys with constraints also addresses a performance bottleneck related to indexing data, as discussed later in this article.

The modified table structure solves the problem of distinguishing user types, but what if you now are told that users may have more than one user type?

# If You Store a Comma-Delimited List of Foreign Keys in a Single Column . . .

Consider the case of a user needing to belong to both the Admin and Manager categories. Since you already have a USER_TYPE_ID column in the USERS table, you might think about storing all applicable USER_TYPES for a given user there. To allow that, you need to remove the FOREIGN KEY constraint and change the column's data type from a numeric to a string. Then, in the application, you collect all of the USER_TYPE_IDs associated with this user into a list and store it in the USERS.USER_TYPE_ID column. Correct?

Wrong! This is a really bad idea. It introduces another performance bottleneck that relates to the scalability of your application. If you redefined USER_TYPE_ID to varchar(50), what happens when your list of IDs grows larger than 50 characters? (If you answered, "you increase the character limit," somewhere a database administrator just fell down dead. Now clap your hands, Peter.)

The correct approach removes the USER_TYPE_ID column from the USERS table and creates a third table that stores only the USER_ID and USER_TYPE_ID. This gives you a place to associate a single USER_ID with many USER_TYPE_IDs without violating any constraints. This type of table is called an *association table, link table,* or *intersect table*. In this case, it acts as an intermediary between the USERS and USER_TYPES tables. Listing 11-9 creates the new association table, named USERS_2_USER_TYPES.

*Listing 11-9. Creating the USERS_2_USER_TYPES table*

```
CREATE TABLE USERS_2_USER_TYPES(
    USER_ID int NOT NULL,
    USER_TYPE_ID int NOT NULL,
    CONSTRAINT PK_USERS_2_USER_TYPES PRIMARY KEY CLUSTERED ( USER_ID ASC, USER_TYPE_ID ASC
));
```

```
ALTER TABLE USERS_2_USER_TYPES WITH CHECK
    ADD CONSTRAINT FK_USERS_2_USER_TYPES_USERS FOREIGN KEY(USER_ID)
    REFERENCES USERS (USER_ID);
ALTER TABLE USERS_2_USER_TYPES
    CHECK CONSTRAINT FK_USERS_2_USER_TYPES_USERS;
ALTER TABLE USERS_2_USER_TYPES WITH CHECK
    ADD CONSTRAINT FK_USERS_2_USER_TYPES_USER_TYPES FOREIGN KEY(USER_TYPE_ID)
    REFERENCES USER_TYPES (USER_TYPE_ID);
ALTER TABLE USERS_2_USER_TYPES
    CHECK CONSTRAINT FK_USERS_2_USER_TYPES_USER_TYPES;
```

Figure 11-6 shows that the new table contains two columns, each with a matching FOREIGN KEY constraint:

- USERS_2_USER_TYPES.USER_ID [FK] is defined by USERS.USER_ID [PK].

- USERS_2_USER_TYPES.USER_TYPE_ID [FK] is defined by USER_TYPES.USER_TYPE_ID [PK].

The primary key of USERS_2_USER_TYPES combines both foreign keys. A primary key made up of more than one column in a table is called a *compound primary key*, or *composite key* (denoted as CPK).

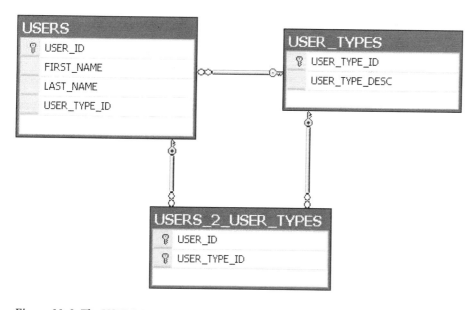

*Figure 11-6. The USERS, USERS_2_USER_TYPES, and USER_TYPES tables*

Storing data in this manner describes a *many-to-many relationship*. Each record in USER_TYPES can be linked to many records in USERS, and each record in USERS can be linked to many records in USER_TYPES.

Before you can continue developing your application, three database tasks must be accomplished:

- You need to create records in USERS_2_USER_TYPES that match the current one-to-many relationship between USERS and USER_TYPES.

- You must drop the FOREIGN KEY constraint FK_USERS_USER_TYPES (shown in Figure 11-6) that still exists between USERS and USER_TYPES.

- Once that constraint is gone, you can drop the column USER_TYPE_ID from the USERS table, as it is no longer needed.

Listing 11-10 shows how to accomplish these tasks, and Figure 11-7 shows the final versions of the tables.

*Listing 11-10. Migrating data from USERS to USERS_2_USER_TYPES*

```
INSERT INTO USERS_2_USER_TYPES
    ( USER_ID, USER_TYPE_ID )
SELECT USER_ID, USER_TYPE_ID
FROM USERS;
// Verify data before continuing

ALTER TABLE USERS DROP CONSTRAINT FK_USERS_USER_TYPES;
ALTER TABLE USERS DROP COLUMN USER_TYPE_ID;
```

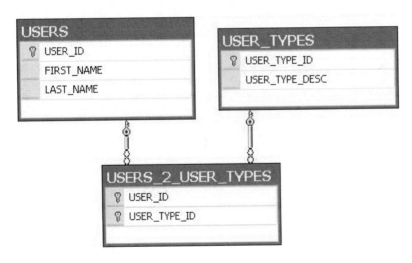

*Figure 11-7. The final versions of USERS, USER_TYPES, and USERS_2_USER_TYPES*

Your next task will be to update how your application manages user records using these three tables.

# If You Use SELECT MAX( ID ) to Get the Primary Key of a Newly Inserted Record . . .

Using USERS_2_USER_TYPES as an association table requires the following process:

1.  Create a record in the USERS table.

2.  Get the value of that record's USER_ID.

3.  Insert a record into USERS_2_USER_TYPES for each USER_TYPE_ID associated with the new USER_ID.

Many developers have been taught to use the SQL function MAX() to obtain the primary key for an inserted record. The MAX() function returns the largest numeric value in a specified column. Given that each new record receives a larger numeric value than the one before, it seems like a safe method, but it isn't. This is because the MAX() function in SQL is not thread-safe.

Most likely, you won't see any problems with this method until your application is in production, and then only if you have a significant number of concurrent users. It also depends on whether or not your database uses single, dual, or more core processors. If problems surface with incorrectly associated records, this use of the MAX() function could be the culprit.

With many concurrent users, an issue can occur where two or more threads (or requests) nearly simultaneously perform an INSERT. Listing 11-11 shows how a first thread can perform SELECT MAX(USER_ID) FROM USERS, but it may not always return the USER_ID for the record that it inserted. If it returns the USER_ID created by the second or subsequent thread's INSERT, then incorrect values will be entered into the association table.

*Listing 11-11. Multiple INSERT requests using SELECT MAX(ID)*

```
Thread1 INSERT SELECT MAX(ID) ID=1
Thread2 INSERT SELECT MAX(ID) ID=2
Thread3 INSERT SELECT MAX(ID) ID=4
Thread4 INSERT SELECT MAX(ID) ID=3
```

Requests will not always be processed in the order they were received. In Listing 11-11, the INSERT requests for threads 1 and 2 were processed simultaneously, as were threads 3 and 4. Thread 4 completed its INSERT and requested MAX(ID) before thread 3 was processed. Now thread 4 has returned a value for ID that was expected to be returned by thread 3 and vice versa. Consider the impact when processing hundreds or thousands of concurrent requests.

Getting an inserted primary key depends on how your database handles creating primary keys. MySQL and SQL Server use auto-incrementing numeric values. Oracle and PostgreSQL use sequences. Depending on how a table was created, DB2 can use either auto-incrementing numeric values or sequences. Any of them can accept a user-defined value (i.e., a UUID) as a primary key.

Listing 11-12 shows the wrong way to get a new primary key.

*Listing 11-12. The wrong way to retrieve a new USER_ID*

```
INSERT INTO USERS( FIRST_NAME, LAST_NAME )
    VALUES ( 'Adrian', 'Moreno' );
    SELECT MAX( USER_ID ) FROM USERS AS NEW_ID;
INSERT INTO USERS_2_USER_TYPES ( USER_ID, USER_TYPE_ID )
    VALUES ( NEW_ID, 1 )
```

Listings 11-13 and 11-14 show the correct ways to retrieve a new primary key.

*Listing 11-13. The right way to retrieve a new USER_ID*

```
// Check your documentation for correct function name
INSERT INTO USERS( FIRST_NAME, LAST_NAME )
    VALUES ( 'Adrian', 'Moreno' );
    SELECT SCOPE_IDENTITY() AS NEW_ID;
INSERT INTO USERS_2_USER_TYPES ( USER_ID, USER_TYPE_ID )
    VALUES ( NEW_ID, 1 )
```

*Listing 11-14. An even better way to retrieve a new USER_ID*

```
INSERT INTO USERS( FIRST_NAME, LAST_NAME )
    VALUES ( 'Adrian', 'Moreno' );
INSERT INTO USERS_2_USER_TYPES ( USER_ID, USER_TYPE_ID )
    SELECT SCOPE_IDENTITY(), 1
```

Consult your documentation for the functions specific to your database, or check out my article here:

```
http://www.iknowkungfoo.com/blog/index.cfm/2008/6/1/Please-stop-using-SELECT-MAX-id
```

Using the correct thread-safe database function to retrieve a new USER_ID solved only half of your problem. You still need to isolate each pair of database INSERT statements from the others to further ensure data integrity.

## If Your Only Transactions Are Between You and a Cashier . . .

Your boss is one of those "Just Do It!" kinds of managers. Things need to get done, and they need to get done now. Rather than hassling you to add a new user type to the database, he logs in to the code source control system and alters the Manage User form. Hard-coding another user type option in this form shouldn't hurt anything, right?

The USER_TYPES table contains five records, but your form now shows six. Someone logs in, creates a new user, selects that sixth user type, and submits the form. Per Listing 11-15, the system creates the new record in USERS, selects the new USER_ID, and attempts to enter a new record into USERS_2_USER_TYPES.

*Listing 11-15. The wrong way to create related records*

```
INSERT INTO USERS( FIRST_NAME, LAST_NAME )
    VALUES ( 'Adrian', 'Moreno' );

INSERT INTO USERS_2_USER_TYPES ( USER_ID, USER_TYPE_ID )
    SELECT SCOPE_IDENTITY(), 6
    // USER_TYPES.USER_TYPE_ID = 6 does not exist
```

Since the USER_TYPE_ID column in the USERS_2_USER_TYPES table has a FOREIGN KEY constraint restricting it to values of USER_TYPES.USER_TYPE_ID, the database will throw an error and refuse to insert the record. Your user sees an error message and backs up to where she started. Looking at the user list, she sees the new user's name and believes everything is OK.

So the INSERT into the USERS table completed, but the INSERT into USERS_2_USER_TYPES did not. Essentially, you have a new user with no user type. You need to ensure that if one of a series of related INSERTs fails, then the database backs out of those INSERTs that completed correctly, as if none of them had ever occurred. Listings 11-16 and 11-17 show two ways to write such a process, called a *transaction*.

*Listing 11-16. The right way to create related records using a transaction in plain SQL*

```
BEGIN TRY
    BEGIN TRANSACTION
        -- Create the new User
        INSERT INTO USERS( FIRST_NAME, LAST_NAME )
        VALUES ( 'Adrian', 'Moreno' );
        -- Create the association record
        INSERT INTO USERS_2_USER_TYPES ( USER_ID, USER_TYPE_ID )
        SELECT SCOPE_IDENTITY(), 6;
        -- If both inserts run, then commit the data to the database
    COMMIT
END TRY
BEGIN CATCH
    -- USER_TYPES.USER_TYPE_ID = 6 does not exist
    -- An error was thrown, meaning at least one insert failed.
    -- The data from any successful insert must be removed
    ROLLBACK
    -- Everything looks the way it was before the insert was attempted
END CATCH
```

*Listing 11-17. The right way to create related records using a CFTRANSACTION*

```
<cftransaction action="begin">
    <cftry>
        <cfquery name="qCreateUser" datasource="#variables.DSN#">
            INSERT INTO USERS( FIRST_NAME, LAST_NAME )
            VALUES ( 'Adrian', 'Moreno' );
            INSERT INTO USERS_2_USER_TYPES ( USER_ID, USER_TYPE_ID )
            SELECT SCOPE_IDENTITY(), 6
        </cfquery>
```

```
        <cfcatch type="database">
            <!--- An insert failed, rollback any successful insert --->
            <cftransaction action="rollback" />
        </cfcatch>
    </cftry>

    <!--- All inserts were successful, commit the data --->
    <cftransaction action="commit" />
</cftransaction>
```

Transactions give an extra layer of security to your insert, update, and delete operations, as data is flying in and out of the database.

There are a couple of potential performance bottlenecks in the database when using transactions:

- On occasion, a transaction being run by one request can impact the speed of a query being run by another.

- If you often use a database that automatically commits transactions like MySQL, and then begin using a database that doesn't like SQL Server (leaving off the commit command), you can stack up uncommitted transactions, causing a "database heart attack" (not that I've ever done that ...).

Consult your documentation for best practices. Also, remove your boss's login account from source control.

Now that you can safely create, update, and delete data in your database, you need to ensure that your application and database are using the most optimal methods to store and read data.

# If You Think the Difference Between Char and Varchar Is Typing Three More Letters . . .

Take a look at how the USERS table could be built with char, in Listing 11-18.

*Listing 11-18. The bad way: creating the USERS table using char*

```
CREATE TABLE USERS(
    USER_ID int IDENTITY(1,1) NOT NULL,
    FIRST_NAME char(50) NOT NULL,
    LAST_NAME char(50) NOT NULL,
    CONSTRAINT PK_USERS_USER_ID PRIMARY KEY CLUSTERED ( USER_ID ASC )
)
```

Now compare the char version with the version that uses varchar, in Listing 11-19.

*Listing 11-19. The good way: creating the USERS table using varchar*

```
CREATE TABLE USERS(
    USER_ID int IDENTITY(1,1) NOT NULL,
    FIRST_NAME varchar(50) NOT NULL,
    LAST_NAME varchar(50) NOT NULL,
    CONSTRAINT PK_USERS_USER_ID PRIMARY KEY CLUSTERED ( USER_ID ASC )
)
```

The two differ only in the data types of the name columns. Each takes a maximum of 50 characters, so at first glance, it doesn't seem to matter whether you use char or varchar. However, their subtle differences can make a big impact on the database.

The char data type has a fixed length. When you define a column as char(50), every non-null record uses the full 50 characters, padding the value with blanks. This can severely increase the amount of data you store, slow down text searches, and impede your application at the oddest times. Depending on the database, when you read a value from a char column, you may or may not get the blank spaces along with the text you stored.

For example, if you were to search the last name column (Listing 11-20), you might not get any matches. But if you use LIKE and the SQL wildcard character (Listing 11-21), you get a match. This happens because the value stored in USERS.LAST_NAME for the records in question is actually 'Smith[+45 *spaces* ]. You could alter the first query to make it work (Listing 11-22), but this will not perform well.

*Listing 11-20. The wrong way to search on a char column, but the right way to search on a varchar column*

```
SELECT USER_ID, FIRST_NAME, LAST_NAME FROM USERS WHERE LAST_NAME = 'Smith'
```

*Listing 11-21. The right way to search on a char column*

```
SELECT USER_ID, FIRST_NAME, LAST_NAME FROM USERS WHERE LAST_NAME LIKE 'Smith%'
```

---

░ **Note** Although Listing 11-21 uses technically valid syntax, a search using the LIKE operator with a wildcard avoids table indexes, causing a considerably slower read than a search using only the = operator.

---

*Listing 11-22. The wrong way to search on a char column without a wildcard*

```
// Check your documentation for the proper trim() SQL function for your database
SELECT USER_ID, FIRST_NAME, trim(LAST_NAME)
    AS LAST_NAME FROM USERS WHERE LAST_NAME = 'Smith'
```

The varchar data type is variable length, so it stores only the number of characters inserted, up to the limit specified in the column's definition. No unnecessary extra data — spaces — gets stored, and the original query (Listing 11-20) works correctly.

In general, char stores a maximum of 255 characters. varchar has a much higher limit, which differs per database.

Defining the wrong data type can create a performance bottleneck in the database by limiting the amount of data you can store. If you need to store pages of text data in a single record, look for the text data type.

# If You Think UTF-8 Is One of Those TV Channels You Used to Get with Rabbit Ears . . .

Many databases ship with Latin-1 (ISO-8859-1) as their standard character set, which allows you to correctly store any character in the Latin alphabet. This includes characters like *a*, *b*, *c*, *æ*, *ñ*, and *ü*, but not characters found in Japanese or other non-Latin base languages. If you retrieve data from a database and instead of the text you expect, you see a series of question marks, boxes, or diamond-wrapped question marks, the text data probably doesn't conform to the character set of the database table or column from which it was retrieved.

UTF-8 is a character encoding that allows your database to correctly store text from a broader range of alphabets. Japanese, written Chinese, Hebrew, and Thai (see Figure 11-8) are just a small sampling of the languages that cannot be handled by the Latin-1 character set.

| Latin-1 (ISO-8859-1) | a, b, c, æ, ñ, ü |
|---|---|
| UTF-8 | |
| Japanese | 私, わたし, ワタシ |
| Written Chinese | 人, 日, 木 |
| Hebrew | ג ,ב ,א |
| Thai | อ, เอ, ม |

*Figure 11-8. Latin-1 and UTF-8 characters*

If your application needs to serve an international community and your database does not support UTF-8, then you have a problem related to the type of data you can store. If your database supports UTF-8, but your application server of choice does not, then you could be limited to an English-only user interface, as well as restricted to storing only certain types of data.

A subset of Unicode, UTF-8 encompasses the ASCII character set, so you don't need to worry about corrupting existing text if you upgrade your database's character encoding. Depending on your needs, you can convert the entire database, individual tables, or individual columns. For example, instead of using char or varchar in SQL Server, use nchar or nvarchar, respectively, to store Unicode character data. Consult your database's manual for Unicode settings and data types.

# If You Use More Than One Query to Read Data from Multiple Tables . . .

Suppose that, working with the original USERS and USER_TYPES tables, where each user can have only one user type, you want to retrieve all of the users, grouped by user type. The output looks something like this:

```
Admin
    Joe Smith
    Jane Doe
Manager
    Tom Smith
    Harry Palmer
Supervisor
    Richard Brown
```

Listing 11-23 shows the approach taken by many developers: run a query to get all of the possible user types, then loop over that record set and run a query that returns a record set of users for each user type.

*Listing 11-23. The wrong way to get users sorted by user type*

```
<cfquery name="userTypes" datasource="#dsn#">
    SELECT USER_TYPE_ID, USER_TYPE FROM USER_TYPES
</cfquery>

<ul>
    <cfoutput query="userTypes">
        <li>#userTypes.USER_TYPE#
            <cfquery name="users" datasource="#dsn#">
                SELECT USER_ID, FIRST_NAME, LAST_NAME
                FROM USERS
                WHERE USER_TYPE_ID = #userTypes.USER_TYPE_ID#
            </cfquery>

            <ul>
            <cfloop query="users">
                <li>#users.FIRST_NAME# #users.LAST_NAME#</li>
            </cfloop>
            </ul>
        </li>
    </cfoutput>
</ul>
```

This technique will perform one `userTypes` query, plus a `users` query for each record returned by `userTypes`, as follows:

3 user types = 4 total queries

8 user types = 9 total queries

$x$ user types = $(x + 1)$ total queries

Even under a small number of concurrent users, this can cost you a considerable amount of unnecessary database traffic, slowing down your application. This performance bottleneck will be even more apparent under a heavy load.

A much faster and more succinct approach uses a single query that joins the two tables together and groups the data by user type. Listing 11-24 shows this approach.

*Listing 11-24. The right way to get users sorted by user type*

```
<cfquery name="users" datasource="#dsn#">
    SELECT
        a.USER_ID, a.FISRT_NAME, a.LAST_NAME,
        b.USER_TYPE_ID, b.USER_TYPE
    FROM
        USERS a
    LEFT JOIN
        USER_TYPES b
    ON
        b.USER_TYPE_ID = a.USER_TYPE_ID
    ORDER BY
        b.USER_TYPE, a.LAST_NAME, a.FIRST_NAME
</cfquery>

<ul>
    <!--- The "group" attribute allows us to display data
        grouped by one column --->
    <cfoutput query="users" group="USER_TYPE">
        <li>#users.USER_TYPE#
            <ul>
            <!--- A nested CFOUTPUT displays data within grouped records --->
            <cfoutput>
                <li>#users.FIRST_NAME# #users.LAST_NAME#</li>
            </cfoutput>
            </ul>
        </li>
    </cfoutput>
</ul>
```

Rather than doing the hard work of manipulating data from multiple queries in your application code, let the database do all the data manipulation, leaving to your application the simple task of displaying data. Using a single query that joins the two tables by USER_TYPE_ID, you get exactly the same results as you did with multiple queries. Using nested `cfoutput` tags with the `group` attribute in the outer `cfoutput` tag, users can be easily displayed grouped by USER_TYPE.

---

▨ **Note** Tyson Vanek of WebApper.com posted an example of this type of performance bottleneck. He was able to take a 24-second (24,000 ms) process and convert it to run in only 24 ms—improving performance by 1000 times, just by crafting better SQL. Read the entire article here: `http://www.webapper.com/blog/index.php/` `2009/08/04/improve-coldfusion-performance-by-1000x-believe-me-its-possible`.

---

Learning to properly join tables can reduce the amount of redundant data you store, as well as the time and resources needed to retrieve the data. Learning how to have the database sort data as it is stored provides additional benefits.

# If the Only Index Your Database Knows Is Next to Your Middle Finger . . .

Open almost any book, and toward the front, you will find a table of contents, which gives you the basics of what that book contains. If you flip to the back of the book, you will often find an index of the topics it covers. The index will tell you the specific page or pages that reference each item listed. Without the index, you would need to go through the book page by page to find a specific piece of information, which would take a considerable amount of time and really affect your productivity. Indexes matter just as much to databases.

Suppose that your database has grown since your application launched, and your search form begins taking a long time to return results. Odds are that your form searches one or more unindexed or incorrectly indexed tables, requiring each search request to look through every row of each table looking for a match in a specific column. The more poorly indexed the table and records, the longer it takes the search to find matches, causing more and more requests to stack up.

In order to see what would happen if you hadn't created a primary key on the table USERS_2_USER_TYPES, create a new version, as shown in Listing 11-25.

*Listing 11-25. Creating an alternate association table, USERS_2_USER_TYPES_V2*

```
CREATE TABLE USERS_2_USER_TYPES_V2(
    USER_ID int NOT NULL,
    USER_TYPE_ID int NOT NULL,);

INSERT INTO USERS_2_USER_TYPES_V2
    ( USER_ID, USER_TYPE_ID )
SELECT USER_ID, USER_TYPE_ID
FROM USERS
ORDER BY
    USER_ID DESC  // Turn the contents upside down;

CREATE INDEX IDX_U2UT2_USER_TYPE_ID ON USERS_2_USER_TYPES_V2 ( USER_TYPE_ID );
```

Table 11-1 shows that adding a standard index (denoted IDX) to the USER_TYPE_ID column does not change the physical structure of the table, nor does it alter its contents (any more than the index of a book changes its contents). It just creates an internal listing of every distinct value of the indexed column in the USERS table, as well as which records contain each value. This index allows the database to sort through its data blocks and find matches from either column much faster. As the number of records increases, the amount of time used to return search results should remain trivial.

*Table 11-1. Contents of the USERS table with indexes on FIRST_NAME and LAST_NAME*

| USER_ID | USER_TYPE_ID |
|---------|--------------|
| 4 | 3 |
| 3 | 1 |
| 2 | 2 |
| 1 | 1 |

To get a list of user IDs grouped by user type, join the USERS table with the USERS_2_USER_TYPES_V2 table on the USER_TYPE_ID column.

With just an index on the USER_TYPE_ID column in the USERS_2_USER_TYPES_V2 table, the database still must sort through all records to get each group of users. By creating a clustered index (denoted IDX_CL), you not only index your data, but you also tell the database to store each new record in the data blocks closest to similar records. Listing 11-26 shows how to add a clustered index to the USERS_2_USER_TYPES_V2 table.

*Listing 11-26. Adding a clustered Index to the USERS_2_USER_TYPES_V2 table*

```
DROP INDEX IDX_U2UT2_USER_TYPE_ID ON USERS_2_USER_TYPES_V2;
CREATE CLUSTERED INDEX IDX_CL_U2UT2_USER_TYPE_ID
    ON USERS_2_USER_TYPES_V2 ( USER_TYPE_ID );
```

Table 11-2 shows that with a clustered index on USER_TYPE_ID, records are indexed and additionally stored grouped by USER_TYPE_ID.

*Table 11-2. The USERS_2_USER_TYPES_V2 table with a clustered index on USER_TYPE_ID*

| USER_ID | USER_TYPE_ID [IDX_CL] |
|---------|-----------------------|
| 3 | 1 |
| 1 | 1 |
| 1 | 2 |
| 4 | 3 |

Now the database can easily skip entire blocks of data as it hunts down matches for users by user type. Since a clustered index rearranges the order of records in a table, each table can have only one. Looking back, you may want to change how you indexed and keyed the original USERS_2_USER_TYPES table.

▨ **Caution** You must be careful to not overindex or incorrectly index a table, as either could have a serious impact on the speed of INSERT, UPDATE, and DELETE statements. Many modern database servers offer performance-monitoring features that can help identify frequently executed, slow queries, as well as missing indexes and other tuning options.

# If You Run Calculations on Data Using Your Application Code . . .

So you've built this system and the customers use it. The boss drops by and asks you to create reports to show how many items have been shipped this month, along with their cost versus retail and sales tax. You may come up with something that looks like Listing 11-27.

*Listing 11-27. The wrong way to generate a report*

```
<cfif state eq "TX">
    <cfset salesTax = 0.0825>
<cfelse if . . .>
    <!--- else if for each state --->
</cfif>

<cfquery name="getOrders" datasource="#someDSN#">
    SELECT PRODUCT_ID, QTY_SOLD
    FROM ORDERS
    WHERE ORDER_DATE BETWEEN '2008-01-01' AND '2008-01-31'
</cfquery>

<cfset products = structNew()>
<cfoutput query="getOrders">
    <cfquery name="productInfo" datasource="#someDSN#">
        SELECT PRODUCT_COST, RETAIL_PRICE
        FROM PRODUCTS
        WHERE PRODUCT_ID = #getOrders.PRODUCT_ID#
    </cfquery>
```

```
    <cfif not structKeyExists( products, getOrders.PRODUCT_ID )>
        <cfset products[ getOrders.PRODUCT_ID ] = structNew()>
        <cfset products[ getOrders.PRODUCT_ID ].totalSold = getOrders.QTY_SOLD>
        <cfset products[ getOrders.PRODUCT_ID ].totalRetail =
            products[ getOrders.PRODUCT_ID ].totalSold
                * productInfo.RETAIL_PRICE>
    <cfelse>
        <cfset products[ getOrders.PRODUCT_ID ].totalSold =
            products[ getOrders.PRODUCT_ID ].totalSold + getOrders.QTY_SOLD>
        <cfset products[ getOrders.PRODUCT_ID ].totalRetail =
            products[ getOrders.PRODUCT_ID ].totalSold
                * productInfo.RETAIL_PRICE>
    </cfif>
    <cfset products[ getOrders.PRODUCT_ID ].totalCost =
        products[ getOrders.PRODUCT_ID ].totalSold * productInfo.PRODUCT_COST>

</cfoutput>
```

This code aggregates all of the orders for the month of January 2008 by looping over them to create a struct of structs. Each key in the main struct is a PRODUCT_ID. Each product's struct contains an increasing tally of the number sold, the total cost, and the total retail value. Once this data is compiled, it will be displayed as an HTML table using another overly complex looping technique.

This performance bottleneck will become more apparent once this report is run for an entire year and your company offers a few thousand products. Instead of a hundred orders in a month, you are receiving thousands. The getOrders query returns 100,000 records, and you loop over that result set, calling 100,000 productInfo queries. Memory on the application server is running out as the products struct grows, and the bottleneck in the application has created a massive bottleneck in the database as the number of productInfo requests stack up.

Listing 11-28 shows how you can refactor the calculations into the database level, so that the database does the heavy lifting.

*Listing 11-28. The right way to generate a report, by making the database do the work*

```
SELECT
    a.PRODUCT_ID,
    SUM( a.QTY_SOLD ) AS TOTAL_QTY,
    b.PRODUCT_COST,
    b.RETAIL_PRICE

FROM
    ORDERS a

LEFT JOIN
    PRODUCTS b ON b.PRODUCT_ID = a.PRODUCT_ID

WHERE
    ORDER_DATE BETWEEN '2008-01-01' AND '2008-01-31'
```

```
GROUP BY
    a.PRODUCT_ID,
    b.PRODUCT_COST,
    b.RETAIL_PRICE
```

This gives you the total sold per product in January, with the cost and retail value for each product. Listing 11-29 shows a simple way to aggregate the total cost and retail value contained in this record set.

*Listing 11-29. Aggregating the data generated by Listing 11-28*

```
SELECT
    EXPR1.PRODUCT_ID,
    EXPR1.TOTAL_QTY,
    ( EXPR1.TOTAL_QTY * EXPR1.PRODUCT_COST ) AS TOTAL_COST,
    ( EXPR1.TOTAL_QTY * EXPR1.RETAIL_PRICE ) AS TOTAL_RETAIL

FROM (
    SELECT
        a.PRODUCT_ID,
        SUM( a.QTY_SOLD ) AS TOTAL_QTY,
        b.PRODUCT_COST,
        b.RETAIL_PRICE

    FROM
        ORDERS a

    LEFT JOIN
        PRODUCTS b ON b.PRODUCT_ID = a.PRODUCT_ID

    WHERE
        ORDER_DATE BETWEEN '2008-01-01' AND '2008-01-31'

    GROUP BY
        a.PRODUCT_ID,
        b.PRODUCT_COST,
        b.RETAIL_PRICE

) AS EXPR1

ORDER BY

    EXPR1.PRODUCT_ID
```

The record set generated by the inner SELECT is aliased as EXPR1. The outer SELECT calculates data using the results contained in EXPR1. Just as in the USERS by USER_TYPE example, the database handles all of the data manipulation, and the application code focuses on simply displaying data.

SQL has many data-aggregation functions like SUM, AVG, MIN, and COUNT. Learn how to use these functions to manipulate data ahead of time, rather than altering the data at the application level.

# If the Contents of a Table Depend on the Phase of the Moon . . .

If you have to consult a list taped to your monitor in order to query your database, you have problems. Consider the following:

- If ColumnA in Table1 contains a numeric value and ColumnB contains a text value less than ten characters in length

- If ColumnA in Table1 is NULL and ColumnB contains a numeric value

- If ColumnA in Table2 contains a positive number, join to the primary key of Table3, but if it contains a negative number, get its absolute value and join to the primary key of Table4

- If ColumnC in Table5 has the value "foo", then check if ColumnD's value is "wibble", "narf", or "point"

I've often had to work with very odd database setups, where development was done at such a rapid pace that existing tables were reused to store data they were never meant to store. I've run into dates in the middle of a sentence stored in a varchar column, and been given the task of sorting the table's data on that date. I've had to normalize data contained in a single table, requiring the creation of 15 new tables. I've even had to pick name/value pairs out of an ever-increasing cloud of text data.

# Build It Correctly from the Beginning

Take the time to build your database as correctly as possible, and you'll sail through developing your application. Let the application ask the database to manipulate data, so the application can concentrate on business logic and the presentation of data. The database doesn't need to be 100% perfect up front, but it does need some of the basics done correctly.

If you don't separate tasks between your application and your database, you might have a performance bottleneck.

# PART 4

# Communication and Integrating with Other Technologies

# CHAPTER 12

■ ■ ■

# An Introduction to Consuming and Deploying Web Services in ColdFusion

## by Ben Nadel

*Web services are a primary means of transporting data from one place to another, from one application to another, across the Internet. ColdFusion makes web services easy to create and even easier to consume. This article steps you through Ben Nadel's experimentation with web services.*

When I started looking into web services, I was very intimidated. I didn't know anything about them or how they worked, and I just assumed that they were very complicated. But we tend to overestimate complexity when we don't know much about something. Often, when we stop and explore it rather than fret, we realize that there is no magic here—no secret sauce. It is just a lot of the same stuff that we're used to, only expressed with a different terminology and context.

So what is a web service? At its most basic level, a web service allows one machine to get usable information from another machine over a network. That's it. Don't get caught up and bogged down in all the fancy terminology. Don't worry about things like SOAP and REST and WSDL. And if the type of communication that you build doesn't involve SOAP or REST, that's totally OK—you've still built a valid web service.

Here are brief definitions of these terms, for those who are new to web services:

- WSDL (Web Service Definition Language) is the definition of what a web service can do. It's like the contract. The XML file defines what can and can't be invoked on the web service. See http://www.w3schools.com/WSDL/wsdl_intro.asp and http://en.wikipedia.org/wiki/Web_Services_Description_Language for further information.

- SOAP (Simple Object Access Protocol) is a protocol that is used to communicate with web services. XML-based, it can be fired over any Internet communication medium, but HTTP is most prevalent. For more on SOAP, see http://www.w3schools.com/soap/soap_intro.asp and http://en.wikipedia.org/wiki/SOAP.

- REST (Representational State Transfer) is a different protocol that is not only used in web services, but often uses the common HTTP GET/POST methodology. Web services that use REST are based on resources rather than a WSDL file. For example, http://example.com/locations/ might be a resource that returns a list of locations that are available on the system. To read up on REST, check out http://en.wikipedia.org/wiki/Representational_State_Transfer.

Now that we've all relaxed a bit, I would like to talk about web services in the context of Jewish law. (He's gonna do what?!?) Here at Epicenter Consulting, we have a client who happens to be a fairly religious Jew. And, in accordance with Jewish law, he is not supposed to work or actively make money during Shabbat, the time of the week that falls roughly between Friday's sunset and an hour after Saturday's sunset. Normally, this would not be an issue to us as developers; however, this client happens to run an e-commerce web site and, to abide by Jewish law, he wants his site to be inactive during Shabbat.

To make this easy for our client and for other developers, we decided to create http://www.ShabbatClock.com. This web site provides a public web service that allows people to get Shabbat times based on a passed-in ZIP code and date. I built and tested all of the code in this article in this context.

# Deploying a Web Service from a CFC

Let's talk about deploying our own web services first. The easiest way to do this in ColdFusion is to set the access attribute of a cffunction tag contained in a web-accessible CFC to remote (Listing 12-1).

*Listing 12-1. ColdFusion component method as a web service*

```
<cfcomponent>

    <cffunction name="WebServiceMethod" access="remote" returntype="struct"
    returnformat="json" output="false" hint="I am a publically accessible method that
    returns objects in JSON format.">

        <!--- Function logic here. --->

    </cffunction>

</cfcomponent>
```

This gives the outside world access to the cffunction as a web service. In addition to granting remote access, a web service must also define the format in which the data will return. To do this, supply the returnformat attribute. In Listing 12-1, I have chosen to return the data using JavaScript Object Notation (JSON), but I could have also used Web Distributed Data Exchange (WDDX) or plain. (Plain is allowed only when the function is returning a simple value.)

Note that this function is part of a ColdFusion component. Only functions contained within a cfcomponent tag can be used as web services. Functions contained in a CFM page cannot be used as web services.

# Using a Remote Proxy Object

While you can grant remote access to any function in your application (outside `Application.cfc`), that might not always prove the smartest decision. Your application probably contains a lot of business logic that extends beyond any single method call. It is often considered a best practice to create what's known as a *remote proxy*.

A remote proxy is an object that grants remote access to its methods and acts as a middleman between the web service consumer and the targeted application. Using a remote proxy allows you to add logic specific to a web-service—which might not be required for internal invocation, such as logging and security—to a method call.

`ShabbatClock.com` provides a remote proxy in the form of `API.cfc`, a ColdFusion component located in the root of the web site (Listing 12-2).

*Listing 12-2. API.cfc*

```
<cfcomponent output="false" hint="I provide remote access to public
    functionality of this site.">

    <cffunction name="GetShabbatSunsetFromZipCode" access="remote"
        displayname="" returntype="struct" returnformat="json" output="false"
        hint="I return the Shabbat-adjusted sunset information for the
        given zip code and date.">

        <!--- Define arguments. --->
        <cfargument name="ZipCode" type="string" required="true"
          hint="The zip code for which we get the sunset.">
        <cfargument name="Date" type="date" required="true"
            hint="The date on which we are getting the sunset.">

        <!--- Define the local scope. --->
        <cfset var LOCAL = {}>

        <!--- Create a return struct. --->
        <cfset LOCAL.Return = APPLICATION.Service.
          GetShabbatSunsetFromZipCode(
          ARGUMENTS.ZipCode, ARGUMENTS.Date)>

        <!--- Echo back the zip code. --->
        <cfset LOCAL.Return.ZipCode = ARGUMENTS.ZipCode>

        <!---
        Check to see if the internal method call worked properly
        (as this call might hit a web service, it might fail).
        If it was a failure, add the appropriate error message.
        --->
        <cfif LOCAL.Return.Success>
            <!--- Copy sunset time. --->
            <cfset LOCAL.Return.Error = "">
        <cfelse>
            <!--- Set the error message. --->
```

```
            <cfset LOCAL.Return.Error = "Sunset time could not be
                determined. Try a different zip code.">
        </cfif>

        <!--- Return out. --->
        <cfreturn LOCAL.Return>
    </cffunction>

</cfcomponent>
```

You'll notice that the remote-access method of the remote proxy object isn't really doing much more that turning around and calling a local method in the application. But a few important and not so obvious points need to be discussed.

When you invoke a web service on a ColdFusion component, that component gets instantiated again and again for every single web service call. There is no ability to remotely access methods on cached objects; therefore, with every request, ColdFusion must create a new CFC instance and execute the requested method. Furthermore, during the instantiation of the target component, you cannot implicitly make use of any constructor functions other than the pseudo constructor (the code inside the `cfcomponent` tag but outside any `cffunction` tags).

Using a remote proxy object allows us to keep our web service objects extremely lightweight, which minimizes the overhead of instantiation and gets around the lack of constructors. And once the web service object is instantiated, it has access to the local application, allowing us to utilize all the cached objects to which standard methods calls would have access. The downside of a remote proxy object is that we can't pass in dependency objects, which forces us to refer to the Application scope directly. This breaks the rules of encapsulation, but since these rules are being broken only in our remote proxy objects, the effects are kept to a minimum.

Once the web service method invokes the local `GetShabbatSunsetFromZipCode()` method, it does some additional error checking and adds an error message, if necessary. Here, we see that by using a remote proxy, we can add additional processing logic that would not be required from within the standard application.

# Deploying a Web Service from a Standard ColdFusion Page

Setting a method's access to `remote` is perhaps the easiest way to publish a web service, but it is not the only way. We can provide web service functionality from a standard ColdFusion page as well. To demonstrate this, I have created `api.cfm`, a standard ColdFusion template in the root of the web site (Listing 12-3).

*Listing 12-3. api.cfm*

```
<!--- Make sure there is a method. --->
<cfparam name="URL.Method" type="string">

<!--- Param the return format. --->
<cfparam name="URL.ReturnFormat" type="string" default="json">

<!--- Create a default return value (this will be overridden by
 the selected methods). --->
<cfset objReturn = "">
```

```
<!--- Check to see which method we have selected. --->
<cfswitch expression="#URL.Method#">
    <cfcase value="GetShabbatSunsetFromZipCode">

        <!--- Param the rest of the URL variables. --->
        <cfparam name="URL.ZipCode" type="string">
        <cfparam name="URL.Date" type="date">

        <!--- Invoke the web service locally. --->
        <cfset objReturn = CreateObject( "component", "api" )
            .GetShabbatSunsetFromZipCode(URL.ZipCode, URL.Date)>

    </cfcase>
    <cfdefaultcase>

        <!--- Selected method not found. --->
        <cfthrow type="API.MethodNotFound">

    </cfdefaultcase>
</cfswitch>

<!--- Because this CFM page is acting as a local proxy for our web
    service functionality, we currently have a native ColdFusion
    object in our return variable. We need to get this into the
    return format of the desired type. --->

<cfswitch expression="#URL.ReturnFormat#">
    <cfcase value="json">
        <!--- Convert to JSON. --->
        <cfset strReturn = SerializeJSON( objReturn )>
    </cfcase>

    <!--- If nothing else matched, we are gonna return WDDX. --->
    <cfdefaultcase>
        <!--- Convert to WDDX xml. --->
        <cfwddx action="cfml2wddx" input="#objReturn#" output="strReturn">
    </cfdefaultcase>
</cfswitch>

<!--- Now that we have the return value ready, let's return it. We
    want to make sure that we don't return ANYTHING but the value.
    The easiest way to do that is to convert the string to binary
    and stream it back to the client.--->

<cfcontent type="text/plain" variable="#ToBinary( ToBase64( strReturn ) )#">
```

There's a lot more involved in this methodology because we need to explicitly build out a lot of the functionality that ColdFusion provides automatically for remote-access method calls. In the end, though, this page is returning JSON or WDDX data in the same way that our remote proxy object did. In fact, this ColdFusion template is acting as a remote proxy to our remote proxy object. Also, take a look at the line that gets the sunset data:

```
<!--- Invoke the web service locally. --->
<cfset objReturn = CreateObject( "component", "api" )
    .GetShabbatSunsetFromZipCode(URL.ZipCode, URL.Date)>
```

You can see that this template is actually instantiating our remote proxy object and locally executing its remote method. We could have accessed our cached Service object directly, but since the remote proxy object has additional logic in it for web-service–specific calls, if we wanted to bypass it, we would need to duplicate that logic in this template.

As far as the actual web services go, that's really all there is to it. The explanation may have seemed a bit complex, but when you look at the code, it's pretty straightforward. However, depending on your application architecture and the way in which the web services are being invoked, you may need to make a few tweaks to the page request processing flow in order to allow the web services to be accessed.

The most obvious issue is that the OnRequest() application event method cannot be used with CFC-based web service calls. The OnRequest() event method works by cfincluding the template to be executed, and CFCs simply cannot be included into CFM templates.

Far trickier and less obvious is the fact that when CFC-based web service calls are invoked using WSDL methods, neither the Form scope nor the URL scope exists in the ColdFusion request. For developers who have rightly assumed that the Form and URL scopes always exist, debugging this problem can be a complete nightmare.

Luckily, to get around both of these issues, all we need to do is add a bit of logic to our Application.cfc's OnRequestStart() event method (Listing 12-4).

*Listing 12-4. Application.cfc adjustments for remote method calls*

```
<cffunction name="OnRequestStart" access="public" returntype="boolean"
 output="false" hint="I run pre-page events.">

    <!--- Define arguments. --->
    <cfargument name="Page" type="string" required="true"
     hint="I am the page template that was requested.">

    <!--- Define the local scope. --->
    <cfset var LOCAL = {}>


    <!--- Check to see if this is a CFC-based web service call. If so, we
     need to take special precautions in how we process the request. --->
    <cfif REFindNoCase( "\.cfc$", ARGUMENTS.Page )>

        <!--- Since this is a web service call, we need to get rid of the
         OnRequest() event method. --->
        <cfset StructDelete( VARIABLES, "OnRequest" )>
        <cfset StructDelete( THIS, "OnRequest" )>

        <!--- Check to see if we need to exit out of the OnRequestStart()
         method call. When a CFC is called using a WSDL (web service
         definition language) conversion, there is a URL or FORM scope.
         Therefore, if there is no FORM scope, exit out of this method. --->
        <cfif NOT IsDefined( "FORM" )>
```

```
            <cfreturn true>
        </cfif>

    </cfif>

    <!--- .... Rest of event logic .... --->

    <!--- Return out. --->
    <cfreturn true>
</cffunction>
```

If we are calling a CFC-based web service method, then no matter what, we delete the OnRequest() event method from the Application.cfc object. Don't worry—the Application.cfc object gets instantiated for every single request, so deleting the OnRequest() method will affect only this unique page request. Then we check to see if the Form scope exists. If it does not, we know this request was made with WSDL and we exit from the OnRequestStart() event method. Technically, you need to exit from the OnRequestStart() method only if the OnRequestStart() logic references the URL or Form scope. However, I find it best to put this logic in place, even if it's not needed, so that in the future, I can update the OnRequestStart() method without breaking my web service calls.

With that last piece of logic in place, your web services are published and completely accessible.

# Invoking Web Services in ColdFusion

Publishing a web service is only half of the fun. The other half is actually invoking (also known as *consuming*) the web service. Just as there are several ways to publish a web service, there are several ways to invoke one. In order to make sure that web services at ShabbatClock.com were working properly, I created a test page that invoked them using the various techniques available in ColdFusion.

---

■ **Note** The following examples include username and password values because I was testing on a secure development server. Once live, you would not need these to be passed in, assuming the web services were made available via anonymous access.

---

## Using the cfinvoke Tag

The first technique I tested uses ColdFusion's cfinvoke tag (Listing 12-5).

*Listing 12-5. Invoking a web service with the cfinvoke tag*

```
<cfinvoke
    webservice="#strWebRoot#shabbatclock/site_v1/www/API.cfc?wsdl"
    method="GetShabbatSunsetFromZipCode"
    username="********"
    password="********"
    returnvariable="objSunset"
```

```
refreshwsdl="true">

    <!--- Send web service arguments. --->
    <cfinvokeargument name="ZipCode" value="10016">
    <cfinvokeargument name="Date" value="08/27/2008">

</cfinvoke>
```

The `cfinvoke` tag calls the ColdFusion component directly and invokes the remote-access method using the component's WSDL file. Because this method requires the WSDL file, we need to put `?wsdl` at the end of the web service URL. If you put this form of URL in your web browser, you will see that it returns an XML definition of the web services contained in the given component. The `cfinvoke` tag uses this XML definition to properly call the web service and handle the return data.

WSDL might seem a little intimidating, but don't worry—you don't need to know anything about it at all. When you access a component using the `?wsdl` flag, ColdFusion creates the WSDL file for you automatically, based on the component code. The one tricky thing to understand is that ColdFusion creates the WSDL file only if it doesn't already exist. Therefore, if you change your web service API, you must be sure to refresh the WSDL file; otherwise, ColdFusion will continue to serve up the old version, which won't accurately define the web service that is actually in place. Luckily, ColdFusion makes refreshing a WSDL file extremely easy. All you need to do is add the attribute `RefreshWSDL` to the `cfinvoke` tag when you want the WSDL file to be refreshed.

---

■ **Note** Use the `RefreshWSDL` attribute only when developing. It should not be needed once in production.

---

When you invoke a web service using WSDL technology, ColdFusion does an awesome thing: It automatically converts the returned value into a ColdFusion-native data type. If you look at the definition of `GetShabbatSunsetFromZipCode()` in Listing 12-1, you will see that it returns a struct. Well, since this method is being accessed using `cfinvoke` and WSDL, ColdFusion automatically converts the returned data back into a native ColdFusion struct. Therefore, when using the code in Listing 12-5, you can treat the return variable, `objSunset`, as a true ColdFusion struct.

## Using the CreateObject() Function

The next technique consumes a web service using ColdFusion's `CreateObject()` function (Listing 12-6).

*Listing 12-6. Using the CreateObject() function*

```
<!--- Define the web service meta arguments. --->
<cfset objAPIArguments = {Username = "********", Password = "********" }>

<!--- Create our web service object. This will act as if it were a
   locally instantiated object. But, instead of pointing to our
   own library, it points to a remote web service object. --->
<cfset objAPI = CreateObject(
   "webservice",
```

```
"#strWebRoot#shabbatclock/site_v1/www/API.cfc?wsdl",
objAPIArguments)>

<!--- Invoke the web service using proxy object. --->
<cfset objSunset = objAPI.GetShabbatSunsetFromZipCode(
  "10016", "08/27/2008")>
```

Like the cfinvoke methodology, the CreateObject() technique also uses a WSDL implementation, so we need to add the ?wsdl flag to the web service URL. ColdFusion implicitly interprets the WSDL and sends the correct SOAP packet to the web service, without you needing to do any of the work. The difference here is that CreateObject() doesn't return a web service result; rather, the CreateObject() method returns a local proxy to the actual web service. This is like having a reference to a locally instantiated object, only when you call methods on it, you are actually calling methods on the remote web service. This can be really useful if you plan on caching the web service proxy object for use in multiple web service calls.

Just as with the other implementations, when you use the web service proxy object, values returned from its methods are converted into native ColdFusion objects. So, just as with our first example, the objSunset value, which is returned here, is an actual ColdFusion struct.

None of the web services discussed in this article have optional arguments. However, if they did, we could use a cached proxy object in conjunction with the cfinvoke tag to make calls with omitted arguments (Listing 12-7).

*Listing 12-7. Invoking a web service with optional arguments*

```
<!--- Create our web service proxy object. --->
<cfset objAPI = CreateObject(
  "webservice",
  "#strWebRoot#shabbatclock/site_v1/www/API.cfc?wsdl")>

<!--- Invoke the web service using CFINVOKE. --->
<cfinvoke webservice="#objAPI#" method="MethodWithOptionalArgument"
  returnvariable="objReturn">

    <!--- Omit optional agrument. --->
    <cfinvokeargument name="ID" value="" omit="true">
</cfinvoke>
```

As you can see in Listing 12-7, the web service proxy object, objAPI, is used as the value for the webservice attribute of the cfinvoke tag. The web service method is then invoked using cfinvoke, and the optional argument, ID, is explicitly not sent, as defined by the omit attribute.

## Using the cfhttp Tag

While invoking web services via WSDL and SOAP has some great benefits, it's not the only way to call a web service. In fact, it's not even the only way to call a CFC-based web service. Both CFC- and CFM-based web services can be accessed using standard HTTP protocols. To test this, the technique shown in Listing 12-8 uses ColdFusion's cfhttp tag to invoke the web service.

*Listing 12-8. Using the cfhttp tag to invoke a web service*

```
<!--- Invoke the web service using CFHTTP.
 Note: This methodology works for both GET and POST requests.
 The only difference is that with GET methods, you have to
 use URL parameters and with POST methods, you have to use
 FormField CFHTTPPARAMs. --->

<cfhttp url="#strWebRoot#shabbatclock/site_v1/www/API.cfc" method="post"
     username="********" password="********" result="objPost">

    <!--- Pass in Method. --->
    <cfhttpparam type="formfield" name="Method"
     value="GetShabbatSunsetFromZipCode">

    <!--- Pass in the method arguments. --->
    <cfhttpparam type="formfield" name="ZipCode" value="10016">
    <cfhttpparam type="formfield" name="Date" value="08/27/2008">

    <!--- When using CFHTTP, we have the option to override the
        return format. We can do this because using CFHTTP circumvents
        ColdFusion's built-in conversion functionality. Even though this comes
        back as JSON, we are going to ask for WDDX. --->
    <cfhttpparam type="formfield" name="ReturnFormat" value="wddx">
</cfhttp>

<!--- We have asked for the web service information to be returned
    in WDDX format. Now, let's take that WDDX information and convert it to a
    native ColdFusion object (this is the automatic step we miss when we don't
    use CFINVOKE or CreateObject()). --->
<cfwddx action="wddx2cfml" input="#Trim( objPost.FileContent )#"
    output="objSunset">
```

As you can see, using this methodology adds a bit of overhead when compared to the equivalent WSDL-based methods. Instead of using cfinvokeargument tags, we are now using cfhttpparam tags. Now, among those cfhttpparam tags, we are passing along the ReturnFormat in which we want to receive the response. If you look back at the GetShabbatSunsetFromZipCode() method (Listing 12-2), you will see that we have defined the return format to be JSON. One of the benefits (if you can call it that) of using cfhttp to invoke a web service is that we have the option to override the return format. So here, instead of JSON, I am requesting that the data come back as WDDX. Note that if you want the data to come back in JSON format, you could omit this cfhttpparam altogether.

Once the web service call has returned, I take the WDDX data and convert it to a ColdFusion struct. So, obviously, the biggest drawback of using cfhttp to invoke a web service is that ColdFusion does not do any implicit data type conversion for you.

## Invoking a CFM-Based Web Service

So far, all of these techniques have been used to invoke CFC-based web services. When it comes to CFM-based web services, our options are quite limited. cfhttp is really the only way to invoke a CFM-based web service. Remember the CFM proxy file (`api.cfm`) created in Listing 12-3? Listing 12-9 demonstrates how to use `cfhttp` to invoke that CFM-based web service.

*Listing 12-9. Invoking a CFM-based web service*

```
<!--- Invoke the web service using CFHTTP. This time, however,
 we are going to hit the proxy CFM page rather than the
 ColdFusion component. The CFM proxy page expects a GET
 method with URL parameters. --->

<cfhttp url="#strWebRoot#shabbatclock/site_v1/www/API.cfm" method="get"
 username="********" password="********" result="objGet">

    <!--- Pass in Method. --->
    <cfhttpparam type="url" name="Method" value="GetShabbatSunsetFromZipCode">

    <!--- Pass in the method arguments. --->
    <cfhttpparam type="url" name="ZipCode" value="10016">
    <cfhttpparam type="url" name="Date" value="08/27/2008">

    <!--- Make sure this comes back as WDDX. --->
    <cfhttpparam type="url" name="ReturnFormat" value="wddx">

</cfhttp>

<!--- We have asked for the web service information to be returned
 in WDDX format. Now, let's take that WDDX information and
 convert it to a native ColdFusion object (this is the automatic
 step we miss when we don't use CFInvoke or CreateObject()). --->

<cfwddx action="wddx2cfml" input="#Trim( objGet.FileContent )#"
 output="objSunset">
```

Because of the way we coded our `api.cfm` web service proxy file, this technique looks almost identical to the one in Listing 12-8. The only real difference is that we are calling a CFM page rather than a CFC. We are also using a `GET` method rather than a `POST` method, but that's only because our CFM page is expecting URL values, not form values. And, just as with the previous example, this technique has the same benefits (overriding `ReturnFormat`) as well as the same shortcomings (lack of implicit data conversion).

# Error Handling

I will touch just briefly on error handling. Unlike executing local methods, invoking a remote web service is not 100% dependable. The remote server may go down. The remote web service may have an error. The API may have changed, and you might have an outdated method of invocation. The request may simply time out. In any of these scenarios, you must accept the very real possibility that a web service call may throw an exception. Therefore, it is important that your web service uses a try/catch or some other method to gracefully handle any errors that may result.

## And Finally...

I know that this was a lot of information to cover, but I hope that this introduction has taken away some of the mystery surrounding web services and some of the hesitation you might be feeling about getting involved with them. As you can see from all of these examples, there's not a whole lot going on. And on top of that, there's clearly no right or wrong way to build or consume web services. Really, the hardest part of web services is that third parties might depend on them. Once you make an API public, changing it can have a very negative fallout for those consuming them. But other than that, web services are not that difficult. Go get your hands dirty, and feel free to contact me if you have any questions.

■ ■ ■

# CHAPTER 13

# Web Services and Complex Types

## by Nathan Mische

*ColdFusion is noted for being the great bridge between different technologies. This becomes quite clear when dealing with building web services, where developers must often send information between applications that use a wide variety of technologies. Building web services for consumption by other ColdFusion applications is simple, as it does many of the complex web development tasks: There is no need for special processing of input parameters or return values, for example, because ColdFusion can handle all of the data mappings behind the scenes. But what must be done to publish web services generated by other technologies or consumed by other programming languages, especially those that involve complex types? Nathan Mische tackles these cases and describes how you can make your web services truly accessible to all.*

## Consuming Web Services

A web service's WSDL (Web Service Definition Language) file defines as messages the names and data types of input parameters and the return values for a web service operation. The WSDL data types for these messages map to corresponding ColdFusion data types. Primitive data types, including `xsd:dateTime` or `SOAP-ENC:string`, map directly to ColdFusion data types, such as date and string, while complex types map to ColdFusion structures. ColdFusion structures offer a lot of flexibility for data representation since structures can hold simple key value pairs, arrays, or even other structures. Unfortunately the complex types don't map automatically to structures, and figuring out how to represent a complex type as a structure can pose a bit of a challenge at times.

## Passing Complex Types as Input Parameters

To illustrate how to map complex types to ColdFusion structures, we will walk through a few examples of calling a fictional web service that expects a complex type as an input parameter. The WSDL snippet in Listing 13-1 shows the definition of a complex type named `Customer`; a `CustomerUpdateInput` message definition using this data type and an operation, `UpdateCustomer`, which uses the `Customer` complex data type through the `CustomerUpdateInput` message.

*Listing 13-1. Customer complexType*

```
...
<s:complexType name="Customer">
  <s:sequence>
    <s:element minOccurs="1" maxOccurs="1" name="fname" type="s:string" />
    <s:element minOccurs="1" maxOccurs="1" name="lname" type="s:string" />
    <s:element minOccurs="1" maxOccurs="1" name="active" type="s:boolean" />
  </s:sequence>
</s:complexType>
...
<wsdl:message name="CustomerUpdateInput">
  <wsdl:part name="updateParams" type="tns:Customer" />
</wsdl:message>
...
<wsdl:operation name="UpdateCustomer">
  <wsdl:input message="tns:CustomerUpdateInput" />
</wsdl:operation>
...
```

To give a better sense of the XSD definition of the `Customer` data, Listing 13-2 shows the `Customer` complex type as an XML snippet.

*Listing 13-2. Customer XML*

```
<customer>
    <fname>John</fname>
    <lname>Doe</lname>
    <active>true</active>
</customer>
```

To call the `UpdateCustomer` operation, you first need to create a ColdFusion structure to represent the `Customer`. In this case, we create a structure with three keys that correspond to the three elements of the `Customer`. The code in Listing 13-3 shows how a call to this web service might be coded.

*Listing 13-3. Calling the UpdateCustomer Operation via ColdFusion*

```
<cfscript>
    stCust = StructNew();
    stCust.fname = "John";
    stCust.lname = "Doe";
    stCust.active = true;
    custService = CreateObject("webservice",
        "http://some.site.com/customerService.asmx?wsdl");
    custService.UpdateCustomer(stCust);
</cfscript>
```

# Nested Complex Types

Let's consider a more complex example in which one of the elements of the Customer type is itself a complex type. The WSDL snippet in Listing 13-4 shows the type definitions for the Customer and Address complex types.

*Listing 13-4. Customer and Address Complex Types*

```
<s:complexType name="Customer">
    <s:sequence>
        <s:element name="fname" type="s:string" />
        <s:element name="lname" type="s:string" />
        <s:element name="active" type="s:boolean" />
        <s:element name="address" type="tns:Address" />
    </s:sequence>
</s:complexType>

<s:complexType name="Address">
    <s:sequence>
        <s:element name="address1" type="s:string" />
        <s:element name="address2" type="s:string" />
        <s:element name="city" type="s:string" />
        <s:element name="state" type="s:string" />
        <s:element name="zip" type="s:string" />
    </s:sequence>
</s:complexType>
```

As you can see, the address element of the Customer complex type has been defined as another complex type, Address. Listing 13-5 shows an XML document conforming to this schema.

*Listing 13-5. Customer XML*

```
<customer>
    <fname>John</fname>
    <lname>Doe</lname>
    <active>true</active>
    <address>
        <address1>123 Main Street</address1>
        <address2>Apt 1A</address2>
        <city>Brooklyn</city>
        <state>NY</state>
        <zip>12345</zip>
    </address>
</customer>
```

In order to represent nested complex types, we simply need to create a set of nested ColdFusion structures. Calling the UpdateCustomer operation from Listing 13-1, using these new Customer and Address complex types would look something like Listing 13-6.

*Listing 13-6. Calling the UpdateCustomer Operation via ColdFusion*

```
<cfscript>
    stCust = StructNew();
    stCust.fname = "John";
    stCust.lname = "Doe";
    stCust.active = true;
    stCust.address = StructNew();
    stCust.address.address1 = "123 Main Street";
    stCust.address.address2 = "Apt 1A";
    stCust.address.city = "Brooklyn";
    stCust.address.state = "NY";
    stCust.address.zip = "12345";
    custService = CreateObject("webservice",
      "http://some.site.com/customerService.asmx?wsdl");
    custService.UpdateCustomer(stCust);
</cfscript>
```

## Arrays

Up until this point, the elements in our complex type definitions have used the default occurrence constraint of 1, which means the web service expects exactly one of each element. Depending on the technology and tools used to generate the WSDL, each of the element definitions may actually have the `minOccurs` and `maxOccurs` attributes explicitly set to 1, as Listing 13-7 demonstrates.

*Listing 13-7. minOccurs and maxOccurs*

```
<s:complexType name="Customer">
    <s:sequence>
        <s:element minOccurs="1" maxOccurs="1" name="fname" type="s:string" />
        ...
    </s:sequence>
</s:complexType>
```

While these occurrence attributes default to 1, other valid values exist. If a complex type can contain repeating elements, the `maxOccurs` attribute may have a value higher than 1 or be unbounded if the type can contain an unlimited number of elements. Take, for example, the `Customer` complex type in Listing 13-4. Changing the `maxOccurs` attribute for the address element to unbounded would allow consumers of this web service to provide an unlimited number of `Customer` addresses. Listing 13-8 shows what the XSD schema definition would look like in this case, and Listing 13-9 shows a sample XML document adhering to this schema.

*Listing 13-8. Customer Complex Type with Multiple Addresses*

```
<s:complexType name="Customer">
  <s:sequence>
    <s:element minOccurs="1" maxOccurs="1" name="fname" type="s:string" />
    <s:element minOccurs="1" maxOccurs="1" name="lname" type="s:string" />
```

```
    <s:element minOccurs="1" maxOccurs="1" name="active" type="s:boolean" />
    <s:element minOccurs="1" maxOccurs="unbounded" name="address"
            type="tns:Address" />
  </s:sequence>
</s:complexType>

<s:complexType name="Address">
  <s:sequence>
    <s:element minOccurs="1" maxOccurs="1" name="address1" type="s:string" />
    <s:element minOccurs="1" maxOccurs="1" name="address2" type="s:string" />
    <s:element minOccurs="1" maxOccurs="1" name="city" type="s:string" />
    <s:element minOccurs="1" maxOccurs="1" name="state" type="s:string" />
    <s:element minOccurs="1" maxOccurs="1" name="zip" type="s:string" />
  </s:sequence>
</s:complexType>
```

*Listing 13-9. Customer XML*

```
<customer>
    <fname>John</fname>
    <lname>Doe</lname>
    <active>true</active>
    <address>
        <address1>123 Main Street</address1>
        <address2>Apt 1A</address2>
        <city>Brooklyn</city>
        <state>NY</state>
        <zip>12345</zip>
    </address>
    <address>
        <address1>456 Main Street</address1>
        <address2>14th Floor</address2>
        <city>New York</city>
        <state>NY</state>
        <zip>13579</zip>
    </address>
</customer>
```

ColdFusion uses arrays to represent repeating elements in a complex type. To represent the repeating addresses in Listing 13-9, the address key of our data structure becomes an array of structures. Listing 13-10 shows how to make a call to UpdateCustomer using this new complex type.

*Listing 13-10. Calling the UpdateCustomer Operation via ColdFusion*

```
<cfscript>
    stCust = StructNew();
    stCust.fname = "John";
    stCust.lname = "Doe";
    stCust.active = true;
    stCust.address = ArrayNew(1);
```

```
    stCust.address[1] = StructNew();
    stCust.address[1].address1 = "123 Main Street";
    stCust.address[1].address2 = "Apt 1A";
    stCust.address[1].city = "Brooklyn";
    stCust.address[1].state = "NY";
    stCust.address[1].zip = "12345";
    stCust.address[2] = StructNew();
    stCust.address[2].address1 = "456 Main Street";
    stCust.address[2].address2 = "14th Floor";
    stCust.address[2].city = "New York";
    stCust.address[2].state = "NY";
    stCust.address[2].zip = "13579";
    custService = CreateObject("webservice",
        "http://some.site.com/customerService.asmx?wsdl");
    custService.updateCustomer(stCust);
</cfscript>
```

## Attributes

In addition to elements, complex types may also define attributes. Let's extend our running example a bit further and add an address type attribute to our **Address** complex type. The WSDL snippet in Listing 13-11 shows how to define this, and Listing 13-12 shows a sample XML document.

*Listing 13-11. Customer Complex Type with Multiple Addresses*

```
<s:complexType name="Customer">
  <s:sequence>
    <s:element minOccurs="1" maxOccurs="1" name="fname" type="s:string" />
    <s:element minOccurs="1" maxOccurs="1" name="lname" type="s:string" />
    <s:element minOccurs="1" maxOccurs="1" name="active" type="s:boolean" />
    <s:element minOccurs="1" maxOccurs="unbounded" name="address"
        type="tns:Address" />
  </s:sequence>
</s:complexType>

<s:complexType name="Address">
  <s:sequence>
    <s:element minOccurs="1" maxOccurs="1" name="address1" type="s:string" />
    <s:element minOccurs="1" maxOccurs="1" name="address2" type="s:string" />
    <s:element minOccurs="1" maxOccurs="1" name="city" type="s:string" />
    <s:element minOccurs="1" maxOccurs="1" name="state" type="s:string" />
    <s:element minOccurs="1" maxOccurs="1" name="zip" type="s:string" />
  </s:sequence>
  <s:attribute name="type" type="s:string" />
</s:complexType>
```

*Listing 13-12. Customer XML*

```
<customer>
    <fname>John</fname>
    <lname>Doe</lname>
    <active>true</active>
        <address type="home">
        <address1>123 Main Street</address1>
        <address2>Apt 1A</address2>
        <city>Brooklyn</city>
        <state>NY</state>
        <zip>12345</zip>
    </address>
        <address type="work">
        <address1>456 Main Street</address1>
        <address2>14th Floor</address2>
        <city>New York</city>
        <state>NY</state>
        <zip>13579</zip>
    </address>
</customer>
```

To pass this new attribute to a web service call, we need to add an additional key to the structure used to model the complex type. This attribute key will exist at the same level as the child elements for a given element. In practice, this means that you do not need to make a distinction between child elements and attributes for a given element. ColdFusion will handle mapping these to their appropriate representation when calling the web service. Listing 13-13 shows a structure built to represent the code in Listing 13-12.

*Listing 13-13. Calling the UpdateCustomer Operation via ColdFusion*

```
<cfscript>
    stCust = StructNew();
    stCust.fname = "John";
    stCust.lname = "Doe";
    stCust.active = true;
    stCust.address = ArrayNew(1);
    stCust.address[1] = StructNew();
    stCust.address[1].type= "home";
    stCust.address[1].address1 = "123 Main Street";
    stCust.address[1].address2 = "Apt 1A";
    stCust.address[1].city = "Brooklyn";
    stCust.address[1].state = "NY";
    stCust.address[1].zip = "12345";
    stCust.address[2] = StructNew();
    stCust.address[2].type= "work";
    stCust.address[2].address1 = "456 Main Street";
```

```
        stCust.address[2].address2 = "14th Floor";
        stCust.address[2].city = "New York";
        stCust.address[2].state = "NY";
        stCust.address[2].zip = "13579";
        custService = CreateObject("webservice",
            "http://some.site.com/customerService.asmx?wsdl");
        custService.UpdateCustomer(stCust);
</cfscript>
```

# Going to the Source

At times, structuring an input parameter for a given operation when working with particularly complex or uncommonly structured types may pose a challenge. Even when following the preceding guidelines you may receive error messages saying that a web service operation with the given parameters could not be found. These error messages usually indicate that you have not passed the proper parameters to the web service. You may need to examine the Java code that ColdFusion calls behind the scenes. In this section we will walk through a few examples that show just how to do this.

Listing 13-14 contains the full WSDL that we will use for the first example.

*Listing 13-14. A Sample WSDL*

```
<?xml version="1.0" encoding="UTF-8"?>
<wsdl:definitions
    targetNamespace="http://example.com/customer.wsdl"
    xmlns:s="http://www.w3.org/2001/XMLSchema"
    xmlns:soap="http://schemas.xmlsoap.org/wsdl/soap/"
    xmlns:tns="http://example.com/customer.wsdl"
    xmlns:wsdl="http://schemas.xmlsoap.org/wsdl/">

    <wsdl:types>
        <s:schema elementFormDefault="qualified"
        targetNamespace="http://example.com/customer.wsdl">

            <s:complexType name="Customer">
                <s:sequence>
                    <s:element minOccurs="1" maxOccurs="1" name="fname"
                        type="s:string" />
                    <s:element minOccurs="1" maxOccurs="1" name="lname"
                        type="s:string" />
                    <s:element minOccurs="1" maxOccurs="1" name="active"
                        type="s:boolean" />
                    <s:element minOccurs="1" maxOccurs="unbounded"
                        name="order" type="tns:OrderNumber" />
                    <s:element minOccurs="1" maxOccurs="unbounded"
                        name="address" type="tns:Address" />
                </s:sequence>
            </s:complexType>
```

```
        <s:complexType name="OrderNumber">
            <s:simpleContent>
                <s:extension base="s:string" />
            </s:simpleContent>
        </s:complexType>

        <s:complexType name="Address">
            <s:sequence>
                <s:element minOccurs="1" maxOccurs="1" name="address1"
                    type="s:string" />
                <s:element minOccurs="1" maxOccurs="1" name="address2"
                    type="s:string" />
                <s:element minOccurs="1" maxOccurs="1" name="city"
                    type="s:string" />
                <s:element minOccurs="1" maxOccurs="1" name="state"
                    type="s:string" />
                <s:element minOccurs="1" maxOccurs="1" name="zip"
                    type="s:string" />
            </s:sequence>
            <s:attribute name="type" type="s:string" />
        </s:complexType>

    </s:schema>
</wsdl:types>

<wsdl:message name="CustomerUpdateInput">
    <wsdl:part name="updateParams" type="tns:Customer" />
</wsdl:message>

<wsdl:portType name="CustomerPortType">
    <wsdl:operation name="UpdateCustomer">
        <wsdl:input message="tns:CustomerUpdateInput" />
    </wsdl:operation>
</wsdl:portType>

<wsdl:binding name="CustomerSoapBinding" type="tns:CustomerPortType">
    <soap:binding transport="http://schemas.xmlsoap.org/soap/http" />
    <wsdl:operation name="UpdateCustomer">
        <soap:operation soapAction="http://example.com/UpdateCustomer"
            style="document" />
        <wsdl:input>
            <soap:body use="literal" />
        </wsdl:input>
        <wsdl:output>
            <soap:body use="literal" />
        </wsdl:output>
    </wsdl:operation>
</wsdl:binding>
```

```
<wsdl:service name="CustomerService">
    <wsdl:port name="CustomerPort" binding="tns:CustomerSoapBinding">
        <soap:address location="http://example.com/customer" />
    </wsdl:port>
</wsdl:service>

</wsdl:definitions>
```

This WSDL continues our running example. You will notice that the `Customer` complex type now has an additional attribute, `order`, which it defines as a complex type, `OrderNumber`. We have already covered how to handle the `fname`, `lname`, `active`, and `address` elements in our structure, but how do we handle the `order` element and its `OrderNumber` complex type? Given the occurrence constraints in the WSDL, we know we will need to create an array of structures for this element, but what keys should those structures have? Taking a look at the Java code ColdFusion uses to call this web service can help here. To do that, create a simple ColdFusion template to generate the Java web service proxy/stub objects ColdFusion uses to call the web service. Listing 13-15 shows such a template. Note that you must save the Java proxy/stub objects using ColdFusion's `CreateObject()` function; you cannot do this using `cfinvoke`. This example assumes the WSDL in Listing 13-14 is available at `http://localhost/ExampleWSDL.wsdl`.

*Listing 13-15. generateStubs.cfm*

```
<cfscript>
    wsargs = {savejava="yes"};
    custService = CreateObject("webservice",
        "http://localhost/ExampleWSDL.wsdl",wsargs);
</cfscript>
```

Calling this template will cause ColdFusion to save the Java `webservice` proxy/stub objects to the `cfusion\stubs` folder. On a default ColdFusion multiserver Windows installation, this folder is `C:\JRun4\servers\cfusion\cfusion-ear\cfusion-war\WEB-INF\cfusion\stubs\`. The `stubs` folder may contain several subfolders whose names begin with WS and end with a series of numbers. If so, you will need to identify the WS stub folder that has the proxy/stub objects for the web service in question. You can do this in a few ways. First, you can look for a folder with the timestamp closest to when you called the template. Second, the various WS stub folders will contain folder trees based on the target namespace used in the WSDL. In this example, the namespace is `http://example.com/customer.wsdl`, so the WS stub folder will contain the following folder tree: `com/example/customer_wsdl`. Finally, you can look for the folder containing a Java file named for the WSDL service. In this example, the service has the name `CustomerService`, so you could look for the folder that contains a file named `CustomerService.java`.

Once you have located the correct stub folder, inspect the files to determine how to call the web service. First, locate the file named for the WSDL port type. In this example, the port type is named `CustomerPortType`, so locate `CustomerPortType.java`. Listing 13-16 shows the contents of this file.

*Listing 13-16. CustomerPortType.java*

```
/**
 * CustomerPortType.java
 *
 * This file was auto-generated from WSDL
 * by the Apache Axis 1.2.1 Jun 14, 2005 (09:15:57 EDT) WSDL2Java emitter.
 */

package com.example.customer_wsdl;
public interface CustomerPortType extends java.rmi.Remote {
  public void updateCustomer(com.example.customer_wsdl.Customer updateParams)
      throws java.rmi.RemoteException;
}
```

Looking at this file, we can see that the updateCustomer operation expects a parameter of type com.example.customer_wsdl.Customer. And Customer is actually a JavaBean, which is just a Java object that follows certain conventions, one of which is that properties are accessible via getter and setter methods. As it turns out, the stub folder has a Java file for the Customer class. (As noted before, all of these Java files were saved in the stubs folder on our ColdFusion server.) We want to look at this Customer JavaBean, which will be in the Customer.java file, to begin determining how to build our ColdFusion structure. You will see a couple of constructors, some getters and setters, and a few other methods. To determine how to build your structure, though, you only really need to look at the fields defined for the JavaBean. Listing 13-17 shows these fields for the Customer JavaBean.

*Listing 13-17. Customer.java*

```
/**
 * Customer.java
 *
 * This file was auto-generated from WSDL
 * by the Apache Axis 1.2.1 Jun 14, 2005 (09:15:57 EDT) WSDL2Java emitter.
 */

package com.example.customer_wsdl;
public class Customer  implements java.io.Serializable {
    private java.lang.String fname;
    private java.lang.String lname;
    private boolean active;
    private com.example.customer_wsdl.OrderNumber[] order;
    private com.example.customer_wsdl.Address[] address;
    ...
}
```

We can see that our structure will need keys named fname, lname, active, order, and address. The fname, lname, and active keys will have simple values while the order and address keys will contain arrays, as the square brackets indicate. The arrays will, in turn, hold structures. To determine what keys those structures should have, we need to look at the OrderNumber and Address beans. Listing 13-18 shows the fields for the OrderNumber bean.

*Listing 13-18. OrderNumber.java*

```
/**
 * OrderNumber.java
 *
 * This file was auto-generated from WSDL
 * by the Apache Axis 1.2.1 Jun 14, 2005 (09:15:57 EDT) WSDL2Java emitter.
 */

package com.example.customer_wsdl;
public class OrderNumber  implements java.io.Serializable,
    org.apache.axis.encoding.SimpleType {
        private java.lang.String _value;
    ...
}
```

OrderNumber has one field, _value, so our structure will have one key named **_value**, which should contain the value we want to pass to the web service. Putting this all together, a call to this web service would look something like Listing 13-19.

*Listing 13-19. Calling the UpdateCustomer Operation via ColdFusion*

```
<cfscript>
    stCust = StructNew();
    stCust.fname = "John";
    stCust.lname = "Doe";
    stCust.active = true;
    stCust.order = ArrayNew(1);
    stCust.order[1] = StructNew();
    stCust.order[1]._value = "123-45";
    stCust.address = ArrayNew(1);
    stCust.address[1] = StructNew();
    stCust.address[1].type= "home";
    stCust.address[1].address1 = "123 Main Street";
    stCust.address[1].address2 = "Apt 1A";
    stCust.address[1].city = "Brooklyn";
    stCust.address[1].state = "NY";
    stCust.address[1].zip = "12345";
    stCust.address[2] = StructNew();
    stCust.address[2].type= "work";
    stCust.address[2].address1 = "456 Main Street";
    stCust.address[2].address2 = "14th Floor";
    stCust.address[2].city = "New York";
    stCust.address[2].state = "NY";
    stCust.address[2].zip = "13579";
    custService = CreateObject("webservice",
        "http://localhost/scribblecf/webservices/WSDLToJava/ExampleWSDL.wsdl");
    custService.UpdateCustomer(stCust);
</cfscript>
```

# When Structures Are Not Enough

Occasionally you may run into a web service operation that doesn't actually take a structure for complex types. Take the WSDL in Listing 13-20, for example.

*Listing 13-20. A Sample WSDL*

```
<?xml version="1.0" encoding="UTF-8"?>

<wsdl:definitions
    targetNamespace="http://example.com/customer.wsdl"
    xmlns:s="http://www.w3.org/2001/XMLSchema"
    xmlns:soap="http://schemas.xmlsoap.org/wsdl/soap/"
    xmlns:tns="http://example.com/customer.wsdl"
    xmlns:wsdl="http://schemas.xmlsoap.org/wsdl/">

    <wsdl:types>
        <s:schema elementFormDefault="qualified"
            targetNamespace="http://example.com/customer.wsdl">

            <s:element name="CustomerQuickAdd">
                <s:complexType>
                    <s:sequence>
                        <s:element minOccurs="0" maxOccurs="1" name="fname"
                            type="s:string" />
                        <s:element minOccurs="0" maxOccurs="1" name="lname"
                            type="s:string" />
                    </s:sequence>
                </s:complexType>
            </s:element>

            <s:element name="CustomerQuickAddResponse">
                <s:complexType>
                    <s:sequence>
                        <s:element minOccurs="1" maxOccurs="1"
                            name="customerQuickAddResult" type="s:int" />
                        <s:element minOccurs="0" maxOccurs="1"
                            name="errorMessage" type="s:string" />
                    </s:sequence>
                </s:complexType>
            </s:element>

        </s:schema>
    </wsdl:types>

    <wsdl:message name="CustomerQuickAddSoapIn">
        <wsdl:part name="parameters" element="tns:CustomerQuickAdd" />
    </wsdl:message>
```

```
<wsdl:message name="CustomerQuickAddSoapOut">
    <wsdl:part name="parameters" element="tns:CustomerQuickAddResponse" />
</wsdl:message>

<wsdl:portType name="CustomerSoap">

    <wsdl:operation name="CustomerQuickAdd">
        <wsdl:input message="tns:CustomerQuickAddSoapIn" />
        <wsdl:output message="tns:CustomerQuickAddSoapOut" />
    </wsdl:operation>

</wsdl:portType>

<wsdl:binding name="CustomerSoap" type="tns:CustomerSoap">

    <soap:binding transport="http://schemas.xmlsoap.org/soap/http"/>

    <wsdl:operation name="CustomerQuickAdd">
        <soap:operation soapAction="http://example.com/CustomerQuickAdd"
                style="document" />
        <wsdl:input>
            <soap:body use="literal" />
        </wsdl:input>
        <wsdl:output>
            <soap:body use="literal" />
        </wsdl:output>
    </wsdl:operation>

</wsdl:binding>

<wsdl:service name="Customer">
    <wsdl:port name="CustomerSoap" binding="tns:CustomerSoap">
        <soap:address location="http://example.com/customer.asmx"/>
    </wsdl:port>
</wsdl:service>

</wsdl:definitions>
```

Looking at this WSDL, you might assume that it accepts a structure with two keys, fname and lname, and returns a structure with two keys, customerQuickAddResult and errorMessage. This assumption, however, would prove incorrect.

If we generate the Java proxy/stub objects using the technique outlined in Listing 13-15 and get the port type from the Java class— CustomerSoap.java, in this case— we can see that this operation expects a series of parameters. Listing 13-21 shows the CustomerSoap.java file with some minor formatting changes for readability.

*Listing 13-21. CustomerSoap.java*

```
/**
 * CustomerSoap.java
 *
 * This file was auto-generated from WSDL
 * by the Apache Axis 1.2.1 Jun 14, 2005 (09:15:57 EDT) WSDL2Java emitter.
 */

package com.example.customer_wsdl;
public interface CustomerSoap extends java.rmi.Remote {
    public void customerQuickAdd(
        java.lang.String fname,
        java.lang.String lname,
        javax.xml.rpc.holders.IntHolder customerQuickAddResult,
        javax.xml.rpc.holders.StringHolder errorMessage
    ) throws java.rmi.RemoteException;
}
```

We can now see that this operation expects four parameters, two simple strings, and two Java objects. To call this web service operation, we need to instantiate the two Java objects. Listing 13-22 shows a call to this service.

*Listing 13-22. Calling a Web Service Operation with Java Objects*

```
<cfscript>
    intHolder = CreateObject("java","javax.xml.rpc.holders.IntHolder").init();
    stringHolder = CreateObject("java",
        "javax.xml.rpc.holders.StringHolder").init();
    custService = CreateObject("webservice",
        "http://localhost/scribblecf/webservices/WSDLToJava/ExampleWSDL2.wsdl");
    custService.CustomerQuickAdd("First", "Last", intHolder, stringHolder);
</cfscript>
```

# WSDL2Java

The method shown in Listing 13-15 for viewing the Java source code of the web service proxy/stub objects only works in versions of ColdFusion 8 and higher. However, if you are using ColdFusion MX 6.1 or 7, don't despair. ColdFusion uses the Apache Axis platform under the hood for working with web services. Axis includes the WSDL2Java utility, which ColdFusion 8 uses to generate the proxy/stub objects in the preceding examples. If you are on earlier MX versions of ColdFusion, you can call the WSDL2Java utility directly to generate proxy/stub objects that you can then inspect. And ColdFusion 8 and later versions can also use the WSDL2Java utility. For more information, see the list of links at the end of this article.

# Working with Complex Return Values

When working with complex return values, you access the elements of the returned type using dot notation, much as you do when working with structures. For example, if a web service operation returned a complex Customer type as defined in Listing 13-8 and we assigned that result to a variable named custResult, we could access the various elements, as in Listing 13-23.

*Listing 13-23. Accessing Complex Type Return Elements*

```
<cfoutput>
    First Name: #custResult.fname#<br>
    Last Name: #custResult.lname#<br>
    Active: #custResult.active#<br>
    Address Line 1: #custResult.address[1].address1#<br>
    Address Line 2: #custResult.address[1].address2#<br>
    City: #custResult.address[1].city#<br>
    State: #custResult.address[1].state#<br>
    Zip: #custResult.address[1].zip#<br>
</cfoutput>
```

However, the variable custResult in Listing 13-23 is not a ColdFusion structure. If you call IsStruct() on this variable, it will return false and you cannot use any of the other structure functions to process this variable. Listing 13-24 shows what a complex return value may look like if dumped.

*Listing 13-24. cfdump of a Complex Return Value*

```
object of com.example.webservices.Customer

Class Name: com.example.webservices.Customer
Methods:
    equals(java.lang.Object) returns boolean
    getActive() returns java.lang.Boolean
    getAddress() returns com.example.webservices.Address[]
    getDeserializer(java.lang.String, java.lang.Class, javax.xml.namespace.QName) returns
org.apache.axis.encoding.Deserializer
    getFname() returns java.lang.String
    getLname() returns java.lang.String
    getSerializer(java.lang.String, java.lang.Class, javax.xml.namespace.QName) returns
org.apache.axis.encoding.Serializer
    getTypeDesc() returns org.apache.axis.description.TypeDesc
    hashCode() returns int
    setActive(java.lang.Boolean) returns void
    setAddress(com.example.webservices.Address[]) returns void
    setFname(java.lang.String) returns void
    setLname(java.lang.String) returns void
```

As you can see, this return value is a Java object. Inspecting the dump output of a complex return value can give some insight into how the complex type is structured. In general, properties of a complex type have corresponding getters in the return object and can be accessed using familiar dot notation. For example, we can see in Listing 13-8 that our sample complex type defines an `fname` property. In the dump output of this complex return type we can see the Java object has a corresponding `getFname()` method. This property of the return value can, in turn, be accessed in ColdFusion via dot notation as in Listing 13-23. To determine the structure of nested complex types we can simply dump the nested element. For example, to get more details on the structure of the address element we can dump `custResult.address[1]`. Finally, while dumping complex return values can provide useful details, in some cases you may have to consult the WSDL or even use the WSDL2Java utility to determine how to process the returned value.

# Publishing Web Services

When publishing ColdFusion web services, structures and queries are represented as complex types. While using ColdFusion structures and queries as parameters for web services is technically valid, the complex types used to represent these data types can prove problematic for clients written in languages other than ColdFusion. Therefore you should consider alternatives, especially when designing a web service for public consumption.

Consider the ColdFusion web service in Listing 13-25.

*Listing 13-25. A Web Service with a ColdFusion Structure Parameter*

```
<cfcomponent>
    <cffunction name="UpdateCustomer" access="remote" returntype="void"
        output="false">
        <cfargument name="updateParams" type="struct">
        <!--- update the customer --->
    </cffunction>
</cfcomponent>
```

Listing 13-26 shows the schema definition for the ColdFusion structure defined as the input to the `UpdateCustomer` operation.

*Listing 13-26. The XML Schema Definition for a ColdFusion Structure*

```
<schema elementFormDefault="qualified"
    targetNamespace="http://xml.apache.org/xml-soap">
    <import namespace="http://rpc.xml.coldfusion"/>
    <complexType name="mapItem">
        <sequence>
            <element name="key" nillable="true" type="xsd:anyType"/>
            <element name="value" nillable="true" type="xsd:anyType"/>
        </sequence>
    </complexType>
```

173

```
<complexType name="Map">
    <sequence>
        <element maxOccurs="unbounded" minOccurs="0" name="item"
            type="apachesoap:mapItem"/>
    </sequence>
</complexType>
</schema>
```

This complex type definition does not give much information to the consumer. We can see that it is a collection of items with keys and values, but what do those keys and values represent? The WSDL defines them as xsd:anyType, which means they could contain other complex types or strings or anything. A better approach would define exactly what the operation expects, and we can do this in ColdFusion using a component.

Assume we want the UpdateCustomer operation to accept a type with three elements: fname, lname, and active. We can create a ColdFusion component to represent this type, as in Listing 13-27.

*Listing 13-27. A Complex Type Defined in ColdFusion*

```
<cfcomponent output="false" displayname="Customer">
    <cfproperty name="fname" type="string">
    <cfproperty name="lname" type="string">
    <cfproperty name="active" type="boolean">
</cfcomponent>
```

We can then modify our web service to use this new Customer component for the argument type, as in Listing 13-28.

*Listing 13-28. A Web Service with a Component Parameter*

```
<cfcomponent>
    <cffunction name="UpdateCustomer" access="remote" returntype="void"
        output="false">
        <cfargument name="updateParams" type="Customer">
        <!--- update the customer --->
    </cffunction>
</cfcomponent>
```

Listing 13-29 shows the definition of the Customer complex type that results from using the Customer component as an argument type. The change has greatly clarified the definition of what our operation expects.

*Listing 13-29. The Customer Complex Type*

```
<complexType name="Customer">
    <sequence>
        <element name="active" nillable="true" type="xsd:boolean"/>
        <element name="fname" nillable="true" type="xsd:string"/>
        <element name="lname" nillable="true" type="xsd:string"/>
    </sequence>
</complexType>
```

While a ColdFusion structure can suffer from a lack of information in its WSDL definition, a ColdFusion query has the opposite problem of too much complexity. ColdFusion queries are represented by the QueryBean complex type. As Listing 13-30 demonstrates, this WSDL type is in fact quite complex and may prove challenging for consumers to construct or parse.

*Listing 13-30. The QueryBean Complex Type*

```
<complexType name="QueryBean">
    <all>
        <element name="data" nillable="true"
                type="intf:ArrayOf_SOAP-ENC_Array" />
        <element name="ColumnList" nillable="true"
                type="intf:ArrayOf_SOAP-ENC_string" />
    </all>
</complexType>
<complexType name="ArrayOf_SOAP-ENCArray">
    <complexContent>
        <restriction base="SOAP-ENC:Array">
            <attribute ref="SOAP-ENC:arrayType"
                    wsdl:arrayType="SOAP-ENC:Array[]" />
        </restriction>
    </complexContent>
</complexType>
<complexType name="ArrayOf_SOAP-ENC_string">
    <complexContent>
        <restriction base="SOAP-ENC:Array">
            <attribute ref="SOAP-ENC:arrayType"
                    wsdl:arrayType="xsd:string[]" />
        </restriction>
    </complexContent>
</complexType>
```

If you are developing a web service for consumption by a variety of technologies, you may want to consider using arrays of components instead of ColdFusion queries for your web service parameters. Doing this in ColdFusion is pretty simple. Assume we want to modify the UpdateCustomer operation in Listing 13-28 to accept multiple customers. We will call this new operation UpdateCustomers. To accept an array of Customer complex types, we just need to modify our component, as demonstrated in Listing 13-31.

*Listing 13-31. Accepting Multiple Complex Types*

```
<cfcomponent>
    <cffunction name="UpdateCustomers" access="remote" returntype="void"
            output="false">
        <cfargument name="updateParams" type="Customer[]">
        <!--- update the customers --->
    </cffunction>
</cfcomponent>
```

The type `Customer[]` can be broken up into two parts. The first is the `Customer`, which is the component that we're returning. The second portion contains the brackets, which says that the type should be an array that contains the `Customer` component. You can read about this in more detail in Michael Dinowitz's companion article, "Type Validation When Returning an Array of Components," which is article 14 in this collection. The code in Listing 13-31 will generate a WSDL with an array complex type, as in Listing 13-32. This array complex type will then be used as the parameter to the `UpdateCustomers` operation.

*Listing 13-32. WSDL with an Array Complex Type*

```
<complexType name="Customer">
    <sequence>
        <element name="active" nillable="true" type="xsd:boolean"/>
        <element name="fname" nillable="true" type="xsd:string"/>
        <element name="lname" nillable="true" type="xsd:string"/>
    </sequence>
</complexType>
<complexType name="ArrayOfCustomer">
    <complexContent>
        <restriction base="soapenc:Array">
            <attribute ref="soapenc:arrayType"
                wsdl:arrayType="impl:Customer[]"/>
        </restriction>
    </complexContent>
</complexType>
```

The same square brackets can be used to return arrays of complex types from web service operations as well. See Listing 13-33 for an example.

*Listing 13-33. Returning Multiple Complex Types*

```
<cfcomponent>
    <cffunction name="GetCustomers" access="remote" returntype="Customer[]"
        output="false">
        <!--- get customers and return as an array of Customer components --->
    </cffunction>
</cfcomponent>
```

# Other Resources

I hope this article helps you tackle some of the issues that may come up when dealing with complex types in web services. Here are some other resources and blog posts you may find helpful.

Tom Jordahl, the man behind ColdFusion's web service implementation and one of the original implementers of Apache Axis, has a series of very helpful blog posts, many of which served as source material for this article.

- "Array Types in ColdFusion Web Services": `http://tjordahl.blogspot.com/2008/04/array-types-in-coldfusion-web-services.html`

- "Reprint: Consuming Web Service Complex Types in ColdFusion": `http://tjordahl.blogspot.com/2008/04/reprint-consuming-web-service-complex.html`

- "Using WSDL2Java to Figure Out CFML Arguments to a Web Service": `http://tjordahl.blogspot.com/2008/07/for-some-reason-i-havent-actually-even.html`

- "Special Axis Types and ColdFusion": `http://tjordahl.blogspot.com/2008/07/special-axis-types-and-coldfusion.html`

Adobe has a couple of TechNotes on using the WSDL2Java utility in CFMX 6.1 and 7.

- "Creating Webservice Stubs with WSDL2Java in ColdFusion MX 6.1": `http://www.adobe.com/go/ea87b65`

- "Creating Webservice Stubs with WSDL2Java in ColdFusion MX 7": `http://www.adobe.com/go/eaf0396`

Charlie Arehart has a post on ColdFusion 8's ability to save Java web service proxies.

- "CF8 Hidden Gem: New Option to Save Java Source for Web Service Proxy—with createobject only": `http://carehart.org/blog/client/index.cfm/2007/10/11/cf8_hiddengem_createobject_savejava`

If all else fails you can always consult the documentation. The ColdFusion Developer's Guide has a whole chapter devoted to using web services:

- "Using Web Services": `http://livedocs.adobe.com/coldfusion/8/htmldocs/webservices_01.html`

■ ■ ■

# CHAPTER 14

# Type Validation When Returning an Array of Components

## by Michael Dinowitz

*This article was born out of an editorial question on Nathan Mische's "Web Services and Complex Types,"
which is Chapter 13 in this book. At the end of that article, Nathan tries to explain the concept of type
validation when returning an array of components, which is a side issue of one of his code examples. It
didn't make sense to interrupt the flow of Nathan's article to explain it clearly, but it is an important
concept nonetheless. Michael agreed to write a companion piece that provides an explanation, and so this
article was born.*

## Validating a Component

The `type` attribute in `cfargument` and the `returntype` attribute in `cffunction` are designed for validation;
they check the value that has been passed to make sure it fits some criteria and if not, they throw an
error. These attributes have specific names for each type or format of data being validated except one:
component names. When a `type` or `returntype` has a value other than one that is predefined, ColdFusion
assumes that the value is for a component reference. This is straightforward when the component
named is being passed in or out. Listing 14-1 gives a simple example of a `returntype` that contains a
component reference.

*Listing 14-1. returncustomer Function*

```
<cffunction name="returncustomer" returntype="customer" output="false">
    <cfset var customervar=createobject('component', 'customer')>
    <cfreturn customervar>
</cffunction>
```

In Listing 14-1, `customervar` is assigned a reference to the `customer` component, which is what the
`returntype` is expecting for validation.

# Validating an Array of Components

This works well when we're passing a single component, but what if we want to pass multiple components, such as multiple customers? We could load all of the customer components into a structure or array and return that, but what of validation? We can validate the return as an array or structure, but not as a component. This validation, however, may be too general for some people, especially those working with web services. What we really need is to validate the component "inside" the structure or array. This is easier than you might think, but it uses an undocumented syntax. Listing 14-2 shows how you might validate a component inside an array.

*Listing 14-2. Validating a Component Inside an Array*

```
<cffunction name="returncustomer" returntype="customer[]" output="false" hint="">
    <cfset var customerarray=arraynew(1)>
    <cfset var customervar=createobject('component', 'customer')>
    <cfset customerarray[1]=customervar>
    <cfreturn customerarray>
</cffunction>
```

Listing 14-2 contains the same customer component as in Listing 14-1, but rather than returning it directly, we're adding it to an array and returning the array. The `returntype` is slightly different than that in Listing 14-1. By adding square brackets to the component name, we are telling ColdFusion that the variable being returned must be a component contained within an array. This has a few limitations.

- It only works with arrays, not with any other complex data types.

- It only works with one-dimensional arrays.

- If an array has nested arrays, the component must be on the top-level array.

- The array returned can contain any values as long as the value in Position 1 is the component being validated.

As we move more and more to object-oriented ColdFusion, the ability to do this sort of validation becomes more useful. A data access object (DAO) might get a record from a database and load it into a component specifically designed for that information (a bean). Multiple records being returned would result in multiple beans. Being able to pass all of these beans inside an array gives more options for those who want purer OO. Of course, as we've seen in Chapter 13 using the bracket syntax for a `returntype` is extremely useful and informative when dealing with web services.

■ ■ ■

# CHAPTER 15

# Sending E-mail the Right Way

## by Mark A. Kruger

*As a means of communication, e-mail can be very effective. It's cheaper and faster than the post office, and a well-written e-mail can grab the attention of your boss, customer, or client. There's only one problem: Once you send that e-mail, how do you know it arrived at its destination? Mark Kruger has put together a fascinating tale of an e-mail and what it faces on the path from sender to recipient, with strategies to ensure that your e-mails will complete the journey.*

If you are a ColdFusion developer, sooner or later someone will ask you to create an application that includes e-mail as an integral part. Practically every web application needs to send e-mail as much as it needs SQL. Whether the task requires a simple Contact Us form or a newsletter sent to tens of thousands every day, successful delivery of your e-mails is vital.

Do you remember playing in a downpour as a child? Were you ever fascinated by the water rushing down the street? My brother and I would find a small chunk of wood and drop it in the flow of water by the curb. To successfully reach the storm drain, our small craft would have to navigate all sorts of obstacles. Sometimes we would have to help it get past a snag so it could continue on its journey.

Think of e-mail as that pretend boat. In almost every web application, some component launches e-mails out onto the river that is the Internet and lets the flow of protocols take it to its destination. Just like our little chunk of wood, the e-mail has obstacles along the way that it must overcome. Sometimes e-mail has difficulties getting through. You might find yourself on the phone with a frustrated user trying to figure out why he or she can't get your ColdFusion e-mail, but can get the same e-mail from Microsoft Outlook just fine.

Most of the e-mail on the Internet is spam, which accounts for the difficulty in sending e-mail. And because most e-mail is spam, dozens of techniques try to figure out whether to deliver a given message or discard it as unwanted. For example, our company e-mail server uses seven different technologies to mitigate spam: Sender Policy Framework (SPF), DomainKeys Identified Mail (DKIM), SpamAssassin (`http://spamassassin.apache.org/`), custom filtering, Real-Time Blacklists (RBLs), greylisting, and abuse detection. Understanding the rapids that your little e-mail boat will have to navigate might give you some insight into how to get legitimate e-mails delivered. You can control some of the obstacles directly, influence some of them indirectly, and still others will remain completely outside of your control. Even so, you can do some things to give your e-mails a fighting chance. Incidentally, I am not going to discuss how to follow the American CAN-SPAM laws for mass marketing—that's between you, your mom, and possibly your attorney. Instead, I will focus on the technical aspects of sending e-mail and I will assume that you follow the rules, which by now have become well-established.

---

■ **Note** The FCC publishes some information on CAN-SPAM: http://www.fcc.gov/cgb/consumerfacts/canspam.html.

---

# The From Conundrum

Before you respond to an e-mail, take a moment to consider who it says it is from. Remember that most of the obstacles you will encounter are really in place to prevent unsolicited e-mail from nefarious marketers who want to question your manhood and get you to refinance your house. Spam e-mail commonly features a deceptive practice called e-mail address spoofing, wherein a spammer can send from any e-mail address he likes through his own SMTP server. Since a spammer doesn't care whether you reply (after all he just wants you to click on his link), he can "fire and forget." The e-mail arrives claiming a return address from a person who actually has no clue that the spammer has used his e-mail address.

This practice can cause many problems for the innocent user and domain. Often, irate people reply to spam and castigate the e-mail address's user, who has nothing to do with the message at all. Bounced messages from the bulk send operation show up in the spoofed e-mail's inbox. In the worst case, the domain of the spoofed e-mail could end up on a blacklist through no fault of its own. To counter this problem, several technologies have evolved that take aim at making sure the From field of an e-mail doesn't spoof or break any of the other rules of polite e-mail.

Still, sending from a domain you do not control has its uses at times. Many applications allow a user to fill out a form on a Web site and send an e-mail that appears to come directly from the user's address instead of from the Web site's domain. Applications like Refer a Friend and Contact Us forms have the legitimate goal of wanting to allow the recipient to click on the Reply button and send a message back. Of course, simply sending from the user's address will run afoul of those spam-busting obstacles intended to stop spoofing. More on that in a moment. Fortunately, this particular obstacle has an easy workaround. Take the following illustration as an example.

Sally sends a greeting card from cfmusecards.com. She enters her e-mail address (sally@earhairsalon.com) and sends a card to her friend nancy@nosehairsalon.com. The card arrives and looks like it is from Sally, but is it really? In fact, it may say it has come from an address at cfmusecards.com on behalf of Sally. The Reply To address can contain Sally's e-mail address, allowing a correct, non-spoofed From address but still showing Sally's name and allowing the user to reply directly to Sally. ColdFusion accomplishes this using the replyTo attribute of the cfmail tag—as in the example shown in Listing 15-1.

*Listing 15-1. The replyTo Attribute of cfmail*

```
<cfmail from="Sally <greetings@cfmusecards.com>"
    replyto="sally@earhairsalon.com"
    to="nancy@nosehairsalon.com"
    subject="Sally Has Sent You a Greeting Card">

    Hey Nancy - check out these dancing hamsters. Pretty neat, huh?
    http://cfmusecards.com/dancinghamsters

</cfmail>
```

If you send a message like this and then look at the headers, you will see something like the following, though you will probably have to poke around a bit in your e-mail client to find it (see Listing 15-2).

*Listing 15-2. Headers Using `replyTo`*

```
From: Sally <greetings@cfmusecards.com>
Reply-To: sally@earhairsalon.com
To: nancy@nosehairsalon.com
```

If you click on the Reply button, you will actually send e-mail to Sally even though the e-mail did not originate from her domain. To be really tricky, add a Sender address into the header using `cfmailparam` (see Listing 15-3).

*Listing 15-3. cfmailparam*

```
<cfmail from="sally@earhairsalon.com"
    replyTo="sally@earhairsalon.com"
    to="nancy@nosehairsalon.com"
    subject="Sally Has Sent You a Greeting Card">
<cfmailparam name="Sender" value="greetings@cfmusecards.com">

Hey Nancy - check out these dancing hamsters. Pretty neat, huh?
http://cfmusecards.com/dancinghamsters

</cfmail>
```

This results in a header that looks like Listing 15-4.

*Listing 15-4. Headers Using cfmailparam*

```
Sender: greetings@cfmusecards.com
Reply-To: sally@earhairsalon.com
From: sally@earhairsalon.com
To: nancy@nosehairsalon.com
```

When viewed in Outlook, the From address now indicates the message came from greetings@cfmusecards.com on behalf of sally@earhairsalon.com. Some e-mail list servers handle addressing in exactly this way. Semantically, it tells the whole story. Domain A sent the e-mail on behalf of a user on domain B.

In addition to the `sender` and the `replyTo` attributes, `cfmail` also offers the `failTo` attribute. This e-mail address catches any bounces for this e-mail. So using the `from`, `sender`, `replyTo`, and `failTo` attributes (and some creative labeling) you can allow the user to reply to an address from outside your domain, and you can handle bounces in an orderly fashion that does not affect a real person's e-mail address.

Of course, other hurdles exist to getting your e-mail out the door, beyond getting the addressing right. The e-mail will still have to jump through a variety of hoops just so Sally can tell Nancy about those dancing hamsters.

First, your e-mail goes to the relay server, either an actual e-mail server or an SMTP daemon running on the web server. The relay server verifies that relaying is allowed and then forwards the message on to the next server, which handles the message based on its own rules. In this case, the sending or originating server is not ColdFusion; it is the SMTP server to which ColdFusion relayed the message. The receiving server is the e-mail's destination server, and it usually determines whether a message is worthy of delivery. The receiving server will probably use more than one technique to evaluate the message, but likely looks at three basic categories: the origin of the message, the behavior of the sending server, and the content of the message. It's these three categories I'll look at in this article.

# Checking E-mail Origins

The first category of technologies used by the receiving server focuses on the idea of a known good sender. The receiving server uses these techniques to see whether the sending server has a place on the "nice list" and has permission to send e-mail from the domain in question.

## Sender Policy Framework (SPF)

SPF is the easiest of these technologies to understand. It uses Domain Name Server (DNS) and requires two things. First, a special TXT record, a sort of DNS comment field, has to exist on the DNS server. The record must contain a set of rules dictating the server or servers allowed to send e-mail on behalf of the users of a domain. The rules can check criteria as simple as IP addresses or as complicated as multiple matches on different types of DNS records, such as A, MX, or PTR records. Additional information tells the receiving server whether to reject or flag messages that fail to meet the standard. Here's a sample SPF record for our fictitious `cfmusecards.com` domain:

```
cfmusecards.com. TXT "v=spf1 mx ip4:192.168.1.1 -all"
```

The rule set begins at `v=spf1` followed by a space. The first item in the rule is `mx`. The `mx` indicates that the server identified in the MX record for the domain does allow relay. The `ip4:192.168.1.1` entry indicates that SMTP from this IP address is also allowed to relay. Finally, the `all` indicates that everything else should be rejected. In plain English this rule says, "Allow the mail server and one other IP address to relay mail for this domain. Reject mail coming from anywhere else."

The other requirement, an SPF-aware e-mail server, will look up the rule set; apply it to the sender; and then pass, flag, or fail the e-mail message. Most of the giant e-mail providers such as Yahoo, Hotmail, and Gmail honor SPF. If you send out an e-mail newsletter or (legitimate) bulk marketing e-mail, you should implement SPF for your domain. Fortunately, you can implement SPF even without an SPF-aware e-mail server, simply by adding the appropriate TXT record to your DNS server. If you relay ColdFusion e-mail from your web server's SMTP daemon, you should take the time to add an SPF record that includes the A record rule or the web server IP address.

There is one gotcha, though. If users for your domain normally relay their e-mail through other servers, they will suddenly begin to have problems. For example, if a user relays e-mails from Outlook through her own e-mail server from her ISP, those e-mails will suddenly fail because your rules won't allow relaying through just any e-mail server anymore—whether the user has authenticated or not. Using a VPN or adding authenticated SMTP relay abilities to your corporate mail server can mitigate this, but only with changes to the user's Outlook to relay differently.

For more information see `http://www.openspf.org/`.

# DomainKeys Identified Mail (DKIM)

DKIM has the same goal as SPF, but takes a far more sophisticated approach. It is also much harder to implement. DKIM has a public and private key, just like in PGP. The private key resides on the sending server and the public key gets added to the DNS server with a special syntax and the TXT record type. The relay server creates a signature from the content of the sent e-mail and places this signature into the e-mail as a header prior to sending it. The receiving server gets the public key from DNS, unpacks the signature header, and compares the contents to the key it got from DNS. If they match, then the receiving server knows the e-mail originates from a legitimate source for that domain.

Of course, this ingenious method has a downside—difficult implementation. It requires additional software on both the outgoing server and the incoming server. Both servers have to work together for the encrypted header to mean anything, and the long and cryptic DNS entry is sometimes difficult to get exactly right.

The upside? Yahoo. If you need to get e-mail through to Yahoo users, DKIM can help. As the driving force behind this technology, Yahoo signs all of its outgoing messages. Signing messages sent to Yahoo accounts ensures their delivery and earns them a spiffy "DomainKeys verified" label in the Yahoo inbox. Since Yahoo accounts for a high percentage of the e-mail on the Internet, it may be worth your while to invest in this technology.

Both SPF and DKIM focus on verifying the legitimacy of the sending server. This known good approach has a counterpart that focuses on known bad domains—the domains on the naughty list.

For more on DKIM see `http://www.dkim.org/`.

# Real-Time Blacklists (RBLs)

The term blacklist can refer to several things. Some blacklists identify bad IP addresses or domains, other blacklists identify domains linked to by spam e-mails, and others even identify blocks of suspect IP addresses. The receiving server checks an incoming e-mail against one or more lists and accepts or rejects the e-mail based on the results of the check. Virtually all e-mail servers contain features that allow you to use a blacklist, many offering tight integration.

I advise trying very hard never to become blacklisted. Unfortunately, while blacklists serve a legitimate purpose, the folks who run them do not generally subscribe to the theory of innocent until proven guilty. So once you hit a list, prepare for some real wrangling to get your domain or IP removed. Of course, you can usually stay off blacklists by following the rules, not sending out unwanted e-mail, and implementing things like SPF and DKIM to legitimize your e-mail.

Some large e-mail domains maintain their own internal blacklists. Yahoo, for example, will exclude e-mail from a domain for its own reasons. If the giant providers are important to your e-mail effort, you should examine their published rules for senders and attempt to configure your process accordingly.

# Checking Sender Behavior

In addition to tweaking your From field, you can apply other techniques for making sure that your e-mail server follows the rules. Most e-mail servers have rules for denying excessive bounce messages and blocking excessive connection attempts and e-mail harvesting. Typically, none of these rules affect legitimate e-mail, though you may want to investigate if rate is limiting your send process. Many servers, however, also employ a technique called greylisting, which might leave you scratching your head.

Greylisting isn't too hard to understand. A receiving server that uses greylisting has a whitelist of domains from which it has previously accepted e-mails. Any e-mails from these domains pass through the greylist hurdle, although they might still fail for some other reason. When a message from a brand-new domain arrives, the server responds with a 451 error, message deferred, effectively greylisting the message. While the SMTP standard defined this message to allow a busy e-mail server to say "try again later," the greylist technique uses it to see how badly the relaying server wants to deliver the message.

It turns out that spammers care more about quantity than about quality. They tend to kick off a few million messages and then go back to playing World of Warcraft in a basement hideaway (under a comic book shop, no doubt). Spammers don't usually resend messages that fail to get through the first time, and greylisting takes advantage of that fact to legitimize a domain. If the sending server attempts to deliver that same deferred message a few minutes later, the e-mail server places the domain on the whitelist and allows both that message and subsequent messages from that domain. Greylisting is not just for giant e-mail domains such as Yahoo. At our company, we have reduced the total number of messages that we actually accept by 70 percent using this very effective technique. Of course, on the downside, messages have to get through that hurdle and are not always delivered in real time.

How do you mitigate the impact of greylisting on your e-mail send operations? You can do very little about it other than counseling patience to your users. You might take advantage of the way some domains process rules. For example, if you use DKIM, Yahoo likely will not greylist you. Still, you will likely end up explaining the process to your users at some point, as they pound their desks waiting for e-mail delivery.

For more on greylisting see `http://www.greylisting.org/`.

## Checking the Content

SPF, DKIM, blacklisting, and greylisting really deal with how e-mail servers interact with each other. These solutions attempt to verify the origin and legitimacy of a sending server. Another group of technologies, typically known as spam filters or sometimes Bayesian filters, examine the content of your e-mails.

A spam filter generally has a dictionary of spam patterns, much like a virus scanner has a dictionary of virus patterns. Using the dictionary, a filter examines incoming mail messages against the patterns and scores the likelihood that a message contains spam.

This score then becomes a factor in accepting or rejecting the message. Bayesian filters have some advantages. For example, they tend to improve over time because they collect known bad spam messages and use them to keep the dictionary up-to-date. Bayesian filtering also causes most of the false positives that occur on e-mail servers. For that reason, most of them also flag possible spam, delivering it but usually placing it in a junk e-mail folder for examination by a real user. This trains the dictionary and keeps it up-to-date, but still requires manpower.

For a monthly fee, companies like Postini and Trend Micro will set up filters that they monitor and tweak constantly. E-mail headed to your domain must pass through these filters to get to you. Theoretically, this minimizes false positives while still giving you the advantages of filtering. While good strategy, this tactic means that your messages will have to hop through another server to get where they are going.

How do you lessen the impact of filters on your e-mail? Unfortunately, e-mail filtering requires a running battle just like SEO. No magic bullet exists but a few best practices may help:

- Only send legitimate content about legitimate subjects. If possible, avoid sales and marketing speak. Make your content valuable to the user.

- Use the Name field in addressing your e-mail. (Sally `<sally@nosehairsalon.com>`).

- Avoid excessive or obscure-looking links in the message body.

- Avoid any appearance of obfuscation. For example, don't use any links that might appear deceptive or dishonest.

- Test your e-mails—both online and desktop tools can assist you with this. In our company, we created a web service that passes messages to our SpamAssassin server and returns a score.

- If you send HTML e-mail, make sure it contains content and not just images. Use well-formed, semantic HTML that identifies the nature of your content rather than just its layout.

- If you send HTML e-mail, make it multi-part and include a plain text section.

- Use fully qualified domain names in URLs and image tags. Avoid using IP addresses.

- Do not include any forms or JavaScript.

- Check out some of the published tips for individual giant e-mail domains such as Yahoo and Hotmail. For example, Yahoo publishes some best practices: `http://help.yahoo.com/l/us/yahoo/mail/postmaster/postmaster-15.html`.

- Make changes to your messages on a regular basis to stay ahead of the curve on filtering. This becomes especially important if your messages feel like marketing.

## Miscellaneous Commandments

The following tips will help as well:

- Handle your bounces. Make sure to have a process in place to remove bad e-mails from your lists. Large e-mail domains detest repeat e-mail sent to the same bad e-mail address over and over again.

- Make sure that the sending server has a reverse lookup PTR record.

- Do not allow an open relay. Use authentication and secure your mail server. If just anyone can relay through your mail server, you probably deserve to be blacklisted. And spanked.

Of course, this process has many other nuances far beyond the scope of this article. Search the Web for more information. Yahoo, Hotmail, and AOL all have excellent checklists that can help you identify your weak spots.

As you can see, understanding end to end how e-mail works is an important skill set. The Byzantine labyrinth of technologies and protocols can seem difficult to navigate, but a little effort will go a long way toward helping your delivery success rate.

███

# CHAPTER 16

# ColdFusion and Microsoft Exchange

## by Terry Ryan

*In December 2005, Ben Forta posted a question on his blog: "What would you want from ColdFusion Microsoft Exchange integration?" People responded in droves. Putting the two products together makes a lot of sense. Both ColdFusion and Exchange are heavily used as part of many companies' intranet solutions, so being able to leverage them at the same time would be extremely useful. There has always been a way to do it: kludge together some socket operation while creating a WebDAV request by hand. It's neither fun nor easy, but eventually it works.*

*Fast-forward to ColdFusion 8 and 9 and the ColdFusion Exchange tags. These features were heavily influenced by the responses to Ben's post. In this article, we'll take a look at what Adobe has put together to allow you to integrate ColdFusion and Exchange.*

What exactly can you do with the ColdFusion Exchange tags? You can connect to a user's mailbox and interact with that user's appointments, contacts, tasks, and mail. *Interact* in this context, means creating, reading, updating, and deleting contacts, tasks, and appointments. Mail works a little differently. You can read it, but you can't really send it with the Exchange tags. However, cfmail can still do that job for you.

## ColdFusion and Exchange Integration Requirements

Before you get started, you'll need a few things:

- A ColdFusion server of at least version 8
- An Exchange Server 2003 or 2007
- Internet Information Services (IIS) enabled on that Exchange Server

- An e-mail account that has access to Outlook Web Access (if your organization already has an Outlook Web Access server, most of the work has already been done for you)

- On any firewalls between the two servers, access to port 80 (HTTP) or port 443 (HTTPS) allowed (Adobe's *ColdFusion Developer's Guide* details how to configure this)

You will probably need help from your organization's Exchange administrators to perform all of the configuration steps. But even if you don't need their help, I suggest dropping your Exchange administrators a line before you do this. Depending on your organization's Exchange configuration, the servers you connect to might not be getting a lot of traffic on those ports. If your administrators are doing a good job of monitoring security, they might be alarmed by the sudden influx of connections from one address. Exchange administrators can cripple your quota, create phantom appointments, or fake e-mail from you to your boss. Trust me, you don't want them angry with you.

# ColdFusion Exchange Tags

People who work with Exchange like to point out that it is basically a database. However, the new ColdFusion Exchange tags don't really work on the same programming metaphor as other database operations. If anything, these tags most resemble `cfftp`. As with `cfftp`, you can do a single operation, or you can create a connection, perform multiple operations, and then close the connection. Additionally, you can store this connection in a shared scope, reuse it, and even use the `cfdump` tag to dump it. However, even if it works like `cfftp`, when returning data from Exchange, ColdFusion transforms it to the ColdFusion query format we've come to know and love.

ColdFusion has several tags for dealing with Exchange. Instead of having one monolithic `cfexchange` tag, the features have been broken up into more manageable tags by Exchange item type and function. Let's explore those tags.

## Using cfexchangeconnection

The first thing you need to do is fire up an Exchange connection. We use the `cfexchangeconnection` tag to make that happen (see Listing 16-1).

*Listing 16-1. Connecting to Exchange*

```
<cfexchangeconnection action = "open" connection = "exConn"
    server = "#mailhost#" mailboxName = "#mailbox#"
    username = "#username#" password = "#password#">
```

This is pretty basic. We're opening a connection to a specific server and mailbox with a specific username and password. The `connection` attribute designates the name of the reusable connection variable. For the rest of our requests, we reuse exConn to communicate with the Exchange Server.

Everything has a beginning and an end, except for Exchange connections. If you don't close them, they'll stay open on the Exchange Server side indefinitely. Therefore, always close your connections when you're finished with them. Listing 16-2 shows how to close your Exchange connection.

*Listing 16-2. Closing the connection*

```
<cfexchangeconnection action = "close" connection = "exConn">
```

Closing connections is important for other reasons as well. The Exchange Server will support only so many open connections before performance suffers. Your Exchange administrators are probably going to be wary of you connecting to their servers. So don't tick them off by eating up all of their connections.

# Using cfexchangecalendar, cfexchangecontact, and cfexchangetask

I've lumped the `cfexchangecalendar`, `cfexchangecontact`, and `cfexchangetask` tags together because they allow you to do similar things:

- Create items (`action="create"`)

- Search for items (`action="get"`)

- Update items (`action="modify"`)

- View files attached to items (`action="getAttachments"`)

- Delete files attached to items (`action="deleteAttachments"`)

- Delete items (`action="delete"`)

## Creating an Item Structure

For the `create` and `modify` actions, you need to build a structure containing the information, as shown in the example in Listing 16-3. Each item type has its own list of valid keys for that structure. The canonical list is available in Adobe's *ColdFusion Developer's Guide* ((http://help.adobe.com/en_US/ColdFusion/9.0/CFMLRef/index.html).

*Listing 16-3. An example of a contact structure*

```
<cfset contact = structNew()>
<cfset contact['FirstName'] = "Terrence">
<cfset contact['LastName'] = "Ryan">
<cfset contact['email1'] = "terry@numtopia.com">
<cfset contact['JobTitle'] = "I.T. Director">
<cfset contact['Company'] = "The Wharton School">
<cfset contact['WebPage'] = "http://www.numtopia.com/terry">
<cfset contact['BusinessAddress'] = structNew()>
<cfset contact['BusinessAddress']['Street']= "3733 Spruce Street Suite 200">
<cfset contact['BusinessAddress']['City'] = "Philadelphia">
<cfset contact['BusinessAddress']['State'] = "PA">
<cfset contact['BusinessAddress']['Zip'] = "19130">
<cfset contact['BusinessAddress']['Country'] = "USA">
```

The structure is the same whether you are creating or updating an item. Each key value is optional, but at least one must be set. Most key values will be strings, but there are a few exceptions:

- Addresses in contacts are structures.

- Date fields in calendar items and task items are ColdFusion-formatted dates.

- Calendar items have several fields, related to recurring appointments and sensitivity, that take specific keywords.

- Priority and status in task items also take a list of specific keywords.

- Various number values require specific ranges of integers.

## Creating and Getting Items

Now that we've created the structure for an item's data, it's quite easy to create the item. Listing 16-4 shows some code for creating a new Exchange contact.

*Listing 16-4. Creating an Exchange contact*

```
<cfexchangecontact action = "create" contact = "#contact#" connection = "exConn"
    result="contactUID">
```

Getting existing items is also pretty straightforward, as shown in Listing 16-5.

*Listing 16-5. Getting a list of tasks*

```
<cfexchangetask action = "get" name = "taskList" connection = "exConn">
```

Listing 16-5 will return your normal, run-of-the-mill ColdFusion query. The columns that are returned are particular to each item type. See your trusty *ColdFusion Developer's Guide* for full details. By default, this query will return a maximum of 100 records. There is a way to increase that limit using the `cfexchangefilter` tag, as you'll see in the discussion of that tag.

## Getting a UID

In Listing 16-4, notice that we added an attribute named `result` to the `cfexchangecontact` tag. This attribute captures the unique identifier (UID) of the newly created Exchange item. The UID is necessary for performing targeted operations that affect the content of existing items. It must be passed into the `modify`, `getAttachments`, `deleteAttachments`, and `delete` actions.

There are only two ways to get a UID:

- Capture it using the `result` attribute of a `create` action.

- Grab it from a query returned by the `get` action.

## Updating and Deleting Items

Armed with a UID and a contact structure, we can now update an item (see Listing 16-6). It's pretty much just the same as creating one, except that we are using the UID to target the contact we want.

*Listing 16-6. Updating a contact*

```
<cfset contact = structNew()>
<cfset contact['FirstName'] = "Terrence">
<cfset contact['LastName'] = "Ryan">
<cfset contact['email1'] = "terry@numtopia.com">
<cfset contact['JobTitle'] = "I.T. Director">
<cfset contact['Company'] = "The Wharton School">
<cfset contact['WebPage'] = "http://www.numtopia.com/terry">
<cfset contact['BusinessAddress'] = structNew()>
<cfset contact['BusinessAddress']['Street']="3733 Spruce Street Suite 200">
<cfset contact['BusinessAddress']['City'] = "Philadelphia">
<cfset contact['BusinessAddress']['State'] = "PA">
<cfset contact['BusinessAddress']['Zip'] = "19130">
<cfset contact['BusinessAddress']['Country'] = "USA">
<cfexchangecontact action = "modify" contact = "#contact#" connection = "exConn"
        uid="#contactUID#">
```

Once you have the UID, deleting an item is incredibly simple, as shown in Listing 16-7.

*Listing 16-7. Deleting an item*

```
<cfexchangecontact action= "delete" connection= "exConn" result="contactUID">
```

## Working with Attachments

Working with files attached to items requires a UID. Using the UID, we target an item, call the getAttachments action, and then work with the files on the local file system. This will do two things:

- Create a query displaying the details of the files attached.

- Download the files from Exchange to the ColdFusion server, if an attachmentPath attribute is set.

Listing 16-8 shows an example of getting attachments from an Exchange item.

*Listing 16-8. Getting the attachments from an Exchange item*

```
<cfexchangecontact action = "getAttachments" name = "contactAttachments"
    uid = "#contactUID#" connection = "exConn" attachmentPath = "#path#">
```

If you don't set attachmentPath, you can evaluate the details of the attachments before downloading them. If you do set attachmentPath, you'll need to wait for the files to transfer over. After the files have been downloaded, you can work with them as you would any other files.

Deleting attachments is even easier. But be careful, because it's almost too easy. Calling the `deleteAttachments` action will delete all attachments on the item in one shot; you cannot delete just one attachment. Listing 16-9 shows an example of deleting attachments.

*Listing 16-9. Deleting all attachments of an Exchange item*

```
<cfexchangecontact action = "deleteAttachments" uid = "#contactUID#"
    connection = "exConn">
```

# Using cfexchangemail

Most of the actions that you can perform on other types of items will also work with `cfexchangemail`. `delete`, `deleteAttachments`, `get`, and `getAttachments` work the same as they do for the other types of items. However, `create` and `modify` will not work at all. It makes sense, because from a workflow standpoint, you don't create e-mail. You receive it—someone else created it. Likewise, you don't really modify e-mail. You might forward a copy, or reply with the original edited inline, but seldom do you ever actually modify the e-mail in your inbox.

There are also actions that are unique to the `cfexchangemail` tag, including the following:

- Get extra details about meeting requests (`action="getMeetingInfo"`)

- Move messages between folders (`action="move"`)

- Set particular attributes about a message (`action="set"`)

## Dealing with Meeting Requests

Meeting requests have extra information that is not visible in the query returned from a `get` action. You get to this information with the `getMeetingInfo` action. But in order to perform this action, you need a meeting UID, which must come from a `get` query. It may seem very convoluted, but it looks something like Listing 16-10.

*Listing 16-10. Reading meeting requests*

```
<cfexchangemail action="get" name="inbox" connection="exConn" folder="Inbox">
    <cfexchangefilter name="timeReceived" from="#start#" to="#end#">
</cfexchangemail>

<cfloop query="inbox">
    <cfif len(meetingUID) gt 1>
    <!--- meetingUID is a column returned by the get operation above  --->
        <cfexchangemail action = "getMeetingInfo" meetingUID = "#meetingUID#"
                name = "meetingRequest" connection = "exConn">
    </cfif>
</cfloop>
```

## Moving Mail Items

Mail items can be moved, but this can be a little dangerous. To understand why, note first that you use the same techniques that you use to get a message, which means heavy use of `cfexchangefilter`, as shown in Listing 16-11.

*Listing 16-11. Moving a mail item to the Deleted Items folder*

```
<cfexchangemail action="move" destinationFolder="Deleted Items"
        connection="exConn">
   <cfexchangefilter name = "uid" value="#messageUID#">
</cfexchangemail>
```

Using loosely written or unspecific filters means that you risk moving large chucks of e-mail unwittingly. Therefore, I recommend filtering on the UID using `cfexchangefilter` tag (discussed shortly) when performing move operations, as in Listing 16-11.

## Setting Attributes on Mail Items

You cannot modify mail items completely, but you can modify the following attributes of the mail message:

- Whether or not the message is marked as read
- The importance of the message
- The sensitivity of the message

You manipulate all this through a structure, as shown in Listing 16-12.

*Listing 16-12. Setting a mail item*

```
<cfset message = StructNew()>
<cfset message['IsRead'] = "no">
<cfset message['Importance'] = "high">
<cfset message['Sensitivity'] = "private">

<cfexchangemail action="set" message="#message#" uid="#messageUID#"
        connection="exConn">
```

# Using cfexchangefilter

You may have noticed that the `cfexchangefilter` tag was referenced several times in the previous examples. It must be called with an action of `get` as a child tag of the `cfexchangecalendar`, `cfexchangecontact`, `cfexchangemail`, or `cfexchangetask` tag, or alternatively, as a child of the `cfexchangemail` tag with an action of `move`. This tag lets you refine searches against the Exchange mailbox store.

You can filter only a single attribute of an Exchange object for each call of `cfexchangefilter`. You can search with either a single value or a date range. Listings 16-13 and 16-14 show examples of filtering.

*Listing 16-13. Filtering on a wildcard search—all appointments with a subject related to something called Max*

```
<cfexchangecalendar action = "get" name = "calendar1" connection = "exConn">
    <cfexchangefilter name="subject" value="Max">
</cfexchangecalendar>
```

*Listing 16-14. Filtering on a date range—all appointments starting within the next seven days*

```
<cfexchangecalendar action = "get" name = "calendar2" connection = "exConn">
    <cfexchangefilter name="startTime" from="#now()#" to="#DateAdd('d', 7, now())#">
</cfexchangecalendar>
```

It's also possible to stack filters to build complex queries that filter on multiple fields, as shown in Listing 16-15.

*Listing 16-15. Stacking filters to find every event this week that was Flag Day*

```
<cfexchangecalendar action = "get" name = "calendar3" connection = "exConn">
    <cfexchangefilter name="startTime" from="#now()#" to="#DateAdd('d', 7, now())#">
    <cfexchangefilter name = "AllDayEvent" value = "TRUE">
    <cfexchangefilter name = "subject" value = "Flag Day">
</cfexchangecalendar>
```

Of course, you can search any item type, as shown in Listing 16-16.

*Listing 16-16. Searching for my Ben Forte contact*

```
<cfexchangecontact action = "get" name = "contactList" connection = "exConn">
    <cfexchangefilter name = "displayAs" value = "Forta, Ben">
</cfexchangecontact>
```

Note that the value filters are implicitly wildcard, so searching for a `displayAs` value of `"Forta, Ben"` will yield just Ben Forta, but setting the filter to `"Ben"` will yield Ben Forta and Ben Nadel.

# ColdFusion and Exchange Interaction Best Practices

You have the basics down and can now use ColdFusion to interact with Exchange. However, there are some thorny issues when dealing with Exchange. Here are some tips to help you handle them.

## Connections

When doing more than one operation at a time, I recommend that you reuse a connection instead of making ad hoc connections for each call. Creating the connection is relatively expensive—about twice as long as a single tag call.

Additionally, if you are accessing the same user's mailbox in your application, I strongly recommend putting that connection into the Session scope, so that you can reuse it.

Finally, I have to reiterate: close those connections down when they are done. In the case of Session-stored connections, close them in the onSessionEnd method of your Application.cfc.

## Service Accounts

If you plan on incorporating Exchange connectivity into your application, I recommend creating or obtaining a dedicated service account for this purpose, instead of passing an actual user's credentials. It will be easier for the Exchange administrators to keep track of it. It will also be easier for you to troubleshoot. Suppose a connectivity problem is due to a change in Active Directory password policy—try tracking that down! Also, you won't need to cache a real user's password someplace where it could be accidentally exposed through debugging or error messages.

## SSL

Speaking of exposing sensitive data, you should take advantage of the https connection instead of passing the username and password over an HTTP connection. There may be a few issues with this, however.

It's possible that your Exchange administrators do not have an SSL certificate on the HTTPS port of the Exchange Server, especially if you don't have dedicated Outlook Web Access servers and need to connect to back-end Exchange Servers. Even if they are secured with a certificate, since they're not public, they may be using an organizational certificate instead of a public certificate issued by a certificate authority. If this is the case, you will need to import the certificate into the cacert file of your installation of JRun or ColdFusion. For details on how to do this, see the *ColdFusion Developer's Guide*.

# Conclusion

The ColdFusion development team members have really outdone themselves with the Microsoft Exchange integration in ColdFusion. Not only is it a powerful, much-requested feature, but it's actually much easier to use than any other programmatic interface I've seen for Exchange, including Microsoft .NET Exchange APIs. So get to programming! I look forward to the day that I can replace Outlook with a desktop client written with Adobe AIR and ColdFusion.

# CHAPTER 17

■■■

# BlazeDS

## by John Mason

*When Adobe introduced BlazeDS, a free, open source messaging system, there was a lot of buzz in the ColdFusion community—and some confusion. While eager to try the product, some ColdFusion developers did not understand its capabilities or the differences between BlazeDS and LiveCycle Data Services (LCDS), Adobe's commercial messaging system. This article dispels any confusion you might have and presents BlazeDS as a free alternative to LCDS.*

Adobe's release of BlazeDS, an open source messaging system with some of the features of LCDS, has generated considerable discussion. I will briefly explain what BlazeDS is and, more important, what it is not. We will also explore how Blaze relates to LCDS and then demonstrate how to use BlazeDS with a ColdFusion event gateway in a simple but useful example.

## Messaging Patterns

Servers and applications have to find ways to communicate with each other. Several messaging patterns have been developed for that purpose over the years. Web developers most often work with a pull model, also called request/response. A client browser requests a web page, and the server responds with an HTML-formatted document that the browser processes and then displays. The browser essentially initiates the communication and pulls the information it needs from the server.

Look at all the progress that stems from this idea. Naturally, a pull methodology implies that a push exists as well. Streaming, for example, is a push technology. The client doesn't know what it needs, so it can't directly request it as in the pull. But it can subscribe to a channel that has the information it needs. Think of a news channel on TV. You don't know what the news is, but you do know that the channel has the information you are looking for. The news station publishes content over the channel to you and anybody else tuned in. It's a fairly simple idea, but you can do a lot with it.

Pull patterns include the common POST and GET requests in the HTTP protocol. We work with these all the time. Web services follow a pull pattern where the client makes a request and the server provides a standardized XML/SOAP response. Remote Objects and common Remote Procedure Call (RPC) methods in the Flex world also serve as pulls. For example, we can invoke a ColdFusion CFC method as if it were an ActionScript object.

Streaming is the most common push pattern. The HTTP protocol has had specifications for streaming since version 1.1 in the late 1990s, and BlazeDS does provide HTTP streaming in addition to Action Message Format (AMF) streaming. AMF is a specification that Adobe developed over the years and published in December 2007. AMF serializes data into a binary format, which is very useful for sending large amounts of data and provides a much faster transmission.

## BlazeDS vs. LCDS

Built on Java, the BlazeDS messaging service infrastructure contains pull patterns, pull patterns that look and feel like push, and a couple of push or streaming patterns. It also has a proxy service that allows Flex applications to access services outside their domains. Using AMF serialization with these patterns provides speed and performance when sending or receiving messages. BlazeDS does not, however, have the Real Time Messaging Protocol (RTMP) found in LCDS. This is an important drawback because the HTTP and AMF streaming that BlazeDS provides is not reliable for many real-world applications. You need RTMP, and more specifically RTMP tunneling, to make a dependable push pattern work. Hence, the confusion about whether or not BlazeDS has push technology. It does, but LCDS is superior with RTMP.

LCDS also scales better than BlazeDS. This capacity is what you pay for when you purchase LCDS. Depending on the Java Virtual Machine's (JVM) configuration and memory heap size, you can service a few hundred clients with BlazeDS. With LCDS, however, you should be able to run that into the thousands. But before you get discouraged by this, BlazeDS still has a lot of benefits, as you will soon see. It provides some very useful tools, and, as opposed to LCDS, costs nothing to use.

## What's in a Name?

The names of these products and the fact that they offer similar features also causes confusion. Here's a short description of each that should help:

- LiveCycle ES (Enterprise Suite) integrates several products, and includes features like PDF generation, digital signing, and data services. You can purchase the various products separately or the entire suite.

- The data services component of LiveCycle ES is naturally called LiveCycle DS (LCDS). This product used to be named Flex Data Services (FDS), which, of course, causes still more confusion.

- BlazeDS has remoting, proxy, and messaging services. You will find these same services in LCDS. However, BlazeDS left several items out, such as RTMP, message queuing, lazy loading, and data synchronization.

- LiveCycle DS Community Edition is really BlazeDS with a paid Adobe support subscription.

- Finally, LiveCycle Express is a single-CPU version of LCDS that can be installed with ColdFusion 8.

## Enterprise Service Bus (ESB)

Several people have noted with LCDS and BlazeDS that we are looking at an enterprise service bus architecture. What is an ESB, what benefits does it bring, and why would we want to use one?

Typically, clients and services communicate directly with each other, as illustrated in Figure 17-1.

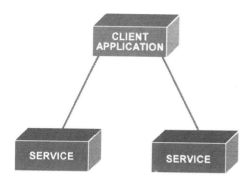

*Figure 17-1. Client and services*

For this to work, the clients have to know the location of the services and their methods of communication. If the services move, then the clients need modifications to properly take note of the change. Take a Flex application that reads data from a web service. If the web service location changes, the Flex application may require an update, which can be a time-consuming and messy process.

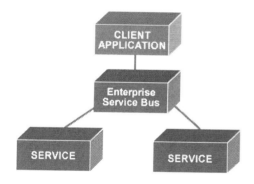

*Figure 17-2. Enterprise service bus*

Figure 17-2 shows how a service bus injected between the clients and the service providers can decouple them. Now the clients only have to know how to connect to the service bus. They may not even really know what the service providers are or from where the services are coming. This is called service location transparency.

A service bus also provides a clear service-oriented architecture (SOA) where you have three distinct players: service provider, service broker, and service requestor. This concept is similar to model-view-controller (MVC) architecture in that by separating these functions, we gain greater flexibility for growth and change. The services can move or change in many ways and not disrupt anything for the end clients. So thinking of BlazeDS or LCDS as part of an ESB can help a ColdFusion or Flex developer see why she might want to use it.

## Installing BlazeDS with ColdFusion

ColdFusion 8 can be installed with a single-processor version of LCDS called LiveCycle Express. You can start using this version of LiveCycle, but bear in mind that it's a limited version. BlazeDS, on the other hand, has no restrictions and is free to use. So in many situations, you will want to use BlazeDS instead.

BlazeDS is easier to use and set up when it is integrated with ColdFusion, and it runs off the same JVM. Follow the installation guide at `http://opensource.adobe.com/wiki/display/blazeds/Installation+Guide`. BlazeDS will install on ColdFusion 7, but requires version 7.0.2 or higher to run. This article assumes you have BlazeDS installed and integrated with ColdFusion.

# Messaging Framework

BlazeDS has three basic frameworks for handling communication: remote, proxy, and messaging. The remote framework calls things like remote objects, and if you have been doing any Flex development, you have probably used remoting services. Proxy frameworks allow Flex applications to call services outside their domain without a `crossdomain.xml` policy file. We won't review the remote and proxy frameworks in this article. I have a recorded presentation and sample code of all the BlazeDS functions at `http://labs.fusionlink.com`. We will instead focus in this article on the messaging service.

The message framework in BlazeDS has an asynchronous message pattern. Senders (producers) of messages don't send their messages to specific receivers (consumers), but rather to a destination that handles the routing, filtering, and forwarding of messages. This framework, also called subscribe/publish or producer/consumer, is a part of a larger architecture called message-oriented middleware (MOM). Do not confuse client/server and producer/consumer. The client can be a producer or a consumer, or both. The same holds true with the server. The client/server distinction exists at the physical level. The producer/consumer distinction is logical.

Consumers and producers communicate through the service destination via channels, shown in Figure 17-3.

*Figure 17-3. Channels*

These channels are accessed through adapters, which work like the network adapter on your computer. The `messaging-config.xml` configuration file contains three basic adapters: cfgateway, ActionScript, and JMS. As you might suspect, you need the cfgateway adapter for ColdFusion to access a destination with an event gateway. The ActionScript adapter similarly allows a Flex application to communicate. Adapters conveniently keep the ColdFusion event gateway or Flex applications from needing to know details of communicating with the messaging service. You can also create your own adapters to expand the capabilities of BlazeDS.

The channel will format the message and deliver it to the endpoint. The endpoint translates the message into a Java object that the message broker inside the service destination can understand. The message broker deals with the routing and queuing of the messages.

BlazeDS gives us several channel types:

- HTTP

- AMF

- AMF with polling

- AMF with long polling

- HTTP streaming

- AMF streaming

All of these channels have nonsecure versions and secure SSL versions. HTTP and AMF channels do typical request/response calls like web services. The HTTP channels send data as text. Since AMF sends binary-encoded data, it provides better performance. I would encourage you to use it whenever possible.

The streaming channels could provide a push strategy, but a variety of issues such as proxy servers, reverse proxies, and firewalls can delay or disrupt a stream, making these channels unreliable. The RTMP protocol was designed to address these problems, but once again it's not included with BlazeDS. You can, however, use a polling channel as a fallback where streaming does not work.

Polling is really a pull strategy but has the look and feel of a server-side push. Polling puts a greater load on the server than streaming because of the increased chatter between client and server. Depending on your application, you could use a piggyback method to create a pseudo-poll framework or to make a standard poll method more efficient. I'm not going to go over piggybacking here, but it is an option in certain circumstances.

In standard polling, shown in Figure 17-4, the subscriber simply sends a series of requests to the service. The service, in turn, sends back either an acknowledgment or a message (if one exists in the queue).

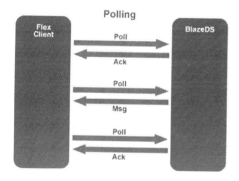

*Figure 17-4. Polling*

The client and server chat continuously with each other, which is not an efficient use of resources. Processing may also feel slow to the user, depending on the timing of each request cycle. The cycle may run every five seconds, so the user could see a delay between sending a message and receiving it. See Figure 17-5. Long polling tries to solve these problems.

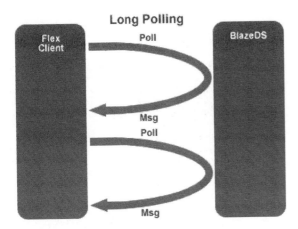

*Figure 17-5. Long polling*

When the client sends a request to the service, the service waits until a message is in queue to send a response. This decreases the chatter and greatly increases the responsiveness. Connections still open and close several times, but long polling looks and feels a lot like a server push. Frankly, your users will not know the difference. This doesn't scale as well as streaming, but in many cases that will not be an issue.

In streaming, as in long polling, the client makes a request to the server, but the response is held open by the server. The server then streams information out over the wire. In this case, the server takes on the responsibility of keeping the communication running by sending very small pings over the line. This prevents HTTP time-outs and other factors from trying to close down the stream. So in a proper stream, there is only one request and a very long response that never closes until the client or server turns it off. While the line is open, the server pushes data out to the client.

## Running BlazeDS with a ColdFusion Event Gateway

Now let's set up a simple example with a ColdFusion event gateway and see what it can do. Let's say we have a web site throwing several errors that we want to track down and debug in real time. Though cferror can catch these exceptions and then e-mail them to us, we find this slow and frustrating and would prefer to see these errors in real time as they pop up. With BlazeDS, we can do this fairly easily. Instead of sending these errors via e-mail, we send them through an event gateway to BlazeDS. In turn, BlazeDS forwards them to a Flex or AIR application. This will be similar to the Linux tail function showing us the errors in real time.

First, we need to create the BlazeDS destination with its associated channel and endpoint. We open our messaging-config.xml file and simply put in a new destination node called siteerrors.

```
<destination id="siteerrors"/>
```

Take a look at Listing 17-1. The destination will use the available adapters and the default channels. We could stop here, but we will go a step further and tell the destination to listen for the ColdFusion gateway and to use long polling first, then fall back to standard polling if that doesn't work. You could also put streaming as the first choice for those who are able to connect via streaming. If the stream can't be established, then BlazeDS will simply fall back to a poll. Again, we are also going to use AMF with our channel since it's more efficient.

*Listing 17-1. Destination Properties*

```
<destination id="siteerrors">
<properties>
    <gatewayid>errorsgateway</gatewayid>
</properties>

<channels>
    <channel ref="cf-longpolling-amf"/>
    <channel ref="cf-polling-amf"/>
</channels>
</destination>
```

In Listing 17-2 you can see that the channel endpoints are typically defined in the services-config.xml file. You may or may not have these definitions in place, or they may have slightly different identification labels. The key is to have a channel that has both polling and long polling formats. You can name them anything you like.

*Listing 17-2. Defining the Channel Endpoints*

```
<channel-definition id="cf-longpolling-amf"
    class="mx.messaging.channels.AMFChannel">
    <endpoint uri="http://{server.name}:
        {server.port}/{context.root}/flex2gateway/cfamflongpolling"
        class="flex.messaging.endpoints.AMFEndpoint"/>
    <properties>
        <polling-enabled>true</polling-enabled>
        <polling-interval-seconds>5</polling-interval-seconds>
        <wait-interval-millis>60000</wait-interval-millis>
        <client-wait-interval-millis>1</client-wait-interval-millis>
        <max-waiting-poll-requests>200</max-waiting-poll-requests>
    </properties>
</channel-definition>

<channel-definition id="cf-polling-amf"
      class="mx.messaging.channels.AMFChannel">
    <endpoint uri="http://{server.name}:
        {server.port}{context.root}/flex2gateway/cfamfpolling"
        class="flex.messaging.endpoints.AMFEndpoint"/>
    <properties>
        <polling-enabled>true</polling-enabled>
        <polling-interval-seconds>3</polling-interval-seconds>
        <serialization>
            <instantiate-types>false</instantiate-types>
        </serialization>
    </properties>
</channel-definition>
```

The URL for these endpoints can vary. With BlazeDS running on top of Tomcat, your URL might contain **messagebroker** instead of **flex2gateway**. The channel id and the last part of the endpoint URL can be anything you like, as long as it's unique.

Channel properties are fairly easy to understand. They deal with the polling times, time-outs, and so on. After we set this up, we just restart ColdFusion and we have an active BlazeDS destination service. It's important to note that we can start the ColdFusion service at the command line to see if the destination loads up correctly without errors. This also allows us to see any problems as messages are published.

Now we need a ColdFusion event gateway to link up our destination to ColdFusion. See Figure 17-6.

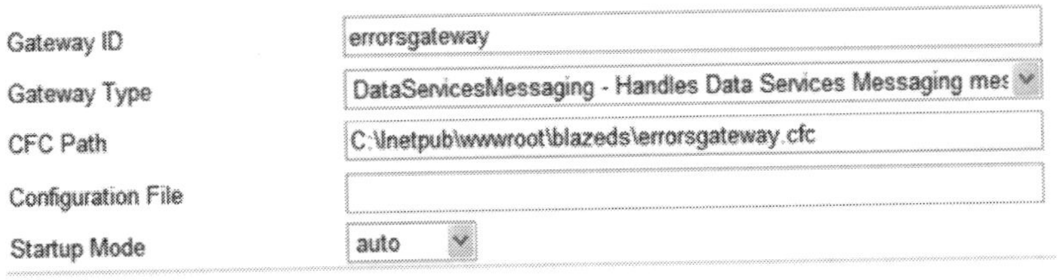

| Gateway ID | errorsgateway |
| Gateway Type | DataServicesMessaging - Handles Data Services Messaging mes ▾ |
| CFC Path | C:\Inetpub\wwwroot\blazeds\errorsgateway.cfc |
| Configuration File | |
| Startup Mode | auto ▾ |

*Figure 17-6. Event gateway*

Since we are just publishing from ColdFusion, our **errorsgateway.cfc**, shown in Listing 17-3, is really simple:

*Listing 17-3. A Simple Event Gateway (errorsgateway.cfc)*

```
<cfcomponent output="false">
</cfcomponent>
```

If we wanted the gateway to be a consumer, then we would have a method in our CFC called **onIncomingMessage** with a structure as the single argument variable.

The gateway should auto-start when we add it. Be patient. It may take a minute. Once the gateway is up and running, we can publish messages from ColdFusion to BlazeDS with the **SendGatewayMessage()** function. So we can put this code into a **cferror** page, inside an **onError** method in an **Application.cfc**, or in a **cfcatch** block to send these error messages to BlazeDS.

Say we are using this code inside a **cfcatch** block to alert us to a failed login attempt:

*Listing 17-4. The Message Structure*

```
<cfset body = structNew()>
<cfset body.detail = "A failed login detected with #form.username#
    as a username from #cgi.remote_addr#">
<cfset body.message = "Failed Login">
<cfset body.type = "Information">
<cfset message = StructNew()>
<cfset message.body = body>
<cfset message.Destination = "siteerrors">
<cfset SendGatewayMessage("errorsgateway", message)>
```

The message is a structure that contains the location of the destination and the message body. In Listing 17-4, the message body is also a structure, but it can be whatever you like. You could use an array or query just as easily.

Now we have both the destination service and the publisher. But we need a Flex application to subscribe to and read the messages. Let's create a new Flex project in Flex Builder. We won't bother with the server technology wizard provided in the setup utility. For simplicity, we'll just point the builder arguments to our `services-config.xml` file. When we have established the project, right-click and go to the project's Properties, then to Flex Compiler. See Figure 17-7. Under Additional compiler arguments, we will add a couple of parameters.

*Figure 17-7. Additional compiler arguments*

First, a services variable will point to our `services-config.xml` file. This file will help tell Flex how to properly talk to BlazeDS. The `context-root` variable is also needed for the project to successfully compile. I would normally recommend doing this inside ActionScript instead. For one thing, your `services-config` may not match the one running on your ISP's server. As a result, many Flex developers control these variables internally with ActionScript and avoid pointing to a `services-config` file. We are simply using this method here because it's easier to set up and you can follow along.

The Flex `mx:Consumer` tag consumes messages sent via BlazeDS. In Listing 17-5 we will use this tag to subscribe to and consume the service feed. The messages will populate an `ArrayCollection`, which in turn will be the `dataProvider` for our `DataGrid`. If you click on an item in the `DataGrid`, then the bottom `TextArea` will display the `DETAIL` node of our message structure.

*Listing 17-5. Consuming the Message*

```
<?xml version="1.0" encoding="utf-8"?>
<mx:Application
    xmlns:mx="http://www.adobe.com/2006/mxml"
    layout="absolute"
    creationComplete="init()">

    <mx:Script>
        <![CDATA[
            import mx.messaging.events.MessageEvent;
            import mx.messaging.messages.AsyncMessage;
            import mx.messaging.messages.IMessage;
            import mx.collections.ArrayCollection;
            import mx.events.ListEvent;

            [Bindable]
            public var messages:ArrayCollection = new ArrayCollection;
```

```
        public function init():void{
           consumer.subscribe();
         }

        private function messageHandler(message:IMessage):void{
            //The zero index makes certain the newest message is on top
            messages.addItemAt(message.body,0);
        }

    ]]>
  </mx:Script>

  <mx:Consumer id="consumer" destination="siteerrors"
      message="messageHandler(event.message)"/>

  <mx:Panel title="Errors" width="100%" height="100%">
      <mx:DataGrid id="errorslist" width="100%" dataProvider="{messages}">
          <mx:columns>
              <mx:DataGridColumn width="100" dataField="TYPE"
                  headerText="Type" />
              <mx:DataGridColumn dataField="MESSAGE"
                  headerText="Message" />
          </mx:columns>
      </mx:DataGrid>
      <mx:TextArea id="msgDetails" width="100%" height="100%"
          htmlText="{errorslist.selectedItem.DETAIL}"/>
  </mx:Panel>

</mx:Application>
```

When you run this Flex application, you should see something like the following.

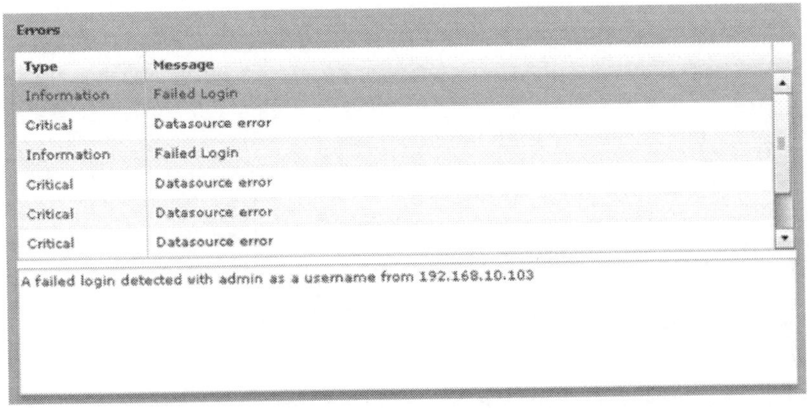

*Figure 17-8. Example Flex application*

An error caught by the `cfcatch` will get sent through the event gateway to BlazeDS, which in turn will send those messages to the Flex application, as in Figure 17-8. We now have a very simple but handy tool to see site errors as they happen in real time. We don't have to hit refresh on the browser or anything—the polling will run in the background and the messages will display as they come over the wire. You could give this application to your support staff or programmers so they can see these errors as well, which would help diagnosis problems people encounter with your ColdFusion application. This could also make a very useful AIR application.

See Listing 17-6. If you wanted the Flex client to publish messages, you could use the `<mx:Producer>` tag.

```
<mx:Producer id="producer" destination="siteerrors"/>
```

Then you could format the same message structure and publish it to the service.

*Listing 17-6. Publishing the Message*

```
private function send():void{
    var message:IMessage = new AsyncMessage();
    message.body.DETAIL = "Detail of the message";
    message.body.MESSAGE = "Error message name";
    message.body.TYPE = "Information";
    producer.send(message);
}
```

A couple of things to note: ColdFusion is not case sensitive, where Flex is. ColdFusion uppercases the variable names in the background because of the Java environment. That can throw you when you try to call a variable as `message.body.detail` instead of `message.body.DETAIL`.

# Concluding Thoughts

A true push strategy with BlazeDS is not really practical for many applications, but you can simulate it fairly well. Once again, your users will not know the difference. If you really want to use RTMP instead, then I would encourage you to either obtain the full version of LiveCycle DS or use the LiveCycle Express edition that comes with ColdFusion 8.

Because of the open source license, developers have started to provide solutions to the missing elements in BlazeDS. For example, lazy loading in LiveCycle DS allows you to initialize only the objects you need. BlazeDS does not have this feature. Digital Primates has developed a solution called dpHibernate, which creates proxies for your real objects with Hibernate. The real object does not actually load until you touch its proxy. When dealing with a large collection of objects, lazy loading can be extremely handy.

The idea of using BlazeDS as part of an enterprise service bus pattern should also pique your interest. ESB has several definitions, and it is a bit of a buzzword these days. I only gave a very simple definition, but I hope you can see that by decoupling these functions your application's infrastructure will be more flexible to changes and more stable in the long run.

I hope this article encourages you to give BlazeDS a run. Adobe only recently joined the open source community with BlazeDS and some other projects. It is up to us to show that the community will provide feedback and support for their efforts. Often the examples for messaging involve chat systems, and I believe this tendency limits people's views of messaging and it capabilities. As a result, I made a point in this article to show a more businesslike problem that BlazeDS can easily solve. Others exist, and clearly messaging will become a more commonly used tool as we move forward with rich Internet applications.

# PART 5

# Object-Oriented Programming (OOP)

■ ■ ■

# CHAPTER 18

# Object-Oriented Programming: Why Bother?

## by Brian Kotek

*Unless you've been living under a rock, you've heard about the increasing focus on object-oriented programming (OOP) in the ColdFusion world. With the advent of ColdFusion Components (CFCs) in ColdFusion MX 6, and the constant improvement to CFCs in every version of ColdFusion since, OOP has not only become possible for ColdFusion developers, but is rapidly becoming the de facto standard for building applications. Why is this? And if you haven't drunk the OOP Kool-Aid yet, why should you care? In this article, I'll start with a brief overview of the fundamentals of OOP. Then I will focus on some reasons for taking the time to learn about it.*

## OOP Fundamentals

I'll try to keep the jargon to a minimum, but unfortunately, a few ideas simply must be covered before any real discussion of OOP can take place. To begin with, *object-oriented programming* should probably be called *class-oriented programming*. When you build an OO application, you start by creating classes. Think of classes as blueprints for objects.

Consider the schematics for a BMW 650i. The schematics are generic and apply to any BMW 650i that could exist. The schematics can be compared to a class in an OO application. You can equate constructing a real, individual—and gorgeous—650i from those schematics to invoking (or instantiating) an object.

In ColdFusion, CFCs take the place of classes. You may write the code for a CFC called Car, but it isn't actually very useful until you use `CreateObject()` to create an actual, individual instance of your Car CFC. Now you have an object that can actually do something!

Objects contain data and behavior, and an OO application does its work by having objects send messages to each other.

The big three elements of OOP are inheritance, polymorphism, and encapsulation.

# Inheritance

*Inheritance* is what you have when an object (the child object) extends or takes on the properties of another object (also known as the *parent* object). Inheritance allows you to create a hierarchy of objects that begin with very general things and progress to very specific things.

For example, you might create an object called `Product`, and within it you might have very general data and behavior that applies to any type of product — data like `productName` or behavior like `calculatePrice()`.With the `Product` class definition as your base, you could then create a more specific child object such as `DownloadableProduct`, which would extend `Product`. `DownloadableProduct` might be an MP3 file or a piece of software, and it might have data and behavior specific to it, such as `fileSize`.

The crucial thing to understand is that `DownloadableProduct` inherits the data and behavior of its parent object `Product`. This eliminates a great deal of code duplication, because anything common to all of your products can be coded once in `Product`, and it will be inherited by all objects that extend `Product`.

# Polymorphism

*Polymorphism* is primarily a side effect of inheritance (in some OO languages, it is possible to gain polymorphism in other ways, but since ColdFusion doesn't support these other ways, I won't complicate the discussion). It sounds fancy, but all it really means is that you can treat child objects that extend a base object just like the base object itself.

To make this clearer, let's continue with the `Product` object example. All objects that extend our `Product` object can respond to the message `calculatePrice()`, because `calculatePrice()` is defined in the `Product`. This means that, from the standpoint of other objects, it doesn't matter which child of the `Product` class they are dealing with—a `DownloadableProduct` or a `PhysicalProduct`. They can call `calculatePrice()` on either one. `DownloadableProduct` and `PhysicalProduct` are said to be *polymorphic*, because from the point of view of any objects that need to interact with them, they both behave the same way.

To put it another way, other objects only need to know that they are dealing with a `Product`. Which specific kind of product they are actually interacting with is completely hidden.

# Encapsulation

The idea of hiding information from the rest of the system forms the third, and in my opinion, the most important, element of OOP: *encapsulation*. Encapsulation comes in many forms. Traditionally, encapsulation refers to hiding the internal implementation of an object from external objects.

In our example, the way a `Product` handles the message `calculatePrice()` is hidden from the outside world. We might start with something simple, such as an internal price variable, and when `calculatePrice()` is called, the object just returns the numeric `price` variable. But because we've hidden the formula by which a `Product` determines its price behind the `calculatePrice()` message, we are free to change it. As our business grows, the simple `price` variable might be replaced with a much more complex series of calculations involving discounts or tiered pricing for larger customers.

In other words, when things are encapsulated, they are hidden. And when things are hidden, they can be changed with minimal impact on the rest of the system. As long as `Products` keep responding to `calculatePrice()` by returning a number, the internal way in which a `Product` actually determines its price can be changed as often as necessary. This is the power of encapsulation.

However, encapsulation actually goes far beyond merely hiding the internal implementation of an object. We already touched on another demonstration of encapsulation when we talked about polymorphism. Because all of our `Products` can respond to `calculatePrice()`, the specific kind of product the system is dealing with is hidden. All of the child objects of Product are hidden behind the base Product object. If the rest of the system only knows about the base Product object, we are free to add or remove specific kinds of products at will.

In essence, any time you are hiding information from the rest of the system, you are leveraging encapsulation. It may take a while to fully wrap your head around this fundamental element of OOP. In traditional OO languages like Java, it is possible to encapsulate object creation, different sets of rules, and entire families of objects. Encapsulation forms the basis of most of the design patterns that are employed when creating well-designed OO systems.

# So What?

I've talked about the fundamental elements of OOP, but why should we ColdFusion developers care? OOP is hard to learn, and it can add complexity to our applications. So why should we bother?

The most common reason cited for using OOP is flexibility. OOP systems are designed to be easy to change. We all know change will happen. Most of the effort in a software project is not actually in building it, but in maintaining it. By encapsulating things that are subject to variation, OOP helps make it easier to cope with change.

I believe this is true, but it is deceptively difficult to prove. Couldn't a well-designed procedural system be made to handle change? Sure it could. Constructs like CFCs give us some helpful tools to manage change, and it is certainly possible to build flexible systems without OOP. I would argue that it is riskier and takes much more care to do so, but no one can deny that it is possible.

In my opinion, the most overpowering reason to learn OOP is your career. Whether you agree or disagree that OOP systems are more flexible than procedural ones is irrelevant. As far as the software development industry is concerned, this debate is already over. OOP has won. Someday, a different approach to software design may come along, but objects are going to rule the field for many years to come. Developers who choose to cling to procedural development will find themselves increasingly marginalized. If you want to continue to be a viable software developer, you simply must learn OOP.

ColdFusion is a wonderful language for learning OOP. Procedural coders can easily begin using CFCs. They can first be leveraged in small ways, and over time, they can become the foundation for entire applications.

Though ColdFusion is a loosely typed language that doesn't offer every OOP feature, all of the essential elements are available, as they are in Java. CFCs allow us to begin thinking in an OO way. They are very capable OOP constructs that can be used with large and complex applications. And the beauty of ColdFusion is that if or when it is needed, we can use the underlying Java platform to perform OOP feats that ColdFusion alone cannot. We've really have the best of both worlds: a rapid language with good OOP capabilities in ColdFusion Markup Language (CFML), and the underlying power and complexity of Java if we really need it. That sounds like a sweet spot to me.

# Where Do I Start?

I hope this overview of OOP helps fuel your desire to learn more about it. Not only is it now a career necessity, but once you "click" with OOP, it really does make it easier to manage change. And, dare I say it, planning and building OOP-based applications is actually fun!

There are many blogs and articles out there that can help you get started, as well as dedicated mailing lists like CFCDev (http://groups.google.com/group/cfcdev). I also recommend reading as much as you can on the subject in books such as the following:

- *Object Technology: A Manager's Guide* by David A. Taylor (Addison-Wesley Professional, 1997)

- *Head First Object-Oriented Analysis and Design* by Brett D. McLaughlin, Gary Pollice, and David West (O'Reilly, 2006)

- *Fundamentals of Object-Oriented Design in UML* by Meilir Page-Jones (Addison-Wesley Professional, 1999)

With all of these resources at your fingertips, there's never been a better time to take on the challenge.

# CHAPTER 19

■ ■ ■

# The Object-Oriented Lexicon

## by Hal Helms

*Learning object-oriented programming brings a whole slew of concepts and terminology that many ColdFusion developers are unprepared for. When we did the object-oriented and frameworks issue (Fusion Authority Quarterly Update Volume 1, Issue 2), I asked Hal Helms to write a lexicon as an easy reference. This was probably the hardest chapter in the whole book to write, and it caused great contention between members of our staff due to the differing philosophical opinions on various items.*

Many of the definitions here are based on Java, the 500-pound gorilla of object-oriented programming (OOP). To apply them to ColdFusion, you may need to go beyond the definitions or limit their scope. This lexicon is meant to give you a basic understanding of the terminology, not to bring you the dogmatic "truth."

**abstract class:** A superclass that is not meant to be instantiated. Abstract classes can have real methods and properties that will be used by their subclasses. Languages that implement the concept of abstract classes usually provide a mechanism for ensuring that they cannot be instantiated; however, ColdFusion does not provide such a mechanism.

**abstraction:** The process of removing details of something in order to reduce it to a set of essential characteristics. By simplifying the thing being modeled, the programmer reduces the original's complexity (without sacrificing the original's essential correctness, we hope). Abstraction is a concept used in many OO techniques, such as abstract classes, base classes, and interfaces.

**aggregation:** A design in which a class holds objects as instance variables. For example, a `Department` class might hold an array of `Employee` objects as well as a `Manager` object (see Figure 19-1). Aggregation often increases the flexibility of a design as it allows for polymorphic variations, which nonobject types do not. You could, for example, provide a subclass of `Employee` to the `Department` class with no ill effects (see *Liskoff Substitution Principle*).

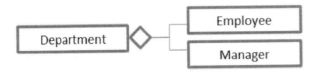

*Figure 19-1. Department aggregates Employee and Manager*

**API (application programming interface):** Implements the principle of information-hiding by providing a public, well-defined, stable set of methods that expose the intended functionality of a class. APIs can be written on the small scale (e.g., a class's public methods) and the large scale (e.g., a published API for an entire application composed of many classes).

**argument:** A value passed to a method.

**base class:** A class that is extended by other classes; also called a superclass. (See also *inheritance.*)

**class:** A type specification, or blueprint, used to instantiate objects. (Contrast with the *abstract class*, which cannot be used to instantiate objects.) Classes typically have methods and instance variables. ColdFusion refers to classes as components (CFCs).

**class variable:** A variable shared by all instances of a class. For every class instance, the value of the variable is the same. If one instance changes the value of this variable, the variable's value will be changed for all instances. For example, a class defining a 2010 Mercedes SL-550 might have a `carsRegistered` variable that tracks the number of these cars registered. All instances of this class will have the same value for this variable.

**component:** See *class.*

**composition:** A stronger form of aggregation in which the class cannot exist without its composite parts. A `Triangle` class would be composed of three individual `Line` objects (see Figure 19-2); remove any of these `Line` objects, and the `Triangle` object is incoherent. The compositing class often handles the instantiation of composite parts itself.

*Figure 19-2. Triangle is composed of Line*

constructor: A special method responsible for object creation. To get around the lack of true constructors in ColdFusion, a best practice is to provide an init method that programmers agree to call when creating objects, as in this example:

```
<cfset hal = CreateObject('component', 'ColdFusionProgrammer').init()>
```

Constructors, like other methods, can take arguments. (See "Tipical Charlie—How Do I Call Thee, CFC?" in *Fusion Authority Quarterly Update Volume 1, Issue 2* for more on object instantiation.)

design pattern: A time-tested architectural solution to a recurring problem. The term was coined by Christopher Alexander, a building architect, and was adopted by the Gang of Four (Erich Gamma, Richard Helm, Ralph Johnson, and John Vlissides) in their seminal work, *Design Patterns: Elements of Reusable Object-Oriented Software* (Addison-Wesley, 1994). There are often several design patterns for a single recurring problem. The choice of design pattern depends largely on the context of the problem and the trade-offs involved in choosing one design pattern over another. Used properly, design patterns allow the architect to adopt best-practice solutions while avoiding short-term fixes that might have pitfalls.

domain model: The set of classes (and/or interfaces) that model a business or organization. Domain models are, to a large degree, independent of any specific application. Domain models are commonly expressed in Unified Modeling Language (UML) diagrams.

dynamic typing: A feature of a language in which a variable's (data) type is determined at runtime. Ruby, Smalltalk, and ColdFusion are examples of dynamically typed languages. Dynamic typing is sometimes referred to as weak typing. Dynamically typed languages are not type-safe. (Contrast with *static typing*.)

encapsulation: The architectural practice of designing components such that their public functionality is exposed only through an API, rather than through direct manipulation of the component's internals. Such information-hiding is key to the nature of OOP. A class is an example of encapsulation—its internals are hidden, and desired functionality is exposed through public methods. On a larger scale, design patterns such as Facade are also based on the idea of encapsulation, where an entire subsystem of functionality is hidden behind a single API.

Encapsulation makes writing code easier. Team members need to know only the component's API and not its internal representation. Encapsulation also makes maintaining code easier, as a component's implementation details may undergo significant changes without affecting other parts of a program that make use of the encapsulated component.

information-hiding: Closely related to encapsulation, the principle that a component's implementation should be hidden, allowing the designer to expose functionality through an API.

inheritance: A mechanism whereby a more specific class borrows the methods and variables from a more general class. For example, a Vehicle class may define certain methods and instance variables common to all vehicle types. That base class might then be extended by more specific types of vehicles, such as Car and Motorcycle, which automatically inherit Vehicle's methods and properties. We say that the Vehicle class is a *superclass* to Car and Motorcycle. It could also be said that Car and Motorcycle are *subclasses* to Vehicle.

Language designers must choose between offering single inheritance (where a class can extend only one other class) and multiple inheritance (where a class can extend many classes). Multiple inheritance has proven problematic and has fallen into disuse. Interfaces provide many of the advantages of multiple inheritance without the drawbacks.

Inheritance is a powerful but overused aspect of OOP. In their book, *Design Patterns: Elements of Reusable Object-Oriented Software,* the authors advise architects to "prefer composition to inheritance." (See also *base class, superclass, subclass,* and *interface.*)

init: A method used as a best-practice work-around for lack of true constructors in ColdFusion components.

instance variable: Also known as a property, a variable defined by a class as belonging to a particular instance of that class. While all instances of a class have these variables, the value of these variables may be different for each instance. For example, all members of the Vehicle class may have a vin variable, but each Vehicle object will have a different value for this variable. Contrast with *class variable.*

instantiation: The process of creating an object from a class. Objects are, therefore, also called *class instances.* In ColdFusion, instantiation is done with the CreateObject function, the cfinvoke tag, or the NEW operator (in ColdFusion 9).

interface: (1) The set of method signatures associated with a type. The type's interface provides a specification for these methods, but not the implementation.

(2) In some statically typed languages (such as Java and C#), a language construct that defines one or more methods and their arguments but does not include their implementation or instance variables and cannot be instantiated. Classes can implement interfaces, thereby gaining the advantage of multiple typing without the problems associated with multiple inheritance.

Liskoff Substitution Principle: Formulated by Barbara Liskoff, a principle that states that a language should ensure that a subtype can always be safely substituted for a more generic type. For example, a ColdFusionProgrammer class that extends a Programmer class can safely be passed to any method expecting a Programmer (e.g., as an argument). The Liskoff Substitution Principle guarantees polymorphism. (See also *inheritance.*)

message-passing: The idea that an object performs its functions by being sent a message. In most OO languages, this phrase is identical to "calling a method on the object."

method: A service provided by an object. In ColdFusion, methods are implemented with the `cffunction` tag or the `function` keyword (in `cfscript`). Methods can take arguments. In some languages, methods can be called directly on a class, rather than on an object (see *static methods*). Methods can, but need not, return a value to their callers.

object: A particular instantiation of a class.

overloading, method: A mechanism afforded by some OO languages (such as Java and C#) that allows multiple implementations of the same-named method, but with different method signatures. The language compiler determines which implementation to call based on the unique combination of argument types. Constructors can also be overloaded in supporting languages. Dynamically typed languages, like ColdFusion, do not support method overloading.

The following is a Java example showing constructor overloading:

```
public class VehicleManager(
    public Vehicle getVehicle(int vin){
        // return vehicle based on vehicle identification number
    }

    public Vehicle getVehicle(String tag){
        // return vehicle based on tag
    }
}
```

overriding, method: A mechanism whereby a subclass redefines the meaning of a same-named method in a superclass.

The following is a ColdFusion example showing method overriding:

```
<cfcomponent displayName="Programmer">
    <cffunction name="program" access="public">
        <cfreturn "Generic programming">
    </cffunction>
</cfcomponent>

<cfcomponent displayName = "ColdFusionProgrammer" extends="Programmer">
    <cffunction name="program" access="public">
        <cfreturn "ColdFusion programming">
    </cffunction>
</cfcomponent>

<cfset hal = CreateObject('component', 'ColdFusionProgrammer')>
<cfoutput>#hal.program()#</cfoutput>
```

The code shown here outputs the string "ColdFusion programming." ColdFusion supports method overriding, but not method overloading.

polymorphism: The ability of objects belonging to different types to respond to method calls of methods of the same name, each one according to an appropriate type-specific behavior. The programmer (and the program) does not need to know the exact type of the object in advance, so this behavior can be implemented at runtime (this is called late binding or dynamic binding).

The following adds another class, AjaxProgrammer, to the example shown for method overriding:

```
<cfcomponent displayName = "AjaxProgrammer" extends="Programmer">
    <cffunction name = "program" access = "public">
        <cfreturn "Ajax programming">
    </cffunction>
</cfcomponent>
```

The following creates three objects:

```
<cfset joe = CreateObject('component', 'Programmer')>
<cfset hal = CreateObject('component', 'ColdFusionProgrammer')>
<cfset mike = CreateObject('component', 'AjaxProgrammer')>
```

Finally, the same method can be called on each of these objects:

```
<cfoutput>
        #joe.program()# produces "Generic programming"
        #hal.program()# produces "ColdFusion programming"
        #mike.program()# produces "Ajax programming"
</cfoutput>
```

The same method call produces different results for each of the objects in a polymorphic language. (See *overriding, method.*)

properties: See *instance variable*. In ColdFusion, anything in a component's Variables scope and This scope is a property of the component.

static method: Also called a class method, in languages such as Java, a method that can be called on a class rather than an object.

The following is a Java example calling a static method:

```
Integer.parseInt("4");
```

The parseInt method is a static method to the Integer class (rather than to an instance of the class).

static typing: A language mechanism where variables are declared to be of a specific type at design time. Statically typed languages (e.g., Java and C#) check for type safety during the compilation phase. The term *static typing* is often used interchangeably with *strong typing*, although there are subtle differences between the two.

subclass: A class that extends another class. (See also *inheritance*).

subtype: A type that is a more specific version of another type. In ColdFusion, subclasses are synonymous with subtypes. In languages with interfaces, all subclasses are subtypes, but not all subtypes are subclasses. For example, an `HourlyPayStrategy` class may implement the `PayStrategy` interface, but not extend any class (see Figure 19-3). `HourlyPayStrategy` is, therefore, a subtype of `PayStrategy`, but is not a subclass. (See also *inheritance* and *interface*.)

*Figure 19-3. HourlyPayStrategy implements PayStrategy interface*

superclass: A class that is extended by another class; also called a base class. (See also *inheritance*.)

supertype: A type that is a more generic version of another type. In ColdFusion, superclasses are synonymous with supertypes. In languages with interfaces, all superclasses are supertypes, but not all supertypes are superclasses. For example, `ColdFusionProgrammer` may extend `Programmer`, making `ColdFusionProgrammer` both a subclass and a subtype of `Programmer` (see Figure 19-4). (See also *subtype* and *inheritance*.)

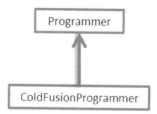

*Figure 19-4. ColdFusionProgrammer extends Programmer class*

**type (data type):** In non-OO languages, the kind of information a variable can hold. In OO languages, types are more closely associated with the methods that can be called on a variable.

**type promotion:** The mechanism whereby polymorphic languages can treat a subtype as a supertype. Assume a method, x, that expects an argument of type Y. Further assume a class, Z, that extends Y. If an object of type, Z, is sent to the method, x, it will be type-promoted to type Y. In Figure 19-5, an object of type, ErrorsAndOmissionsPolicy, can be sent to any method expecting either a CommercialInsurancePolicy or an InsurancePolicy. Similarly, an object of type, CommercialInsurancePolicy, can be sent to any method expecting an InsurancePolicy object. Types can be promoted automatically, but they cannot be demoted (e.g., you could not send a CommercialInsurancePolicy object to a method expecting an ErrorsAndOmissionsPolicy). (See also *Liskoff Substitution Principle* and *inheritance.*)

*Figure 19-5. ErrorsAndOmissionsPolicy extends CommercialInsurancePolicy, which extends InsurancePolicy*

**type safety:** In common usage, indicates the assurance that no type mismatching will occur. If, for example, a method advertises that it accepts an argument of type, X, a language is said to be type-safe if it can ensure, prior to runtime, that only variables of type X (or type-promotable to type X) will be passed to that method. (See also *type, subtype, supertype,* and *Liskoff Substitution Principle.*)

**UML (Unified Modeling Language):** An Object Modeling Group (OMG) standard object modeling and type specification language. The UML consists of 13 different diagram types, the most common of which is the Class diagram. UML is currently at version 2.0.

---

■ **Note** Special thanks to Sean Corfield and Michael Dinowitz for their insights and corrections.

---

■■■

# CHAPTER 20

# Design Patterns: Exposing the Service Layer

## by Peter Bell

*Peter Bell is known in the community for his focus on meta programming, code generation and domain specific modeling. However this article is focused on application architecture - specifically some design considerations when creating a domain model that can be accessed by multiple view technologies such as HTML, AJAX and Flex.*

As web technology changes, developers may wish to add new front-end interfaces, such as an Ajax call, a Flex front-end or a SOAP or RESTful API, to an existing application. However, they often find that their application's existing architecture does not easily adapt to the change, and that mistakes they have made in setting up that architecture are compounded when the application has multiple front ends.

Here are some ideas on designing web applications that support multiple front-ends so that when you need to add new ways of accessing your information like an AJAX request or a Flex front-end, you won't have to re-architect your entire application.

## Model-View-Controller (MVC)

Hopefully, you are already breaking your application into Model, View and Controller concerns. The model is the meat of the application. It consists of business objects containing all of the key business rules for your application, which you may want to expose to your AJAX, Flex or web service calls. Views are responsible for displaying a snapshot of the model in HTML. For example, your views might display a list of users or a form for adding a new product to your store. The controller is responsible for taking web requests from users, combining the values of the Form and URL scopes with any cookie or session data, calling methods within the model and passing any resulting data to be displayed by the view template or passing the data back as an XML or JSON packet if it is a request from an AJAX call.

It is often useful to create a collection of Service or Manager components to act as an interface for interacting with the model. These components provide an easy way to access the functionality that relates to the business objects. For example, UserService.cfc might have methods that return a list of users and delete a user from the system.

There are two approaches to designing this service layer:

- Design the services based on business functions or groups of business objects. For example, DiscussionGroupService would manage the topics, threads and comments within a discussion group.

- Create one service class for every business object, so that a discussion group application would contain TopicService, ThreadService and CommentService, for handling interactions with the three different objects.

The first approach can often create a cleaner, more intuitive interface. However, I typically just generate one service class for every business object, effectively treating it as a repository for the kind of class methods that you might put in your business objects if you were programming in Java. This second approach may not create an ideal architecture, but it allows for much easier and more consistent code generation and can create "good enough" applications in much less time.

Whichever approach you take, you will typically have a collection of service CFCs acting as the interface to access your model. Your controller methods will call methods on those CFCs to tell the model what to do and/or to retrieve information from the model. The model will often return rich business objects for your view templates to display. For example, if you have a article.list controller action, the details of the syntax will vary with the framework you are using, but it will probably look something like Listing 20-1.

*Listing 20-1. A Controller Method Calling the Model*

```
public void list( event ) {
  event.setValue( "articleList" , ArticleService.getAll() );
}
```

This works well when you just use a single HTML front-end interface. When you start to support multiple front ends, things get a little more complicated for three reasons:

- Firstly, not all front end interfaces support sessions, so you have to do a little more work to implement security if you're not limited to HTML requests.

- Secondly, you need to handle the return of XML or JSON data

- Thirdly, you might need to make sure that your various front end interfaces are sharing data correctly so if you update a setting using Flex, that is reflected immediately for visitors to the HTML version of your site.

Let's look at each of those issues in turn.

## Handling Sessions

The first issue you run into is session handling. Let's take a simple example. Some web applications have an administrative interface that allows for the management of pages in the site, usually through a page secured by authentication. An administrative user logs in, and for the rest of the session you can identify the administrative user by a unique key stored in the Session scope - often his or her user ID. Listing 20-2 illustrates the concept.

*Listing 20-2. Standard Code Allowing User to Delete a Page*

```
public string function deletePage( pageId ) {
  if ( !structKeyExists( session, "userId" ) ) {
    redirectTo( "/login" );
  }
  else {
    var user = UserService.getbyId( session.userId );
    if ( user.isAllowedTo( "Page", "delete" ) ) {
      return PageService.delete( pageId );
    }
    else {
      return "permission denied";
    };
  };
};
```

The problem with handling requests from multiple front ends is that not all of them provide access to a usable Session scope. Just looking for session.userID between requests won't always work, so you need to roll your own way to persist state between requests.

In practice, this is pretty easy to do. Create a unique session ID using the createUUID() function when a user authenticates, then return that UUID. Add it to an object cached within Application scope, associating the session to a given user ID. Then require a UUID for all method calls that need to be secured, comparing the UUID against the session object, which also handles avoiding duplicate keys and killing sessions after a time-out period. So, if a site user wanted to delete a page, as in Listing 20-2, there would be two method calls required. First, he'd need to authenticate using his credentials (often a username and password) to get a valid session key, as shown in Listing 20-3. Then he'd have to pass that session key, as shown in Listing 20-4.

*Listing 20-3. Getting a Valid Session Key*

```
validateSiteUser( string username, string password ) {
  var siteUser = UserService.getValidatedUser( username, password );
  if ( siteUser.exists() ) {
    return siteUser.getSessionUUID();
  } else {
    return "Invalid credentials";
  };
}
```

*Listing 20-4. Passing a Session Key*

```
deletePage( pageId, sessionUUID ) {
  // Load the user
  var siteUser = UserService.getbySessionUUID( sessionUUID );
  // Validate session key
  if ( siteUser.isValidSiteUser() ) {
    // Validate security
```

```
  if ( siteUser.isAllowedTo( "Page", "delete" ) {
    PageService.delete( pageId );
    return "Page deleted";
  }
  else {
    return "Permission denied";
  };
}
else {
  return "Please authenticate";
};
}
```

You do need to remember that all of your remote requests need to pass the session UUID every time they call a service method. Also, all of your remote methods must understand a "session expired" error code, so that they know to re-authenticate the user, either by asking for user input or by passing stored credentials the user previously entered into the remote system.

## Returning Data

There are two issues to address when returning data. The first is to return the right format such as XML or JSON and the other is to handle any business logic relating to formatting (such as prepending monetary values with a $ sign or formatting dates in a locale appropriate way).

Regarding business logic, please see Chapter 32, "Separating Layout from Logic," where I address the importance of having methods within your business objects to handle any formatting that needs to be applied irrespective of the front-end interface being used. Obviously you don't want to have methods on the business object returning HTML specific markup such as Hello world, but you may well want to have a product.displayPrice() method that returns the price to two decimal places with a $ sign (e.g. "$95.99") or an event.displayStartDate() method that returns the start date of an event in the appropriate locale for the end user.

In terms of the overall format, you can either use a .cfm template to create the output or you can write a script to generate it. Let's imagine that we are trying to return an XML packet containing information on a list of product objects. Listing 20-5 shows an example of how we could do that using a .cfm template:

*Listing 20-5. productXMLdisplay.cfm*

```
<productList>
    <cfoutput query="productList">
        <product name="#Name#" title="#Title#" />
    </cfoutput>
</productList>
```

Listing 20-6 shows an example that does the same thing as a script through string concatenation—this would be part of the product object (or more likely a base class the product object extends or a utility class that it delegates to internally) so you could call product.asXML() to return an XML representation of the product object.

*Listing 20-6. product.asXML()*

```
public string function asXml( ) {
  var XMLString = "<product ";
  var propertyNameList = "name,title";
  var i = 0;
  var propertyName = "";
  for ( i=1; i lte listLen( propertyNameList ); i++ ) {
    propertyName = listGetAt( propertyNameList ), i );
    XMLString = XMLString & '#propertyName#="#get( propertyName )#" ';
  }
  return XMLString & "/>";
}
```

## Accessing the Application

Providing they are calling the same ColdFusion application, your various front-end interfaces will share the same application scope. However, depending on your application architecture, you might also need to make sure that if you are using a Dependency Injection framework such as LightWire or ColdSpring, it is also shared between the various front end interfaces.

The solution to this is fairly straightforward. If you are rolling your own framework, make sure that the beanFactory is saved in the application scope so both your remote and HTML applications get their beans by calling `application.beanFactory(beanName)`. If you are using a framework, check the framework documentation for how to handle remote service calls.

# Conclusion

When we first move from writing simple applications to enforcing a Model-View-Controller separation, it is easy to make mistakes in the exact interfaces between the model, view and controller. As you start to develop applications with multiple front-ends, you will find those mistakes become problematic very quickly. Hopefully the ideas above will help you to jump-start your development of applications capable of supporting multiple front end interfaces.

# CHAPTER 21

# Beans and DAOs and Gateways, Oh My!

## by Sean Corfield

*When you decide to incorporate object-oriented programming and design patterns into your ColdFusion toolbox, the most confusing set of concepts is the whole notion of "beans and DAOs and gateways and services." It seems like so much work just to do something that you used to do with a couple of tags – and everyone seems to have strong, and differing, opinions on how best to implement these concepts.*

*In this article, I'm going to try to demystify why we might want to introduce a number of layers into our applications and then review the options available to us, along with some pros and cons. My hope is that after reading this article you'll feel less intimidated by the terminology and less worried about making the wrong decision about how to structure your application.*

## A Four-Layer Cake

The simplest way to write an application is just to mix all the code together on a page-by-page basis. We've all done it, and I think we all know that it can lead to duplicated code and, ultimately, to an unmaintainable mess as the application grows.

Few people disagree with the idea that it's a good thing to separate out database code, business logic code, and presentation code. The core principles behind Fusebox addressed this by using file naming conventions to emphasize the separation into qry files (for database queries), act files (for actions – business logic) and dsp files (for display / presentation code).

This is essentially the same principle as the Model-View-Controller design pattern, although that focuses on separating presentation code, application control code, and "everything else."

As we adopt object-oriented principles, we start to represent concepts in our applications using ColdFusion Components (CFCs). We are told that encapsulation is a good idea, so we write CFCs that have getXyz() and setXyz() methods to provide access to our xyz properties. Following the common Java terminology, we refer to these as beans. Then we have to deal with getting that data in and out of the database, and we need to decide what to do with our application's logic.

What we end up with is a somewhat inevitable series of layers in our applications, as shown in Figure 21-1.

**Four Layer Cake**

*Figure 21-1. Four Layer Cake*

Each layer has a pretty clearly defined purpose:

- Presentation – The HTML shown to the user, along with the minimal code necessary to display data and loop over sets of data.

- Control – The logic that routes requests (links and form submissions), interacts with the model (business logic), and selects the appropriate views (presentation) to display.

- Business Logic – This is (or should be) the core of your application, containing all of your business objects and the operations they can perform or have performed on them.

- Database Access – This contains all of the SQL operations necessary to get your business objects' data in and out of the database.

This approach allows us to change our presentation layer or to refactor and optimize the database without changing the core of our application. It also makes our business logic more testable, since we don't have to deal with either the database or the user interface in our testing and can therefore more easily automate our testing. The layered approach often allows us to reuse more of our code across multiple projects because it leads to code that has fewer dependencies on its environment.

# A Review of Recipes

So how do we go about creating those layers? There's no "One True Way," which some people find very frustrating and others find very liberating. I'm going to look at four possible recipes for building the bottom three layers: Control, Business Logic, and Database Access. The four recipes I'm going to review sit on a continuum from big, richly functional objects to small, specialized objects. In the ColdFusion world, the latter end of the continuum is the one that seems more familiar to developers, but I hope this article will make you take a closer look at other possibilities as well. I'll walk through each recipe first and then look at some pros and cons of each.

We'll start with a familiar recipe, shown in Figure 21-2. For each table in your database, write a bean that represents a row in the table and then write an object that handles the database operations for that bean. We often call this a Data Access Object, or DAO. Next write an object that handles database operations that span multiple rows or multiple tables. We often call this a Gateway Object. Then write an object that contains your business logic for that bean. We often call this a Service Object or a Manager Object. Finally, write a controller that is used to wire the user interface to the service or manager. You'll see this approach in sample applications for frameworks as well as on many blogs and mailing lists.

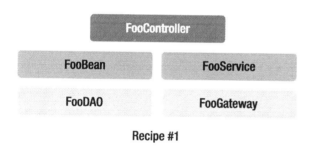

*Figure 21-2. The First Recipe*

The second recipe, shown in Figure 21-3, will look, on the surface, like a simple variant of that first recipe. Instead of five objects in the mix, there are only four, with the functions of the DAO and the gateway blended together. Don't be fooled by that apparent similarity – the real differences run much deeper than that. While there is still a bean for every table in the database, the Gateway Objects handle database operations for related groups of tables and thus related groups of beans. The Service Objects are also not tied to individual beans but instead contain business logic that operates across multiple objects. Business logic that operates on a single bean is usually written as part of that bean rather than as part of some Service Object. Finally, the Controller Objects interact with the Service Objects and with the beans, in line with how the business logic shifts between the first recipe and this recipe.

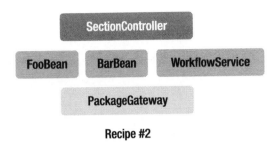

*Figure 21-3. The Second Recipe*

Our third recipe, shown in Figure 21-4, typically has fewer ingredients but can be cooked up as a simple variant of either the first or second recipes. The first scenario, a variation on the first recipe, combines beans and DAOs so that the beans themselves know how to get their own data in and out of the database. This is usually referred to as an active record, and I'll talk more about that in the next section. The second scenario, a variant of the second recipe, combines the Gateway Objects and the beans. These rich Business Objects know not only how to get their own data in and out of the database but also how to perform database operations that span multiple rows on the table with which they are associated. In both cases, the Service Objects and Controller Objects are unchanged from whichever recipe you used as the basis for Recipe 3.

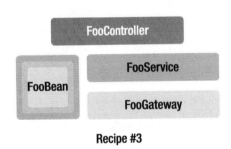

*Figure 21-4. The Third Recipe*

The fourth and final recipe, shown in Figure 21-5, has the fewest ingredients. In the ideal world of this recipe, there are only business objects. Each Business Object knows how to interact with the other Business Objects it needs to get its job done, and it knows how to get its data in and out of the database. The intent of this approach is to create a set of collaborating objects, each of which is wholly responsible for an aspect of the application's model. This recipe leads to an application model with fewer, larger objects than any of the other recipes. The design techniques applied in this recipe are often referred to as Object Think. When you are applying this design technique, you put yourself into the role of each object and ask, "What are my responsibilities?" and "What do I know about?" The first question helps you identify what behavior an object should have (what methods it should implement), and the second question helps you identify what attributes an object has as well as what other objects need to be available to this object (its dependencies).

Recipe #4

*Figure 21-5. The Fourth Recipe*

Even these four basic recipes have a number of variants so that there really is a continuum of approaches to building the basic layers in an application. Let's look at some of the pros and cons of each of these recipes and then we'll take a closer look at some of the ingredients, as well as the calorie content of your objects.

As you might expect, each approach has different tradeoffs, and understanding those can help you make more-informed decisions about which approach will best suit you - and your application.

The simplest recipe to learn and use is the first one. Starting with a database model, it's an almost mechanical process to build the beans and DAOs, as well as the basic query methods in the Gateway Objects. Indeed, there are a number of code generation tools that can automate this exact process, such as Brian Rinaldi's Illudium PU-36 Code Generator (`http://cfcgenerator.riaforge.org/`).

Even though you can't entirely automate the creation of your Service and Controller Objects, the rules for naming each layer are fairly straightforward: a Something bean, SomethingDAO, SomethingGateway, SomethingService, and SomethingController. The most obvious downside to this recipe is that it creates a lot of objects, and, to the novice, it can look like an awful lot of work to do something that used to be so simple. (It wasn't really so simple, but it was something we were used to.) I've started referring to this recipe as the 5:1 Syndrome because you typically have five objects for every database table. While the automation of code generation can offset the tedium of initially creating all those objects, the repetitive nature of the code can lead to maintenance issues, and there are certainly a lot more lines of code in this recipe than in the other three.

Now let's turn our attention to the fourth recipe. For many people this represents a complete shift in thinking because it is totally object-centric: it's all about responsibilities and behavior, with data taking a back seat. Once you start thinking in objects, this becomes a very natural way to design objects. In some ways, it's the ideal way to design an object-oriented system, but it has a couple of serious downsides. Remember the four layer cake we talked about? One of the key aspects of that layering is separating the database access out of your application logic so that you can refactor and optimize your database more easily. The cake model also makes it easier to test the business logic independent of any database. Unfortunately, this fourth recipe scores badly on both of those measures because the objects are tightly integrated with the database access. It can also be very hard to establish how the dependencies need to be set up so that objects can collaborate without creating separate manager objects to help orchestrate the interactions between otherwise smart business objects.

Next, we'll consider the active record recipe and its variants. Ruby on Rails has made this approach very popular, and the simplicity of integrating the bean and its database access is very appealing to a number of people. As a variant of the first recipe, this approach has much the same pros and cons: it is simple to learn, and it lends itself to automatic generation of beans and their associated database access code, but it still leads to a lot of objects (perhaps the 4:1 Syndrome).

Just as with the first recipe, this can look like a lot of additional work to do something that ought to be fairly straightforward. It also has an additional downside in common with the fourth recipe: blending the database code into the beans makes it harder to refactor and optimize your database without affecting your application code, and it also makes it harder to test your application code in isolation. If the second recipe is used as a basis for "active records," the result is much closer to the fourth recipe so the same concerns that tight integration with the database can make life harder for us apply again.

Finally, let's consider the second recipe, which blends aggregate and single object persistence into Gateway Objects and endeavors to create smart objects and workflow-based services. This clearly does not suffer from tight coupling between beans and database access. It also doesn't have the problem seen in the fourth recipe in terms of dependencies because it embraces the need for service objects as a way to handle cross-object workflow.

If it doesn't have those downsides, what could possibly be wrong with this approach? The other recipes are all fairly easy to understand in terms of structure. In the first recipe, the organization of code is almost mechanical. In the fourth recipe the goal is to create richly-functional, self-contained objects with no services or managers being necessary. This recipe sits in the middle ground with no hard and fast rules. That makes it more difficult to teach and, for a lot of people, much more difficult to learn.

My personal preference, of all four approaches, is that second one. It has no artificial structure imposed by dogmatic rules but instead tries to take the most natural shape based on the Business Objects and their workflow, as an organic design. It maintains the separation of the database access code that allows the database to be refactored without changing the business logic. It is amenable to unit testing, partly because of that data layer separation but also because it separates workflow from beans: it is easier to test a self-contained bean than one that has complex dependencies on other beans, and it is easier to test workflow in isolation when you can mock up beans on which that workflow can operate.

# What Are Those Ingredients?

I've deliberately glossed over a number of terms in the preceding sections that I will now cover in more depth. So far I've generally used DAO and Gateway to indicate separate concepts, and that really dates back to some guidelines that I published in 2003 and updated in 2004, as part of the original Mach-II Development Guidelines (*Web Technology Group Mach-II Development Guidelines*, `http://livedocs.adobe.com/wtg/public/machiidevguide`). Those guidelines were written when object-oriented programming was still a very new concept to most ColdFusion developers, and I was trying to provide simple rules of thumb that would help focus on the object while still providing a pigeonhole for `cfquery` style results.

If we look further than the ColdFusion community, we see that although both terms exist, they are actually used almost interchangeably. The term DAO comes primarily from the book *Core J2EE Design Patterns* by Deepak Alur, John Crupi, and Dan Malks. It is intended to be an object that provides all forms of data access for a given business object (or sometimes a group of closely-related objects). It's a natural name to give to such an object, but in other design pattern literature this same pattern is called a Data Gateway or Table Data Gateway (*Patterns of Enterprise Application Architecture*, by Martin Fowler). In this respect, the second recipe more closely follows the design patterns in common usage outside the ColdFusion community.

Data Access Object is described as an object that encapsulates a data source and implements the access mechanism required to work with it. The data source can be any sort of data provider, including a database, LDAP, or even business service that might be accessed remotely. The intent is that the DAO provides a simple, consistent interface that completely hides the specific access mechanism. In our common usage, this is usually referred to as CRUD (Create, Read, Update, Delete) and most frequently the data source being encapsulated is a database, so it is the SQL code that is being hidden. In theory, a DAO could encapsulate an LDAP repository or a remote data service and still provide a CRUD interface. Along with the basic CRUD interface, the DAO typically provides aggregate query operations and sometimes bulk update and delete operations.

Martin Fowler describes a Table Data Gateway as a specific form of the Gateway design pattern that "holds all the SQL for accessing a single table or view: selects, inserts, updates, and deletes" (http://www.martinfowler.com/eaaCatalog/tableDataGateway.html). A Gateway is a "base pattern" and describes an "object that encapsulates access to an external system or resource" (http://www.martinfowler.com/eaaCatalog/gateway.html).

Fowler goes on to give examples for the Table Data Gateway that look very similar to the previously mentioned DAO and, in closing, references the *Core J2EE Design Patterns* book for further reading. Fowler's Table Data Gateway is a DAO that encapsulates a database table.

As can be seen from this information, DAO and Gateway is a somewhat artificial distinction to be making in ColdFusion if we want to speak the same language as other computing communities. It will be interesting to see whether this distinction goes away over time – in other words, whether we shift from favoring recipe #1 to recipe #2.

Active Record is another design pattern that is explained in depth in Fowler's book. He describes it as an "object that wraps a row in a database table or view, encapsulates the database access, and adds domain logic on that data." Again, this is focused on encapsulating database access rather than some arbitrary external source of data. Fowler makes the observation that an Active Record is "a Domain Model in which the classes match very closely the record structure of an underlying database." In other words, while the Active Record encapsulates the database access, hiding the SQL, it does not hide the structure of the database.

Fowler goes on to say that Active Record suits domain logic that "isn't too complex," but if your "business logic is complex, you'll want to use your object's direct relationships, collections, inheritance, and so forth," and he notes that this "will lead you to use Data Mapper instead." The Data Mapper is a "layer of software that separates the in-memory objects from the database," and it is responsible for transferring data between the two while keeping them isolated from each other. This is the core idea behind an Object-Relational Mapping (ORM) tool such as Hibernate, Reactor, or Transfer. Fowler recommends using a Data Mapper to allow "the database schema and the object model to evolve independently."

After reading this section, you should have a better understanding of how the different patterns (recipes) relate to each other and some of their strengths and weaknesses. Now we'll take a look at a common pitfall with all these patterns.

# Eating Well or Poor Diet?

A term you may have heard, often in disparaging tones, is anemic domain model. This is considered an anti-pattern, which is something you should try to avoid in your design. In order to avoid it, you need to know what it is. Many consider it good practice in object-oriented design to create richly functional business objects that contain data and all of the associated logic for that data. This is your domain model.

An anemic domain model's Business Objects really only contain data (and getters and setters), and the business logic is instead in other objects, typically Service or Manager Objects. A symptom of this is code that calls getters on an object to retrieve data, performs some operation on that data, and then calls setters on the same object to update the data. It's likely that the operation should be part of the object that already contains the data, and the code should just ask the object to perform that operation directly on its own data.

If your code exhibits these symptoms I just described, your beans are probably just acting as data containers and all your business logic is in your Service or Manager Objects. In other words, your domain model is anemic. You need to feed your beans some more logic and turn them into proper business domain objects.

The anemic domain model anti-pattern is easy to fall into for two reasons. The first is simply that most of us in the ColdFusion community have a procedural coding background where our data and our code have historically been separate. If we wrap our data in an object and we wrap our code in another object, we may be taking the first baby steps on the path to OO, but in reality we have an anemic domain model.

The second reason can be born out of our choice of recipe. The 5:1 Syndrome in the first recipe can lead to an anemic domain model, particularly if you auto-generate your code. When you start out with beans that are auto-generated as data containers, it's often easier to just add logic to your Service Objects and leave the generated beans alone. The same can be true of using an ORM framework. When the framework automatically manages your beans and their basic database access, it's often easier to add your business logic elsewhere.

The two most popular CFML-based ORM frameworks – Reactor and Transfer – both provide ways for you to add your business logic to your beans, where it should be. Reactor auto-generates some empty components that extend the Active Record beans that it also generates. You can add your business logic to these components and Reactor will not overwrite them. Transfer uses the Decorator design pattern to allow you to add your business logic to the beans that it generates.

The main difference is that Reactor expects your business logic components to have particular names and be in the same directory where it generates code, whereas Transfer lets you use any name and location for your Decorator code. Either way, it's still a change of habit for most people so it requires effort to avoid the anemic domain model.

Hibernate works natively on your beans so you can put your business logic directly into those beans and work with a rich domain model, without having to worry about adding business logic somewhere else, just to suit the ORM.

# Real-World Web Applications

Despite all the best intentions regarding design patterns and the goal of cultivating well-fed business objects, the reality of most of the applications we build is that we are often building simple data management applications. These applications contain pages that list record sets in summary form, pages that display the details of a single record and pages that let us edit a single record. There simply isn't much business logic in these applications so our domain model is often going to look somewhat anemic; we have no business logic to feed to our beans!

Even in such applications, we will probably have validation logic, and that may be a good candidate to add to our beans in an effort to create the habit of writing business domain objects instead of dumb data containers.

Web applications are evolving all the time, and more sophisticated systems are appearing on the web, especially with the advent of richer user interfaces that make it possible to build more complex applications that are still highly usable. This provides us with both the opportunity and the challenge of designing more complicated domain models, composed of smart objects that collaborate to get their work done.

I hope this article has provided some illumination and guidance on how to meet that challenge and take advantage of the opportunity before you.

■ ■ ■

# CHAPTER 22

# SOA for the Rest of Us

## by Dave Konopka

*Examples of service-oriented architecture (SOA) systems abound in this Web 2.0 world. Twitter is a perfect example. Twitter is both a web site and a service exposed as a web-accessible API. All sorts of clients allow users to interact with the Twitter service without ever visiting the Twitter web site. A variety of mashups also extend Twitter—linking photos, offering search capabilities, and even posting geographic info to tweets.*

*However daunting the term SOA may seem, it represents a relatively simple approach to application design. Using some basic SOA concepts, you can build reusable modularized applications that you, your coworkers, and web developers the world over can extend. And ColdFusion includes a collection of features that make launching SOA-guided applications extremely easy. This article should help you introduce some SOA practices into your own projects.*

## SOA Components

Let's take a closer look at what constitutes SOA. It boils down to the guiding principle that you should build applications from separate, independent blocks called *services*. These services expose functions honed down to specific pieces of focused work, closely matching actual business processes. They should be accessible to all sorts of systems, regardless of their technology platform. The complexity of SOA emerges in the implementation of these principles.

Two parties interact in an SOA environment: the *service provider* and the *service consumer*. A service provider offers a set of services. Each service offers a set of functions, and each function performs some isolated operation. The consumers access and build on top of provider services. A consuming system could be an end-user web application that contacts multiple provider services for its operations, a Flex administrative application that supplements the web site, or even a separate service provider that relies on your services for data that it supplies to its own consumers.

## SOA vs. OOP

You have probably become familiar with the concepts of object-oriented programming (OOP). In its simplest form, a ColdFusion Component (CFC) represents OOP implementation in ColdFusion. A CFC typically has properties that describe it and methods that perform actions using those properties. To use a CFC, you can call `CreateObject` to create an instance of the object. Then, with that object, you can get and set properties and call functions to perform operations on the properties.

SOA focuses particular attention on functions. A service is a collection of related functions, each as specific as possible. Remember that these functions are building blocks for other applications. If a service function performs multiple steps, odds are a developer using your service later on will not need or want one of those steps to fire. If that developer has no access to the individual steps that make up that function, this might make your service unusable. By breaking operations down to their simplest components, you empower developers to pick and choose what best suits their applications.

For instance, you might build a directory service for your organization that exposes employee contact information. The service would include functions that get contact information for a specific employee, add a new employee to the system, and remove an employee from the system. These building block functions would have uses in different applications across your organization. The same functions could power an employee management application, an internal company phone book, and an external company web site. All of these consuming applications could access the same employee contact data with no need for any code rewrites.

Services are a bit like objects without property state. A service should not use cookie or session scopes. Each function should take in any data it needs to perform its work through its arguments. You do not need to instantiate a service. All of the functions of a service should offer complete access individually. This lack of state reduces the number of dependencies that your service introduces into consuming systems.

In an OOP design, an employee contact info object would typically include an init function that takes an employee ID. That init function would return a self-contained object with employee data and the functions to change that data. Let's look at an Employee CFC from a typical object-oriented application, in Listing 22-1.

*Listing 22-1. Employee OO CFC example*

```
<cfcomponent>
    <cfset this.FirstName = "">
    <cfset this.LastName = "">
    <cffunction name="Init">
        <cfset this.FirstName = "James">
        <cfset this.LastName = "Smith">
        <cfreturn this>
    </cffunction>
    <cffunction name="GetFullName">
        <cfreturn this.FirstName & " " & this.LastName>
    </cffunction>
</cfcomponent>
```

In contrast to the OO approach, every function in a contact data service would require an employee ID as an argument. The get employee info function would require this ID in order to return information about that employee. The update employee function would require the ID, along with the contact information that needs updating.

Using CFCs as objects allows a flexible approach to organizing business logic. When you use a CFC as an object, you can extend it, and both add to and override its functionality. You have multiple options when it comes to techniques for invoking your objects.

This approach, however, requires the CFC code on every server where you invoke it. For a simple, single-server web application, it's easy enough to include a group of CFCs with the application. But this approach starts to break down as you create other applications that depend on your system. Every new application that deploys will need an additional copy of your CFCs installed on any number of servers. Every time your core system CFCs change, you will need a mechanism to update the consuming applications. Listing 22-2 contains an example of a Service CFC.

*Listing 22-2. Service CFC example*

```
<cfcomponent>
    <cffunction name="GetEmployeeContactInfo" access="remote"
        returnformat="json">
        <cfargument name="EmployeeId">
        <cfset EmployeeObj =
            CreateObject("cfc.Employee").init(employeeid=arguments.EmployeeId)>
        <cfreturn EmployeeObj.GetContactData()>
    </cffunction>
</cfcomponent>
```

# SOA Code Organization

SOA and OOP are not mutually exclusive methodologies. You can build a service layer on top of any existing web application. And even for a new application built from scratch, you can avoid locking all of your logic into service components. You should still build the logic of your application into components, which I'll call the *model*. You can even use the same application frameworks you already know for your model. Some frameworks (such as ColdSpring) may even provide additional support for SOA. Extend the model by building out a service layer of components exposed as web services that make use of the underlying model components to perform their operations.

To expose a service layer to the general public in addition to an internal API for your organization, consider creating a second service layer. Your concerns for an external API will not always match those for an internal service API. Since your model does the actual work, creating an additional, separate set of components that expose web service methods costs little. It will provide you with flexibility as you support both APIs.

# Web Services

SOA design also distinguishes itself by allowing access to services over standard communication channels, of which HTTP is one of the most common. Most organizations block proprietary ports but leave HTTP's port 80 open, and just about every programming platform includes some form of support for accessing and sending data over HTTP. Simple Object Access Protocol (SOAP) and Representational State Transfer (REST) are the two prevalent modes of web service communication, and we will focus on these modes in this article.

SOAP web services accept and return XML messages. The messages adhere to a strict protocol. A consumer can send a message to a SOAP web service to invoke a function. The service function parses the message, executes the function, and then returns specially formatted XML data to the consumer. You can create a .NET SOAP web service, publish it on the Internet, and then execute the function in ColdFusion code without any knowledge of the inner workings of the .NET code. It's worth noting that while SOAP promotes interoperability, you will need to do quite a bit of hand-holding to transfer complex data types between different platforms.

Luckily, you will never need to worry about XML messages again. ColdFusion takes care of all the work involved with managing SOAP web services. Simply setting the function property access="remote" will allow you to publish a CFC as a web service. There's nothing else to do to the component to have it instantly become accessible as a web service.

REST web services offer another popular technique for exposing services over HTTP. REST web services do not use XML. Instead, they are accessible by HTTP URL requests. Generally, you request data from a REST service in much the same way that you access a web page by using a URL. You can pass data to a REST service using POST or PUT actions. Yahoo, Flickr, and Facebook all expose APIs using REST services. While RESTful web services do not require formatted messages by design, they do often expose and expect data in XML or a similar format.

ColdFusion includes a few features that make it easy to work with REST services. The cfhttp tag allows you to make HTTP requests to access a REST service. You can include POST data by setting method="Post" on the cfhttp tag and including cfhttpparam tags with form data. Response data can be stored in a variable and parsed according to data format.

You can expose a REST service as easily as a SOAP web service. You can access remote CFC functions by URL. Argument values can be passed via query string parameters. Set access="remote" for any function, and the function becomes available as a REST-style service accessible by the URL path to the file followed by the string ?method=functionname&argument1=value&argument2=value. REST services can also accept form post data. These simplified data-transmission options make REST a more popular option than the more complex SOAP services.

## Data Formats

Now that we've gone over some options for transmitting data in and out of a service, let's take a closer look at the data itself. When you transfer complex data types across systems, you will run into problems translating those data types. The consuming system must map your data to its own data types.

ColdFusion does not support exactly the same data types that other systems do. You can expect simple types like strings and numerics to translate. However, more complex data types like cfquery results may result in data that is difficult for consumers of your web service to parse.

Untyped structs and queries do not translate well over remote function calls. It is best to use value objects when returning complex data. A value object in ColdFusion is a CFC with typed properties (see Listing 22-3). This typing ensures clarity for the structure of your data and will make it easier to consume the data in other environments.

*Listing 22-3. Value object example*

```
<cfcomponent alias="com.EmployeeVO">
    <cfproperty name="FirstName" type="string">
    <cfproperty name="LastName" type="string">
    <cfproperty name="EmployeeId" type="numeric">
    <cffunction name="init" access="public" returntype"employeeObj">
        <cfreturn this>
    </cffunction>

    <cfset this.FirstName=''>
    <cfset this.LastName=''>
    <cfset this.EmployeeId=''>

</cfcomponent>
```

You can get a performance boost when you pass larger data sets from ColdFusion 8 or 9 to Flex by using arrays of structures instead of instantiating value object CFCs. Set structure values using property names as keys, much as you would with CFC value objects. And then set an additional structure key named __type__ to the alias of the object that you wish to map the structure to on the Flex side. ColdFusion will automatically convert the struct to a typed object that Flex understands (see Listing 22-4).

*Listing 22-4. Return struct example*

```
<cfset EmployeeStruct = StructNew()>
<cfset EmployeeStruct["FirstName"] = "">
<cfset EmployeeStruct["LastName"] = "">
<cfset EmployeeStruct["EmployeeId"] = "">
<cfset EmployeeStruct["__type__"] = "com.EmployeeVO">
```

By default, a remote service returns data in Web Distributed Data Exchange (WDDX) format. Few platforms will interpret this data natively. Consider the likely users of your services, and tailor the data to suit them. Simplify the data types where possible. You can usually assume that other Adobe products can interpret more advanced data types returned from a ColdFusion web service, but there are no guarantees when transmitting data between platforms. Err on the side of simplicity to ensure compatibility with the broadest spectrum of clients. For more information about building web services with complex data types, see Chapter 13, "Web Services and Complex Types" by Nathan Mische.

ColdFusion 8 introduced new tools for working with JavaScript Object Notation (JSON) data. JSON, a lightweight data format, allows easy interchange between different technology platforms. SerializeJSON() and DeserializeJSON() convert data in and out of JSON format. Remote CFC functions can also export JSON-formatted data instead of WDDX-formatted data by simply setting the returnformat property to "json". You can override this property when you call a function by passing in a new returnformat property. JSON libraries exist for most programming platforms. This makes JSON a great choice for formatting service output data. JSON also integrates easily with JavaScript, which makes it an attractive format for functions that you plan to consume in a browser with AJAX code. For more information about using JSON with ColdFusion, check out Chapter 34, "Working with JSON and CFAJAXPROXY in ColdFusion" by Raymond Camden.

# Security

Earlier, I mentioned that services should not maintain any sort of state. This presents a challenge for securing services. The typical model for securing a web application goes something like this:

- A user provides a username and password through a web form.

- The application verifies the credentials. If the credentials pass, the application sets a property in the session scope.

- The session scope ties to a cookie token value, which the client browser stores. Every request triggers a check of the session for the logged-in flag.

- The client stays logged in as long as the session remains active.

Without a session scope or browser cookies, we need to adjust the security scenario a bit for services. One of the easier approaches enables HTTP basic authentication at the web server level for the folder where you store your services. The web server will then prompt consumers for a username and password when they access the services. The **cfinvoke** tag includes a username and a password function that will send credentials through to the web server on each request.

You could also implement custom authentication for your services—for instance, with security tokens. First, create a login service method. This method should accept a username and password, and pass back a unique token value for valid credentials. On the server side, you would store this token in a database. Every service method would then require the token as an additional argument. A private security function would be called at the top of every service method to validate the token. For a valid token, the service function executes as expected. Otherwise, the function can abort. The security check function should also update the token's last access time. After a short period of inactivity—15 minutes or so—the token expires, and further requests with that token fail. Listing 22-5 shows an example of this authentication system.

*Listing 22-5. Some authentication functions*

```
<cffunction name="Login" access="remote" returntype="string"
    hint="Returns a session token if username and password is valid">
    <cfargument name="Username">
    <cfargument name="Password">
    <cfset var my = StructNew()>
    <cfset my.SecurityToken = "FAILED">

    <!--- Call custom function to validate supplied credentials --->
    <cfif CredentialsAreValid(username=arguments.Username,
        password=arguments.Password)>
        <!--- Call custom function to create a
            new token for the user in the database --->
        <cfset my.SecurityToken =
            CreateNewSecurityToken(username=arguments.Username)>
    </cfif>
    <!--- Return security token, or FAILED string --->
    <cfreturn  my.SecurityToken>

</cffunction>

<cffunction name="SecurityTokenIsValid" access="remote" returntype="boolean"
    hint="Validates a security token.">

    <cfargument name="SecurityToken">
    <cfargument name="Username">
    <cfset var my = StructNew()>
    <cfquery name="my.qryTokenLookup" datasource="TokenDatabase">
        SELECT token
        FROM SecurityTokens
        WHERE username = <cfqueryparam cfsqltype="cf_sql_varchar"
            value="#arguments.Username#">
        AND token = <cfqueryparam cfsqltype="cf_sql_varchar"
            value="#arguments.SecurityToken#">
```

```
        AND lastupdate_timestamp > <cfqueryparam cfsqltype="cf_sql_date"
            value="#DateAdd("m",-20,Now())#">
    </cfquery>
     <cfif my.qryTokenLookup.RecordCount EQ 1>
        <!--- Call custom function to update the
            lastupdate_timestamp to track session activity --->
        <cfset UpdateSecurityTokenTimestamp(username=arguments.Username,
            securitytoken=arguments.SecurityToken)>
        <cfreturn true>
    <cfelse>
        <cfreturn false>
    </cfif>

</cffunction>
```

ColdFusion currently does not include support for WS-Security SOAP header security standards. Some other platforms require encrypted messages with an accompanying certificate in the SOAP message headers adhering to WS-Security standards. While crafting your own SOAP messages by hand might solve this, I suggest looking to Java packages for help.

If you pass usernames, passwords, or any other sensitive data to a web service over HTTP, remember that the data transmits in clear text. I cannot overstate the importance of securing your services by obtaining an SSL certificate and setting up HTTPS to encrypt requests to and from your services. If you do set up HTTPS without using a trusted certificate provider for your SSL certificate, ColdFusion consumers will likely have trouble accessing the secured services. In this case, consumers will need to register the certificate to the Java keystore on their web server in order to make a secure connection to your services.

## Error Handling

How will your services handle errors and exceptions? When you invoke a CFC directly, you can use try/catch statements to trap and handle exceptions. But with services, errors may occur on a completely different system than the consuming application. Make sure to build in error logging. Create a logging component that logs messages either to a file or a database table. Also, consider having the component fire off an e-mail message to you when errors do occur. This will help you to respond quickly when problems leave your consumers hanging.

When exceptions occur, call your custom error handler component, but do not throw the exception back to the client. For SOAP services, you could return AxisFault errors. For REST services, you could rely on HTTP error codes. But keep your services generic. Establish a consistent standard for the data that your service returns. Return a success/failure message, a detailed results message, and any results data for a success. Consistency will help consumers react to the results of your service functions, and so will including as much description as possible with your failure messages. Do not return error codes unless you document them well and your consuming applications can use them. Listing 22-6 contains an example of this error handling code.

*Listing 22-6. Sample error handling code*

```
<cffunction name="HandleError" access="public" returntype="void">
    <cfargument name="ErrorObject">

    <!--- Call custom function to write the details
        of the error to a database --->
    <cfset LogErrorToDatabase(ErrorObject = arguments.ErrorObject)>
    <!--- Call custom function to email the details
        of the error to service administrators --->
    <cfset NotifyAdministrators(ErrorObject = arguments.ErrorObject)>

</cffunction>
```

You can now use this method throughout your service code:

```
<cfset ServiceResults = StructNew()>
<cfset ServiceResults.Success = true>
<cfset ServiceResults.Message = "">
<cfset ServiceResults.Detail = "">

<cftry>
    ...

    <cfcatch type="database">
        <cfset HandleError(cfcatch)>
        <cfset ServiceResults.Success = false>
        <cfset ServiceResults.Message = "Request failed">
        <cfset ServiceResults.Detail = "Your request failed because of a
            database error. The error has been logged and administrators
            have been notified.">
    </cfcatch>
</cftry>
```

# Discoverability

Another key to a viable SOA system is that clients can actually find your services. It also helps to offer metadata explaining what each function expects and returns.

ColdFusion automatically generates documentation for CFCs. Developers can view this documentation by browsing to any CFC file path. The documentation includes all the functions exposed by the CFC, the parameters expected, and the type of data returned.

Make sure you set descriptive hint properties for your remote functions and arguments. These hints display in the generated documentation. This happens automatically, and the information is constantly updated without any effort on your part.

# Service Interfaces

Your service components become a contract as soon as you publish them. Whether your consumers are applications within your organization, applications available to the general public on the Web, or a mixture of both, consumers will depend on your services. Think carefully before changing the names of functions, the parameters expected by a function, or the format of return data. Applications that you do not control will require fixes every time you break the interface of your services by making such changes. Good practice suggests that instead of making such modifications, you should extend your service layer with new services and functions as new needs arise. Always make an effort to preserve existing services and data conventions.

Writing a lot of automated unit tests for your service layers can help protect your consumers. The MXUnit framework (`http://mxunit.org/`) excels at managing unit tests for your functions. Unit tests help ensure that the functions are accessible and work as expected. Write as many tests as you can to ensure that the data is handled and returns as you expect. MXUnit allows you to group tests into suites that you can run in bulk. Whenever you make a change to any part of your underlying application or to your service layer, run your automated test suite. This should shake out most problems before they have a chance to affect clients.

As you begin to use SOA for your projects, remember that SOA remains a set of guiding principles, not steadfast rules. You don't need to rebuild an application from the ground up to create a useful API and expose your system to the world.

# CHAPTER 23

■■■

# How Base Classes Can Help You Generate Your Applications

## by Peter Bell

*Base classes don't just make your applications leaner and quicker to develop. They can also be a great first step toward generating more of your code. This article examines what base classes are, why you should care, and how they can be used as a starting point when generating code for your applications.*

## Base Class Basics

One of the biggest problems with object-oriented programming is that it takes a lot more typing than "the good old way." What is worse, a lot of the typing is repetitive, dull, and error-prone. For example, Data Access Objects (DAOs) are commonly used to hold your "single-record" queries (create, read, update, and delete against a single record). If you look at a DAO for a user (Listing 23-1) and compare it to a DAO for a product (Listing 23-2), you'll see they are similar.

*Listing 23-1. Part of a simple user DAO*

```
<cffunction name="getUser" returntype="query" output="false" hint="I return a recordset
    containing the requested User based on the provided User ID">
    <cfargument name="UserID" type="numeric" required="yes" hint="The ID of the User
        to return">
    <cfset var Local = StructNew()>
    <cfquery name="Local.GetUser" datasource="#variables.datasource#">
        SELECT UserID, FirstName, LastName
        FROM tbl_User
        WHERE UserID = <cfqueryparam value = "#arguments.UserID#"
            CFSQLType = "CF_SQL_INTEGER">
    </cfquery>
    <cfreturn Local.GetProduct>
</cffunction>
```

*Listing 23-2. Part of a simple product DAO*

```
<cffunction name="getProduct" returntype="query" output="false" hint="I return a
    recordset containing the requested product based on the provided product ID">
    <cfargument name="ProductID" type="numeric" required="yes" hint="The ID of the
        product to return">
    <cfset var Local = StructNew()>
    <cfquery name="Local.GetProduct" datasource="#variables.datasource#">
       SELECT ProductID, Title, Price
       FROM tbl_Product
       WHERE ProductID = <cfqueryparam value = "#arguments.ProductID#"
       CFSQLType = "CF_SQL_INTEGER">
    </cfquery>
    <cfreturn Local.GetProduct>
</cffunction>
```

Base classes are one way to avoid much of the repetitive typing. Imagine that ProductDAO and UserDAO both extend a BaseDAO (using the extends property of cfcomponent). You could then create a base getbyId() method that both DAOs could use. It would probably look something like Listing 23-3.

*Listing 23-3. getbyId base method used by both DAOs*

```
<cffunction name="getbyId" returntype="query" output="false" hint="I return a recordset
    containing the requested object based on the provided Id">
    <cfargument name="Id" type="numeric" required="yes"
      hint="The Id of the object to return">
    <cfset var GetRecord = "">
    <cfquery name="GetRecord" datasource="#variables.datasource#">
        SELECT #variables.FieldNameList#
        FROM #variables.TableName#
        WHERE #variables.IdFieldName# = <cfqueryparam value = "#arguments.Id#"
            CFSQLType = "CF_SQL_INTEGER">
    </cfquery>
    <cfreturn GetRecord>
</cffunction>
```

Now, instead of writing nearly identical getUser() and getProduct() methods, you can let the base class do the heavy lifting using its generic getbyId() method, and just set the field name list, the table name, and the name of the Id field in the init() method for the UserDAO and ProductDAO, respectively. For example, Listing 23-4 shows what the init() method for the ProductDAO might look like.

*Listing 23-4. A sample ProductDAO init() method*

```
<cffunction name="init" returntype="ProductDAO" access="public" output="false" hint="I
    initialize the Product DAO with Product specific parameters.">
    <cfscript>
        var Arguments = StructNew();
        Arguments.FieldNameList = "ProductID,Title,Price";
        Arguments.TableName = "tbl_Product";
```

```
        Arguments.IdFieldName = "ProductId";
        Super.Init(argumentCollection=Arguments);¹
    </cfscript>
    <cfreturn This>
</cffunction>
```

This method, in turn, would call the `BaseDAO` `init()` method using the `Super.Init()` call. Note the explicit passing of the object-specific parameters to the base class `init()` method to provide for encapsulation and validation. Listing 23-5 contains the `BaseDAO` `init()` method that was called in Listing 23-4.

*Listing 23-5. BaseDAO init() method*

```
<cffunction name="init" returntype="BaseDAO" access="public" output="false" hint=
        "I return the initialized Base DAO.">
    <cfargument name="FieldNameList" type="string" required="true">
    <cfargument name="TableName" type="string" required="true">
    <cfargument name="IdFieldName" type="string" required="true">
    <cfscript>
        variables.FieldNameList = arguments.FieldNameList;
        variables.TableName = arguments.TableName;
        variables.IdFieldName = arguments.IdFieldName;
    </cfscript>
    <cfreturn This>
</cffunction>
```

This might not be worth the effort if there were only one method in a DAO. But since there are `get()`, `insert()`, `update()`, and `delete()` methods, being able to set just a few properties, instead of having to cut and paste all of the methods, can save you a lot of time. In addition, having only one copy of each query means that you need to update the code in only one place if you want to make a systematic change, such as adding a `LastUpdatedDate` property whenever you do an update.

With base classes, adding a new object becomes much easier. If you need an `ArticleDAO`, for example, just take a copy of the `ProductDAO`, change a few well-named properties in the DAO's `init()` method, and you're finished.

Of course, you can do the same for your business objects, service objects, controller objects, and gateway objects, which will make your application much quicker to code.

# It's All About the API

Creating a base class is very easy. Creating a good base class is not. The difficult part lies in coming up with the appropriate base methods with just the right arguments to be easy enough for simple cases, but flexible enough to cover most of the special cases as well.

One of the best ways to write an application programming interface (API) is to examine the APIs that other people have written. It makes sense to look initially at the popular frameworks to see how they work. Want to come up with an API for your controllers? Look at Model-Glue, ColdBox, FW/1, Mach-II, and Fusebox 5 (specifically lexicons). Interested in an API for your DAOs and gateways? Check out the documentation for Hibernate, Transfer, and Reactor.

# A Simple Example

Let's take a simple example of a base get method for returning 0 to *n* records from a single database table based on a filter clause. There are no joins, group bys, aggregates, calculations, or aliases in this example.

Even for this simple case, we need to be able to set which field names to return, a where filter, and an order by clause. We're getting records from a database using a filter (the WHERE clause), so let's call this method getbyFilter(). What might this base method look like? Take a look at Listing 23-6.

*Listing 23-6. getbyFilter base method*

```
<cffunction name="getbyFilter" returntype="query" output="no" hint="I return a recordset
    containing all of the records matching the provided filter.">
    <cfargument name="Filter" type="string" required="no"
        default="#variables.DefaultFilter#" hint="The SQL Where clause (excluding the
        actual word 'WHERE').">
    <cfargument name="FieldNameList" type="string" required="no"
        default="#variables.DefaultFieldNameList#" hint="The field names to be selected by
        the query.">
    <cfargument name="OrderBy" type="string" required="no"
        default="#variables.DefaultOrderBy#" hint="The sort order of the query.">
    <cfset var GetbyFilter ="">
    <cfquery name="GetbyFilter" datasource="#variables.datasource#">
        SELECT #arguments.FieldNameList#
        FROM #variables.TableName#
        WHERE #arguments.Filter#
        ORDER BY #arguments.OrderBy#
    </cfquery>
    <cfreturn GetbyFilter>
</cffunction>
```

There are all kinds of issues with this code. Some are simple. For example, this will break if the Filter or OrderBy arguments are of zero length. Others are more profound. For instance, the query doesn't have any cfqueryparam tags, so the important associated security and performance benefits are lost. However, this is just a simple example, so please bear with me.

First, notice that all of the arguments are optional. So, if we just wanted to get a default field list with any default filters in the default order for (say) a product, we would call ProductDAO.getbyFilter(). As long as ProductDAO extends BaseDAO, it will return the default product list.

Second, notice that all of the variables holding the configuration data for a given object (in the cfquery) are in the Variables scope. (The Variables scope is private within a CFC.)

# The Variables Define the API

What does that tell us? If we use this base getbyFilter() method, and it works for most of our needs, all we need to do when adding a new object DAO is to define the object-specific parameters we saw earlier: data source, table name, default filter, default field name list, and default order by. Then we will have provided all of the information required to implement the DAO for that object, other than the few special cases we'll always need to code by hand. We have gone from needing to copy, modify, and debug what might be hundreds of lines of code for a real-world class to just setting a few properties, simplifying and speeding the development process.

## Composition or Inheritance?

An object-oriented purist might suggest using composition instead of inheritance. How would that work? Instead of having the classes like ProductDAO and ArticleDAO inherit the methods like getbyFilter() from a base class, they would include another object that would contain those methods. So, ProductDAO and ArticleDAO would be composed with a DAOHelper class by including the following code within their init() methods:

```
<cfset variables.DAOHelper = MyFactory.create("DAOHelper")>
```

where MyFactory is the code responsible for creating objects.

We would then need to add very simple methods to the ProductDAO and ArticleDAO for each composed method. For example, ProductDAO.getbyFilter() would have just this line:

```
<cfreturn variables.HelperDAO.getbyFilter(argumentCollection=Arguments)>
```

where Arguments was a structure of all of the arguments passed to the DAO method.

With composition, we have the benefit that if the DAOHelper.getbyFilter() API changed, we might need to edit only the getbyFilter() methods in our other DAOs, rather than in every single place that called those DAOs (simplifying maintenance). The downside of composition is that now we're back to having to put a simple implementation of every single method into every single DAO, which is a lot of typing. It also means that if we want to add a new method to our DAOs, we must add a simple wrapper method to every single DAO.

While we should usually favor composition over inheritance, in this case, inheritance is the appropriate tool for the job. How do I know when to use inheritance rather than composition? I like my code to pass three key tests:

- Is it a DAO? A product DAO very clearly is a DAO—that is the essence of what it is and does.

- Are the functions I am inheriting cohesive with the intent of the class? For example, an order should be able to return its status, but should it really know how to send an e-mail when its status changes? Clearly, the ability to perform create, read, update, and delete (CRUD) operations is essential to a DAO, so the base methods are cohesive.

- Is the API to the methods likely to change? If it is likely to change, I will use composition to hide the likely interface changes within the composing class. In this case, the API to the base methods is my core DAO API and is very unlikely to change, so I am comfortable exposing those classes through inheritance, rather than encapsulating them with composition

# Types of Methods

We can classify most methods with only a few method types. For example, getProductsinCategory() and getNewestUsers() are really just types of getbyFilter(). getUserbyEmail() and getProductbySKU() are really just types of getbyAttribute(). As you become more comfortable working with base classes, you can replace most of your custom methods with a couple of static parameter or runtime property settings and a call to a base method. For example, if you had a getbyAttribute(AttributeName, AttributeValue) base method, you might have a getProductbySKU() method (Listing 23-7).

*Listing 23-7. getProductbySKU() method*

```
<cffunction name="getProductbySKU" returntype="query" output="no" hint="I return a
    recordset containing the product with the requested SKU.">
    <cfargument name="ProductSKU" type="string" required="yes"
        hint="The Product SKU">
    <cfreturn variables.getbyAttribute( "SKU" , arguments.ProductSKU )>
</cffunction>
```

As you substitute parameters and base method calls for your methods, it becomes much easier to use metaprogramming to generate those methods. But what is metaprogramming, and how can you use it?

# Metaprogramming

Metaprogramming is all about writing programs that write programs, so we don't have to do the extra coding. What we have just done is a type of metaprogramming called *dynamic programming*. We have written generalized code that will do different things for different objects, so that we can just provide different parameters to our dynamic code, instead of needing to write different code for each similar problem.

In theory, all programming could be called dynamic programming, unless you're just writing HTML. In practice, dynamic programming usually refers to programming that is more dynamic than that commonly being written at the time. It is a relative measure, rather than an absolute measure.

The other type of metaprogramming is application generation (or code generation). The difference between dynamic programming and application generation is that when you write a code generator, you are writing code that creates a file that is saved to the file system and then executed. The benefit of code generation is that the actual code you run is simpler. It may also perform better. The downside of code generation is that you now must manage all of the generator code, either as part of your project or as a separate dependency.

It is quicker to prototype a new class of solution using dynamic programming than to write and maintain an application generator. You can use simple patterns to generalize the behavior of your code and can quickly change your code if you didn't capture the correct API the first time around. Once you have a solid working prototype using dynamic programming, you can then examine whether the application would benefit from generated code. For instance, you may decide to generate a set of object-specific DAOs instead of using your base class.

The good news is that you need only three things to generate an application: an application generator (which is usually pretty simple), a template, and the metadata required to create the instances you want to generate.

If you have written a base method, you already have the most difficult two of those three things! How? The base class acts as the template, with a few syntactic tweaks depending on the template language you are using, and the object-specific parameters define the metadata. Drop those parameters into a database or an XML file, run it against your template, and you will be up and generating your DAOs within a few hours!

## Summary

Base classes are a great way to prototype applications, and in many cases allow for cleaner, more maintainable production code. Even if you outgrow the capabilities of your base classes for reasons of flexibility or performance, if you think of them as "prototype templates" for your application generator, and think of the properties as the metadata, you'll be able to leverage what you learned in building your base classes, and you will be up and generating applications in no time at all.

## Resources

Here are some resources for learning more about base classes

- Wikipedia, "Superclass": http://en.wikipedia.org/wiki/Base_class

- Bell, Peter, "The Benefits of Base Classes": http://www.pbell.com/index.cfm/2006/6/25/The-Benefits-of-Base-Classes

- Wikipedia, "Fragile Base Class": http://en.wikipedia.org/wiki/Fragile_base_class

And here are some code generator resources:

- CF Template: http://cftemplate.riaforge.org/

- Illudium PU-36 Code Generator: http://code.google.com/p/cfcgenerator/

- Rooibos (Bean Code) Generator: http://rooibos.maestropublishing.com/

# PART 6

# ColdFusion Frameworks

■ ■ ■

# CHAPTER 24

# An Introduction to Frameworks

## by Jared Rypka-Hauer

*Within minutes of the first ColdFusion framework (Fusebox) being announced on CF-Talk, questions arose: Why bother? What do we need a framework for? Isn't it just more work? The questions have not been resolved, despite the fact that Fusebox is now in its fifth iteration. So we asked Jared Rypka-Hauer to take on frameworks—explain what they are and why they are useful, and delve into the differences among the many frameworks available to the ColdFusion community.*

I'll never forget my first experience with ColdFusion. I bought a copy of Ben Forta's now-ubiquitous WACK (Web Application Construction Kit) book at the suggestion of a friend and had the ColdFusion server installed and serving up the responses to queries within minutes. In less than three days I had a corporate text paging system up and running using the typical 5–10 ColdFusion tags and our group's Lotus Notes database. That was around 1998. Today we like to think that ColdFusion is less about simple scripts and more about real programming, yet I could still sit down with someone and have him reading data from a database and displaying master/detail pages within minutes. Our beloved language has become far more flexible and is able to cater to advanced techniques without sacrificing the simple, old-fashioned techniques we've come to both love and hate.

While we should not allow ourselves to forget that ColdFusion, at its most fundamental level, is about making complicated things easy, we shouldn't shackle ourselves, either. We need to continue discussing advanced techniques and building our skills on the programming side of things. Frameworks are a fundamental part of advanced techniques and, fortunately, the concepts behind using any given framework are portable from one language to almost any other.

## Can Someone Just Tell Me What They ARE Already?

Before we go digging through information about which frameworks are available, I want to address a common misconception. Frameworks aren't magic, nor are they terribly difficult to learn. A framework is simply a collection of code and a particular methodology for blending that code into your own applications, creating a more organized application while saving you some time and effort. Frameworks answer questions such as where to put the business logic of your application, where to place your display files, and what directs the framework to take actions or display pages when an event or file is called. By taking care of many of the mundane aspects of application logic, frameworks give us much faster time-to-production on a site and a better shot at being consistent when writing our applications. All frameworks have the following two things in common:

- Core files (that generally come in a zip file)

- Instructions on how to get your code to work with the code provided by the framework

The various frameworks out there can be divided into the following two basic groups:

- Frameworks intended to deliver HTML content to a browser

- Frameworks (or libraries) intended to provide services and support your applications

# Frameworks that Focus on HTML and the User Interface

The first category of frameworks focuses on connecting back-end systems with your user interface (UI).

- Fusebox

- Model-Glue

- Mach-II

- ColdBox

Most of the time, at least in the ColdFusion world, a framework used to deliver content will receive its instructions in the form of URL or form variables and XML config files. For example, URL variables such as `fuseaction=blog.showentry&entryId=122` (Fusebox) or `event=blog.showentry&entryId=122` (Mach-II, ColdBox, and Model-Glue) tell the code in the framework to look in a particular XML file, look up `blog.showentry` to get further instructions, and finally, to run the code associated with the `blog.showentry` fuseaction or event handler(s). That code is written by the developer and will (in this case) fetch the blog entry from the database and display it, along with any pods and special links (such as del.icio.us links), and perhaps update a view counter. The way this code is blended with the code supplied by the framework can reduce development time. And by creating a common language of sorts (in terms of framework-specific terminology), frameworks can also facilitate communication with other developers.

Most frameworks also include certain settings that turn caching on and off to accelerate performance when the site is in production, change the way pages are reloaded or not, and alter other actions the framework itself takes as it processes requests.

## Fusebox

Fusebox is a procedural framework that takes all the information provided by the developer via two or more XML files and compiles a complete page of CFML for each distinct fuseaction URL variable. These pages, once compiled, are used for subsequent requests unless the developer informs the framework otherwise. Fusebox contains facilities to make using CFCs (ColdFusion Components) quite easy, so "procedural framework" isn't meant to imply that object-oriented practices have no place in Fusebox applications.

Fusebox 5.5.1, which was released in March 2008, offers more tools than previous versions for using CFCs, along with many new enhancements to the framework that make application management that much easier. For example, application startup hooks have been added (AppInit and fusebox.appinit. cfm) that control tasks the application must perform the first time one of its pages are requested; also, the XML files have been made optional by adopting a set of conventions for locating code instead. Fusebox applications have a reputation for being incredibly fast and performing extremely well under load. And because the process of compiling a whole page out of several smaller chunks of code only happens once (at least in production mode), there's actually very little of the framework involved in the request after the first run of the fuseaction. It doesn't do quite as well in situations where you may have dynamic execution paths, but for sites with static layouts and very little need for dynamic event handling, Fusebox is very hard to beat.

When should you use Fusebox? Well, that's easy. You should use Fusebox if you're still developing your applications in a page model but want to make a move toward more modular applications, or if you want to use a framework but have a mixed-ability team with persons that might not be comfortable with an object-oriented approach. You can organize your applications into various architectural patterns, such as Model-View-Controller (MVC), more easily with something like Fusebox than you can by rolling up your own architecture—and you can learn a lot about application architecture in the process.

Fusebox is also quite handy for the following:

- Podded static layouts with dynamic content

- Sites requiring support for plug-ins

- Sites migrating directly from a procedural page model (things such as `blogentrylist.cfm` or `blogentrydetail.cfm` become `index.cfm?fuseaction=blog.showentrylist` or `index.cfm?fuseaction=blog.showentrydetail`)

## Model-Glue

Model-Glue is a relative newcomer to the frameworks scene, with a version 3.0 released in August 2009 after an initial 1.0 release in 2005. It has gained rapid acceptance in the ColdFusion community because it makes the transition to a purely object-oriented framework much easier than rolling your own object-oriented application architecture. Originally written by Joe Rinehart, who made a great effort to provide rich features while keeping the framework as simple as possible, it's gained enough ground (and features) that it's now supported by a team of volunteers led by Dan Wilson. In Model-Glue, events replace pages and are triggered via an event variable passed through the URL or form. If at one point you had a page called `blogentrylist.cfm` you would, in the Model-Glue world, have an event that looks like `index.cfm?event=blog.showentrylist` instead.

Model-Glue is also based on MVC. A developer creates an application by writing CFCs that comprise the model section and CFM templates that comprise the views. He then writes CFCs that extend the framework's core controller CFC to provide interaction between the two. When an event is requested, any number of controller methods are fired that access data in the application or session scopes, the database, or from other data sources. Events also include views to render the final output to the browser. For more detail on how this all works, see the Model-Glue Fundamentals article in Chapter 27 of this collection.

The other guiding design principle behind Model-Glue is the concept of implicit invocation (II). This means that if the `getProductsList` message is broadcast, for example, all controller methods configured in the Model-Glue config files' `<controller>` section listening for the `getProductsList` method will fire. To put it in more tangible terms, if `clean the kitchen` is a message broadcast by the `mom.isTired` event, then any subtasks (such as `sweep the floor` and `load the dishwasher`) registered under the `KidController` will fire. Implicit invocation abstracts a larger task, such as `products.list,` into smaller tasks, such as `get products query` and `render products list page,` by making it the listener's responsibility to respond instead of the broadcaster's responsibility to delegate explicitly.

When should you use Model-Glue? If you're familiar with CFCs and want to take a crack at an object-oriented framework, Model-Glue is definitely a bit easier for the newbie to get his or her head around than Mach-II. Model-Glue finds its strength in simplicity and a limited number of XML files that make it possible to see what the entire application is doing step-by-step without looking anywhere else.

# Mach-II

Mach-II was originally created as an advanced version of Fusebox in 2003 and is currently at version 1.8. Like Model-Glue, Mach-II is an implicit invocation framework. It provides some extended functionality beyond that of Model-Glue, such as programmatic access to its event queue, plug-in points, and filters that are used to alter the instructions to be executed as a request is processed. This adds up to a potentially more powerful framework. But at first blush, Mach-II is more complex and harder to understand than the alternatives and, consequently, may be harder to implement according to best practices.

The core components of a Mach-II application are listeners, filters, and the event, and you tie these CFC-based objects together using a rich XML syntax. Mach-II event handlers can check the status of anything in the environment, access the currently queued batch of instructions waiting to be processed and change its contents, call upon objects in the model to get data in or out of a database or other data store, redirect the application's flow from the current event to a new event, and any number of other tasks. The framework's richness is largely due to the number of options available when building your own application in Mach-II, which, in many ways, bears some similarity to a J2EE application's structure. So it fits well in the same sort of environment in which J2EE thrives.

You should try Mach-II if you're accomplished with CFCs and want to take a crack at something new. Or, if you are familiar with computer science terminology and Java design patterns, it should feel very homey. If you're familiar with Model-Glue and want to add another tool to your toolbox, it's a good next step. It does provide some industrial-strength functionality, but it's often a toss-up between Model-Glue and Mach-II in terms of choice for a project. It usually comes down to developer preference. Mach-II has many options and can yield many CFC files, but is quite powerful.

# ColdBox

ColdBox, written by Luis Majano and originally released to the public in 2006, favors convention over configuration and can be used without a config file by placing CFCs in particular directories using a particular naming convention—just like the no-XML approach offered by Fusebox 5.5. It has a very robust feature set, lots and lots of extension points (including a plug-in API), and a strong internal event model. And some say that its biggest claim to fame is the volumes of documentation out there on ColdBox, most of which, remarkably, was created by Luis himself.

ColdBox does basically everything the other frameworks do, with one significant difference: Without plug-ins or some other sort of modification it's not implicit invocation. It's explicit invocation, which means you have to abide by naming conventions to guide your application's execution path through each request. Is this better or worse? Neither, really. But it is different and worth mentioning.

Generally people either love ColdBox or hate it based on whether convention over configuration rings true for them. ColdBox, like most other frameworks, has the capacity to be simple or extremely robust and complex depending on how it is used. It is, however, best used by those with at least minimal experience with CFCs.

# Back-End and Service Frameworks

Some frameworks aren't intended to deliver HTML-based content to the end user. They're designed to make it easier to interact with databases and provide services to your applications and clients, while lessening the code required by the developer. These include

- ColdSpring

- Reactor

- Transfer

This type of framework receives instructions via code written by the developer rather than through a URL or form variable. By calling some fairly simple code, the framework can be set up to access data sources such as databases and libraries of other objects. Most of the time, the code required looks something like the following:

```
<cfset reactor=createObject("component","reactor.reactorFactory").init("reactorConfig.xml")>
<cfset User = reactor.createRecord("User").load(url.userId)>
```

In this case, I'm creating an instance of the `ReactorFactory` (which is used to create instances of other objects that represent rows in your database), and then accessing all the data in the `User` table for a record that has an ID value of 1. Reactor is configured via an XML file, which is the file referenced in the first line of the snippet (`reactorConfig.xml`). ColdSpring also uses an XML file for configuration and has very similar syntax to the first line of the snippet. Transfer is also similar in syntax, but uses two XML config files rather than one.

These frameworks reduce the amount of code a developer has to write to get a particular subsystem within an application up and running, like reading from or saving data to a database (Reactor, Transfer) or managing the CFCs that provide services to your actual application code (ColdSpring).

## ColdSpring

ColdSpring is meant to manage CFCs in the application or server scopes and to make it much easier to interconnect various CFCs than if you were writing all the code by hand. ColdSpring also makes remoting a lot easier when providing ColdFusion services to Flash or Flex movies and Ajax clients. In addition, ColdSpring provides tools to use aspect-oriented programming (AOP), which is far beyond the scope of this introductory article. Suffice it to say that AOP can be a very valuable tool for injecting standard behaviors into your CFCs.

## Reactor

Reactor, a framework authored by Doug Hughes and now managed by Mark Drew, is used to read and save data from a database—it has a robust code-generation library that allows you to read a record from a database in as little as five lines of CFML. It features one XML configuration file and can read records from a table across link tables; read, save, and delete records; and aids in creating a CFC-based object model out of your database schema. Obviously this means that your objects are directly related to your database design, and Reactor may not always be suitable. But in a majority of situations Reactor is an ideal tool to get you off the ground with an object-oriented framework by creating your objects for you and giving you quick and easy access to your database.

## Transfer

Transfer, a framework authored by Mark Mandel, is also used to read and save data from a database. Like Reactor, it can read records from a table across link tables, and read, save, and delete records. Transfer provides options for adding your business object methods to your persistence code either by specifying methods directly in one of the XML configuration files or by using the decorator design pattern, keeping business methods separate but allowing Transfer to blend the resulting code. Transfer features a sophisticated caching system and, like Reactor, now offers integration with Model-Glue:Unity for scaffolding and generic data messages. Transfer is worth considering as an alternative to Reactor.

# Summary

As you can see, ColdFusion has an active and involved developer community and a growing and robust set of development tools. In terms of HTML-based UI frameworks, there is enough variety to provide a solution for almost any preference. And as for back-end or service frameworks, we have a powerful set of tools at our disposal, all of which are written by developers to solve pain points experienced by developers. The future is shaping up brightly for ColdFusion programmers with a wealth of powerful tools at our disposal and an array of options that should fit nearly any project.

::: :::

# CHAPTER 25

# Fusebox 5 Fundamentals

by Sean Corfield

Updated by Jeff Peters

*Fusebox 5.5 is the latest release of ColdFusion's oldest and most popular application framework. This article introduces Fusebox. And for those who have been using Fusebox 4, 4.1, or 5, it covers what's new in Fusebox 5.5.*

## Fusebox—What and Why

Let's start by defining what we mean by an *application framework* in the context of Fusebox. An application framework is a set of files that provides two things:

- Reusable code that is common across most web applications

- A standardized structure for your applications so that maintenance is easier

Fusebox has been designed specifically to help you build more maintainable applications, regardless of your skill level with ColdFusion. Whether you write procedural code or object-oriented (OO) code, and whether you are a novice or an expert, Fusebox can support your style of programming. This makes Fusebox particularly attractive to development teams with members who have varying skill levels or use different programming styles, encompassing both procedural and OO approaches.

Fusebox tries hard not to enforce a particular programming style, but it strongly encourages best practices such as separating display code, database code, and other business logic. Fusebox supports the widely used Model-View-Controller (MVC) design pattern, but does not force you to use it. Fusebox supports using ColdFusion Components (CFCs) in your application, but again, does not force you to do so.

# Fusebox Concepts

The basic metaphor behind Fusebox is a practical, everyday one: the electrical circuits in your home. In the same way that electricity flows into your house through a central fusebox and is then routed to individual circuits that control related appliances, the Fusebox application framework has a central control point— the fusebox—and organizes code into circuits containing related functionality.

For example, a task manager application might have a circuit that handles user identity and a circuit that handles tasks. As the application grows, new circuits can be incorporated, each containing a group of related functionality. If you build a new application, you may be able to reuse a circuit from a previous application, such as user identity.

All requests come through the central fusebox by way of a standard URL or Form variable, often called `fuseaction`. The value of this variable specifies which circuit to route the request to and which fuseaction to invoke within that circuit. Here's an example that specifies that the `login` fuse action within the `user` circuit should be executed:

```
index.cfm?fuseaction=user.login
```

Within a fuseaction, you can specify that Fusebox execute multiple operations, using verbs in an XML file for each circuit. This could be as simple as including a ColdFusion source file using the `include` verb, or as complex as conditional and looping control logic, using the `if` and `loop` verbs, for example. Fusebox has a very small set of verbs that allows you to perform basic control logic. This makes the Fusebox syntax easy to learn.

Versions of Fusebox prior to 4 used a file called `fbx_switch.cfm` to define the actions, and didn't have formalized verbs. Fusebox 4 introduced the XML vocabulary with formalized verbs, and used the `circuit.xml` file to contain them. As of Fusebox 5.5, you can choose to omit the XML file and use either a CFC or a directory containing `.cfm` files to represent a circuit, as long as you follow a convention for organizing your code. This makes Fusebox 5.5 a good choice for programmers who like the style of earlier Fusebox versions, as well as those who prefer the XML-based style. For example, the preceding fuseaction example could be implemented as `user.cfc` with a `login()` method or as a `user` directory with a `login.cfm` file. This convention-over-configuration approach follows the lead of frameworks such as Ruby on Rails.

In keeping with the electrical metaphor, Fusebox refers to any included ColdFusion files as *fuses* to emphasize their intended small, atomic nature. In addition, Fusebox encourages the use of a file-naming convention to remind developers to separate their code appropriately. Files containing display logic (and HTML) are usually given the prefix `dsp` (for display) or `lay` (for layout); files containing database queries are usually given the prefix `qry` (for query); and files containing other business logic are usually given the prefix `act` (for action).

In the first few releases of the Fusebox framework, all of this was very much just convention, with only a few core files in the framework. With Fusebox 4, the structure became more formalized with the introduction of XML files to specify the fusebox itself—the set of circuits in the application and the various parameters of the framework—and to specify the fuseaction code in each circuit.

Returning to our task manager application, we might choose to organize our code like this:

```
Application.cfm
index.cfm
fusebox.xml
user/
    circuit.xml
    dsp_login.cfm
    … other CFML fuse files
task/
    circuit.xml
    dsp_task_list.cfm
    qry_task_list.cfm
    qry_update_task.cfm
    … other CFML fuse files
```

In this structure, the `index.cfm` file includes the main Fusebox core file, the `fusebox.xml` file specifies where to find the user and task circuits (and other application parameters), and the `circuit.xml` files specify the various fuseactions in the circuits.

Here, we have just two circuits: one containing all of the fuses related to user identity and the other containing all of the fuses related to task management. We can see a display fuse in the user circuit that would contain the login form. In the task circuit, we see query fuses that fetch tasks and update a task. There would be a number of other fuse files that contain the rest of the logic and display code for the application, but the preceding outline should give you a sense of how a Fusebox application is structured.

As noted, Fusebox 5.5 offers the option of omitting `fusebox.xml` and instead having circuits determined by convention. A no-XML version of the same task manager application might look like this:

```
Application.cfm
index.cfm
user/
    showLogin.cfm
    dsp_login.cfm
    … other CFML fuse files
task/
    showTaskList.cfm
    addTask.cfm
    dsp_task_list.cfm
    qry_task_list.cfm
    qry_update_task.cfm
    … other CFML fuse files
```

Still another approach to the same application is to use CFCs to contain circuits, which might look like this:

```
Application.cfm
index.cfm
controller/
    user.cfc
        showLogin() method
    task.cfc
        showTaskList() method
        addTask() method
model/
    m_user.cfc
    m_task.cfc
    qry_task_list.cfm
    qry_update_task.cfm
    … other CFML fuse files
view/
    v_user.cfc
    v_task.cfc
    dsp_login.cfm
    dsp_task_list.cfm
    … other CFML fuse files
```

Operations on tasks might be protected by a security check. We might require that users are logged in before they can use the task manager. We may want to execute the `user.authenticate` fuseaction prior to any fuseaction in the task circuit, for example. Fusebox provides an easy way to do this by specifying `prefuseaction` and `postfuseaction` operations on each circuit:

```
<prefuseaction>
    <do action="user.authenticate"/>
</prefuseaction>
```

Fusebox would then automatically run this fuseaction before executing any other fuseaction in the task circuit. `user.authenticate` would check that the user is logged in and, if not, would cause a redirect to the `user.login` fuseaction. This modularity can allow developers to reuse whole circuits in other applications.

In the no-XML approaches, a circuit CFC may contain a `prefuseaction()` method, and a circuit directory may contain a `prefuseaction.cfm` file.

## Fusebox Benefits

The simple structure and organization of a Fusebox application make maintenance easier by allowing any developer who is familiar with the framework to pick up the code and get a sense of its purpose just by looking at the circuit layout and, within each circuit, the available fuseactions. Similarly, the file-naming convention allows developers to quickly locate code and make changes in a systematic way.

Fusebox has been around long enough that there is a wealth of information out there about the framework, so it is easy to learn how to use it and get support from the community.

Books about Fusebox are available from Proton Arts (`http://protonarts.com/`) as well as other technical booksellers.

The Fusebox web site (`http://fusebox.org/`) has documentation about the framework and forums where you can engage with the large Fusebox community if you need assistance. There are also several mailing lists, three of which are linked from the home page of the web site, as well as an extensive resources list on the web site.

## A Fusebox Glossary

Here are definitions of some common Fusebox terms:

- **circuit**: A group of fuseactions, often self-contained, that implement a coherent subset of an application's functionality. Each circuit typically addresses a specific concept from the application's domain, such as user management, shopping cart, or invoicing.

- **FLiP (Fusebox Lifecycle Process)**: A project management approach to planning, architecting, coding, and testing a Fusebox application. FLiP focuses on building an HTML prototype of the web site with the client and using that to drive the architecture of the Fusebox application that will power the site.

- **fuse**: A ColdFusion file that is executed by the `include` verb. Each fuse contains a simple piece of ColdFusion code that does just one job: executes a database query or displays some HTML or performs some specific business operation. Fuse files are typically named with a prefix that indicates which type of job they do: `act` (action), `dsp` (display), `qry` (query), `lay` (layout), and so on.

- **fuseaction**: A named handler for a specific request within a given circuit. A fuseaction defines the verbs that are executed in order to perform that request.

- **lexicon**: A collection of one or more related verbs. Each lexicon is stored in a separate directory underneath the `lexicon/` directory within each application. A lexicon is made available within a circuit by declaring its location in the `circuit` tag, using an XML namespace, e.g., `<circuit xmlns:prefix="location/">`, which tells Fusebox that verbs with the specified prefix (`<prefix:myverb/>`) can be found in the `lexicon/location/` directory.

- **verb**: An individual XML tag in the `circuit.xml` file that is compiled to ColdFusion Markup Language (CFML) by executing the verb's implementation in the appropriate lexicon. A verb may be built in (such as *set* or `include`), or it may be part of a user-defined lexicon.

269

- **XFA (eXit FuseAction)**: A fuseaction that represents an exit point from a given web page. Exit points are links and form actions that take you from one page to another. It is considered good practice not to hard-code links into pages, but instead use variables to create those links, with those variables usually set in the fuseaction that includes the display fuse. This allows display fuses to be reused when only the destinations of links change.

# What's New in Fusebox 5 and 5.5

The first section of this article should make you feel comfortable about choosing the Fusebox application framework for your projects. The remainder of this article focuses on what's new in Fusebox 5 and 5.5 and why existing Fusebox developers will want to upgrade.

## Compatibility

The first and most important thing to note about Fusebox 5.5 is that it is designed to be completely backward compatible with Fusebox 5, Fusebox 4.1, and Fusebox 4. If you have an existing Fusebox 4.1 application, it should not require any changes to run on this new release of the framework.

## Coding Styles

Five different styles can be used to write applications under Fusebox 5.5:

- XML for circuits and fuseactions

- CFCs as circuits, with methods for fuseactions

- Implied circuits, with CFCs for fuseactions

- Implied circuits, with CFMs for fuseactions

- Implied circuits, with XML for fuseactions

### XML for Circuits and Fuseactions

The XML for circuits and fuseactions style is used by Fusebox 4 and 5.0. It uses `fusebox.xml` to define circuits and a `circuit.xml` in each circuit's directory to define fuseactions. For example, the `navigation.showMenu` fuseaction would require the navigation circuit to be defined in the circuits section of `fusebox.xml`, and the `showMenu` fuseaction to be defined in the fuseactions section of `circuit.xml` in the appropriate directory according to `fusebox.xml`. Listings 25-1 and 25-2 show an example of an application structured in this way.

*Listing 25-1. fusebox.xml in an application using XML for circuits and fuseactions*

```
<fusebox>
  <circuits>
    <circuit alias="navigation" path="nav/" parent="/" />
  </circuits>
...
</fusebox>
```

*Listing 25-2. nav/circuit.xml in an application using XML for circuits and fuseactions*

```
<circuit access="public">
  <fuseaction name="showMenu" />
    <include template="dspMenu" />
  </fuseaction>
</circuit>
```

## CFCs As Circuits, Methods for Fuseactions

The style of CFCs as circuits, with methods for fuseactions uses a CFC named for the circuit, with a method named for each fuseaction within the circuit. For example, the navigation.showMenu fuseaction would be defined by the showMenu() method within the navigation.cfc file. Listing 25-3 shows an example of this application style.

*Listing 25-3. navigation.cfc in an application that uses CFCs as circuits and methods for fuseactions*

```
<cffunction name="showMenu">
  <cfinclude template="dspMenu.cfm" />
</cffunction>
```

## Implied Circuits, CFCs for Fuseactions

The style of implied circuits, with CFCs for fuseactions uses directories named for each circuit, allowing Fusebox to infer circuit names from the directories within an MVC style. Fuseactions are defined as CFCs within the circuit subdirectory of the controller directory. For example, the navigation.showMenu fuseaction would be defined by the showMenu.cfc file within the navigation subdirectory of the controller directory: /controller/navigation/showMenu.cfc. A method called do() is used within each fuseaction CFC to execute the desired CFML. Listings 25-4 and 25-5 give examples of this application style.

*Listing 25-4. controller/navigation/showMenu.cfc in an application that uses implied circuits and CFCs for fuseactions*

```
<cffunction name="do">
  <cfset myFusebox.do("v_navigation.showMenu") />
</cffunction>
```

*Listing 25-5. view/v_navigation/showMenu.cfc in an application that uses implied circuits and CFCs for fuseactions*

```
<cffunction name="do">
  <cfinclude template="dspMenu.cfm" />
</cffunction>
```

## Implied Circuits, CFMs for Fuseactions

The style of implied circuits, with CFMs for fuseactions uses directories named for each circuit, allowing Fusebox to infer circuit names from the directories. Fuseactions are defined as CFML files with the name of the fuseaction as the file name. For example, the `navigation.showMenu` fuseaction would be defined by the `showMenu.cfm` file within the navigation directory. Listing 25-6 shows an example of this application style.

*Listing 25-6. /navigation/showMenu.cfm in an application that uses implied circuits and CFMs for fuseactions*

```
<cfinclude template="dspMenu.cfm" />
```

## Implied Circuits, XML for Fuseactions

The style of implied circuits, with XML for fuseactions uses directories named for each circuit, allowing Fusebox to infer circuit names from the directories. Each circuit directory contains a `circuit.xml` file to define fuseactions, much as with the traditional XML style. Listing 25-7 shows an example of this application style.

*Listing 25-7. /navigation/circuit.xml in an application that uses implied circuits and XML for fuseactions*

```
<circuit access="public">
  <fuseaction name="showMenu" />
    <include template="dspMenu" />
  </fuseaction>
</circuit>
```

# Multiple Applications

Prior to Fusebox 5, releases of the Fusebox framework assumed that you built monolithic applications, and that each individual Fusebox application was also a separate ColdFusion application. Fusebox stored information about your application in the `application.fusebox` data structure. This made it hard to write Fusebox applications that integrated well with each other, because they couldn't share application data or session data. This made it difficult to have single sign-on across multiple applications, for example.

By default, Fusebox 5.*x* uses `application.fusebox` for information about your application, but you can override this by setting the `FUSEBOX_APPLICATION_KEY` variable in `index.cfm` before you include the framework runtime file. This allows you to have multiple Fusebox applications sharing a single ColdFusion application name without overwriting each other.

## Application Initialization

Just as ColdFusion MX 7 introduced `Application.cfc` and a way to write code that executes just once at application startup through the `onApplicationStart()` method, Fusebox 5 introduced a portable way to do this within the framework. Fusebox 4.1 introduced an optional file called `fusebox.init.cfm`, which is executed automatically at the start of each request. Fusebox 5 introduced an optional file called `fusebox.appinit.cfm`, which is executed automatically when the first request is made for the application. Like ColdFusion MX 7's `onApplicationStart()` method, the code in `fusebox.appinit.cfm` is executed inside a lock to ensure it is thread-safe. Fusebox 5.*x* also provides a way to execute code at application startup—as fuseactions specified in the XML files, within the framework itself.

Fusebox 5.5 offers direct integration with `Application.cfc`. Your `Application.cfc` can extend `fusebox5.Application` and have access to framework event methods such as `onFuseboxApplicationStart()`.

## Custom Lexicons

Custom lexicons represent a major extension in Fusebox 5.*x*. In order to explain them, we need to cover in a little more detail the machinery that Fusebox uses to handle requests.

The first time a specific request comes into the framework, Fusebox locates the appropriate circuit and the fuseaction within it, and then converts the XML for that fuseaction into ColdFusion code, which it writes to a parsed directory. Subsequent requests for that fuseaction are handled by simply including the generated file.

Each fuseaction is specified in the XML file as a sequence of verbs to be executed. For example, see the task manager application in Listing 25-8.

*Listing 25-8. Task manager application*

```
<fuseaction name="showall">
  <set name="max" value="20" />
  <include template="qry_task_list" />
  <xfa name="view" value="task.showtask" />
  <include template="dsp_task_list" contentvariable="body" />
  <include template="lay_main" />
</fuseaction>
```

Here, we have three verbs in use: `set`, `include`, and `xfa`. The `set` verb generates code that sets a variable (called `max`) to the specified value (20, in this case). The `include` verb generates code that includes the specified file (with a `.cfm` extension appended automatically). The `xfa` verb is a special case of the `set` verb that generates code to set an XFA (eXit FuseAction) variable to the specified value. (XFAs are kept in a special structure variable called `xfa`.) The generated code from this fuseaction will be stored in `parsed/task.showall.cfm` (based on the name of the circuit/fuseaction).

The XFA variable is used in a display fuse to construct a link to another page:

```
<a href="#myself##xfa.view#&amp;taskId=#taskId#">View this task</a>
```

The `myself` variable is usually set in `fusebox.init.cfm` and refers to the base URL of the Fusebox `index.cfm` page, as shown here:

```
<cfset self = "index.cfm">
<cfset myself = self & "?" & myFusebox.getApplication().fuseactionVariable & "=">
```

This technique allows the fuseaction to determine where the links inside the display fuse will actually go, so display fuses can be reused more easily.

In Fusebox 4, the built-in verbs were all handled magically inside the framework, and there was no way to add new verbs. Fusebox 4.1 introduced an experimental mechanism called *lexicons* that allowed Fusebox developers to create their own verbs as ColdFusion files and specify their location (using the `<lexicons>` section in the `fusebox.xml` file). User-defined verbs could not have nested child verbs and were, overall, quite a pain to write.

Fusebox 5.*x* takes this basic idea and integrates it into the core of the framework. Apart from `do`, which is more of a compiler directive, there are no magic built-in verbs. All of the standard verbs in Fusebox 5.*x* exist as ColdFusion files that are executed by the framework. User-defined verbs are just like those standard verbs, except that they must be introduced using an XML namespace in each circuit that needs them.

The skeleton application for Fusebox 5.*x* shows an example of this as well as providing almost a dozen verbs that mimic tags within the ColdFusion language. Here is a simple example of Fusebox 5.*x* syntax:

```
<circuit access="public" xmlns:cf="cf/">
```

This introduces the XML namespace `cf` and defines the path for it: `cf/`. The path is relative to the `lexicon/` directory within your application root and doesn't need to match the namespace name. Once the XML namespace has been declared, whenever Fusebox sees a verb in the `cf` namespace, such as the `dump` verb found in the following code, it will look in `lexicon/cf/` for the implementation file.

```
<cf:dump label="Attributes Scope" var="#attributes#">
```

Fusebox expects to find `dump.cfm` in the `lexicon/cf/` directory and will execute it much like a custom tag is executed in ColdFusion. Each verb is run twice: first with an execution mode of `start` when the tag is opened, and then again with an execution mode of `end` when the tag is closed. The ColdFusion file that implements the verb generates ColdFusion code and writes it to the parsed file using convenience methods such as `fb_appendLine()`:

```
fb_appendLine('<cfdump #fb_.label# var="#fb_.verbInfo.attributes.var#">');
```

The skeleton application for Fusebox 5.*x* includes several Fusebox verbs that mimic ColdFusion tags, such as `try`/`catch`, `switch`/`case`/`defaultcase`, and others. These are good examples of how to extend the Fusebox XML language in any way you want. For a more complex example, refer to these blog entries, which shows what it might look like to have a set of Model-Glue style verbs for use within Fusebox:

```
http://corfield.org/entry/Fusebox_5_in_a_ModelGlue_style
```

http://corfield.org/entry/Fusebox_5__The_Power_of_Custom_Lexicons

Note that the example does not use Model-Glue code at all; it merely emulates it as a Fusebox 5.*x* custom lexicon.

You might wonder why you would want to duplicate ColdFusion tags in the Fusebox grammar. The built-in Fusebox grammar is deliberately very simple, so that you are not tempted to put too much logic into your fuseactions. The original guiding principle for Fusebox was that all logic belonged in fuses instead. However, with the increasing use of CFCs in Fusebox applications, there are a number of situations where the simple Fusebox grammar gets in the way of writing clean code. For example, although you could *invoke* a component's method directly within a fuseaction, if the method could throw an exception that you wanted to handle gracefully, Fusebox 4.1 forced you to create an action fuse and place the invocation in there, surrounded by your try / catch logic. This made the application flow harder to read, since you were forced to open a fuse just to see the method call, as well as required to put conditional checking into your fuseactions. Fusebox 5.*x* allows you to keep simple control logic like this directly in the fuseaction, making it easier to follow the application flow. Compare the examples in Listings 25-9 and 25-10.

*Listing 25-9. Fusebox 4.1 code*

```
<!--- Showquote Fuseaction --->
<fuseaction name="showquote">
  <include template="actGetQuote" />
    <if condition="len(stockPrice) neq 0">
      <true>
         <include template="dspStockQuote" />
      </true>
      <false>
          <include template="dspQuoteFailed" />
       </false>
    </if>
</fuseaction>

<!--- actGetQuote.cfm --->
<cftry>
    <cfinvoke component="#application.stockTracker#" method="getQuote"
             returnvariable="stockPrice">
        <cfinvokeargument name="symbol" value="#attributes.symbol#">
    </cfinvoke>
    <cfcatch type="any">
        <cfset stockPrice = "">
    </cfcatch>
</cftry>
```

*Listing 25-10. Fusebox 5.x code*

```
<fuseaction name="showquote">
    <cf:try>
        <invoke object="application.stockTracker" method="getQuote"
                returnvariable="stockPrice">
            <argument name="symbol" value="#attributes.symbol#" />
        </invoke>
        <include template="dspStockQuote" />
        <cf:catch type="any">
            <include template="dspQuoteFailed" />
        </cf:catch>
    </cf:try>
</fuseaction>
```

By providing extensibility through optional lexicons in this way, Fusebox 5.*x* retains the small, easy-to-learn grammar of Fusebox 4.1 while offering increased expressiveness to those developers who need it, especially those using CFCs extensively.

Of course, if you use the no-XML approach offered by Fusebox 5.5, the issue of extending the XML grammar goes away, since you can simply write CFML directly (in the circuit CFC or .cfm files).

## XML Grammar

In addition to the major new language features introduced by the custom lexicons, Fusebox 5.*x* provides a number of smaller improvements to the language as defined in Fusebox 4.1. In Fusebox 5.*x*, there are no restrictions on nesting of if and loop verbs as there were in Fusebox 4.1, and Fusebox 5.*x* now supports the same five styles of loops that ColdFusion itself supports (query, collection, condition, list, and from/to).

There has been a lot of development in the area of CFC support in Fusebox 5.*x*. In addition to the once-per-application initialization hooks discussed in the previous section, a new argument verb has been added as a child to the instantiate and invoke verbs to provide a much cleaner syntax for working with CFCs and that is more in line with ColdFusion's own syntax. You can specify unnamed (positional) arguments, as in Listing 25-11, or named arguments, as in Listing 25-12.

*Listing 25-11. Specifying unnamed (positional) arguments with the argument verb*

```
<invoke component="util.myCFC" method="doSomething">
    <argument value="firstArg" />
    <argument value="2" />
</invoke>
```

*Listing 25-12. Specifying named arguments with the argument verb*

```
<invoke component="util.myCFC" method="doSomething">
    <argument name="arg1" value="firstArg" />
    <argument name="arg2" value="2" />
</invoke>
```

The do and include verbs have a similar extension so that parameters can be passed into fuseactions and fuses. Listing 25-13 shows an example of passing in the name of a fuseaction that the user login code can redirect to once a user has successfully authenticated.

*Listing 25-13. Passing parameters to the do and include verbs*

```
<prefuseaction>
    <do action="user.authenticate">
        <parameter name="returnAction" value="task.#myFusebox.thisFuseaction#" />
    </do>
</prefuseaction>
```

This will set the variable returnAction to the value of the current circuit (task) and fuseaction for the duration of the user.authenticate fuseaction.

## The Fusebox Grammar

The following verbs are built into Fusebox 5:

- do: Execute another fuseaction as part of the current fuseaction. do may have optional parameter children (new in Fusebox 5).

- if: Conditionally execute other verbs. if may contain a true group and/or a false group.

- include: Include a fuse file. include may have optional parameter children (new in Fusebox 5).

- instantiate: Instantiate a CFC that was previously declared in the <classes> section of the fusebox.xml file. instantiate may have optional argument children (new in Fusebox 5).

- invoke: Invoke a component's method. invoke may have optional argument children (new in Fusebox 5).

- loop: Repeatedly execute a group of other verbs.

- relocate: Relocate to a new URL—similar to cflocation in ColdFusion.

- **set**: Set a variable to a given value—similar to `cfset` in ColdFusion.

- **xfa**: Set an XFA variable to a given fuseaction.

## Dynamic Do

The **do** verb is one of the most used in the Fusebox 5 grammar. Therefore, it was desirable to have an analog for its behavior available even when not using XML under Fusebox 5.5. The result is the so-called *dynamic do*, which is actually a method named `do()` on the `myFusebox` object. A fuseaction called `navigation.showMenu` could be called using the syntax `myFusebox.do("navigation.showMenu")`. Listing 25-14 shows an example of using the dynamic do.

*Listing 25-14. An example of the dynamic do*

```
<cfscript>
  if (loginSuccessful){
    myFusebox.do("navigation.showMenu");
  }
</cfscript>
```

## Application.cfc Support

Fusebox 5.5 provides direct support of `Application.cfc` by adding the `fusebox5.Application` CFC. This new object is then used as the **super** when writing `Appliction.cfc`; that is, `Application.cfc` extends `fusebox5.Application.cfc`. Functions in the `Application.cfc`, such as `onRequestStart()`, simply call their **super** (e.g., `super.onRequestStart()`) first to ensure the Fusebox code is executed.

## The event Object

Long-time Fuseboxers are familiar with the use of the Attributes scope to contain all variables, regardless of whether they were originally defined in the URL, Form, or Attributes scope. This approach breaks when using CFCs, as the Attributes scope is not available to CFC methods. Fusebox 5.5 uses the **event** object to serve this purpose. All variables in Fusebox 5.5 applications are available as properties of the **event** object. You can then use the syntax `event.getValue(myVar)` to access the variables. So the variable that originates as `form.userID` can be accessed as `event.getValue("userID")`.

The **event** object has several methods that simplify its use:

- `getAllValues()`

- `getValue()`

- `init()`

- `removeValue()`

- `setValue()`

- valueExists()
- xfa()

## The myFusebox Object

Several changes have been made to the myFusebox object as of Fusebox 5.5:

- The showDebug property, if true, shows debug data at the bottom of all pages.
- The getApplicationData() method returns the application's complete data structure.
- The getOriginalCircuit() method returns the original circuit object for the request.
- The getOriginalFuseaction() method returns the original fuseaction object for the request.
- The variables() method returns the entire top-level variables structure.

## Search-Engine-Safe URLs

Fusebox 5.5 simplifies the creation of search-engine-safe (SES) URLs. Fusebox itself will interpret SES URLs based on the queryStringStart, queryStringSeparator, and queryStringEqual settings in fusebox.xml or the FUSEBOX_PARAMETERS structure. To create an SES URL based on the same settings, use the following syntax:

```
<cfset event.xfa("xfaName","circuit.fuseaction","argumentName1","value1",
                                "argumentName2","value2") />
```

This syntax allows for an arbitrary number of arguments to be added to the URL. For example, to set an XFA named success to go to the fuseaction security.login, and pass the argument userID with a value of "Smith", use this command:

```
<cfset event.xfa("success","security.login","userID", "Smith") />
```

When the application uses the generated XFA, the result is a URL that looks something like this:

```
http://www.myapp.com/index.cfm/fuseaction/security.login/userID/Smith
```

## Runtime Control

In addition to the changes in the Fusebox language itself, there are a number of improvements in the control you have over the runtime behavior of the framework.

Fusebox 5.*x* provides a new execution mode that reloads only individual circuits that have changed, without resetting application data on each request. You can also tell Fusebox 5.*x* to remove all the previous parsed files or to regenerate all public fuseactions in the entire application—both of which can be useful when you are upgrading a production web site to ensure that you have all the latest code running.

Stephen Judd has created a very useful extension for Firefox (`https://addons.mozilla.org/en-US/firefox/addon/6664`) that lets you easily and automatically control the execution of your Fusebox 5.*x* application. (He also has a version of the extension for Fusebox 4.)

The new runtime change that will most likely appeal to the largest number of Fusebox developers is the addition of a debug mode for the framework. Just add the following line to your `fusebox.xml` file, and debugging information will be displayed at the end of each page you request:

```
<parameter name="debug" value="true" />
```

The debugging information shows every fuseaction executed and every fuse included, as well as the time taken to get to each entry and a count of any repeated fuseactions and fuses. This can be very helpful in identifying bottlenecks in your application, as well as debugging unusual behavior, because you can see the execution path through your code.

# Why Upgrade?

Since Fusebox 5.5 is backward compatible with Fusebox 5 and Fusebox 4.1, we might as well ask, "Why wouldn't you upgrade?" Well, an upgrade is going to mean that you need to test your applications completely on the new framework release, so there is always a cost associated with any upgrade.

The next question might be, "If it's backward compatible, what benefits will I get from simply running my Fusebox 4.1 application on it?" That's a good question. If you really aren't planning to change your codebase to take advantage of the new features, you won't get much benefit from an upgrade. However, being able to simply enable tracing and debugging in `fusebox.xml`, and get timing information about your application with no code changes, might be sufficient incentive to encourage you to upgrade, even without changing your codebase.

Finally, you might just find the changes discussed appealing enough to make this an easy decision. Perhaps the ability to use some of the sample verbs from the new Fusebox 5 skeleton application, such as `cf:dump`, might be reason enough. Maybe the new CFC-related syntax or the parameters on `do` and `include` verbs will entice you. Maybe you're interested in the option to avoid XML altogether. Or perhaps the attraction is the option to perform all your per-application initialization directly within the framework in a thread-safe manner.

Fusebox 5 and 5.5 are the first releases of Fusebox that are backward compatible with the previous major release. It protects your investments—both intellectual (knowledge of Fusebox 4.*x*) and physical (your Fusebox 4.*x* codebase)—while offering increased functionality in a number of important areas. The completely rewritten core files provide a solid basis for future development, assuring you of continued growth and richness of the Fusebox framework. There has never been a better time to be a Fusebox developer.

# CHAPTER 26

■ ■ ■

# Mach-II Fundamentals

## by Matt Woodward

*Mach-II was created in 2003 by Ben Edwards and Hal Helms. Originally, they thought this would be a new, CFC-centric branch of Fusebox, and they called it Fusebox MX. They changed the name to Mach-II when they realized that it was very different from Fusebox. Mach-II was the first truly object-oriented framework that was created for ColdFusion. In 2007, Ben Edwards and Hal Helms passed the torch to Peter Farrell, Matt Woodward, and Kurt Wiersma, who have been stewards of the framework ever since. The Mach-II web site has an active community of participants who help to guide the framework, and the motto "We're community-driven" is something they stress greatly in their documentation. In this article, Matt Woodward gives a clear, comprehensive introduction to Mach-II, discusses where Mach-II fits in the CFML framework landscape, and demonstrates Mach-II in action through a few simple examples.*

Despite their reputation in some circles, frameworks exist to make our lives as developers easier. A good framework helps create the basic "plumbing," or flow, of an application so we don't need to keep reinventing that wheel. In addition, the framework's core files can be leveraged to make common tasks easier and less repetitive. Your application will use the framework's application programming interface (API) to simplify and accelerate common development tasks. Most frameworks revolve around a specific design pattern, which helps developers organize their code in a consistent, recognized way. This means that the organization of the application code itself becomes a common language among developers, in addition to the programming language of the application.

In the past few years, there has been a bit of a framework explosion in the ColdFusion Markup Language (CFML) community. Many developers are finding it difficult to understand what all the various CFML frameworks do, let alone which framework or combination of frameworks might be right for their needs. This article covers the Mach-II framework.

After introducing the framework, we'll install it, examine the organization of a basic Mach-II application, and see some simple Mach-II code in action. We'll also look briefly at the incredibly powerful and flexible plug-in and filter architecture that's built in to Mach-II.

## Introducing the Mach-II Framework

Mach-II is an application development framework that is designed to handle application logic and flow, and also helps make applications easier to maintain. The purpose of application development frameworks such as Mach-II can be contrasted with more specialized frameworks such as Transfer, which is an object-relational mapping (ORM) framework, and ColdSpring, which is an inversion of control (IoC) framework. Mach-II uses the Model-View-Controller (MVC) design pattern, which is a tried-and-true method of separating the application's business logic (model), user interface (view), and overall flow (controller) into discrete components. This makes applications easy to develop and maintain.

Since Mach-II is designed to be singular in purpose and focus solely on the logic and flow of the application, it does not incorporate other frameworks directly. However, Mach-II's extensible architecture allows for easy and seamless integration with frameworks such as ColdSpring and Transfer. In fact, the combination of Mach-II with ColdSpring has become so popular that Mach-II ships with a ColdFusion Component (CFC) that allows you to easily integrate the two frameworks.

Mach-II was the first object-oriented (OO) framework for CFML and has proven very successful in a large number of high-traffic web applications, including Adobe.com. Version 1.8 of Mach-II was just released as this article was being written, and version 1.9 and 2.0 are already planned and underway. You can download the framework code, sample applications, and documentation from `http://www.mach-ii.com`.

Because of its OO nature, in order to use Mach-II productively, developers should be familiar with basic concepts of OO development.

In addition to its use of the MVC design pattern, Mach-II is an event-driven, implicit invocation framework (hence the "II" in Mach-II!) that encourages the development of highly cohesive, loosely coupled components. These concepts are fundamental to how Mach-II works, so let's examine each one briefly.

> *Event-driven*: The event object is at the heart of the Mach-II request life cycle. Mach-II automatically puts all the request's form and URL variables into the event object, and your application can programmatically put data into and pull data from the event object. The ability to access everything from a single event object is an extremely convenient way to deal with the event's data. For example, when a form containing username and password fields is submitted in a Mach-II application, these form fields are automatically added to Mach-II's event object.

> *Implicit invocation architecture*: In an implicit invocation architecture, the application announces events, rather than explicitly invoking procedures. This causes objects that have registered an interest in the event to invoke methods. For example, an announcement of the `processLoginAttempt` event might implicitly cause a `checkLoginCredentials` method to be invoked in a login object. This approach keeps the application's flow extremely flexible.

> *Highly cohesive, loosely coupled components*: Because of its event-driven, implicit invocation architecture, Mach-II naturally encourages good development practices by promoting the use of highly cohesive, loosely coupled components. A component with high cohesion does one thing and does it well. Components are loosely coupled when they know as little about one another—particularly the inner workings of one another—as possible. Combined, these concepts lead to the creation of components that are easy to debug and reuse.

> ■ **Note** One might ask how loose coupling differs from encapsulation. Loose coupling refers to creating objects that are not dependent upon one another. Encapsulation is typically used to describe how well inner implementations of and data contained within objects are hidden in the outside world, particularly the data aspect. (Some people use the terms *encapsulation* and *data-hiding* interchangeably.) There is some crossover between loose coupling and encapsulation, but they aren't literally the same.

In addition to basic MVC functionality, Mach-II also includes the following:

- Industrial-strength caching (`https://greatbiztoolsllc.trac.cvsdude.com/mach-ii/wiki/IntroToCaching`) and logging (`https://greatbiztoolsllc.trac.cvsdude.com/mach-ii/wiki/IntroToLogging`) packages

- Environment configuration (`https://greatbiztoolsllc.trac.cvsdude.com/mach-ii/wiki/EnvironmentSpecificProperties`), so your code will "know" if it's in a development environment versus a production one and use the correct settings

- A full-featured form tag library (`https://greatbiztoolsllc.trac.cvsdude.com/mach-ii/wiki/MachII1.8SpecificationFormTagLib`) including data binding

- A view tag library (`https://greatbiztoolsllc.trac.cvsdude.com/mach-ii/wiki/MachII1.8SpecificationViewTagLib`) to make common view page tasks much easier

- An HTML helper library (`https://greatbiztoolsllc.trac.cvsdude.com/mach-ii/wiki/HTMLHelperProperty`) that manages JavaScript, CSS, and other HTML assets for you

There are many more new features in Mach-II 1.8, and more coming in Mach-II 1.9 and 2.0, so be sure to join the Mach-II mailing list (`http://groups.google.com/group/mach-ii-for-coldfusion`) and check the wiki for the latest information.

Now let's take a look at how some of these concepts are realized in the context of a Mach-II application. Understanding the abstract concepts is very important, but they will make more sense through actual coding.

# Installing Mach-II

Installing Mach-II is as simple as downloading the framework files from `http://www.mach-ii.com` and dropping the `MachII` directory contained in the zip file into your web server or virtual host root, or create a mapping for `MachII`. As long as `MachII.` and `/MachII` references in your code get you to the `MachII` directory on your web server, you've successfully installed Mach-II.

In addition to the framework code itself, you can also download two additional packages to help with your Mach-II development. The first is an application skeleton that gives you a head start on building your Mach-II applications. The skeleton also verifies that you've installed Mach-II (and even ColdSpring) correctly, so it's a quick and easy way to make sure everything is in its right place. Just place the contents of the skeleton zip file in your web server or virtual host root, and you're finished. You can then run your application in a browser to test your installation. You'll see the messages shown in Figure 26-1 if you've installed Mach-II correctly.

## Skeleton Installation Success!

You have successfully installed the Mach-II application skeleton.

### ColdSpring Configuration Status

Warning

ColdSpring is not installed or incorrectly configured. If you expected ColdSpring to work, check your configuration. This Mach-II skeleton is compatible with ColdSpring 1.2RC1 or higher. If you didn't install ColdSpring, maybe you should download and install ColdSpring.

### Next Steps

Just a few more thing to convert this skeleton to your application.

- Open the Application.cfc file and change this.name to the name of your application.

Start building your Mach-II application. The Mach-II configuration file is found at /config/mach-ii.xml

- Add and edit any event-handlers.
  - Note: The current defaultEvent property is home.
  - Note: The home event-handler simply calls the home view. This view is found at /views/home.cfm
- Add any listeners.
- Add any event-filters.
- Add any plugins.

### Need Help?

- Check out the Mach-II Frequently Asked Questions (FAQs) at the Mach-II website.
- Join the Mach-II listserv at Google Groups where you can ask questions and seek advice from other Mach-II developers.

*Figure 26-1. Mach-II installation screen for a good installation of Mach-II*

The last piece of the Mach-II puzzle is the Mach-II Dashboard, shown in Figure 26-2. The Dashboard is itself a Mach-II application that can be incorporated in any other Mach-II application, and it adds powerful development and monitoring tools to your applications.

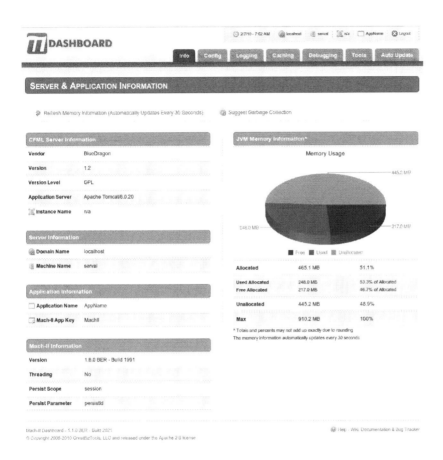

*Figure 26-2. The Mach-II Dashboard*

The Dashboard gives you real-time information about things such as memory usage and caching and logging statistics, and also allows you to reload discrete components in the application as they change during development. The Dashboard includes development tools such as a regex tester and a CFC generator to make your development life easier. Beginning with Mach-II 1.9, the Mach-II core files, skeleton, and Dashboard will be incorporated into a single download to get you up and running with Mach-II even more quickly.

Now that you know how to install Mach-II, let's dig in. The Mach-II core files consist of numerous CFCs, but don't let that scare you away if you're new to CFCs. Mach-II is very simple to learn, and you don't need to know anything about the inner workings of the core files in order to use it. All you need to learn is the framework's API, which is very logical and straightforward.

# The Mach-II Application Skeleton

Before we look at specific code examples, let's see how a basic Mach-II application is organized and how the various application files work together. If you start with the Mach-II skeleton, the basic Mach-II application directory structure will look something like Figure 26-3.

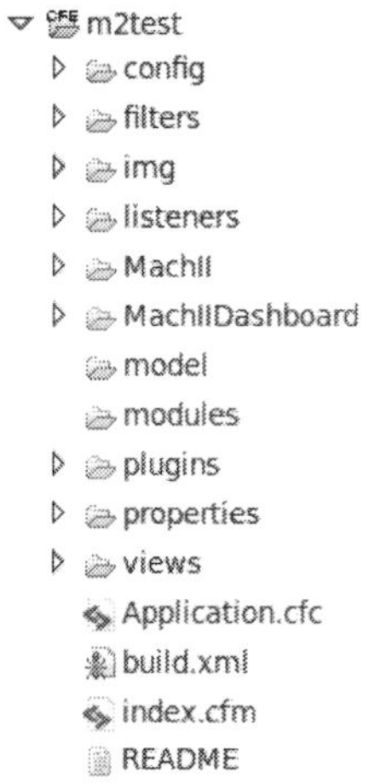

▽ ☷ m2test
  ▷ 🗁 config
  ▷ 🗁 filters
  ▷ 🗁 img
  ▷ 🗁 listeners
  ▷ 🗁 MachII
  ▷ 🗁 MachIIDashboard
    🗁 model
    🗁 modules
  ▷ 🗁 plugins
  ▷ 🗁 properties
  ▷ 🗁 views
    ✎ Application.cfc
    🔨 build.xml
    ✎ index.cfm
    📄 README

*Figure 26-3. Mach-II directory structure*

At minimum, a basic Mach-II application will include `Application.cfc`, `index.cfm`, `mach-ii.xml` (the Mach-II configuration file), a listener CFC, and a view page. Technically, the listener object is optional, but if you want your application to do anything beyond displaying simple view code, you'll be creating listeners to add functionality.

Mach-II is what's known as a front-controller framework, which means that all requests coming into a Mach-II application are routed through `index.cfm`. One of the first things you'll notice is that `index.cfm` is empty. This is because the `OnRequestStart()` method in `Application.cfc` handles request processing in Mach-II applications. The `index.cfm` file still needs to exist, however, because otherwise a 404 error would be thrown without it. So `index.cfm` serves as the entry point for all requests, but the actual request handling is done in `Application.cfc`.

When a request is made to `index.cfm` and `OnRequestStart()` in `Application.cfc` is triggered, Mach-II (in conjunction with your application's code, of course!) determines how to service the request based on the application's XML configuration file. As you'll see shortly, the display code that generates what the user sees is contained in view pages, rather than in the pages that are called directly by a URL.

# Mach-II's XML Configuration File

The `mach-ii.xml` file contained in the `config` directory can be thought of as the application's road map. This declarative configuration file outlines the details of every event in the application and contains important configuration settings. Listing 26-1 shows the `mach-ii.xml` file from the Mach-II skeleton.

*Listing 26-1. mach-ii.xml (configuration file)*

```xml
<?xml version="1.0" encoding="UTF-8"?>

<!DOCTYPE mach-ii PUBLIC "-//Mach-II//DTD Mach-II Configuration 1.8.0//EN"
    "http://www.mach-ii.com/dtds/mach-ii_1_8_0.dtd" >

<mach-ii version="1.8">
    <!-- INCLUDES -->
    <includes>
        <!-- <include file="./mach-ii_coldspringProperty.xml" /> -->
    </includes>

    <!-- PROPERTIES -->
    <properties>
        <property name="applicationRoot" value="/CHANGEME" />
        <property name="defaultEvent" value="home" />
        <property name="eventParameter" value="event" />
        <property name="parameterPrecedence" value="form" />
        <property name="maxEvents" value="10" />
        <property name="exceptionEvent" value="exception" />

        <!-- CACHING RELATED -->
        <!-- this will create an unnamed cache that caches data
        for 1 hour in the application scope -->
        <!-- <property name="caching" type="MachII.caching.CachingProperty" /> -->

        <!-- LOGGING RELATED -->
        <!-- this will log to the screen -->
        <!-- <property name="logging" type="MachII.logging.LoggingProperty" /> -->
    </properties>

    <!-- LISTENERS -->
    <listeners>
        <!-
        <listener name="yourListenerName" type="fully.Qualified.Dot.Delimited.Path.To.CFC">
            <parameters>
                    <parameter name="yourParameterName" value="yourParameterValue" />
            </parameters>
        </listener>
        -->
    </listeners>

    <!-- MESSAGE SUBSCRIBERS -->
    <message-subscribers>
        <!-- see the messagePublisher event handler below for an example of what would
        call this -->
        <!-
        <message name="needStuff" multithreaded="true" waitForThreads="true"
        timeout="10">
```

287

```
        <subscribe listener="listener1" method="method1" resultArg="stuff1" />
        <subscribe listener="listener2" method="method2" resultArg="stuff2" />
        </message>
        -->
</message-subscribers>

<!-- EVENT-FILTERS -->
<event-filters>
    <!-
    <event-filter name="yourEventFilterName"
                  type="fully.Qualified.Dot.Delimited.Path.To.CFC">
        <parameters>
                <parameter name="yourParameterName" value="yourParameterValue" />
        </parameters>
        </event-filter>
        -->
</event-filters>

<!-- PLUGINS -->
<plugins>
    <!-
    <plugin name="yourPluginName" type="fully.Qualified.Dot.Delimited.Path.To.CFC">
    <parameters>
    <parameter name="yourParameterName" value="yourParameterValue" />
    </parameters>
    </plugin>
    -->
</plugins>

<!-- EVENT-HANDLERS -->
<event-handlers>
<event-handler event="home" access="public">
    <!-- <notify listener="SomeListener" method="doSomething"
     resultArg="resultOfSomething" />   -->
    <view-page name="home" />
    </event-handler>

    <!-- sample event handler that uses caching and the default cache
    (data cached for 1 hour in application scope) -->
    <!-
    <event-handler event="useCache" access="public">
    <cache>
        <notify listener="SomeListener" method="getDataForCache" resultArg="
          cachedData" />
    </cache>
    </event-handler>
    -->
```

```
    <!-- sample event handler that uses message/subscriber listener notification -->
    <!--
    <event-handler event="messagePublisher" access="public">
    <publish message="needStuff" />
    </event-handler>
    -->

    <event-handler event="exception" access="private">
    <view-page name="exception" />
    </event-handler>
</event-handlers>
<!-- SUBROUTINES -->
<subroutines>
    <!--
    <subroutine name="yourSubroutineName">
    </subroutine>
    -->
</subroutines>

<!-- PAGE-VIEWS -->
<page-views>
    <page-view name="home" page="/views/home.cfm" />
    <page-view name="exception" page="/views/exception.cfm" />
</page-views>

</mach-ii>
```

The nine sections in the configuration file are as follows:

- includes: Contains a list of additional XML files to include. This allows you to split up your XML configuration file into multiple files for easier management.

- properties: Contains general application settings, both those required by Mach-II and those defined by the developer. In addition to basic name/value pairs, properties can be CFCs.

- listeners: Contains the instance name and specific CFC path for the application's listener objects.

- message-subscribers: Used to declare multiple listener methods that are called as a result of a single notification.

- event-filters: Contains information about the application's filters, which are used to preprocess events and potentially to take action (such as short-circuiting the event) before allowing event execution to proceed.

- plugins: Contains information about the application's plugins. Similar to filters, plugins can be used to take action at any of nine plugin points during the course of an event: preProcess, preEvent, postEvent, preView, postView, postProcess, onSessionStart, onSessionEnd, and handleException.

- event-handlers: Contains information about the application's event handlers. The event handler contains the details of what occurs during that event.

- **subroutines**: Contains a list of subroutines. Subroutines are a handy way to execute blocks of XML within event handlers. This can reduce redundancy of XML between event handlers that leverage the same blocks of XML.

- **page-views**: Registers the view pages. Each has a name (an alias that is called via the **view-page** command in Mach-II) and the specific location of the CFML page that will be called.

You can add XML configuration sections, such as modules that allow you to break your application into multiple large portions, as well as caching, logging, and many other features. Here, we'll look at the more commonly used sections in a bit more detail.

## Properties

Six properties are required by all Mach-II applications:

- **applicationRoot**: The root directory of the application relative to your web server or virtual host's root directory.

- **defaultEvent**: The default event that is announced if an event name isn't specified in the URL.

- **eventParameter**: The URL variable that contains the event parameter name. Typically this is **event**, so the URL will be something like **index.cfm?event=doSomething**.

- **parameterPrecedence**: Because Mach-II automatically puts all URL and form variables in the event object, this property determines which scope (URL or Form) takes precedence if a URL and form variable have the same name.

- **maxEvents**: The maximum number of events that can be announced in a row. This is basically a safeguard against infinite event announcement loops.

- **exceptionEvent**: The event that is announced when an exception occurs.

You aren't limited to these six properties, however. You can add your own as needed by specifying additional name/value pairs. For example, to store your data source name as a Mach-II property, simply add the line shown in Listing 26-2 to the properties section.

*Listing 26-2. Storing your data source name as a Mach-II property in mach-ii.xml*

```
<property name="dsn" value="MyDatasourceName" />
```

When you need something more than a name/value pair to be available as a property, you have a couple of options. First, properties can be declared as arrays, structs, or any combination of the two directly in the XML configuration file. Listing 26-3 contains an example of declaring a struct as a property.

*Listing 26-3. Declaring a struct as a property in mach-ii.xml*

```
<property name="myStruct">
    <struct>
        <key name="key1" value="value1" />
        <key name="key2">
            <value>value2</value>
        </key>
    </struct>
</property>
```

You may also use CFCs as properties by creating a CFC that extends `MachII.framework.Property`, as shown in Listing 26-4. This is a great way to make things like user-defined function (UDF) libraries available across your entire application, or when you need something more complex than a name/value pair.

*Listing 26-4. Creating a CFC that extends MachII.framework.Property*

```
<property name="udfs" type="path.to.udfCFC" />
```

Regardless of their type, properties are available throughout your application by calling `getProperty("propertyName")`.

Learn more about properties at the Mach-II wiki: `https://greatbiztoolsllc.trac.cvsdude.com/mach-ii/wiki/NewPropertyDatatypes`.

# Listeners

The listeners you create extend the base listener object contained in the framework core files so that they are loaded into the server's memory when the application initializes. This provides a significant speed benefit because, the listeners don't need to be created each time they're used. Listeners are very important in Mach-II applications because they are the objects that listen for specific events and take action when those events are announced.

Learn more about listeners at the Mach-II wiki: `https://greatbiztoolsllc.trac.cvsdude.com/mach-ii/wiki/IntroToListeners`.

# Event Filters

Event filters are a way to inject additional functionality at the beginning of specific events. One example is a `CheckLogin` filter. If a user isn't logged in and attempts to access a secure portion of the application, the `CheckLogin` filter can short-circuit the event and send the user to the login page before the event proceeds.

Learn more about event filters at the Mach-II wiki: `https://greatbiztoolsllc.trac.cvsdude.com/mach-ii/wiki/IntroToFilters`.

## Plugins

Plugins are similar to filters in that they allow for the injection of functionality into the event. Unlike filters, which are executed only on events to which they are explicitly added, plugins run on every request. For example, you could use a plugin to add logging to every request. Plugins also provide more granular access to specific points within the request life cycle.

Learn more about plugins at the Mach-II wiki: `https://greatbiztoolsllc.trac.cvsdude.com/mach-ii/wiki/IntroToPlugins`.

## Event Handlers

The details of each application event are listed in the `event-handler` section of the configuration file. For example, if you want an event called `showWeather` to call a listener method that retrieves weather data and then display this data on a view page, you would register this functionality in an event handler.

Event handlers can be declared public, meaning the event can be announced via the URL, or private, meaning the event can be announced only by code within the application. You'll see specific examples of event handlers later in this article.

## Page Views

Last but not least is the `page-views` section, wherein all view pages are declared. If you were wondering where the display code for the user interface is contained, you've come to the right place!

When page views in a Mach-II application are called via the `view-page` command, they are called by an alias, so the `page-views` section is where you will create all of your page aliases and map them to the actual CFML pages to which they correspond. Changing the page that is displayed when a particular alias is called is as simple as changing the CFML page referenced by the alias.

Whew! That was a lot of information, and it all probably still seems rather abstract at this point. Now let's take a look at a couple of specific examples of Mach-II in action: first, a basic Hello World application that illustrates how views are used in Mach-II, and then a listener in a slightly more real-world Mach-II event.

# Hello Mach-II

What kind of introductory article would this be without a Hello World example? Not only is this traditional, it's also a great way to show how view pages are called in Mach-II. If you want to follow along, download the Mach-II framework and the application skeleton from `http://www.mach-ii.com`, put the `MachII` core folder in your web or virtual host root (see the "Installing Mach-II" section earlier in this article), and unzip the application skeleton files into a directory in your web root called `HelloMachII`.

The first step in any Mach-II application is to update `Application.cfc` with the application name, which is `HelloMachII` in this example), as shown in Listing 26-5.

*Listing 26-5. Updating Application.cfc with the application name*

```
<cfset this.name = "HelloMachII" />
```

That's all we'll need to update in `Application.cfc` for this simple example.

Next, we'll update a couple of the properties in mach-ii.xml with the settings that are appropriate for our application. In this case, we only need to worry about the first two properties, as shown in Listing 26-6.

*Listing 26-6. Updating the first two properties in mach-ii.xml*

```
<property name="applicationRoot" value="/HelloMachII" />
<property name="defaultEvent" value="sayHello" />
```

Next, scroll down in the mach-ii.xml file to the <event-handlers> node and add a new event handler for the default event, as shown in Listing 26-7.

*Listing 26-7. Adding a new event handler for the default event*

```
<event-handler event="sayHello" access="public">
    <view-page name="hello" />
</event-handler>
```

Finally, in the <page-views> section of the configuration file, create a page-view entry for the hello page referenced in the event handler, as shown in Listing 26-8.

*Listing 26-8. Creating a page-view entry for the hello page*

```
<page-view name="hello" page="/views/hello.cfm" />
```

All that's left is to create the hello.cfm page and save it in the views directory, as shown in Listing 26-9.

*Listing 26-9. Creating hello.cfm*

```
<html>
   <head>
       <title>Hello Mach-II!</title>
   </head>

   <body>
       <h3>Hello Mach-II!</h3>
   </body>
</html>
```

Congratulations! You just created your first Mach-II application. Now fire up your favorite browser and go to the following URL (adjust as appropriate for your environment):

http://localhost/HelloMachII

If you don't specify an event in the URL, the default event is called—sayHello in this case. You can also call http://localhost/HelloMachII/index.cfm?event=sayHello and see the exact same results.

How does this all work? Remember from the beginning of the article that Mach-II is an event-driven framework, so rather than calling CFML pages directly, events are announced via the URL. In this case, the event sayHello was announced, and this tells Mach-II to execute the code for the sayHello event handler. Inside that event handler, we're telling Mach-II to show a static view page that outputs "Hello Mach-II!"

This is a very simple example, but all events in Mach-II applications work in this same way. Since this isn't terribly useful, let's step through a slightly more involved example that uses a listener and the Mach-II event object you've been hearing so much about.

# Let's Get Personal

In the previous example, Mach-II said hello to itself, but it isn't terribly difficult to get Mach-II to say hello to you by name. As an added bonus, we'll even get Mach-II to report the time.

We're going to create a listener called TimeListener that will tell us the current date and time. Using the code from the previous example, open the mach-ii.xml configuration file and go to the <listeners> section. Add a reference to the TimeListener that we'll be creating in a moment, as shown in Listing 26-10.

*Listing 26-10. Adding a reference to the TimeListener*

```
<listener name="timeListener" type="HelloMachII.listeners.TimeListener" />
```

Remember that when you reference the location of the TimeListener CFC, you must provide a fully qualified path—HelloMachII.listeners.TimeListener in this case.

Now let's add a new event handler to the mach-ii.xml file below the sayHello event handler, as shown in Listing 26-11.

*Listing 26-11. Adding a new event handler to the mach-ii.xml file*

```
<event-handler event="showPersonalGreeting" access="public">
    <notify listener="timeListener" method="getCurrentDateTime"
        resultArg="currentDateTime" />
    <view-page name="personalGreeting" />
</event-handler>
```

Note that because we want to show the current date and time in our personalized greeting, we need to notify our TimeListener and call its getCurrentDateTime method. We then tell Mach-II to put the result of this method call into the event object as a variable called currentDateTime. This is accomplished via the resultArg attribute of the notify command. You'll see how to retrieve this variable from the event object on our final view page.

The last step in updating the mach-ii.xml file is to add a view page to the page-views section, as shown in Listing 26-12.

*Listing 26-12. Final Step in Updating the mach-ii.xml File*

```
<page-view name="personalGreeting" page="/views/personalGreeting.cfm" />
```

Finally, we must create two files: the personalGreeting.cfm view page and the TimeListener CFC. Let's get the hard stuff out of the way and create the TimeListener, which we'll save in the listeners directory. Listing 26-13 shows the TimeListener CFC,

*Listing 26-13. TimeListener.cfc*

```
<cfcomponent displayname="TimeListener" output="false" extends="MachII.framework.Listener"
    hint="TimeListener for Hello Mach-II app">

    <cffunction name="configure" access="public" output="false" returntype="void"
        hint="Configures this listener as part of the application">
        <!--- don't need to do anything here for now --->
    </cffunction>

    <cffunction name="getCurrentDateTime" access="public" output="false" returntype="date"
        hint="Returns the current date/time">
        <cfreturn Now() />
    </cffunction>
</cfcomponent>
```

Take a look at the configure method on line 2 of Listing 26-13. Because your listener object extends the listener object from the core files, and because you declare all of your listeners in the XML configuration file, Mach-II kindly calls your listener's configure method when the application first initializes, so if you need to do any initial setup within your listener, that's the place to do it. Note that listeners are required to contain a configure method, but the method can be empty if you don't need anything to happen when the listener is initialized by Mach-II.

As you can see, the getCurrentDateTime method (line 5) merely returns the result of a call to Now(). Overkill to say the least, but it does illustrate in a basic way how listener methods are called. The result of this call gets put in the event object via the resultArg attribute of the notify command, as shown in Listing 26-14.

*Listing 26-14. Notify command*

```
<notify listener="timeListener" method="getCurrentDateTime" resultArg="currentDateTime" />
```

Since this data is now in the event object, we'll be able to access it on our view page. The event object is an extremely powerful part of Mach-II. Imagine more complex events that are pulling data from various sources, be it from form variables, URL variables, or data returned from calls to listeners. Rather than needing to keep track of all this data as individual variables, Mach-II uses the event object to contain all the data relevant to the current event. You are then able to easily access this data from a single place.

Finally, we will create a very simple view page. as shown in Listing 26-15. On this page, you will enter your name and click Say Hello. Mach-II will dutifully respond by greeting you by name and telling you the current date and time.

*Listing 26-15. personalGreeting.cfm*

```
<cfif event.isArgDefined("firstName")>
    <cfset firstName = event.getArg("firstName")>
<cfelse>
    <cfset firstName = "Stranger">
</cfif>

<html>
    <head>
        <title>Hello <cfoutput>#firstName#</cfoutput>!</title>
    </head>

    <body>
        <cfoutput>
            <p>Hello #firstName#! The current date/time is↵
#event.getArg("currentDateTime")#.</p>
        </cfoutput>

        <form action="index.cfm?event=showPersonalGreeting" method="post">
            Enter your first name:
                <input type="text" name="firstName" size="30" />
                <input type="submit" value="Say Hello" />
        </form>
    </body>
</html>
```

Take a look at Listing 26-15. You'll notice that both the form data (the firstName text input on line 15) and the result of the call to the listener method (the currentDateTime variable on line 12) are contained in the event object. Mach-II puts all form and URL variables in the event object automatically, and listener-created data is put into the event object via the result-arg attribute in the notify command. In both cases, the data is retrieved from the event using the event object's getArg() method, which we see in the event.getArg("currentDateTime") call that retrieves the data that was returned by the TimeListener. On line 1, we use the event object's isArgDefined() method to see if firstName has been set in the event object. If it has not been set, we set the local variable firstName to a value of "Stranger".

Now the moment you've all been waiting for! Go to the following URL:

http://localhost/HelloMachII/index.cfm?event=showPersonalGreeting

Enter your name, hit Say Hello, and feel the Mach-II love.

I hope this example gives you some basic insight into how listeners and the event object interact in the Mach-II request life cycle. With these skills in hand you'll find yourself creating real-world Mach-II applications in very short order.

# Conclusion

Mach-II is a proven, extensible framework designed to help developers build applications that are flexible and highly maintainable. It is an excellent choice for experienced OO developers or those who want to begin OO development. It encourages best practices, such as tight cohesion and loose coupling of components, as well as use of the MVC design pattern. Mach-II also integrates well with other popular frameworks such as ColdSpring and Transfer. It offers numerous features—such as caching, logging, environment awareness, and form and view tags with data binding—that help you build robust CFML applications quickly and easily.

# CHAPTER 27

■■■

# Model-Glue Fundamentals

## by Joe Rinehart

## Updated by Ezra Parker

*In the Model-Glue documentation, they lament that there is no book on Model-Glue. They say that the framework is so small that it wouldn't fill a book. This article is our answer to that lack.*

Back in 2004, I started writing Model-Glue, a framework for object-oriented ColdFusion development, as a fun exercise. I had been doing a lot of Flash MX development, and I really liked its simple event system. When I started writing the code that became Model-Glue, I wanted to see if there was a way to organize ColdFusion code in the same way, because Flash's system of broadcasters and listeners made a lot of sense to me. After releasing an early version, I was pleasantly surprised to find that it also made sense to a lot of other developers. In fact, some have said that Model-Glue is now their tool of choice for doing object-oriented ColdFusion development.

But why would you bother learning Model-Glue in the first place? You may have been writing ColdFusion applications successfully for years without a framework. You may think that frameworks solve a problem you simply don't have.

Ask yourself the following questions:

- Have you ever had to trace through source code to find when and where a certain query is run?

- Would you benefit from being able to look at a single file to see how access control is applied to your application, instead of needing to wrap each page in security code?

- Are you interested in using the same business logic to power HTML, Flex, Flash, and AJAX applications?

If you've answered yes to any of these three questions, you're ready to learn Model-Glue. This article will introduce you to the Model-Glue framework, teaching you about the problems the framework solves, its core philosophies, how to get started, and even a bit of Model-Glue history.

# A Recipe for Spaghetti

Why does Model-Glue exist in the first place? When the idea of a web-enabled application burst onto the scene in the late 1990s, the architecture was fairly primitive. In fact, it was downright scary. It seemed like everyone who had figured out how to write well-architected client-server and desktop applications forgot everything they had learned in the past 20 years and started from scratch. Instead of having separate tiers for business logic and presentation code, web applications were nothing more than loosely associated collections of hundreds of little scripts, all acting independently of one another. From an architectural perspective, web applications looked less like applications and more like shell scripts producing text output.

As the application servers processing these scripts evolved, they began to allow the scripts to share information. ColdFusion introduced concepts like session, application, and client scopes. These allowed each of the hundreds of little scripts to change data that all of the other scripts would use, and many ColdFusion developers lost a lot of sleep worrying about concurrency issues and misuse—or lack of use— of the cflock tag.

Writing a single script to add new functionality was easy. You would define your algorithm and implement it at the top of the script. Then, further down in the file, you would write some display code to send some HTML to the browser.

Maintaining the same script when something went wrong was infinitely more difficult. There was no way to see how the script interacted with the system as a whole. It was impossible to find out what other scripts might be updating the same shared scope values as your script. Developers felt like their code had become a jumbled tangle of pasta, often described by the term *spaghetti code*.

At about the same time, many of the application servers began to allow code reuse. In ColdFusion, tags like cfinclude and cfmodule let developers encapsulate small portions of business logic or presentation script, reusing them throughout their application. With the introduction of ColdFusion Components (CFCs), we could even use object-oriented programming to encapsulate both data and logic in a stateful manner.

These mechanisms alone didn't solve the spaghetti code problem, but they did provide some central functionality, so we could use an interface and not worry about what was inside. I guess you could call this spaghetti code with meatballs. I generally think meatballs are a tasty addition to a bowl of pasta. When they're not homemade, though, I don't ask what's inside. That's how code reuse works—if you didn't write a module, you should be able to rely on its interface without investigating the internals.

But how can you be writing spaghetti (with meatballs!) if you're using includes, custom tags, and CFC-based APIs? Ask yourself this: What have they done to solve the original problem of the script-based approach to web application development? Other than removing the duplication of logic from the top of each script, there's not much difference. Each page is still a separate .cfm file, acting as its own little world, invoking pieces of logic as necessary. Every page explicitly scripts together the invocation of business logic and presentation script in a procedural manner.

This may work very well for small applications, but it's a lousy way to write large, complex applications. It's an even worse way to write applications where the mechanisms to invoke a specific piece of logic may change. That's because when change happens, you'll be stuck editing each page in your application that may invoke a given piece of logic. That means you'll need to somehow know which pages invoke which pieces of business logic.

While some developers may be enlightened to the point of code clairvoyance, I'm simply not one of them. I felt a need for a framework that separated the invocation of logic, such as retrieving a list of contacts from a database, from any page needing to use such a list. That way, if the manner in which the application asks for a list of contacts changes, I need to change my code in only one place.

# Fun with Front Controller

So what's really needed to detangle the knot of spaghetti code? I'm sure there are multiple answers, but my favorite is a concept called *Front Controller*. Front Controller states that all requests will go through a single pipeline. That pipeline will control which business logic will be invoked. Once it's done with business logic, it will decide which presentation script to render, resulting in HTML that's sent to the browser.

It's a simple solution, and I'm a big fan of simple solutions. In general, Front Controller frameworks provide you with a central place to configure each page, or event, in the application. In a Model-Glue application, this is the ModelGlue.xml file. ModelGlue.xml gives you a bird's-eye view of the application. Each page is defined with an event-handler tag. Within each event-handler tag, you define exactly which business logic needs to execute, and then which presentation scripts need to run.

How does this help the spaghetti problem?

First, it applies an external controller, not even based in ColdFusion code, to decide which logical functions to execute and which presentation code to render. This forces you not only to separate your business logic from your presentation code, but also to create code that doesn't know anything about its context. A query to retrieve contacts doesn't know if it's being used to display a list of contacts for editing or to provide data for a drop-down list in a form. It's well encapsulated, knowing only about its one job and doing that job very well. Any event handler that needs the query can simply state that it needs a list of contacts, and this function will provide such a list. In other words, each little piece of business logic is completely separate from all of the other little pieces. They're entirely decoupled from both each other and the actual context of their invocation. In fact, in a really well-architected Model-Glue application, the business logic doesn't even know Model-Glue exists!

Second, this decoupling allows applications to be rearranged very quickly but with minimal impact. When you use Model-Glue, you treat each piece of business logic and presentation code as a stand-alone unit. Then, using ModelGlue.xml, you arrange these units into pages. Since they don't know anything about each other, you can safely rearrange them at your leisure (or, as the case more often may be, at your clients' demand, once they realize what they really wanted in the first place).

Now that you know what Model-Glue can do for you, we'll walk through a standard exercise in web development. We're going to build a form, validate user input, and return a result to the user.

# Installing Model-Glue

Before you can begin using Model-Glue, you need to install the framework. Assuming you've already installed ColdFusion MX 7 or higher, installing Model-Glue is straightforward. All applications on a single server can share the same copy of the framework, so you don't need to repeat this process each time you begin a new Model-Glue application.

Installing Model-Glue also requires the installation of ColdSpring, as the Model-Glue framework uses ColdSpring internally.

First, download the latest stable version of each of the two frameworks from http://www.model-glue.com and http://www.coldspringframework.org.

Second, unpack the Model-Glue zip file. Inside, you'll find directories named ModelGlue, modelglueactionpacks, modelglueapplicationtemplate, and modelgluesamples.

If you're using a standard installation of ColdFusion, you can simply copy the ModelGlue directory into your web server's root directory.

If you've set up virtual servers, or need to use ColdFusion's mapping capabilities, copy the ModelGlue directory to wherever you like and create a ColdFusion mapping with a logical name of /ModelGlue pointing to the ModelGlue directory. If you choose to go with a mapping, and you're using

ColdFusion 8 or higher, you can create an application-specific mapping in `Application.cfc` by adding the following line outside any functions, replacing `path/to/ModelGlue` with the appropriate path for your system:

```
<cfset this.mappings["/ModelGlue"] = "path/to/ModelGlue" />
```

Finally, take the same approach with the extracted ColdSpring directory. You may place the directory in your web server's root directory (making sure that `coldspring` is the entire directory name, without any version number or identifier), or copy it wherever you like and create a `/coldspring` mapping pointing to this location.

That's it. The framework is installed.

# Starting a New Model-Glue Application

Every Model-Glue application begins with a copy of what's called the *application template*. This is just a collection of files like `Application.cfc` and `ModelGlue.xml`, as well as a suggested directory structure for creating basic Model-Glue applications. You'll find the application template in the `modelglueapplicationtemplate` directory of the zip file you downloaded from Model-Glue web site.

There are two ways to create a new application: manually or by using a supplied Ant task that automates the process. We'll explore the manual process first.

## Creating the Application Manually

To create a new application by hand, copy the contents of this directory to wherever you would like to build your application. I'll be placing them in a subdirectory named `mgfundamentals` that I can then browse to at `http://localhost/mgfundamentals`. All of the instructions from this point forward assume you'll use the same naming.

After the files have been copied, we need to do a few find-and-replace operations to give our new application a unique application name and properly configure Model-Glue:

- Open `mgfundamentals/Application.cfc`. Perform a find-and-replace to change all instances of `modelglueapplicationtemplate` to `mgfundamentals`. (Note that `Application.cfm` is also supplied for those that prefer not to use `Application.cfc`—in which case, that would be the file to modify.) Save and close the file.

- Open `mgfundamentals/RemotingService.cfc`. Perform the same find-and-replace operation, and then save and close the file.

- Open `mgfundamentals/config/ModelGlue.xml` and `mgfundamentals/config/ColdSpring.xml`. Once again, perform the same find-and-replace operation. After saving these `.xml` files, leave them open; we're going to explore them in just a moment.

Now that you've configured these four files, you should be able to run `http://localhost/mgfundamentals`. You should receive a message stating that "Model-Glue 3 seems to be up and running." If you don't, make sure that you've installed the framework as described, and double-check your changes to `Application.cfc` (or `.cfm`), `ColdSpring.xml`, `ModelGlue.xml`, and `RemotingService.cfc`.

Optionally, you may remove some files that are not needed: `Application.cfm` (assuming you are using `Application.cfc`), `build.properties`, `build.xml`, and `readme.txt`.

## Automating Application Creation

Since performing manual find-and-replace operations can get a little tedious, Model-Glue also supplies an Ant task that will automate this procedure for you.

---

■ **Note** Apache Ant is a Java-based build tool that is configured using XML. Ant it is built into Eclipse, so developers using ColdFusion Builder or CFEclipse will be able to easily run Ant tasks directly in their development environment. See `http://ant.apache.org` for more details on Ant.

---

In order to use Ant to create a new Model-Glue application directory, first create an Eclipse project for the `modelglueapplicationtemplate` directory, and then open `modelglueapplicationtemplate/build.xml`.

You need to change two Ant properties (configuration parameters):

- On line 21, the `newApplicationName` property defines the name of the new application. The **value** attribute needs to be changed to reflect the name we have selected for our new application—in this case, `mgfundamentals`.

- On line 22, the `newApplicationDirectory` property specifies the location where the new application directory will be created. Change the **value** attribute of this property to the path where you wish the new directory to be created, including the directory name itself. If you wish, you can reference the `newApplicationName` property from the preceding line by prefacing the property name with `${` and following it with `}`, as in this example:

```
<property name="newApplicationName" value="mgfundamentals" />
<property name="newApplicationDirectory"
value="c:/inetpub/wwwroot/${newApplicationName}" />
```

Once you save the modified `build.xml` file, you can run the Ant task in Eclipse by right-clicking the file in the Navigator view and selecting Run As ➤ Ant Build, or by using the keyboard shortcut Alt-Shift-X + Q. In the Eclipse Console view, you should see a couple of status messages ending in "BUILD SUCCESSFUL." Now you should be able to run the new Model-Glue application at `http://localhost/mgfundamentals` as in the manual process. Optionally, you can delete the `Application.cfm` (assuming you are using `Application.cfc`), `build.properties`, and `readme.txt` files (`build.xml` will not be copied to the new directory).

# Model-Glue XML Files in a Nutshell

Right now, if you've done what I've suggested so far, you should be looking at a browser window that lets you know that Model-Glue seems to be up and running. If not, you'll want to review the previous section before moving forward.

You can switch back to the editor you've used to make changes to ColdSpring.xml and ModelGlue. xml (I prefer the free XMLBuddy plugin for Eclipse), and follow along as we examine these files.

## ColdSpring XML Configuration File

We'll look at the ColdSpring.xml file first, in Listing 27-1. (A portion of this file that is not relevant for this exercise has been omitted here for the sake of brevity.)

*Listing 27-1. ColdSpring.xml*

```
<beans>
<!-- This is your Model-Glue configuration -->
   <bean id="modelglue.modelGlueConfiguration"
class="ModelGlue.gesture.configuration.ModelGlueConfiguration">

        <!-- Be sure to change these to false when you go to production! -->
        <property name="reload"><value>true</value></property>
        <property name="debug"><value>true</value></property>

        <!-- Name of the URL variable that states which event-handler to run -->
        <property name="eventValue"><value>event</value></property>

        <!-- Default event-handler -->
        <property name="defaultEvent"><value>page.index</value></property>

        <!-- Execute this event when the requested event is missing. Won't work if
generationEnabled=true and in development mode! -->
          <property name="missingEvent"><value>page.missing</value></property>

         <!-- Execute this event when an error occurs. -->
         <property name="defaultExceptionHandler"><value>page.error</value></property>
         <!-- Controls reloading -->
         <property name="reloadPassword"><value>true</value></property>
         <property name="reloadKey"><value>init</value></property>

        <!-- Where to find necessary files -->
        <property name="configurationPath"><value>config/ModelGlue.xml</value></property>
         <property name="applicationMapping"><value>/mgfundamentals</value></property>
         <property name="viewMappings"><value>/mgfundamentals/views</value></property>
        <property name="helperMappings"><value>/mgfundamentals/helpers</value></property>

         <!-- Generate unknown events when in development mode?  (reload=false) -->
         <property name="generationEnabled"><value>false</value></property>
```

```
        <!-- Set the default cache timeout in seconds -->
        <property name="defaultCacheTimeout"><value>60</value></property>

        <!-- Scaffolding config -->
        <!-- Turning this off will disable any scaffold generation. Turning this on
requires the reload setting above to also be on.-->
        <property name="rescaffold"><value>true</value></property>
        <!-- Where do you want generated views to be saved to? -->
        <property name="generatedViewMapping"><value>views</value></property>
        <!--This directory structure should already exists. ModelGlue will create the
Scaffolds.xml file and overwrite as needed.-->
        <property
name="scaffoldPath"><value>config/scaffolds/Scaffolds.xml</value></property>
        <!-- What scaffold generation patterns should ModelGlue use if you do not specify in
the <scaffold type=""> attribute? .-->
        <property
name="defaultScaffolds"><value>list,edit,view,commit,delete</value></property>

        <!-- See documentation or ModelGlueConfiguration.cfc for additional options. -->
    </bean>
<!-- Put definitions for your own beans and services here -->
</beans>
```

A ColdSpring XML configuration file is made up of one or more bean tags, each representing a CFC that is specified in the class attribute of the tag. For our purposes, the bean we are interested in has an id attribute of modelglue.modelGlueConfiguration, and it is used to define the configuration settings of a Model-Glue application. This configuration block tells the framework where to find things like view files, whether it should reload itself, and whether or not to display the framework's debugging information at the bottom of every page. Each of these individual settings is defined in a property tag that has a name attribute, which identifies the particular setting. Each property tag contains a value tag, which in turn contains the setting's specific value.

## The Model-Glue XML Configuration File

Next, take a look at ModelGlue.xml, in Listing 27-2.

*Listing 27-2. ModelGlue.xml*

```
<?xml version="1.0" encoding="UTF-8"?>
    <modelglue>

        <controllers>
            <controller id="Controller" type="mgfundamentals.controller.Controller">
                <!--
                <message-listener message="message" function="controllerFunction" />
                -->
            </controller>
        </controllers>
```

```
<event-types>
<!-- Sample Event Type:
 You can use before, after or both.
    <event-type name="templatedPage">
        <before>
            <results>
                <result do="SomethingThatShouldRunBefore"/>
            </results>
        </before>
        <after>
            <results>
                <result do="SomethingThatShouldRunAfter"/>
            </results>
        </after>
    </event-type>
 -->
</event-types>

<event-handlers>
<!--
Sample Event Handler:
    <event-handler name="eventname">
        <broadcasts>
            <message name="message" />
        </broadcasts>
        <results>
            <result name="resultName" do="otherEvent" />
        </results>
        <views>
            <include name="body" template="content.cfm" />
        </views>
    </event-handler>
-->

<!-- A homepage for your application. -->
    <event-handler name="page.index">
        <broadcasts />
        <results>
            <result do="template.main" />
        </results>
        <views>
            <include name="body" template="pages/index.cfm" />
        </views>
    </event-handler>

<!-- An error event to show when an error occurs, much like <cferror>. -->
    <event-handler name="page.error">
        <broadcasts />
        <results>
            <result do="template.main" />
        </results>
```

```
            <views>
                <include name="body" template="pages/exception.cfm" />
            </views>
        </event-handler>

    <!-- A "404" event to show when the requested event isn't defined. -->
        <event-handler name="page.missing">
            <broadcasts />
             <results>
                <result do="template.main" />
             </results>
             <views>
                <include name="body" template="pages/missingEvent.cfm" />
             </views>
          </event-handler>

    <!-- Private events:  can't be accessed through a URL -->
        <event-handler access="private" name="template.main">
            <views>
                <include name="main" template="templates/main.cfm" />
            </views>
        </event-handler>
    </event-handlers>

</modelglue>
```

This file is divided into three sections: `controllers`, `event-handlers`, and `event-types`. Let's look at each of these sections.

## The controllers Block

The `controllers` block defines a series of CFCs that will be loaded into the Application scope when the application is initialized. When the `reload` setting in the `ColdSpring.xml` file is set to `true`, this will happen on every page request. When you move your application to a production environment, you'll want to change this to `false`.

Each `controller` tag requires two attributes. The first, `id`, is a unique name for the controller. The second, `type`, is the path of the CFC to load; it is in the same format as the component path used in the `createobject()` function. Each controller CFC is an extension of the `ModelGlue.gesture.controller.Controller` CFC, inheriting framework-specific functionality.

These controller CFCs replace what's at the top of many traditional ColdFusion pages. They'll collect input from the browser, such as form data, and ask a model CFC to act on this data.

Each `controller` tag contains a series of `message-listener` tags. It's easiest to think of a message as a given page's way of announcing that something has happened or needs to happen. A `message-listener` tag relates a message to a function on a controller CFC. When the appropriate message is broadcast, the function will run.

Multiple `message-listener` tags can listen for the same message, causing multiple functions to run. You can even have multiple controllers listening for the same message.

## The event-handlers Block

When we talked about Front Controller, I stated that ModelGlue.xml will "provide you with a central place to configure each page" in your application. This central place is the event-handlers block. As we discuss the tags, you should refer to the Sample Event Handler section in the ModelGlue.xml file (Listing 27-2).

Inside the event-handlers block, each event handler defines one page in the application. To run a given event, you append the event handler's name attribute to the URL. To run the home page of our copy of the application template, we can use http://localhost/mgfundamentals/index.cfm?event=page.index.

The broadcasts tag serves as a container for a series of message tags. Any event handler can broadcast as many messages as needed. When it runs the event handler, Model-Glue will broadcast these messages in the order that they are listed, and any message-listener tags in the controllers block will run their related functions.

The views tag is a container for include tags, which state which presentation scripts (.cfm) should be run as part of this event handler. An include tag functions much like the familiar cfinclude tag.

The first attribute, name, gives a name to the view's content after it has been rendered. When a subsequent view is rendered, it can display the content from any prior view by name. This makes creating site-wide templates very easy.

The template attribute names a file in the mgfundamentals/views directory to include. To make it easier to organize large sites, you're free to use subdirectories, such as mgfundamentals/views/myModule. You could then use a template attribute such as myModule/dspNavigation.cfm to include the dspNavigation.cfm file in the myModule subdirectory.

The remaining child tag of the event-handler block is the results tag. Much like broadcasts and views, it serves as a container. This time, it contains result tags. A result tag states that another event handler should be run as a result of executing the current event handler.

One common use case for the result tag is to apply a site-wide template (another way to accomplish this task is to use an event type, as described in the next section). One event handler could generate content, such as a list of contacts, displaying the list with an include tag that has a name attribute of body. A second event handler may display the details of a single contact, again giving the rendered content the name body. A third event handler, named template, may then render an include that provides navigation and look and feel, and displays the content of the body view. Adding a result tag with a do attribute of template would cause the template event handler to run after either the contact list or detail events, wrapping the rendered content with a consistent look and feel.

You could also use results to conditionally control the flow of your application. For example, if a user fills out a form with invalid data, it's good to redisplay the form. However, if the user entered valid data, you may want to redirect the user to a new page. To handle this use case, you can use what are known as *named results*. When you give a result tag a name attribute, the event handler indicated in the do attribute will execute only when a listener function in a controller specifically adds a result of the same name.

If you find it hard to understand the result tag without an example, don't worry. We're almost ready to start coding, and we'll use results in our code.

## The event-types Block

The event-types block is used to specify common broadcasts, views, and/or results that should be executed before or after one or more event handlers. The event-types block can contain any number of event-type tags, which in turn will contain a before tag, an after tag, or both.

You can think of the `before` and `after` tags as shared `event-handler` tags that will run before and after any event handler that is assigned to that particular event type. Each `before` or `after` tag will contain a `broadcasts`, `views`, or `results` tag, or any combination of these three elements.

As an example of a common use of event types, many applications require a security check before allowing access to certain events. This task is a perfect fit for an event type with a `before` tag, which can be used to broadcast a message and then respond with a redirection result if the security check fails.

An `after` tag can be used as a less verbose method than a result to apply site-wide templates or shared layouts, or to execute a commonly used function after one or more event handlers.

# Your First Model-Glue Application

OK, let's stop talking about theory and write a small application. We're going to build a form that allows you to enter a word, click a submit button, and see the word in all uppercase. It's not very thrilling, but you'll learn how to create a page, validate form or URL data, and do something with that data.

First, we need to add two new event handlers to our application: one for the form and one for handling the form. This is just like the classic model of a `form` page and an `action` page. In `ModelGlue.xml`, add two `event-handler` tags named `uppercaser.form` and `uppercaser.action` just below the `event-handlers` tag, as shown in Listing 27-3.

*Listing 27-3. Event-handler tags for the form*

```
<event-handler name="uppercaser.form">
</event-handler>

<event-handler name="uppercaser.action">
</event-handler>
```

You can run these by using a URL such as `http://localhost/mgfundamentals/index.cfm?event=uppercaser.form` or `http://localhost/mgfundamentals/index.cfm?event=uppercaser.action`, but nothing will happen yet.

## Setting Up the Form

Let's start our form by creating a file in the `/views` directory named `frmUpperCaser.cfm`, as shown in Listing 27-4. It asks for a word, displays any validation messages, and, if available, displays the uppercased version of the word.

*Listing 27-4. frmUpperCaser.cfm*

```
<form action="index.cfm?event=uppercaser.action" method="post">
    <input type="text" name="phrase">
    <input type="submit" value="Go">
</form>
```

```
<cfif event.exists("validationError")>
    <cfoutput>
        <p style="color:red">#event.getValue("validationError")#</p>
    </cfoutput>
</cfif>
```

You'll notice that Listing 27-4 looks just like any normal `.cfm` template, except that all of its data is coming from a variable named `event`. The event is a CFC instance containing the combination of the Form and URL scopes, as well as any additional data that is set inside a listener function. In this case, we'll ask the event if it contains a validation error. If it does, we'll show it.

Also note that the `action` attribute of the `form` tag points to the `uppercaser.action` event. When the submit button is clicked, we'll post to the other event handler that we've created.

Now that we've created our form, we need to instruct our `uppercaser.form` event to include it. We use the `views` and `include` tags in `ModelGlue.xml` to do this, as shown in Listing 27-5.

*Listing 27-5. Including the form*

```
<event-handler name="uppercaser.form">
    <views>
        <include name="body" template="frmUpperCaser.cfm" />
    </views>
</event-handler>
```

Now, when you run `http://localhost/mgfundamentals/index.cfm?event=uppercaser.form`, you'll see our form. If you click Go, not much happens—Model-Glue just runs the empty `uppercaser.action` event handler.

## Adding Functionality

Let's add some functionality to the action event. First, the event handler must broadcast the fact that it needs something. In this case, it needs the contents of the phrase text input to be uppercased. In `ModelGlue.xml`, we'll add a message to the event handler indicating this, as shown in Listing 27-6.

*Listing 27-6. Adding a message to the event handler*

```
<event-handler name="uppercaser.action">
    <broadcasts>
        <message name="needUpperCasedPhrase" />
    </broadcasts>
</event-handler>
```

Now, if you submit the form, nothing will happen, as there is nothing listening for the `needUpperCasedPhrase` message yet. It's time to add a `message-listener` tag to our controller. When we're finished, our `controller` tag at the top of `ModelGlue.xml` looks like Listing 27-7.

*Listing 27-7. Controller tag*

```
<controller name="Controller" type="mgfundamentals.controller.Controller">
    <message-listener message="needUpperCasedPhrase" function="UpperCasePhrase" />
</controller>
```

If you try submitting the form now, you'll get an error. It will indicate that the method `UpperCasePhrase` doesn't exist in our controller CFC, located in `controller/Controller.cfc`. This makes sense, since we haven't written the function yet. Let's do that now. The code for the function is shown in Listing 27-8.

*Listing 27-8. UpperCasePhrase function*

```
<cffunction name="UpperCasePhrase" output="false">
    <cfargument name="event" required="true" />

    <!--- Get the "phrase" value from the form --->
    <cfset var phrase = arguments.event.getValue("phrase") />
     <!--- Upper case the phrase --->
     <cfset var upperCasedPhrase = uCase(phrase) />
     <!--- Set the upper-cased phrase into the event --->
    <cfset arguments.event.setValue("upperCasedPhrase", upperCasedPhrase) />

    <!--- Add a line to the debugging trace, showing that it worked --->
    <cfset arguments.event.addTraceStatement("User", "Phrase is: " & upperCasedPhrase,↵
 "UpperCasePhrase") />

</cffunction>
```

As you can see, the listener function receives one argument, usually named event. This is the same object that is referenced in the views. It contains all of the data from the Form and URL scopes, as well as any data added by prior listener functions.

The listener function first asks the event for the contents of the phrase text input. Then it uppercases the phrase. Next, it sets the uppercased phrase into the event so that a view template will be able to access its value. Finally, it adds a line to the debugging trace showing that the phrase has been uppercased.

Now we need to add a view template showing the uppercased phrase. That's easy enough. First, add `dspUpperCasedPhrase.cfm`, shown in Listing 27-9, to the /views directory.

*Listing 27-9. Adding dspUpperCasedPhrase.cfm to the /views directory*

```
<cfoutput>
    <p>Upper-cased phrase: #event.getValue("upperCasedPhrase")#</p>
</cfoutput>
```

Next, we'll change our `uppercaser.action` event handler in `ModelGlue.xml` to include the new view file, as shown in Listing 27-10.

*Listing 27-10. Including the new view file in the uppercaser.action event handler*

```
<event-handler name="uppercaser.action">
    <broadcasts>
        <message name="needUpperCasedPhrase" />
    </broadcasts>
    <views>
        <include name="body" template="dspUpperCasedPhrase.cfm" />
    </views>
</event-handler>
```

Now when you run the form, enter a phrase, and click Go, you're shown the uppercased phrase. Thrilling stuff!

# Finishing Up

To finish our exercise, we need to add form validation. When the user doesn't enter a phrase, we would like to take the user back to the form. We'll do this by first adding a `result` tag to the `uppercaser.action` event handler that states that Model-Glue should redirect to the `uppercaser.form` event-handler whenever a result named `validationError` is added. Listing 27-11 contains this code to add to `ModelGlue.xml`.

*Listing 27-11. Returning to the form when there's a validationError result*

```
<event-handler name="uppercaser.action">
    <broadcasts>
        <message name="needUpperCasedPhrase" />
    </broadcasts>
    <views>
        <include name="body" template="dspUpperCasedPhrase.cfm" />
    </views>
    <results>
        <result name="validationError" do="uppercaser.form" redirect="true" />
    </results>
</event-handler>
```

Now, we'll modify our listener function to perform basic validation, adding a validation message and the `validationError` result if the inputted phrase is zero length. Listing 27-12 showcases this basic validation.

*Listing 27-12. Adding basic validation to the listener function*

```
<cffunction name="UpperCasePhrase" output="false">
    <cfargument name="event" required="true" />

    <!--- Get the "phrase" value from the form --->
    <cfset var phrase = arguments.event.getValue("phrase") />
```

```
    <!--- Upper case the phrase --->
    <cfset var upperCasedPhrase = uCase(phrase) />

    <!--- Validate the form --->
    <cfif not len(trim(phrase))>
        <cfset arguments.event.setValue("ValidationError", "Please enter a phrase.") />
        <cfset arguments.event.addResult("validationError") />
    </cfif>

    <!--- Set the upper-cased phrase into the event --->
    <cfset arguments.event.setValue("upperCasedPhrase", upperCasedPhrase) />

    <!--- Add a line to the debugging trace, showing that is worked --->
    <cfset arguments.event.addTraceStatement("User", "Phrase is: " & upperCasedPhrase,↵
 "UpperCasePhrase") />
</cffunction>
```

Now we have form validation, and our uppercaser functionality is complete.

The simplicity of this example is a clear illustration of how Model-Glue provides an advantageous architecture.

First, notice that we could reuse our form and results templates in any other event handler. It would be a cinch to add a form for uppercasing a phrase to any page by just including the frmUpperCaser.cfm template.

Second, the mechanism by which the phrase is uppercased is separate from the pages in the application. Any page can ask for a phrase to be uppercased by broadcasting the needUpperCasedPhrase message. The event handler itself has no idea how the phrase is uppercased; it simply trusts that the operation will happen.

Through this system of decoupling, applications become more flexible. As change inevitably occurs, the application can respond quickly, with fewer chances for errors.

# Conclusion

Model-Glue solves the problems of spaghetti code by separating your application into clearly defined layers. Views do nothing but render HTML. Controllers receive data from the URL and Form scopes, ask for actions to be performed on the data, and return a result to the view.

The portion of the application that performs the action on the collected data is often referred to as the *business model*. In our sample application, the entirety of the model was the UCase() function. In other words, we just wrote a full Model-View-Controller (MVC) application without really thinking about it.

When Model-Glue separates the model from the presentation script, it does so in such a way that no page knows which functions are being executed on the controller CFCs. In fact, all a page does is broadcast a message. The event handler itself has no idea how many controller methods will execute. This system of implicit invocation allows applications to be rearranged, scaled, and reused, while changing as little functional, tested code as possible.

That about wraps it up. I hope this has been useful, and that you've learned a bit about Model-Glue specifically and seen how MVC and implicit invocation work. If you would like to learn more, see the following:

- The Official Model-Glue web site (`http://www.model-glue.com`)

- Ray Camden's blog (`http://www.coldfusionjedi.com`), which has numerous posts under the Model-Glue category

- Dan Wilson's blog (`http://www.nodans.com`), which also has many posts under the Model-Glue category, including a step-by-step tutorial for creating a Model-Glue application

■■■

# CHAPTER 28

# ColdSpring Fundamentals

## by Chris Scott

### Updated by Kurt Wiersma

*The ColdSpring framework, originally developed by Chris Scott and Dave Ross, was created to help developers manage their components and any dependencies (objects or data that the components depend on). Modeled on Java's popular Spring framework, ColdSpring has been widely accepted by object-oriented developers in the ColdFusion community—in two separate surveys of the community, about a third of the respondents said they use ColdSpring. All of the popular MVC frameworks support ColdSpring integration, including Model-Glue, Fusebox, Mach-II, and ColdBox. Indeed, Model-Glue uses ColdSpring internally to configure the framework itself. In this article, Chris Scott explains what ColdSpring does and how you might use it in your development.*

There are two questions that people are always asking me about the ColdSpring framework:

- What is ColdSpring?

- What is the problem that ColdSpring tries to solve?

I hope to answer those questions in this article, but I will also talk about a whole lot more. We will consider how we work, what we think about when we design software systems, how we test our systems, and what goes into designing our application architecture.

ColdSpring is more than just a solution to a simple problem. It allows you to think about your applications in an entirely new way. But first, let's start with the central issue that ColdSpring addresses.

## The Problem of Dependency in System Design

Unless the system we design is fairly simplistic, complexities are going to arise. Certain components will need to know some bit of data, such as the name of a data source or the current tax rate for a purchase, to run properly. Sometimes we need more than just simple data, and our components depend on each other to run.

For example, we may abstract the `cfmail` tag into a MailService component in order to maintain one point of reference to our mail server. Now we can just use the MailService whenever we want to send an e-mail in our application. We've gained an important ability to move mail servers by simply changing one component, but we've also created a new dependency. Any component that uses the MailService now depends on it and requires it to operate. This is not really bad, except that we will need to decide what to do about the settings that the MailService needs to operate. The MailService itself depends on things like the mail server address and perhaps a default from address. This isn't really a big issue when we are talking about only a few collaborating objects, but what if we are talking about 10, 20, or a 100?

Our system is going to grow somewhere, and so is the complexity of creating all the components and supplying them with the data they need to get their jobs done. This is the essence of the problem that ColdSpring aims to solve.

ColdSpring (`http://www.coldspringframework.org/`) was designed mainly to abstract away everything to do with creating your application's model components. When you ask ColdSpring for a component, ColdSpring automatically supplies that component with the data or objects it needs to function. And the great thing is that it doesn't matter how complex your CFC's dependencies are. You might have an object that performs user authentication, which depends on a session façade and a Data Access Object (DAO), which needs a data source and that MailService we talked about, which in turn needs a mail server address along with some default values for our e-mail messages. ColdSpring will do everything for you and return the user authentication object ready to use. But that's just the beginning.

ColdSpring allows you to add functionality into existing components through a powerful aspect-oriented programming (AOP) framework. It also lets you automatically make your model components available for remote method calls, via ColdSpring remote proxies. These topics could fill up their own articles, but in this one, we're going to cover ColdSpring's core focus: managing components.

# ColdSpring and Component Management

We like to speak of ColdSpring's core as a container, not a framework, because at its heart, it's more like a factory. A *factory* is a type of object that creates other objects, which can be retrieved from the factory with simple methods. This allows you to encapsulate the complexities of creating those objects inside the factory. It is easier for other objects to work with the objects created by the factory because they don't need to be concerned with how those objects are created.

Typically, factories are designed to create specific sets of objects, since creating a generic factory can be difficult. Even when designing a simple factory, we still need to figure out how the objects the factory creates will get their dependencies. ColdSpring solves this problem by using what is known as *dependency injection*, which really means that it takes on the responsibility of resolving the dependencies for the objects it creates.

How does ColdSpring do this? Let's go back to our MailService, which requires a mail server address. We could simply hardwire the address into it, but that would not make for a very reusable component. So we need to supply the service with the mail server address when we create it. We can do this in one of two ways: provide the address as an argument to an init method, known as a *constructor-arg*, or create a setter method for it. The factory will then provide this data upon creation of our MailService, "injecting" the CFC with the dependencies it needs. If we use a constructor-arg, we call this *constructor injection*; if we use a setter, it's known as *setter injection*.

When we want to work with a MailService, we simply ask the ColdSpring factory, known as the *bean factory*, for the object. With a single call, `getBean("MailService")`, the calling code will never need to configure a MailService again.

This type of factory is also known as an *inversion of control* (IoC) container, because the control of configuring the components is taken away from our objects and their consumers, and held by the factory. Because ColdSpring uses IoC, our components never know they are being managed by ColdSpring, and have no dependencies on the framework at all.

The ColdSpring bean factory also manages objects as singletons. When we want only one copy of a particular object in our application, we call it a *singleton*. (See `http://www.allapplabs.com/java_design_patterns/singleton_pattern.htm` for more about the singleton pattern.) In fact, you will probably find yourself using ColdSpring most often for objects that you would like to create once and persist across many requests. ColdSpring makes this completely transparent to you. If an object has not been created, it will be created when getBean() is called; if it already exists, you will receive the same object.

Let's see what this actually looks like in practice. First, it is important to understand a small bit of semantics. As we have discussed, ColdSpring can use setters to inject objects with their dependencies. The JavaBean pattern mandates that objects expose their properties through associated getter and setter methods. Following this pattern, if we define a property for an object when configuring ColdSpring, it will expect to find a setter method for the property in that object. In a sense, we can say that ColdSpring views our objects as beans, so we carry that terminology into ColdSpring's XML configuration file. A typical configuration file may look like Listing 28-1.

*Listing 28-1. A sample ColdSpring XML configuration file*

```
<beans>
    <bean id="AuthService" class="com.foo.AuthService ">
        <property name="userDao">
            <ref bean="UserDao" />
        </property>
        <property name="mailService">
            <ref bean="MailService" />
        </property>
    </bean>
    <bean id="UserDao" class="com.foo.UserDao">
        <property name="datasource">
            <value>fooData</value>
        </property>
    </bean>
    <bean id="MailService" class="com.foo.MailService">
        <property name="mailserver">
            <value>127.0.0.1</value>
        </property>
        <property name="defaulFrom">
            <value>foo@bar.com</value>
        </property>
    </bean>
</beans>
```

Our XML file has one bean element for each of our components. The id attribute represents the name we will use to retrieve our bean through a call to getBean(), such as getBean(" AuthService "). The class attribute is the file name of the CFC we want ColdSpring to create. We define each bean's dependencies as properties, which can themselves be references to other beans. For example, on lines 4 and 7 in Listing 28-1, the UserDao and MailService beans are defined as properties (or dependencies) of the AuthService bean. This may seem like a bit of extra work, but you can set up extremely complex relationships in this way, and retrieve the objects through a single getBean() call.

# Some Development Concepts

Now that you've seen how ColdSpring can help you manage components, you should understand how ColdSpring can help you to architect your application. To explain this, I'll first need to discuss some more general development concepts that complement ColdSpring perfectly.

## Unit Testing

Unit testing is the process of writing snippets of code to validate the functionality of a module, such as a CFC. These snippets of test code are known as *test cases*. To assist in creating and running these test cases, you can use a framework like MXUnit (`http://www.mxunit.org/`), which is based on the Java testing framework JUnit.

Unit tests are generally applied to our model components —the objects that make up our core business logic— rather than our views. How would we create our unit tests? We would write a test for each component. That test creates an instance of the component and runs various test routines against each of its methods. In these test routines, we make assertions on the results of method calls, which are used to determine if a component has passed or failed the test. Ideally, we would create tests for every CFC in our model, which may sound like an enormous amount of work. However, all these tests, collected together in a test harness, give us the ability to change a piece of code and immediately see the repercussions throughout our model. There's a programming methodology called *agile software development* that stresses the importance of individual working units of code and the ability to freely refactor code—to perform structural changes while preserving the code's functionality. (See `http://www.martinfowler.com/articles/newMethodology.html` for more about agile methods.) With a test harness in place, we can easily check to see if our code is still working as expected, and we are encouraged to experiment.

## Test-Driven Development

One of the big questions is when to write your unit tests. Maybe we want to work on a subset of our application and then write tests for that group of components. Perhaps we would rather work through a slice of our application, such as a login process, and then write tests for those components. The technique known as *test-driven development* (TDD) stresses the importance of writing tests as early on in our development process as possible —to think of our tests first, in accordance with specific use cases, and then create components to satisfy those tests.

TDD stresses the mantras of KISS (keep it simple stupid!) and YAGNI (you ain't gonna need it!). Your components should concentrate on passing the test, or satisfying the functionality that those tests require. The result is components that are more focused and less dependent on others to get their job done—in other words, more encapsulated. Instead of thinking about the entire system and how a CFC satisfies the requirements of a large system, we focus on how a CFC performs a very specific task and leave out anything that is not required. This can be a strange and possibly unsettling way to develop software, and truthfully, I believe a balance can be achieved. But thinking about testability early and concentrating on specific design goals often results in focused components.

## Too Many Dependencies Can Spoil the Model

When model objects use many other objects to get their jobs done, they are dependent on those objects. As components become more and more dependent on other components, our model can become very brittle. Small changes to one part of our model tend to propagate throughout our components, and large changes can make our application fall apart altogether, forcing us to redesign entire sections. Sometimes the dependencies between our components are holding our model together. This can be very dangerous, as it makes our model less flexible.

We sometimes think of code that spreads functionality throughout our model components as *spaghetti* code, as our components become entangled with one another. Spaghetti is sticky and tends to hold itself together, but when we start pulling on it to make changes, it falls apart into a great big mess. We should be very wary of this kind of code, as it resists change. We can get lost in the maze of a highly dependent domain model for hours before being able to accomplish even the simplest fixes.

## Back to ColdSpring

You may be wondering where this tangent about unit testing and avoiding spaghetti code is going right now. Unit testing and TDD can really help to break your code down into cohesive functional units, avoiding the spaghetti mess. This is where we get back to ColdSpring.

ColdSpring specializes in taking these units and organizing them into larger groups, perfectly complementing the concepts of TDD. In other words, we can use ColdSpring to wire together components from different functional layers into modules that deal with specific business areas.

# Using ColdSpring to Architect Your Application in Logical Tiers

Most of us begin by building applications that are too procedural, too dependent, and in need of a marinara. ColdFusion had no real facilities for object-oriented programming (OOP) until relatively recently, and before CFCs, most of us just used `cfswitch` statements to try to alleviate the issues inherent with procedural systems.

However, as CFCs have gained popularity, people have begun to see the need for true OO patterns like Model-View-Controller (MVC) to assist in separating applications into logical tiers. Some excellent frameworks like Mach-II and Model-Glue have been introduced to help us get a handle on these new paradigms. These frameworks are good, but they still do not address the core problems in our applications. We know to put our user interface code in our views and our logic on our model, but where do we go from there? We often find ourselves just shifting the spaghetti into one unit that we call our "model." We need to apply the same concept of a tiered architecture to our model as well, and this is where a framework like ColdSpring can really help.

Let's take a look at what this means in the real world. Most web applications need to store data of some kind, usually in a database. Saving data beyond the scope of your application's memory is known as *persistence*. Objects like DAOs and table gateways can help us put persistence into its own tier. This gives us a great degree of flexibility and makes the job much less painful if we need to change the way we store our data, such as switching our database from SQL Server to Oracle, or our storage scheme to an Lightweight Directory Access Protocol (LDAP) system.

Our application may also require more generalized services, like a caching system, a notification system, or a security strategy. These types of components represent functionality required by many parts of our model, so we may want to put these auxiliary services in their own tier. This would be our auxiliary services tier. Some people call these pieces of functionality *aspects*, which is a concept we find in AOP (a subject for yet another article).

Finally, our application probably does something like sell books or reserve hotel rooms. Thus, it deals with *domain objects*—the people, places, and things on which our systems operate. We can place these objects in a separate tier as well.

If we think of our model in terms of these three tiers, we may also want to design façades for logical areas of our model. A *façade* is a type of object that provides a simple set of functions that hides the complexity of a system made up of a larger body of code. Façades give the clients of our model—whether Flex applications or Mach-II applications—a simple API to consume and greatly simplifies its use. (See `http://www.allapplabs.com/java_design_patterns/facade_pattern.htm` for more about this pattern.)

What is so powerful about this type of *n*-tiered architecture? At each layer, the components can be designed to perform only the task at hand. Persistence objects are designed to handle nothing but fetching and saving objects. File I/O objects know nothing more than how to read and write to a file. These components are easy to test, and if we build a solid test harness, we can feel more confident when making changes, because we have a system in place to see the results of those changes immediately.

However, using traditional programming paradigms, there is a problem with this type of architecture. You have probably noticed that there could be a lot of objects involved. We are going to end up with a lot of initialization code. We may think that there's no point. Why break out a query into its own CFC if we haven't actually been thinking in terms of a separate data tier in the first place? Well, let's get back to ColdSpring.

As we have already discussed, the ColdSpring bean factory specializes in configuring our components for us. Using ColdSpring, we don't need to write all of the initialization code. If we have a UserService, which acts as a façade, and needs a UserGateway and UserDAO, as well as a SessionService, and perhaps a NotificationService to work, all we have to do is add setters for those components, register them with ColdSpring, and identify each bean's dependencies. When our application needs to use the UserService, we call `getBean('UserService')`, and that's it. ColdSpring abstracts away the complexities of initialization, resolving dependencies, and managing the objects as singletons.

ColdSpring provides a very simple paradigm. If we want to use an object, we ask ColdSpring for it, and we get it completely ready to use. From this basic idea, we can begin to think about our architecture in terms of separate units of work, logical tiers. We can think about testing early and build ourselves a safety net, giving us more confidence to experiment with changes in our systems. Whether we test components individually or in groups of collaborating components, we can use ColdSpring just as we would in application code.

I have always viewed ColdSpring as part of a way of thinking about applications. By now, you should know what ColdSpring is and the problem it solves. But I hope I've also sparked some interest in looking deeply at your system's architecture, considering TDD and other methodologies, and becoming a better developer.

# CHAPTER 29

# Reactor Fundamentals

**by Doug Hughes**

## The Origin of Reactor

*A few years ago, I was deep in the throes of crunch time. All programmers are familiar with this point in a project. This is where it sinks in that there really are only two weeks remaining to get all that work done. Luckily, we weren't very far from our goal. One of the major reasons we weren't in over our heads was that we were using a code generator to build (and rebuild) our database abstraction layer. This article looks at some of the advantages of using generated database abstraction layers, what Reactor is, and some basic examples of Reactor usage.*

What is a database abstraction layer? Essentially, it's a set of object-oriented components used to access data in a database. For example, you might have one set of objects that read data from your database in order to populate other objects that you use in your application.

One of the programmers on the project was using a code generator that could generate a range of components when pointed to a database. These components became our project's database abstraction layer; as our database schema changed, we would regenerate objects.

Let's say we had a table of users. We would open a separate ColdFusion application that was configured to use our data source, select the User table from a list of tables, choose the types of objects we wanted to generate, and hit the proverbial go button. The tool would then generate all of the objects we required. From there, we would add our own customizations and integrate them into the application we were building.

I estimated that we generated 152 files in the 720 hours we worked on the project. If we assume that it would have taken an average of one hour to write each of those generated files by hand, then generating them saved us 20% of our project development time. The time saved generating the database abstraction layer allowed us to complete the project on schedule.

Don't forget that database abstraction layers also tend to be very repetitive. All of the files for one class of object tend to be very similar. The only notable differences between objects of the same type are the table and column names. Because of this, developers tend to get lazy, which leads to a cut-and-paste style of programming. For example, a developer might write one of these files by hand. Each subsequent time the developer creates one of these files, he copies the first file, does a find-and-replace for the table name, and then quickly changes the column names.

From firsthand experience, I know that this is a bug-prone way to write code. I can't tell you how many times I've missed a comma, typed something wrong, or forgotten something. There is such a range of things that can go wrong! This development process leads to code that may work sometimes, but is actually rife with subtle bugs, or bugs that are only rarely encountered. The bottom line is that cut-and-paste is not a realistic way to write database abstraction layers.

However, the repetitive nature of database abstraction layers means they're a ripe area for code generation. The nice thing about generating a database abstraction layer is that a program is responsible for all the semantics. A generator is a lot less likely to write code rife with subtle bugs. Any bugs you do run into will typically be consistent across the abstraction, and they can be easily fixed in one location within the generator.

Once that project ended, I found that I hated to write database abstractions by hand. Unfortunately, I didn't have any rights to the generator we used, and besides, I thought I could improve upon it. This was the genesis of the Reactor framework.

# A Look at Reactor

Before we look at a Reactor example, let's take a step back. One of the handiest features in ColdFusion is how easy it is to query data from a database. We're all familiar with code that looks like Listing 29-1.

*Listing 29-1. A sample traditional query*

```
<cfquery name="getUsers" datasource="myDSN">
    SELECT *
    FROM User
</cfquery>

<cfoutput query="getUsers">
    <p>#firstName# #lastName#</p>
</cfoutput>
```

This is how we all wrote code a few years ago. Query data and output it, all within one .cfm file. The ease with which you can query and manipulate data in ColdFusion is not only one of its greatest strengths, but also its Achilles' heel.

Take a minute and read over that fragment of code and ponder what might go wrong. Go ahead—I'll wait for you!

You probably came up with at least one problem. I saw several, including the hard-coded database source name, the query commingled with display logic, and the procedural, spaghetti nature of the code.

Today, a range of frameworks are available to help you with some of these problems. For example, ColdSpring can help you configure your data source. Model-Glue, Fusebox, Mach-II, and others can help you separate your application's logic from its presentation tier. Reactor will help you create a reusable set of object-oriented components that you can use to access your database.

Reactor leverages a range of design patterns to solve common problems that arise when abstracting database access. The following are some of the more recognizable design patterns:

*Data Access Objects (DAOs)* : DAOs are objects used to interact with a single record in a database. Traditionally, DAOs have methods to create, read, update, and delete a record (called CRUD for short).

*Table data gateways (gateways)* : Gateway objects are used to interact with multiple rows of data in a database. For example, you might have a `SELECT` statement to get all the users in your `User` table.

*Active Records*: The Active Record design pattern is a relatively new pattern in which an object, sometimes referred to as a *bean* (which is another design pattern in and of itself), knows how to read, write, and delete itself from a database. Because this object is also a bean, it provides methods to get and set its data.

Reactor is really an API. On the fly and as needed, it generates objects that leverage these design patterns (and others) to make accessing and manipulating data in your database very easy.

Reactor essentially becomes a layer between your application and a database, so it is frequently called an object-relational mapping (ORM) framework. That's not 100% correct, but I won't get into the semantics of it. I call Reactor an inline dynamic database abstraction API. In a nutshell, this means that Reactor is an API that will generate your database abstraction layer.

# Installing Reactor

To begin using Reactor, you need to download and install it. The best place to get Reactor is the Subversion repository. However, there are some zip files of the latest code made available both officially and unofficially. Instructions for downloading Reactor are available on the Reactor project site (`http://trac.reactorframework.com`).

Once you've downloaded Reactor, you'll be interested in three directories:

`/Documentation`: This folder contains the Reactor documentation. At the moment, the documentation is incomplete, but it still contains a wealth of valuable information. If you get Reactor from Subversion, look under `/Documentation/Documentation/!SSL!`, as this is where RoboHelp places generated documentation.

`/ReactorSamples`: This folder contains two sample applications: a Contact Manager sample inspired by the Mach-II and Model-Glue samples, and a more complex ReactorBlog sample, which is currently being run on `DougHughes.net`.

`/Reactor`: This is the core framework itself.

The simplest way to use Reactor is to extract the `/Reactor` folder into your web root. Alternatively, you could place Reactor outside your web root and create a mapping named `/Reactor` that points to the location of your `/Reactor` directory. That's all you need to do to install Reactor!

# Some Simple Reactor Examples

Now that you have Reactor installed, let's look at Listing 29-2, which is Reactor's equivalent to the query in Listing 29-1.

*Listing 29-2. A simple Reactor example*

```
<cfset Reactor =
    CreateObject("Component", "reactor.reactorFactory").init(expandPath("reactor.xml"))>
<cfset users = reactor.createGateway("User").getAll()>
<cfoutput query="users">
    <p>#firstName# #lastName#</p>
</cfoutput>
```

The first line simply creates a `ReactorFactory` object. In design pattern parlance, a *factory object* is an object that will instantiate and return another object to you. This line creates the factory and configures it using a simple XML file that you'll see in the next section. The second line does a few things. First, it asks the Reactor factory for a gateway object for the `User` table. Remember that gateway objects work with sets of data in your database. Reactor gateway objects have a `getAll()` method, which returns all the records in a table. Thus, calling `getAll()` on the `User` gateway returns a query of users. The remaining chunk of code simply outputs the data from the table.

Let's look at another example. What if you wanted to select a particular user from your database and put the user's data into a form? Listing 29-3 shows how you might do that.

*Listing 29-3. Selecting a user from the database and putting that data into a form*

```
<cfset Reactor =
    CreateObject("Component",  "reactor.reactorFactory").init(expandPath("reactor.xml"))>
<cfset User = reactor.createRecord("User").load(userId=1)>

<cfform name="UserForm" action="edituser.cfm">
    <cfinput type="hidden" name="userId" value="#User.getUserId()#">
    <p>
        First Name: <cfinput type="text" name="firstName" value="#User.getFirstName()#">
    </p>
    <p>
        Last Name: <cfinput type="text" name="lastName" value="#User.getLastName()#">
    </p>
    <p>
        <cfinput type="submit" name="Submit" value="Submit">
    </p>
</cfform>
```

As in Listing 29-2, the first line simply creates the `ReactorFactory` object, and the second line creates an object. (Actually, it would be best to instantiate the `ReactorFactory` into the Application scope or another location that exists for the life of your application.) In this case, it creates a record object for the `User` table. A record object is an object that implements the Active Record design pattern. Our record has getters and setters corresponding to the column names in the `User` table. For this example, let's assume that we have only `userId`, `firstName`, and `lastName` columns.

Record objects have a `load()` method that loads data from the database. There are a couple of ways to use this method, but Listing 29-3 shows the most common usage. The `load()` method can accept any number of name and value arguments. In Listing 29-3, we pass in `userId=1`, which tells the `load()` method to load the user whose user ID is 1. (Obviously, this is a contrived example. The user ID value is most likely to be provided dynamically, rather than hard-coded.)

Behind the scenes, the records use DAOs and other objects known as Data Transfer Objects (DTOs) to populate the record with data.

Once the record is loaded, we can access and manipulate data in the record with its getters and setters. The form in Listing 29-3 uses the getters on the `User` record to get the record's user ID, first name, and last name.

The preceding examples just scratch the surface of the functionality that Reactor provides.

# How Does Reactor Work?

The heart of Reactor is the `ReactorFactory`, which provides a number of methods to generate and return types of objects. The `ReactorFactory` is configured by an XML file. The XML file defines basic configuration information, such as the data source to use and where to write generated files. In addition, it provides a mechanism for defining relationships between objects. Listing 29-4 shows an example of a configuration file.

*Listing 29-4. Sample Reactor configuration file*

```
<reactor>
    <config>
        <project value="Scratch" />
        <dsn value="Scratch" />
        <type value="mssql" />
        <mapping value="/data" />
        <mode value="development" />
    </config>

    <objects>
        <object name="User" />
    </objects>
</reactor>
```

This file is made up of two sections: `config` and `objects`.

The `config` section contains configuration options. This is not technically necessary, as you can use an inversion of control (IoC) container, such as ColdSpring, to configure this information. However, for our examples, it's easier to leave this here. The `config` section contains the following tags:

> `project`: This is similar to an application name. It uniquely identifies your application so that generated code does not conflict between applications. A side effect is that changing your application name midstream will break everything. When you start a new application, set this name, and don't change it later.

> `dsn`: This sets the ColdFusion data source that Reactor will use to access your database.

`type`: This sets the type of database you are working with. The following options are supported (support for other databases is in the works):

- `mssql` for Microsoft SQL Server 2000 or 2005

- `mysql4` for MySQL 4 (views are not supported in MySQL 4)

- `mysql` for MySQL 5 and later

- `db2` for IBM DB2

- `oracle` for Oracle 9*i* and later

- `postgres` for PostgreSQL

`mapping`: This tag defines a relative path to a directory where Reactor will write its generated files. The name `mapping` is a bit misleading, in that this does not need to actually be a mapping in your ColdFusion server. You should be aware that the directory identified by the mapping setting must already exist, as Reactor won't create this directory for you.

`mode`: This defines the circumstances under which Reactor will generate files. This tag accepts one of three values:

- `always`, so that Reactor always generates files

- `development`, so that Reactor generates files when the database or configuration changes

- `production`, so that Reactor never generates files unless they do not already exist

The last section of the configuration file is, by far, the most interesting section. The `objects` tag defines objects in your database and their relationships to other objects. Technically, in the example in Listing 29-4, the `objects` tag is not required, because it doesn't define relationships between the `User` table and any other tables in your database. However, it's a good practice to define all of your tables, even if they have no relationships.

# Slightly More Interesting Reactor Examples

Let's make this a bit more interesting now. Let's say that we add an `Address` table to our database. The `Address` table will have the `addressId`, `street`, `city`, `state`, and `zip` columns. Let's further update our `User` table so that it has an `addressId` column, which is a foreign key to the `Address` table's `addressId` column. Thus, one could say that a `User` *has one* `Address` by virtue of the foreign key relationship between the two objects.

Wouldn't it be nice if you could easily get the user's address from a `User` record object? Reactor makes this very simple! First, you need to establish a relationship between the `User` and `Address` tables in your configuration file. Let's edit the configuration file as shown in Listing 29-5.

*Listing 29-5. Sample Reactor configuration file (version 2)*

```
<reactor>
    <config>
        <project value="Scratch" />
        <dsn value="Scratch" />
        <type value="mssql" />
        <mapping value="/data" />
        <mode value="development" />
    </config>

    <objects>
        <object name="User">
            <hasOne name="Address">
                <relate from="addressId" to="addressId" />
            </hasOne>
        </object>

        <object name="Address" />
    </objects>
</reactor>
```

The objects section of the file now effectively tells Reactor that a User has one Address by virtue of the addressId column in both tables.

When we make this configuration change, if we're running Reactor in development mode, the next time we request a User record, it will have two new methods: getAddress() and setAddress(). These methods get and set an Address record into the User record. With these new methods, we can do something fun, like the code in Listing 29-6.

*Listing 29-6. Something fun*

```
<cfset Reactor =
    CreateObject("Component", "reactor.reactorFactory").init(expandPath("reactor.xml"))>

<cfset User = reactor.createRecord("User").load(userId=1)>

<cfoutput>
    #User.getFirstName()# #User.getLastName()#<br>
    #User.getAddress().getStreet()#<br>
    #User.getAddress().getCity()#, #User.getAddress().getState()#↵
 #User.getAddress().getZip()#
</cfoutput>
```

The code in Listing 29-6 outputs a formatted address for the user. We used User.getAddress() to get the user's address. However, aside from the configuration change, we didn't need to write a single line of code to do that. Furthermore, Reactor caches the Address object on the first call to getAddress(). That means that the code in Listing 29-6 runs only two simple queries against our database.

Reactor supports one-to-one, one-to-many, and many-to-many relationships. As an example of a one-to-many relationship, let's drop the addressId column from the User table and add a userId column to the Address table, making it a foreign key to the User table's userId column. This change lets one record in the User table relate to multiple addresses in the Address table. Before this change takes effect, we need to update our Reactor configuration, as shown in Listing 29-7.

*Listing 29-7. Sample Reactor configuration file (version 3)*

```
<reactor>
    <config>
          <project value="Scratch" />
          <dsn value="Scratch" />
          <type value="mssql" />
          <mapping value="/data" />
          <mode value="development" />
    </config>

    <objects>
        <object name="User">
            <hasMany name="Address">
                <relate from="userId" to="userId" />
            </hasMany>
        </object>

        <object name="Address" />
    </objects>
</reactor>
```

This change tells Reactor that a user has many addresses. Now when we ask Reactor for a User record, it will no longer have the getAddress() and setAddress() methods. Instead, it will have a getAddressIterator() method.

# Using Iterators

An Iterator is a Reactor-specific object that interacts with sets of data. It is similar to a gateway, but instead of simply returning sets of data, it will let you interact with that data. For example, Iterators have methods to return data as a query or to return an array of records. Furthermore, Iterators apply several techniques, such as lazy loading of records (objects are loaded only when needed) and caching data, to help maintain peak performance.

Listing 29-8 shows an example of an Iterator in use.

*Listing 29-8. Sample Iterator*

```
<cfset Reactor = CreateObject("Component",
"reactor.reactorFactory").init(expandPath("reactor.xml"))>

<cfset User = reactor.createRecord("User").load(userId=1)>
<cfset AddressIterator = User.getAddressIterator()>

<cfoutput>
    <p>#User.getFirstName()# #User.getLastName()#</p>
```

```
    <cfloop condition="#AddressIterator.hasMore()#">
        <cfset Address = AddressIterator.getNext()>
        <p>
        #Address.getStreet()#<br>
        #Address.getCity()#, #Address.getState()# #Address.getZip()#
        </p>
    </cfloop>
</cfoutput>
```

When Listing 29-8 is run, Reactor will recognize that the configuration and database schema have changed, and it will regenerate all the necessary files before instantiating and returning the User record. Furthermore, the Address record is regenerated, but not until the first time it's requested.

Listing 29-8 outputs the user's name, which you've seen several times now, and then all of the addresses associated with the user.

The new getAddressIterator() method on the User record returns an Iterator object that (potentially) holds multiple Address records. Conveniently, the Iterator object has two methods that make it easy to loop over the records in the Iterator: hasMore() and getNext().

The Iterator knows how many records it is holding (just ask its getRecordCount() method). It also knows the index of the last record it returned. The hasMore() method simply compares the two to see if there are any more records in the Iterator. The getNext() method simply gets the next record based on the current index, and then increments the index.

All in all, Iterators make it easy to work with sets of records.

# Learning More About Reactor

We've looked at some of the advantages of using generated database abstraction layers, what Reactor is, and some basic examples of Reactor usage. Sadly, in such a short article, there isn't enough space to cover topics such as customization of Reactor-generated objects, many-to-many relationships through linking tables, cascading saves (which, in my highly biased opinion, are awesome), data validation, or any of Reactor's smaller but really handy features.

If you're interested in getting started with Reactor, you should first visit http://trac.reactorframework.com. (Right now, this page is only a rough skeleton, but it should help you get started.)

The best resource for help with the framework is the Reactor mailing list. Instructions on joining the list can be found at http://trac.reactorframework.com/wiki/ReactorMailingList. The Reactor category on my blog at http://www.doughughes.net is useful, but contains some out-of-date material. There is incomplete documentation on the framework at http://livedocs.reactorframework.com.

Good luck with Reactor.

# CHAPTER 30

■ ■ ■

# Developing Applications with Transfer

## by Mark Mandel

*First released in November 2005, Transfer is a ColdFusion object-relational mapping (ORM) framework that is still in use today. In fact, Mark Mandel, the creator of Transfer, is constantly updating the ORM, which is now on version 1.1. Sean Corfield has called Transfer "a very low overhead ORM, in terms of raw performance." (http://corfield.org/entry/The_Other_ORM). In this article, Mark Mandel explains what an ORM framework is, how Transfer works, and how to get started with your Transfer application.*

Developing all the back-end code that manages the data in a database-driven, object-oriented (OO) system can be a very long and repetitive process, and the codebase can become quite immense.

At an object level, we must write all the get and set methods for each of a table's columns in the system. If the application also incorporates objects composed of structures or arrays of other objects, we must write code to manage these collections and to match them back to the proper database tables correctly.

At the database level, consider the onerous task of writing all the SQL statements to do the basic create, read, update, and delete operations on the tables. Then factor in the code that takes the queries for the database tables and maps them to the objects themselves. This may require massaging the data that comes from the SELECT statements so that it can populate an object, or retrieving data from an object for INSERT, DELETE, or UPDATE statements.

There is also the problem of system maintenance. Changing a single database table column causes changes in the object representing the table, the SQL that is used to map it, and the code that is used to map the SQL to the object. This sort of maintenance can add up quickly. Any major updates to a database structure, or the refactoring of a codebase or database, can add hours—if not days—to development time.

What if there was a way to automate this entire process, and still allow enough flexibility to match a wide variety of requirements?

Object-relational mapping (ORM) software was developed to solve exactly this problem. When configured, ORM software will generate all the SQL statements required to manage data within the database itself. It will also take the data from the database and map it to and from the objects that represent that data. This often incorporates representing and managing the relational database tables through a series of collections of child objects within a parent object, which can be a relatively complicated operation when done manually.

ORMs will often also automatically generate the objects that represent the data, and provide functionality to extend the generated object, allowing customization. An extensive suite of capabilities often manages the model aspect of a given application, depending on the specific ORM solution. This article discusses Transfer, a powerful ORM solution for ColdFusion.

# Transfer—An ORM for ColdFusion

Transfer is an ORM for ColdFusion that has been in development since 2005. At a core level, the information in Transfer's two XML configuration files allows Transfer to interact with the required database tables, generate its ColdFusion code as a series of `.transfer` files, and build and populate TransferObjects, which represent the data stored in the database.

TransferObjects, or the objects in your Transfer application, resolve to a ColdFusion Component (CFC) type: `transfer.com.TransferObject`. While a Transfer application will often use only CFCs of this type, it is possible to provide more specific CFC typing using Decorators, as discussed later in this article.

Transfer is supported on four databases: Microsoft SQL Server 2000 and later, MySQL 4.1 and later, PostgreSQL 8.1 and later, and Oracle 9*i* and later.

One of Transfer's key features is a caching layer. Transfer maintains a cache of the requested TransferObjects in its system, thus greatly reducing your database traffic and speeding up your system's performance. This caching layer is highly configurable through the object configuration file, including configuration options for the ColdFusion scope the cache resides in, the number of TransferObjects to be cached, and/or the duration a TransferObject is cached.

The configurable nature of Transfer gives us a wide variety of application development options and great deal of flexibility, while still providing ease of development.

# Installing and Configuring Transfer

As in many other ColdFusion frameworks, to install Transfer, the `/transfer/` directory needs to be in the web root of your application, or a mapping called `transfer` must point to the Transfer directory.

## The Transfer Data Source Configuration File

The data source configuration file, shown in Listing 30-1, provides Transfer with the required information to connect to the correct ColdFusion data source.

*Listing 30-1. Data source configuration file (datasource.xml)*

```xml
<?xml version="1.0" encoding="UTF-8"?>
<datasource
        xsi:noNamespaceSchemaLocation="../../transfer/resources/xsd/datasource.xsd"
        xmlns:xsi="http://www.w3.org/2001/XMLSchema-instance">
    <name>tBlog</name>
    <username></username>
    <password></password>
</datasource>
```

This configuration file should be fairly self-explanatory. It simply gives the name of the ColdFusion data source, and the username and password, if required.

On line 2 of Listing 30-1, there is a declaration for a **datasource.xsd** XML schema file. This is useful when developing with an XML editor, as it allows the editor to validate the XML and provide auto-completion and code hinting.

While the name of the data source configuration file can be anything you like, I suggest naming it **datasource.xml** to make things simple.

## The Transfer Object Configuration File

Transfer requires information about how to map tables in the system database to objects that it is going to generate and populate, and it gets this through the object configuration file. Listing 30-2 shows an example of an object configuration file.

*Listing 30-2. Object configuration file (transfer.xml)*

```xml
<?xml version="1.0" encoding="UTF-8"?>

<transfer xsi:noNamespaceSchemaLocation="../../../transfer/resources/xsd/transfer.xsd"
        xmlns:xsi="http://www.w3.org/2001/XMLSchema-instance">
<objectDefinitions>
    <package name="user">
        <!-- User details -->
        <object name="User" table="tbl_User">
            <id name="IDUser" type="numeric"/>
                <property name="Name" type="string" column="user_Name"/>
                <property name="Email" type="string" column="user_Email"/>
        </object>
    </package>

    <package name="system">
        <!-- Different categories for Blog Posts -->
        <object name="Category" table="tbl_Category">
            <id name="IDCategory" type="numeric"/>
                <property name="Name" type="string" column="category_Name"/>
                <property name="OrderIndex" type="numeric"
                        column="category_OrderIndex"/>
        </object>
    </package>

    <package name="post">
        <!-- A Blog Post -->
        <object name="Post" table="tbl_Post" decorator="tblog.com.Post">
            <id name="IDPost" type="numeric"/>
            <property name="Title" type="string" column="post_Title"/>
            <property name="Body" type="string" column="post_Body"/>
            <property name="DateTime" type="date" column="post_DateTime"/>
```

```
            <!-- Link between a Post and the User who wrote it -->
            <manytoone name="User">
                <link to="user.User" column="lnkIDUser"/>
            </manytoone>
            <!--   Link between a Post and its array of Comments   -->
             <onetomany name="Comment">
                <link to="post.Comment" column="lnkIDPost"/>
                <!--  Specifying the collection is an array and is ordered by the dateTime
                  property of the Comment  -->
                <collection type="array">
                    <order property="DateTime" order="asc"/>
                </collection>
            </onetomany>

            <!--  Link to the many Categories that Posts can fall under. This is provided by
              an intermediate table between the Category table and the Post table.  -->
             <manytomany name="Category" table="lnk_PostCategory">
                 <link to="post.Post" column="lnkIDPost"/>
                 <link to="system.Category" column="lnkIDCategory"/>
                 <!--  Specifying the collection is an array and is ordered by the orderIndex
                   property of the Category -->
                 <collection type="array">
                     <order property="OrderIndex" order="asc"/>
                 </collection>
            </manytomany>
        </object>

        <!-- A comment for a blog post -->
        <object name="Comment" table="tbl_Comment">
            <id name="IDComment" type="numeric"/>
            <property name="Name" type="string" column="comment_Name"/>
            <property name="Value" type="string" column="comment_Value"/>
            <property name="DateTime" type="date" column="comment_DateTime"/>
        </object>
    </package>

 </objectDefinitions>
</transfer>
```

I suggest naming this file transfer.xml; however, there is no restriction on what the name of this file should be.

# Mapping Objects to Tables

As you can see in Listing 30-2, several core XML elements allow objects to be mapped to tables:

- package elements provide organization to the structure of the document, and become part of the class name used to retrieve generated objects from Transfer.

- object elements map an object type to a table and give that object a name. There may be more than one object in a package, such as the post package defined in Listing 30-2, which contains the Post and Comment objects.

- id, a subelement of object, defines the primary key for that object. id generates get and set methods corresponding to the name attribute of the object with that id element. For example, the id element in the final object tag from Listing 30-2 tells Transfer that getIDComment() will be generated on the Comment TransferObject.

- property elements in an object map columns to properties generated on the object. The property element also generates get and set methods corresponding to each of its configurations. For example, Listing 30-2 tells Transfer to generate the getTitle() and setTitle() methods on the Post TransferObject.

In Listing 30-2, we have an object of type user.User. The name of this type is derived by combining the package element's name and the object element's name. This User TransferObject maps back to the tbl_User table in the database. The table's primary key column, IDUser, maps back to an ID of the same name on the User object. The object has two properties, Name and Email, which map back to the columns user_Name and user_Email, respectively, in the tbl_User table.

Finally, when you build your object configuration file, remember that XML is case-sensitive, while names of objects (in quotes) may be either uppercase or lowercase. Whatever names you give, keep them consistent, or you'll get caught in the XML case-sensitivity trap. It can often be handy to use an XML editor to validate your XML against the XML schema that is provided for the object configuration file.

## Object Composition

In terms of object-oriented programming (OOP), composition represents a "has-a" relationship, where a single object is made up of multiple subobjects, and these subobjects have a closely related or dependent relationship with their parent. In terms of a pure OO definition, subobjects can have no independent existence without their parent; however, in this case, this is largely dependent on your application design. (For more information about composition, see our definition in Chapter 19, "The Object-Oriented Lexicon.") In Listing 30-2, The Post TransferObject is composed of a User TransferObject representing the author of the Post, an array of Comment TransferObjects representing all the comments that have been made on the Post, and a second array of Category TransferObjects representing the categories to which the Post belongs.

As shown in Listing 30-2, Transfer can also generate and manage object composition, and this is done through several XML elements in the configuration file.

The names of these elements echo the relationships that are found in a relational database: one-to-many, many-to-one, and many-to-many.

## Many-to-One Composition

The use of a ManyToOne element allows an instance of a TransferObject to contain a single TransferObject. In Listing 30-2, the Post object is configured to contain a single User TransferObject. While this may seem like a one-to-one relationship, at a database level, it is actually many-to-one, as many Posts can share one User.

This many-to-one composition on a TransferObject is controlled by the lnkIDUser foreign key on the tbl_Post table, which points to the primary key of IDUser on the tbl_User table. This also generates the getUser(), setUser(), removeUser(), and hasUser() methods on the Post object for managing the User record associated with the Post.

## One-to-Many Composition

A OneToMany element allows an instance of a TransferObject to contain multiple TransferObjects as a collection of objects, which can be set as either an ordered or unordered array, or as a struct. In Listing 30-2, the Post object contains an array of Comments ordered by the date they were created.

This one-to-many composition is controlled by the foreign key lnkIDPost on the tbl_Comment table, which points to the primary key IDPost on the tbl_Post table. The array of Comments is ordered by the Comment object's DateTime property.

This configuration will generate getComment(), getCommentArray(), containsComment(), findComment(), and sortComment() methods on the Post object to manage the Comments within a Post, and setParentPost(), getParentPost(), removeParentPost(), and hasParentPost() methods to manage the Comment's connection to its parent Post.

## Many-to-Many Composition

A ManyToMany element allows an instance of a TransferObject to contain multiple child TransferObjects, including multiple instances of the same type of TransferObject. It also allows child TransferObjects to belong to more than one parent. These child TransferObjects can be contained in an ordered or unordered array, or a struct, similar to a OneToMany collection. In Listing 30-2, a Post can contain multiple categories, and since the relationship is many-to-many, different Posts can all belong to the same Category.

This many-to-many composition is controlled at the database level through the interim table lnk_PostCategory, which contains a foreign key to the tbl_Post table, lnkIDPost, and a foreign key to the tbl_Category table, lnkIDCategory. The array is also configured so that it is ordered by the OrderIndex found on the Category.

This configuration will generate the getCategory(), getCategoryStruct(), containsCategory(), sortCategory(), addCategory(), removeCategory(), findCategory(), and clearCategory() functions on the Post TransferObject to manage the Post's connection to specific categories.

# Lazy Loading

Transfer also supports lazy loading of composite objects. This means that one-to-many, many-to-one, and many-to-many collections can be configured to load their data only when it is requested, a feature that can be very important for application performance.

By default, Transfer does not lazily load its composite elements. To configure lazy loading, add the attribute lazy to the composite element, and set its value to true. For example, Listing 30-3 shows how to set the configuration of the Comment collection found inside a Post (Listing 30-2) to lazily load.

*Listing 30-3. Lazy loading of the comment collection*

```
<object name="Post" table="tbl_Post">
    …
    <onetomany name="Comment" lazy="true">
        …
    </onetomany>
</object>
```

In the configuration shown in Listing 30-3, the Comment of the Post will be loaded only if any of the methods generated for the OneToMany configuration element, such as getCommentArray(), are called.

# Decorators

Where a generic transfer.com.TransferObject is not acceptable, or where you need to add a high level of custom ColdFusion code to an object, you might want to set a Decorator in the object configuration file.

A Decorator, based on the Decorator design pattern, is a CFC that extends transfer.com.TransferDecorator. When it's configured, an instance of the Decorator containing the generated TransferObject is returned instead of the TransferObject requested by Transfer.

Transfer allows the specified Decorator to automatically extend all the public methods of the generated TransferObject it contains. This means that the CFC designated as Decorator has access to all the methods that are generated for the TransferObject, as well as the ability to overload those methods, and overwrite or extend the default functionality. This is very similar to the usual inheritance hierarchy; however, in this case, it is functionality that is provided by Transfer, and not by an extends attribute on a CFC.

In Listing 30-2, the Post TransferObject is configured with a Decorator of type tblog.com.Post. Therefore, when a request is made for the Post TransferObject, a CFC of type tblog.com.Post is returned. Listing 30-4 shows an example of a Post Decorator CFC.

*Listing 30-4. Post Decorator CFC*

```
<cfcomponent hint="Post Decorator" extends="transfer.com.TransferDecorator"
            output="false">
    <cffunction name="getNumberOfComments" access="public"
                hint="Custom function for retrieving how many Comments a Post has"
                returntype="numeric">
        <cfreturn ArrayLen(getCommentArray())>
    </cffunction>
</cfcomponent>
```

The Decorator in Listing 30-4 leverages the getCommentArray() method generated by Transfer for the Post TransferObject. Transfer makes this method available to the Decorator CFC so that it is able to return the number of Comments the Post has.

# Using Transfer

Once the configuration files have been written, you will be able to take full advantage of Transfer's ability to manipulate the data held in the database.

## Creating the TransferFactory

To begin using Transfer, you must create a singleton of the `transfer.TransferFactory` CFC. This means that there will be only one instance of the `TransferFactory` in the entire application. Usually, you'll create an instance of the `TransferFactory` within the ColdFusion Application scope, but this depends on your application design.

The `TransferFactory` CFC takes three arguments on its `init` function:

- The relative path to the data source configuration file, often called `datasource.xml`

- The relative path to the `Transfer` object configuration file, often called `transfer.xml`

- The relative path to where Transfer will write the `.transfer` files.

Listing 30-5 is an example of the `transfer.TransferFactory` CFC.

*Listing 30-5. transfer.TransferFactory CFC*

```
application.transferFactory = createObject("component", "transfer.TransferFactory").init(
  "/tblog/resources/xml/datasource.xml", "/tblog/resources/xml/transfer.xml",
  "/tblog/definitions");
```

The `TransferFactory` CFC has two public methods that allow interaction with Transfer: `getDatasource()` and `getTransfer()`. `getDatasource()`, shown in Listing 30-6, simply returns a CFC with the properties of the configured ColdFusion data source from the data source configuration file. This CFC is useful for custom SQL that is not generated by Transfer, and therefore needs the data source details for the `cfquery` to run properly.

*Listing 30-6. getDatasource() method*

```
datasource = application.transferFactory.getDatasource();

 <cfquery name="qPosts" datasource="#datasource.getName()#"
        username="#datasource.getUsername()#" password="# datasource.getUsername()#">
    <!--- query here --->
 </cfquery>
```

On line 2 of Listing 30-6, the `Datasource` CFC provides the information to execute a `cfquery` tag.

The `getTransfer()` returns the `transfer.com.Transfer` CFC. This CFC is the primary gateway to the main functionality of Transfer, and it is covered in the following sections.

## Creating a New Object

To create an object, you invoke the `new()` method with the TransferObject's class name as an argument. This class name is derived from the package element names and the object name, as defined in the configuration XML. Listing 30-7 shows an example of the `new()` method.

*Listing 30-7. Example of the new() method*

```
transfer = application.transferFactory.getTransfer();
post = transfer.new("post.Post");
```

In Listing 30-7, we are requesting a new instance of the `Post` TransferObject defined in Listing 30-2. We pass in the argument of `post.Post`, because it is a combination of the `name` attribute on the package configuration element and the name of the `Post` object element.

The code in Listing 30-7 will generate the required ColdFusion code for the `Post` TransferObject, and return a new `transfer.com.TransferObject`–or perhaps a new Decorator, depending on the configuration—along with all the methods required to manage the object. Therefore, once the `Post` TransferObject has been created, values can be set and retrieved on it, as shown in Listings 30-8 and 30-9.

*Listing 30-8. Example of setting values on a TransferObject*

```
post.setTitle(form.title);
post.setBody(form.Body);
```

*Listing 30-9. Example of getting values from a TransferObject*

```
<h2><a href="displayPost.cfm?ID=#post.getIDPost()#">#post.getTitle()#</a></h2>
```

In Listing 30-8, the `Title` and `Body` properties of the `Post` TransferObject are being set for form values. In Listing 30-9, the `IDPost` and `Title` properties from the `Post` Object are being used to display the `Post`'s `Title` and a link to the `Post` in HTML.

## Saving an Object

Persisting the properties of an object to the database is a simple operation that can be done via the `create()`, `update()`, and `save()` methods that are found on the Transfer CFC.

To explicitly insert a record into the database, you invoke the `create()` method, passing the TransferObject to be inserted as an argument. Listing 30-10 shows an example that inserts a `User` from the configuration in Listing 30-2 into the database.

*Listing 30-10. Using the create() method to insert a record*

```
transfer = application.transferFactory.getTransfer();
user = transfer.new("user.User");

user.setName(form.name);
```

```
user.setEmail(form.email);

transfer.create(user);
```

In Listing 30-10, the Name and Email properties of the User TransferObject are set. When the object is passed to the Transfer CFC's create() method, Transfer inserts the User into the tbl_User table, as configured in Listing 30-2, with the columns populated with the values stored in the User TransferObject. Transfer generates the required SQL INSERT statement and executes it against the configured database.

To update a record in the database, you call the update() method with the TransferObject to be updated. Transfer will generate the appropriate SQL UPDATE statement to update the values in the designated database table. Listing 30-11 shows an example that will update the categories that a Post TransferObject contains.

*Listing 30-11. Using the update() method*

```
transfer = application.transferFactory.getTransfer();
//clear out the categories
 post.clearCategory();

//loop through the categories and add them back in
categories = listToArray(form.category);
len = ArrayLen(categories);
for(counter = 1; counter lte len; counter = counter + 1)
 {
     category = transfer.get("system.Category", categories[counter]);
     post.addCategory(category);
 }
transfer.update(post);
```

In Listing 30-11, when calling the update() method with the Post as the argument, Transfer will update column values of the tbl_Post table with the values from the Post TransferObject. Transfer will also update the values of the ManyToMany table in Listing 30-2 with the primary key stored in the Post TransferObject and the primary key stored in the categories added to the Post in Listing 30-11.

While these are specific methods for explicitly inserting or updating data within the database, Transfer also provides a save() method that automatically determines whether the create() or update() method is necessary. This will depend on whether the TransferObject has been persisted in the database.

The save() method works exactly like the create() and update() methods, as demonstrated in Listing 30-12.

*Listing 30-12. Using the save() method*

```
transfer = application.transferFactory.getTransfer();
post = transfer.new("post.Post");
post.setTitle(form.title);
post.setBody(form.Body);
transfer.save(post);
```

In Listing 30-12, the **save()** method will intelligently call the **create()** method on the Transfer CFC to insert the new **Post** TransferObject, which has not yet been persisted, into the database. This contributes to code reuse, as the same ColdFusion can be used to create a new TransferObject or to update a TransferObject that is already persisted in the database.

# Retrieving an Object

To retrieve a TransferObject from the database by its primary key, you invoke the **get()** method, passing the class name and primary key value of the TransferObject as arguments. Listing 30-13 shows an example that retrieves a **Post** TransferObject with all its **Comments**, **Categories**, and **User**.

*Listing 30-13. Using the get() method*

```
transfer = application.transferFactory.getTransfer();
post = transfer.get("post.Post", url.id);
```

Like the **new()** method, **get()** will generate all the appropriate ColdFusion for the **Post** TransferObject and any of its composite children, and return the appropriate Decorator or TransferObject. It will also generate the required **SELECT** statement to populate the TransferObject with its required data. In Listing 30-13, the **Post** TransferObject is queried on aspects of its composite elements.

Listing 30-14 displays the details of all the **Comments** in the **Post** that has been retrieved.

*Listing 30-14. Example of composition methods*

```
<ul>
<!--- show all the comments in the post --->
<cfscript>
   comments = post.getCommentArray();
      len = ArrayLen(comments);
</cfscript>
<cfloop from="1" to="#len#" index="counter">
   <cfset comment = comments[counter]>
     <li>
       #comment.getName()# wrote on
       #DateFormat(comment.getDateTime(), "dd mmm yy")#
       #TimeFormat(comment.getDateTime(), "hh:mm:ss tt")#
       :<br/>
      #comment.getValue()#
      </li>
</cfloop>
</ul>
```

In Listing 30-14, the **Post** TransferObject contains all the **Comment** TransferObjects within it as an array, which can be retrieved and looped through.

Sometimes, retrieving a TransferObject by its primary key is not appropriate, and therefore it is also possible to retrieve a TransferObject from the database by a unique property value. This is done by calling the **readByPropertyValue()** method, which takes the class name of a TransferObject, a property

341

name, and a property value as arguments, and retrieves the TransferObject by the given property and its value for that class. Listing 30-15 shows an example of using the readByProperty() method.

*Listing 30-15. Using the readByProperty() method*

```
post = transfer.readByProperty("post.Post", "Title", "My First Post");
```

In Listing 30-15, we retrieve a Post TransferObject by its Title property, whose value is "My First Post".

You can also retrieve a TransferObject by multiple property values that translate to an unique record, by using the readByPropertyMap() method. This method takes the class name of the TransferObject and a struct with keys corresponding to the properties of a TransferObject and the value of the key used for retrieval. Listing 30-16 shows this in action.

*Listing 30-16. Using the readByPropertyMap() method*

```
map = StructNew();
map.title = "My First Post";
post = transfer.readByPropertyMap("post.Post", map) ;
```

In Listing 30-16, we again retrieve the Post TransferObject by its Title property. However, the property to retrieve is set from the map struct, seen on line 1, and its value of "My First Post", set on line 2.

Finally, it is also possible to retrieve TransferObjects using Transfer's SQL-like query language called Transfer Query Language (TQL), and Transfer's readByQuery() method. TQL is a query language that uses the configuration provided by your transfer.xml file to abstract the SQL side of querying your database, allowing you to focus on your object model. Listing 30-17 shows a quick example of what is possible with TQL.

*Listing 30-17. Using TQL*

```
query = transfer.createQuery("from post.Post as post where post.title = :title);
query.setParam("title", "My First Post");
post = transfer.readByQuery(query);
```

In this example, we retrieve the Post TransferObject by its Title property, with the value of "My First Post", which is set via the :title property in the TQL statement used to retrieve the Post TransferObject.

If any of these methods do not find a TransferObject in the database, they will return a new object of the same class as the requested TransferObject. This contributes to code reuse, as you can run the same ColdFusion when creating a new TransferObject and when updating TransferObjects that are already persisted in the database.

## Deleting an Object

Deleting a TransferObject from the database is another simple operation. Invoke the delete() method, passing in the TransferObject to be deleted as an argument, and the record represented by the TransferObject will be deleted from the database. Listing 30-18 shows an example.

*Listing 30-18. Deleting a User TransferObject*

```
transfer = application.transferFactory.getTransfer();
user = transfer.get("user.User", form.userid);
transfer.delete(user);
```

In Listing 30-18, we retrieve the User TransferObject from the database and then delete the User from the database. Transfer generates the required DELETE statement to delete the User from the table.

# Using List Queries

Transfer also allows simple list operations on tables. By default, these list queries alias the column names of the tables with the configured property names and allow for ordering by a single object property.

To return a list of all records for a given class, call the list() method with the TransferObject class as an argument. Listing 30-19 shows an example of using the list() method.

*Listing 30-19. Using the list() method*

```
query = getTransfer().list("post.Post");
```

Listing 30-19 will return a query of all the records in the tbl_Post table, as configured in Listing 30-2 for the post.Post TransferObject.

You can also return a list of records, filtered by a given property value. Invoke the ListByProperty() method, while passing in the class of the TransferObject, and the name and value of the property to filter, as arguments. For example, Listing 30-20 will return a query of all posts with the Title of "My First Post".

*Listing 30-20. Returning a query of all posts with a title of "My First Post"*

```
query = transfer.listByProperty("post.Post", "Title", "My First Post");
```

Transfer also allows you to query for a list of records, filtered by a set of property values. You do this by invoking the listByPropertyMap() method, which takes two arguments: the class name of the TransferObject and a struct with key/value pairs corresponding to the properties of a TransferObject and the value of the key to filter by. Listing 30-21 shows an example.

*Listing 30-21. Using the listByPropertyMap() method*

```
map = StructNew();
map.title = "my first post";
query = getTransfer().listByPropertyMap("post.Post", map);
```

Like the previous example, Listing 30-21 returns a query for all Posts with the Title "My First Post". However, here the struct passed in to the listByPropertyMap() method delineates that the query be filtered by its Title—by the key title and the value found therein.

Finally, you can retrieve list queries with the listByQuery() method. For example, using the same technique demonstrated previously, you can use TQL to quickly query the database for Posts whose dates are after 1/1/2009, as shown in Listing 30-22.

*Listing 30-22. Using the listByQuery() method*

```
query = getTransfer().createQuery("from post.Post as post where post.date > :date);
query.setParam("date", "1/1/2009", "date");
result = getTransfer().listByQuery(query);
```

# Other Transfer Functionality

Transfer is not limited to the features discussed in this article. It offers a wide variety of other functionality to help map objects to database tables and manage the model space of application development. Here are some of the features provided by Transfer:

- *Primary key management:* A full suite of tools is available for managing the value of the primary key of a TransferObject.

- *Nullable properties:* Set properties to have NULL values, so that they will be entered into the database as NULL.

- *Configurable caching:* A wide range of caching options allow you to configure caching at the object level.

- *An event model in which observers can be set:* You can capture create, update, and delete events in Transfer by setting CFCs as listeners to Transfer events.

- *An Object.clone() method:* Clone a TransferObject; changes made to the clone are not reflected in the cache until the clone is saved.

- *Automatic cache synchronization:* If TransferObjects have been discarded from the cache or are clones, calling the create(), update(), save(), or delete() method on them will synchronize them with their cached version automatically.

- *Configurable conditions on collections:* Filter out certain TransferObjects from composite collections.

- *Ignore on insert and/or update:* Configure properties to be ignored when generating INSERT and/or UPDATE SQL statements.

- *Refresh on insert and/or update:* Configure properties to refresh their values after an INSERT and/or UPDATE.

- *TransferObject proxies:* Use object proxies to further control object loading.

- *Get TransferObject metadata from Transfer:* Retrieve metadata outlining the structure of a TransferObject class.

- *Transferdoc*: User this tool to introspect TransferObject classes and document the methods that are generated on them.

- *Cache Monitor*: Use this tool to monitor the state of the cache for fine-tuning.

# Conclusion

Transfer is a powerful, highly configurable ORM solution that can greatly reduce the amount of time spent developing the model aspect of an application, assist in mapping that model to a given database, and give the developer a high degree of flexibility to facilitate a wide variety of development requirements.

Transfer generates the CFCs that represent your data, as well as the SQL statements that map the objects to your database and update that data. It handles object composition, generates basic list queries, and provides a configurable caching layer that gives you a large increase in performance in your application.

Transfer's configuration and extension possibilities, including the object configuration file and the use of Decorators, means that while Transfer generates many aspects of an application for you, you still have a high degree of control over your application, and no limitation on extending the generated base.

These resources will help you learn more about Transfer:

- Transfer home page (`http://www.transfer-orm.com/`)

- RIAForge home page (`http://transfer.riaforge.org`)

- Transfer mailing list (`http://groups.google.com/group/transfer-dev/`)

- CompoundTheory blog articles on Transfer (`http://www.compoundtheory.com`)

All of the code examples in this article were derived from the blog example that can be downloaded from `http://www.compoundtheory.com/?action=transfer.examples`.

■ ■ ■

# CHAPTER 31

# FW/1: The Invisible Framework

## by Sean Corfield

*Just when you thought we'd seen all possible frameworks in ColdFusion, Framework One (FW/1) comes along. In this article, Sean Corfield talks about this framework's conception, a reponse to the increasing complexity of popular application frameworks, and its ease of implementation and use.*

ColdFusion has always been about simplicity. We build web applications using ColdFusion Markup Language (CFML) because its faster and easier to use than other languages. The rich set of tags and the built-in functions let us quickly create solutions for our clients without having to worry about technical minutiae.

Accessing a database is simple. Sending e-mail is simple. CFML simply lets you do your job.

Such simplicity comes with a price. Because you can just start coding without thinking too much about it, you can easily create a tangled ball of string, hard to debug and hard to maintain. To solve that problem, a variety of frameworks have appeared over the years. All of the popular frameworks work by routing requests through a centralized system that examines URL variables to determine what to do next, calling components and including templates to generate the HTML sent back to the user.

Fusebox, the granddaddy of these frameworks, was in its early days extremely simple. Your `index.cfm` page contained a big `cfswitch` statement, and each `cfcase` branch used `cfinclude` to pull in some business logic (e.g., a query) and a display page. Teamed with a naming convention, Fusebox brought structure and maintainability to your application. Over time, Fusebox grew and became more sophisticated, and more complicated. With version 4.0, it introduced XML as the way to specify application flow instead of just code. For a lot of people, this made Fusebox too complex to bother with, and they stayed with Fusebox 3.0.

Other frameworks began to appear. Mach-II and Model-Glue both used XML to specify application flow, and they also relied a lot more on ColdFusion Components (CFCs). They have also evolved and become much more sophisticated and much more complicated. Model-Glue 2.0 introduced a dependency on ColdSpring. Both Mach-II and Model-Glue now have a rich set of features that go far beyond their humble origins. Somehow, we all seemed to get used to the idea that in order to write even a simple Hello World! app, we needed to write half a page of XML and have a directory containing thousands of lines of third-party code.

ColdBox came along promising "No XML" and promoting conventions over configuration. In theory at least, it offered the simplest, quickest way to build your applications. It could find your display files using conventions and automatically call the appropriate business logic along the way. But ColdBox is itself massive. The core framework has more than 50,000 lines of code in 200 files and a feature set so rich that it has a 400+ page book describing how to build applications with it, as well as one-day and two-day training courses.

I conceived Framework One (FW/1 ) in the summer of 2009 as a reaction to the increasing complexity of the popular application frameworks. I wrote the initial specification on July 17, with this goal:

*Create an extremely lightweight convention over configuration framework.*

The specification containsed just a dozen bullet points. I wrote the first version of the framework in four hours on July 19, published it to RIAForge (`http://fw1.riaforge.org`) and created the FW/1 mailing list (`http://groups.google.com/group/framework-one/`). Today, the FW/1 mailing list has 130 subscribers, and numerous web sites based on FW/1 are in production. FW/1 is in use by more than 10% of respondents in the CFUnited's State of the CF Union survey (January 2010), making it the next most popular framework behind Fusebox, Model-Glue, ColdBox, and Mach-II.

# What Happened to ColdFusion's Simplicity?

Let's take a quick trip back to ColdFusion MX 7 and look at something Adobe provided that should have had a huge impact on how we built applications.

## Initialization with Application.cfc

For years, we built applications that automatically included two files: `Application.cfm` and `OnRequestEnd.cfm`. The latter didn't have universal popularity. The former laid at the heart of many applications, where all of the initialization took place for application and per-request variables (and often session data, too).

A number of techniques evolved for managing application initialization, and then, in ColdFusion MX 7, Adobe introduced a new, more structured way to handle application, session, and request initialization: `Application.cfc`. This single file could replace both `Application.cfm` and `OnRequestEnd.cfm`, and it provided us with methods where we could safely write our initialization code without messy conditional logic. It also provided the mysterious `onRequest()` method, which allowed us to intercept the page request and do anything we wanted. In short, it provided complete control over the entire application life cycle.

But we didn't really do much with it. In fact, `onRequest()` probably caused more confusion than it saved, because it also intercepted requests for CFC methods via Flex or AJAX. And, to be honest, other than helping us clean up our `Application.cfm` files, `Application.cfc` didn't really do enough for us in terms of automating anything in our application.

The frameworks all advertised integration with `Application.cfc` so that you could hook into the various initialization points in the application life cycle, but they didn't really take advantage of `Application.cfc`. The frameworks just absorbed it into their massive bulks and continued on their merry way—a missed opportunity.

## Convention over Configuration

About the same time as ColdFusion MX 7 was released, another community released a new web application framework: Ruby on Rails. Tired of all the XML used for configuring applications, this community began a movement to adopt conventions as an alternative way to locate parts of an application and determine its general flow. Ruby on Rails is the classic example of convention over configuration, and the approach has gained popularity in the web application world ever since it was introduced.

In the CFML world, ColdBox was the first popular framework to use this approach, and Fusebox offered a convention-based way of building applications with its 5.5 version. However, ColdBox still uses an XML file for certain core configuration settings, and both ColdBox and Fusebox add quite a bit of overhead and complexity beyond their simple conventions.

All the same, the question must be asked: Could convention over configuration, combined with the basic life cycle management of `Application.cfc`, offer a return to ColdFusion's simple roots?

The idea behind such conventions is that the URL determines the behavior of the request. Consider this URL:

```
http://mydomain.com/index.cfm/product/list
```

An intuitive convention for this URL would have the framework locate a section called `product` in your application and invoke or include an item called `list`. This convention could look for `product.cfc` in a particular folder and call the `list()` method, then look for a `product` folder somewhere containing a `list.cfm` display page. An extension to `Application.cfc`, with these conventions implemented in the `onRequest()` method, could make this happen automatically.

Here's another example:

```
http://mydomain.com/index.cfm/product/detail/id/123
```

This would invoke or include an item called `detail` in the product section and pass it `id=123`.

This simple approach automates the workflow of your application, wiring pieces together with no action needed by the developer. This, and a desire to avoid the complexity of existing frameworks, led to the creation of FW/1.

# Getting Started with FW/1

FW/1 is a single CFC that your `Application.cfc` extends. It implements the conventions described in the previous section, and then gets out of your way. It has a very simple API. It's designed to be invisible.

To get started with FW/1, download the FW/1 zip file from `http://fw1.riaforge.org` and unzip it into an empty folder.

---

■ **Note** If you configure the folder containing the unzipped FW/1 bundle as a new web root and browse to it, you'll see an introductory application and a number of sample applications that start off with the simple Hello World! example shown here and increase in complexity. These include two versions of a simple contact manager, one of which shows how to create an AJAX-based application that degrades gracefully when JavaScript is disabled. The introductory application also shows how to combine individual FW/1 applications as subsystems of a larger application. The samples provide concrete examples of FW/1 applications.

---

Follow these steps to try out FW/1:

1. Create a new folder under your web root for your sample application, such as **fw1test**, and copy **org/corfield/framework.cfc** from the FW/1 folder into your application folder.

2. Create an **Application.cfc** file in your application folder that contains the code in Listing 31-1.

*Listing 31-1. The cfcomponent Syntax*

```
<cfcomponent extends="framework" output="false">
    <cfset this.name = "fw1test" />
</cfcomponent>
```

3. Create an empty **index.cfm** file in your application folder.

4. Create a **views** folder and inside that create a **main** folder.

5. Inside that **main** subfolder, create a **default.cfm** file containing the string 'Hello World!'.

Browse to your new application folder—for example, **http://localhost/fw1test/**—and you should see the words "Hello World!" displayed. Congratulations—your first FW1/ application is running!

As you might guess from this exercise, the default action for the framework is **main.default**, and you can invoke that directly using either of the following URLs (assuming your web server supports so-called search engine-safe, or SES, URLs):

```
http://mydomain.com/index.cfm?action=main.default
http://mydomain.com/index.cfm/main/default
```

Let's add a little business logic to show how FW/1 automatically executes that for you.

Create a **controllers** folder. Inside that folder, create a **main.cfc** file containing the code found in Listing 31-2.

*Listing 31-2. main.cfc*

```
<cfcomponent output="false">
    <cffunction name="default">
        <cfargument name="rc" />
        <cfset rc.theTime = now() />
    </cffunction>
</cfcomponent>
```

Edit **views/main/default.cfm** and add the following line after Hello World!

```
It is <cfoutput>#dateFormat( rc.theTime, 'medium' )#!</cfoutput>
```

Reload the page in your browser, and you should see something like this:

`Hello World! It is Jan 24, 2010!`

To process the `main.default` action, FW/1 automatically found your `main.cfc` application controller and called the `default()` method. Then it found your `main/default.cfm` view and included that.

What about that `rc` variable? It's a simple struct containing the URL and form variables passed into your application. FW/1 passes it as an argument to each controller method and makes it available as a local variable in each view it includes. The initials `rc` stand for request context. You'll also notice that the controller CFC does not extend another CFC—it's just a regular, simple, independent component.

You can read the complete Getting Started guide at `http://fw1.riaforge.org/wiki`, along with the rest of the FW/1 documentation.

# A Real Application

Hello World! is not very exciting, but most applications don't fit in a single article that aims to introduce readers to a framework. Here, we're going to look at a simple to-do list application that shows how you might structure a real-world FW/1 application.

For this application, you'll need a simple database table:

```
id         int          auto-increment (primary key)
name       varchar(255)
complete   int          default 0
```

Your `Application.cfc` will look like the code in Listing 31-3.

*Listing 31-3. Application.cfc*

```
<cfcomponent extends="framework" output="false">
    <cfset this.name = "fw1todo" />
    <cfset variables.framework = {
        defaultSection = 'todo',
        defaultItem = 'list'
    } />
</cfcomponent>
```

The `variables.framework` struct specifies any nondefault behavior for FW/1. In this example, it specifies the default section name to be `todo` and the default item to be `list`. That means that when no action is specified in the URL, FW/1 will execute the `todo.list` action.

Your `controllers/todo.cfc` file will look like the code in Listing 31-4.

*Listing 31-4. controllers/todo.cfc*

```
<cfcomponent>

    <cffunction name="init">
        <cfargument name="fw" />
        <cfset variables.fw = arguments.fw />
        <cfreturn this />
    </cffunction>

    <cffunction name="add">
        <cfargument name="rc" />
        <cfif not len( trim( rc.name ) )>
            <cfset rc.message = 'Name is required' />
            <cfset variables.fw.redirect( 'todo.new', 'message' ) />
        </cfif>
    </cffunction>

    <cffunction name="endAdd">
        <cfargument name="rc" />
        <cfset variables.fw.redirect( 'todo.list' ) />
    </cffunction>

    <cffunction name="endDone">
        <cfargument name="rc" />
        <cfset variables.fw.redirect( 'todo.list' ) />
    </cffunction>

</cfcomponent>
```

The first thing to note here is the init() method—the constructor—passes a single argument called fw (the instance of FW/1). This is how controllers can get access to the FW/1 API. The add() method performs validation; if the name field is missing from the request context, it sets a message in the request context and redirects to the todo.new action, preserving the message key in the request context. The endAdd() and endDone() methods are called at the end of requests for the todo.add action and the todo.done action, respectively, and they redirect back to the list of todo items.

You will need a services/todo.cfc file that looks like the code in Listing 31-5.

*Listing 31-5. services/todo.cfc*

```
<cfcomponent>

    <cffunction name="add">
        <cfargument name="name" />
        <cfset var newItem = 0 />
        <cfquery name="newItem" datasource="todo">
            insert into todo ( name )
            values ( <cfqueryparam cfsqltype="cf_sql_varchar" value="#arguments.name#" /> )
        </cfquery>
    </cffunction>
```

```
    <cffunction name="done">
        <cfargument name="id" />
        <cfset var item = 0 />
        <cfquery name="item" datasource="todo">
            update todo
            set complete = 1
            where id = <cfqueryparam cfsqltype="cf_sql_integer" value="#arguments.id#" />
        </cfquery>
    </cffunction>

    <cffunction name="list">
        <cfargument name="showcomplete" default="false" />
        <cfset var items = 0 />
        <cfquery name="items" datasource="todo">
            select * from todo
            where complete = <cfqueryparam cfsqltype="cf_sql_integer"
value="#arguments.showcomplete#" />
        </cfquery>
        <cfreturn items />
    </cffunction>

</cfcomponent>
```

FW/1 automatically calls service methods that match the action, after the controller method has been called. The request context is passed as an argument collection, and the service can pull named arguments out of the request context (and ignore the rest).

Services do not need to return a value. Services are completely independent of the framework itself—they are just regular, simple components.

You will need two view files: one is the default view, the list of to do items, and the other is a form to enter new todo items.

Listing 31-6 shows views/todo/list.cfm.

*Listing 31-6. views/todo/list.cfm*

```
<cfparam name="rc.showcomplete" default="false" />
<cfoutput>
    <p><a href="#buildURL( 'todo.new' )#">Add New Item</a></p>
    <p>Things To Do:</p>
    <cfoutput query="rc.data">
        <form action="#buildURL( 'todo.done' )#" method="post">
            <input type="hidden" name="id" value="#id#" />
            <cfif complete>
                Done
            <cfelse>
                <input type="submit" value="Done" />
            </cfif>
            #name#
        </form>
    </cfoutput>
```

```
    <cfif rc.showcomplete>
        <p><a href="#buildURL( 'todo.list')#">Show to do items</a></p>
    <cfelse>
        <p><a href="#buildURL( 'todo.list&showcomplete=true')#">Show completed items</a></p>
    </cfif>
</cfoutput>
```

This shows the buildURL() API method creating FW/1 URLs. It also shows how the request context passes to a view and gets used. rc.showcomplete is an optional URL variable that determines whether to show completed todo items or active todo items. rc.data is the result of the list() service call—another convention.

Listing 31-7 shows views/todo/new.cfm.

*Listing 31-7. views/todo/new.cfm*

```
<cfoutput>
    <p>New To Do</p>
    <cfif structKeyExists( rc, 'message' )>
        <p>Error: #rc.message#</p>
    </cfif>
    <form action="#buildURL( 'todo.add' )#" method="post">
        <p>Name: <input name="name" type="text" /></p>
        <input type="submit" value="Add" />
    </form>
</cfoutput>
```

This view displays the optional error message (set in the add() controller method if validation fails), and then the simple form for the new todo item.

Finally, we have a layout that is automatically called by FW/1 for each view in the todo section. Listing 31-8 shows layouts/todo.cfm.

*Listing 31-8. layouts/todo.cfm*

```
<cfoutput>
    <h1>FW/1 To Do List</h1>
    <div>
        #body#
    </div>
</cfoutput>
```

The variable body is automatically passed to the layout. It contains the rendered view.

Once you have these six files in place (and your empty index.cfm), you have a simple to-do list application. For http://mydomain.com/, the default action is todo.list, so FW/1 calls:

- (no matching controller method)

- services/todo.cfc: list()—the result is automatically stored in rc.data

- views/todo/list.cfm

- layouts/todo.cfm

You can click the add new item link or the show completed items link. The latter requests `todo.list` with `showcomplete=true`. The former requests `todo.new`, and FW/1 calls:

- (no matching controller method)
- (no matching service method)
- `views/todo/new.cfm`
- `layouts/todo.cfm`

When you fill out the form and submit it, FW/1 calls:

- `controllers/todo.cfc`: `add()`, which redirects back to the form if validation fails
- `services/todo.cfc`: `add()`, which adds the new to-do item
- `controllers/todo.cfc`: `endAdd()`, which redirects back to the list view

Now you have an item in your list and can click the Done button. FW/1 calls:

- (no matching controller method)
- `services/todo.cfc`: `done()`, which updates the item
- `controllers/todo.cfc`: `endDone()`, which redirects back to the list view

# Beyond the Basics

While FW/1 is intentionally simple so that you can get on with building your application without worrying about the complexity of a framework, it provides a lot more functionality than the preceding example might suggest. For example, layouts can nest so that you can have a specific layout for an individual action, which is then wrapped in a layout for that section, which is then wrapped in a default layout for the whole application.

If you like using a bean factory (ColdSpring, LightWire, or something you've rolled yourself), FW/1 lets you do that to automatically wire dependencies into the controllers and services, or even to manage the controllers and services directly.

If you don't like the simplistic conventions for handling services, you can always call them directly from the controller methods yourself. Listing 31-9 contains a version of the `todo` controller that assumes a `todo` service (with methods `create()`, `markDone()`, and `getAll()`) is managed by a bean factory and autowired in.

*Listing 31-9. to-do controller that assumes a to-do service*

```
<cfcomponent>

    <cffunction name="init">
        <cfargument name="fw" />
        <cfset variables.fw = arguments.fw />
        <cfreturn this />
    </cffunction>
```

```
<cffunction name="setTodoService">
    <cfargument name="todoService" />
    <cfset variables.todoService = arguments.todoService />
</cffunction>

<cffunction name="add">
    <cfargument name="rc" />
    <cfif not len( trim( rc.name ) )>
        <cfset rc.message = 'Name is required' />
        <cfset variables.fw.redirect( 'todo.new', 'message' ) />
    <cfelse>
        <cfset variables.todoService.create( rc.name ) />
        <cfset variables.fw.redirect( 'todo.list' ) />
    </cfif>
</cffunction>

<cffunction name="done">
    <cfargument name="rc" />
    <cfset variables.todoService.markDone( rc.id ) />
    <cfset variables.fw.redirect( 'todo.list' ) />
</cffunction>

<cffunction name="list">
    <cfargument name="rc" />
    <cfparam name="rc.showcomplete" default="false" />
    <cfset rc.data = variables.todoService.getAll( rc.showcomplete ) />
</cffunction>
```

```
</cfcomponent>
```

Or, if you don't like bean factories, you could just create the service in the controller's constructor (and omit the setToDoService() method), as in Listing 31-10.

*Listing 31-10. Creating the Service in the Controller's Constructor*

```
<cffunction name="init">
    <cfargument name="fw" />
    <cfset variables.fw = arguments.fw />
    <cfset variables.todoService =
                createObject( 'component', 'model.ToDoService' ).init() />
    <cfreturn this />
</cffunction>
```

The point here is that FW/1 has some opinions about how your code should be organized, but it still allows you to manage your business logic in whatever way you feel most comfortable.

You can read more about how to develop applications with FW/1 here:

http://fw1.riaforge.org/wiki/index.cfm/DevelopingApplicationsManual

# Summary

FW/1 is designed to be invisible. You should be able to build applications by following a simple set of conventions without needing to learn about configuring a framework or reading an API reference manual (although one is provided!). FW/1 1.0 was released on January 4, 2010, after six months of prerelease testing.

Take it for a spin—and recapture the simplicity of ColdFusion!

Note I would like to thank Ryan Cogswell for his contributions to the FW/1 code base, Dutch Rapley for his contributions to the FW/1 documentation, and Javier Julio for his contributions to the FW/1 sample applications. Also, thanks to everyone on the FW/1 mailing list who has supported and evangelized the framework, as well provided critical feedback to make the framework robust and ready for production use!

▓ **Note** I would like to thank Ryan Cogswell for his contributions to the FW/1 code base, Dutch Rapley for his contributions to the FW/1 documentation, and Javier Julio for his contributions to the FW/1 sample applications. Also, thanks to everyone on the FW/1 mailing list who has supported and evangelized the framework, as well as provided critical feedback to make the framework robust and ready for production use!

PART 7

# Designing the User Interface

■ ■ ■

# CHAPTER 32

# Separating Layout from Logic

## by Peter Bell

*When architecting a web application, one of the hardest problems is cleanly separating presentation from programming. In this article, Peter Bell of SystemsForge looks at why this is a problem and then introduces three techniques that can help to make your code more maintainable by reducing duplication and more clearly separating presentation and programming concerns.*

## Why Does Separation Matter?

There are four key benefits to improving the separation between your markup and your scripts: more maintainable business calculations, less formatting duplication, template simplification, and better support for specialization within your development team.

### More Maintainable Business Calculations

A lot of ColdFusion programmers still have business calculations embedded in their display templates. They might display (price * quantity) to show the total price or `firstName & " " & lastName` to display a full name. I'm hoping most of our readers have already given up this evil practice, because:

- Putting business calculations in your views means you are going to have to duplicate them if you have multiple views of the same object.

- Mixing them in with your presentation code makes them much harder to find and maintain as your application grows and changes. It is much easier if they were well encapsulated in a single place.

- If you want to implement a non-HTML front end (Flex, AJAX, Web service, etc.) you'll have to replicate your business calculations yet again if they are embedded in your HTML views.

## Less Formatting Duplication

Have you ever written an application that uses `dateFormat()` in its views? `dateformat()` is a great function and very easy to use, but what happens if you build a large application with hundreds of views and then need to quickly internationalize it or change it from an American to a European date format for a new client? Because you have repeated your formatting rules for dates (perhaps "MM/DD/YYYY") all over your view screens, that would be a pretty painful change to make.

The same goes for currencies, times, and even phone numbers. How much work would it be to change the display of all your US phone numbers to use an xxx.xxx.xxxx instead of (xxx) xxx-xxxx format?

## Template Simplification

While interspersing HTML content with CFML tags is usually a great way to lay out a page, sometimes string concatenation is cleaner. If you're laying out a product page, you're going to want to use CFML to add simple logic, loops and variables to your HTML, but if you're building up a list of page links for a "Page 1 of 4" kind of navigation, it is much easier to do that using string concatenation.

If you build up complex content with lots of variables and very few static characters in your CFML templates, it can make your views very hard to read as the intent of your view gets mixed up with the implementation. For example, you might end up with a page containing both a display of page links at the bottom of a table (your intent) and a series of calculations that figures out how many page links to display and what URLs to use to access them, while keeping track of elements such as records per page, order by and user-selected filters (your implementation). Such a combination would be both hard to follow and hard to maintain as your business needs (and your application layout) changed.

## Better Support for Specialization

The skills required to write complex logic in code are quite different from those required to select the right font, color and spacing to make a page look great. While some web developers excel at both, it is usually a good idea to create applications with a clear separation of concerns so designers can focus on layout and programmers can focus on logic.

# Three Helpful Techniques

These three techniques — business objects, custom data types, and view CFCs — will help you improve the separation of your programming from your presentation.

## Business Objects

ColdFusion developers are starting to embrace object-oriented programming concepts, but they still have a way to go. For example, the Table Gateway pattern (sometimes just called a "Gateway") is still frequently used for returning a collection of data as a recordset. It is a simple approach that yields good performance, it works well if you are building simple applications where the object properties you display exactly map to the fields in your database, or if you choose to place most of your business logic within the database as views or stored procedures and you're treating ColdFusion as a simple templating language. But as soon as you start having calculated properties such as `User.age` or `Product.discountedPrice`, you are left with the problem of where to put your business logic.

There are four common answers to this question:

- You could put the business logic in the view template. If you do this, you're mixing up your presentation templates with business logic, you'll have to duplicate the logic for every view screen, and your logic isn't available to non-HTML applications.

- You could break the view code out into functions included into your view code to act as "view helpers" (scripts which can be called by your view templates to simplify logic in the templates) which would allow you to reuse the logic across views but wouldn't help with non-HTML applications.

- You could write some code to loop over your recordset and add all of the calculated properties to it. However, as you have more calculated properties, this can become difficult to maintain.

- You could just put the logic in your business object – exactly where most object-oriented programmers would expect to find it. Unfortunately, in the past, ColdFusion developers have been loath to use business objects for returning all of their recordsets because of the performance cost of instantiating business objects in ColdFusion, but with the much faster object creation performance in Railo, OpenBD, and ColdFusion 9 there is really no reason to be concerned about this any more for most use cases.

## Custom Data Types

Once you start using business objects instead of putting all of your business logic into your display templates, you'll typically start using a syntax like #User.getAge()# for displaying your properties in list and detail pages. However, if you add custom data types to the mix you can make your code base much easier to maintain and substantially increase its DRY (Don't Repeat Yourself) factor.

Custom data types are a way of efficiently describing the intent of your business objects' properties. If I tell you I want to have a Holiday business object with a startDate property, you're probably already thinking about displaying it using #DateFormat(startDate, "MM/DD/YYYY")#, validating it using isValid( "date" , startDate ) to make sure it is a well-formed date, and using some combination of a text box and/or a date picker to edit its value. If I talk about a User.usPhoneNumber property, you might display it using an (xxx) xxx-xxxx mask and validate that it is a ten-character integer when stripped of all non-numeric characters. Clearly, you don't want to treat every date or phone number exactly the same. You'd probably validate User.dateofBirth differently from HistoricEvent.date - one is much less likely than the other to be valid if it is 7/4/1776! But it is equally clear that there are collections of display formatting, form fields and validations that are often used for certain types of properties.

Custom data types are a way of encapsulating these commonalities, allowing you to substantially decrease the code required to build forms, lists and detail screens. They also make it much easier for you to make universal changes to the way you handle dates, phone numbers or any other heterogeneous collection of properties within an application.

At SystemsForge, we put three methods into a generic business object HTML helper that decorates our business objects with display(), field() and process() methods. We've also added validate() and title() methods to a base business object. So while User.getAge() will still return the age, User.displayAge() displays a well-formed age using your customized display rules for ages, User.fieldAge() displays the form field(s) that you use for ages, User.processAge() turns the age form field(s) into a single string for processing by the bean, User.validateAge() calls a validation library to confirm that the age is valid and User.titleAge() displays the title of the age property, making the title something that can be edited by non-technical users instead of just programmers.

In ColdFusion, it takes a little tap dancing to implement custom data types in a way that performs well. In Java you could just create an object for each property so you'd be able to call methods like User.age.display() and User.age.field(). In ColdFusion, creating that many objects would be slow. The solution is to create a CFC for handling each data type (string.cfc, date.cfc, currency.cfc, usPhoneNumber.cfc, etc). You then instantiate each of those just once in your application (the Singleton pattern for those interested in design patterns) and then you put these data type objects into all of your business objects. If you are constructing your business objects manually you're going to have to add them either as parameters you pass into the init() method, or by calling setter methods on the object to save the data type objects in the variables scope of each object that needs them. However, you're probably going to want to use LightWire (or possibly ColdSpring) to inject them automatically into your business objects.

It is also important to allow each data type to have parameters that can be set on a property-by-property basis, so you can set the length of the text box for a Product.fieldTitle() or choose whether to return a date picker from the User.fieldDateofBirth() method. Listing 32-1 gives the simplest example of this technique by showing what a string custom data type would look like.

*Listing 32-1. A String Custom Data Type*

```
component name="string.cfc" {

    public string  field( string propertyName, string  propertyValue,
                          string  dataTypeProperties ) {
        var properties = setProperties( dataTypeProperties );
        return '<input type="text" name="#propertyName#"  size="#properties.size#"
                    maxlength="#properties.maxLength#" value="#propertyValue#" />';
    }

    public string function display( string propertyValue, string dataTypeProperties ) {
        var properties = setProperties( dataTypeProperties );
        return propertyValue;
    }

    public string process( string propertyName, input  input, string dataTypeProperties ) {
        var properties = setProperties( dataTypeProperties );
        return input.get( fieldName );
    }

    private struct function setProperties( string dataTypeProperties,
                                           string defaultPropertyList ) {
        /* This allows you to set arbitrary properties for different data types from a
        delimited list. So if you want to be able to set the size and maxlength for a string,
        you'd pass in dataTypeProperties = "size=20|maxLength=50" and this will set size and
        maxLength properties that can be used by the other methods.   */
        var propertyValuePair = "";
        var i = 0;
```

```
        for ( i = 1; i lte listLen( defaultPropertyList , "|" ); i++ ) {
            propertyValuePair = listGetAt( defaultPropertyList, i, "|" );
            if ( !structKeyExists( dataTypeProperties, listGetAt( propertyValuePair, 1, "=" ) )
                && listLen( propertyValuePair, "=" ) == 2 ) {
                dataTypeProperties[ listGetAt( propertyValuePair, 1, "=" ) ]  =
                                    listGetAt( propertyValuePair, 2, "=" );
            };
        };
        return dataTypeProperties;
    }
}
```

Now, that might seem a lot of code just to be able to display a property and a text box for editing. But now let's think about a slightly more useful data type - say date. Let's say that our application is intended primarily for the US market. If that is the case, we would probably format most of our dates using #dateFormat( date , "MM/DD/YYYY" )#. With custom data types, there would be a date.cfc with the displayValue() method in Listing 32-2.

*Listing 32-2. displayValue method in a date.cfc*

```
public string function display( string propertyValue, string dataTypeProperties ) {
    var properties = setProperties( dataTypeProperties );
    return dateFormat( propertyValue, "MM/DD/YYYY" );
}
```

Now instead of having the display code in hundreds of places throughout all of your views, that formatting rule is in exactly one place – in the date.cfc. If you then decided to internationalize the application, all you'd need to do would be to replace that one line of code with a function that returned a localized date such as lsDateFormat( propertyValue ) and you'd have localized date display for your entire application. Same would go for currencies if you had a money custom data type with a display method that initially returned $ #propertyValue#. Again you'd only have to change this in one place to support multiple currencies instead of having to add logic to display the correct currency symbol throughout all of the views in your application.

## View CFCs

In the first two techniques, you've abstracted your business calculations and data type-specific layout and form logic. There are still a number of common view calculations that need to be handled such as creating links for paging through a recordset. I have tried several different approaches to abstracting the calculations from the templates. I've found the idea of using view CFCs as view helpers to be one of the most useful.

Let's start with displaying a list, a pretty common use case. Imagine you have a User object with firstName, lastName and email. A simple table to display a list of users might look like Listing 32-3.

*Listing 32-3. CFML Template For Displaying a User Object*

```
<table border=1 class="bodytext">
    <tr>
        <td><strong>First Name</strong></td>
        <td><strong>Last Name</strong></td>
        <td><strong>Email</strong></td>
    </tr>
    <cfloop condition="#UserIterator.hasMore()#">
        <cfset User = UserIterator.getNext()>
        <tr>
            <td valign="top">#user.displayFirstName()#</td>
        </tr>
    </cfloop>
</table>
```

The only unusual piece is the cfloop which is saying that while there are more users in the user iterator (which contains an array of user objects), the loop should continue and the User = UserIterator.getNext() should take the next business object from the user iterator. Conceptually this is similar to a cfoutput query="userList" - but it returns a business object instead of the fields from the query so you can put any business logic into the business object instead of having to repeat it in all of your views.

Now let's try to generalize this. If we had a comma-delimited list of the property titles (First Name,Last Name,Email) and the property names (firstName,lastName,email), we could replace Listing 32-3 with the code in Listing 32-4.

*Listing 32-4. CFML Template For a Generalized Display*

```
<table border=1 class="bodytext">
    <tr>
        <cfloop list="#propertyNameList#" index="propertyName">
            <td><strong>#Object.title( propertyName )#</strong></td>
        </cfloop>
    </tr>
    <cfloop condition="#ObjectIterator.hasMore()#">
        <cfset Object = ObjectIterator.getNext()>
        <tr>
            <cfloop list="#propertyNameList#" index="propertyName">
                <td valign="top">#Object.display( propertyName )#</td>
            </cfloop>
        </tr>
    </cfloop>
</table>
```

This code starts by looping over the properties to display, displaying the appropriate title (Object.title( propertyName )) for each to create the column headers for the table. For a user object it might display "First Name", "Last Name" and "Email". It then loops over all of the objects to be displayed and for each one displays the values (Object.display( propertyName )) in the table, starting a new row (<tr>) for each object.

Now if we want to add or remove properties or change the titles of given properties, we can do that without having to edit the list view. All we need to do is edit the list of properties.

However, if you want to add the ability to create page links – something like "[1]-[2]-[3]-[4]" at the bottom of the table, you start to run into problems. Adding the logic to calculate that inside the template would make it much harder for designers to work with.

We really want to be able to just say what we're trying to display within the template. It would be ideal if we could just have a #pageLinks# variable created for us dynamically each time a user accesses a template. I've been wrapping each CFM template that needs custom logic within a CFC. Because the CFM template has access to the local scope of the CFC in which it is included, it is easy to add methods like displayPageLinks() or displayBackURL() to the CFC. Then the designer can just put #displaypPageLinks()# and #displayBackURL()# wherever he or she wants without worrying about how the methods actually work, as they are taken care of by a different person working on a different file.

So you might have a list.cfc with a render() function that is called to display the list, and any number of other functions that do the necessary calculations to generate strings like page links and URLs. Listing 32-5 shows a sample list.cfc and Listing 32-6 shows a sample list.cfm that might be cfincluded within the list's render() method, allowing the designer to customize the layout without having to worry about how the view logic works.

*Listing 32-5. Sample List.cfc*

```
component name="List" {
    public List function init() {
        variables.templatePath = "/projectname/layouts";
        return this;
    }

    public void function render( any model ) {
        include template="#variables.templatePath#/list.cfm";
    }

    public string function displayPageLinks( ) {
        var returnString = "";
        // add logic here to concatenate the appropriate page display links for paging
        return returnString;
    }

    // other view helper methods here
}
```

*Listing 32-6. Sample List.cfm*

```
<div align="center">#displayPageLinks()#</div>
    <table border=1 class="bodytext">
        <tr>
            <cfloop list="#propertyNameList#" index="propertyName">
                <td><strong>#Object.title( propertyName )#</strong></td>
            </cfloop>
        </tr>
```

```
        <cfloop condition="#ObjectIterator.hasMore()#">
            <cfset Object = ObjectIterator.getNext()>
            <tr>
                <cfloop list="#propertyNameList#" index="PropertyName">
                    <td valign="top">#Object.display( propertyName )#</td>
                </cfloop>
            </tr>
        </cfloop>
    </table>
<div align="center">#displayPageLinks()#</div>
```

The basic concept of CFCs as view helpers isn't limited to common problems like displaying lists or forms. Wherever you have a layout template that is starting to get confused with a bunch of layout calculations, you can write a view helper with a render() method that cfincludes the template, and you can then call the CFC's methods to take care of any concatenations or calculations.

# Conclusion

Whether you are just getting started with object-oriented programming or are looking to move the maintainability of your code to the next level, the combination of business objects, custom data types, and view helpers provides a really powerful framework for making your code DRYer and more maintainable while helping you separate the layout from the logic in your applications.

■ ■ ■

# CHAPTER 33

# Creating Dynamic Presentations in ColdFusion

## by Wally Kolcz

*Presentations, love them or hate them, are a fact in most businesses. Being stuck in a primarily Microsoft office, my colleagues and I were usually forced to work with PowerPoint whenever the need for a presentation arose. PowerPoint is a good piece of software, but it has its limitations, especially if you want to present remotely. Sharing a PowerPoint presentation over the web has unique challenges and does not allow for a very interactive or engaging presentation.*

*Now, I have to admit that when I first saw Macromedia Breeze (now Adobe's Acrobat Connect presentation service), I was a little jealous that I was unable to create such an appealing, Flash-based presentation online without subscribing to the service. Since I wasn't a Flash genius at the time, creating something sharp, interactive, and easily reusable would have taken me forever. But, thanks to Adobe ColdFusion 8 and 9, that has all changed, and this article explains how.*

## Overview

With ColdFusion's `presentation` tags, you can easily create and deploy beautiful, Adobe Acrobat Connect-style presentations in as little as two to four lines of code. There are three separate elements to the new tag series:

- `Cfpresentation`: the main presentation wrapper that controls the look and interface of the presentation

- `Cfpresenter`: allows you to add different presenters and their personal/business information to each slide

- `Cfpresentationslide`: generates each slide in your presentation

With these tags you can incorporate HTML-based slides for text and images, Flash animations, and audio and video files, and even render live web sites into your slides. Slides can contain not only static information but also dynamic data such as sales numbers or membership numbers, which will then show real, up-to-date information to your audience.

Since your presentations are done programmatically, you can quickly edit or add to your presentation or remove slides from the show. In this article, I'm going to use some of the more interesting attributes to build my example presentation, but that is by no means all of them. Half the fun of this new series of tags is that you can play with them till you get the right look and feel for your presentation. By the end of the article, you shall see how easy it is to create dynamic presentations with ColdFusion 8.

Well, with no further ado, on to the details about the tags.

# cfpresentation - The Shell

You start your presentation with the `cfpresentation` tag, which sets the main parameters of the presentation, such as color, the name of the presentation, whether to show notes, a working search area that searches the text in your slides, an outline that lists all your slides in order, drop shadow color, text color, and more. There are 16 possible attributes, and in Listing 33-1 I use 12 of them to set the style of the presentation.

*Listing 33-1. Setting the Presentation Style*

```
<cfpresentation backgroundcolor="0x006633" control="normal" controllocation="right"
        primarycolor="0x009933" directory="/presentation" overwrite="yes"
        shadowcolor="0x000000" shownotes="yes" showoutline="yes" showsearch="yes"
        textcolor="0xFFFFFF" title="My First Presentation">
</cfpresentation>
```

Listing 33-1 creates a shell for the presentation. The code tells the renderer to create a presentation called 'My First Presentation' (`title`) that has a dark green background specified using a hexadecimal color code (`backgroundcolor`), an interface color of a lighter green (`primarycolor`), and white text (`textcolor`), with a shadow (`shadowcolor`). To set a color, you can express it as—for example, for dark green—either `0x006633` or `##006633` (just don't forget the second #!).

The `directory` attribute tells ColdFusion whether to save the presentation to the server. If you do not specify a directory, ColdFusion runs the presentation directly in the client browser from files written to a temp directory on the server. To save the presentation, specify an absolute path or a directory relative to the CFM page. Please note that ColdFusion does not create the directory; it must already exist!

The `overwrite` attribute tells ColdFusion to overwrite the file when saving should a file of the same name exist in that directory.

The `control` attribute applies to a panel that houses the notes, search, outline, and presenter information. You have two options: `normal`, which creates a full-sized information panel; and `brief`, which creates a stub that includes the basic play / pause / sound controls, with the option of expanding it to `normal`. You can also set the placement of the control (`controllocation`) to either left or right.

You also have these options:

- Showing notes (`shownotes`) that are read from your individual slides

- Showing a search engine (`showsearch`) that allows your viewers to search for specific information and scans the text of your slides for matches

- Showing the outline (`showoutline`), a slide-by-slide list that allows your audience to jump around or go back to certain slides for review

# cfpresenter - The People

With the shell of the presentation in place, you can add presenters to your slides. It's always nice to put a face to a name.

With any presentation, you can include multiple presenters for the series and one presenter per slide. With the `cfpresenter` tag, you can add a lot of interesting information for each presenter, including the person's name, email address, photo, job title, company logo, and a biography that mentions related experience, the presenter's current position in the company, or maybe just some fun facts about the person.

Here's how you would add a presenter:

```
<cfpresenter name="Wally Kolcz" email="wkolcz@isavepets.com" image="images/me.jpg"
    title="ColdFusion Web Developer"
    biography="Wally has been a ColdFusion Web Developer for many years.">
```

Notice that the name you give your presenter doesn't follow the traditional naming convention of an ID name without blank spaces. ColdFusion can still match the name, with spaces, to the right person and show the person properly. This threw me off the first time, since I come from a discipline of never, ever adding spaces in an ID. If you happen to concatenate the name – for example, name="WallyKolcz" – it will appear on your slide that way and not make much sense. Also note that the bio can be as long as you like.

A slide does not need to contain a presenter, but adding one makes your slides more informative as to who is presenting and, if you use audio for voice, who is speaking.

To add multiple presenters to your presentation, you must include all your presenters after the beginning `cfpresentation` tag, and then include them in each slide in which you would like them to appear. So if my presentation had multiple presenters, Listing 33-2 shows how I would add them to the list.

*Listing 33-2. Adding Multiple Presenters*

```
<cfpresentation title="My First Presentation"...>

    <cfpresenter name="Wally Kolcz" email="wkolcz@isavepets.com"
        image="images/me.jpg" title="ColdFusion Web Developer"
        biography="Wally has been a ColdFusion Web Developer for many years.">
    <cfpresenter name="Siobhan Kolcz" email="skolcz@isavepets.com"
        image="images/skolcz.jpg" title="Web Designer"
        biography="Siobhan is Wally's right-hand lady who makes all our web sites look
wonderful">

</cfpresentation>
```

# cfpresentationslide - The Message

Now that you have the shell of your presentation and a presenter, it's time to add your slides.

The `cfpresentationslide` tag takes up to 12 different attributes. For this example, I am going to use a simple HTML-based slide and add only a slide title, myself as a presenter, notes, and a duration of 15 seconds (see Listing 33-3).

*Listing 33-3. Creating a Slide*

```
<cfpresentationslide title="my First Slide" presenter="Wally Kolcz"
                    notes="This is my first slide." duration="15">
    Hello World. Welcome to my first presentation and slide!
</cfpresentationslide>
```

Anything in between the beginning and ending `cfpresentationslide` tags is included in your slide. It can use normal HTML markup, CSS, images, dynamic data with `cfquery` or `query` of queries, charts and graphs, and more. Anything that can be put on a normal HTML/CFML page can be added to the slide. If you don't specify the font size, the presentation reduces the size of the font to fit inside the slide area.

You can also control the look of your slide by using the margin attributes (`leftmargin`, `rightmargin`, `topmargin`, `bottommargin`) and scaling to reduce the size of the display.

You can include ColdFusion code in your slide to incorporate dynamic information, using `cfquery`, `cfloop`, `cfoutput`, etc., or you can use the `cfchart` series of tags to create pie charts, line graphs, etc. (see Listing 33-4).

*Listing 33-4. Using cfchart in Your Slide*

```
<cfpresentationslide>
    <h3>Total Sales</h3>
    <cfchart format="jpg" chartwidth="500"show3d="yes">
        <cfchartseries type="pie" query="members" itemcolumn="activeMembers"
            valuecolumn="premier">
    </cfchart>
</cfpresentationslide>
```

Want to make your slides a little more than plain HTML? The `audio`, `video`, and `src` attributes of `cfpresentationslide` can transform your presentation from just words and images on a slide to interactive, engaging content.

The `audio` attribute allows you to add the path of an audio file that will play on your slide while it is running. Currently, ColdFusion supports only the MP3 audio format in a presentation.

```
<cfpresentationslide title="All About Me" audio="me.mp3" duration="15">
```

The `video` attribute, like `audio`, allows you to easily add the path to a video file that plays in the slide's body.

```
<cfpresentationslide title="Save A Pet" presenter="Wally Kolcz" duration="15"
    video="pets.flv">
```

Note that ColdFusion does not allow both audio and video on a single slide. You'll have to choose one or the other.

The `src` attribute allows you to add the path to a Flash animation file (SWF) or to an HTML page created elsewhere on your web site. The Flash animation retains its interactivity, so if your animation allows the user to click a button or add text, the user will be able to interact with it in the presentation. This attribute also lets you add a URL to a live web site that ColdFusion can render inside your slide; however, links inside the rendered web site are not active. I think having the web site render inside your slide is a very neat feature because it keeps you from having to screen-capture a web site and add it as an image file. It also saves on file size, as opposed to including an image file.

- SWF: `<cfpresentationslide title="slide 1" src="presentation/slide1.swf">`

- HTML Page: `<cfpresentationslide title="slide 2" src="/slide2.htm">`

- URL: `<cfpresentationslide title="slide 3" src="http://www.isavepets.com">`

You can combine the various attributes to make a more informative slide. For example, the following code uses an audio file to describe a rendered web site:

```
<cfpresentationslide title="Help Save Pets" presenter="Wally Kolcz" audio="mySite.mp3"
    duration="5" src="http://www.isavepets.com/">
```

# Putting It All Together

Listing 33-5 shows how to create a complete presentation with one presenter and one slide with just three tags.

*Listing 33-5. My First Presentation*

```
<cfpresentation backgroundcolor="0x006633" control="normal" controllocation="right"
    primarycolor="0x009933" directory="presentation" overwrite="yes"
    shadowcolor="0x000000" shownotes="yes" showoutline="yes" showsearch="yes"
    textcolor="0xFFFFFF" title="My First Presentation">

    <cfpresenter name="Wally Kolcz" email="wkolcz@isavepets.com"
        image="/people/wally.jpg" title="ColdFusion Web Developer"
        biography="Wally has been a ColdFusion Web developer for many years.">

    <cfpresentationslide title="My First Slide" presenter="Wally Kolcz"
                    notes="This is my first slide." duration="15">
        Hello World. Welcome to my first presentation and slide!
    </cfpresentationslide>

</cfpresentation>
```

# The Amazing Potential

With a little imagination and good use of a front-end interface, database, `cfoutput`, or `cfloop`, you can easily build an application that will let your coworkers create and manage dynamic presentations on the fly. I developed a little intranet application that allows some of my bosses to create and manage their own online presentations using a simple interface and a back-end database. It populates the presenter with his personal information, and the presenter can simply add new slides to the database that render when the presentation runs.

The `cfpresentation` tag series allows you to create interactive presentations easily while having to learn only three new tags. The presentations should go over well with the people in your organization. As always, don't tell your bosses just how easy it was to create; instead, let them think you are a genius.

■ ■ ■

# CHAPTER 34

# Working with JSON and cfajaxproxy

## by Raymond Camden

*Integrating Ajax with ColdFusion took a big leap forward with the introduction of two features: JSON (JavaScipt Object Notation) support and the addition of cfajaxproxy. In this article, Raymond Camden shows how JSON support and cfajaxproxy can make your Ajax ColdFusion development much easier.*

## Working with JSON

ColdFusion 8 and 9 added so many new tools to our programming toolbox that many experienced developers may have actually felt themselves falling behind simply trying to learn all the new tags and functions at their disposal. In this article, Raymond Camden discusses two features that were added in ColdFusion 8: JSON (JavaScript Object Notation) support and the addition of cfajaxproxy, which he considers the most powerful tag ever added to ColdFusion — yes, even more powerful than cfdump. Let's begin our journey with a look into JSON.

JSON is a lightweight data interchange format that was designed to be easy for humans to read and write and for machines to parse and generate. It is usually used to transfer objects and data structures across network connections in a process called serialization.

JSON is a text format that is language-independent but based on a subset of JavaScript, so when we use JSON, ColdFusion may be transforming your ColdFusion objects into their JavaScript equivalents. The most common alternative to using JSON is to represent your objects and data structures using XML formats, such as WDDX.

Many years ago, before web services and SOAP were popular, ColdFusion added WDDX support to the language. This lets you take any ColdFusion datatype and convert it into WDDX, a flavor of XML created by Allaire for the purposes of syndication and data sharing. WDDX never really took off, although it was added to other languages such asPHP, but it was and still is a handy way to convert dynamic data into a string-based representation. The alternative to this is to create XML from the data yourself. While this gives you more control over the resulting XML, it does require a bit more work on your part. (For developers looking for an easy tool to convert ColdFusion data into XML, please see my `toXML ColdFusion` component, at `http://www.coldfusionjedi.com/projects/toxml/`). Both the custom and WDDX types of XML suffer from verbosity. While you can work around this, the typical XML representation of data can be a bit too big. This becomes an issue when working with XML over Ajax.

Let's take a look at a few examples. First, in Listing 34-1 I've converted a simple array with four elements into XML.

*Listing 34-1. First XML Example: A Simple Array with Four Elements*

```
<people>
    <person>
      Jacob
    </person>
    <person>
       Lynn
    </person>
    <person>
       Noah
    </person>
    <person>
       Mazie
    </person>
</people>
```

Listing 34-2 contains a query with two rows and two columns.

*Listing 34-2. Second XML Example: A Query with Two Rows and Two Columns*

```
<?xml version="1.0" encoding="UTF-8"?>
<people>
    <person>
       <ID>
          1
       </ID>
       <NAME>
          Raymond
       </NAME>
    </person>
    <person>
       <ID>
          2
       </ID>
       <NAME>
          Jacob
       </NAME>
    </person>
</people>
```

Not terribly bad, but remember that both the array and the query are rather small. Now let's look at the array from Listing 34-1 and the query from Listing 34-2 converted to JSON (Listings 34-3 and 34-4).

*Listing 34-3. Listing 34-1 Converted to JSON*

```
["Jacob","Lynn","Noah","Mazie"]
```

*Listing 34-4. Listing 34-2 Converted to JSON*

```
{"COLUMNS":["ID","NAME"],"DATA":[[1.0,"Raymond"],[2.0,"Jacob"]]}
```

It is rather easy to see that in both cases, the JSON is slimmer than the equivalent XML. If the original data set were larger, the differences would be even more dramatic. A while back, I performed the same comparison with a four-column query of 100 rows. The XML ended up being close to 8000 characters long, whereas the JSON was around 1800. That's a huge difference and really speaks to the greater trimness of JSON over XML.

So now that you know why someone would use JSON, let's talk about how you can work with JSON in ColdFusion. ColdFusion provides three JSON-related functions:

- `serializeJSON`, which will convert ColdFusion data to JSON.

- `deserializeJSON`, which will convert a JSON string to ColdFusion data.

- `isJSON`, which will tell you if a string is valid JSON.

Let's start with a simple example (Listing 34-5).

*Listing 34-5. An Example Using serializeJSON*

```
<cfset data = queryNew("id,name")>
<cfset queryAddRow(data, 1)>
<cfset querySetCell(data, "id", 1)>
<cfset querySetCell(data, "name", "Raymond")>
<cfset queryAddRow(data, 1)>
<cfset querySetCell(data, "id", 2)>
<cfset querySetCell(data, "name", "Jacob")>

<cfset data2 = ["Jacob", "Lynn", "Noah", "Mazie"]>

<cfset json1 = serializeJSON(data)>
<cfset json2 = serializeJSON(data2)>

<cfoutput>#json1#</cfoutput>
  <p>
<cfoutput>#json2#</cfoutput>
```

Listing 34-5 creates two variables. The first variable, `data`, is a query and is filled with two rows. The second variable, `data2`, is an array. I convert both of these variables into JSON using `serializeJSON`. Notice that I didn't have to do anything but pass the variable to the function. ColdFusion handles looking at the data and converting it correctly. I've already shown you the output. We can take these results and convert them right back into ColdFusion, as seen in Listing 34-6.

*Listing 34-6. Using DeserializeJSON to Convert JSON Output into ColdFusion Data*

```
<cfset newData = deserializeJSON(json1)>
<cfset newData2 = deserializeJSON(json2)>

<cfdump var="#newData#">
<cfdump var="#newData2#">
```

If you run Listing 34-6, you will notice something odd. (Be sure you add this code to the end of Listing 34-5.) The variable `json1` was created from our query, but when it's converted from JSON back into a native ColdFusion variable, we no longer have a query. Instead we have a structure with two keys: `columns` and `data`. The `deserializeJSON` function has an optional second parameter, `strictMapping`, that determines how it should deserialize the JSON data. The value of `strictMapping` is `true` by default and tells ColdFusion to convert the information as strictly as possible from JSON. Since JavaScript doesn't have a `query` datatype like ColdFusion, the JSON representation of a ColdFusion query looks more like a structure. Therefore, when converting back, you end up with a structure. By setting `strictMapping` to `false` (see Listing 34-7), you end up with a native ColdFusion query.

*Listing 34-7. Setting strictMapping to False When Using DeserializeJSON*

```
<cfset newData = deserializeJSON(json1,false)>
```

Now let's take a look at the last JSON-related function, `isJSON`. This is rather simple, so our example (Listing 34-8) will also be simple.

*Listing 34-8. An Example Using isJSON*

```
<cfset data = ["Jacob", "Lynn", "Noah", "Mazie"]>

<cfset jsonString = serializeJSON(data)>

<cfif isJSON(data)>
    data is JSON
<cfelse>
    data is NOT JSON
</cfif>
<p>
<cfif isJSON(jsonString)>
    jsonString is JSON
<cfelse>
    jsonString is NOT JSON
</cfif>
```

Running Listing 34-8 will return:

```
data is NOT JSON

jsonString is JSON
```

# Special Considerations with JSON Serialization

When you serialize a ColdFusion `datetime` value, the result is a string that works more easily with JavaScript. The format will be:

```
Name of Month, Day Number Year Hours:Minutes:Seconds
```

The current time represented in JSON is:

```
"February, 13 2010 23:59:38"
```

When you serialize a ColdFusion component, you may end up seeing something odd: {}. The reason for this? SerializeJSON will only work with the *This* scope values of CFCs. If your CFC contained a variable in the *This* scope named NAME with a value of "Raymond", you would see this:

```
{"NAME":"Raymond"}
```

Obviously, this means that true CFC serialization isn't possible, which makes sense. There would be no way to convert methods of CFCs into JavaScript functions, nor would it be possible to do the reverse. As I've mentioned in the past when talking about CFC serialization in general (whether to XML or JSON), you should write a method of the CFC that will create this serialization for you. While you would not be able to treat it like a true JavaScript object, you could at least pass it around as a string. Your CFC would need a corresponding deserialization method as well.

When converting ColdFusion queries, you can use the second, optional parameter to `serializeJSON`, `serializeQueryByColumns`. The default value for this parameter is `false`, and you have seen the result of this conversion. When `serializeQueryByColumns` is set to `true`, the resulting JSON looks a bit more like WDDX. The string represents an object with three columns: ROWCOUNT, COLUMNS, and DATA. ROWCOUNT is obviously the number of records in the query; COLUMNS is an array of column names; and DATA is the actual data, represented as a structure with keys based on the column name.

# Working with cfajaxproxy

I began by declaring that the `cfajaxproxy` tag was the most powerful tag in the ColdFusion language. It is now time to back that up. At a very basic level, the `cfajaxproxy` tag creates a connection between the client (your browser and specifically, JavaScript) and your ColdFusion back-end (specifically, a CFC). It has always been possible to communicate with ColdFusion using Ajax. In the past you would do something like this:

1. Create your CFC method (`getSomething()`)

2. Create code, possibly another method, to convert the result of the first step into XML

3. Write Ajax code to point to your CFC and call the method that returned XML

4. Parse the XML into something useful for JavaScript

By itself, that isn't too terribly difficult, but there are some extra steps there that can be a bit painful, especially in step 2. You have to build a second method just to wrap your original result in XML. That can be made easier using the tool I mentioned before (`toXML.cfc`), but it still means more work on your part.

379

cfajaxproxy takes all of this and makes it as easy as pie. Before digging into the syntax, let's look at a rather simple example so that you can see cfajaxproxy's power. First, in Listing 34-9, I'll build a simple ColdFusion component.

*Listing 34-9. A Simple ColdFusion Component*

```
<cfcomponent output="false">

    <cffunction name="sayHello" output="false" access="remote" returnType="string">
        <cfargument name="name" type="string" required="false" default="Nameless">
        <cfreturn "Hello, #arguments.name#">
    </cffunction>

</cfcomponent>
```

This component has one method, sayHello, that simply echoes back a name. Note that the method has an access setting of remote. As you can probably guess, Ajax calls will require CFCs with remote methods. Now let's look at a template (Listing 34-10) that uses this code.

*Listing 34-10. A Template that Uses the Code in Listing 34-9*

```
<cfajaxproxy cfc="test1" jsclassname="testcfc">

 <script>
    function callBackEnd() {
      var namevalue = document.getElementById('name').value;
      var mycfc = new testcfc();
      alert(mycfc.sayHello(namevalue));
     }
 </script>

 <form>
        <input type="text" id="name"> <input type="button" value="Test"
             onclick="callBackEnd()">
 </form>
```

If you run Listing 34-10 in your browser, you will be presented with a simple text box and a button. Enter your name, hit Test, and you will see: "Hello, Ray" (or whatever name you supplied.) I hope you are impressed by the simplicity of the code. I count a grand total of 13 lines.

The JavaScript makes up 5 lines. For those of us who are writing Ajax, it should be pretty evident that this is an extreme improvement over doing Ajax the manual way. So what's going on here? The first line creates the connection. I tell cfajaxproxy that my CFC is named test1. I tell it that the JavaScript class name is testcfc. The first argument should be obvious. The second argument simply creates a class name for the JavaScript. What do I mean by that? Notice that I create an instance of testcfc in the callBackEnd function. Where did I define testcfc? I didn't. cfajaxproxy defined it for me behind the scenes. This JavaScript class is a virtual mirror of the CFC code. To call the CFC method, I only need to treat it like any other normal JavaScript function: mycfc.sayHello().

Now that I've shown you a simple example, let me delve into the details. I mentioned that the CFC method had to be remote. This is part of the normal security/access restrictions for CFCs. If you've written web services, you know that you can only expose remote methods. The same rule applies here. You do not need to make every method remote. But if you want to call the method directly from JavaScript, then it must be defined as remote.

Notice that I didn't have to convert my CFC method to XML or even JSON. Why? Time for a bit of history. When ColdFusion MX was released and CFCs were introduced, you could invoke all CFCs with remote methods directly from the browser. When you did this, the method would return the data wrapped in WDDX. In ColdFusion MX 7, this behavior was changed. If the returnType was XML, then ColdFusion wouldn't WDDX-ify the result. In ColdFusion 8 and 9, CFC methods can now supply a `returnFormat` attribute. You can also pass a returnFormat argument via the URL querystring (or via Form post). If you pass the `returnFormat` as an argument, it overrides the setting in the method. The `returnFormat` value can be:

- WDDX

- JSON

- plain

If you run my demo code with Firebug (`http://www.getfirebug.com/`), you'll see requests being made to your CFC with `returnFormat=json` automatically applied. Here is a full example URL:

```
http://localhost/ajaxproxy/test1.cfc?method=sayHello&returnFormat↵
=json&argumentCollection=%7B%22name%22%3A%22Ray%22%7D&_cf_nodebug=true&_cf_nocache=true
```

There is a lot going on there, but the main things to notice are:

- The CFC you defined in the `cfajaxproxy` tag

- The method as called in the JavaScript line

- The `returnFormat=json`

- The arguments that are passed in are URL encoded

In this case, the method had an argument named `name` with a value of `Ray`.

One last point of interest: I was able to wrap my call to the CFC inside an alert. By default, calls to the CFCs are synchronous. Later on I'll show how you can change that behavior. Let's now take a deeper look at the attributes of `cfajaxproxy`:

- `cfc`: The CFC that your Ajax code will be communicating with. Like `createObject()` calls, this is a dot notation path to the CFC.

- `bind`: An expression that ties the front-end client to a CFC method, URL, or other JavaScript calls. Bindings will not be discussed in this article.

- `jsclassname`: The name of the JavaScript class that corresponds to the CFC. This is optional and will default to the name of the CFC.

- `onError` and `onSuccess`: The names of functions to call when an error or a successful call is made. However, these two attributes are only used with bindings.

The only attributes I'll be using in this article are CFC and JSClassName. Now let's look at the JavaScript functions available in the class created by `cfajaxproxy`:

- **setAsyncMode**: Sets calls to be asynchronous. This means that you can fire off a code and continue executing other JavaScript code. You will need to use `setCallBackHandler`.

- **setCallbackHandler**: Specifies which function to call when the remote call is done. This automatically sets calls to be asynchronous.

- **setErrorHandler**: The name of the function to call if an error is thrown in the remote call.

- **setForm**: Copies form values into the arguments passed to the remote call.

- **setHTTPMethod**: Allows you to set the HTTP method to be GET or POST. GET is the default.

- **setQueryFormat**: Specifies how the CFCs should return query information. This isn't covered in this article.

- **setSyncMode**: The opposite of `setAsyncMode`. It sets calls to the CFC to be synchronous. This is the default.

# A More Complex Example

Now that I've covered some of the basics, let's look at a more complex example. This code is a search interface to my blog. The back-end ColdFusion component is the simplest so I'll show that first, in Listing 34-11.

*Listing 34-11. Backend ColdFusion Component to Search Interface*

```
<cfcomponent output="false">

    <cffunction name="search" access="remote" returnType="query" output="false">
        <cfargument name="search" type="string" required="true">
        <cfset var q = "">

        <cfquery name="q" datasource="coldfusionjedi">
            select    id, title, posted
            from      tblblogentries
            where  title like <cfqueryparam cfsqltype="cf_sql_varchar"
                                            value="%#arguments.search#%">
            or  body like <cfqueryparam cfsqltype="cf_sql_longvarchar"
                                        value="%#arguments.search#%">
        </cfquery>

        <cfreturn q>
    </cffunction>

</cfcomponent>
```

This CFC has one method, `search`, which will search my blog entry database. As with my earlier CFC, notice that my code doesn't have anything Ajax-y about it. It is a simple query-based method that takes a search term as an argument. The front end is a bit more complex. Here is the code, in Listing 34-12.

*Listing 34-12. Frontend to Search Interface*

```
<cfajaxproxy cfc="test" jsClassName="blog">

  <script>
    function arrayFind(arr, x) {
      for(var i=0; i < arr.length; i++) {
        if(arr[i]==x) return i;
      }
    }
    function handleResults(results) {
      //find the positions of our columns
      idcol = arrayFind(results.COLUMNS, "ID");
      titlecol = arrayFind(results.COLUMNS, "TITLE");

      //find our results div
      resultsdiv = document.getElementById("results");
      resultsdiv.innerHTML = '';
      for(var i=0; i < results.DATA.length; i++) {
        var newresult =
          "<a href='http://www.coldfusionjedi.com/index.cfm?mode=entry&entry=" +
            results.DATA[i][idcol];
        newresult += "'>" + results.DATA[i][titlecol] + "</a><br>";
        resultsdiv.innerHTML+=newresult;
        }
    }

    function searchBlog() {
      //get the search value
      var searchterm = document.getElementById("search").value;
      //if blank, return
      if(searchterm == '') return;
      //make an instance of the connection to the blog
      var blogCFC = new blog();
      //name the function to call when done
      blogCFC.setCallbackHandler(handleResults);
      blogCFC.search(searchterm);

      resultsdiv = document.getElementById("results");
      resultsdiv.innerHTML = 'Loading...';

    }
  </script>
```

```
<form>
    <input type="text" id="search" name="search"> <input type="button"
            value="Search" onClick="searchBlog()">
</form>

<div id="results">
</div>
```

There is a lot going on in Listing 34-12, so let's tackle it line by line. The first line defines the connection between the front-end JavaScript and the CFC on the back-end. Once again I'm using a CFC named test (sorry, not feeling very imaginative) and a JavaScript class name of blog. Let's skip to the form at the end of the file. The form has one text field named search. The button will run searchBlog, a JavaScript function that I'll describe later. The last thing on the page is an empty div with the ID of results. So what happens when you search?

The searchBlog function begins by simply checking that you've actually entered something into the form. If you have entered something, the function creates an instance of the CFC. Since I had already told cfajaxproxy to use a JavaScript class name of blog, all I need to do is this:

```
var blogCFC = new blog();
```

After I've made an instance, I set the callback handler to a function named handleResults. This means that when the CFC code is done running, it should send the results to handleResults. This automatically makes the call asynchronous as well. Next I actually call the search method described in the CFC I just mentioned. I pass in the search term to the method. Finally, the function updates the empty div at the bottom of the page with a "Loading..." message.

Let me restate what I've done here. I've told the JavaScript code to asynchronously call a method, handleResults, that is defined in my CFC. Basically, "fire this method and, when done, run my function." Now let's look at the handler results function. A callback function, it will always take one argument, the result of the CFC call. I've named this value results in my function. I was honestly unsure exactly how the result would look. Luckily ColdFusion ships with an Ajax-based debugger. I enabled it in the ColdFusion Administrator and then hit my template with ?cfdebug=1 in the URL. This let me see the result data as it was returned from the CFC.

The format was JSON, of course. ColdFusion's Ajax code automatically converts the JSON into a native JavaScript variable. This variable contained two main parts. The first part was an array of columns. The second part was a datastructure named data that contained the actual query data. The query data stores information in the same order as the columns array, so the first thing I did was store the positions of the ID and TITLE columns. I wrote a simple arrayFind function to make this easier for me. Once I know the position of my ID and TITLE columns, I can loop over my data.

For each item in the data field, I created HTML to display a link to the blog entry returned in the results. This HTML is then printed back out in the div tag at the bottom of the page.

# Conclusion

ColdFusion has been the glue between the browser and the server for many years now and has always put the focus on practical, easy-to-use solutions for development problems. ColdFusion 8 and 9 continue the trend, and we now have what is perhaps the simplest and most practical approach to Ajax development I've ever seen. With native JSON support and simple connections between JavaScript and CFCs, your development will take off in ways you've never seen before.

■ ■ ■

# Prototyping for Interface Driven Architecture: Easing the Transition from Prototype to Application

## by Doug Boude

*Interface-Driven Architecture (IDA), as developed by Hal Helms and Clark Valberg, is the idea that one develops the interface design of the application before one actually builds the code for the backend. Having a client sign off on a clickable prototype should make planning the client's application much simpler. Doug Boude relates his experience on a real-life project using IDA, and explains how some preplanning on aspects of the interface architecture would have made things simpler still.*

## Introduction

"Yes, I got the job!" I said excitedly to myself as I hung up the phone. The project I was just awarded was one that had started life using the Interface Driven Architecture methodology (developed by Hal Helms and Clark Valberg), and I had been invited to step in and perform all of the nuts and bolts work that come during the latter phases. The client and original designer had been working for quite some time on the application's user interface, meticulously laying out every screen with every field and label in place so that when it came time for actual architecture and coding, scope creep would be virtually non-existent. This fact, of course, helped give me a sense of security that the project would proceed relatively smoothly and without a hitch since we had only to think about the back end of it all and not the front... or so I thought.

## The Challenges

Step one was to transfer the clickable prototype to my team's development box so we could start bringing this baby to life. Since we were using an MVC framework, it became necessary to first separate the prototype into individual view templates. It was at this 'simple' step that a lot of ideas began to come to mind for how to make it easier next time.

The challenges (there are no problems, only challenges) lay first in the fact that although the prototype had been styled using CSS (to a degree), there was no consistency in the names used for the classes, and many classes were exact duplicates of one another. Second, since an IDE had been used to mock up the prototype, most of it consisted of auto-generated tables, sometimes nested up to seven levels deep in order to achieve the desired layout. As we were waist deep in code, it became clear to us that sections of the prototype had not been fully built out, so we were left to adlib it and come up with what we felt would suffice… an open door for scope creep if the client didn't agree with our judgment. Finally, when developing the prototype itself, the designer had not considered the use of AJAX. Although the project charter called for the use of AJAX to make the interface more intuitive and user friendly, no asynchronous functionality had been mocked up in the design. The team and I were left, again, to judge where asynchronous functionality could best be leveraged, resulting in a redesign, however minor, of the already approved interface.

It cost money that wasn't budgeted to get a designer to clean up the CSS and re-work some of the more elaborate table nesting into a CSS-friendly layout, but we got past it and completed the project. With better planning, these unforeseen challenges could have been prevented.

# Suggestions

For the benefit of the reader wishing to leverage the benefits of Interface Driven Architecture, here are a few things to keep in mind when initially creating the prototype.

## CSS

If you're not halfway decent at CSS, bring someone in who is OR invest the time to become halfway decent. This will be one of your greatest assets as you build out this and future prototypes, as CSS allows you to modify layout, look, and feel in just a few minutes as opposed to hours. Also, from the beginning, keep your style classes categorized and commented within your CSS file. For example, in our project we created four groups of styles: Global styles, to be used in a global manner, such as 'body', 'p', 'detailTextHeader', 'detailTextNormal', and 'h1'; Table styles, for laying out tables throughout the application, such as 'tableBackgroundGreyLight', 'tableBorderSolidUnderlined', and 'tableDataGrid'; Form Styles, and finally Link styles. Of course, divide them up as it makes sense for your project. Whatever you do, though, use an existing style if it meets your need rather than make up new ones as you go, possibly creating duplicate styles with different names.

## Tables

I can't emphasize enough how much to your advantage it will be to avoid using tables whenever possible. They do have their place, and they were definitely used in the example project above; but leverage the power of DIV tags! It's nothing short of amazing what a somewhat CSS-savvy individual can do with layout in short order when the template has its content organized within DIVs. Doing so also opens the door for dynamic look and feel, simply by swapping out style sheets on the fly. For a sample of what you can do with CSS, you should check out CSSZenGarden.com. Also, for a good supply of helpful tutorials on getting up to speed with CSS, check out Joe Gautreau's blog at www.twoninemedia.com. One more thing: if you're using an IDE to create your interface, don't forget that you can just as easily drag and drop a DIV or SPAN element as you can a table element!

## Complete Your Prototype

It's easy to avoid mocking up certain things, like backend administrative pages, action pages with messages, or anything else the designer feels should just be intuitive on the part of the coders. Do not make any assumptions in this area, however, and make sure that the prototype leaves little to nothing to the imagination of the coders and architect. What may seem like a "no brainer" to the designer could actually influence the application's architecture, possibly resulting in something overlooked that will require backtracking later.

## AJAX

AJAX is the absolute bomb in my book, and it can result in the assimilation of several separate templates into a single, more intuitive one. If the prototype designer, however, isn't aware of Ajax' capabilities or how it generally functions, they won't know how to incorporate it into the prototype. This potentially puts the coders in a difficult position, as their incorporation of Ajax can actually nullify the need for certain other templates or processes. Educate your prototype designer about AJAX: what it can do, how it works, and what it looks like within a living, breathing application.

# Conclusion

Working on projects that are following the Interface Driven Architecture methodology are, from my hands-on perspective, nothing short of a joy. Scope creep is almost entirely contained and controlled within the initial phase of distilling a client-approved clickable user interface, and that in itself is worth my weight in gold (that's a lot of gold, by the way). In order to ensure that the remaining steps (architecture and coding) go as smoothly as possible, it is important to give as much time and attention to the underlying design of the prototype as to what it looks like in its rendered state. Maintain the CSS from the beginning; utilize DIV tags in lieu of tables whenever possible; ensure that no portion of the prototype is left to anybody's imagination; and if you are one of the enlightened ones who sees and believes in the beauty that AJAX can lend to a user interface, make sure the designer knows and understands the same beforehand.

# PART 8

# Development Tools

■■■

# CHAPTER 36

# Turbo Charging Eclipse

## by Mike Henke

*Eclipse's widespread use across multiple programming communities is perhaps partly due to its versatility and flexibility. Developers can customize their user interface with different views and can even add custom plug-ins for a highly personalized interface. However, Eclipse may need fine-tuning to be efficient and quick to respond. Mike Henke has experimented with different settings on his Eclipse installation to find the secrets to a faster, happier IDE. This article describes his recipe for a turbo-charged Eclipse.*

You made the leap to the Eclipse integrated development environment (IDE), and now you get the benefit of tight integration between the systems you use daily. You have CFEclipse or ColdFusion Builder for CFML, Subclipse for source control, Mylyn as your ticket repository, SQL Explorer as a SQL editor, CSS, XML, and Aptana as a Javascript editor. Everything is easily accessible and you are more productive, except Eclipse seems slower and a bit unstable. You have learned to accept the quirkiness to get all the advantages of Eclipse, but Eclipse should not be slow or unstable, so this article will help you.

I initially researched Eclipse tuning after installing the Flex Builder plug-in. I would get an OutOfMemoryException when building a Flex project. I am not an Eclipse or Java virtual machine (JVM), expert, but I have done a lot of research, read many articles on these subjects, and made numerous trials, errors, and retrials. I have achieved performance gains and better stability, though these may not always materialize. It really depends on your computer system.

This article will help you learn how to improve Eclipse startup time, stability, and performance. It will also point you toward choosing the correct package option, a pre-configured starting point for the editor, based on your proposed use for Eclipse. We'll also set some Eclipse preferences, identify any plug-in performance issues at startup, tune the eclipse.ini file for the Sun JVM, and finally show how to switch Eclipse to another JVM.

# The Right Eclipse Package

Ideally, you should start off with the right Eclipse package. Why have C/C++ extensions and features if you are coding web pages? Eclipse comes in several packages, to which you can add additional features through plug-ins such as CFEclipse. Here are five you might be interested in:

- Eclipse IDE for Java Developers: The essential tools for any Java developer, including a Java IDE, a client for Concurrent Versions System (CVS), an XML editor and Mylyn.

- Eclipse IDE for Java Enterprise Edition (EE) Developers: Tools for Java developers creating Web and Java Enterprise Edition (JEE) applications, including a Java IDE, tools for JEE and JavaServer Faces (JSF), Mylyn and others. Requires Java 5 or higher.

- Eclipse IDE for C/C++ Developers

- Eclipse for Rich Client Platform and Plug-in Developers: A complete set of tools for developers who want to create Eclipse plug-ins or rich client applications. It includes a complete SDK, developer tools, and source code.

- Eclipse Classic 3.3.2 - The classic Eclipse download: the Eclipse platform, Java development tools, and a plug-in development environment, including source and documentation for both users and programmers.

I started with Eclipse Classic. You might want to start with the Eclipse IDE for Java EE Developers. It has database tools as well as typical web development editors.

# Preparing for Turbo Charging

I recommend starting the turbo charging process with a pristine version of Eclipse. I also find it useful to regularly back up my current Eclipse folder in case I need to revert back without any hassle, so you may want to back up your Eclipse folder before we start. Switching to a fresh Eclipse instance could seem a little intimidating, but you can make this easier by exporting and importing your existing update sites from the Update Manager. If you aren't using Eclipse yet, skip the next paragraph and go to Getting Eclipse.

The Update Manager contains a list of default sites and other sites you have added for installing and updating features, as shown in Figure 36-1. Exporting your list will help speed up the transition process and lessen the burden of transferring to a fresh instance of Eclipse. The Update Manager is found at **Window ➤ Preferences ➤ Install/Update ➤ Available Software Sites**. Click **Next**, then select the **Export sites** button. Importing follows the same process but uses the **Import sites** button. Please export your update site list now, and then you can import it when you are in your fresh instance of Eclipse.

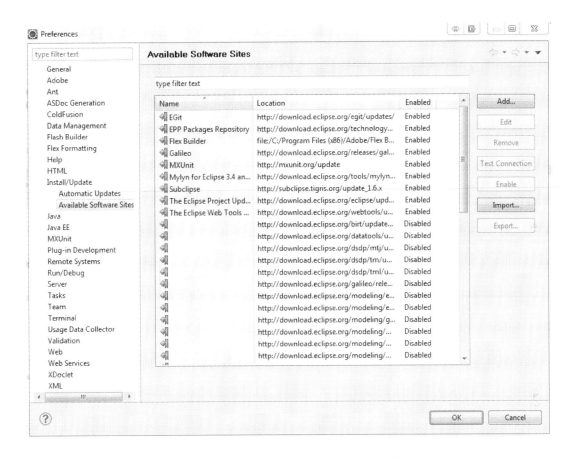

*Figure 36-1. Exporting and Importing Your List of Sites for Installing and Updating Features*

# Getting a Fresh Instance of Eclipse

To download a fresh instance of Eclipse, first remove the Eclipse folder for your existing instance. Download the proper package for you (see the section on The Right Eclipse Package). Unzip the file and place it in the same location as your old Eclipse installation. To start, use the eclipse.exe file in the Eclipse folder or create a shortcut.

# Setting Eclipse Preferences

Now that you have the fresh Eclipse instance, let's set some Eclipse preferences to make startup a little faster before we dive into plug-in performance and tuning `eclipse.ini`:

- **Window ➤ Preferences ➤ General ➤ Editors** - Make sure you have chosen *Close editors automatically.*

- **Window ➤ Preferences ➤ General ➤ Startup and Shutdown** - Uncheck *Refresh workspace on startup.* On this screen you can also review the items listed under *Plug-ins activated on startup.* I uncheck all the plug-ins I don't use, like Eclipse Monkey and most Aptana plug-ins.

- **Window ➤ Preferences ➤ General ➤ Capabilities** - Disable any capabilities of the Eclipse Platform that you never use, as shown in Figure 36-2. For instance, using the `Advanced...` button, I disabled both Plug-in Development and CVS support. Disabled items disappear from the Eclipse user interface completely, including views, perspectives, and preference pages.

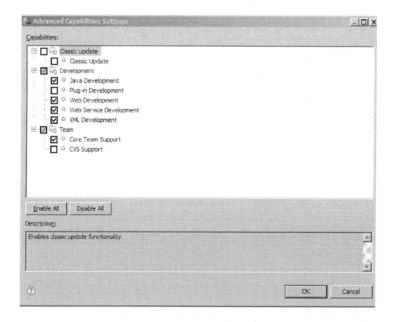

*Figure 36-2. Example of Disabling Capabilities in Eclipse (3.4)*

- **Window ➤ Preferences ➤ General** - Toggle on *Show heap status* and *Always run in background,* as shown in Figure 36-3. These don't tweak performance, but we will use the heap status to monitor memory and the *Always run in background* option will keep processes from bringing Eclipse to a screeching halt.

Close projects you aren't using. The resources within the project stay offline until opened. Running with all but the current project closed should use less memory and help with startup time and performance.

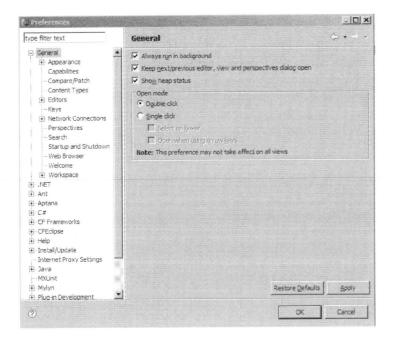

*Figure 36-3. Example of Window ➤ Preferences ➤ General*

# Installing Core Tools

We will use the Runtime Spy to benchmark and troubleshoot any issues with slow startup.

1. Add the Core Tools update site URL listed below to your Update Sites list (Help ➤ Software Updates ➤ Find and Install) and click `Install...`.

2. After restarting Eclipse, copy the sample `.options` file from `<eclipse_folder>\plugins\` or `.eclipse.core.tools_1.0.2` and paste it into the Eclipse folder.

These steps will enable all available Runtime Spy options. I put my Eclipse folder under Program Files in Windows, as shown in Figure 36-4. On Ubuntu, I chose `usr/lib/eclipse`.

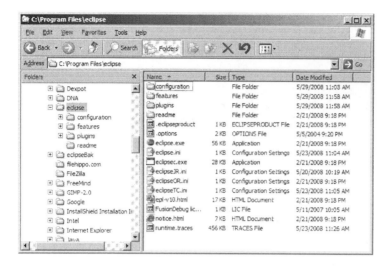

*Figure 36-4. My Eclipse Folder After I Pasted the .options File into it*

## Refresh Eclipse Data

Before we run our tests, we'll run the `clean` command, as shown in Figure 36-5. (For a list of those options, see `http://help.eclipse.org/stable/index.jsp?topic=/org.eclipse.platform.doc.isv/reference/misc/runtime-options.html`). This command will clear Eclipse's cached data. Initially, you may notice a decreased startup time, but Eclipse will rebuild the data to have current data to work with. Before running the command, make sure to close Eclipse if you have it open.

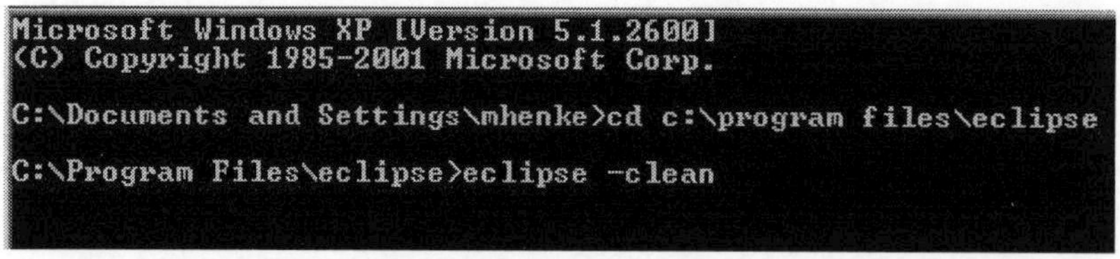

```
Microsoft Windows XP [Version 5.1.2600]
(C) Copyright 1985-2001 Microsoft Corp.

C:\Documents and Settings\mhenke>cd c:\program files\eclipse

C:\Program Files\eclipse>eclipse -clean
```

*Figure 36-5. Running the Clean Command*

Restart and then close Eclipse so we build fresh cache and don't exaggerate our initial benchmark test slowness.

# Initial Benchmark

Now we'll start our initial benchmark and see if we actually improve the Eclipse system startup time. Make sure you have installed Core tools, a process that was described above in the Installing Core Tools section.

Navigate to your Eclipse folder via the command line.

```
cd <eclipse_installation_folder>
eclipse -debug
```

Another command line window will open up with statistics, as shown in Figure 36-6. Jot down the numbers for Time to load bundles, *Starting application*, and *Application Started*. These should display at the bottom. We have our benchmark now, but don't close Eclipse.

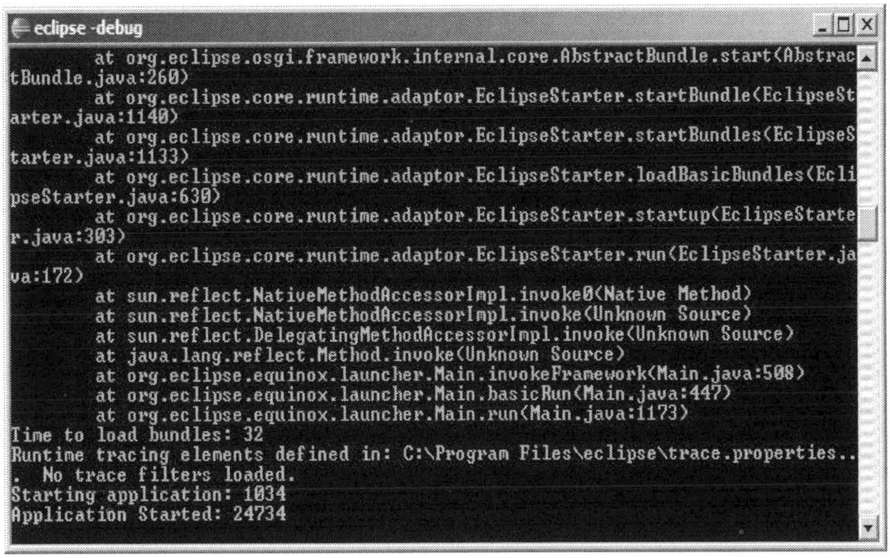

*Figure 36-6. Recording our Benchmark Times*

## Diagnosing Plug-in Issues

We can use the Runtime Spy to troubleshoot any plug-in performance issues. Open the Runtime Spy perspective (Window ➤ Open Perspective ➤ Runtime Spy). The Runtime Spy allows great insight into what Eclipse is doing, as shown in Figure 36-7.

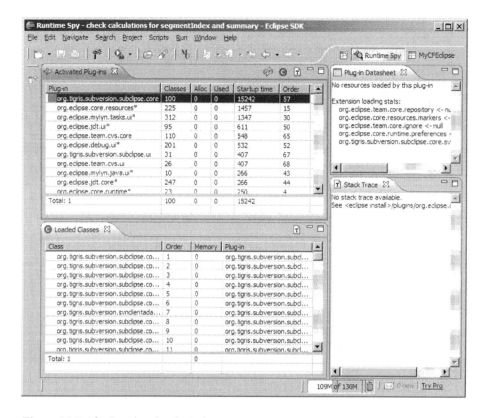

*Figure 36-7. The Runtime Spy in Action*

We will use the Activated Plug-ins view and sort by Startup time. If the Activated Plug-ins view displays *Plug-in monitoring is not enabled,* it means either that you are missing the `.options` file in the Eclipse folder or that you forgot the `-debug` switch.

Any plug-in name with an asterisk next to it loads during startup. In Figure 36-7, I see that `org.eclipse.team.cvs.core` loads at startup, but I don't use that feature, so I will disable it in the Capabilities window (see Setting Eclipse Preferences above). Examine the other items that appear here. Disable any plug-in that you don't use, and try to reduce the number of plug-ins that run on startup. Plug-ins use resources and should not be activated until you need them; activating them only when you need them will help speed up your instance of Eclipse (see Setting Eclipse Preferences).

For more detail on the Runtime Spy, please refer to the reference section at the end of the article.

## eclipse.ini

You may need to adjust the settings I suggest here to better suit your own needs. Be careful; the `.ini` file can cause errors over misplaced returns and spaces. Remember that each argument has to be on a separate line. Before modifying the `eclipse.ini` file, please back it up. I copied mine and named the copy eclipseOrg.ini so that the "Org" would remind me that this is the untouched original. You'll find the eclipse.ini file in the Eclipse folder. As a first pass, modify it so that it looks like Listing 36-1.

*Listing 36-1. Intermediate eclipse.ini (This version of your eclipse.ini file will be temporary, and may be unstable for regular usage)*

```
-nosplash
-vmargs
-XX:+AggressiveHeap
-XX:+AggressiveOpts
-XX:+UseParallelOldGC
-XX:ParallelGCThreads=2
-XX:ThreadPriorityPolicy=1
-Xverify:none
```

Start Eclipse normally. You should notice that no splash screen appears. This is good news: it means that the new ini settings work. You can take out the -nosplash argument later if you want to see the splash screen. I found the -XX:+AggressiveHeap command unstable, so we will use it only to obtain what the Sun JVM thinks are the optimal memory settings for your computer system and then will not use it for our final turbo-charged eclipse.ini file. Once Eclipse has started, write down the heap maximum and minimum, which will be shown as in Figure 36-8. Mine were 130m and 900m. You can mouse over the heap status display to get this information.

*Figure 36-8. Show Heap Size displays heap values*

For the turbo-charged eclipse.ini below, I removed the AggressiveHeap argument and added the vm, Xms, and Xmx options. The Eclipse documentation recommends specifying a Java VM, which we do here with the vm option. Notice that the option is broken into two lines. If you don't do this, the vm command will not work. The Xms option sets initial heap size. Use the lower value you obtained from the heap status, the 130m I got earlier. The Xmx option sets the maximum heap size. Use the high value you obtained from the heap status, in Listing 36-2 the 900m value.

*Listing 36-2. My Turbo Charged eclipse.ini*

```
-nosplash
-vm
C:\Program Files\Java\jdk1.6.0_06\bin\javaw.exe
-vmargs
-Xms130m
-Xmx900m
-XX:+AggressiveOpts
-XX:+UseParallelOldGC
-XX:ParallelGCThreads=2
-XX:ThreadPriorityPolicy=1
-Xverify:none
```

Let's run our benchmark test again in the command line.

```
cd <eclipse_installation_folder>
eclipse -debug
```

Compare the numbers. I see gains, as shown in Table 36-1, and hope you do too.

*Table 36-1. Benchmark Speeds Measured in Milliseconds on my Windows XP Laptop*

| | turbo-charged eclipse.ini first test | turbo-charged eclipse.ini second test | eclipse-SDK-3.3.2-win32 eclipse.ini first test | eclipse-SDK-3.3.2-win32 eclipse.ini second test |
|---|---|---|---|---|
| Time to load bundles | 15 | 16 | 16 | 15 |
| Starting application | 640 | 625 | 1094 | 938 |
| Application Started | 5640 | 5641 | 10328 | 8245 |

# Switching Eclipse from the Default JVM

Eclipse will use the first JVM reference it finds in the environment path variable unless the eclipse.ini specifies something else. Usually the default JVM is from Sun but I have heard good comments about BEA JRockit. For specific benchmarks published on JRockit, check out the comparisons at http://www.shudo.net/jit/perf/ and at http://weblogic.sys-con.com/node/135863/print.

For some reason, BEA links to download JRockit weren't working but after numerous searches, I did find a place to download JRockit JDK: http://www.securityfocus.com/bid/24004/solution.

I unzipped the file to C:\BEA. I copied my turbo-charged eclipse.ini into my Eclipse folder and named it eclipseTC.ini, then modified the eclipse.ini to use the JRockit JVM. Listing 36-3 is what I did.

Notice again that the -vm option is on two lines. Also I removed some Sun-specific JVM options and added a couple of JRockit options.

*Listing 36-3. JRockit eclipse.ini*

```
-nosplash
-vm
C:\BEA\jrockit-jdk1.6.0_01\jre\bin\javaw.exe
-vmargs
-Xms128m
-Xmx900m
-XXaggressive
-Xverify:none
-XgcPrio:pausetime
```

To verify that Eclipse is actually using JRockit rather than the old JVM, check the Configuration Details (**Help ➤ About Eclipse SDK ➤ Configuration Details**). It should list the JRockit as the VM. I didn't see any performance gains when checking the JRockit `eclipse.ini` using Runtime Spy, so I switched back to my turbo-charged `eclipse.ini` setup.

# Conclusion

Eclipse is a great IDE, but with different plug-ins it can become slower and unstable. We have shown some techniques to improve start up and stability through modifications of the `eclipse.ini` file and using the Runtime Spy.

Details on particular options follow in the "Eclipse Runtime Commands and Various JVM Options" section at the end of this article. For more information, see the articles referenced in the following pages. We used some of the options they discuss in setting up your turbo-charged Eclipse and others in your new turbo-charged `eclipse.ini` file.

# References

## More Learning

- Eclipse.ini – Eclipsepedi: `http://wiki.eclipse.org/Eclipse.ini`

- Tune Eclipse's startup performance with the Runtime Spy, Part 1: `http://www.ibm.com/developerworks/java/library/os-ecspy1/`

- Keeping Eclipse Running Clean: `http://www.eclipsezone.com/eclipse/forums/t61566.html`

- Picking the right Eclipse distribution: `http://www.ibm.com/developerworks/opensource/library/os-eclipse-dist/`

- Eclipse - a Tale of Two VMs (and Many Classloaders): `http://www.eclipsezone.com/articles/eclipse-vms/`

- Core Tools Home: http://www.eclipse.org/eclipse/platform-core/index.php

- Eclipse Runtime Options: http://help.eclipse.org/help33/index.jsp?topic=/ org.eclipse.platform.doc.isv/reference/misc/runtime-options.html

## SUN JVM Information

- The most complete list of –XX options for Java 6 JVM: http://www.md.pp.ru/ %7Eeu/jdk6options.html

- Java Garbage Collection Tuning: http://www.folgmann.com/en/j2ee/gc.html

- Turbo-Charging Java HotSpot Virtual Machine, v 1.4x to Improve the Performance and Scalability of Application Servers: http://java.sun.com/developer/ technicalArticles/Programming/turbo/

- Java Tuning White Paper: http://java.sun.com/performance/reference/ whitepapers/tuning.html

- Tuning Garbage Collection with the 1.4.2 Java™ Virtual Machine: http://java.sun.com/docs/hotspot/gc1.4.2/

## BEA JRockit Information

- About BEA Jrockit: http://edocs.bea.com/jrockit/geninfo/diagnos/ aboutjrockit.html

- BEA JRockit Command-Line Reference: http://edocs.bea.com/jrockit/jrdocs/ refman/optionXX.html

## Products/Downloads

- Eclipse Downloads: http://www.eclipse.org/downloads/

- Eclipse Core Tools Update Site: http://eclipse.org/eclipse/platform-core/downloads

- JRockit JDK downloads: http://www.securityfocus.com/bid/24004/solution

# Eclipse Runtime Commands and Various JVM Options

Material has been obtained from the links below the main titles and in the article references section. Some terms may be Java-centric; feel free to research unknown terms.

# Eclipse Runtime Commands

`http://help.eclipse.org/help33/index.jsp?topic=/org.eclipse.platform.doc.isv/reference/misc/runtime-options.html`

## -clean

If set to "true", -clean will wipe clean any cached data used by the OSGi framework and Eclipse runtime. This will clean the caches that store bundle dependency resolution and Eclipse extension registry data. Using this option will force Eclipse to reinitialize these caches.

## -debug

If set to a non-null value, -debug puts the platform in debug mode. If given a string value, this command interprets it as the location of the .options file. This file indicates what debug points are available for a plug-in and whether or not they are enabled. If a location is not specified, the platform searches for the .options file in the install directory.

## -vm <path to java executable> (Executable, Main)

When passed to the Eclipse executable, this option locates the Java VM used to run Eclipse. The path must be the full file system path to an appropriate Java executable. If you do not specify a path, the Eclipse executable uses a search algorithm to locate a suitable VM. In any event, the executable then passes the path to the actual VM used to Java Main, using the -vm argument. Java Main then stores this value in eclipse.vm.

## -vmargs [vmargs*] (Executable, Main)

When passed to Eclipse, this option customizes the operation of the Java VM used to run Eclipse. If specified, this option must come at the end of the command line. Even if not specified on the executable command line, the executable will automatically add the relevant arguments (including the class being launched) to the command line passed into Java using the -vmargs argument. Java Main then stores this value in eclipse.vmargs.

# JVM Options

These arguments may not be available for all VM versions and platforms; consult your VM documentation for more details.

## -Xms

The Xms is the initial/minimum Java heap size within the VM.

## -Xmx

The Xmx is the maximum Java heap size within the VM.

## -Xverify:none

The -Xverify:none skips the class verification stage within the VM.

# Sun JVM OPTIONS

http://java.sun.com/performance/reference/whitepapers/tuning.html

## -XX:+AggressiveHeap

The -XX:+AggressiveHeap option inspects the machine resources (size of memory and number of processors) and attempts to set various parameters for optimal performance on long-running, memory allocation-intensive jobs. It was originally intended for machines with large amounts of memory and a large number of CPUs. In the 1.4.1 version and later of the J2SE platform I have found it useful even on four-processor machines. This option uses the throughput collector (-XX:+UseParallelGC) along with adaptive sizing (-XX:+UseAdaptiveSizePolicy). Aggressive Heap requires at least 256MB physical memory. The size of the physical memory determines the size of the initial heap. The algorithms attempt to use heaps nearly as large as the total physical memory.

## -XX:+UseAdaptiveSizePolicy

A feature available with the throughput collector in the J2SE platform, version 1.4.1 and later releases, this is on by default. Adaptive sizing keeps statistics about garbage collection times, allocation rates, and the free space in the heap after a collection. The runtime then makes decisions regarding changes to the sizes of the young generation and tenured generation so as to best fit the behavior of the application. Use the command line option -verbose:gc to see the resulting sizes of the heap.

## -XX:+UseParallelGC

Use the Parallel Scavenge garbage collector.

## UseParallelOldGC

Use the Parallel Old garbage collector.

## -XX:+AggressiveOpts

This turns on point performance optimizations. These will probably be on by default in upcoming releases. This flag groups minor changes to JVM runtime compiled code, not distinct performance features (such as BiasedLocking and ParallelOldGC).

-XX:+AgressiveOpts allows you to try the JVM engineering team's latest performance tweaks for upcoming releases. Note: this option is experimental! The specific optimizations enabled by this option can change from release to release and even from build to build. You should reevaluate the effects of this option prior to deploying a new release of Java.

## ParallelGCThreads

Number of parallel threads parallel gc will use.

## ThreadPriorityPolicy

*ThreadPriorityPolicy=0:* Normal. VM chooses priorities appropriate for normal applications. On Solaris, NORM_PRIORITY and above map to normal native priority. Java priorities below NORM_PRIORITY map to lower native priority values. On Windows, applications are allowed to use higher native priorities. However, with ThreadPriorityPolicy=0, VM will not use the highest possible native priority, THREAD_PRIORITY_TIME_CRITICAL, as it may interfere with system threads. Linux ignores thread priorities because the OS does not support the static priority in SCHED_OTHER scheduling class, the only choice for non-root, non-realtime applications.

*ThreadPriorityPolicy=1:* Aggressive. Java thread priorities map over to the entire range of native thread priorities. Higher Java thread priorities map to higher native thread priorities. Use this policy with care, as sometimes it can cause performance degradation in the application and/or the entire system. On Linux, this policy requires root privilege.

# JRockit JVM Options

`http://edocs.bea.com/jrockit/jrdocs/refman/optionXX.html`

## -XXaggressive

The XXaggressive collection of configurations makes the JVM perform at a high speed and reach a stable state as soon as possible. To achieve this goal, the JVM uses more internal resources at startup; however, it requires less adaptive optimization once the goal is reached. We recommend you use this option for long-running, memory-intensive applications working alone.

## -XgcPrio:pausetime

With this option, a thread-local area is split into chunks and, when a new chunk is reached, the subsequent chunk is prefetched.

## CHAPTER 37

■ ■ ■

# An Introduction to ColdFusion Builder

## by Jacob Munson

*If you haven't heard, Adobe is working on an Integrated Development Environment (IDE) for ColdFusion. Old timers will remember ColdFusion Studio, released with early ColdFusion versions. But Macromedia stopped developing new features for ColdFusion Studio around ColdFusion 5. Some versions of Dreamweaver had features that made it a good ColdFusion editor, but more recent releases have not seen any new ColdFusion features other than updated syntax dictionaries. The continued lack of developer support from Adobe has caused many prominent ColdFusion developers to ask for a fully supported ColdFusion development environment. Adobe heard the message and answered with ColdFusion Builder, based on the Eclipse development platform.*

*As of this writing, Adobe has not released a final version of ColdFusion Builder. It has released three betas so far, and this article will discuss Beta 3. You can get your own copy of the most recent public beta at http://labs.adobe.com/technologies/coldfusionbuilder/.*

## Why Eclipse?

Many developers expressed disappointment when Adobe announced a new IDE based on Eclipse instead of Dreamweaver or HomeSite. This is understandable, as a respectable segment of the ColdFusion community currently use either HomeSite or Dreamweaver. However, if you consider that Flex Builder is based on Eclipse, Adobe's decision makes more sense. Adobe can use the same developers to work on both Flex Builder and ColdFusion Builder, and lessons learned working on one can benefit the other. Also, as many ColdFusion developers currently use CFEclipse, making a transition to ColdFusion Builder would be relatively trivial for them.

But why not base ColdFusion Builder on HomeSite? Adobe has announced that it will no longer support HomeSite, largely because it was written with Delphi, and Adobe no longer wants to support that language[1].

---

[1] http://forta.com/blog/index.cfm/2009/7/24/On-Eclipse-ColdFusion-Builder-And-IDEs

Adobe has stated that it is not interested in turning Dreamweaver into a developer's IDE. Adobe would prefer that Dreamweaver stay designer-focused, and so Adobe doesn't want to bog it down with IDE features like a ColdFusion debugger. That said, the current version of ColdFusion Builder omits designer features that many CF developers love to use in Dreamweaver. In the short term, Adobe is probably not going to try to duplicate many of Dreamweaver's features in ColdFusion Builder but will expect people to use Dreamweaver for design work and ColdFusion Builder for coding. However, over time I think ColdFusion Builder will be fleshed out with designer features that ColdFusion developers would use. Additionally, there are thousands of existing Eclipse plug-ins that developers can leverage to add functionality they miss from Dreamweaver.

# Installation

You can install CFB on Windows or on a Mac, currently the only officially supported operating systems. However, if you are running Linux, Mark Mandel has directions for getting it working (see `http://www.compoundtheory.com/?action=displayPost&ID=432`).

As part of the installation, you will have to decide which type of ColdFusion Builder installation you need, Standard or Plugin. If you do not have Eclipse or Flex Builder installed, you should choose Standard. If you already have Flex Builder, you can install ColdFusion Builder as a plug-in to your existing Eclipse or ColdFusion Builder install, which will allow you to easily switch between Flex and ColdFusion development within the same IDE. If you are currently using CFEclipse, you cannot install CFB as a plug-in to your existing Eclipse; the installer will give you an "incompatible" error. In this case, choose the Standard installation, which will give you a new Eclipse installation.

# Learning Eclipse

This article will not go into a step-by step guide to Eclipse. You'll find such a guide in the article *CFEclipse CFExplained* by Robert Blackburn in the *Fusion Authority Quarterly Update* Volume 1 Issue 1.If you have never used Eclipse before, it can be a steep learning curve before you feel comfortable. But don't give up! There is a LOT to like about Eclipse and ColdFusion Builder, as I will show you.

## Projects

Eclipse has a lot of functionality based around projects. But for me, the main thing I do with projects is just find and open files. Projects are a way to group files that pertain to applications or web sites. They can help you focus on the specific files you need and ignore other files not related to your current work. To get started with projects, click `Window ➤ Show View ➤ Navigator`, where you will interact with all of your projects. As you can see in Figure 37-1, after you have created a number of projects this looks a lot like a File Explorer. But it's better than a plain file explorer, because you can have files spread all over your hard drive and network shares but easily get to all of them if you group things into projects.

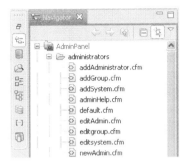

*Figure 37-1. Navigator View*

A lot of new Eclipse users don't like the focus on projects, but in ColdFusion Builder a lot of extra functionality works directly with Projects. Like me, you will probably really like them after a while. Though if you really prefer a plain File Explorer, you can have that too. Click `Window` ➤ `Show View` ➤ `File` (if you don't see it in the list, click `Other` and then type 'File' in the filter text box).

## Rearranging Your Workspace

I almost never like the default layout that you get with an IDE. With Eclipse, you can move things around to your heart's content. Click and drag on almost any tab or toolbar, and you can move it to a different place (this does not work for *all* of them, unfortunately). Also, you can minimize and maximize any view (including the Editor view), which will create these cool button areas that you can tuck away until you need them. As you can see in Figure 37-1, I have most of my views organized in a shortcut bar on the left of my workspace.

There are a lot of hidden features in views that don't open by default, so take some time exploring the `Window` ➤ `Show View` area to look for cool stuff that you might want to use on a regular basis.

## Ask for help

If you get stuck , you can try looking in the Help system (`Help` ➤ `Help Contents`). Adobe has provided a lot of information there, including generic Eclipse help. If you can't find an answer to your question in Help, try the ColdFusion Builder forums, located here: `http://forums.adobe.com/community/labs/coldfusionbuilder/`

# ColdFusion Server Integration

Much of the cool stuff you can do with ColdFusion Builder involves interactions with your ColdFusion servers. Many useful tools are at your disposal. You can directly view and edit databases through your configured Data Sources, use the ColdFusion Administrator and Server Monitor from within ColdFusion Builder, and start and stop your ColdFusion server, to name a few. In order to use many of these tools, you need to enable Remote Development Services (RDS) on your ColdFusion server. If you want to interact with remote servers, you will need to install the ColdFusion Builder Admin Server Components on your server if you are using ColdFusion 7 or 8 (CF9 comes with the Admin Components pre-installed), which are available from the ColdFusion Builder download page. This article will not cover remote server configurations and will only be working with a locally installed ColdFusion server.

## Configuring Your Server

Before you can leverage all of the RDS-based features, you need to set up a server in ColdFusion Builder. The default workspace layout has a group of tabs at the bottom of the window. Look for the one named Servers, and select it. Right click in the pane below the tab and click `Add Server` in the drop-down menu that displays. The first screen allows access to many values, but I was able to get the server configuration working by entering only the values in Figure 37-2.

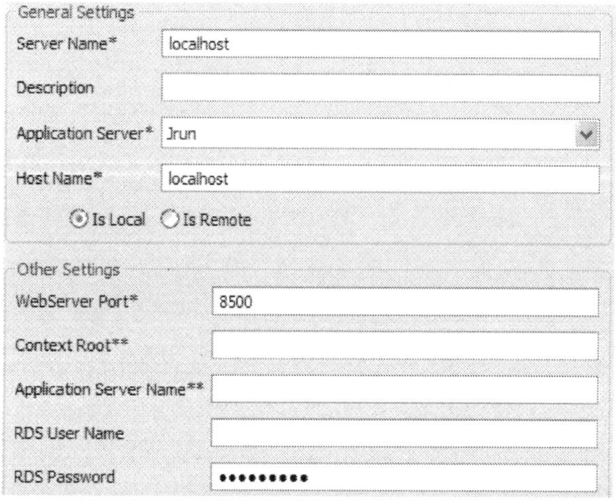

*Figure 37-2. Configuring Your Server*

Of course, you may have to change some values to match your server setup, like the port and host name. On the second page (Local Server Settings) browse to your CF install directory for the Server Home value, and CFB should automatically find and enter your Document Root. If not, browse to the directory in which your web server is set up to serve your CFM files. Next, choose your ColdFusion version from the drop-down. I also selected the `Use Windows Service to Start/Stop Server` check box, but this option will probably appear differently on a Mac. Finally, I left the URL Prefix and Virtual Host Settings tabs unchanged.

You will want to add or change settings to match your setup. I will say this: watching the CFB forums on Adobe's labs site, I have seen a lot of people struggle with these settings, especially when setting up remote servers. I think the labels and descriptions in this wizard have room for improvement. If you get stuck, check the forums to see if you can find an answer. You will know you have success when you see "Running" in the Status column next to your server name on the Servers tab. On the Console tab, you should see a message like this: "Server is available. Getting server settings from Server".

# RDS Dataview

Using the RDS Dataview (see Figure 37-3), you can browse your data sources to view table settings and Views or write queries. I don't imagine this tool will completely replace your favorite database client tool, but it will let you quickly look up settings, or write a quick query, without having to leave CFB. If you left the workspace in its default layout, you will see a tab named RDS Dataview in the upper-right corner of your workspace. If you can't find it, click Window ➤ Show View and you'll find it in the drop-down list.

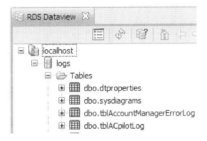

*Figure 37-3. RDS Dataview*

If you expand the tree under your server name, you should see all of the data sources you have set up in your ColdFusion server. If you expand a data source, you can view all of the data source's tables and other database information. You can quickly see all of each table's columns, as well as data types and some other helpful information. If you right-click a table, you can open it to view its contents. This window will also allow you to write queries against the data source, and when they execute, the result set will appear in the same window. This can come in very handy for quickly viewing data in your database.

# Services Browser

This useful tool allows you to reference the CFCs that ColdFusion Builder finds on your server – local or remote, as long as the server has been set up in CFB. If you expand the tree under your server name, you will see a list of CFCs. If Services Browser is properly configured, you will see all of the CFCs from your various projects. Interestingly, you will also see CFCs used to provide access to native ColdFusion tags, like cfmail, cfpop, and cfquery, through remote services. Expanding each CFC, you can see all of its functions and any arguments that it accepts.

You can also right-click on one of these functions and click insert CreateObject (or a similar menu item for cfinvoke), and ColdFusion Builder will create the full code snippet you need to call this particular CFC function, including the names of argument values that you will need to supply – a very handy feature. The Services Browser can also be used to view web services and their methods.

# CF Admin and Server Monitor

You can access the ColdFusion Administrator and the Server Monitor directly from the Servers View in ColdFusion Builder (see Figure 37-4). Open your Servers View, right-click on your server name, and then you can click either Launch Server Monitor or Launch Admin Page. Both of these will open up an internal web browser in CFB to work with these tools. The nice thing is that the browser becomes just another tab in your workspace, so you can keep coding and quickly reference your ColdFusion Administrator or Server Monitor in that tab when you need to.

*Figure 37-4. ColdFusion Administrator and Server Monitor*

# CFC Wizard

Using the CFC Wizard, you can create a CFC skeleton, complete with functions. To access this wizard, open up your Navigator view and right-click a project or folder where you want to create your new CFC. Select New ➤ ColdFusion Component. Enter a CFC name and, optionally, a Hint and Display name. If you want this CFC to extend an existing CFC, you can click the Browse button next to "Extends" and find the parent CFC. You can also specify that the CFC will implement a component or interface. If you are using ColdFusion 9, you can specify that ColdFusion Builder should generate the CFC using the new script component syntax instead of the traditional tag syntaxClick Next, and you can add properties to your CFC, including getters and setters. Finally, you can add functions, including all of the attributes you might want to assign for the function, including return type and format, and access level. After you've added a function, you can assign arguments to it.

In short, rather than having to type out a *lot* of code to create a skeleton CFC, you can use this wizard to quickly create a new CFC with all the basic elements in place.

# CF Builder Extensions

You can write your own extensions to ColdFusion Builder in ColdFusion. You can build just about anything you can imagine doing with ColdFusion into ColdFusion Builder as an extension. Quite a few extensions already exist; some come with ColdFusion Builder, pre-installed in its /extensions directory.

ColdFusion Builder provides an Extensions View to manage installed extensions. Extensions are distributed as Zip files. RIAforge (`http://riaforge.org`) has a category for ColdFusion Builder Extensions, and as of this writing has 29 extensions hosted there. You can install a new extension by clicking the plus sign (+) button in the top-right corner of the Extensions view. Navigate to the downloaded zip file and then click Open. The first screen displays information about the Extension. Click Next and you'll see a second screen showing the license agreement for the extension. Click Accept and then Next. You'll need to associate Extensions with a ColdFusion server, because they run from that server when you execute them in CFB.

If you followed along, you have already configured a server in ColdFusion Builder. Select this server from the Select Server drop-down menu. ColdFusion Builder will automatically pre-fill your web server root in the Select install location field. Extensions have to run from your web root folder, but you can create a new directory for them if you want. If you don't, ColdFusion Builder will create a new directory in your web root for each extension that you install. Select your install directory and then click Next. The final screen shows a summary of the options you chose. After you click Finish, you should get an "Installation Successful" message.

## Building an Extension

Building your own extension is a little tricky but not too difficult. ColdFusion Builder's Help system has a lot of good documentation for building extensions, but it is lacking in a couple of areas. I found it helpful to download extensions and see how they work. Let's create a simple extension that will let you right-click a file in the Navigator and then get a code line count for that file, excluding comments and empty lines.

Every extension has two components: a definition file called `ide_config.xml` and a handler, stored in a subdirectory called "handlers" within your extension's directory. First, create the `ide_config` file with the code in Listing 37-1.

*Listing 37-1. Creating the ide_config File*

```
<application>
  <name>Count Code Lines</name>
  <author>Jake Munson</author>
  <version>0.1</version>
  <email>yacoubean@gmail.com</email>
  <description>This counts the lines of code for a selected file, excluding extra white↵
space.</description>
  <license>Just promise not to destroy the world.</license>

  <menucontributions>
    <contribution target="projectview">
      <menu name="Count Code Lines">
        <filters>
          <filter type="file" pattern="(?i).+\.cf(m|c)" />
        </filters>
        <action name="Count Lines" handlerid="countLines" showresponse="false" />
      </menu>
    </contribution>
  </menucontributions>
```

```
<handlers>
  <handler id="countLines" type="cfm" filename="countLines.cfm" />
</handlers>
</application>
```

The first few lines of Listing 37-1 define the Extension info that displays to the user during installation. Real functionality starts with the menucontributions line. In the first contribution tag, `target="projectview"` tells ColdFusion Builder to put my Extension in the right -click menu of the navigator. Next, a menu tag defines the name that displays in the right-click menu. The filters tags define the file types for which the extension will be visible (in this case, .cfm and .cfc files). The action tag specifies the handler that needs to run when the user clicks my menu item. At the bottom of the code you can see the handler definition. As you can see, the handler's id matches the `handlerid` attribute in the action tag above and the filename attribute will match the name of the .cfm file that performs the work.

Next, create the handler file, countLines.cfm, in the handlers directory, but leave this file blank for the moment. Also, create a second file in the handlers directory called countCodeLines.cfc, which I will explain later. At this point, I advise installing your extension to make sure everything works. Make a zip file that contains your .xml file and the handlers directory with the blank countLines.cfm. Follow my directions in the extensions introduction to install your extension. Hopefully it works. If it does, you will see your new extension's menu item when you right-click on a .cfm file in the Navigator. Of course, nothing will happen yet when you click it.

One handy trick I have learned is that you can edit your installed extension from its installed directory and see your changes in real time without having to reinstall. From here on out, we will be editing those files. Open ide_config.xml, countLines.cfm, and countCodeLines.cfc in ColdFusion Builder, from the location where you installed the extension in your web root. Next, let's look at countLines.cfm (Listing 37-2).

*Listing 37-2. countLines.cfm*

```
<cfsetting showdebugoutput="false">

<cfset XMLDoc = xmlParse(ideeventinfo)>
<cfset fileToCount = XMLDoc.event.ide.projectview.resource.XmlAttributes.path>
<cfset countObj = new countCodeLines()>
<cfset numLines = countObj.countLines(fileToCount)>

<cfheader name="Content-Type" value="text/xml">
<response showresponse="yes">
  <ide>
    <dialog width="310" height="250" />
    <body>
      <![CDATA[
      <cfoutput>
      The selected file has <strong>#numLines[1]#</strong>
      total lines. After removing blank lines and comments,
      the file has <strong>#numLines[2]#</strong> lines of
      code.
```

```
    </cfoutput>
    ]]>
    </body>
  </ide>
</response>
```

That first line of code in Listing 37-2 is very important. When I first started out, I left the `cfsetting` tag out only to find out that extensions will NOT run without it. The next line creates an XML document object from the data that CFB sends to the extension. All communications between ColdFusion Builder and your extension use XML. The `ideeventinfo` variable in the second line of code holds the data that ColdFusion Builder sends to the extension when the user clicks your extension menu item. You can cfdump the XML object in your output section if you want to see what it looks like.

The next three lines are where the extension counts the lines of your file. The `fileToCount` variable gets the file name from the XML object. The next line creates a new `countCodeLines` object, which just tells ColdFusion to look in the handlers directory for a cfc with the same name. Finally, the `numLines` variable is created from the `countObj.countLines` function, which I will explain later.

The last part of the code displays the message to the user, in this case a dialog box. All of the code from the `cfheader` line to the closing response tag is XML, which gets sent back to ColdFusion Builder. As you can see, you can define the height and width of the dialog box. The message to be displayed is inside the body tags, and it tells the user the total line count from the selected file, as well as the count ignoring blank lines and comments.

Lastly, let's look at Listing 37-3, `countCodeLines.cfc`, which counts the lines of a file. I won't go into detail here, since it's basic ColdFusion code.

*Listing 37-3. countCodeLines.cfc*

```
<cfcomponent output="false">
  <cffunction name="countLines" access="public" returntype="array">
    <cfargument name="filePath" required="true" type="string">

    <cfset numLines = arrayNew(1)>
    <cfset numLines[1] = 0>
    <cfset numLines[2] = 0>

    <cffile action="read" file="#filePath#" variable="theFile">

    <!--- Count total lines --->
    <cfloop list="#theFile#" index="i" delimiters="#chr(13)##chr(10)#">
      <cfset numLines[1]++>
    </cfloop>

    <!--- Remove any CFML or HTML comments --->
    <cfset theFile = reReplace(theFile,"<!--.*?-->","","all")>
```

```
<cfloop list="#theFile#" index="curLine" delimiters="#chr(13)##chr(10)#">
  <cfif trim(curLine) neq ""> <!--- Ignore blank lines --->
    <cfset numLines[2]++>
  </cfif>
</cfloop>

<cfreturn numLines>
</cffunction>
</cfcomponent>
```

As you can see, the function returns an array containing two numbers, the total line count and the compressed line count.

To run the function, right-click on a ColdFusion file in the Navigator, as seen in Figure 37-5. You'll see a new menu item called Count Code Lines (which is taken from the extension name), and under that is Count Lines.

*Figure 37-5. Right-click Menu*

If you click the Count Lines command, you'll get back a dialog box like the one shown in Figure 37-6.

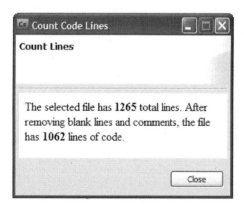

*Figure 37-6. Line Count Results*

That covers the basics of writing an extension. In addition to or instead of putting the extension's menu items into the right-click menu for the Navigator View, you can put them in the right-click menu from within a file, if that would be more appropriate for your needs. You can also have the results from running your extension show up in a tab within the workspace, or they can go into the currently selected editor (if you are doing work on the contents of an editor). There are a lot of possibilities. I encourage you to explore the help and to search the ColdFusion blogs. There are a few good blogs with examples to help get you started.

# Debugging Applications

ColdFusion Builder provides a built-in debugger that lets you inspect variables and applications states in real time and step through the code line by line. Getting the debugger to work can be tricky, especially if you want to debug with a remote server instead of on your local machine. In this section, I will use a locally installed ColdFusion 9 server to debug.

## Configuring Your Application for Debugging

Before you can debug a ColdFusion page, you have to configure a couple of settings. First, you have to attach your CFB project to the server on which the code runs. If you followed the directions in the ColdFusion Server Integration section, you should already have your server configured in ColdFusion Builder. Now, open the Navigator view and right-click on your project name and then click `Properties`. On the Properties dialog, select `ColdFusion Server Settings` from the list on the left. On the right side, in the "Select a Server" section, click the `Servers` drop-down box and select your server, and then click `OK`.

Secondly, you have to make sure your ColdFusion server accepts debugging sessions. In your ColdFusion Administrator, choose `Debugger Settings` in the Debugging & Logging section. Enable "Allow Line Debugging" and then submit your changes. You will have to restart your ColdFusion server before the change will take effect.

At this point you can begin debugging your pages in this project. As shown in Figure 37-7, click the down arrow next to the little green bug in your tool bar, select `Debug as`, and then `ColdFusion Application`. This switches you to the Debugging perspective with several views open by default.

*Figure 37-7. Switching to the Debugging perspective*

As an example, create a file to debug containing the code in Listing 37-4.

*Listing 37-4. Code Example for Debugging*

```
<cfloop from="1" to="20" index="i">
  <cfset thisDate = dateAdd("d",i,now())>
  <cfif year(thisDate) lt 2010>
    <cfoutput>#thisDate#</cfoutput><br />
  </cfif>
</cfloop>
```

Suppose you want to see what is happening to the variable `thisDate` throughout the loop. Set a breakpoint on the line that sets the variable value, and then start the debugger as described above. To set a breakpoint, double-click the line number next to the line you are curious about (you can also right-click in the left margin and select `Toggle Breakpoint`). You should see a little blue dot appear next to the line number. This blue dot indicates a breakpoint. After you start the debugger, ColdFusion Builder will launch your page in a browser, but it will pause execution at your break point. ColdFusion Builder will switch to the debugging perspective, where you can step through the code using the buttons in the top-left pane. The top-right pane has a Variables tab, where you will see the contents of variables that are available in the current context at any given time. Your code view is also displayed, as well as the Outline view.

To step through your code, you can click the `Step Over` button in the top-left view. This button is the second button from the left in Figure 37-8.

*Figure 37-8. The Step Over button*

Each time you click this button, ColdFusion Builder will execute the current line and move to the next line of code. The `Step Into` button will execute the current line, and if the line contains any included code (CFCs, UDFs, etc.), the debugger will step into that included code. Step over will execute included code without stepping through it.

In the Code view, a small blue arrow indicates what line the debugger is currently waiting for your permission to process. As you step through the code, the Variables view will change to reflect any variable values that have changed. You will see any new variables that become available from code that has been processed. Variables that are no longer available will disappear from this view. In this example, the variable `thisDate` will appear in the Variables view, and it change as you step through the code.

You can see an example of this in Figure 37-9. When you are finished debugging, you can click the `Continue` button to stop debugging and let ColdFusion finish processing the application.

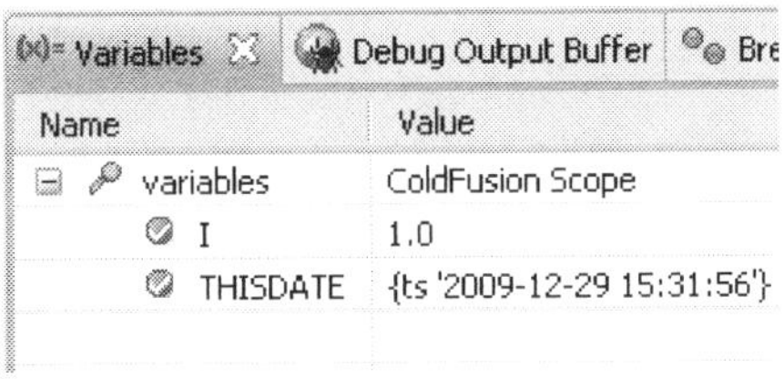

*Figure 37-9. The Variables view will change to reflect any variable values that have changed.*

This powerful tool allows you to observe what is happening as your page executes, instead of trying to dump variable values to the page at the right times. The step debugger gives you much greater control over and visibility into what your application is doing at runtime.

Keep page timeouts in mind as you debug. If you keep a page suspended for a long time as you debug, your ColdFusion server will time out as if you are running a normal page request. If you expect long debug sessions, you might want to put a cfsetting tag in your page to temporarily increase the timeout to allow enough time to complete your debugging.

# Conclusion

ColdFusion Builder offers a lot that did not fit in this article, like the Tag Wizard, the Outline View, page previews inside ColdFusion Builder, and many others. Take the time to explore and learn this great new tool that Adobe has provided for us, and be sure to check out the ColdFusion Builder forums at Adobe's ColdFusion Builder labs site (linked in the article introduction). Also, keep an eye on the official ColdFusion Builder blog for updates (`http://blogs.adobe.com/cfbuilder/`). Finally, Charlie Arehart gave an excellent presentation for the CFMeetup group titled "Hidden Gems in ColdFusion Builder" where he talks about a lot of deeper tips and tricks that I didn't cover here. You can find that by going to his UGTV page (`http://www.carehart.org/ugtv/list.cfm`) and searching for ColdFusion Builder.

■ ■ ■

# The ColdFusion Debugger Explained: Interactive Step Debugging for ColdFusion 8 and 9

## by Charlie Arehart

*Charlie Arehart has long been known for his support of debuggers and monitors for ColdFusion when they were available only through third-party vendors. Now that Adobe has created a debugger for ColdFusion 8 and 9, who else would we get to cover it but Charlie?*

Many CFML developers have felt that the one thing missing from their arsenal of tools was an interactive step debugger. Until now, step debugging in ColdFusion required FusionDebug, a third-party tool I introduced to readers in *Fusion Authority Quarterly Update* Volume 1, Issue 2. ColdFusion 8 now includes its own CFML step debugger, and in this article I'll introduce readers to the concept of step debugging and to the tool in ColdFusion 8 without presuming you've used FusionDebug. In the sidebar included with this article, I'll explain why developers, even those who dismiss debuggers, should give them serious consideration. I think perhaps you'll see some aspects of the tool that exceed your expectations.

## What Is Interactive Step Debugging?

Interactive step debugging has nothing to do with the debugging output at the bottom of your CFML page. Have you ever wished you could watch as your program executes from line to line? That's exactly what a step debugger does for you. You can set breakpoints on any line of CFML code, and in the case of the ColdFusion 8 debugger (CF8 debugger), set it to stop on a line of code in error. You can step into your include files, custom tags, functions, and CFC methods; watch the values of expressions and variables; and much more.

Such tools are common in languages such as Java, .NET, Javascript, Flex, and Flash. CFML developers who have not used those languages may not even have noticed that they've lacked a debugger. ColdFusion 4 and 5 did have interactive debugging by way of ColdFusion Studio (now HomeSite+). But Macromedia/Adobe chose not to carry that feature forward into ColdFusion MX. In 2006, Integral GmbH introduced FusionDebug, a tool that brought step debugging to ColdFusion MX. And now Adobe has included a debugger in ColdFusion 8, which works in all editions of the product.

While FusionDebug is a commercial product and the CF8 debugger is free, note that FusionDebug also works with ColdFusion 6 and 7. The two tools are very similar, though, and I'll discuss the differences at the end of the article.

Both CFML debuggers allow you to trigger the debugging session not only in the development environment, but also in any browser, or indeed from any kind of client that can make requests to CFML pages—CFM or CFC files—on your server. Naturally, this powerful feature may cause some concerns about security, which we'll address later.

## Why Use a Step Debugger?

What advantages does a debugger offer over cfoutput, cfdump, and other such techniques? Here are just a few ways in which interactive step debugging can solve problems a CFML developer might otherwise find very difficult.

- *You can't always use cfoutput or cfdump.* Cfdump and cfoutput create no output when OUTPUT="no" has been set in cfcomponent or cffunction, or when cfsilent has been used, possibly in frameworks and complex applications. In both cases, you may try to disable those features. But that may introduce errors or unexpected results due to other code that was relying on them, so it isn't always an option. You could also use cftrace or cflog to send output to a file, but this is nowhere near as simple as viewing variables in the debugger.

- *Sometimes you are outputting to Flex, Ajax, or web services—not a browser.* You can't always reasonably add debugging output to code that is called by a Flex or Ajax client, or a web service. Cfdump typically creates a big HTML table, an issue if the client is expecting XML. The CFML debuggers, however, can debug CFML pages requested from Flex, Flash, Flash Remoting, Ajax, or web services clients. In fact, they can intercept any kind of requests for a CFML page including scheduled tasks, event gateways, the new cfthread, or events in Application.cfc, such as onSessionEnd or onApplicationEnd.

- *You can intercept and debug a request from any user—on remote machines or in production!* The CFML debuggers can intercept and show the step-by-step execution of any CFML page run by anyone in any manner. It's not limited to requests you trigger yourself. You can use it to debug someone else's request, which allows debugging of strange problems on production or test servers that you can't recreate in development. For example, a real end user can run a request that's causing a problem while you watch. Of course, this capacity is a two-edged sword. You can't currently limit debugging to be shown only for requests from some given user, so it will impact anyone who makes the request while you have debugging enabled. But the CF8 debugger only intercepts the first request received. Another person can request the same page while the other is being debugged and that request will not be debugged. The debugged user, meanwhile, would see the page hang until the developer responded to let the page proceed. There are performance and security impacts in enabling debugging, so you should think carefully about leaving it enabled continually in production.

- *There's no need to change your code.* If you use cfoutput and cfdump, you have to remember to remove those tags when you are done debugging. How often do we see code still showing debug output?

- *There's no need to have write access to the code.* What if you need to debug some code that is protected so that you can't edit it anyway? Debuggers don't require you to have write access. When you're in production or on a server where you don't have edit permissions, this can be a valuable benefit.

- *You don't need to enable ColdFusion's debugging output.* Similarly, if you don't have access to turn on ColdFusion 8's debugging output, you can still use the debugger.

- *Cfdump will not always suffice to solve a problem.* When you are at a breakpoint, you can see the value of *all* variables in *all* scopes. The CF8 debugger has a very easy-to-use tree view of the scopes, including query results. And since you can see everything, you may be able to learn something about the variables or make connections that you might not have thought of otherwise.

- *You can discover the flow of execution of the request.* Debuggers will display a clear visual representation of the flow of a request. You can readily see whether the code went into a certain IF statement or loop, or if it included a file or called a custom tag or method. This is also a great way to introduce a new developer to your code or to CFML in general.

- *The debugger stops on error.* This capability in the CF8 debugger puts you in the editor at the line and page where the error occurred. This especially helps if you have debugging output disabled or restricted.

- *You can view the stack trace during execution.* Output from traditional ColdFusion debugging shows at the end of the page request what files were called to run the entire request. But that doesn't really help you understand which were opened just to get to a particular line of code. In the CFML debuggers, the stack trace pane displays all the files you opened to get to any breakpoint.

# Getting Started with the CF8 Debugger

Like FusionDebug, the CF8 debugger is an Eclipse plug-in, leveraging the underlying debugging capabilities built into Eclipse. Flex Builder, too, is an Eclipse plug-in that functions in the same manner. If you don't use Eclipse currently, you may worry about having to switch editors. First, note that you don't need to give up your favorite CFML editor, be it DWMX, CF Studio, HomeSite+, or CFEclipse. Further, you need to know only minimal Eclipse functionality—which is very easy to learn—to use the CF8 debugger. You can just use the Eclipse-based debugger to debug and then go back to your favorite editor if you prefer.

To get started you will need two things: the Eclipse IDE (Integrated Development Environment), which is a free download available at http://www.eclipse.org, and the ColdFusion 8 Eclipse extensions, a free zip file found at Adobe.com at http://www.adobe.com/support/coldfusion/downloads. html#cfdevtools.

Download and install the Eclipse IDE. (Note that you might already have it if, for instance, you have Flex Builder or CFEclipse.) The CF8 debugger is supported on Eclipse version 3.1.2 or 3.2. Installing Eclipse is beyond the scope of this article, but the good news is that it's really just a matter of saving the provided Eclipse directory onto your file system and running the Eclipse executable (such as Eclipse.exe on Windows). The Eclipse site explains installation on all supported operating systems.

Now download and install the ColdFusion 8 extensions for Eclipse. The process is very easy, and you'll find instructions on the installation in the ColdFusion 8 manual, *Installing and Using ColdFusion*, in the chapter "Installing Integrated Technologies," available online at http://livedocs.adobe.com/ coldfusion/8/htmldocs/othertechnologies_11.html.

The next step involves enabling debugging in the ColdFusion Administrator (separate from the traditional debugging), setting the port on which the debugger will listen, and enabling ColdFusion RDS (Remote Development Services). See "Setting up ColdFusion to Use the Debugger" in the chapter of the *ColdFusion Developer's Guide* entitled "Using the ColdFusion Debugger." There you will also see discussion of a minor difference in setup for ColdFusion's multiple instance (Multiserver) or J2EE configurations vs. the standalone server configuration. This chapter can be found at http://livedocs.adobe.com/coldfusion/8/htmldocs/help.html?content=usingdebugger_1.html.

Finally, you'll need to configure Eclipse itself in a couple of ways that are discussed in the same chapter. This involves configuring a connection to your server via RDS in the ColdFusion 8 Eclipse plug-ins interface, configuring mappings if ColdFusion and Eclipse are not on the same machine, and switching to the Eclipse Debug perspective. While FusionDebug does not rely on the ColdFusion RDS feature, the CF8 debugger does. All of these steps are described in the documents mentioned in the preceding paragraphs, including the "Using the ColdFusion Debugger."

Besides the Adobe documentation, there's a very nice Adobe Developer Center article by Brian Szoszorek, "Using the ColdFusion 8 Step-Through Debugger for Eclipse," which walks carefully through the configuration and setup of the Admin and the debugger with ample screenshots. It's available online at `http://www.adobe.com/devnet/coldfusion/articles/debugger.html`.

I will address some aspects of these configuration features later in the article.

## First Stop: Setting a Breakpoint

Now that you've configured both the debugger and ColdFusion itself and you've started the debugger, open the file you wish to debug in the Eclipse environment. You can begin by telling the tool that you want to stop execution on a given line of CFML code. This is called setting a breakpoint. Just right-click on the line of code in the Eclipse editor and choose Toggle Breakpoint. In FusionDebug you could right-click anywhere on the line, but in the CF8 debugger you must be sure to place the mouse over the line number (if shown) or over the area just to the left of that (see Figure 38-1). You can also use the shortcut Ctrl-Shift-B.

When the CFML template you're working with is requested and that line of code would be executed, the program halts and the debugger interface reflects that execution has halted. It will open the file if it's not already open and show the line of code on which execution has stopped.

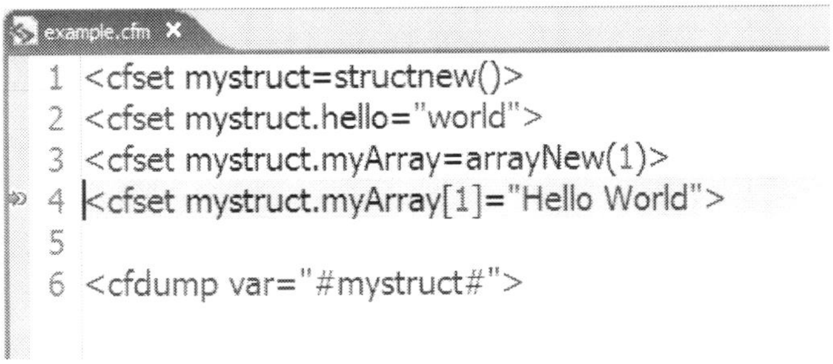

```
example.cfm ✕
  1  <cfset mystruct=structnew()>
  2  <cfset mystruct.hello="world">
  3  <cfset mystruct.myArray=arrayNew(1)>
» 4  <cfset mystruct.myArray[1]="Hello World">
  5
  6  <cfdump var="#mystruct#">
```

*Figure 38-1. Simple sample code*

The blue dot to the left of the line shows where a breakpoint has been set, and the blue arrow and shading on the line indicates that control has halted on that line. Those familiar with FusionDebug will notice that this part of the interface is the same. In fact, both debuggers are really leveraging underlying features of the Eclipse interface and its built-in debugging functionality. Still, without the CF8 debugger or FusionDebug it wouldn't be possible to debug CFML requests using Eclipse alone.

You may wonder what happens when a user requests a page that is being debugged. He'll generally see the page request waiting in the browser, as if the request is just taking a long time. Both CFML debuggers can intercept a request from any user, not just the user who initiated the debugging session. This is a two-edged sword. The good news is that you can use this feature to intercept a request other than one you initiated. How often have you tried to understand why a problem occurred in production or testing, but were unable to recreate it locally? The debugger can also intercept a request made by something other than a browser, such as web services, Flex, or Ajax. Find more on that in the sidebar, "Why Use a Step Debugger?"

Using this feature also means that anyone on that server being debugged will be affected when you set a breakpoint. This certainly speaks to taking caution about setting breakpoints in production. Still, it's nifty that you can. But remember—with power comes responsibility.

Here's another area where the CF8 debugger differs from FusionDebug: FusionDebug intercepts all requests from all such users, which means you may see several different requests piling up in the interface, ready for you to debug. The CF8 debugger works differently. It stops only the first request it receives for a given page. All other requests for that page are ignored by the debugger while the first request is being debugged.

## Observing Program State Information (Variables)

Being able to stop the program in its tracks may seem only mildly interesting, but the real power lies in your ability to learn a lot about what was going on in the program while you are stopped at a breakpoint in the debugger. For instance, you can see all the variables that may have been set either in the program or perhaps in other templates before this one executed.

The CF8 debugger (again, just like FusionDebug) provides a Variables view, which in the case of the code in Figure 38-1, would show what is displayed in Figure 38-2.

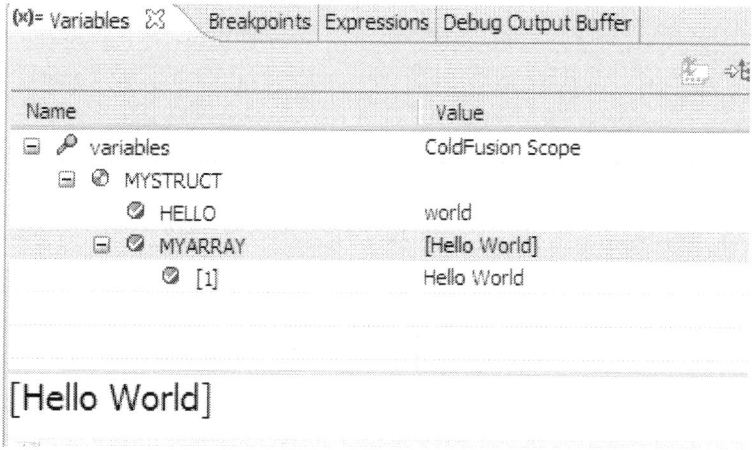

*Figure 38-2. Variables view*

You can see in Figure 38-2 that a structure with a key and an array has been created. You can expand the local Variables scope and any Application, Session, Server, or other scope. (Note that you can configure which scopes are viewable in the Debug Settings preferences page, as discussed in the Adobe documentation referenced throughout this article.) If you were stopped within a method, you could also see the local Variables and This scopes. Isn't that a whole lot easier than putting in cfdumps or cfoutputs and remembering to remove them? As I discuss in the sidebar, there are also situations where you simply can't use cfdump or cfoutput.

If you had a large number of variables, exploring this Variables view would be tedious. Another option is to set a number of watched expressions. This is more like using old-style outputs, except they never send output to the browser; instead, the results are shown inside the debugger. With this

Expressions panel, you can choose to watch any variable or expression. (An expression can be anything you might put on the right side of the = of a cfset or a cfif condition, including variables and functions.) Figure 38-3 shows a few examples.

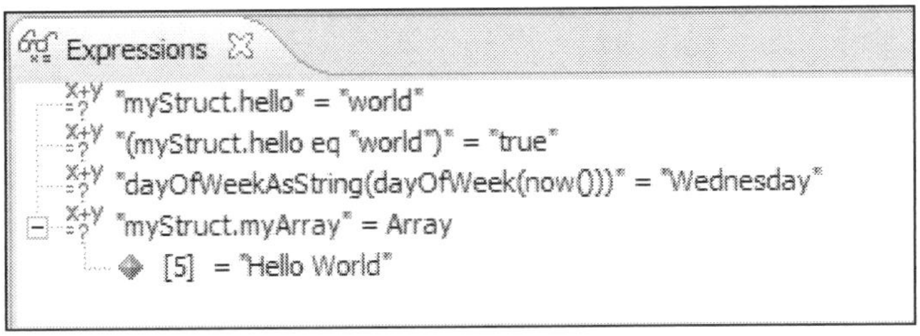

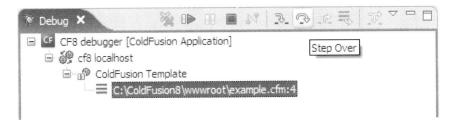

*Figure 38-3. Expressions view*

You can enter expressions by right-clicking in the Expressions view, selecting Add Watch Expression, and typing in the expression manually. Unlike FusionDebug, you cannot highlight an expression in the code editor, right-click, and select Watch Expression. And though the CF8 debugger won't show a Set Variable option when you right-click such a variable within code, you can indeed right-click on a variable in either the variables or expressions pages in order to set that variable on the fly to a new value while debugging an application.

## Stepping Through Lines of Code

While it is useful to stop at some point in the program and view all of the information as we did in the preceding paragraphs, the ability to step through your code is one of the debugger's most important and fundamental features.

Consider again the code in Figure 38-1 where we were stopped on line 4. How would we tell the debugger to proceed? Notice the icons at the top of the Debug pane of the debugger interface in Figure 38-4.

*Figure 38-4. Debug pane*

These icons tell the program whether and how to continue executing code. The Step Over button selected in Figure 38-4 is perhaps the most commonly used, though the one to the left of it is Step Into, which is discussed later. When you select Step Over, the debugger simply executes the next line of code (line 6 in Figure 38-1).

All the examples so far have talked about things you can do while stopped at a breakpoint. These apply to code you've reached by stepping through code as well.

## Understanding the Stack Trace

The debug pane also provides a representation of the stack trace for a current request, which is especially helpful when the line being executed is embedded deep within a multi-file page request. For instance, consider the code in Figure 38-5, which is an application built in Fusebox 5.

```
    dsp_productdetails.cfm  ✕
  ●  1  <cfou www.root project/fb41bookstore/view/pages/dsp_productdetails.cfm
     2
     3  <font size="1">#GetFileFromPath( GetCurrentTemplatePath() )#</font>
     4
  ▶  5  <h2>#product.getName()#</h2>
     6
     7  #product.getDescription()#<br><br>
     8  <a href="#mySelf##xfa.addToCart#&productid=#product.getProductID()#">Add to
     9
    10  </cfoutput>
```

*Figure 38-5. Fusebox sample code*

Let's see how the Debug view (stack trace) appears at this point in this sample application (see Figure 38-6).

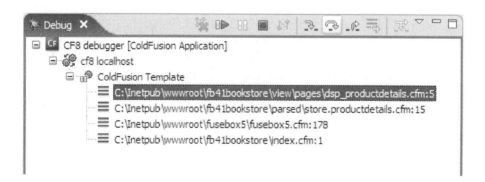

*Figure 38-6. Debug (stack trace) view of Fusebox application*

This reflects not only that we're stopped on line 5 of dsp_productdetails.cfm, but also that we got there from store.productdetails.cfm, which must have called or included dsp_productdetails.cfm page on its own line 15, and so on. It's great to be able to see, at any point of execution in our request, how we got to where we are based on which files were called. Note that you can double-click on any of the lines shown in that stack trace to jump to the indicated file and line of code.

## Stepping into Other Files

Getting back to stepping through code, we can see in Figure 38-5 that the debugger is stopped on line 5, which is about to call something called product.getDescription(). This looks like a CFC (represented by product) calling a method called getDescription. But can the debugger help us make sure that this is a CFC? Yes, it can. Look at Figure 38-7, which shows that I've selected the path of the products variable in the Variables view, and I can see that it is indeed a CFC. If I expand it, I can see various metadata, such as the actual file path where the CFC exists. This can be powerful information when you're trying to understand your location in a complex, multi-file environment.

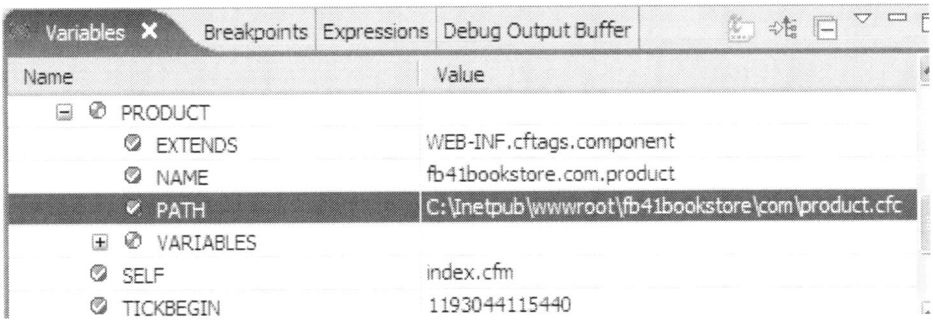

*Figure 38-7. Variables view showing CFC metadata*

Since the next line of code is a call to a CFC method, we can follow the flow of execution into that file. We can also do this with custom tags, included files, and so on. If we were to use Step Into, the icon just to the left of Step Over, then the debugger would open product.cfc (in the location indicated in Figure 38-7) and stop at the first line of CFML within that.

You could use the Step Return button to execute the current file without further stepping. When you've stepped into a file, it will run the remainder of the file that was stepped into (unless there were any remaining breakpoint in the file) and then stop before execution of the next line of CFML code in the calling page. The Step Return button is enabled in Figure 38-6 and is to the right of Step Over and Step Into.

The left-most of those icons, which looks like a green arrow, is called Resume. It would let the request run to completion unless it hit another breakpoint.

## Stopping on an Error

It's great to set a breakpoint and stop on a particular line of code, but sometimes you don't know exactly where you're getting an error. Is it possible to get the debugger to stop when an error is reached? Yes!

Simply enable the option "Break on a CFML runtime exception" in the Eclipse interface's Window ➤ Preferences ➤ ColdFusion ➤ Debug Settings. I've had mixed success with this feature, because sometimes it doesn't stop when an error occurs. It could be a problem of configuration on my system, so your mileage may vary.

# Configuration and Security

A few configuration and security issues ought to at least be mentioned. Three configuration pages in the Eclipse interface are devoted to the CF8 debugger or related features. Select Window ➤ Preferences, and from that dialogue choose the ColdFusion section to find the Debug Mappings, Debug Settings, and RDS Configuration pages.

## Configuring RDS in both Eclipse and ColdFusion's Administrator Page

I mentioned that the CF8 debugger relies on ColdFusion's RDS security. RDS is the same feature used to control access to files, databases, and CFCs on a ColdFusion server when they are accessed from editors such as ColdFusion Studio, HomeSite+, Dreamweaver, and Eclipse (with the Adobe Eclipse extensions).

ColdFusion must be configured to support RDS. Further, you need to understand the form of RDS authentication enabled for your ColdFusion server, as you'll need to provide that information in the RDS Configuration interface in Eclipse. The ColdFusion Administrator page—Security ➤ RDS ➤ RDS Authentication—determines the RDS authentication to be used for that server.

- If the "No authentication is needed" option is set, then no password is required. Of course, this configuration is dangerous if your server is accessible over any network, intranet, or Internet.

- If the option is set to "Use a single password only," then you would provide in the Eclipse setting whatever password is defined as the RDS Single Password option on the server.

- If "Separate user name and password authentication" is selected (an option available only on the Enterprise and Developer editions), then both a username and password would be required to access the server via RDS, where the usernames are defined in the Administrator page Security ➤ User Manager.

Discussion of the User Manager interface is beyond the scope of this article. By default there are no configured user accounts. To enable user-based access you must first create user accounts and passwords and assign roles to those accounts. To use the debugger, such a user would need the Allow RDS Access option enabled. He does not need to be given any Admin access. You may notice an available sandbox role that you could allow called Debugging and Logging ➤ Debugging, but that's for accessing the debugging page in the Admin console.

If you're having any problems getting the CF8 debugger to work, first confirm whether the RDS setup on Eclipse is working for the connection to the server. Look at the tool in Window ➤ Show View ➤ Other ➤ ColdFusion and then use either the RDS Fileview or RDS Dataview tools to confirm that you can connect to the server using one of them. If not, then you won't be able to debug.

In the CF8 debugger, it's possible to enable multiple developers to debug a single server. To do this, set the previous RDS configuration using multiple user accounts. Additionally, a setting in the

ColdFusion 8 Administrator, Debugging & Logging ➤ Debugger Settings ➤ Maximum Simultaneous Debugging Sessions, which defaults to five, also controls how many developers can debug at once or how many single developers can start multiple debugging sessions.

## Configuring the Multiserver or J2EE Configuration

There are a couple of final points to make regarding the use of ColdFusion in the Multiserver or J2EE configurations (as opposed to the perhaps more commonly used Standalone configuration of ColdFusion).

First, with the Standalone edition, when you enable the debugger in the ColdFusion 8 Administrator, ColdFusion automatically modifies the `jvm.config` for the server. With the Multiserver or J2EE configurations, ColdFusion requires that you make the change yourself, adding the following string to the end of the Java args line:

```
-Xdebug -Xrunjdwp:transport=dt_socket,server=y,suspend=n,address=5005
```

Use whatever port you would have entered in the ColdFusion Admin page for enabling line debugging. And whenever you modify your `jvm.config`, be sure to first make a backup of the file. Otherwise the ColdFusion server won't start if you make a mistake.

Second, in the Multiserver configuration, each instance (the ColdFusion instance, the admin instance, and any new instances you create) will by default share a single `jvm.config`. That's acceptable in simple setups, but when using the debugger you may find that you need to create a separate `jvm.config` for each instance. Some do that anyway, perhaps to create different configurations (and therefore different `jvm.config` files) for each instance with different JVM memory, different garbage collection, or even different JVMs. You can find a couple of blog entries discussing how to set up different `jvm.config` files for each instance at

```
http://mkruger.cfwebtools.com/index.cfm/2006/4/17/multiserver
http://www.alagad.com/go/blog-entry/cf7-cf8-jrun-and-the-jvm
```

Third, if you want to use the Sandbox security feature in the Multiserver or J2EE configuration, you'll need to enable a Java security manager (`java.lang.SecurityManager`), which is also done by defining the JVM arguments in the `jvm.config file`. For JRun, this is the Java args line in the `jrun_root/jvm.config` file.

```
-Djava.security.manager -Djava.security.policy="cf_root/WEB-
INF/cfusion/lib/coldfusion.policy" -Djava.security.auth.policy="cf_root/WEB-
INF/cfusion/lib/neo_jaas.policy"
```

# Differences Between the Debugger and FusionDebug

The focus in this article has been on the CF8 debugger, but along the way I've mentioned a few ways in which the debugger compares and contrasts with FusionDebug. Let's do a quick recap here. First, the CF8 debugger runs only on ColdFusion 8, where FusionDebug works with ColdFusion 6, 7, and 8. On the other hand, you can use the CF8 debugger with the free Developer edition of ColdFusion, but then you can't use it for multiple developers (or rather, you can't use it for anymore than ColdFusion will support for making requests against the Developer edition, which is localhost plus two IP addresses.)

431

Some of the advantages of the CF8 debugger are related to use by multiple developers. I've mentioned that the debugger does permit multiple developers to debug a single ColdFusion server and that it uses RDS to control such access. An administrator can control debugger access using a single RDS password shared by all, or separate RDS accounts per user in the Enterprise or Developer editions. For some, the fact that the debugger requires RDS access may be a disadvantage. They've been conditioned to regard RDS as something that should be disabled. But since the debugger is primarily a developer tool as is RDS, this shouldn't be as much of a concern. (Certainly for public production or central test environments, however, it may be something to consider carefully due to the security implications of enabling RDS on such public servers.)

Related to the multiple developer feature, the CF8 debugger only stops the first user making a certain request, while FusionDebug lets you intercept all requests for a page from all users. That could be an advantage or a disadvantage. You may wish that the CF8 debugger allowed you to see the requests of more than the first user hitting a page. Or you may be annoyed that FusionDebug lets you intercept the requests of any user hitting a page.

But the debugger adds something that FusionDebug lacks, which I haven't mentioned previously: The debugger adds another tab next to Variables and Breakpoints called Debug Output Buffer, which shows the HTML or other content generated to that point in the flow of execution. Very handy. Also, as I mentioned, the debugger lets you stop on an error.

# Summary

That's a lengthy review of features, benefits, and challenges in using the ColdFusion 8 debugger. I do hope that the introduction to step debugging and the debugger interface and features will help you get started. For more on step debugging in CFML, you may want to review the series of blog entries I've written on FusionDebug, at `http://carehart.org/blog/client/index.cfm/fusiondebug`, or my previous article in *Fusion Authority Quarterly Update* Volume 1, Issue 2.

# CHAPTER 39

■■■

# Getting Started with Subversion

## by Jim Pickering

*When I first decided to commission a three-part Subversion series for Fusion Authority Quarterly Update, Volume 2, Issue 4, my aim was to fill a gap in documentation that existed at the time. The ColdFusion community was becoming more interested in source control at the time, but the documentation for Subversion was slim and not very well written. Jim Pickering's introduction to Subversion was one of the clearest I have come across, and it is better than most documentation I have read since. He has updated and expanded his article for this anthology.*

I am not one to experiment with open source projects, but when I see an opportunity to work more efficiently, sometimes I find that it is worth my time. When I tried Subversion, the open source version control system touted as an alternative to CVS (Concurrent Versions System), it didn't disappoint. All of the buzz is true. And despite a complex and intimidating appearance, getting started was pretty simple and fast. I did not need to know about all of the bells and whistles in order to install Subversion and take advantage of the efficiency gains. Once I became familiar with the basics, I was able to set up Subversion and get back to work quickly.

In this article, I will describe how to set up Subversion on a Windows server, create your first repository, and set up your client/development machine. You will learn the key features to take advantage of this impressive technology.

## Introducing Subversion

Subversion exists to "...take over the CVS user base," according to the Subversion site's FAQ (`http://subversion.apache.org/faq.html`). The FAQ also states that "Subversion is very similar to CVS, but fixes many things that are broken." As of February 17, 2010, Subversion has become *Apache Subversion* and can be found at the new web site: `http://subversion.apache.org/`. Subversion is often referred to as SVN.

Subversion runs as a server on Windows, Linux, Unix, BeOS, OS/2, and Mac OS X. I typically follow the path of least resistance, because I seek to get up and running quickly, so my Subversion server runs on Windows Server 2003. The Windows version of Subversion can use either the Apache HTTP server or its own web server, called SVNServe. SVNServe runs parallel to Microsoft Internet Information Services (IIS), and is the easiest and fastest way to get started. Apache HTTP server integration is for those who need the ability to configure custom settings, which are limited with SVNServe. I'll leave the Apache HTTP server integration for your own exploration.

433

With Subversion, I can check out any of my projects on any computer with Internet access, and have a fully updated copy of the site. When I say "check out," I'm not talking about a system like Dreamweaver's, where a file gets locked and only one person can work on it until it is unlocked. With Subversion, to *check out a site* means to download a working copy of the site. This is done only once with Subversion, and then only the changes to the files are uploaded to the repository via the Commit command, and downloaded via the Update command.

With Subversion, an entire web team can work on the same file at the same time, and Subversion will keep track of everything. I can make changes to ColdFusion files (`.cfm` and `.cfc`) and upload them to the Subversion repository via the Commit command at work. Then, on my home computer, where the site is already checked out, I can update my local copy of the files, which downloads the changes, and continue working. No more messing with multiple files named with different version numbers. No more risking overwriting files and losing work.

You can work with a team of developers, and Subversion will keep a running history of everything since day one. If a mistake is made, you can use the Revert command to go back to any version in history that you want—you can even view the previous version before you decide.

All of this sounds great, but you may be wondering just how brutal the learning curve is. In my opinion, it is more difficult locating the correct Subversion installer files to download than it is to learn how to use Subversion.

# Setting Up Subversion on a Windows Server

There are two parts to getting the entire system in place: the server side and the client side. On the server side, we'll set up Subversion and create a repository. On the client side, we'll set up TortoiseSVN (for Windows). We will connect to the Subversion repository, check out a site, and then go over the most useful features and commands for Subversion.

---

■ **Note** For Mac users, SCPlugin is a very popular GUI for Subversion that integrates into the Mac OS X Finder. It works similar to TortoiseSVN on the PC. It supports Mac OS 10.4 Tiger, 10.5 Leopard, and 10.6 Snow Leopard. However, as of January 25, 2010, Snow Leopard setup requires some extra steps, which are detailed at http://scplugin.tigris.org/ds/viewMessage.do?dsForumId=1525&dsMessageId=2441924.

---

Here is the list of software we'll use:

> *Subversion for Windows*: Download `Setup-Subversion-1.6.6.msi`, which has the Windows Installer with the basic Win32 binaries (includes binaries for Apache 2.2.*x*). The latest version is Subversion 1.6.9, but there is no Windows Installer (`.msi`) version yet. Also, versions 1.6.7 and 1.6.8 were never released. Get it from http://subversion.tigris.org/servlets/ProjectDocumentList?folderID=8100.

> *TortoiseSVN*: For Windows only, this integrates a GUI for Subversion into Windows Explorer for Windows XP/Vista/2000/2003/2008. You will install TortoiseSVN on the Windows server and on your Windows client machine, too. I have found that it is better if the TortoiseSVN versions match on the server and the client. The latest version, which supports Subversion 1.6.6 is

TortoiseSVN-1.6.7.18415-win32-svn-1.6.9.msi. Get if from
http://tortoisesvn.net/downloads.

*SVNService*: This makes SVNServe run as a Windows service. (The .NET
Framework is required.) The most recent version at the time of printing is
SVNServiceSetup-0.6.0.msi. This version supports Windows Server 2008. Get it
from http://svnservice.tigris.org/servlets/ProjectDocumentList?folderID=
7805&expandFolder=7805&folderID=0.

Once all of the software is downloaded, use the following procedure to install Subversion on a
Windows server. It is important to install the software in the order listed.

1.  Install Subversion by running the .msi file on your Windows server.

    •   During the installation, you can choose a hard disk drive other than C:\. I
        keep my web root on a drive separate from C:\. The Subversion repositories
        will be right at home on the same drive.

    •   There is no need to create a repository or a project during installation, so
        skip those steps.

2.  Install TortoiseSVN (Windows-only) by running the .msi file on your Windows
    server.

3.  Create a directory to store your repositories. Typically, it is called svnrepos, but
    you can name it anything you want. You can put it anywhere, too. I put mine
    on the same drive as my web root, which is not on drive C:.

4.  Install SVNService by running the .msi file on your Windows server. Right-click
    and choose Run As Administrator or use an administrator command prompt
    to launch the .msi file, for best results.

5.  After finishing the installation of SVNService, run SVNServiceAdmin (Start ➤
    All Programs ➤ SVNService ➤ SVNServiceAdmin). Provide the following
    information:

    •   Browse to the location of your repository directory (typically *X*:\svnrepos,
        where *X* is the drive of your choice).

    •   Browse to the location of your bin (or binary) of Subversion (typically
        C:\Subversion\bin).

    •   For the listen host, put 0.0.0.0 if you want to connect remotely to
        Subversion. If you leave the default value of localhost, it will bind to
        127.0.0.1 and not allow remote connections.

    •   The listen port is 3690 by default. You can change it to anything you want,
        but using the default is easiest. Make sure, if you're connecting remotely, to
        open the port you use in your firewall. Contact your network administrator
        for more information on that.

6.  Restart your server.

After installing TortoiseSVN, when you right-click any folder or file in Windows Explorer, you will see a TortoiseSVN option on the menu, which will open a submenu full of SVN commands, as shown in Figure 39-1. For convenience, the parent menu also will include options like SVN Update and SVN Commit, if the file or folder you right-clicked has been changed. Notice the Help option in the TortoiseSVN menu, which is very informative not for only learning TortoiseSVN, but also for learning Subversion.

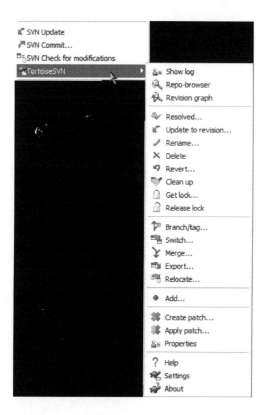

*Figure 39-1. The TortoiseSVN options in the Windows Explorer menu*

## Creating Your First Repository

Once SVNServe and TortoiseSVN are installed, browse to the SVNRepos directory and create folders for your repositories. It is generally best to create a separate repository for each site in your web root, so that each site has separate revision numbers. If two or more sites are imported into a single repository, they share revision numbers, which is confusing. I will use a HelloWorld site as a sample project. You can replace HelloWorld with your project's name, if desired.

To begin, create a HelloWorld project folder in SVNRepos. Then right-click your new project folder and select TortoiseSVN ➤ Create Repository Here, as shown in Figure 39-2.

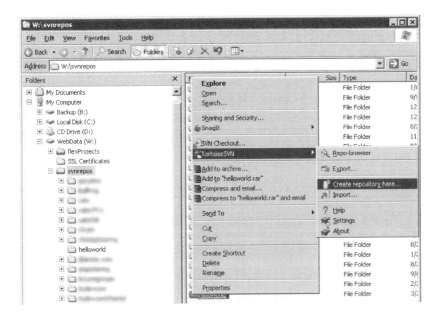

*Figure 39-2. Choosing to create your repository*

TortoiseSVN will ask what type of repository you want to create: Berkeley database (BDB) or Native Filesystem (FSFS)). Choose Native Filesystem (FSFS) and click OK.

Now that your repository exists, it's time to set permissions. Open the `conf` folder created inside `/SVNRepos/Helloworld`. You will see three files: `authz`, `passwd`, and `svnserve.conf`. You don't need to do anything to the `authz` file.

In the `passwd` file, you set logins for each developer to have access to this particular repository. Simply follow the examples provided in the file:

- The # is used for commenting out a line.

- Make sure [`users`] is not commented out.

- Add your username = password.

The options in the svnserve.conf file control access to the repository for unauthenticated and authenticated users. There are three settings:

- anon-access controls anonymous access. If set to none, no one can access the data, If set to read, anyone can download the data from the repository, but they can't upload changes back to it; it is read-only. If set to write, anyone can download or upload the data.

- auth-access is for authenticated users. The same rules as for anon-access apply.

- password-db = passwd controls the location of the password database file.

Instead of removing the # signs between the paragraphs of text commented out, I like to type my own code at the bottom of the file beneath the comments, which keeps the settings together. I like remote access to authenticated users and no anonymous access, so my settings are as follows:

- anon-access=none

- auth-access=write

- password-db=passwd

For each repository you create, you can copy these the authz, passwd, and svnserve.conf files from one conf folder and paste them in the other conf folder.

## Importing a Web Site Project into a Repository

The SVNRepos folder is not your repository, but rather holds all of the repositories that you create. The HelloWorld folder inside svnrepos is the first repository.

The next step in our example is to import our web site project into the HelloWorld repository. Before we import the site, we need to do a little rearranging.

If you already have existing web sites in your web root on the server, I recommend renaming the web root folder by adding _backup (or whatever distinguisher you prefer) to its name, and then creating a new folder using the same name your web root had originally. As far as IIS is concerned, your web root still exists, but it is empty. Now we move to the HelloWorld project folder in the webroot_backup.

Inside of each project folder contained in your backup web root, you will need to do some reorganizing. An SVN repository consists of three default folders that are manually created: branches, tags, and trunk. branches and tags are SVN-specific folders, which are discussed in the next two articles. trunk holds the files and folders of your web site.

Create a trunk folder in your HelloWorld project folder, and then drag and drop everything else inside trunk, so that trunk is the only folder inside the HelloWorld project folder. Create the tags and branches folders. Do this for every project folder you intend to import into Subversion.

This is how to import your HelloWorld site into the repository you just created:

1. In your backup web root folder, right-click the HelloWorld folder and select TortoiseSVN ➤ Import, as shown in Figure 39-3. This opens the Import dialog box.

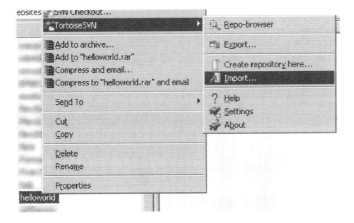

*Figure 39-3. Choosing the TortoiseSVN Import option*

2. In the Import dialog box, enter the URL for your repository. For this example, enter svn://[*servername*]:3690/Helloworld. The server name can be localhost, 127.0.0.1, or a fully qualified domain name. Port 3690 is the default port for SVNServe.

3. In the Import Message area of the dialog box, you can enter a log message. Log messages are displayed for every version change, and are used to help decipher what changes were made. You can enter anything you want or nothing at all. I recommend that you type something like **Initial Trunk Import**, as shown in Figure 39-4, so that it logs this action.

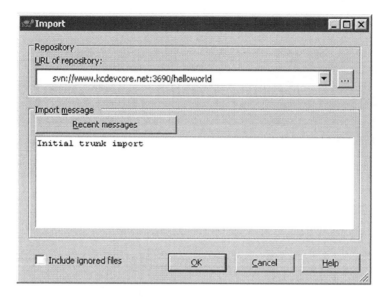

*Figure 39-4. The Import dialog box*

**4.** Click OK to begin the Import. You'll be asked to log in. Be sure to check the Save Authentication check box, as shown in Figure 39-5, or it will ask you to log in quite frequently.

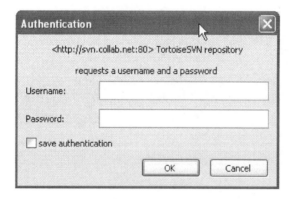

*Figure 39-5. The Authentication dialog box*

**5.** When the process completes, repeat it for each of your sites.

When all your sites have been imported, you can move to the client machine setup.

## Setting Up the Client Machine

Thus far, you have installed SVNServe, your Subversion server. You have created a HelloWorld repository, and imported the site into the repository. Now it is time to install TortoiseSVN (for Windows) on your client/workstation. Just run the installer that you downloaded.

After the client software is installed, you must check out a working copy of your site from the repository to your web root. This is required once for each site, as it downloads the code from the server back to your client machine or testing server. Right-click to display the TortoiseSVN submenu and choose SVN Checkout. This opens the Checkout dialog box, as shown in Figure 39-6.

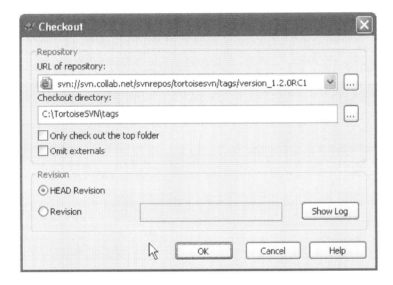

*Figure 39-6. The Checkout dialog box*

The dialog box asks for the URL of the repository and a checkout directory. The repository URL typically looks like this for localhost: svn://localhost:3690/repository/trunk. Always use svn:// and the default port 3690 (unless you changed it).

The checkout directory is the destination directory. It is the local path, like E:\wwwroot\HelloWorld.

The Revision area of the dialog box gives you two choices: HEAD Revision and Revision, with a text box to indicate the revision number. Typically, you will want to use the default setting, HEAD Revision. HEAD means you are getting the latest, or youngest, revision.

Click OK to start the checkout process. If you set permissions, you will need to log in before the download starts, unless you checked the Save Authentication check box in a previous step.

Once authorized, the site will download to the specified location. If your project folder, like HelloWorld in this example, is not created, TortoiseSVN will ask you if you want to create it. Click Yes.

After a working copy of the site is checked out, the code again exists in your web root, just as it did before. You can use your code as you've always done, with your favorite integrated development environment (IDE), like Dreamweaver or CFEclipse. The difference is the new TortoiseSVN icon overlays on your files, which help you identify the status of your files at a glance. Figure 39-7 shows an example.

## register.cfm

*Figure 39-7. The check mark icon overlays the register.cfm site in Subversion*

Table 39-1 displays a few of the more common icon overlays and what they mean.

*Table 39-1. Common Subversion Icon Overlays*

| Icon | Description |
| --- | --- |
| | Working copy is normal. |
| | File has been modified and needs to be committed. This icon changes as soon as you start editing a file. |
| | A conflict occurred. The file should be adjusted, saved, and then marked resolved, prior to committing. |
| | File or folder will be added to repository on next commit. |
| | File or folder will be deleted from repository on next commit, or a file in the repository is missing in a folder. |

# Updating, Committing, and Resolving with Subversion

Three commands that you will use most often with Subversion are Update, Commit, and Resolved.

When your code works the way you want it, then you are ready to commit your code. You should always do an update before you commit. When you choose Update, Subversion syncs any changes in the repository with your version of the code, and syncs dates between the files on your machine with the repository. If you are on a team, when you update your code, others' changes will be downloaded to your files, so you will want to retest your code before you commit to ensure that it still works. Figure 39-8 shows an Update command executed in Subversion.

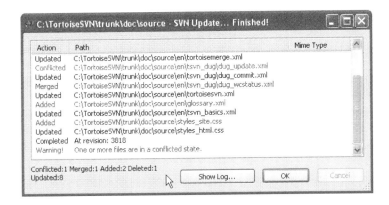

*Figure 39-8. An Update command in Subversion*

When you use the Commit command, you check the file names of files that you changed, and while it is optional, I suggest that you also write a log message to describe the changes, such as the one shown in Figure 39-9. This is a great discipline to learn, because one day you will want to go back in the history of revisions and restore a file from weeks or months earlier. In this case, the log message will be your guide to identifying the revision you seek to restore—or as Subversion sees it, the previous version to which you are reverting.

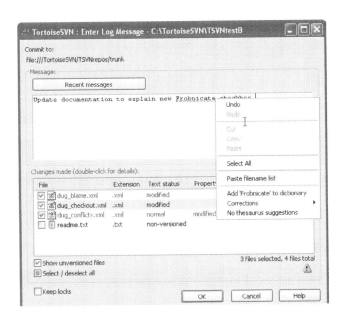

*Figure 39-9. Writing log messages in Subversion*

Subversion's magic works by merging all of the copies of each file into a single file. One developer changes lines of code at the top of a file, and another changes lines near the bottom. When they are merged, it creates one working file. As long as multiple developers don't change the same line of code, the merging is seamless. If multiple developers do change the same line of code, Subversion can handle what is known as a *conflict*.

When you update your code, you might get a conflict. Subversion adds its own code to the file where the conflict is and creates two versions of the code block in question: a copy of the code called mine and a copy of the code that is the latest revision from the repository. Here's how to fix a file with a conflict:

1.  Remove the code you don't need (including the code labels Subversion adds), and keep the code you want to use.

2.  Save the file.

3.  Right-click the file and select TortoiseSVN ➤ Mark Resolved.

The Mark Resolved command tells Subversion that you fixed the conflict and changes the status of the file, so you can commit the file to the repository.

## Always More to Learn

You may never need to know any more about Subversion than what I have shared in this article, and you can already reap the benefits of this amazing, open source application. However, if you want to learn more about Subversion, the next articles provide advanced information.

Also, a good place to start learning is with the freely available online book *Version Control with Subversion* (http://svnbook.red-bean.com/). While it can be lengthy and overwhelming, the first few chapters are a quick read and provide a really good primer on how Subversion works. Also, as mentioned earlier, the TortoiseSVN Help option provides some of the most thorough, accurate, and helpful information that I have found on Subversion, other than the free book.

■ ■ ■

# CHAPTER 40

# Subversion in the Workflow

## by Boyan Kostadinov

*Using source control isn't just learning the software; it's acquiring work habits that may feel foreign to you or to your company. Making changes in how you work can seem threatening, but making the right changes can bring a wonderful boost of productivity to a company. In this part of our Subversion trilogy, Boyan Kostadinov tackles the question of how to incorporate Subversion into your company's workflow.*

It is very likely that you have heard of Subversion, commonly referred to as SVN. You might have been told how wonderful it is, how you need version control, and how Subversion will save you time and make you more organized and efficient. But you have not tried it. Maybe you have downloaded it, but it sits there, unused. Why? Maybe Subversion seems too complex, the idea of switching over scares you, or you have your own system of file organization and it is too hard to change. On top of that, there are all those strange terms: branches, trunks, tags. What do you do?

In this article, I am going to address all of those issues. We will look at the advantages of using Subversion, examine the terminology that seems confusing, and talk about using the tool in a real-life environment. This article is a companion to the "Getting Started with Subversion" article in this collection, so I will assume that you know what Subversion is and have already installed it as described in that article.

## The Advantages of Subversion

Using a version control system will not write your project, make you dinner, or groom your cat. However, there are a few very good reasons for using a version control system:

- *Improve Productivity and Speed Up Your Development Life Cycle.* Once you start using a version control system, you can easily keep track of changes, Revert to previous versions and create an alternate code base. You will find it easier to create patches for previous and/or deployed versions.

- A *Distributed Development Environment.* If you work on the same project from two different locations (at the office and at home, for example), a common place for your source code will make working on your project much easier.

- *Clear Version History.* No more wondering who made a change, why, or when. SVN supports and even encourages log messages with each committed change.

# Terminology

Once you start working with SVN, you will need to be familiar with some of the terminology used in version control software. Here is a short description of the terms used:

- *branch* – a copy of the main development code that you made in order to make some change or to work on a new version of your application.

- *Commit* – the action of saving the latest changes in your project to the repository.

- *Checkout* – the action of getting an initial copy of your project from the repository.

- *locking* – the process of allowing only one user at a time access to a file inside the repository.

- *repository* – the location where SVN stores all information related to your project. The repository usually contains a trunk, one or more branches, and one or more tags.

- *revision* – a number by which SVN identifies a specific set of changes committed to the repository.

- *tag* – a snapshot of a certain trunk, most commonly created when you want to create a major or minor version of your application.

- *trunk* – the location where the main development for your project is stored.

- *Update* – the action of retrieving the latest changes to your project from the repository.

- *working copy* – the local development copy of your code that you have checked out from SVN.

# Using Subversion

Before version control systems came along, it was somewhat difficult to work in more than one environment. If you wanted to work on the same code at the office and at home, you had to make a copy of the whole code base, take it with you, work on it at home, and remember to bring back the change. Furthermore, new functionality was developed by creating a copy of the code base, writing the new code, and eventually replacing the old code. Keeping track of what changed from one release to the next was nearly impossible.

SVN is an intermediate step between development and releasing your code to a production environment. The cycle goes from your development environment to the repository, possibly to a testing environment, and finally to production.

Subversion in Your Workflow This article assumes that you have a working copy of SVN already installed on your machine and that the main SVN directory is called Projects. There are various tools to interact with SVN, but the most common one is TortoiseSVN. For the sake of simplicity, this article also assumes that you have TortoiseSVN installed and working.

While the next few sections on creating a repository and importing code have been covered in greater detail in the "Getting Started with Subversion" article in this collection, I felt that they were necessary for our later discussion of the workflow issues. Those who already know this material can skip to the "Committing Your Code and Updating from the Repository: Some Tips" section of this article.

# Creating Your First Repository

Before you can start using SVN, you need to create a repository for your project. Using TortoiseSVN the process is simple:

1. Create an empty directory inside the Projects directory to act as the repository location for your project.

2. Under Windows, right-click on the directory, go to the TortoiseSVN menu, and click "Create repository here."

3. TortoiseSVN will ask about the type of repository you want to create. Leave at the default Native Filesystem (FSFS) and click OK.

You are done and now have your first repository.

The next step is to create certain predefined directories inside your repository—the trunk, the branches, and the tags. This is done by browsing to the main repository location with your SVN client and creating the needed directories, or by using the SVN command line tools. TortoiseSVN allows you to browse the repository by selecting the Repo Browser option, entering the repository location, right-clicking on the repository location, and selecting Create folder. You would do so for each of the predefined directories.

# Setting Up Your Project

Now that you have created your first repository, you will need to checkout a working copy for your development.

## Starting with a Blank Project

Using TortoiseSVN, select an empty directory, right-click, and select SVN Checkout from the menu. This will prompt you for the address of the repository for which you can enter the file system URL in HTTP format (for example, `file:///c:/projects/test/`). At this point you have created a working copy of your test project in a directory of your choice. The working copy should already contain the predefined directories you created above—trunk, branches, and tags. Now you can start adding code, images, or other files to the trunk of your working copy.

## Importing Existing Code

Importing existing code requires nothing more than creating a new blank project, checking out a working copy, and adding all your existing code to your working copy directory.

# Creating Your First Revision

Once you have set up your working copy and added your code, it is time to add those files to the repository by committing them. Under Windows, right-click on the directory and select SVN Commit. TortoiseSVN will present you with a log window where you will see all the files and directories you have added with the status Non-versioned. Enter a log message, such as "Initial Commit of the code base," and click OK.

## Committing Your Code and Updating from the Repository: Some Tips

Once you have made changes to your project, you can Commit those changes to the repository. The steps you take are the same as those you took when you committed your initial code to the repository. A log message is always a good idea when you Commit changed files. Furthermore, SVN can be set up so that it does not allow you to Commit your changes unless you enter a log message.

How often should you Commit? That depends on your mode of development and how you work on a project. Some people believe that changes should be committed only when you have a complete feature worth committing. For example, if you are working on your project one module at a time, you might not want to Commit every single change to the code, but rather Commit the full module once it is complete. However, the advantage of frequent Commits is having the latest changes in your repository when you need to work on the project from a different location. Your needs should determine how often you Commit your code.

# Branching and Tags

As explained in the Terminology section, branches start as a copy of your main development tree (the trunk) when you need to create new features or a new version in your application, but do not want those changes to be available in the main application just yet. Branches are also helpful when you have multiple developers working on the same application. In that scenario, each developer can create her own branch, work on a module for which she is responsible, and when done, Merge the changes with the main development code base.

## Creating Branches and Tags

To create a branch under Windows, right-click on the directory holding your working copy, look under the TortoiseSVN menu, and select the Branch/tag option. This will prompt you to enter the location of the branch/tag where the code from the trunk will be copied. Assuming that you have created the trunk, branches, and tags directories, you should point your SVN client to a sub-directory inside the branches directory. The directory name does not have to exist yet, as the Branch/tag command will create it. Note (and this applies to both tags and branches) that after you create a branch, you have to run an Update to get the latest branch to appear in your working copy. Also, your working copy will still point to the original trunk unless you switch the location of your working copy to point to the branch you just created. Point your working copy to the newly created branch using the Relocate command.

■ **Note** Tags are meant to store major or minor versions of your application as it becomes ready for release or upgrade. You would create a tag by following the same procedure as described for creating branches.

# Synchronizing Changes Between Branches and the Trunk

Once development is finished on a certain branch, it is time to merge the branch with the main development tree using the Merge command. Essentially, Merge takes all the changes that you have made in the branch and applies them to the trunk. When merging, you would specify the trunk as the source of the merge and the selected branch as the destination. At this point you can also specify which revision of the branch to merge with which revision of the trunk. SVN clients, such as TortoiseSVN, allow you to see a difference between the two development paths and do a simulated run of the merge called a dry run. A dry run is recommended to make sure that your Merge settings are correct. Once you are satisfied that the correct action will be taken, perform the merge. Remember that after every merge, you need to Commit to the repository for the changes to take effect.

## Resolving Conflicts

Conflicts can occur when two or more developers change the same piece of code and the repository does not know which is the latest copy. If you try to Commit some code but another developer has already made changes to the same file, your SVN client will tell you that it cannot Commit your changes because there is an unresolved conflict. Resolving conflicts can be painful and slow, depending on how much code has been changed. You will have to use a diff tool to figure out what has changed between your working copy and the copy in the repository. Luckily, TortoiseSVN comes with a built-in diff tool, but you can also use something like WinDiff. When comparing two files, the SVN client allows you to select the file to use to resolve the conflict. Under Windows, TortoiseSVN allows you to right-click on the conflicted files and select either "Resolve using theirs" or "Resolve using mine." You can set up your repository to require locks as an alternative to dealing with conflict resolution. Locks allow write access to each file in the repository to only one user at a time. Locks, however, have to be requested and released and can cause inexperienced (and even experienced) users grief while trying to use SVN.

## Creating Patches

Patches are another somewhat advanced feature of SVN. They are meant to be used when changes in one branch need to be persisted in another branch or in the trunk. Here is a scenario where using a patch will make your development efforts much easier. Let's say that you have deployed the first version of your application and your client is using it. Time goes by and the client finds an issue with the application. "No big deal," you say, and you pull up the branch from SVN, fix the issue, and give it a new, patched version.

That is all great, except that now you need to apply the same fix to the main development tree (the trunk). This is done by creating a patch from your branch that you can apply to the trunk or to any of the branches or tags. Create Patch and Apply Patch are options available under the TortoiseSVN file menu. To create a patch, before you Commit the code back to the repository, select the development location from which the patch will be created and choose the Create Patch option. This will show you which files have changed since the last Commit and allow you to save the differences as a patch file. To apply the patch, navigate to where you want the patch applied and choose the Apply Patch option. Select the patch file and you will see a dialog with all the changed files. Finally, select all the files in the TortoiseSVN diff list, and click Apply, and you're done.

# Taking Advantage of Advanced SVN Features in Your Workflow

There are three main advanced features of SVN that you can take advantage of in your workflow, each of which I'll cover:

- Reverting to a previous version
- Working with locks
- Exporting from SVN

## Reverting to a Previous Version

Reverting refers to backtracking your changes to a previous revision already stored in Subversion. You might need to revert if the latest changes you have made have broken the application. Any good SVN client makes this fairly straightforward. In TortoiseSVN, just select the local development directory and use the Revert option. You will need to pick a previous revision number and off you go.

## Working with Locks

Locks, like the Read-Only attribute in file systems, allow or disallow file editing. Once somebody has reserved a lock on a file, another user cannot change and Commit the same file until the first user has released the lock, which can be aggravating. Instead of locking my files, I Update them before I Commit to the repository. Then I always know if there is a conflict before I Commit my code, and I have to resolve it before I can Commit.

## Exporting from SVN

Exporting is nothing more than taking a copy of your SVN development tree and decoupling it from SVN. This means that the files will no longer be associated with a version in SVN. The practice is most commonly done when you are ready to release a version of your application.

# Conclusion

SVN is a very powerful tool and can save both development time and unforeseen headaches when used correctly. It has many more features than I could cover in this article, including continuous integration (with tools such as CruiseControl), bug tracking integration (with Trac), and pre-Commit and post-Commit hooks. You can read more about SVN and its features at http://subversion.tigris.org and http://tortoisesvn.tigris.org, and in the "Advanced Subversion" article in this collection (Chapter 41). If you haven't started using SVN, I hope that this article has helped you decide to try it out.

# CHAPTER 41

# Advanced Subversion

## by Kevin Jones

*This article is the final piece in our Subversion trilogy, adding content beyond the standard introduction to Subversion. You've set up your Subversion server and you're up and running (Chapter 39, "Getting Started with Subversion"). You've integrated Subversion into your workflow (Chapter 40, "Subversion in the Workflow"). Well, where do you go from here? What does Subversion offer for the more experienced user? Kevin Jones gives us the benefit of his extensive experience.*

Subversion differs from other source control systems in its greater stability and advanced feature set, yet it remains simple to use.

Subversion is simple: Check out your code, change it, and commit it. Even so, Subversion does allow us to do advanced operations. Some of these you may choose to adopt and some you may not. The particular features you choose will depend on how many of your team members are using Subversion and whether all of them agree that these particular features are beneficial.

In this article, I will discuss some of Subversion's more advanced features: merging, branching, tagging, and properties. We will dive a little bit deeper into how Subversion works and unmask some of its hidden power.

## Branching

It is common for different people to work on different features of the same code base once a team has expanded beyond two people. This sounds simple, but it can be tricky to execute in certain situations. For example, Bob and Sally, your top developers, may be working on different features, but there is always the chance that they may end up working on a piece of code that their features share. How can two users easily work on the same code without interrupting each other's work?

Unlike other version control systems, Subversion does not use a lock as its primary mechanism for ensuring consistency in the code base. Therefore, Bob and Sally can freely check out, modify, and commit the same file at the same time. If Sally commits her code first, Bob will have to update to get Sally's changes before he can commit. When Bob updates, Subversion will attempt to merge both of their changes.

Subversion will look at the lines that Sally changed, and, if Bob hasn't changed those lines, it will merge in Sally's changes. If Bob and Sally changed the same line, or added lines at the same place, this will result in a conflict. Subversion won't know how to merge the changes together, and it won't let Bob commit the file until the conflict is marked as resolved. Bob and Sally will now work together on how to merge their changes so both of their features will work properly.

This can be a slow and tedious process. If Bob and Sally are working on large features that span multiple files, there may be a lot of conflicts. Fortunately, Subversion solves this with branching. It copies the existing main codebase and creates a branch. Sally and Bob can develop their own features on separate branches. When they complete their features, they will merge their changes from their branches back to the trunk. (We will go into the trunk in greater detail in the next section.) There may be conflicts, but they can merge all of their changes at once rather than having to do a merge every time they commit (see Figure 41-1).

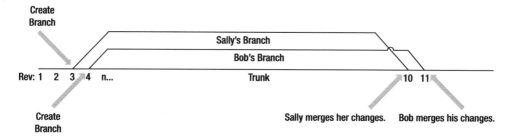

*Figure 41-1. Branching*

Branching is useful for multiple releases. Say Sally is working on a minor update for the latest version of a product, but Bob is working on features for the next major release. Sally would work on a release branch while Bob continues to do his work on the trunk. Later, Sally would merge the changes on the release branch back to the trunk so that the next major release will include the change.

## Creating a Branch

There are two ways to create a branch. You can either branch the working copy or branch on the server, which is the most efficient method. When Subversion creates a branch on the server side, it doesn't actually copy the data – it just points the branch back from the original location. This means that Subversion will create it almost instantly, regardless of the size of the repository. To branch on the server side, use the copy command in the SVN client program. The two required parameters are the source of the new branch and its location. You can optionally specify a message for the revision that created the branch:

```
> svn copy --message "Created a new branch for bug fixes."
http://svn.mydomain.com/product/trunk http://svn.mydomain.com/product/branches/BugFixes
```

This example takes the trunk URL and creates a branch called BugFixes.

This may be impractical, though. If you are working on a feature or bug fix and it occurs to you that you should probably have created a separate branch for your work, you may want to create a branch from your working copy instead. To do this, you would still use the SVN client tool and the copy command, but your working copy would be the source instead of another path in the repository:

```
> svn copy --message "Created a new branch from my messy working copy."
trunk http://svn.mydomain.com/product/branches/MessyStuff
```

As when you created a branch on the server, this will create a copy of your existing trunk, but then it will apply your working copy's changes to the new branch. In this case, `trunk` is a relative physical path to your working copy.

## Successful Branching

When done properly, branching is an extremely effective and efficient way of maintaining a large codebase. However, it can cause some clutter in your repository, which is why it's a good idea to have a policy about branching for your team.

The typical layout for a repository has three subfolders: branches, tags, and trunk (see Figure 41-2).

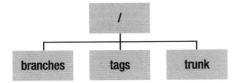

*Figure 41-2. Repository Layout*

All branches will go into the branches folder, tags go in the tags folder, and the main codebase, or trunk, is in the `trunk` folder. This helps keep your repository organized. A tag is a branch that gives a snapshot of a released version of the code. If you ever need to look at the source for a given version of the released software, you can check out the tag for that version. I'll be exploring this concept more deeply in the section on tagging that follows.

When you create branches that correspond to a version of your software, this methodology is called *software version branching*. It's common to release a minor update for software before the next major version release. You can easily do this with software version branching. Some teams don't use a trunk but rather rely solely on branches. For example, instead of having a `/trunk` path in your repository, you would have two top-level directories named `/releases` and `/devreleases`. In `/devreleases`, you would have branches for all versions currently being developed. Once a version is released, it is copied to the `/releases` folder, where it will be treated as a tag. The tag is then copied back to the `/devreleases` with a new version number and development continues (see Figure 41-3).

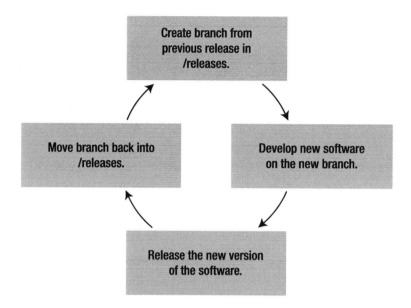

*Figure 41-3. Branch Cycle*

A developer implementing a feature can create a branch for it and merge it back to the trunk later on. These are *task branches*. They are good to use when a developer doesn't want to interrupt the trunk code. Some people enforce a policy where everything is developed in a branch and then merged into the trunk. This may sound overbearing, but it may be useful when many developers are working on a given repository where there is a lot of activity.

There are several different methodologies of branching, and I won't say one is preferred. I do recommend that you choose a methodology that is comfortable for both you and all of the members of your team.

# Tagging

When a piece of software is released, there is no guarantee that it will be bug free. In fact, that is almost never the case. Often bugs are submitted by clients or customers, and they need to be addressed. Let's say a customer has discovered a show-stopping bug that needs to be patched as soon as possible. However, in the background, development has continued since the release. You don't want to release all of your new features because they haven't been tested properly yet or are still incomplete. What you need is code that is identical to what was released.

Subversion solves this using tagging. Tagging is common among other source control systems; however, in Subversion, a tag is just a conceptual idea. A tag is a branch that reflects the code of a shipped release or a snapshot of the code. When you release a version of your code, you tag your code. This way, when a troublesome bug arises, you can easily create a new branch from your tag. As far as Subversion is concerned, a tag is just a branch, but the users of Subversion have chosen to treat it specially.

You should never commit changes to a tag. Rather, create a branch from it, fix the bug in the branch, and then release the branch. After the release, you can merge the changes from the branch back to the trunk. Since the new branch was released to address that nasty bug, we should tag that release too (see Figure 41-4). This way, we always have a snapshot of released code.

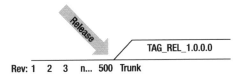

Rev: 1   2   3   n...   500   Trunk

*Figure 41-4. Tagging*

Creating a tag is done exactly the same way as creating a branch. You would use the `svn copy` command to create a tag:

```
> svn copy --message "Tagging 2.0 release of code." http://svn.mydomain.com/product/trunk
http://svn.mydomain.com/product/tags/REL_2.0
```

When tagging, make sure users know it is a tag by either prefixing the name with TAG or putting it in a tags folder. Unlike other version control systems, tags are mutable in Subversion. This means that the tag can still be committed, but that defeats the purpose of a tag. As far as Subversion is concerned, there is no difference between a branch and a tag.

# Switching

Once you have created a branch or tag, you'll need to change your working copy to point to the new branch or tag. You would use the svn switch command to change your working copy and pass it the URL you want to relocate:

```
> svn switch http://svn.mydomain.com/product/branches/BobsBranch
```

This changes our working copy to the new location specified. Optionally, you can specify a target parameter that defines where the switch will take place other than the current directory.

# Merging

Branching makes development easy, but eventually everyone's work is going to have to be brought back together. Also, if you are working on a branch for a long time, you may want to pull other developers' work into your branch to make sure your changes don't have a negative impact on their work.

Let's say you have a simple JavaScript function that alerts a user that he or she is about to permanently delete something, and it is in a file named `common.js`:

```
function confirmDelete()
{
return confirm("Do you want to delte this record?");
}
```

Quality Assurance (QA) has informed you that "delete" is spelled improperly. Unfortunately, this slipped by QA initially, and the code already shipped. However, you have fixed this on the release branch so that it will be shipped in the next minor update. All is well now, but the change needs to be merged back into the trunk so that the next major release doesn't have the same typo.

Before you merge, you'll need to know the revision number of the commit(s) that you want to merge. You can do this easily by running svn log common.js:

```
> svn log common.js

------------------------------------------------------------------------
r1274 | kjones | 2007-12-07 00:16:00 -0500 (Fri, 07 Dec 2007) | 1 line

Fixed typo in delete confirmation.
```

The fix for the typo was revision 1274. If you want to merge the changes from revision 1274, you will need to merge the changes between revisions 1273 and 1274.

The Subversion merge command takes a source directory, including two revision numbers to specify a range, and a path to the working copy. Make sure that your working copy is pointed to the location in your repository where you would like your merge to take effect. In this case, you want trunk. You will run a `Switch` command to change your working copy to the trunk.

```
> svn switch http://svn.mydomain.com/product/trunk
```

Then you will run the merge using the `merge` command:
```
> svn merge --revision 1023:1024
http://svn.mydomain.com/product/branches/REL_1.0.3.0
U common.js
```

After the merge, open the code, scan through it and make sure everything is okay. Once you have verified that everything looks normal, commit it using the svn `commit` command:

```
> svn commit –message "MERGE: Merged revisions 1023 to 1024 from branch↵
REL_1.0.3.0 to trunk."
```

Note that the commit message is very specific, and it includes a revision number range and the merge source. Subversion doesn't handle merge history as well as it could. It doesn't keep track of the revisions merged, nor does that information show up in the file history. Including the revision history in a special commit message helps keep a record of merge history and prevents potential problems such as merging the same revision more than once or merging the wrong revision range. This can have serious side effects, such as accidentally putting in code that was taken out previously.

One way to avoid incorrect merges is to do a dry run. A dry run allows you to run the merge and see what will change without actually doing the merge. This helps identify problems such as accidentally applying a revision more than once, or it may prevent a conflict before it occurs. To do a dry run, specify the --dry-run option when using the merge command:

```
> svn merge --dry-run --revision 1023:1024
http://svn.mydomain.com/product/branches/REL_1.0.3.0
```

There is always the chance of a conflict, though. Let's say you've fixed the typo on the release branch. However, now that your minor release has been released, you decide it needs to be merged back into the trunk, so you attempt to merge revision 1024 into the trunk:

```
> svn merge --revision 1023:1024
http://svn.mydomain.com/product/branches/REL_1.0.3.0
C common.js
```

Notice however, that instead of the usual U that indicates an update, we have a C for conflict. When a conflict occurs, Subversion marks the file in a conflicted state. When a file is in a conflicted state, it cannot be committed until it is marked as resolved. Subversion also creates four files for each conflicted file, common.js, common.js.mine, common.js.r1024 and common.js.r1056. The first file is a copy of the file with both changes in it:

```
function confirmDelete()
{
<<<<<<< .mine
return confirm("Are you sure you want to delete this record?");
=======
return confirm("Do you want to delete this record?");
>>>>>>> .r1024
}
```

This shows the changes from both revisions. In this case, revision 1056 is the revision on the trunk where the other developer implemented the new wording. The first revision is your working copy, the part after <<<<<<<. Your working copy changes end at =======. The revision that conflicted with yours is between ======= and >>>>>>>. This is called a *diff*.

The second file, common.js.mine, is a copy of your file before you tried to merge it. The third file, common.js.r1024, is the file as it was before you modified it. The fourth file is the file as it is from the trunk.

In order to resolve the conflict, the original file, common.js, needs to be changed to the proper way. At this point, you can do a svn log command on the trunk to see who made this change and discuss it with them. Once a decision is reached and the file is as it should be, it needs to be marked as resolved before it can be committed. In our case, we want to keep the trunk changes. This is done using the svn resolved command:

```
> svn resolved common.js
Resolved conflicted state of 'common.js'
> svn commit common.js --message "Merging revisions 1023 to 1024 from ¬
branch REL_1.0.3.0 to trunk."
Sending /trunk/scripts/common.js
Transmitting file data .
Committed revision 1057.
```

Now we have committed our changes and resolved the conflict.

It may seem intimidating at first, but once you start to get the hang of it you'll immediately recognize the benefits.

# Blame Game

Sometimes, you'll be implementing a feature or a bug fix and you will come across something that you don't understand or doesn't seem right, and you want to know who specifically wrote the line or lines of code in question.

One way to do that is to look through every commit of the file, but that can be lengthy and tedious. Subversion makes this easy with the blame command, which allows you to see the author of each line of the file and tells you which revision it came from:

```
> svn blame common.js
614 kjones function confirmDelete()
614 kjones {
1056 bob return confirm("Are you sure you want to
delete this record?");
614 kjones }
```

The blame command returns three columns. The first column is the revision number that caused the line to be in its current state. The second is the author, and the third is the line itself. We can see that at revision 1056, Bob committed a new confirmation message. I can later do a log on that revision and see his commit message and other changes.

Keep in mind that in Subversion, everything counts as a change. If all the user did was change the white space or reformat the code, this will show up in the blame. That is why it is generally a good idea to log the revision number and see the commit message, or check out the revision before that commit to see exactly what changed in that commit.

# Properties

One of Subversion's most interesting features is its extensive property system. Subversion allows you to apply abstract information to a file using a key and value pair system. Like the files themselves, the properties are versioned. Optionally, they may not be versioned, so that a specific property only applies to a single revision of a file. Properties may be useful for some sort of internal management. If you practice peer reviews, then using properties is a good way to indicate that a specific revision of a file has been peer reviewed.

Assign a property to a file with the svn propset command. You specify a key, then its value, and finally where to apply the property:

```
> svn propset myproperty "property value" trunk/web/home.cfm
```

The only restrictions are on the property key. Subversion uses XML internally to manage properties, so the key must be a valid XML NAME. Loosely, an XML NAME is a string containing alphanumeric characters, periods, hyphens, underscores, and commas. Like changes to the working copy, properties are not automatically changed on the repository. They must be committed using svn commit.

Properties can also be binary data, not just text. This may be useful in some situations. For example, certain files may need to have a checksum file attached to them for security purposes. This can be done by applying the `--file` option on the `propset` command and specifying a path to the file of the binary object instead of a text value. In the following example, `trunk/web/importantfile.cfm.md5` is the path to a file that is a binary object containing this checksum:

```
> svn propset checksum --file trunk/web/importantfile.cfm.md5 ¬
trunk/web/importantfile.cfm
```

If you only want the property to be specific for a revision and not to carry across future revisions, use the `--revprop` option. You must also specify which revision to apply the property to with the `--revision` command:

```
> svn propset peerreview --revprop --revision 5 "This revision was ¬
reviewed by kjones and jthompson on 12/07/2007"
```

However, unlike versioned properties, revision properties are immediately applied and undoable once set.

Once you have your properties set, you will want to retrieve them and review them. Subversion offers several options for looking at properties. The most important one will be `propget`. This command returns the value of a property for a given file:

```
> svn propget myproperty trunk/web/home.cfm
```

Like `propset`, this can also be applied to revision properties by specifying the `--revprop` option and the `--revision` option. When using a binary object for the value of a property, you may redirect the standard output from the console to a file location. However, the `propget` command adds some arbitrary data to the output to display it in a more readable format, such as appending a new line at the end of the property. The `--strict` option prevents any modifications, and it only returns the raw contents of the property, hence making a file redirection useful:

```
> svn propget --strict checksum trunk/web/importantfile.cfm >
importantfile.cfm.md5
```

This causes the output from `svn` to be redirected into that file rather than being displayed in the console.

Sometimes you don't know what properties are assigned to a file. Subversion provides the proplist command to allow you to list all of the properties. You may also specify the `--verbose` option, which not only lists the properties but their values as well:

```
> svn proplist --verbose importantfile.cfm
Properties on 'importantfile.cfm':
myproperty : This is a property
checksum: ????
```

Notice that the binary property, checksum, displayed question marks. The `proplist` command will not display the values of a property if it contains non-ASCII data to prevent the display of a binary property. You must use the propget command to get the value of a binary property.

Subversion also contains several built-in properties that are either used internally by the program, or may be used by you to enhance your Subversion experience. I won't discuss all of them, but I will touch on some of the important ones. Built-in Subversion properties are prefixed with `svn:`, and Subversion treats these specially. You cannot prefix your own properties this way because you cannot use a colon in a property name, since it is not a valid XML NAME.

Imagine that a repository contains a dependency that projects in other repositories depend on, like a web application depending on common business logic. The developers would need to compile the project, but this common dependency must also be checked out. This can be achieved by checking both of them out in the same directory and ensuring that the compiler is always using relative paths. However, Subversion offers another solution. Subversion can automatically check out another repository or part of a repository and place it in a subfolder when that repository is checked out using the `svn:externals` property. Simply set this property on the base directory of your repository and point it to another repository URL. When you check out one repository, the other repository comes down with it in a subfolder.

Often, when you are working with a compiled project, there are things you don't want to commit, such as Debugging PDB (program database) files or obj files from the result of a compilation. We can tell Subversion to ignore a file or files by using the `svn:ignore` property, which allows you to ignore files based on their names. If I wanted to ignore all files with the PDB extension, I would use a propset on the root of the repository:

```
svn propset --recursive svn:ignore *.pdb
```

Notice the `--recursive` option on propset. This tells Subversion to apply it recursively to all subdirectories as well.

# Where to Go From Here

Subversion is a fantastic tool for anyone to use. I've explored some of its methodologies and techniques, but there is much more. If you are just starting with Subversion, try to become familiar with some of these features. Try them out; create repositories, branches and tags, and experiment. Find a methodology that works for you and your team. If you use it properly, Subversion can make your team much more productive and effective. These resources will give you a place to start.

- *Submerged - The Subversion Blog*: http://blogs.open.collab.net/svn/

- *Version Control with Subversion* - Free online eBook: http://svnbook.red-bean.com/en/1.4/svn-book.html

- *Pragmatic Version Control* - http://www.pragprog.com/titles/svn/

■ ■ ■

# CHAPTER 42

# Automating Your Development with Ant

## by Jim Priest

*Any complex task, such as making an important update or upgrade live, or doing some complex testing on an application, becomes easier and more organized with automation software such as Ant. This program has become extremely popular in many programming communities, and ColdFusion is no exception. In this article, Jim Priest explains how to automate your development with Ant.*

It's 2 AM. You have been working for the past three days finishing up an important update for your client. Tonight, you will upload the changes and be done! You crank up your FTP program and begin uploading files. Uh oh—you just overwrote that critical configuration file. You fix that, and then realize you forgot to upload the new shopping cart CFC! What turned out to be a simple update has gone horribly wrong!

Has this happened to you? If so, it's time to automate!

In this article, we will explore how you can use Ant to automate some of your more common development tasks. Ant (Another Neat Tool) was created by James Duncan Davidson while developing what would become Apache Tomcat, and it is now part of the Apache project. It is free and open source. Since it is written in Java, it is also platform-independent.

We will cover the following:

- Installing Ant
- Using Ant within the Eclipse IDE
- Creating an Ant buildfile
- Copying and zipping files with Ant
- Interacting with Subversion
- Sending e-mail

461

# Ant Installation

This section will explain how to install Ant, allowing you to run buildfiles from the command line. If you are using the Eclipse IDE (such as CFEclipse), see the next section on Eclipse integration.

---

▓ **Note** The examples in this article are done using Windows. If you are on a Mac or Linux platform, you may need to adjust some of the paths accordingly.

---

Downloads are available on the Apache Ant home page (`http://ant.apache.org`). As of this writing, the latest version is 1.8.0. Since Ant is a Java application, you will also need a suitable JDK, as stated in the Ant manual (which is available both online from `http://ant.apache.org/manual/install.html` and within the Ant download):

*For the current version of Ant, you will also need a JDK installed on your system, version 1.4 or later required, 1.5 or later strongly recommended. The later the version of Java, the more Ant tasks you get. If a JDK is not present, only the JRE runtime, then many tasks will not work.*

Once you have downloaded the binary for your operating system, installation is as simple as unzipping the archive to a directory on your computer. Since this is a command-line program, I suggest creating a directory off the root named Ant:

`C:\Ant`

After extracting the files, navigate to the documentation directory (`C:\Ant\docs`) and open `index.html` in your favorite browser. This is a complete copy of the documentation available on the Apache Ant web site.

---

▓ **Tip** In addition to the manual, I encourage you to read "Ant in Anger: Using Apache Ant in a Production Development System" (`ant.apache.org/ant_in_anger.html`). This quick read includes a lot of great Ant information, like best practices, how to keep your buildfiles platform-independent, tips and tricks, and some of Ant's limitations.

---

After installing Ant, you'll need to set a few environment variables. (On Windows, this is done by selecting Settings ➤ Control Panel ➤ System, choosing the Advanced Tab, and clicking Environment Variables.) Set the following:

- Add the `C:\Ant\bin` directory to your path statement.

- Set the `ANT_HOME` environment variable to point to the directory where you installed Ant (`C:\Ant`).

- Ensure you have the `JAVA_HOME` environment variable set. This should be set to the directory where your JDK is installed.

To test your Ant installation, open a command prompt and enter the following:

```
C:\> ant -version
```

Ant should display the current version and compile date.

# Eclipse Integration

If you are currently using ColdFusion Builder, CFEclipse, or Flex Builder, you already have Ant!

The Ant runtime is included in Eclipse, and the latest version of Eclipse 3.5 (Galileo) includes Ant 1.7.1. Ant is available as a view within Eclipse. To access it, select Window ➤ Show View and click `Other`. Expand Ant, select `Ant`, and click OK. You should now have a new Ant view available, as shown in Figure 42-1.

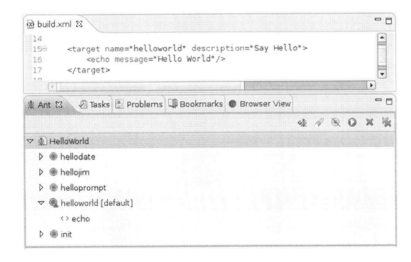

*Figure 42-1. Ant view in Eclipse*

The rest of the examples in this article will use Ant within Eclipse. The examples can be run via the command line as well.

Before we can continue, however, we need to create our first buildfile!

# The Ant Buildfile

By default, Ant will look for a file called `build.xml` when executed. This buildfile is a simple XML document.

## Buildfile Components

The `build.xml` file consists of a few parts: projects, targets, and tasks. These components outline what Ant should do when executed.

### Projects

Each `build.xml` consists of one `project` tag per buildfile. The `project` tag defines the following attributes:

- `name`: The name of the project.

- `default`: The default target to run.

- `basedir`: All activity is relative to the directory specified by `basedir`. If no `basedir` is specified, it defaults to `"."` (the directory where the buildfile resides).

Listing 42-1 brings this all together in a simple Ant project.

*Listing 42-1. A simple Ant project*

```
<project name="Test" default="init" basedir=".">
</project>
```

### Targets

Each project is made up of one or more targets. Each target is a collection of tasks that you want Ant to perform. Each target should be dedicated to one particular goal, such as sending e-mail or deleting files.

A target is represented by a `target` element and has the following attributes:

- `name`: The name of the target (required).

- `depends`: A comma-delimited list of names of other targets on which this target depends. The `depends` attribute ensures that targets are executed in the proper order.

- `if`: The name of the property that must be set in order for this target to execute.

- unless: The name of the property that must *not* be set in order for this target to execute.

- description: A short description of the function of this target.

In Listing 42-2, we define a target named sayHelloWorld. The only required attribute is name.

*Listing 42-2. The sayHelloWorld target*

```
<target name="sayHelloWorld" description="Say Hello">
</target>
```

# Tasks

Tasks do the actual heavy lifting in Ant. Ant has many built-in tasks, and you can also create custom tasks. To complete the sayHelloWorld target we defined in Listing 42-2, we will add an echo task, as shown in Listing 42-3.

*Listing 42-3. Adding a task to our target*

```
<target name="sayHelloWorld">
   <echo message="Hello World!"/>
</target>
```

When this target is executed, the echo task will be run, and "Hello World!" will be printed to the console.

Some of the many Ant tasks available are listed in Table 42-1.

*Table 42-1. Some Common Ant Tasks*

| Task | Description |
| --- | --- |
| exec | Executes a system command such as running batch files or command-line executables |
| copy | Copies a file or fileset to a new file or directory |
| delete | Deletes a single file, all files, and/or subdirectories in a specified directory |
| get | Gets a file from a URL |
| zip/unzip | Zips and unzips files and directories |
| mkdir | Creates a directory; nonexistent parent directories are created, when necessary |
| sshexec | Executes a command on a remote server using SSH |

| Task | Description |
|------|-------------|
| input | Allows user interaction during the build process by displaying a message and reading a line of input from the console |
| sql | Executes a series of SQL statements via JDBC to a database |
| tstamp | Sets the time in the current project, based on the current date and time |
| ftp | Implements a basic FTP client that can send, receive, list, and delete files, and create directories |
| mail | Sends SMTP e-mail |

A complete list of Ant tasks is available in the Ant manual.

## A Hello World Buildfile

Now that you have a basic understanding of the `build.xml` file, by combining the preceding examples, we can write a complete build file, as shown in Listing 42-4.

*Listing 42-4. A sample buildfile*

```
<?xml version="1.0"?>
<project name="HelloWorld" default="helloworld" basedir=".">
  <description>
      This is a sample build file - Hello World
  </description>
  <target name="helloworld" description="Say Hello">
     <echo message="Hello World"/>
  </target>
</project>
```

We have added a few additional elements. The `description` element (lines 3 through 5) contains a brief description of our project. We have also defined a `default` attribute in the `project` tag (line 2), which determines which target will run if no target is defined during execution.

If your buildfile is not displayed within the Ant view, click the small Ant icon. You will be prompted to select your `build.xml` file, as shown in Figure 42-2.

*Figure 42-2. Adding buildfiles*

Once you have selected your `build.xml` file, you can expand it to see each target and task. Default targets will be highlighted. To run your buildfile, click the green arrow in the Ant view toolbar, as shown in Figure 42-3.

*Figure 42-3. Running a selected target*

The default target, `helloworld`, will run automatically, and the `echo` task will output "Hello World" to the console, as shown in Figure 42-4.

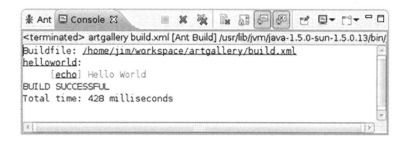

*Figure 42-4. Console output*

Build successful! Now, regardless of how many times we run our buildfile, we will get the same results.

This is our goal: consistent, repeatable results with one click.

# Ant Properties

Ant properties allow you to define variables that you can reuse throughout your buildfile. Each property consists of a name and value. Listing 42-5 shows an example of the `name` and `value` properties.

*Listing 42-5. The name and value properties*

```
<property name="myname" value="Jim Priest" />
```

Once you define a property, you can use it in your tasks, as shown in Listing 42-6.

*Listing 42-6. Using a property defined elsewhere in your buildfile*

```
<target name="helloworld"
        description="Say hello and display name from property">
  <echo message="Hello ${myname}"/>
</target>
```

This echoes "Hello Jim Priest" to the console.

Now let's revisit our Hello World example and add some global properties by defining a new `init` target. First, we'll change our project definition's `default` target to `init`. Next, we'll add a new `myname` property, which defines our username. We'll also introduce a new task, `tstamp`, to provide us with the current date and time, which we'll define as a property named `mydate`. All of these changes have been incorporated into Listing 42-7.

*Listing 42-7. Updated Hellow World buildfile*

```xml
<project name="HelloWorld" default="helloworld" basedir=".">
    <description>
        This is a sample build file - Hello World
    </description>

    <target name="init" description="Set global properties">
        <property name="myname" value="Jim Priest" />
        <tstamp>
            <format property="mydate" pattern="MM/dd/yy hh:mmaa"/>
        </tstamp>
    </target>

    <target name="helloworld" depends="init" description="Say hello and display the current
date and time">
        <echo message="Hello ${myname}. It is ${mydate}."/>
    </target>
</project>
```

Notice the new **depends** attribute for the **helloworld** target in Listing 42-7 (line 11). Each target can depend on another target. In our example, we can't run the **helloworld** target before we set our name and time properties, so the **helloworld** target **depends** on the **init** target. To illustrate this, run the **helloworld** target. You'll see something like Figure 42-5.

*Figure 42-5. Depends order*

You can see in the console that **init** is run first, then **helloworld**, which echoes both of our new properties. To learn more about **depends**, see the "Writing a Simple Buildfile" section of the Ant manual.

# Dynamic Data in Ant

While static properties are quite useful, Ant also provides the **input** task to allow interaction with the user during runtime. Let's add a new **yourname** property to our **init** target and capture user input, as shown in Listing 42-8.

*Listing 42-8. Capturing user input with the new message property*

```
<input message="Please enter your name:" addproperty="yourname"/>
```

And alter the `helloworld` target:

```
<target name="helloworld" depends="init"
        description="Say hello and display the current date and time">
    <echo message="Hello ${myname}. It is ${mydate}. The name you entered is is
${yourname}."/>
  </target>
```

Now when you execute the `helloworld` target, you will be prompted to enter your name. When you do, you should see something like the following in the console:

```
[echo] Hello Jim Priest. It is 03/12/10 08:27PM. The name you entered is John Doe.
```

With these basic Ant concepts under your belt, we can look at some more useful examples.

# Copying and Zipping Files

Manipulating files is one of a developer's more frequent (and error-prone) chores. Here, we will look at interacting with files using Ant. We will grab our local project files, move them to a temporary directory, manipulate them, and finally zip them up and copy them to another directory. In this example, we will be moving the files locally, but you could just as easily copy files from a source control system and move them to a remote location via FTP. Ant's flexibility is one of its strongest assets.

First, in Listing 42-9, we will modify our `init` target to define some new properties.

*Listing 42-9. Defining some new properties for the init target*

```
<target name="init" description="Set global properties">
    <property name="project.fullname" value="Ant Example Shopping Cart Project" />
    <property name="project.name" value="shoppingcart" />
    <property name="project.rootdir" value="/workspace/${project.name}" />
    <property name="project.builddir" value="/temp/build/" />
        <tstamp>
            <format property="project.builddate" pattern="MM/dd/yy hh:mmaa"/>
        </tstamp>
    <property name="build.logfile" value="ant-build.log" />
    <record name="${build.logfile}"/>
</target>
```

In Listing 42-9, we define a project name, our project root, and build directories, as well as a log file name. Notice that we use another property to define the path in our `project.rootdir` property. The `record` task will write the events of the build to the log file we defined in the `build.logfile` property. The `project.builddir` will provide a temporary location to store our files while we prepare them for deployment.

▪ **Note** The backward slashes in the file paths allow the buildfile to run on both Windows and Mac/Linux operating systems.

Notice that in Listing 42-9, we do not declare a physical path: `C:\temp\build`. Instead, we simply refer to a relative path `/temp/build/`. When you declare your project, you define a `basedir`, defined as follows in the Ant documentation:

> *Basedir: the base directory from which all path calculations are done. This attribute might be overridden by setting the "basedir" property beforehand. When this is done, it must be omitted in the project tag. If neither the attribute nor the property have been set, the parent directory of the buildfile will be used.*

We defined the basedir as `"."`, which means all our directories will be relative to the directory from which we are running the buildfile.

Let's move on to the next step, shown in Listing 42-10.

*Listing 42-10. The makeDir target*

```
<target name="makeDir" depends="init" description="Create our temp directory for files">
  <delete dir="${project.builddir}" />
  <mkdir dir="${project.builddir}" />
  <echo message="Build directory created!"/>
</target>
```

In Listing 42-10, we introduce two new tasks: `delete`, to delete the previous build, and `mkdir`, to create a new directory to store our files while we prepare them for deployment. Note that the `makeDir` target depends on the `init` target. As we define each successive target, we will make it depend on the previous one. Let's add a new target, as shown in Listing 42-11.

*Listing 42-11. the copyFiles target*

```
<target name="copyFiles" depends="makeDir"
        description="Copy project files into temporary build dir">
    <copy todir="${project.builddir}">
        <fileset dir="${project.rootdir}">
            <exclude name="build.xml" />
            <exclude name=".project" />
            <exclude name="*.log" />
        </fileset>
    </copy>
    <echo message="File(s) copied successfully!"/>
</target>
```

In Listing 42-11, we copy our project files to our temporary build directory `project.builddir` using the `copy` task (lines 2 through 8). `fileset` defines a group of files for the `copy` task to act upon. We have set it to our project directory using the `project.rootdir` property. We can use the `exclude` tag to define files or directories that we don't want to copy. In lines 4 through 6, we've excluded both the `.project` file Eclipse creates, as well as our `.xml`, `.log`, and `.txt` files.

---

▨ **Caution** Filesets and excludes can contain powerful wildcards, and care should be taken when defining them, especially when deleting files. The Ant manual includes several good examples.

---

Next, we will use Ant's `replace` task to write the current time and date to our `Application.cfc` file, which is shown in Listing 42-12. We do this by first placing a string or token in our `Application.cfc`. This is simply a unique string that Ant will look for and replace with a value during the build.

*Listing 42-12. Application.cfc*

```
<!---
Ant Example - writing to application.cfc
~~~~~~~~~~~~~~~~~~~~~~~~~~~~~~~~~~~~~~~~~~
@@@build-date@@@
~~~~~~~~~~~~~~~~~~~~~~~~~~~~~~~~~~~~~~~~~~
--->
```

Now, in Listing 42-13, we will define the `writeRevision` target, which will modify our `Application.cfc`.

*Listing 42-13. Modifying Application.cfc with the writeRevision target*

```
<target name="writeRevision" depends="copyFiles"
        description="Write info into application.cfc">
   <replace file="${project.builddir}\Application.cfc"
            token="@@@build-date@@@"
            value="${project.fullname} last updated: ${project.builddate}"/>
   <echo message="Application.cfc modified successfully!"/>
</target>
```

In Listing 42-13, we define our token as the same string we placed in `Application.cfc`. When this target is executed, the token will be replaced by the specified string that contains two of the properties we defined earlier in our `init` target. Note that we are manipulating our copy of `Application.cfc` in our temporary build directory, not our original in our project directory. When run, this target will modify our copy of `Application.cfc`, and our token will have been replaced (see Listing 42-14).

*Listing 42-14. Application.cfc (modified)*

```
<!---
Ant Example - writing to application.cfc
~~~~~~~~~~~~~~~~~~~~~~~~~~~~~~~~~~~~~~~~~
Ant Example Shopping Cart last updated: 12/07/10 09:07PM
~~~~~~~~~~~~~~~~~~~~~~~~~~~~~~~~~~~~~~~~~
--->
```

Instead of cluttering your code with conditional logic, you could use this technique to change database source name settings or set other environment variables when you deploy files to production or development servers.

As a final step, we will zip our modified files, move them to our project directory, and delete our temporary build directory.

With the `zip` task, we define a base directory and destination location. Running the `zipFiles` task (see Listing 42-15) will zip our modified files in our temporary build directory, move those files back to our project directory, and delete our temporary files. During each build of your project, you could also copy these files to a directory for backup or a simple version control system.

*Listing 42-15. Running the zipFiles task*

```
<target name="zipFiles" depends="writeRevision"
        description="Zip our build files into our project dir">
    <zip destfile="${project.rootdir}\project.zip" basedir="${project.builddir}" />
    <delete dir="${project.builddir}" />
    <echo message="File(s) zipped!"/>
</target>
```

# Interacting with Subversion

The previous articles covered version control with Subversion. Using the `SVNAnt` task, you can easily interact with Subversion. In this example, we will check out files from Subversion to our temporary build directory.

▓ **Note** See the resources listed at the end of this article for information about how to configure Subversion interaction with Ant.

First, in Listing 42-16, we add some new properties to our `init` target.

*Listing 42-16. Adding properties to our init target*

```
<property name="svn.url" value="http://your.repository.source/svn/${project.name}/trunk" />
<input message="Enter revision (HEAD or number:)" addproperty="svn.revision"
        defaultvalue="HEAD" />
<input message="Enter your SVN username (lowercase)" addproperty="svn.username" />
<input message="Enter your SVN password" addproperty="svn.password" />
```

In Listing 42-16, we define our Subversion repository URL and our Subversion username and password. We will use the `input` task to allow the user to input these values when the buildfile is executed.

Next, in Listing 42-17, we create the `checkoutSVN` target to check out our files from Subversion.

*Listing 42-17. Creating the checkoutSVN target*

```
<target name="checkoutSVN" depends="makeDir"
        description="Checkout code from SVN repository into the local temp directory">

  <svn username="${svn.username}" password="${svn.password}">
    <checkout url="${svn.url}" destpath="${project.builddir}" revision="HEAD" />
  </svn>

  <svn username="${svn.username}" password="${svn.password}">
    <wcVersion path="${project.builddir}" />
  </svn>

  <replace file="${project.builddir}/Application.cfc"
           token="@@@build-date@@@"
           value="Last updated: r${revision.max} - Date: ${svn.builddate}"/>
  <echo message="Files checked out to temp directory successfully!"/>
</target>
```

When our revised `init` target is run, the user will be prompted to enter a revision to check out, as well as a Subversion username and password. We then run the `checkoutSVN` target, using the `svn` task from SvnAnt to execute a Subversion checkout. We will also grab the current Subversion revision number using `wcVersion` and write that to our `Application.cfc`, replacing our existing token.

SvnAnt supports most of the existing Subversion commands usually run on the command line. See the SvnAnt documentation for details.

# Sending E-mail

Sending e-mail from Ant requires two additional libraries that are not included with the main Ant distribution. Installing additional Ant tasks is usually a simple matter of copying the included `.jar` file to the `/lib` directory of your Ant installation. Refer to the installation instructions included with the task.

Once you have the additional libraries installed, you can use the mail task, as shown in Listing 42-18.

*Listing 42-18. Using the mail task*

```
<target name="sendMail" depends="checkoutSVN" description="Send email notification">
    <mail mailhost="your.mailserver.com" mailport="25"
        subject="'${project.fullname}' build at revision ${revision.max}"
        messagefile="${build.logfile}">
        <from address="${email.toaddress}"/>
        <to address="${email.fromaddress}"/>
    </mail>
    <echo message="Mail sent!"/>
</target>
```

This listing will send an e-mail with the contents of the build log file as the mail body. You can also send attachments. The properties email.toaddress, and email.fromaddress could be defined in the init target or submitted by the user using the input task.

# Some Ant Guidelines

Here are some guidelines for your own use of Ant:

- Define your properties in a global init target.

- Check out files from repository (or grab them from local directories using the copy, exec, or source control-specific tasks).

- Clean up and modify files (write dates and revision number, or write application-specific application variables using the replace task).

- Push files to production servers (using the FTP or copy tasks).

- E-mail the results of your build to developers (using the email task).

- Remember your target dependencies.

# Conclusion

Now that we have covered the basic Ant components, you should be able to put together your own buildfile. Remember that the power of Ant lies in its flexibility, so feel free to experiment!

There is a zip file containing all the examples listed in this article, as well as a complete buildfile combining all the techniques discussed here, on the Fusion Authority Quarterly Update site (http://www.fusionauthority.com/quarterly/). The following are some other useful resources:

- Apache Ant project: http://ant.apache.org/

- Ant manual: http://ant.apache.org/manual/index.html

- Ant wiki: http://wiki.apache.org/ant/FrontPage

For more examples and Ant-related tutorials, visit the Ant section on my wiki at `http://www.thecrumb.com/wiki/ant`. For links and more information regarding the additional tasks mentioned in this article, visit `http://www.thecrumb.com/wiki/ant/tasks`. Also visit my blog at `http://www.thecrumb.com`.

# Index

## Symbols

$ dollar sign, in UDF names, 18

_ underscore, in UDF names, 18

## Numbers

301 redirects, 54

403 Forbidden error, 48

## A

abstraction, object-oriented programming and, 217

Acrobat Connect, 369

Action Message Format (AMF), 199

ActionScript adapter, messaging and, 202

Active Record, 237, 323

activePDF, 76

adapters, messaging and, 202

addWatermark action (cfpdf tag), 84

Admin Server Components, for ColdFusion Builder, 409

aggregating data, 139

aggregation, object-oriented programming and, 217

agile software development, 318

Ajax

cfajaxproxy tag and, 379–382, 384

prototypes and, 387

AMF (Action Message Format), 199

AMF channels, 203

anemic domain model, 237

Ant

automating development and, 461–476

build.xml file for, 464–470

copying/zipping files and, 470–473

Eclipse and, 463

e-mail and, 474

guidelines for, 475

installing, 462

Model-Glue framework and, 303

resources for further reading, 462

Subversion and, 473

AOP (Aspect-Oriented Programming), 70, 316

Apache Ant. *See* Ant

Apache Axis, 171

Apache Subversion. *See* Subversion

Apache Tomcat, 461

APIs (application programming interfaces)

base classes and, 251

object-oriented programming and, 218

Reactor framework and, 323

application framework. *See* frameworks

application generators, 254, 321

application programming interfaces. *See* APIs

Application scope, 3, 10, 35, 41

application template, Model-Glue framework and, 302

application variables, 5–13

Application.cfc, 3–13, 348

asynchronous gateways and, 117

benefits of, 13

cffunction tag and, 19

Fusebox framework and, 273, 278

Mach-II framework and, 286

Model-Glue framework and, 302

reference/visual aid for, 15

resources for further reading, 13

Application.cfm, 3, 348

cffunction tag and, 19

converting to Application.cfc, 13

applications

ColdSpring framework and, 318

convention-based application building and, 266, 348

debugging, ColdFusion Builder and, 417

defined within ColdFusion, 3

Fusebox framework and, 265–280

FW/1 (Framework One) and, 347–357

Interface-Driven Architecture prototyping and, 385–387

layering, 231–238

metaprogramming and, 254

Model-Glue framework for, 302–313

multiple, Fusebox framework and, 272

test-driven development and, 318, 319

architecture, ColdSpring framework and, 319

Arguments prefix, 25

Arguments scope

cfargument tag and, 22

UDFs and, 23

arguments, object-oriented programming and, 218

arrays

complex types and, 160, 175

components within, validating, 180

XML vs. JSON and, 376

Aspect-Oriented Programming (AOP), 70, 316

association tables, 126

asynchronous gateways, setting up/using, 117–119

asynchronous processing, 111–116

attachments, Microsoft Exchange and, 193

Attributes scope, 278

audio, slide presentations and, 372

automating development, Ant for. *See* Ant

AVG function, 141

Axis (Apache), 171

## B

back-end frameworks, 263

base classes, 249–255

    object-oriented programming and, 218

    templates and, 255

Base64, 100

basedir, Ant and, 464, 471

Bayesian filters, 186

BEA JRockit, 400, 406

bean factories

    ColdSpring framework and, 316, 320

    FW/1 (Framework One) and, 355

beans, 231–238, 323

best practices

    for e-mail filtering, 186

    for Microsoft Exchange integration with ColdFusion, 196

blacklists, e-mail and, 185

blame command, version control and, 458

BlazeDS, 199–210

    installing with ColdFusion, 202

    messaging framework of, 202–209

    messaging patterns and, 199–202

    sample illustrating, 204–209

    vs. LCDS, 200

blog application (sample), 56

border action, image processing and, 91

branches, version control and, 446, 448, 451–454

    merging changes and, 455–458

    patches and, 449

    software version branching and, 453

    switch command and, 455

    task branches and, 454

breakpoints, CF8 debugger and, 425

build.xml file, for Ant, 464–470

business calculations, 361

business logic

    Fusebox framework and, 265

    FW/1 (Framework One) and, 350, 356

    remote proxies and, 147

    separating presentation from programming and, 362, 366

business logic layer, 232

business objects, 232–238

    custom data types and, 363–365

    separating presentation from programming and, 362, 366

## C

cacert file, 197

caching

    CFCs, 41

    Mach-II framework and, 283

    Transfer framework and, 332, 344, 345

calculations

business calculations and, 361

generating for reports, 139

cameras, extracting information about, 98

CAN-SPAM, 181

CAPTCHA images, 91

case sensitivity, XML and, 335

cf namespace, Fusebox framework and, 274

CF8 debugger, 421–432

breakpoints and, 425

configuration and, 430

Debug Output Buffer and, 432

vs. FusionDebug (summarized), 431

security and, 430

cfabort tag, onError() method and, 52

cfajaxproxy tag, 379–382, 384

cfapplication tag, 3

cfargument tag, 22–25, 179

Arguments scope and, 23

type attribute and, 179

.cfc file extension, 33

CFC Wizard, 412

cfcomponent tag, 33, 34, 39

CFCs (ColdFusion components), 17, 32–46

caching, 41

cfajaxproxy tag and, 380

CFC Wizard and, 412

ColdSpring framework and, 316

creating, 33–39, 380

frameworks and, 260–263

Fusebox framework and, 265, 271

inheritance and, 43–45

object-oriented programming and, 215

onRequest() method, web services and, 12

as properties, Mach-II framework and, 291

properties and, 33, 40

security and, 39

service CFCs and, 225

Services Browser and, 411

terminology and, 33

as view helpers, 365

web services deployed from, 146

cfdocument tag, PDFs and, 75, 78, 86

cfdocumentitem tag, 76, 80

cfdocumentsection tag, 76

cfdump tag, 190, 422, 426

cferror tag, 8

CFEvent structure, 118

cfexchange tag, 190

cfexchangecalendar tag, 191, 195

cfexchangeconnection tag, 190

cfexchangecontact tag, 191–194, 195

cfexchangefilter tag, 192, 195

cfexchangemail tag, 194, 195

cfexchangetask tag, 191–194, 195

cfftp tag, 190

cffunction tag, 17, 19–22, 39, 179

    cfargument tag and, 22

    CFCs and, 34

    cfreturn tag and, 26

    returntype attribute and, 179

    web services deployment and, 146

cfgateway adapter, messaging and, 202

cfhttp tag, web services invocation and,
    153

cfimage tag, 89–92

cfinclude tag, cffunction tag and, 19

cfinvoke tag, 35

    UDF invocation and, 27–30

    web services invocation and, 151

cfinvokeargument tag, 29

cflocation tag, 10, 54

cflog tag, 422

cfloop tag, 26

.cfm files, web services deployed from,
    148–151

cfmail tag, 182

cfmailparam tag, 183

CFM-based web services, invoking, 154

cfobject tag, 35, 36

cfoutput tag

    debugging and, 422, 423, 426

    nested cfoutput tags and, 136

cfpdf tag, 75, 77–88

    DDX and, 86–88

    metadata and, 80–83

    watermarks and, 84

cfpdfform tag, 77

cfpdfparam tag, 77

cfpdfsubform tag, 77

cfpresentation tag, 369, 370

cfpresentationslide tag, 369, 371

cfpresenter tag, 369, 371

cfquery tag, 26, 31

cfreturn tag, 22, 26

CFScript, 17, 39

cfscript tag, 17

cfset tag, 19, 26, 34

cfswitch tag, 112

cftrace tag, 422

cftry/cfcatch blocks

    onError() method and, 9

    onMissingTemplate() method and, 52

    UDF error handling and, 30

channels, messaging and, 202

char data type, 132

character sets, 134

CHECK constraint, 122–125

checkout command, version control and,
    446

children (child components), 33, 43–45

circuit.xml file, 266

circuits, Fusebox framework and, 266, 269, 270

class variables, object-oriented programming and, 218

classes, 33, 218

clean command, Eclipse and, 396, 403

client machine, for Subversion setup, 441

Client scope, 3

clustered indexes (IDX_CLs), 138

code generators, 254, 321

ColdBox framework, 262

ColdFusion

    BlazeDS installation and, 202

    debugging applications and, 417, 421–432

    integrating Microsoft Exchange with, 189–197

    JVM and, 103

    simplicity and, 348

ColdFusion Administrator page, RDS configuration and, 430

ColdFusion Administrator, ColdFusion Builder and, 411

ColdFusion Builder

    CFC Wizard and, 412

    debugging applications and, 417

    downloading, 3

    Eclipse and, 407–409

    extensions for, 412–417

    installing, 408

    projects and, 408

    resources for further reading, 419

    server integration and, 409–412

ColdFusion components. *See* CFCs

ColdFusion structs, 152

ColdFusion Studio, 407, 422

ColdSpring framework, 263, 315–320

    Aspect-Oriented Programming and, 70

    Mach-II framework and, 282

    Model-Glue framework and, 301

ColdSpring.xml file, Model-Glue framework and, 304

commit command, version control and, 443, 446, 448

    branch-to-trunk merges and, 449

    merging changes and, 456

    patches and, 449

    properties and, 458

    resolving conflicts and, 449

Completely Automated Public Turing test to tell Computers and Humans Apart (CAPTCHA), 91

complex types

    arrays and, 160, 175

    attributes and, 162

    nested, 159

    passing as input parameters, 157–164

    return values and, 172

    web services and, 157–177

component.cfc, 39

components
    highly cohesive, loosely coupled, 282
    object-oriented programming and, 218
    validating, 179

composite collections, Transfer framework
    and, 344

composite keys, 127

composition, 335
    vs. inheritance, 253
    object-oriented programming and, 218

compound primary keys (CPKs), 127

Concurrent Versions System (CVS), 433

constructor-arg, 316

constructor injection, 316

constructors, 33, 34–39, 219

consumers
    messaging and, 202
    SOA environment and, 239–247

consuming web services, 151–155

Contact Us form, e-mail and, 181, 182

contacts, creating for Microsoft Exchange,
    192

content, redirection of, 54

control layer, 232

control systems, 433–444
    advanced features and, 451–460
    locking and, 450
    resolving conflicts and, 449

reverting to a previous version and, 450
    terminology and, 446
    workflow and, 445–450

control tables, 125

controllers
    FW/1 (Framework One) and, 352, 355
    ModelGlue.xml file and, 307

convention-based application building,
    266, 348

copy task, Ant and, 465, 472

COUNT function, 141

countCodeLines.cfc file, 414, 415

countLines.cfm file, 414

cpdfformparam tag, 77

create() method, 339

CreateObject() function, 35, 36, 152, 166

createUUID() function, 227

CSS, prototypes and, 386

CVS (Concurrent Versions System), 433


**D**

DAOs (Data Access Objects), 233, 236, 323,
    325

Dashboard, for Mach-II framework, 284

data access layer, 232

Data Access Objects (DAOs), 233, 236, 323,
    325

data aggregation, 139

data formats, 242

data integrity, 126

data source configuration file, for Transfer framework, 332

Data Transfer Objects (DTOs), 325

data types. *See also entries at* type

ColdFusion-native, 152

custom, separating presentation from programming and, 363–365

object-oriented programming and, 224

database abstraction layers, 321

database tables

association tables and, 126

contents of, 142

objects mapped to, Transfer framework and, 335–337

queries, reading from multiple tables and, 135

database users, performance bottlenecks and, 121–142

databases

building correctly from the start, 142

frameworks and, 262

performance bottlenecks and, 121–142

Transfer framework and, 332

DDX (Document Description XML), 77, 79, 86–88

Debug Output Buffer (CF8 debugger), 432

Debug view, CF8 debugger and, 428

debugging

ColdFusion Builder and, 417

ColdFusion debugger and, 421–432

Decorators, 337

default documents, 48

delegation to parent handler, 69

DELETE statement

indexing data and, 139

Transfer framework and, 343

delete task, Ant and, 465, 471

delete() method, 342

dependencies, 315, 318

dependency injection, 316

DeserializeJSON() function, 243, 377, 378

design patterns

object-oriented programming and, 219

Reactor framework and, 323

digital cameras, extracting information about, 98

directories, default documents and, 48

discoverability, for services, 246

DIV tags, prototypes and, 386

DKIM (DomainKeys Identified Mail), 185

DNS (Domain Name Server), 184

do verb, Fusebox framework and, 277, 278

do() method (dynamic do), 278

Document Description XML (DDX), 77, 79, 86–88

documentation, for CFCs, 246

doesNotUnderstand handler (Smalltalk), 63, 72

dollar sign ($), in UDF names, 18

domain models, object-oriented programming and, 219

Domain Name Server (DNS), 184

domain objects, 320

DomainKeys Identified Mail (DKIM), 185

downloads

Ant, 462

asynchronous processing experiment, 115

ColdFusion Builder, 3, 407

Eclipse, 424

JRockit, 400

Mach-II framework, 282, 283

Reactor framework, 323

Subversion, software for, 434

drawing functions, for image processing, 92–96

Dreamweaver, ColdFusion Builder and, 407

DTOs (Data Transfer Objects), 325

duplicate() function, 30

dynamic typing, object-oriented programming and, 219

dynamic data, Ant and, 469

dynamic do (do() method), 278

dynamic page generation, onMissingTemplate() method and, 55–58

dynamic programming, 254

▓ E

echo task, Ant and, 465

Eclipse, 391–406

Ant and, 463

CF8 debugger and, 424, 425

clearing cached data and, 396, 403

ColdFusion Builder and, 407–409

commands/options for, 402–406

configuring RDS and, 430

core tools for, installing, 395

initial benchmark for, 397–400

JVM default, switching from, 400

package options for, 392

plugins, troubleshooting performance of, 397

preferences for, setting, 393

resources for further reading, 401

Update Manager and, 392

eclipse.ini file, 398

e-mail, 181–187, 474

encapsulation, 41

vs. loose coupling, 283

object-oriented programming and, 214, 219

onMissingMethod() method and, 66–68

enterprise service bus (ESB), 200

environment configuration, Mach-II framework and, 283

error handling. *See also* debugging

cferror tag and, 8

global missing template handler and, 47

onError() method and, 8

onMissingMethod() method and, 61, 65

onMissingTemplate() method and, 47–59

services and, 245

UDFs and, 30

web services and, 155

ESB (enterprise service bus), 200

event filters, Mach-II framework and, 289, 291

event gateways, BlazeDS and, 204–209

event handlers

Mach-II framework and, 289, 292, 294

ModelGlue.xml file and, 308

event model, Transfer framework and, 344

event object

Fusebox framework and, 278

Mach-II framework and, 282, 294

event types, ModelGlue.xml file and, 308

examples. *See* sample applications

Exchange. *See* Microsoft Exchange, integrating with ColdFusion

Exchangeable Image File Format (EXIF), displaying model information about, 98

excludes, Ant and, 472

exec task, Ant and, 465

EXIF data, displaying model information about, 98

eXit (FuseAction XFA), 270, 273, 279

explicit invocation, 262

Expressions view, CF8 debugger and, 427

▓ **F**

façades, 320

factories, ColdSpring framework and, 316

factory objects, 324

failTo attribute, 183

fbx_switch.cfm file, 266

files, copying/zipping via Ant, 470–473

filesets, Ant and, 472

Flash animations, slide presentations and, 369, 372

Flash Remoting

onRequest() method and, 12

onRequestStart() method and, 13

Flex, BlazeDS and, 199–209

FLiP (Fusebox Lifecycle Process), 269

FOREIGN KEY constraint, 125, 131

foreign keys (FKs), 123, 126–128

form for uppercasing text (sample), 309–313

Form scope, 150

formatting, reducing duplication and, 362, 363

Framework One. *See* FW/1

frameworks, 259–264, 347

defined, 259, 265

Front Controller frameworks and, 301

URLs and, 58

from attribute, 183

From field, e-mail and, 182, 185

Front Controller frameworks, 301

front-end interfaces, multiple, 225–229

ftp task, Ant and, 466

functions

image processing, 92–96

user-defined. *See* UDFs

fuseactions, 266, 269, 280

Fusebox framework, 260, 265–280

application initialization and, 273, 280

application skeleton for, 274

backward compatibility and, 270, 280

benefits of, 268

ColdFusion tags and, 274

FuseAction XFA and, 270, 273, 279

lexicons and, 273–276

myFusebox object and, 279

naming conventions and, 266

new features with 5/5.5 releases of, 270–280

reasons for upgrading, 280

resources for further reading, 269

runtime control and, 279

terminology specific to, 269

web site for, 269

XML and, 266, 276

Fusebox Lifecycle Process (FLiP), 269

fusebox.appinit.cfm, 273

fusebox.init.cfm, 273

fusebox.xml file, 267, 270, 280

fusebox5.Application, 273, 278

fuses, 266, 269, 280

FusionDebug, 421

vs. CF8 debugger (summarized), 431

RDS and, 424

requests and, 426

FW/1 (Framework One), 347–357

getting started with, 349

resources for further reading, 356

sample applications illustrating, 349

to-do list sample illustrating, 351–355

## G

Gateway Objects, 233, 324

Gateways, 237, 323

get task, Ant and, 465

get() method, 341

getbyFilter() (sample) method, 252

getFname() method, 173

getinfo action (cfpdf tag), 80

get-set methods, onMissingMethod() method and, 66–68

getter methods, 40

global missing template handler, 47

running concurrently with onMissingTemplate() method, 49

setting, 48

greylisting, 185

## H

heap memory, 108

Hibernate framework, 238

Home Site, ColdFusion Builder and, 407

HomeSite+, 422

HTML, frameworks for, 260–262

HTTP, SOA architecture and, 241

HTTP channels, 203

HTTP streaming, 199

HTTPS, Microsoft Exchange and, 197


**I**

I/O functions, for image processing, 100

IDA (Interface-Driven Architecture), 385–387

IDE (Integrated Development Environment)

    ColdFusion and, 407

    Eclipse and, 424

ide_config.xml file, 413

if verb, Fusebox framework and, 277

II (implicit invocation), 261, 282

image processing, 89–100

    cfimage tag for, 89–92

    drawing functions for, 92–96

    I/O functions for, 100

    information functions for, 97

    manipulation functions for, 96

ImageDraw… functions, 93, 95

ImageDrawRect function, 93

ImageDrawText function, 94

ImageGetEXIFMetadata function, 98

ImageGetEXIFTag function, 98

ImageGetHeight function, 97

ImageGetWidth function, 97

ImageInfo function, 97

ImageNew function, 92

ImageScaleToFit function, 96

ImageSet… functions, 93, 96

ImageSetAntialiasing function, 94

ImageSetDrawingColor function, 93

ImageSetDrawingStroke function, 93

implicit invocation (II), 261, 282

include verb, Fusebox framework and, 277

includes, Mach-II framework and, 289

index.cfm, Mach-II framework and, 286

indexes (IDXes), 137

info action, image processing and, 89

information functions, for image processing, 97

information-hiding, object-oriented programming and, 219

inheritance

    CFCs and, 43–45

    vs. composition, 253

    object-oriented programming and, 214, 220

init() method, 34, 37–39, 220

injected methods, 68

input parameters, complex types passed as, 157–164

input task, Ant and, 466, 469, 474

INSERT statement

    indexing data and, 139

    SELECT MAX(ID) function and, 129

    Transfer framework and, 344

instance variables, object-oriented programming and, 220

instances, 33

instantiate verb, Fusebox framework and, 277

instantiation, 33, 34–39, 220

Integrated Development Environment (IDE)

    ColdFusion and, 407

    Eclipse and, 424

Interface-Driven Architecture (IDA), 385–387

interfaces, object-oriented programming and, 220

internationalization

    custom data types and, 362, 365

    UTF-8 character encoding and, 134

interpolation, for images, 96

intersect tables, 126

inversion of control (IoC), 316

invocation, 33

invoke verb, Fusebox framework and, 277

IoC (inversion of control), 316

isDDX tag, 77

isJSON() function, 377, 378

isPDFFile tag, 77

isPDFObject tag, 77

IsStruct() function, 172

items, Microsoft Exchange and, 190, 191–193

Iterators, Reactor framework and, 328

## J

J2EE configuration, 431

Java EE (Java Enterprise Edition), 103

Java security manager, 431

Java Virtual Machine (JVM), 103–110, 400, 403

JavaScript Object Notation (JSON), 146, 149, 243, 375–379

JMS adapter, messaging and, 202

JRockit, 400, 406

JRun, 104, 431

jrun.xml file, enabling metrics logging and, 105

JSON (JavaScript Object Notation), 146, 149, 243, 375–379

JVM (Java Virtual Machine), 103–110, 400, 403

JVM settings, 103

## K

key icon, denoting primary key, 122

## L

languages, UTF-8 character encoding and, 134

layout, separating from logic, 361–368

    developers and, 362

    techniques for, 362–368

lazy loading, Transfer framework and, 336

LCDS (LiveCycle Data Services), 199–200

lexicons, Fusebox framework and, 269, 273–276

libraries, Mach-II framework and, 283

link tables, 126

Liskoff Substitution Principle, object-oriented programming and, 220

list queries, Transfer framework and, 343

list() method, 343

listByProperty() method, 343

listByPropertyMap() method, 343

listByQuery() method, 344

listeners, Mach-II framework and, 286, 289, 291, 294

LiveCycle Assembler, DDX and, 86

LiveCycle Data Services (LCDS), 199–200

LiveCycle DS Community Edition, 200

LiveCycle ES (Enterprise Suite), 200

LiveCycle Express, 200

local prefix, 25

local scope, 22, 23, 25–27

local variables, 25–27

localization, UTF-8 character encoding and, 134

locking, version control and, 446, 450, 451

logging, Mach-II framework and, 283

logging proxy, 71

logic, separating from layout, 361–368

    developers and, 362

    techniques for, 362–368

lookup tables, 125

loop verb, Fusebox framework and, 277

loose coupling, 282

## M

Mach-II framework, 262, 281–297

    application skeleton for, 283, 286

    ColdSpring framework and, 282

    configuration file for, 286–292

    Dashboard for, 284

    Hello page illustrating, 292–296

    installing, 283–285

    resources for further reading, 283

    Transfer framework and, 282

mach-ii.xml file, 286–292

    sections of (list), 289

    updating, 293

Macromedia Breeze, 369

mail task, Ant and, 466, 475

Manager Objects, 233

manipulation functions, for image processing, 96

many-to-many composition, 336

many-to-many relationships, 127

many-to-one composition, 336

mapping objects to tables, Transfer framework and, 335–337

mark resolved command, version control and, 444

maxOccurs attribute, 160

memory, JVM and, 104, 108

merge command, version control and, 449, 455–458

message-oriented middleware (MOM), 202

message-passing, object-oriented programming and, 220

message subscribers, Mach-II framework and, 289

messaging, 199–210

    messaging framework and, 202–209

    messaging patterns and, 199–202

    sample illustrating, 204–209

    unknown messages, onMissingMethod() method for handling, 61–72

messaging-config.xml, 202, 204

metadata

    services and, 246

    Transfer framework and, 344

metaprogramming, 254

method chaining, 36, 38

method injection, 68

methods, 33

    as messages sent to objects, 61–72

    object-oriented programming and, 221

    reference to, 15

    types of, 254

metrics logging, JVM and, 104–110

Microsoft Exchange, integrating with ColdFusion, 189–197

    best practices for, 196

    ColdFusion Exchange tags for, 190–196

    connecting/closing connections and, 190, 196

    e-mail and, 194

Microsoft Outlook, e-mail and, 181, 184

MIN function, 141

minOccurs attribute, 160

mkdir task, Ant and, 465, 471

Model-Glue framework, 261, 299–314

    creating applications with, 302–313

    installing, 301

    resources for further reading, 314

ModelGlue.xml file, 301, 302, 305–309

Model-View-Controller. *See* MVC

MOM (message-oriented middleware), 202

Multiserver configuration, 431

MVC (Model-View-Controller), 201

    Fusebox framework and, 265

    Mach-II framework and, 282

    multiple front-end interfaces and, 225–229

MXUnit framework, 247, 318

myFusebox object, 279

## ▓ N

naming conventions

    CFCs and, 18

    Fusebox framework and, 266

    UDFs and, 18

nchar data type, 134

new keyword, 35, 37

new() method, 339

newinit() method, 38

newsletters, e-mail and, 181

*n*-tiered architecture, 320

nullable properties, Transfer framework and, 344

nvarchar data type, 134

## ■O

object composition, 335

object configuration file, for Transfer framework, 333

Decorators and, 337

XML case sensitivity and, 335

Objective-C, messages and, 61

object-oriented programming (OOP)

base classes and, 249

component validation and, 180

fundamentals of, 213–216

Mach-II framework and, 282

object composition and, 335

reasons for using, 215

resources for further reading, 215

vs. SOA architecture, 239

terminology and, 217–224

object-relational mapping (ORM)

Reactor framework and, 323

Transfer framework and, 331

objects, 33

cloning, Transfer framework and, 344

creating/manipulating, Transfer framework and, 339–343

mapping to tables, Transfer framework and, 335–337

object-oriented programming and, 221

occurrence constraints, 160, 166

omit attribute, 153

onApplicationEnd() method, 10

onApplicationStart() method, 5, 49

onError() method, 8, 52

one-to-many composition, 336

one-to-many relationships, 125

onMissingMethod() method, 38, 61–72

defining, 64

ways of using, 65–72

onMissingTemplate() method, 47–59

cftry/cfcatch block used within, 52

dynamic page generation and, 55–58

how it works, 49–51

method invocation within, 51

onError() method and, 52

reasons for calling, 53–56

reporting errors via, 49

as request handler, 53, 55

running concurrently with global missing template handler, 49

search engine optimization and, 55

URLs and, 58

onRequest() method, 11, 150, 348

disadvantages of, 12

onMissingTemplate() method and, 49, 52

UDFs and, 20

onRequestEnd() method, 11, 49

OnRequestEnd.cfm, 19, 348

onRequestStart() method, 7, 56, 150

    Flash Remoting and, 13

    onMissingTemplate() method and, 49

onSessionEnd() method, 10 197

onSessionStart() method, 6, 49

OOP. *See* object-oriented programming

ORM (object-relational mapping)

    Reactor framework and, 323

    Transfer framework and, 331

Outlook (Microsoft), e-mail and, 181, 184

overloading, object-oriented programming and, 221

overriding, object-oriented programming and, 43, 221

## ▓P

page views. Mach-II framework and, 286, 290, 292, 295

parents (parent components), 33, 43–45

patches, version control and, 449

PDFs, ColdFusion support for, 75–88

    bookmarks and, 76

    checking PDF validity and, 77

    deleting pages and, 79, 88

    embedded forms and, 76

    images and, 76, 79

    indexing PDF content and, 86–88

    metadata and, 79, 80–83, 88

    PDF packages and, 79

    watermarks and, 79, 84

    XMP data and, 88

pdfutils CFC, 88

performance, database bottlenecks and, 121–142

persistence, 319

plugins, Mach-II framework and, 289, 292

polling channels, 203

polymorphism, object-oriented programming and, 214, 222

prefixes

    Arguments prefix and, 25

    local prefix and, 25

    request prefix and, 19

    super prefix and, 43

presentation layer, 232

presentation, separating from programming, 361–368

    developers and, 362

    techniques for, 362–368

presentations, creating, 369–374

primary keys (PKs), 121–132

    compound, 127

    foreign keys and, 125

    managing, Transfer framework and, 344

processddx action (cfpdf tag), 87

producers, messaging and, 202

programming

    Aspect-Oriented Programming and, 70

    metaprogramming and, 254

object-oriented. *See* object-oriented programming

separating from presentation, 361–368

templates and, 255

projects, 408

Ant and, 464

importing into Subversion repositories, 438–441, 447

properties, 33, 40

Ant and, 468

Mach-II framework and, 289, 290

object-oriented programming and, 222

Subversion and, 458–460

propget command, version control and, 459

proplist command, version control and, 459

propset command, version control and, 458

prototypes, 385–387

providers, SOA environment and, 239

proxies, 70, 344

proxy/stub objects, 166, 171

pseudo-constructors, 33, 34

publishing web services, 173–176

push/pull technology, 199

**Q**

queries, 322

Microsoft Exchange and, 192

Reactor framework and, 324

reading from multiple tables, 135

XML vs. JSON and, 376

**R**

RBLs (Real-Time Blacklists), 185

RDS (Remote Development Services), 409

CF8 debugger and, 424

configuring, 430

RDS Dataview, ColdFusion Builder and, 411

Reactor framework, 238, 263, 321–329

how it works, 325

installing, 323

resources for further reading, 329

read action, image processing and, 91

readByProperty() method, 342

readByPropertyMap() method, 342

readByPropertyValue() method, 341

readByQuery() method, 342

Real-Time Blacklists (RBLs), 185

Real Time Messaging Protocol (RTMP), 200

record task, Ant and, 470

redirection, 54

Refer a Friend form, e-mail and, 182

referential integrity, 126

RefreshWSDL attribute and, 152

relocate verb, Fusebox framework and, 277

Remote Development Services (RDS), 409

    CF8 debugger and, 424

    configuring, 430

remote proxies, 147

removeWatermark action (cfpdf tag), 84

replace task, Ant and, 472

replyTo attribute, 182, 183

reports, generating calculations and, 139

repositories, version control and, 446

    creating, 436, 447

    importing projects into, 438–441, 447

    resolving conflicts and, 449

    Subversion installation and, 435

    types of, 437

Representational State Transfer (REST), 146, 241

request errors, 53

request handlers, onMissingTemplate() method as, 53, 55

Request scope, 8, 19, 20

requests

    flow of, debugging and, 423

    Fusebox framework and, 273

    onRequest() method and, 11

    onRequestEnd() method and, 11

    onRequestStart() method and, 7

resize action, image processing and, 90

resizing images, 90, 96

resolved command, version control and, 457

resources for further reading

    Ant, 462

    Application.cfc, 13

    asynchronous gateways, 115

    base classes, 255

    CAN-SPAM, 182

    code generators, 255

    ColdFusion Builder, 419

    composition, 335

    DDX, 86

    doesNotUnderstand handler (Smalltalk), 72

    dynamic multiple inheritance, in Ruby, 72

    Eclipse, 401

    e-mail, 184–187

    façades, 320

    Fusebox framework, 269

    FW/1 (Framework One) and, 356

    JRockit, 402

    JVM, 402

    Mach-II framework and, 283

    Model-Glue framework, 314

    object-oriented programming, 215

    Reactor framework, 329

    SELECT MAX(ID) function, 130

    singletons, 316

    step debugging, 432

Subversion (SVN), 444, 450, 460

Transfer framework, 345

web services, 177

REST (Representational State Transfer), 146, 241

returntype attribute, 179

revisions, version control and, 446

blame command and, 458

your first revision, 448

RIAforge, ColdFusion Builder extensions and, 413

rotate action, image processing and, 91

RTMP (Real Time Messaging Protocol), 200

Ruby

messages and, 64

onMissingMethod() method and, 65

Ruby on Rails, 266, 348

Runtime Spy, 395, 397

## ■ S

sample applications

blog application, 56

form for uppercasing text, 309–313

messaging, 204–209

search interface, 382–384

to-do list, 351–355

UDFs and, 31

save() method, 340

SCPlugin, 434

search engine optimization, dynamic page generation and, 55

search-engine-safe (SES) URLs, 279

search interface (sample), 382–384

security

CF8 debugger and, 430

CFCs and, 39

Microsoft Exchange and, 197

services and, 243

SELECT MAX(ID) function, 129

sender attribute, 183

Sender Policy Framework (SPF), 184

SendGatewayMessage() function, 206

serialization, 375–379

SerializeJSON() function, 243, 377

serializeQueryByColumns parameter, 379

Server Monitor, ColdFusion Builder and, 411

service accounts, Microsoft Exchange and, 197

service buses, 200

service CFCs, MVC and, 225

service consumers, SOA environment and, 239–247

service frameworks, 263

service location transparency, 201

Service Objects, 233

service-oriented architecture (SOA), 201, 239–247

service providers, SOA environment and, 239

services

FW/1 (Framework One) and, 353, 356

SOA architecture and, 239–247

Services Browser, CFCs and, 411

services-config.xml file, 205, 207

SES (search-engine-safe) URLs, 279

session handling, 226

Session scope, 3, 35, 41

sessions

onSessionEnd() method and, 10

onSessionStart() method and, 6

set methods, onMissingMethod() method and, 66–68

set verb, Fusebox framework and, 278

setinfo action (cfpdf tag), 82

setter injection, 316

setter methods, 40

ShabbatClock.com, 146

Simple Object Access Protocol (SOAP), 145, 241

singletons, ColdSpring framework and, 316

site-wide error handler, setting, 48

slide presentations, 369–374

Smalltalk

messages and, 61

onMissingMethod() method and, 65

SOA (service-oriented architecture), 201, 239–247

SOAP (Simple Object Access Protocol), 145, 241

software version branching, 453

source code

input parameters, troubleshooting for, 164–171

spaghetti code and, 300

step debugging and, 421–432

spaghetti code, 300, 319

spam, 181

spam filters, 186

SPF (Sender Policy Framework), 184

spoofing, e-mail and, 182

Spring framework, ColdSpring framework and, 315

sql task, Ant and, 466

sshexec task, Ant and, 465

SSL certificates, Microsoft Exchange and, 197

stack trace, 424, 428

static methods, object-oriented programming and, 222

static typing, object-oriented programming and, 223

step debugging, 421–432

reasons for using, 422

resources for further reading, 432

streaming, BlazeDS and, 199, 203

string concatenation, 362

structKeyExists() function, 67

subclasses, object-oriented programming and, 223

subroutines, Mach-II framework and, 290

subtypes, object-oriented programming and, 223

Subversion (SVN), 433–444

  advanced features of, 451–460

  advantages of, 445

  Ant and, 473

  exporting from, 450

  key commands for, 442

  locking and, 450, 451

  Macintosh and, 434

  patches and, 449

  properties and, 458–460

  repositories for, 436–441

  resources for further reading, 444, 450, 460

  reverting to a previous version and, 450

  setting up on a Windows server, 434–442

  Subversion for Windows and, 434

  terminology and, 446

  using, 446–449

  workflow and, 445–450

SUM function, 141

Sun JVM, 104

super prefix, 43

superclasses, object-oriented programming and, 223

supertypes, object-oriented programming and, 223

SVN. See Subversion

SVNAnt task, 473

SVNRepos folder, 435, 438

SVNServe, 433

SVNService, software for SVNServe, 435

switch command, version control and, 455, 456

■ T

Table Data Gateways, 236, 323

tables. See database tables

tags, version control and, 446, 448, 454

  patches and, 449

  switch command and, 455

targets, Ant and, 464

task branches, version control and, 454

tasks, Ant and, 465

TDD (test-driven development), 318, 319

templates, 254

  global missing template handler and, 47

  merging into PDFs, 79

  onMissingTemplate() method and, 47–59

  simplifying, 362

terminology

  CFCs and, 33

  Fusebox framework and, 269

  object-oriented programming and, 217–224

  Subversion and, 446

test cases, ColdSpring framework and, 318

test-driven development (TDD), 318, 319

text
   drawing on images, 94

   drawing options for, 95

   uppercasing, sample form illustrating, 309–313

   UTF-8 character encoding and, 134

text data type, 134

This scope, 5, 40, 379

This.welcomeFileList variable, 48

threads, JVM and, 104

throw() function, 67

thumbnails, PDFs and, 79

tiered architecture, ColdSpring framework and, 319

to-do list (sample application), 351–355

Tomcat (Apache), 461

TortoiseSVN, 434–444

   icon overlays and, 442

   patches and, 449

   repositories and, 436–441

   software for, downloading/installing, 434

   workflow and, 445–450

toXML.cfc, 375, 379

TQL (Transfer Query Language), 342

transactions, databases and, 130

Transfer framework, 238, 264, 331–345

   installing/configuring, 332–337

   Mach-II framework and, 282

   resources for further reading, 345

   using, 338–344

Transfer Query Language (TQL), 342

transfer.xml file, 334, 342

Transferdoc tool, 345

TransferFactory, 338

TransferObjects, 332, 335–345

trunks, version control and, 446, 449, 452, 453

try/catch blocks, for web services, 155

tstamp task, Ant and, 466, 468

TXT record, e-mail and, 184

type attribute, 179

type promotion, object-oriented programming and, 224

type safety, object-oriented programming and, 224

types. *See* data types

## U

UDFs (user-defined functions), 4, 17–32

   creating, 18–27

   defining, 19

   error handling and, 30

   example illustrating, 31

   executing, 27–30

   output and, 21

   passing parameters and, 27–30

   Request scope and, 8

UI (user interface), frameworks for, 260–262

UML (Unified Modeling Language), object-oriented programming and, 224 underscore (_), in UDF names, 18

Unicode, UTF-8 character encoding and, 134

Unified Modeling Language (UML), object-oriented programming and, 224

unique identifier (UID), Microsoft Exchange and, 192

unit tests

ColdSpring framework and, 318, 319

consumers and, 247

update command, version control and, 442, 446, 448

UPDATE statement

indexing data and, 139

Transfer framework and, 344

update() method, 340

uppercaser for text (sample form), 309–313

URL scope, 150

URLs

convention-based application building and, 349

frameworks and, 58

request error handling for, 53

search-engine-safe, 279

user interface (UI), frameworks for, 260–262

user-defined functions. See UDFs

UserService.cfc, 225

UTF-8 character encoding, 134

UUIDs, createUUID() function and, 227

**V**

val() function, 58

validation

components and, 179

Model-Glue framework and, 312

validation logic and, 238

var keyword, 25

varchar data type, 132

variables

CF8 debugger and, 426

local, 25–27

UDFs and, 18

Variables scope, 18, 40, 67, 252

Variables view, CF8 debugger and, 426

variables.instance, 67

variables.readableFields, 67

variables.writableFields, 67

verbs, Fusebox framework and, 269, 273, 276, 280

Verity, 86

version control systems, 433–444

advanced features and, 451–460

locking and, 450

resolving conflicts and, 449

reverting to a previous version and, 450

terminology and, 446

video, slide presentations and, 372

view CFCs, 365

## W

watermarks, adding to PDFs, 79, 84

WDDX (Web Distributed Data Exchange), 146, 149, 243, 375

web developers, separating presentation from programming and, 362

Web Distributed Data Exchange (WDDX), 146, 149, 243, 375

web forms, e-mail and, 181

Web Service Definition Language. *See* WSDL

web services, 145–156

    CFM-based, invoking, 154

    complex types and, 157–177

    consuming, 157

    deploying, 146, 148–151

    invoking, 151–155

    publishing, 173–176

    SOA architecture and, 241–247

webservice attribute, 153

whitelists, 185

whitespace, UDFs and, 21

WinDiff, 449

working copies, version control and, 446, 447

write action, image processing and, 91

writeToBrowser action, image processing and, 91

WS-Security, 245

WSDL (Web Service Definition Language), 145

    cfinvoke tag, web services invocation and, 152

    consuming web services and, 157

    CreateObject() function, web services invocation and, 153

    RefreshWSDL attribute and, 152

WSDL2Java utility, 171

## X

XFA (eXit FuseAction), 270, 273, 279

xfa verb, Fusebox framework and, 278

XML

    DDX and, 86–88

    Fusebox framework and, 266, 270, 276

    XML elements, Transfer framework and, 335

## Y

Yahoo!, e-mail and, 185, 187

yellow key icon, denoting primary key, 122

## Z

zip/unzip tasks, Ant and, 465, 473

zipFiles task, Ant and, 473

zipping files, using Ant and, 470–473

Made in the USA
Lexington, KY
30 April 2013